Contested Boundaries

Contested Boundaries: A New Pacific Northwest History

Contested Boundaries: A New Pacific Northwest History is an engaging, contemporary look at the themes, events, and people that have shaped the history of the Pacific Northwest over the last two centuries.

Bringing together the best features of a reader and a traditional textbook, this work features 12 stand-alone essays that thematically capture the essential narratives of Washington, Oregon, and Idaho, with features like timelines, illustrations, and sidebars that provide scholarly context.

Centered on the concept of "exclusion," *Contested Boundaries: A New Pacific Northwest History* introduces the region's many different inhabitants – past and present – from Native Americans and women to Asian Americans and Hispanic peoples, and details the political, economic, and social barriers they encountered. It includes well-balanced, inclusive, up-to-date coverage of a variety of important issues for the region, including the environment, gender, ethnicity, and culture. A companion website for students and instructors includes test banks, PowerPoint presentations, student self-assessment tests, useful primary documents, and resource links.

Written by two professors with over 20 years of teaching experience, this work introduces the history of the Pacific Northwest in a style that is accessible, relevant, and meaningful for anyone wishing to learn more about the region's history.

DAVID JEPSEN is a former journalist and corporate marketing professional who has been writing professionally for 40 years. He holds a BA in Communications and a MA in History from the University of Washington. Since 2007, he has taught at Pierce College, the University of Washington Tacoma, and Tacoma Community College, where he is currently a member of the adjunct faculty, teaching both U.S. and Pacific Northwest history. His many writing awards include Honorable Mention for the 2006 Oregon Historical Society Joe Palmer Award for the article *"Old-Fashioned Revival: Religion, Migration and a New Identity for Pacific Northwest at Mid-Twentieth Century"* (2006).

DAVID NORBERG has taught Pacific Northwest history in Washington for nearly 14 years and currently is a full-time member of the history faculty and chair of the Social Sciences Division at Green River Community College, in Auburn, Washington. He holds a BA in History from the University of Washington and a MA in History from Western Washington University. His article, *"The Ku Klux Klan in the Valley, a 1920s Phenomenon,"* published by the White River Valley Museum, shed new light on the conservative backlash in the region following World War I.

Contested Boundaries

A New Pacific Northwest History

David J. Jepsen and David J. Norberg

WILEY Blackwell

This edition first published 2017
© 2017 John Wiley & Sons, Inc

The right of David J. Jepsen and David J. Norberg to be identified as the authors of this work has been asserted in accordance with law.

Registered Office:
John Wiley & Sons, Inc., 111 River Street, Hoboken, NJ 07030, USA

Editorial Office
350 Main Street, Malden, MA 02148-5020, USA

For details of our global editorial offices, customer services, and more information about Wiley products visit us at www.wiley.com.

Wiley also publishes its books in a variety of electronic formats and by print-on-demand. Some content that appears in standard print versions of this book may not be available in other formats.

Library of Congress Cataloging-in-Publication Data applied for.

9781119065487 (hardback)
9781119065548 (paperback)

Cover Design: Wiley
Cover images courtesy of the authors

Set in 10/12pt WarnockPro by Aptara Inc., New Delhi, India

Printed in the United States of America

10 9 8 7 6 5 4 3 2 1

To Jackie, who taught me how to listen.

To Kristine, Alex, and Niko, whose support and encouragement made this work possible.

Contents

List of Illustrations   *xi*
Authors' Biographies   *xv*
Preface and acknowledgments   *xvii*
Introduction   *xix*

Part I   Clash of Cultures   *1*

1   Early Encounters   *3*
    Ships logs tell of a clash of cultures   *5*
    British pursue "every branch" of Puget Sound   *6*
    "Mean huts and wretched sheds" greet explorers   *8*
    Understanding European misconceptions   *9*
    Robert Gray braves entrance to Columbia River   *10*
    Lewis and Clark arrive by land, 1804 to 1806   *13*
    Meeting with Shoshone turns tense   *15*
    Assessing the Corps of Discovery   *20*
  The time of the people   *22*
  Sacagawea: heroism in perspective   *27*
  Explore more   *30*
  Notes   *30*

2   Trade Among Equals   *35*
    Slow beginning for fur trade   *36*
    An "astronomical" tale   *36*
    'Single-minded' pursuit of otter skins   *37*
    Traders establish permanent presence in interior   *39*
    Hudson's Bay Company takes charge   *41*
    Aggressive tactics create "fur deserts"   *42*
    British diversify beyond furs   *44*
    HBC–Native relations – the ties that bind trade   *46*
    From 'bad to worse' and the end of an era   *50*
  Explore more   *52*
  Notes   *53*

3 Making a Christian Farmer   *59*
    In search of a holy life   *60*
    Seeking the "book of heaven"   *61*
    Promising start in God's work   *64*
    Protestants and Catholics compete for converts   *66*
    A day of reckoning at Waiilatpu   *74*
Indian Removal Act of 1830 – a portent of trouble for Northwest natives   *78*
Beyond the written word – the drawings of Father Nicolas Point   *79*
Explore more   *81*
Notes   *81*

4 Building an American Northwest   *87*
    Americans look West   *87*
    Experiencing the Oregon Trail   *89*
    Forging American institutions in Oregon   *93*
    Taming a 'wilderness'   *95*
    Nothing settled – Indian reservations and war   *97*
"Seeing the Elephant" – the Catherine Sager story   *103*
Mother Joseph – a Northwest builder   *104*
Federal boarding schools challenge cultural boundaries   *106*
Explore more   *108*
Notes   *109*
Important Dates and Events   *115*

Part II   People and Place   *117*

5 Riding the Railroad Rollercoaster   *119*
    Unlimited opportunity, limited markets   *121*
    Frenzy of railroad construction   *122*
    Big ideas from flawed men   *124*
    Marketing the "wasteland" as a "friendly place"   *125*
    Making and breaking cities   *128*
    Extraction industry finally on wheels   *131*
    Not all is rosy in rail town   *133*
    Panic exposes poor management   *135*
James J. Hill: from empire builder to noxious weed   *139*
Cashing in on the Klondike Gold Rush   *141*
Explore more   *143*
Notes   *143*

6 Seeking Dignity in Labor   *149*
    Making sense of the Progressive Era   *151*
    Divided union struggles for power   *152*
    At the mercy of predatory "job sharks"   *153*
    A rough and tumble lumber business   *155*
    Arrest and expulsion in Aberdeen   *157*

Running the gauntlet in Everett   *158*
A parade of violence in Centralia   *160*
Looking for answers in a violent past   *163*
The beginning of the end   *165*
R.D. Hume, "pygmy monopolist" on the economic frontier   *169*
Explore more   *172*
Notes   *172*

7   **Dismantling a Racial Hierarchy**   *177*
African Americans – seeking haven from racial oppression   *179*
Early industrialization and demand for substitute labor   *181*
Chinese – the travails of life on "gold mountain"   *184*
The Tacoma Method – organized vigilantism at gunpoint   *186*
Clashing with "mongoloid races" in Idaho's goldfields   *187*
A century and a half of change   *190*
European immigration – overlooked stories of the American West   *191*
Doc Hay and generous medicine – a prescription for cultural acceptance   *192*
Explore more   *194*
Notes   *194*

8   **Liberation in the West**   *197*
Women serve as the moral authority   *199*
Working-class labor in farm yard and factory   *200*
Challenging long hours and low pay   *204*
The dual challenge – female and minority   *205*
Chinese build a presence in a strange land   *207*
The Irish – moving beyond the domestic   *208*
African Americans – finding confidence and self-worth   *209*
Winning the franchise   *212*
Answering the "why" question   *216*
Muller v. Oregon   *218*
Caroline Gleason – debunking the myths of women's work   *220*
Explore more   *222*
Notes   *222*
Important Dates and Events   *227*

Part III   Crisis and Opportunity   *229*

9   **Beyond Breadlines**   *231*
Returning to the not so "Roaring '20s"   *232*
Going from bad to worse   *233*
"Let's call this place Hooverville"   *234*
Out with the old, and in with the New Deal   *237*
Putting Americans to work in the city   *240*
Did the government create a "nation of softies"?   *243*
Pointing towards a new era   *244*

Building the "Eighth Wonder of the World"   *246*
Explore more   *249*
Notes   *249*

10   Marching through Global Conflict   *255*
The winds of war sweep across the Pacific Northwest   *256*
Northwest industries rise to the challenge   *257*
A Critical shortage of workers breaks down barriers   *262*
Japanese Americans challenge new boundaries   *266*
From a World War to a Cold War   *270*
A changed Northwest?   *272*
Women for the defense   *273*
Maggie, Scoop, and the Federal Northwest   *276*
Explore more   *278*
Notes   *279*

11   El Movimiento: Chicanos Unite to Improve Economic Standing   *287*
A rights movement that inspires others   *288*
Braceros, a world war and a war on poverty   *289*
Federal government enters the war on poverty   *292*
California's rising star shines on Yakima Valley   *294*
Workers fight the "slave bill" in Oregon   *296*
El Movimiento comes to campus   *297*
Changing how a university serves its minority communities   *300*
Radio KDNA links with itinerant audiences   *302*
Limited victories in Washington and Oregon   *303*
"Taking off the mask"   *306*
Movin' on up … and outside the Central District   *313*
Explore more   *316*
Notes   *316*

12   The Fractured Northwest   *321*
A new Northwestern economy   *322*
The big business of outdoor recreation   *324*
A region divided by uneven growth   *328*
Politics from left to right   *330*
Environmental politics: resources vs. recreation   *332*
An uncertain future   *335*
From building to breaching dams   *337*
Standoff at the Malheur National Wildlife Refuge   *339*
Explore more   *341*
Notes   *341*
Important Dates and Events   *348*

Bibliography   *349*
Index   *367*

List of Illustrations

I.1	HMS *Discovery* grounded at Queen Charlotte's Island	*1*
1.1	Mt. Rainier from Admiralty Inlet	*4*
1.2	USS *Columbia* encounters HMS *Discovery*	*11*
1.3	Members of Corps of Discovery entertain Puget Sound natives	*14*
1.4	Lewis & Clark Centennial poster	*21*
1.5	Native Peoples playing stick games	*24*
1.6	Chinook camped near Mt. Hood	*25*
1.7	Sacagawea	*28*
2.1	Alexander Mackenzie	*40*
2.2	Colville Chief See-pay	*42*
2.3	Hudson's Bay Company recruitment flyer	*44*
2.4	Fort Nisqually	*45*
2.5	Colville Peoples fishing at Kettle Falls	*49*
2.6	Chief (Spokane) Garry	*51*
3.1	Narcissa and Marcus Whitman	*63*
3.2	St. Mary's Mission	*67*
3.3	Salish Peoples receiving the Sacrament of Communion	*69*
3.4	Catholics and natives at an outdoor altar	*72*
3.5	Monument at the Whitman Mission National Historic Site	*76*
3.6	The "Return of the Hunter"	*79*
4.1	Joel Palmer	*92*
4.2	Army scouts from Warm Springs Reservation	*93*
4.3	Pacific Northwest map from 1863	*95*
4.4	Hop pickers in Yakima	*98*
4.5	Washington Territorial Governor Isaac Stevens	*99*
4.6	Mounted Nez Perce circle Walla Walla Treaty Council	*101*
4.7	Nez Perce dining at Walla Walla Treaty Council	*102*
4.8	Mother Joseph	*104*
II.1	Families posing on logs in Sedro Woolley	*117*
5.1	Northern Pacific Last Spike Ceremony	*123*
5.2	Railroad prospectus promoting Pacific Northwest	*127*
5.3	Chart: Pacific Northwest population 1860–1920	*128*
5.4	Poster celebrating Washington statehood	*130*
5.5	Railroad dining car	*134*

5.6	Railroad poster promoting tourism in Pacific Northwest	*137*
5.7	James Hill	*139*
6.1	IWW Songbook cover	*151*
6.2	IWW "One Big Union" poster	*154*
6.3	Wanted poster	*161*
6.4	Group portrait of Ralph Chaplin and other labor activists	*164*
6.5	The 1903 Seattle streetcar strike	*166*
6.6	Seattle dockworkers on strike in 1919	*167*
7.1	Chinese expulsion poster	*178*
7.2	Miners at Wilkeson coal mine	*182*
7.3	Chinese workers at Bellingham salmon cannery	*185*
7.4	Seattle anti-Chinese riots	*189*
7.5	Chart: European immigration by country of origin 1900	*191*
7.6	Pulsologist Ing "Doc" Hay	*192*
8.1	Women picketing for minimum wage	*200*
8.2	Women packing salmon at Bellingham cannery	*203*
8.3	Native women picking hops	*207*
8.4	Beatrice Morrow Cannady	*210*
8.5	*Votes for Women* newspaper	*213*
8.6	Seattle Waitresses Union in Labor Day parade	*215*
8.7	Women's suffrage political cartoon	*217*
8.8	Caroline Gleason	*221*
III.1	President Franklin Roosevelt at Grand Coulee Dam	*229*
9.1	Ku Klux Klan at Oregon rally	*233*
9.2	Family Welfare publicity photo during Great Depression	*235*
9.3	Seattle Hooverville	*236*
9.4	Ronald Ginther painting of men stealing apples	*238*
9.5	Young men in Civilian Conservation Corps barracks	*239*
9.6	WPA publicity photo at Snohomish County Airfield	*241*
9.7	Violence at lumber workers strike in Tacoma	*242*
9.8	Herd of sheep crossing Grand Coulee Dam	*247*
10.1	Henry J. Kaiser Shipyards in Portland	*258*
10.2	Rollout of Boeing's B-17 "Flying Fortress"	*259*
10.3	U.S. Army poster promoting lumber workers	*261*
10.4	Women's Land Army recruiting poster	*263*
10.5	American Red Cross volunteers distributing food to soldiers	*264*
10.6	Scrap metal drive in Oregon	*268*
10.7	Japanese "hospital workers" at Camp Minidoka	*270*
10.8	Woman working at Rainier Aircraft Training Center	*274*
11.1	Braceros picking potatoes	*290*
11.2	Removal of condemned migrant worker housing	*292*
11.3	César Chávez speaking to labor organizers in Yakima	*296*
11.4	Migrant workers at camp near Zillah, Washington	*298*
11.5	Picketers outside Safeway store in Yakima, Washington	*300*
11.6	Ricardo García in 1971	*305*
11.7	Youth protesters at Seattle City Council meeting in 1963	*314*
12.1	Micron Technology worker in Boise, Idaho	*323*

12.2 Downtown Portland from Tom McCall Waterfront Park   *324*
12.3 REI flagship store in Seattle   *325*
12.4 Downtown Seattle from Elliott Bay   *326*
12.5 Boeing P-8A Poseidon   *328*
12.6 Kshama Sawant at Seattle teachers' strike   *330*
12.7 Hikers at Mount Rainier National Park   *333*
12.8 Signs protesting Wild Olympics Bill   *334*

Authors' Biographies

David J. Jepsen, a former journalist and corporate marketing professional, has been writing professionally for 40 years. He holds a BA in Communications and a MA in History from the University of Washington. He teaches Pacific Northwest and United States history at Tacoma Community College. He writes regularly for academic journals and history museums. David and his wife Jackie live in Gig Harbor, Washington. They have two grown daughters, Jillian and Danielle.

David J. Norberg teaches Pacific Northwest and United States history and is currently the social science division chair at Green River College in Auburn, Washington. He holds a BA in History from the University of Washington and a MA in History from Western Washington University. He periodically writes articles and gives public presentations for local history museums and historical societies. David lives in Tacoma with his wife Kristine and their two sons, Alex and Niko.

Carly Cross photo

Preface and acknowledgments

For much of my 40-year writing career, penning a book has long been a sought-after goal. A monograph, the staple of regional historians, or a modest collection of essays seemed achievable. I never dreamed my first book would be a survey of Pacific Northwest History. But a chance encounter at the Organization of American Historians 2013 annual meeting in San Francisco remade that dream.

Typical for such events, dozens of publishers filled an exposition hall to display their latest titles, while sales reps eagerly explained how theirs would enhance the learning experience in our classrooms. Amidst the din of hundreds of teachers and historians strolling through rows of exhibits, I chatted with a small group of Pacific Northwest historians and professors. We agreed that for all the great history on display, the publishers had failed to address our greatest need – an up-to-date text on regional history. After all, the last new one was released the year Ronald Reagan handed the presidential reins over to the first George Bush, and Booth Gardner occupied the governor's mansion in Olympia.

Some informal research demonstrated the need was bigger than I suspected. Nearly half of the roughly 100 colleges and universities in Washington, Oregon, and Idaho offer Pacific Northwest History at least once in a school year, often more. The remainder focus primarily on state history. Clearly a survey of regional history was sorely needed and long overdue, and I began to explore how I might fill this embarrassing gap in our offerings.

Fortunately, the history division at the publisher John Wiley & Sons saw the same need, and had been searching for an author as far back as 2012. So it's the contribution of Wiley and Sons that I must first acknowledge. Andrew Davidson, then Wiley's senior history editor, shared my vision for a new approach to a regional text, and entrusted the work to a relatively untested writer.

Andrew cautioned that such a hefty undertaking required multiple authors. While initially resistant to the idea, I set about finding a regional historian with the requisite writing skills and willingness to take on what amounted to a two-year commitment. That search led me to David Norberg, currently the social science division chair at Green River College in Auburn, Washington. *Contested Boundaries* is the byproduct of a true collaboration between Dave and me. Importantly, we share fundamental beliefs in what it takes to engage students. His chapters on the North American fur trade and early settlement era in the nineteenth century, and the Great Depression and World War II in the twentieth century reveal his exceptional research and writing talents. His work on the twelfth and last chapter, "The Fractured Northwest," creates a telling snapshot of the region's most recent past, vital if we expect to connect with the rapidly growing number of students born in the twenty-first century.

Even double-teaming the narrative we needed support from many corners. If *Contested Boundaries* finds a long-term home in the classroom, it will be in large part due to fellow historians who willingly shared their time and expertise in reviewing chapters. In addition to adding clarity and balance, they often moved us to rethink what by then had become well-entrenched positions. Our heart-felt thanks go to John Findlay and James Gregory at the University of Washington; Peter Boag and Karen Blair, retired, Washington State University; Patricia Killen, Gonzaga University; Coll Thrush, University of British Columbia; Dan Bush, Green River College; Drew Crooks, independent historian and author; Ed Echtle, independent researcher and historian; David Nicandri, retired director, Washington State Historical Society (WSHS); Ed Nolan, head of special collections at WSHS; and Feliks Banel, producer and historian. A special note of thanks to Stephanie Lile at Bering Street Studios and the University of Washington Tacoma, whose editing skills and well-honed instincts helped put the final touches on an evolving narrative.

The authors and publisher would like to extend special thanks to the Washington State Historical Society for providing us affordable access to their vast collection of photos and images. We share their goal of engaging students, teachers, and the community in bringing to life the colorful histories of Washington State and the Pacific Northwest. To view more WSHS images or visit the Washington State History Museum go to http://www.washingtonhistory.org/.

Finally, I would like to acknowledge the mentorship and longtime support of two University of Washington professors. On the Tacoma campus, Mike Allen provided guidance early in my graduate studies, and confirmed that a 50-something student could indeed succeed in a second career. In Seattle, John Findlay's contributions to regional history extend far beyond his many books and essays. A generation of aspiring historians owe their careers to Professor Findlay. He taught me how to think and write like an historian. He urged me to look past the headline stories and see the subtle nuances that give regional history depth and context.

David Norberg wishes to thank his colleagues at Green River College for their numerous suggestions, encouragement and support: Ed Echtle, friend and fellow historian, who shaped his thinking on the region's past; and Alan Gallay, grad school advisor, whose reminder that he should enjoy his work profoundly affected his research and teaching style.

Finally, both David Norberg and I would like to thank our families for patiently tolerating (most of the time) our prolonged absences while we buried ourselves in libraries and museums or flailed away on our keyboards. To borrow from the politicos, publishing a book takes a family.

Introduction

During Captain George Vancouver's two-month exploration of Puget Sound in spring 1792, he dispatched crews in longboats to chart and map the Sound and pursue the "termination of every branch no matter how small it might appear."[1] On the evening of May 22, a crew under the leadership of Lieutenant Peter Puget was camped on the beach near present day Steilacoom when a contingent of 30 or more Natives approached in six dugout canoes.

By now, three weeks into their exploration, the British had accepted the constant presence of curious Native Peoples. But this visit felt different. There were no women and children among them, and the men were armed with bows. Alarmed, Puget's men grabbed their muskets and darted for cover behind trees. One of the British, likely Puget, stepped forward, drew a line in the sand, and thrust out his hands, signaling the Natives to stop. They hesitated, and appeared briefly to argue among themselves, before returning to their canoes. A peaceful end to a potentially fatal incident.

On January 2, 2016, two and a quarter centuries after Vancouver's expedition, another incident did not end so amicably. Angered over the way in which the Federal Government controlled Western lands, two dozen armed ranchers and anti-government protesters occupied the Malheur National Wildlife Refuge in eastern Oregon. The standoff ended 41 days later with 25 arrests and the death of one militant, LaVoy Finicum, a 55-year-old Arizona cattle rancher. Finicum, who had acted as spokesmen for the militants throughout the occupation, was shot by police during a roadside incident outside the wildlife refuge.

So goes the history of the Pacific Northwest. From Puget drawing a simple line in the sand, to more complex lines drawn by federal regulation, the region offers a rich history of people contesting boundaries set down by others. Boundaries came in all sizes and shapes. International, territorial, and state boundaries gave the region shape but with only minimal intrusion on people's daily lives. Others were writ in code and proved more intrusive: Indian reservations, racial exclusion laws, bans on women voting and wartime internment restricted people's freedom and access to society. Others still were abstruse, persistent, and harder to contest: cultural dominance, racism, class conflict and homophobia – all variations on that line in the sand. Not all barriers were drawn in black and white. Competing interests sometimes resulted in erecting obstacles for some that opened doors for others. Grand Coulee Dam and other hydroelectric projects emasculated a mighty river, destroyed a salmon habitat and harmed a native culture. Yet what boosters called the "Eighth Wonder of the World" created thousands of jobs, opened millions of acres of farmland for irrigation and supplied the region with affordable electricity for generations – a clear case of one group's boundary being another's opportunity.

Contested Boundaries: A New Pacific Northwest History conceptualizes the region's past under the umbrella of Contest. It's a collection of stories about people contesting the political, economic, and social barriers that blocked their path to equality: Native Peoples, African Americans, Asians, women, unskilled workers of all races, and others. We follow them across the centuries as they struggle to hurdle one boundary after another during settlement, industrialization, economic calamity, world war and globalization.

Our coverage is mostly confined to Washington, Oregon, and Idaho. This choice may seem arbitrary but practical reasons dictate we define the region narrowly. The question of where it begins and ends remains open to debate. In addition to the trio of states, some historians include western Montana, southwest British Columbia, Alaska and even Northern California. Others eschew political boundaries altogether, using the geography of the North Pacific Slope to define "Nature's Northwest."[2] More lyrically, the writer Timothy Egan argues the Pacific Northwest is "wherever the salmon can get to."[3] But for our purposes, the debate is mostly academic and irrelevant because wherever one draws the lines, the stories vary only in detail. The legacy of contest and exclusion prevailed throughout the North American West, or as one historian called it, a "contest for property and profit" combined with "a contest for cultural dominance."[4]

A brief note on structure is appropriate here. *Contested Boundaries* is a hybrid that merges an edited collection of essays with elements of a traditional text. Rather than offering a text-like narrative in strict chronological order, *Contested Boundaries* features 12 stand-alone chapters covering the time from when only Native Peoples inhabited the land through the end of the twentieth century. Largely derivative in nature, they provide a synthesis of the superb historical scholarship in regional history published over the last 40 years. We cannot tell every story, and therefore must omit important ones. But we have tried to capture the essential narratives that collectively leave the reader with a vivid picture of the region's past, and importantly, eager to explore further. Historical timelines and brief sidebars highlighting ancillary people and events help to fill potential gaps in our coverage.

Contested Boundaries is divided into three parts. The four chapters in Part I, "Clash of Cultures," opens with an examination of the cultures that indigenous peoples maintained for millennia. The late eighteenth and early nineteenth centuries, when European and American explorers ventured into the region, signaled a dramatic change in their way of life. Some visitors came away with fortunes, and others made claims to ownership. All left behind deadly disease. Enthralled by the promise of riches, traders soon swept into the region, leading to the first permanent contact with indigenous peoples already wracked by disease but still able to negotiate on the trade grounds as equals. In addition to furs, traders returned east with colorful stories about "savages" ready to receive the word of God and don the work clothes of a "civilized" society. Following the trade routes west, Catholics, Presbyterians, and Methodists established missions in the wilderness and committed themselves to recasting native life. Their well-intended, but largely unsuccessful and sometimes tragic quest to transform Native Peoples into Christian farmers drew others west. Soon a great government-sponsored land giveaway, coupled with the wonders of rail transport, triggered a veritable stampede of settlers, erecting new boundaries in every direction.

Part II, "People and Place," explores the monumental impact and boundaries that came with industrialization. By late nineteenth century, Native Peoples had been largely marginalized and "free land" gobbled up. The railroad fostered industrialization and mechanization, which in turn opened up worldwide markets for natural resources, created tens of thousands of jobs, and established the region as a source of "inexhaustible" resources. Promoted as a land where "money grows on trees," the region soon swelled with workers of all races and social classes, many radicalized by the harsh realities of the industrial era. Radicals were begrudgingly tolerated as long as there were enough jobs to go around. But when prices fell, as they inevitably did, and markets closed, jobs disappeared. Soon tolerance gave way to fear, anger, and class conflict. Women also sought to break the ties that bind, and demanded a place side by side with men on the factory floor, in the office and at the polls.

Part III, "Crisis and Opportunity," examines the transformations brought on by the Great Depression, world war, and the economic growth and globalization that marked the second half of the twentieth century. Once known mostly for resource extraction, the region soon gained a new identity – the Federal Northwest. Government projects to create jobs, military contracts to wage war, and newly established national parks to preserve the environment made the federal government the region's biggest employer and largest landowner. And while Uncle Sam offered wealth and prosperity for many, federal ties created unwanted dependence for others and ate away control over the natural resources on which they relied for support. As the twentieth century drew to a close, a proliferating service economy and globalization morphed the Pacific Northwest identity once again. Arguably, the region today is known as much for its coffee and high technologies as for its salmon and airplanes.

Contested Boundaries allows you to define the Pacific Northwest in your own way. Draw the boundaries where they suit you. Accept or reject its many identities. Ask yourself what boundaries block your path to the life you have chosen. Finally, see this book as a beginning not an end. Use it as a launch pad to take you to places where you can further explore the mighty contests of our past and therefore learn more about yourself and your connection with the region.

Notes

1 Richard W. Blumenthal, ed. *With Vancouver in Inland Washington Waters, Journals of 12 Crewmen, April–June 1792* (Jefferson: McFarland & Company, 2007), 46.
2 For a discussion of how nature shaped the Pacific Northwest, see William G. Robbins and Katrine Barber, *Nature's Northwest: The North Pacific Slope in the Twentieth Century* (Tucson, AZ: The University of Arizona Press, 2011).
3 Timothy Egan, *The Good Rain: Across Time and Terrain in the Pacific Northwest* (New York: Knopf Publishers, 1990), 22.
4 Patricia Nelson Limerick, The Legacy of Conquest: The Unbroken Past of the American West, (New York: W.W. Norton & Company), 1987), 27.

Part I

Clash of Cultures

Figure I.1 Natives in canoes, probably members of the Kwakwaka'wakw group of peoples, watch with interest as Captain George Vancouver's ship, *The Discovery*, lies grounded at Queen Charlotte Sound north of Vancouver Island in July 1792. The *Discovery*'s consort, the *Chatham*, was unable to free the *Discovery* although it dislodged from the rocks at high tide. Image provided with permission from the University of Washington Libraries Special Collections (NA 3988).

Contested Boundaries: A New Pacific Northwest History, First Edition. David J. Jepsen and David J. Norberg.
© 2017 John Wiley & Sons, Ltd. Published 2017 by John Wiley & Sons, Ltd.

1

Early Encounters

Three hundred years after Columbus, explorers stake claims, exploit riches and leave disease

Antiquated notions of "discovery" fail to describe the thunderous clash of cultures that occurred when Europeans first ventured into the Pacific Northwest in the late eighteenth century. Whether arriving by sea or by land, explorers encountered Native Peoples whose initial reactions to the newcomers ranged from fear to curiosity to hostility. Even as they encountered new and unknown barriers, most Native Peoples saw the potential of the European possessions, unaware the price included an end to the life they knew.

On June 4, 1792, the British explorer Captain George Vancouver made Puget Sound a birthday present for his King. Nothing could have been more fitting on George III's fifty-fourth birthday than to take possession for Great Britain of "the most lovely country that can be imagined."[1]

On a sunny morning, half way into their two-month stay in Puget Sound, Vancouver and crew rowed ashore near what is now Everett, Washington. Officers with now familiar names like Peter Puget, Joseph Whidbey, and Joseph Baker dined on fish and toasted the King's health with a double allowance of grog for the entire crew. After lunch, with curious natives watching from a safe distance in canoes, Vancouver's ship *Discovery* fired off a twenty-one-gun salute, formally taking possession of the Sound and surrounding territory.[2] It may or may not have troubled Vancouver to know his act of possession would not likely stand up under international law, as Spain had claimed much of the same territory 17 years earlier.[3]

The possession ceremony marks a critical moment in early Pacific Northwest history. It illustrates how European nations engaged in fierce competition to control a region rich in resources and ripe for trade. It also signaled something far more monumental for Native Peoples who may have suspected the cannons sounded the beginning of the end of the life they knew.

Excursions into the North Pacific represent the last chapter in a 300-year story of North American exploration beginning with Christopher Columbus in 1492. Due to its remoteness, nearly three centuries passed before European explorers ventured into the region. The Dutch sailor Vitus Bering, sailing for Russia, explored the Bering Straits in 1728 and the waters off Alaska in 1741, but made no serious stabs south.[4] Spanish

Contested Boundaries: A New Pacific Northwest History, First Edition. David J. Jepsen and David J. Norberg.
© 2017 John Wiley & Sons, Ltd. Published 2017 by John Wiley & Sons, Ltd.

Figure 1.1 This illustration of Mt. Rainier at Admiralty Inlet on Puget Sound was sketched in 1792 by Midshipman John Sykes, not a trained artist, and likely redrawn by a professional artist for publication in in the 1798 Atlas to George Vancouver's Voyages. Reprinted with permission from the Washington State Historical Society.

explorers could claim the deepest history in the region, when Juan José Pérez Hernández explored the coastline in 1774 and traded with Native Peoples. The following year, Bruno de Heceta and Juan Francisco de la Bodega y Quadra explored and claimed it for the King of Spain.[5]

Between 1778 and 1794, Great Britain sent dozens of ships to the North Pacific mostly to trade for furs.[6] The most notable was the third voyage of James Cook from 1776 to 1780. In search of the fabled Northwest Passage, a navigable route across the continent, Cook explored much of the North American coast from what's now Oregon to Alaska and the Bering Straits. At Nootka Sound, the party acquired a supply of sea otter pelts, igniting a global fur trade that Cook would not live to see. After failing to find the Northwest Passage, Cook headed west to explore what are now known as the Hawaiian Islands, where he died in an altercation with natives. Under the command of Captain Charles Clerke, the party first returned to the Bering Strait to continue the search for the Northwest Passage. Failing to find the passage and with northern seas blocked by ice, the expedition sailed south to Canton, China. To everyone's surprise, Chinese merchants paid a fortune for the pelts. Profits were so high, the crew threatened mutiny in order to return to Nootka to acquire more. According to Historian Carlos Schwantes, this rags-to-riches story triggered a steady flow of traders to the region for a generation and "ended the previous pattern of sporadic and haphazard European contact with the Pacific Northwest and its native peoples."[7]

Great Britain and Spain soon butted heads over competing claims at Nootka Sound on Vancouver Island. Fearing a plot to take the island, Spain's Don Esteban José Martínez seized a British fur-trading vessel in 1789, arrested its captain and men and sent them to Mexico City for prosecution.

Spanish actions stirred British passions and almost led to war between the two powerful navies. The countries avoided war, however, after they signed the Nootka Sound Convention in 1790, which limited Spain's territorial possessions, compensated England for damages at Nootka and secured free trade along the Northwest Coast. More important, the convention formalized the possession-taking practice. For centuries explorers seeking possession of territory simply rowed ashore, planted a cross, prayed and buried a bottle containing a written record of the event. Under the Nootka convention, the right of possession now required more documentation, including a published record of the journey, mapping the region and evidence of contact with Native Peoples.[8]

The United States, busy fighting for independence from Great Britain, could only stand by as other countries squabbled over portions of the North American Continent. But with independence achieved, it didn't take long for the fledging country to catch up. Between 1788 and 1814, American vessels repeatedly plowed Northern Pacific waters in search of fur and other goods. Trader Robert Gray sailed into the region twice, first in 1788 and again in 1792. On the second voyage, he netted something far more valuable than otter skins. Gray located and braved the treacherous passage into the Columbia River, the first non-native to do so, helping the United States to lay claim to the waterway and eventually the region itself.

Ships logs tell of a clash of cultures

Excursions via the seas tell only half the story of American intentions. President Thomas Jefferson, after completing the Louisiana Purchase in 1803, wanted to learn more about the interior and western end of North America, as well as establish a foothold there. In 1804, he sent Meriwether Lewis, William Clark and the Corps of Discovery on a two-and-half-year journey across the continent and back to explore, trade and search for the Northwest Passage.

By 1818, America had sufficiently strengthened its claims to the future Oregon Territory to begin to gradually take political control. But putting American ambitions aside, let's focus on a more human story about two cultures – Euro-American and Native American – meeting for the first time. Men hungry for trade and eager to pursue nationalistic goals made assumptions about entitlement to the land, held biases about Native Peoples, and believed unquestionably in the superiority of "civilized" society. Native cultures consisted of a multiplicity of peoples whose geographic isolation insulated them from a rapidly industrializing world of trade and commerce.

We learn about these first encounters from logbooks and the journals explorers and traders kept as part of their jobs. While useful, they should be viewed with a critical eye, because they're the only written record of early encounters. Vancouver made daily entries in his ship's log, recording his observations about the landscape and Native Peoples. So too did several of his officers, especially Lieutenant Peter Puget, ship's surgeon, naturalist Archibald Menzies, and William R. Broughton, commander of the *Chatham*, the *Discovery's* armed consort. Traveling by land from the East, Lewis and

Clark, too recorded their dealings with Native tribes living along the Missouri, Snake, Yellowstone, and Columbia rivers. Collectively they paint a vivid and surprising, yet agonizingly incomplete, picture of the interactions between people from drastically different cultures.

> The skill Native People displayed in trade with Europeans and Americans "was sufficient to tire the patience of any man."[9]

Early encounters on the North Pacific Coast were generally peaceful, because both visitors and many, but not all Native People quickly realized they needed each other. Following the initial shock of the intrusion, events quickly turned to business. The traders needed Native People to trap the prized otter and other animals, a skill-set far beyond most explorers and traders. Conversely, Native People accommodated foreign visitors, often reluctantly, in hopes of accessing a steady flow of their tools, weapons, and other industrialized goods. It was a mutually beneficial relationship.

Later exchanges note that although Native People eagerly engaged in trade, we can forget stereotypical notions about greedy white men taking advantage. Granted, some were initially dazzled by tools like chisels, axes, and knives. Many delighted in and wore colorful European cloth and jewelry, and evidence suggests that others yearned for the power of manufactured weapons for protection against aggressive neighbors. But barter and trade had dominated Native life for centuries. Tribal leaders often drove hard bargains at steep prices. As one crewman aboard the American ship *Columbia* put it, Native People's intransience in trade "was sufficient to tire the patience of any man."[10] (to read more about the fur trade era see Chapter 2, "Trade Among Equals")

Another misconception is that Europeans and Americans entered a pristine land unsoiled by human hands. While no Europeans had previously ventured into Puget Sound, for example, the invisible microbes they carried had. European diseases for which Native Peoples held no immunity devastated large swaths of Native society following the arrival of Spanish and English explorers in the 1770s and 1780s. A smallpox epidemic in 1780–1782 wiped out an estimated 30% of coastal peoples and eventually spread throughout the region. Over 50 years, disease could take up to 90% of a Native population. As Vancouver explored the shores of Puget Sound he met many Native People with pocked faces, walked on beaches littered with skulls, and rowed by large abandoned villages. He strongly suspected smallpox, a disease, which Vancouver wrote, "there is great reason to believe is very fatal to them."[11]

British pursue "every branch" of Puget Sound

The two ships under Vancouver's command, the *Discovery* and *Chatham*, sailed from Falmouth, England, on April 1, 1791, with three tasks: explore the Pacific Coast of South and North America, search for the Northwest Passage, and meet with Spanish officials to implement the recently agreed to Nootka Sound Convention. On April 29, 1792, the *Discovery* and *Chatham* entered the Strait of Juan De Fuca "in very thick rainy weather."[12] A week later, Vancouver set up a base camp in a protected bay just west of present-day Port Townsend. He named it Discovery Bay after his ship.[13] The *Discovery* dropped anchor several times over the next two months, mostly in the North Sound.

What's in a name?

The practice of naming Pacific Northwest places went hand in hand with the European sense of entitlement to "possess" much of the region. The British Captain George Vancouver christened the area surrounding much of North Puget Sound and San Juan Islands "New Georgia" after King George III, one of the few names that didn't stick. Among the approximate two hundred names Vancouver assigned to local places, he named mountains and large bodies of water after friends or fellow naval officers, including Rear Admiral Peter Rainier (Mt. Rainier); the "Right Honorable" Lord Hood (Hood Canal); the Marquess Townshend (Port Townsend); and James Vashon (Vashon Island). Some names recognized accomplishments of his officers: Third Lieutenant Joseph Baker, who first spotted the snowy peak easily visible in the north; Joseph Whidbey, who circumnavigated the Sound's largest island; the ship's clerk, Harry Masterman Orchard (Port Orchard); and, of course Peter Puget, who rowed and charted much of the South Sound.

At each anchorage, Vancouver dispatched boats, under the various commands of Puget, Baker and Lieutenant James Johnstone, to pursue the "termination of every branch no matter how small it might appear."[14] Each boat held six to eight oarsmen. Armed and provisioned with enough supplies and food to last several days, the seamen charted the Sound and surrounding land. Using drop-lines to measure water depth, celestial observations to pinpoint latitude, and a chronometer to measure longitude, they charted hundreds of canals and inlets with impressive accuracy. Persistent northerly winds often made rowing "exceeding laborious" and progress slow.[15]

The moderate climate and scenic beauty immediately impressed the men. Ship's doctor Menzies quickly noticed how the mountain range to the west (later named the Olympics) protected the Sound from "those destructive Gales which drive their furious course along the exterior edge of the Coast." One log entry after another commented on the "enchanting variety" of the surrounding scenery, or the "interesting and picturesque prospect on every side." The climate was "exceeding favorable" in so "high a latitude."[16] The many mountain peaks also captivated Menzies, especially the tallest one to the southeast (Rainier) that "swelled out very gradually to form a most beautiful & majestic Mountain of great elevation ..."[17]

Contact with Native Peoples occurred almost daily. Near the Strait, in northern waters frequently visited by European ships over the previous five years, Native People showed little fear of the British visitors. Some rowed right up to the ships or longboats and exchanged fish or skins for "buttons and trinkets."[18] After the sailors made camp, natives occasionally approached, laid down their bows and arrows, and sat peacefully a few yards away. They'd engage in light trade and then leave, sometimes bedding down on an opposite shore, but within sight of the British.[19]

British approaching Native People in the South Sound required more diplomacy. In mid-May, a seaman saw two beached canoes and rowed to shore. Suddenly four men ran from the woods armed with spears, their gestures and body language vigorously warning the intruders away. They rejected proffered gifts and "spoke loud to us in a guttural kind of lingo and used threatening gestures" to discourage the men from advancing. In a demonstration of restraint, the sailors backed off. "Poor souls," Manby wrote later. "It would have been cruel so soon to commence hostilities, therefore we left them in hopes time would make us better friends …"[20]

Native People in dugout canoes sent similar messages a few days later in Carr Inlet. Three men approached the longboats, but instead of accepting trinkets, they made "menacing signs [they] wanted us to return back the way we came & treated with contempt the alluring presents we held up to them," Manby wrote. Not discouraged, the British tied some copper and buttons to driftwood, left it floating in the water and rowed a short distance away. When the men felt safe, they rowed forward and retrieved the floating gifts. They repeated this water dance twice before the Native men pulled alongside the British and engaged in trade.[21]

The land of the "Poo Poo" men

As George Vancouver's expedition explored Puget Sound in large rowboats in spring 1792, encounters with Native Peoples sometimes turned humorous. On one occasion, as a group of Native People watched the explorers row by, one man stood, pointed north, and repeatedly chanted "Poo poo! Poo poo!" What was he saying? Turn around? Leave this place? Archibald Menzies, ship's surgeon and naturalist, could only shake his head in puzzlement. Eventually, he concluded the insistent man was referring to reports from British hunting rifles or cannons on the ship *Chatham* earlier in the week. It amused him to think, the British were forever to be known to the local people as the "Poo Poo" men. (Richard W. Blumenthal, ed. With Vancouver in Inland Washington Waters, Journals of 12 Crewmen, April–June 1792, 74)

"Mean huts and wretched sheds" greet explorers

About 6 miles south, the explorers entered their first Indian village. As they pulled ashore, the inhabitants ran into the woods "shrieking loud and their dogs yelling to a very great degree." Several huts surrounded a large fire pit. Enclosed on three sides, the huts consisted of "broad planks resting on rafters." Salmon hung on wooden drying racks. Eventually a few elderly men ventured out. Using gestures, the visitors offered pieces of copper and brass bracelets in exchange for salmon and clams, brightening the mood. Native People showed keen interest in British clothing, especially their boots. Soon the visitors enticed the remaining villagers into the open. Most of the men were naked. Women wearing deer and bearskin around their waist and shoulders stayed near their huts, "glittering shells" hanging from pierced ears. To Manby's disappointment, "few of them possessed very engaging features."[22]

During their two-month stay in Puget Sound, the English visited several villages ranging from four or five families to twenty-five or more. Menzies' impression likely reflects the attitudes of the crew. On one hand they admired the quality of the Native craft work, mostly colorful mats and baskets woven from reeds and "perfectly watertight."[23] Yet Manby described their dwellings as "mean huts," and "wretched sheds." He chastised the village men for "lolling about in sluggish idleness," while women busied themselves hanging salmon or weaving.[24]

Vancouver's men, of course, coveted the women, who Puget described as "decently covered, but not distinguishable by any effeminacy or softness of Features." They wore seashell earrings, and strung shells around their necks, wrists, and ankles. Their long, dark hair, often festooned with "Down of Birds," was "Black & filthy as the men's."[25]

Puget's opinion notwithstanding, his crew found the women sufficiently attractive to solicit "their favors." The women refused, according to Puget, "for want of more Secret Opportunity." The men did not appear "at all jealous of the Liberties taken with their women," Puget concluded.[26]

While Puget praised their "honesty" in trade, and "friendly and inoffensive" behavior, it's clear he looked down upon the "uncivilized" nature of village life. Like nearly all Europeans who ventured to the Americas over the three previous centuries, Puget judged Native Peoples by European standards. The "wretched sheds" could not compare to dwellings in London; the women were unattractive when matched with standards of European effeminacy. When Menzies criticized the men for "sluggish idleness," he did not appreciate the division of labor critical to surviving in a subsistence culture.

More than one encounter turned tense with little warning. On May 22 near McNeil Island, men in six or more canoes approached the British camp, bows at the ready, no women among them. Prepared for potential hostilities, the crewmen armed their muskets, several moving for cover behind trees. As the armed Native People walked ashore, one of the British drew a line in the sand, and with hand gestures, made it abundantly clear they must not cross it. Message received, they returned to their canoes and huddled, apparently arguing among themselves and pointing back at the British. A wary Puget "absolutely felt at a loss how to act." He had heard of the incident involving the *Imperial Eagle* five years earlier, when Hoh or Quinault people killed six crewmen. To discourage the Native People from "committing such atrocious action," Puget decided a little demonstration of power was in order, and ordered a crew member to fire the swivel, a small canon mounted on one of the longboats.[27]

The standoff ended peacefully with trade, including their bows and arrows. "By this means," wrote Menzies, "we disarmd them in a more satisfactory manner."[28] Puget, who had nearly ordered his men to open fire, expressed relief for the nonviolent ending, otherwise he feared "it would have proved fatal to their whole Party …"[29]

Understanding European misconceptions

The above incident is telling. First, the fact the Native People argued amongst themselves after the British warned them off, suggests disagreement over how to deal with the strangers. It's reasonable to conclude they weighed the promise of more European goods against the risk of accommodating the newcomers. Conversely, the explorers also seemed conflicted. While prepared for the worst, they silently hoped for the best. Like the incident with the unfriendly Native People a few days earlier, patience and restraint proved the better part of valor.

Later in May, while exploring south of present-day Port Townsend, the sight of human skulls mounted on long poles near the beach shocked Puget's crew. Puget's explanation for this "truly horrid" site illustrates the Europeans' biases and misconceptions about indigenous peoples. In England, skulls of criminals executed for "very capital offenses" were sometimes displayed in public to "deter others from falling into the same Snare." But Puget attributed the practice not to criminal justice, but to "the Barbarity of the Manners and Customs of the Indians."[30] Later, they found human remains in canoes suspended in a tree. Inside were bows and arrows, fishing implements, and clams on sticks. Puget concluded the site represented a form of human sacrifice, perhaps even cannibalism.[31] Vancouver, a more experienced sailor who'd accompanied James Cook on two voyages to the Pacific, speculated the skeletons "were probably the chiefs, priests, or leaders of particular tribes, whose followers most likely continue to possess the highest respect for their memory and remains …" When leaving the site, Vancouver took care to "prevent any indignity" to the burial site."[32]

Vancouver was close. The burial sites tell us much about Native People's belief in an afterlife – a connection between the physical world and spiritual one. Native People treated death as a "journey rather than as a final destination," and supplied the dead, especially tribal leaders, with items needed along the way. While Western societies consider the deceased "dead and gone," according to anthropologist Kathryn McKay, Native People assumed they held a responsibility to care for the dead.[33]

> Enthralled by Puget Sound's natural beauty, George Vancouver nevertheless felt it would be "enriched by the industry of men, with villages, mansions, cottages and other buildings."[34]

To explain British misconceptions, it's important to realize three centuries of contact with Native Peoples colored the attitudes of British explorers. Most explorers studied their predecessors, going back to Columbus. Vancouver, an accomplished seaman who'd initiated contact with Native Peoples throughout the Pacific, held attitudes consistent with the day. Historian Gary B. Nash, writing about European attitudes regarding Native Peoples in the Southern colonies of North America, said colonization and possession taking were "external expressions of goodwill and explanations of mutual benefits" of trade that masked a deep-rooted fear and anticipation of violence.[35] European encounters with Native Peoples around the world often resulted in bloodshed, so the relative absence of violence in Puget Sound likely surprised the explorers. Nevertheless, the line-in-the-sand scene near Indian Island offers evidence of a self-fulfilling prophecy. They expected violence, prepared for it, and almost got it.

Imagining Native Peoples as hostile savages simplified everything for the explorers. It allowed them to predict the future and prepare for it, writes Nash.[36] Also the act of taking possession of land reflects European attitudes regarding the humanity of Native People. Godless savages missed their opportunity to improve on the land and thereby forfeited any right to it, which entitled the British to take possession.[37] To Vancouver, the natural beauty of Puget Sound required only to be "enriched by the industry of men, with villages, mansions, cottages and other buildings, to render it the most lovely country that can be imagined …"[38]

This sense of entitlement helps to explain the European practice of naming geographical places like mountains, islands, and waterways. Not the least curious about what Native People called things, Vancouver assigned names to more than 200 geographic places on the North Pacific Coast.[39]

Robert Gray braves entrance to Columbia River

While Vancouver probed Puget Sound in May 1792, American sea captain Robert Gray sailed south along the Washington Coast in search of the entrance to the "Great River of the West," an achievement that eluded Spanish and British explorers for years.[40] When he approached the river's entrance, Gray was on his second voyage to the Pacific, and had been at sea for nearly five years. Unlike Vancouver's government-sponsored voyage, Gray's journey enjoyed the backing of private sponsors eager to enter the lucrative fur trade. On their first voyage from 1787 to 1790, Gray commanded the *Lady Washington* and John Kendrick the *Columbia Rediviva.* They held what Historian Gordon Speck called "worthless junk and trinkets which cost the merchants virtually nothing but were supposed to return big dividends."[41]

The two ships arrived in the North Pacific in September 1788, engaging in trade tabbed as a "polite form of robbery."[42] That may be so, but one man's worthless trinket is another man's prize, as Vancouver demonstrated in Puget Sound. Gray found the fur trade hard going as they moved from cove to cove, purchasing furs in small batches.[43]

Where Vancouver exercised restraint with Native Peoples, Gray exhibited a short-temper and suspicion. In August, near Tillamook Bay, armed natives greeted a landing party as they rowed ashore for fresh water. Business went smoothly at first until a Tillamook "made off with" a crew member's cutlass. When Gray's demands for its return went unheeded, the argument turned violent, leaving three Tillamook and one crewman dead.[44]

In the spring of 1789, the two captains exchanged ships, Gray commanding the *Columbia* and Kendrick the *Lady Washington.* Kendrick continued to explore northern waters, while Gray headed for Canton, China, to reap the rewards of his

Figure 1.2 The American ship *Columbia* (foreground), under the command of Captain Robert Gray, encounters the British ships *Discovery* and *Chatham* under George Vancouver's command. Gray and Vancouver met April 29, 1792, and discussed the search for the illusive entrance to the "Great Oregon River," later named the Columbia. Reprinted with permission from the Washington State Historical Society.

harvest. But instead of eager buyers like those who had enriched the English and ignited the fur trade, Gray found a glutted market and depressed prices. He did the best he could, trading furs for tea.

Despite the meager returns, the Boston investors funded a second voyage, and six weeks after having returned to Boston, Gray embarked on a return voyage to the Pacific Northwest.[45] This time Gray carried a letter signed by President George Washington stating the two ships were property of United States citizens and that he hoped Gray would "prosper in all his lawful affairs … and should be treated in a 'becoming manner'."[46]

Things didn't go much better for Native People on the second voyage. In response to rumors about a possible Nootka attack, Gray ordered the destruction of deserted dwellings on Vancouver Island in April 1792. Over the next several months, trade negotiations twice turned violent when Gray felt slighted or cheated. In May, north of Nootka Sound Gray's men killed seven Native People and stole their furs.[47]

Few incidences are more telling than the one involving Otto, a Hawaiian Islands boy who was either bought or stolen during the first voyage to China. On June 15 near Nootka, according to the log kept by crewman John Hoskins, Otto attempted to "desert," seeking refuge with a local chief Tootiscootsettle. When Gray discovered the boy missing, he invited the chief to his cabin "under false pretenses," and threatened to take him to sea unless he returned Otto immediately. With few options, the hapless chief gave up the boy. Gray ordered Otto flogged, forced Tootiscootsettle to watch, and promised to flog anyone who aided future deserters.[48]

Gray left a rough wake along much of the northern coast, but he would have likely been little remembered were it not for his pursuit of the Columbia River. How Vancouver and others previously missed the entrance seems mysterious given the presence of multiple clues: drifting logs, discolored water, feeding gulls, and a slew of cross currents. Historian Gordon Speck suggests Vancouver's pride cost the British possible possession of the region. Due to stubbornness, "he threw away what might have clinched England's claim to all of Old Oregon."[49]

Gray would miss no such clues. On May 11, relying on information provided by natives, the *Columbia* waited near the suspected entrance. Early in the morning, a crew dispatched in a sailboat to search for a clear passage reported that they found a way in. Negotiating some of the roughest waters in North America, the *Columbia* bore in "east-northeast, between the breakers" in about 50 feet of water. After crossing the bar, they entered a wide-open bay about a mile wide, villages lining both shores, and soon "vast numbers of natives came alongside."[50]

As Gray's men explored upriver, they took stock of "one of most heavily populated and richest areas north of Mexico."[51] Large villages dotted both banks, but unlike the "mean huts" Vancouver's crew described on Puget Sound, the river dwellers lived in longhouses made of large cedar planks. When one of Gray's crew asked a man the name of his village, he heard something that sounded like "Chinook." As so often happens in history, a simple remark takes on complex meaning. The entire region and all its peoples would ultimately be known as Chinook.[52]

Later reports offer no evidence of the violence that plagued Gray earlier. The traders ventured upriver for about 13 miles, turning around only after being temporarily grounded in shallow water. Further exploration proved the waterway too treacherous for the 83-foot *Columbia*. On May 19, Gray claimed the river for the United States, named it after his ship, and two days later returned to open waters. There are few written details about the claiming ritual. It's reasonable to suggest Gray may have lost interest in the river once he realized the limited trading opportunities. Nevertheless, his persistence helped to position America in competition for control of the Oregon Territory.

Lewis and Clark arrive by land, 1804 to 1806

Meriwether Lewis, William Clark and the Corps of Discovery entered the Pacific Northwest when they crossed the Continental Divide in August 1805. When they ascended Lemhi Pass in the Rocky Mountains, near the current Montana-Idaho border, the expedition had been on the trail for sixteen months. An exhausted Lewis hoped the summit offered grand views of the Columbia River, the known waterway to the Pacific Ocean. But when he and a small advance party summited, the view offered neither river nor ocean. Instead the landscape stretched hundreds of miles in all directions, blocked only by "immence [*sic*]ranges of high mountains still to the West of us," the snow-covered Bitterroots.[53]

After experiencing arguably the biggest surprise of his life, Lewis faced what one historian called the "geography of reality."[54] Instead of a one or two-day jaunt down the Rockies to the Columbia River, the party now faced several more weeks or months on the trail, a sobering welcome to the Pacific Northwest.

> "In all your intercourse with the natives … treat them in the most friendly & conciliatory manner which their own conduct will admit."
> – *Thomas Jefferson's instructions to Meriwether Lewis.*[55]

Like George Vancouver 13 years earlier, Lewis entered the region under the auspices of his government. The mission was the inspiration of Thomas Jefferson, third president, keenly interested in the promise of the interior of the North American continent and the Pacific Coast. Yet his vision would likely not come to pass as long as Louisiana, the massive region between the Mississippi River and the Rocky Mountains, belonged to France. The purchase of the territory for $15 million in 1803 set the stage for exploration.

Louisiana – a bargain at any price

Exploration and trade opportunities in new territories – especially in the Pacific Northwest – remained limited as long as Louisiana, the vast territory between the Mississippi River and the Rocky Mountains, belonged to a foreign power, in this case France.

In 1802, Jefferson dispatched James Monroe and the diplomat Robert R. Livingston to Paris to negotiate with France for the sale of New Orleans, the delta of the Mississippi River and critical to U.S. trade. To everyone's surprise, French diplomats offered to sell a much bigger hunk of real estate – massive Louisiana which stretched from modern-day New Orleans to northwestern Montana. A delighted Monroe agreed to purchase the 828,000-square-mile territory for $15 million, or four-cents per acre, more than doubling the country's size, and clearing the way for exploration of the American West.

Figure 1.3 Encounters between the Corps of Discovery and Native Peoples often involved a cultural exchange. In this Roger Cooke painting, Corps member Private Pierre Cruzatte plays the fiddle while others dance, much to the entertainment of their hosts. Reprinted with permission from the Washington State Historical Society.

Jefferson selected Lewis, his thirty-year-old secretary, to head up the expedition, who then picked Clark as co-captain. Jefferson's written instructions outlined multiple goals for the expedition. Finding "the most direct & practicable water communication across this continent, for the purposes of commerce," the infamous Northwest Passage, topped the list. Additionally, he wanted Lewis to map the Missouri and other rivers with "great pains & accuracy," as well as record information about the climate, flora, fauna, and minerals.[56]

Above all, Jefferson sought hard information on the "people inhabiting the line you will pursue," including the names and sizes of their "nations," their languages, relations with other tribes, traditions and occupations. "In all your intercourse with the natives," Jefferson cautioned, "treat them in the most friendly & conciliatory manner which their own conduct will admit." In other words avoid hostilities unless a Native struck first.[57]

The Corps of Discovery departed from near St. Louis in May 1804, traveling up the Missouri in three vessels; a versatile 55-foot keelboat and two wooden row boats called pirogues. In addition to the leaders, the permanent party included thirty men and officers, interpreters, and Clark's slave, York, as well as Lewis's Newfoundland dog, Seaman. Several soldiers and boatmen accompanied the party as far as the Mandan Village in

North Dakota. The boats carried sufficient supplies to last two years or more, as well as merchandise Lewis intended to either present as gifts or trade for Indian goods or services. The list reads like an inventory of a modern variety store: glass beads, scissors, knives, combs, clothing, kettles, mirrors, tobacco and whiskey.[58]

Traveling up river was slow and laborious and not without danger. Four or five men on each side of the keelboat planted long poles in the river bottom, and literally pushed it against the current. Headed north by northwest, they moved up the Missouri through the current states of Kansas, Nebraska, South Dakota and North Dakota. They spent the winter of 1804–1805 with the Mandan in central North Dakota, who like most Native Peoples on the plains boasted deep experience doing business with Europeans, mostly French traders.[59]

While camped at the Mandan village, Lewis and Clark met Toussaint Charbonneau, a forty-five-year-old Canadian trader, and his fifteen-year-old wife Sacagawea, six months pregnant. Charbonneau, who spoke French and Hidatsa, and Sacagawea, was versant in Hidatsa and Shoshone, joined the Corps as interpreters.

In early April 1805, the Corps eagerly prepared to head west. "We were now about to penetrate a country at least two thousand miles in width, on which the foot of civilized man had never trodden," Lewis wrote.[60] Lewis overstated the case, yet it exemplifies the perception of someone set to enter a vast unknown land.

With the unwieldy keelboat returned to St. Louis, the Corps pulled up the Missouri in six dugout canoes and the two flat-bottom pirogues. It proved slow going until they reached the continental divide and the headwaters of the Missouri at the summit of the Rocky Mountains. From there, all rivers drained down to the Columbia and on to the Pacific. The party snaked their way west through North Dakota and Montana towards the Missouri headwaters.[61] Near the foothills of the Rockies, they faced their most arduous obstacle to date – the Great Falls of the Missouri, a series of five cascading waterfalls stretching for 18 miles upriver. Lewis called it a "sublimly grand spectacle [*sic*]." Ranging from 14 to 50 feet high, and impossible to negotiate in a boat, it forced the crew to construct a crude "truck" out of cottonwood to transport their boats and supplies up the falls.[62]

Meeting with Shoshone turns tense

Lewis and a small party advanced up Lemhi Pass to the summit as the main Corps toiled up the mountains. Given the historical record about the trying weeks ascending the Missouri Falls and Rockies, it's reasonable to conclude that Lewis was more than a little shocked and disappointed when he learned the Columbia was still an unknown distance away – perhaps weeks even months. But the captain could not afford to brood. Reaching the Columbia and the Pacific were unattainable goals without help. Lewis hoped Shoshone living west of the Rockies would provide the horses needed to cross the interior basin and the Bitterroots.

On August 13, Lewis spotted two women, a man and several dogs. They were Shoshone likely gathering berries or roots. Thus began one of the most poignant yet intense encounters of Lewis's odyssey. He immediately set down his gun and pack, unfurled a large American flag, and slowly approached, repeating the words "tab-ba-bone," which Lewis believed meant "white man." Uncertain and afraid, the natives fled. Undeterred, Lewis managed to woo one of the dogs, placed some trinkets and beads in a handkerchief and attempted to tie it around the dog's neck, but it skittered back to its owners. The party followed the trail and soon came across an elderly woman and a girl about twelve years old sitting on the ground, their heads lowered, as if they were "reconciled to die ..."[63]

This is Lewis the diplomat at his best. Desperate to belay their fears, he put down his gun as he advanced, took the elderly woman's hand and helped her to her feet. "Tab-ba-bone," he repeated, "tab-ba-bone." He then pulled up the sleeve of his buckskin and pointed at his white skin. "Tab-ba-bone," he said again, and handed the woman a few beads and other gifts. As the woman appeared to relax, Lewis dabbed vermilion, orange face paint, on her "tawny cheeks," which Sacajawea told him was a Shoshone sign of peace. Using sign language, he then asked her to lead him to her chief.[64]

The group advanced about 2 miles when they saw "a party of about sixty mounted and armed warriors" gallop up to the group.[65] Again, Lewis ordered the party to halt, left his gun behind and approached the apparent leader. The elderly woman spoke excitedly to the chief named Cameahwait and showed him the gifts. This was a critical moment, one Lewis had been anticipating for months. All his goals were now agonizingly close. The man before him possessed everything the expedition needed: food, horses, intelligence about the route to the Columbia; and the manpower to help with the portage. Yet, the Shoshone outnumbered the Americans fifteen to one and could easily have overwhelmed them. The Shoshone war party, the women, and the Americans all likely held their collective breath as Cameahwait approached, placed his hand on Lewis's shoulder and said "ah-hi-e, ah-hi-e," (I am much pleased, I am much rejoiced).[66]

A much relieved Lewis gave the chief an American flag, which he said "was an emblem of peace among white men" and a "bond of union between us." He then distributed gifts to the other chiefs and invited everyone to sit and smoke. Later they hiked to the Shoshone village where they smoked again, ate and danced well into the night (evidence of the significance the Shoshone placed on the Americans, who some believed were "children of the great spirit)."[67]

The success of this encounter provides evidence of the degree to which the Americans and Native People of the interior needed and valued each other. Unlike the sea captains, who could simply return to their ship after brief stays in a village, Lewis was deep in the wilderness, running out of food, lacking means to advance his party and operating in unfamiliar terrain. It's reasonable to argue that without Native assistance, the mission would have failed.[68]

Cameahwait likewise saw in Lewis an opportunity to improve conditions for his people. Native Peoples living in the interior of the Pacific Northwest, including the Shoshone's western neighbors the Nez Perce, survived through hunting, fishing and gathering. Though devastated by the same smallpox epidemic that plagued coastal tribes in the 1780s, the interior tribes thrived on the abundant resources of the region. In summer and fall, they rode east to hunt bison. Living in a nether land between the Pacific Coast and Great Plains, interior tribes had tasted but not dined on the wonders of the industrialized world. At trade fairs and during hunting excursions, they saw how other tribes had reaped the benefits of trading with white men, yet so far, they mostly eluded interior tribes.

Thomas Jefferson and the "empire of liberty"

Among the American leaders who never set foot in the Pacific Northwest, few impacted the region more than America's third president, Thomas Jefferson.

The West fascinated the expansion-minded Jefferson, who believed the country's future lay west of the Appalachians and even beyond the Mississippi River. The settlement of the West – what he called an "empire of liberty," fit nicely with his Republican vision of a population of yeoman farmers living off God's bounty. These attitudes as much as anything prompted Jefferson to accept France's offer to purchase Louisiana and then deploy Lewis and Clark on the Corps of Discovery (Gordon S Wood, *Empire of Liberty: A History of the Early Republic, 1789–1815* (New York: Oxford University Press, 2009), 257–258.)

Importantly, he believed in the possibility of a peaceful coexistence between Euro-Americans and Native Peoples, providing they gave up their "savage" ways and accepted a "civilized" lifestyle, an ominous sign for future native relations (James P Ronda, *Lewis & Clark Among the Indians* (Lincoln, NE: University of Nebraska Press, 1984), 4).

Historian Elliott West argues European trade upset the balance of power among tribes. By the end of the eighteenth century, tribes on the Great Plains like the Blackfeet, Crow, Sioux and Hidatsa acquired guns from Canadian traders, allowing them to expand their territory to the west and prevail in competition for game. Conversely, coastal tribes like the Chinook acquired through the fur trade luxuries like metal tools and clothing.

In a recent account that examines the Lewis and Clark journey from the Native perspective, the primary motivation for cooperation with Lewis and Clark was access to guns "that kill at a great distance … Our enemies to the east and north have [guns] in great numbers and we don't."[69]

Yet in their quest for weapons, interior tribes held a critical bargaining chip – horses. The Shoshone, Nez Perce, and other interior tribes acquired horses from tribes in the Southwest during the first three decades of the eighteenth century, dramatically changing their lifestyle, increasing their mobility and improving their effectiveness on the hunt or in war.

The historian James P. Ronda argues confusion prevailed in most trade negotiations. First, any translation requiring three or four people and three languages, as well as hand signing, was bound to muddle transaction. Take the word "tab-ba-bone" for example. Lewis understood it to mean "Whiteman," yet it more closely translated to "stranger or foreigner."[70]

Second, the nature of the expedition must have puzzled the chiefs. Lewis wasn't carrying guns or other goods for trade. They were on an "advanced mission," paving the way for future trade. Any real return for assisting the explorers would be at least two or more years away. Moreover, the promise of future trade came with strings attached. In one speech after another, Lewis declared that access to a steady supply of American products required warring tribes to make peace. Conflicts between the Shoshone and Blackfeet, for example, or between the Nez Perce and Chinooken, must stop. Trying to influence what Ronda called a "tangled web of band factional politics" must have struck the chiefs as unrealistic at best or even laughable.[71] "Lewis and Clark simply did not understand the nature of tribal and band politics."[72]

In late August, the expedition headed west on the "cruel and unforgiving" Lolo trail over the Bitterroots, a trek made possible only with Shoshone guides and horses.[73] They spent nearly two weeks with the Nez Perce, who helped them build five canoes in ten days for the water route ahead. The men's axes were too small to dig out logs, so the Nez Perce showed them how to burn out a log's center.

With the guidance of two Nez Perce chiefs, the party worked its way down the Clearwater and Snake rivers towards the Columbia. As the explorers approached what came to be known as the Pacific-Plateau trade network near the Dalles in present-day Oregon, contact with Native People increased dramatically. For centuries, trading took place throughout summer and fall. The Yakima, Tenino, Umatilla, Walula, Nez Perce and others traded meat, fish, roots, berries and a growing variety of western goods. At one village, Clark saw thousands of pounds of salmon hanging from racks, dried and readied for trade.[74] Lewis predicted the end of easy terms he found on the plains. Tribes along the lower Columbia familiar with trade with outsiders drove hard bargains.

Most Columbia River tribes appeared welcoming. One evening, a delegation of about two hundred Wanapams, who lived near the confluence of the Snake and Columbia rivers, approached the expedition's camp, singing and dancing to the beat of drums, a traditional opening to trade discussions.[75]

Other encounters struck a less friendly tone. The people in one Umatilla village eyed the newcomers with suspicion and fear. At one point, Clark entered a mat lodge uninvited to see several families huddled in the back. Clark sat down, lit his pipe and passed it around. Soon the villagers relaxed and accepted Clark's gifts. This event seems puzzling at first. Clearly by this point, most Native Peoples had heard of white men. Hearing about the possible presence of some strange creature is one thing, but it's something else entirely when one barges unannounced into your home. Later Sacagawea told Clark the Native People believed he was a god.[76]

> In the winter of 1805–1806, which the Corps of Discovery spent on the Pacific Coast, William Clark counted only "twelve days without rain and only six with sunshine."[77]

With the Pacific Ocean agonizingly close, the explorers spent little time with the tribes along the Columbia. By this time Native People from countless villages crowded the shores, watching the Americans paddle rapidly down river. Occasionally they'd stop to trade for dog or dried fish during brief and often chaotic encounters. Lewis offered medals or other trinkets and gave an abbreviated version of his speech. Private Pierre Cruzatte then played his fiddle while the men danced, and then they'd return to the canoes and paddle away. Given the lack of any translator, Sacagawea did not speak Salish, it's impossible to tell what locals thought of this flotilla of curious aliens. It must have seemed bizarre indeed.[78]

On November 7, 1805, Clark wrote his famous declaration, "Ocian in view O! the joy."[79] A month later he carved his name in a pine tree to record his arrival to the Pacific: "William Clark December 3 1805. By land from the U. States in 1804 & 1805."[80] On December 8, the Corps moved into the newly built Fort Clatsop on the south side of the Columbia. Named after the nearby tribe, "fort" is a generous description for the 50-foot-square log enclosure with seven small cabins and a parade ground 20-foot square.[81]

The men suffered through a long, boring and wet winter. Days filled with hunting and repairing equipment followed nights fighting off fleas, "so troublesome that I have slept but little for 2 night past."[82] Mostly it rained. By the end of the winter, Clark counted "twelve days without rain and only six with sunshine."[83]

Disease and illness were as abundant as the fleas. Dysentery, abdominal infections, dehydration, and venereal diseases plagued the expedition. Typically Clark or Lewis employed the practices common to the day: "purging" with a laxative for intestinal problems, bleeding for infections and a small dose of mercury to cure syphilis or gonorrhea. For most of the trip, Lewis tolerated his men engaging in sexual relations with Native women. The chiefs behaved as if trading the favors of their wives or daughters was part of trade, no different from selling furs or food. But when incidences of sexually transmitted diseases reached almost endemic levels at Fort Clatsop, Lewis asked his men to honor a "vow of celibacy."[84]

In the evenings, the explorers played host to a steady stream of visitors. They exchanged food, smoked and discussed trade. The Clatsop and Chinooks appeared "escessively fond of smoking tobacco," Lewis wrote. They "inhale it in their lungs [and] puff it out to a great distance through their nostrils and mouth. I have no doubt the smoke of the tobacco in this manner becomes much more intoxicating ..."[85]

It seems the presence of the explorers offered Native People a pleasant distraction from tribal life, an early nineteenth century "tourist attraction."[86] But cordial evenings of smoking, sex, and trade could quickly turn sour when a visiting Native tried to steal a gun, tool, or anything of perceived value, a not infrequent occurrence. The sudden disappearance of a rifle or knife dogged the explorers throughout the journey. During a visit with Skilloot People earlier in the fall, Lewis's ceremonial tomahawk pipe disappeared. While Lewis angrily searched the Native canoes, someone's overcoat vanished. The incident rattled Lewis, who never again allowed a large party of Native People into his camp.[87] Eventually they started posting guard on valuables, and clearing the fort at night in order to prevent theft, "which we were more fearful of, than their arrows."[88] At Fort Clatsop, Clark threatened to shoot the next Native inclined to lift anything.[89] In fairness, it should be noted Lewis was not above a little slight-of-hand himself. When Lewis could not extract an acceptable price for a canoe needed for the return trip, he stole one from a Clatsop village.[90]

The Corps was not alone in coping with theft. Vancouver, Gray, fur traders, missionaries, and later settlers all found themselves confronting natives to demand the return of their property. Moreover, Native People regularly stole from other each other, evidenced by the frequent horse raids and abduction of women and children. Understanding these practices requires looking at things from the point of view of Native People, who may have viewed it as tribute for allowing white men to cross through their territory or build forts on their land. Second, Native People living on the barest essentials likely looked at the relative wealth of the white men and concluded no one would miss just one gun or knife.[91] Finally, operating under a tribe's division-of-labor system, some men were tasked with bringing home resources that enhanced a clan's defense and weakened the enemy's. To do so brought one honor and respect. The fact that a significant majority of stolen goods were horses and weapons, adds weight to that explanation.[92]

Lewis's threats notwithstanding, the Corps could not afford to totally alienate Native People whose help they needed to survive the winter. Without trade for essentials, Clark feared it would be a "disagreeable" winter for certain.[93] Nevertheless, Lewis and Clark did not like nor trust the coastal tribes, who they viewed "as habitual thieves tainted with avarice and treachery."[94]

Such attitudes, of course, did not further trade. Native People living near the mouth of the Columbia had been dealing with European and American traders for years. Lewis saw signs of trade everywhere: guns, powder, balls and shot, copper and brass tea kettles, coffee pots, blankets, plates, sheets of copper, brass wire, knives, beads, tobacco and fishhooks. Even a trade jargon permeated Chinookan speech. English words like muskets, powder, shot, knife, file, "dammed rascal," and "son of a bitch" popped up in trade discussions.[95]

Experience, of course, makes for shrewd traders, and the captains often found themselves paying "double and tribble" the value of goods. "Like the New England shopkeeper or the backcountry merchant, the Chinookan knew when to hold his ground and when to sell quickly." It didn't help that after nearly two years in the wilderness, most valuable items were in short supply.[96]

Disease, theft, tough trade and nearly constant rain made for a Corps anxious to put the Pacific Northwest to their backs. On March 23, 1806, Lewis turned possession of the fort over to a Clatsop chief and "bid a final adieu" to the Pacific Coast.[97] As the party moved slowly up the Columbia and to higher elevations, the snow thickened and it became clear they'd left too early. They spent May and most of June with the Nez Perce before heading for home, reaching St. Louis in September.

Assessing the Corps of Discovery

More than two centuries later, the Lewis and Clark Expedition remains one of the most celebrated events in American history. The question is: How should students assess it? Were they American heroes who displayed "undaunted courage," as the historian Stephen Ambrose couched it? Or does James Ronda more accurately describe the captains as diplomatic bundlers and traveling salesmen? Undoubtedly a journey that lasted twenty-eight months over 8,000 miles required courage and heroism under the most trying circumstances. The scientific documentation of the mission was unparalleled in the country's young history. The wealth of knowledge about the landscape, Native Peoples, flora and fauna painted an exciting portrait of America's newly acquired Louisiana Territory and the Pacific Northwest. Additionally, America gained the documentation it needed to strengthen its claims on the region, first during the joint occupancy agreement with Great Britain in 1818 and later when it took full possession in 1846. But it's equally clear efforts to implement Thomas Jefferson's foreign policy thousands of miles removed from the capital were clumsy and to some degree disingenuous. The Americans made promises about trade they would be unable to keep. The era of exploration was nearing its end and soon a new wave of European and American traders arrived hungry for furs and thoroughly unconcerned about promises made by men who came before them.

While historians debate the successes and failures of the Corps, perhaps it's more relevant to examine the Native Peoples, especially in the Pacific Northwest. How should

Figure 1.4 In 1905, Portland hosted the Lewis & Clark Centennial, a world's fair designed to bring business and workers to the city. Note the patriotic tone of the poster as Lewis and Clark march west arm-and-arm with the flag-draped Lady Liberty. Reprinted with permission from the Washington State Historical Society.

THE LEWIS & CLARK CENTENNIAL
PORTLAND – OREGON – 1905

we judge the many tribes who found themselves set upon by strangers from a distant land? Myths abound about Native People and an environment untarnished by "the foot of civilized man."[98] But for people who called the lower Columbia or Pacific Coast home, Lewis's proclamation missed the mark. The Corps engaged with Native Peoples markedly experienced in European trade and prepared to leverage their resources and skills acquired over countless generations. Further, unlike when men came in big ships, there were no attacks or violent deaths, a credit to both sides. Nor should we overlook their countless acts of kindness and support. It's reasonable to argue that offers of food, shelter, guidance, survival skills, horses and portage were as much about decency as trade. Two vastly different cultures fought through misunderstandings and prejudices, displaying kindness as much as cunning. They pushed beyond familiar boundaries and transgressed new ones to find common ground in an unforgiving land.

The time of the people

Broadening the definition of civilization

In early April 1805, when the Corps of Discovery trekked west along the Missouri River, Meriwether Lewis expressed his excitement. "We were now about to penetrate a country at least two thousand miles in width on which the foot of civilized man had never trodden," Lewis wrote in his journal.[99]

Like nearly all Americans in the early nineteenth century, Lewis's narrow definition of civilization blinded him to reality. He was entering a west where a different kind of civilized culture had flourished for thousands of years. Archeological data suggests Pacific Northwest Natives had lived in the region for 10,000 to 12,000 years. The generally accepted theories suggest humans migrated from Siberia during the Ice Age, following herds as they slowly moved north through Asia, crossing east on a massive land and ice bridge covering the Bering Sea, then south into North America. Others may have traveled by sea. Whether by land or sea, DNA extracted from two ancient Siberian skeletons in 2013 shows a genetic match with modern-day Native Americans, supporting the migration theory.[100] Nevertheless, many Native Peoples assert that they didn't migrate at all, but had always been in the Americas.

Anthropologists generally group Native Peoples according to their system of language. Peoples from eight separate language groups populated what are now Washington, Oregon, and Idaho. Due to space constraints, this story focuses on two representative groups – the Coast Salish inhabiting much of Western Washington, and the Sahaptin in the southeastern part of the region near the Columbia River.

The Coast Salish people

More than a dozen Puget Sound tribes fall under a common language system called Coast Salish. Archeological evidence points to a ring of more than 300 villages throughout the region, ranging from a handful of families to several hundred.[101] While we refer to Native Peoples in the past tense, keep in mind that many still live in the region. A clockwise tour around the Sound helps to locate the former homes of the major groups. (Note: the word "tribe" was a European contrivance that many Native Peoples find objectionable as an overly simplistic and inaccurate description of their societies.) The Suquamish, Sklallam, Skokomish, and Chimakum inhabited the Straits of Juan De Fuca, the northwestern reaches of Puget Sound and the Olympic Peninsula. On the northeastern side, the Stillaguamish, and Snohomish, inhabited present-day Skagit and Snohomish counties. Heading south into current King and Pierce counties, the Duwamish and Puyallup thrived on the riches along the eastern shore of the Sound. Members of the Nisqually and Squaxin inhabited the South Sound near the present-day cities of Steilacoom, Olympia, and Shelton. The Twana inhabited parts of Hood Canal, while the Chehalis and Tillamook lived farther south.

Coast Salish in most villages built shelters along the rivers that flowed into Puget Sound and nearby lakes. Made from large cedar planks, a single longhouse was home to several families. Sleeping platforms and storage shelves lined the walls. Dried fish and meat hung from the ceiling. Mats on the earthen floor served as a workplace for preparing food, weaving, and building tools for hunting and fishing. Wood fires provided heat, the smoke escaping through adjustable slats in the roof.[102]

Prior to adopting tribal identities thrust upon them by Euro-Americans, Native Peoples identified with their clan or village. Less reliant on the horse than Native Peoples east of the Cascade Mountains, the Salish moved about in dugout canoes. Throughout the year, they plied Puget Sound, hunting, gathering, and socializing with other clans and villages.[103]

Salmon, other fish, and a variety of mollusks like clams, oysters, and mussels constituted the majority of their diet, but they also dined on water fowl, venison, and other mammals. In addition to hunting, the Salish gathered berries and vegetables natural to the region: raspberries, gooseberries, strawberries, salmonberries, and vegetables like tubers, fiddleheads, and onions.

It's difficult to accurately estimate native population on Puget Sound prior to the arrival of the Europeans.[104] It's clear however, the population dropped precipitously following exposure to European diseases. So when English Captain George Vancouver entered Puget Sound in the spring of 1792, he found a native habitat already under assault by European pathogens.

The peoples of the Plateau

The Native Peoples of the Columbian Plateau, in the Sahaptin language group, made their homes on a massive region along the tributaries of the Columbia and Snake rivers: the Yakama, Klickitat, Wishram, Umatilla, Cayuse and Nez Perce. Any discussion, however, of the dozens of tribes inhabiting the Pacific Northwest interior and elsewhere should begin with a note of caution. While climate and environmental factors led to commonalities among these people, no two cultures were the same and each reacted to outside factors in their own way, especially to the presence of newcomers.[105]

The arrival of the horse thoroughly transformed native culture, dietary habits, migration patterns, and intertribal relations. Introduced by the Spanish on the southern plains in the seventeenth century, large herds reached Northwest Natives in the early decades of the eighteenth century. Mounted Native People could travel farther and longer to hunt game and trade, and carry larger loads back to their home territory. The Nez Perce, for example, often crossed the Bitterroots to hunt bison and trade, sometimes staying for two years or more. The horse also upset the balance of power on the Plateau, giving mounted tribes a clear advantage in war. The ability of Native Peoples to adapt to the horse, and eventually become skilled breeders and riders, evened the playing field in confrontations with neighboring tribes like the Blackfeet, Hidatsa and Shoshone, and to some degree with the U.S. Army in the second half of the nineteenth century.[106]

The hunter-gatherer lifestyle revolved around the seasons. Throughout spring, summer, and into fall, women, children and the elderly roamed the plains on foot, gathering berries, roots, onions, nuts, tubers and mushrooms they later dried or pounded into cakes and stored for winter, providing 50% to 70% of the diet.[107] Men fished and hunted. Displaying skills developed over thousands of years, they used dip nets, gaff hooks, and small spears to catch salmon, steelhead, trout, lamprey eels, and sturgeon. The women cleaned and hung the catch on drying racks and stored them for winter. Salmon was also ground to a powder and mixed with berries to form a high-energy paste that sustained the people while on the move. Bison, deer, antelope, elk, black bear, mountain sheep, dog and a variety of waterfowl provided year-round sources of protein.[108]

In the fall, Native Peoples from throughout the Pacific Northwest traveled to events akin to trade fairs at the Dalles on the Columbia River and other spots. These gatherings provided opportunities to buy or sell food, hides, plants, and medicines. By the late

Figure 1.5 An unidentified group of Native People play a stick game called "alcholoh." During the summer, Natives enjoyed ball and stick games, foot races, and other competitive activities. Paul Kane oil on canvas *ca* 1850. Image provided with permission from the Royal Ontario Museum.

eighteenth century, western goods like beads, clothing, cookware, and weapons that coastal Native Peoples acquired from explorers and maritime traders began showing up in the interior. Beyond trade, Native Peoples shared traditions like music and stories. They did what humans everywhere do. They enjoyed themselves dancing, telling stories, and wagering on sports. Native Peoples gambled on stick games, foot races, horse races and wrestling, many of which served as training ground for young men expected to hunt and fight. The fairs offered a time to unwind, celebrate, and acquire goods needed for the upcoming winter, at which point everyone returned home, dug in, and waited for spring.[109]

For peoples living on both sides of the mountains, winter also marked the beginning of the "winter dance" ritual where young boys and girls sought their "guardian spirits." This "most sacred and mythical ceremony" involved boys at around age ten embarking upon a spiritual quest. They'd venture alone into the wild, fast for days, and wait for a vision in which an animal, plant or other life form gave the boy instructions that would guide his life. The spirit and boy were forever linked.[110]

Spiritual leaders, known as healers or *tewats*, were central to indigenous peoples' view of the world. Believed to hold powers not found among other Natives, healers possessed the power to "remove" ailments from the sick or wounded. The healing ritual began with the healer entering a self-induced trance and leading the village in a dance that could last for days.[111] If the patient healed, the family paid the healer in horses or blankets. Failure could lead to serious consequences as grieving family members vowed to kill the unsuccessful healer, a practice that foretold trouble for missionaries attending to Native Peoples who contracted European diseases.

Figure 1.6 Chinook lounging outside what is likely a temporary summer shelter. Most Chinook lived in substantial longhouses in winter. Mount Hood can be seen in the distance. Paul Kane oil on Canvas. Image provided with permission from the Royal Ontario Museum.

Native Peoples from all language groups sustained their culture and histories through the oral tradition of telling stories or legends. In the evening, village elders gathered around the fire and passed along mythical stores about monsters, cataclysmic events, and the people before they were transformed into humans.[112]

The spiritual beliefs of the Plateau peoples offers a good example. Centered around a theology called *Tamanwit,* the people believed "all things on the earth were placed by the Creator for a purpose."[113] A widely told story among the peoples of the Southern Columbia Plateau involved the heroics of *spilyay*, or Coyote.[114] One of dozens of Coyote stories goes as follows: The Creator of the Earth spoke to Coyote of the coming of "human beings who would be like infants and who would need to be taught how to live here." The animal and plant worlds convened a council at which many volunteered to sacrifice themselves for the humans. Salmon stepped up first, followed by other animals, berries and roots to "sustain Plateau peoples for thousands of years."[115] A related legend tells of a huge monster called *Its-welx* who swallowed all animal life and imprisoned them in its stomach. The sly Coyote allowed the monster to swallow him as well, at which point he slew the monster and freed all its prisoners. He then tore the monster into pieces, throwing them in all directions, each time bringing a tribal people to life and giving it a name.[116]

It's important to note these legends are far more than tall tales. The Coyote legend, for example, served as the foundation of a complex set of spiritual practices that explained human existence. Ethno historian Christopher Miller wrote that myths "can no longer be passed off as quaint stories dreamed up by the childlike imaginations of primitives."[117] It's also important to distinguish native spiritual practices from their faith in a creator. Coyote functioned as a "technician" who served the creator's will, and should not be confused with the creator itself.[118]

This was the civilization that Lewis and Clark and other explorers were about to encounter, initiating a veritable clash of cultures that changed the course of history and challenged our ideas of what "civilized" means for men and women of all cultures.

Sacagawea: heroism in perspective

Among the many legendary figures who took part in the Lewis and Clark Expedition, few generate more fascination and debate than Sacagawea, the Lemhi-Shoshone girl who joined the Corps with her husband, Toussaint Charbonneau, as interpreters.

Sacagawea has remained a transcendent figure for more than two centuries, portrayed as a true American hero. It's believed that her courage, perseverance, knowledge of the land and native languages guided the Corps through a vast American wilderness, and placed her at the center of critical trade negotiations with native chiefs. In a famous Edgar S. Paxson painting, she stands tall with Lewis and Clark, boldly pointing the way west. "Follow my lead," it suggests.

Yet there are few verifiable facts about Sacagawea's life to justify such a towering reputation. Historians disagree even about basic facts like the spelling of her name (Sacagawea, Sacajawea, Sakakawea), or when and where she died (1812 in present-day South Dakota, or 1884 in Wyoming). She left no diary or other written record, and no original paintings or drawings of her face are known to exist, so we can only guess what she looked like. But the biggest questions involve her role in the expedition: Interpreter or guide? Contributor or burden?

In spite of the informational vacuum, Sacagawea's reputation has blossomed to near mythical status. Her likeness has been displayed on stamps, coins, and countless paintings and posters. She is the subject of several novels, feature films, and documentaries. Historical monuments honoring her contributions can be found in Portland, Oregon; Three Forks, Wyoming; Lemhi Pass in Idaho, and Mobridge, South Dakota. A plaque at Mobridge reads, "By her courage, endurance, and unerring instincts, she guided the expedition over seemingly insurmountable obstacles."

Eva Emery Dye, in her 1902 novel, *The Conquest: The True Story of Lewis and Clark*, calls Sacagawea the "Madonna of her race," who led America to the great Pacific Northwest and Asia. "Sacagawea's hair was neatly braided, her nose was fine and straight, and her skin pure copper like the statue in some old Florentine gallery ... To the hands of this girl, not yet eighteen, had been instructed the key that unlocked the road to Asia."[119] Sacagawea "heroine of the great expedition ... stood in the Rocky Mountains pointing out the gates. So had she followed the great rivers, navigating the continent."[120]

Whether inscribed on monuments or fictionalized in novels, such claims far exceed what can be verified, and according to historian James Ronda, "diminish" Sacagawea and complicate efforts to fairly evaluate her genuine contributions, which were not insignificant.[121]

A review of the journals of Lewis and Clark and other expedition members, reveals a much different Sacagawea. Here is what we know with some certainty about her childhood and involvement in the 29-month expedition. Born in the Rocky Mountains, she was about 11 years old when enemies of the Shoshone, the Hidatsa, raided their village and took several captives as slaves, including Sacagawea. The raiders then took their hostages east into Canada at which point they sold Sacagawea, or, according to some accounts, lost her gambling with the French trader Charbonneau. He later married Sacajawea, one of two or three wives.[122]

Lewis and Clark met Charbonneau at their winter quarters at Fort Mandan in 1804. Conversant in French, Hidatsa and some English, he offered his services as an interpreter. While Charbonneau's other wives were left behind, Lewis agreed to include Sacagawea because she spoke Shoshone and could assist in critical negotiations for horses when the party reached the Rocky Mountains.[123] She was 15 years old and six months pregnant at the time. On February 11, 1805, she gave birth to a son, Jean Baptiste Charbonneau. With the infant

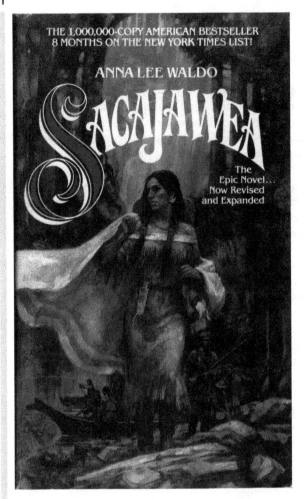

THE 1,000,000-COPY AMERICAN BESTSELLER
8 MONTHS ON THE NEW YORK TIMES LIST!

ANNA LEE WALDO

SACAJAWEA

The
Epic Novel...
Now Revised
and Expanded

Figure 1.7 This larger-than-life portrayal of Sacagawea, which appeared on the cover of the novel *Sacajawea,* typifies her heroic legacy. In all likelihood it bears little resemblance to the real Sacagawea, who was 15 years old and six months pregnant when she joined Lewis and Clark. Book cover from *Sacajawea* by Anne Lee Waldo. Copyright © 1978. Reprinted by permission of HarperCollins Publishers.

strapped on a cradle board on her back, Sacagawea would accompany the Corps to the Pacific Ocean and back.

The record turns cloudy on the trail because Lewis and Clark journals mention her so infrequently. Scattered references to the "Indian girl," "Snake woman" (another name for the Shoshone) "squaw," or "squar," suggest a diminished importance in the eyes of the leaders. But a closer examination speaks to her usefulness and utility. First, because she grew up in a hunter-gatherer society, she helped identify edible plants like mushrooms, roots and nuts, fattening the Corps' scanty food supply and enriching their diet. When the expedition halted for dinner in April 1805, Sacagawea "busied herself" searching for "wild artichokes," and her "good quantity of labour soon proved successful and she procured a good quantity of these roots."[124]

In May the party came across a large deserted campground that Lewis hoped belonged to Shoshone. Sacagawea could tell from "mokersons" left behind they were not her people's but Minnetaree (Hidatsa).[125] As they approached the Rockies, she was able to point out familiar landmarks, confirming the party was on route.

Later in May, tragedy nearly struck when a pirogue carrying valuable supplies and equipment nearly capsized in high winds. Charbonneau, Sacagawea and other men were aboard. According to Lewis, Charbonneau, who was manning the rudder at the time, lost control and panicked (he couldn't swim). He began "crying to his god for mercy," until boatman Pierre Cruzatte "threatened to shoot him instantly if he did not take hold of the rudder and do his duty."[126] They eventually gained control of the boat and bailed sufficient water to tow it to shore, while Sacagawea hurriedly retrieved items from the rushing water. Her quick reactions and steady nerve, in sharp contrast to her husband's distress, impressed Lewis. The "Indian woman" displayed "equal fortitude and resolution with any person onboard at the time," he wrote.[127] Later Lewis named a nearby stream "bird woman's River after our interpreter the Snake woman."[128]

As the expedition approached the headwaters of the Missouri and the highly anticipated union with Shoshone, Sacagawea became "unexpectedly important," according to historian Bernard DeVoto. The tribe's "great herds of horses" would provide the mounts needed to negotiate the rugged trail down the Rockies, over the Bitterroot Mountains and on to the Columbia River.[129]

Although not in the advance party that first encountered the Shoshone in August, her presence proved crucial in a most personal and unexpected way – a Shoshone family reunion. A woman kidnapped in the same raid that took Sacagawea four years earlier recognized her as they entered the village. The women hugged and cried. Later as the party sat down for trade talks, Sacagawea realized the Shoshone Chief, Cameahwait, was her brother. She shrieked and "jumped up, ran & embraced him, threw her blanket over him and cried profusely."[130]

The Shoshone hosted the Corps for several weeks, traded away the much-needed horses and helped guide them down the Rockies. Sacagawea kept busy as the key link in the complex communications chain that moved from English to French to Hidatsa to Shoshone and back again. As the expedition encountered other tribes on the way to the Pacific, Sacagawea could not translate because she could not speak any of the Salish dialects. Yet her very presence – a young native woman with a baby – signaled the Corps' "friendly intention." Wrote Clark, "A woman with a party of men is a token of peace."[131]

Sacagawea's survival skills, steadiness in an emergency, familiarity with the territory, language skills, personal ties with the Shoshone and her mere physical presence collectively point to a valuable contribution to the success of the Corps of Discovery. The mere fact she traversed across the continent for two years with a baby strapped to her back makes her exceptional. Yet it's important to realize that all members of the mission played key roles, demonstrated skills and fortitude, and made personal sacrifices. On a dauntless mission deep in unchartered territory thousands of miles from home, everyone was expected to do their part, and Sacagawea certainly did hers. Does that make her a hero? Perhaps, provided such heroism is placed in the same light as the countless other heroic feats of the members of the Corps of Discovery.

Explore more

Books

To learn more about the impact of European and American exploration in the Pacific Northwest, see *With Vancouver in Inland Washington Waters, Journals of 12 Crewmen, April–June 1792*, Richard Blumenthal, editor. Because it includes journal entries from multiple officers, it's interesting to see how different men responded to the same event. For an American point of view of Northwest exploration, see Frederic W. Howay's *Voyages of the "Columbia" to the Northwest Coast: 1787–1790 and 1790–1793*. Large volumes of literature are available on the Lewis and Clark Expedition, starting with Stephen, E. Ambrose's popular *Undaunted Courage, Meriwether Lewis, Thomas Jefferson, and the Opening of the American West*. For an alternative and less flattering interpretation of the Corps of Discovery check out James P. Ronda's *Lewis and Clark Among the Indians*.

Online

Two of many websites that document native languages and culture include the Lewis and Clark Tribal Legacy Project (http://www.lc_triballegacy.org/) and the Coastal Salish Map (http://coastsalishmap.org/start_page.htm), which documents the host of tribes that flourished throughout the Puget Sound region.

Museums

The Washington State History Museum (http://www.washingtonhistory.org/) features informative and interactive displays on the region's geological formation, as well as the lives of indigenous peoples and their first contact with Europeans and Americans.

Questions for further discussion

How should history judge European and American explorers and their practice of taking possession of foreign lands? Were they brave men driven by greed or loyal patriots serving their countries? How do you explain Native People's reaction to the sudden presence of strange men in big ships? Was there debate within a clan on how to respond? What was that debate, and why were there relatively few incidences of violence between explorers and Native Peoples?

Notes

1 Richard W. Blumenthal, ed. *With Vancouver in Inland Washington Waters, Journals of 12 Crewmen, April–June 1792* (Jefferson, WA: McFarland & Company, 2007), 44.
2 Robert Whitebrook, *Coastal Exploration of Washington* (Palo Alto, CA: Pacific Books Publishers, 1959), 81.
3 William Farrand Prosser, *History of the Puget Sound Country, Its Resources, Its Commerce and Its People* (New York: The Lewis Publishing Company, 1903), 59.
4 Center For the Study of the Pacific Northwest, *European and American Exploration of the 18th-Century Pacific Northwest*, accessed June 19, 2014, http://www.washington.edu.

5 Ibid.

6 Ibid.

7 Carlos A. Schwantes, *The Pacific Northwest, An Interpretive History* (Lincoln, NE: University of Nebraska Press, 1996), 24.

8 Schwantes, *The Pacific Northwest*, 47–48.

9 American crewmen sailing with Captain Robert Gray.

10 Frederic W. Howay, *Voyages of the "Columbia" to the Northwest Coast: 1787–1790 and 1790–1793* (Portland, OR: Oregon Historical Society Press in cooperation with the Massachusetts Historical Society, 1990), 198.

11 Vancouver, George, *A Voyage of Discovery to the North Pacific Ocean, and Round the World in Which the Coast of North-West America Has Been Carefully Examined and Accurately Surveyed* (London: Printed for G.G. and J. Robinson, Paternoster-Row; and J. Edwards, Pall-Mall, 1798), 256.

12 Vancouver, George, *A Voyage of Discovery*, 220.

13 Ibid., 228.

14 Blumenthal, *With Vancouver in Inland Washington Waters*, 46.

15 Ibid., 68.

16 Ibid., 84–85.

17 Ibid., 72.

18 Thomas Manby, *Journal of the Voyages of the H.M.S. Discovery and Chatham* (Fairfield, WA: Ye Galleon Press, 1992), 153.

19 Blumenthal, *With Vancouver in Inland Waters*, 72.

20 Manby, *Journal of the Voyages of the H.M.S.*, 154.

21 Ibid.

22 Ibid.

23 Blumenthal, *With Vancouver in Inland Waters*, 40–41.

24 Ibid., 80.

25 Ibid., 40–41.

26 Ibid., 23

27 Ibid., 74–76.

28 Ibid., 74–76.

29 Ibid., 35.

30 Ibid., 19.

31 Ibid., 26–27.

32 Vancouver, *Voyage of Discovery*, 255.

33 Kathryn McKay, "Recycling the Soul: Death and the Continuity of Life in Coast Salish Burial Practices," master's thesis (University of Victoria, 2002), 16, accessed October 12, 2015, http://web.uvic.ca/.

34 William Farrand Prosser, *History of the Puget Sound Country*.

35 Gary B Nash, "The Image of the Indian in the Southern Colonial Mind," *The William and Mary Quarterly*, 3rd Ser., 29, no. 2. (Apr., 1972): 206.

36 Ibid.

37 Nash, "The Image of the Indian," 210.

38 Prosser, *History of the Puget Sound Country*, 59.

39 Gordon Speck, *Northwest Explorations*. L.K. Phillips, ed. (Portland, OR: Bindfords & Mort, 1970), 138.

40 Howay, *Voyages of the "Columbia" to the Northwest Coast*, 360.

41 Speck, *Northwest Explorations*, 153.

42 Ibid., 156.

43 Howay, *Voyages of the Columbia*, 323.

44 Robert H. Ruby, and John A. Brown, *Indians of the Pacific Northwest* (Norman, OK: University of Oklahoma Press, 1981), 6.

45 Speck, *Northwest Explorations*, 156–160.

46 Kenneth L. Homes, "Pages From Our Past: Captain Gray and Washington Letter," *Eugene-Register Guard*, February 22, 1962.

47 Daniel Wright Clayton, *Islands of Truth: The Imperial Fashioning of Vancouver Island* (Vancouver: University of British Columbia Press, 2000), 128–129.

48 Howay, *Voyages of the Columbia*, 186.

49 Speck, *Northwest Explorations*, 137.

50 Speck, *Northwest Explorations*, 160.

51 "Captain Robert Gray Becomes the First non-Indian Navigator to Enter the Columbia River, which He Later Names, on May 11, 1792," Historylink.org, January 13, 2003, http://www.historylink.org/.

52 "Captain Robert Gray Explores Grays Bay and Charts the Mouth of Grays River in May 1792," Historylink.org, accessed May 12, 2015; http://www.historylink.org/.

53 Stephen, E. Ambrose, *Undaunted Courage, Meriwether Lewis, Thomas Jefferson, and the Opening of the American West* (New York: Touchstone, 1996), 266.

54 John Logan Allen, "Summer of Decision: Lewis and Clark in Montana, 1805," *We Proceeded On* 8, no. 4 (Fall 1976), 10.

55 Bernard DeVoto, ed. *The Journals of Lewis and Clark* (Boston: Houghton Mifflin Company, 1981), 482–483

56 Ibid.

57 Ibid., 483–484.

58 Ambrose, *Undaunted Courage*, 88.

59 Robert V. Hine and John Mack Faragher, *The American West: A New Interpretive History* (New Haven, CT: Yale University Press, 2000), 137.

60 DeVoto, *The Journals of Lewis and Clark*, 91.

61 Ambrose, *Undaunted Courage*, 211–213.

62 DeVoto, *The Journals of Lewis and Clark*, 147–149.

63 Ibid., 189–191.

64 Ibid., 190.

65 Ibid., 191.

66 James P. Ronda, *Lewis and Clark Among the Indians* (Lincoln, NE: University of Nebraska Press, 1984), 142.

67 Ronda, 147.

68 Ibid., xiv.

69 Allen V. Pinkham, Sr., "We Ya Oo Yet Soyapo," in *Lewis and Clark through Indian Eyes*, ed. Alvin M. Josephy, Jr., with Marc Jaffe (New York: Knopf, 2006), 155.

70 Ronda, *Lewis and Clark Among the Indians*, 140.

71 Ibid., 31.

72 Ibid., 174.

73 Ibid., 157.

74 Ibid., 177.

75 Ibid., 165.

76 Ibid., 169.

77 Bernard DeVoto, ed. *The Journals of Lewis and Clark* (Boston: Houghton Mifflin Company, 1981), 312

78 Pinkham, Sr., "We Ya Oo Yet Soyapo," 155 .

79 Ibid., 177.

80 Ibid., 179–180.

81 DeVoto, *The Journals of Lewis and Clark*, 294.

82 Ibid., 295.

83 Ibid., 312.

84 Ibid., *The Journals of Lewis and Clark*, 329.

85 Ibid., 305.

86 Ronda, *Lewis and Clark Among the Indians*, 187.

87 Ibid., 176.

88 DeVoto, *The Journals of Lewis and Clark*, 261.

89 Ibid., 285.

90 Ronda, *Lewis and Clark Among the Indians*, 211.

91 Ibid., 172.

92 Roberta Conner, director, Tamastslikt Cultural Institute, in a telephone conversation with author, Nov. 21, 2014.

93 Ronda, *Lewis and Clark Among the Indians*, 179–180.

94 Ibid., 188.

95 DeVoto, *The Journals of Lewis and Clark*, 307.

96 Ronda, *Lewis and Clark Among the Indians*, 190–192.

97 Ibid., 212.

98 Ibid., 133.

99 DeVoto, *The Journals of Lewis and Clark*, 91.

100 Tia Ghose, "Ancient Siberian Skeletons Confirm Native American Origins," Livescience .com, http://www.livescience.com/41363-ancient-siberian-dna-native-americans.html, accessed February 14, 2016.

101 Tom Dailey, "Coast Salish People of Puget Sound," Coastsalishmap.org, accessed February 13, 2016; http://coastsalishmap.org/start_page.htm; and Native-Languages.org, accessed April 8, 2014, *Native American Tribes of Washington*, http://www.native-languages.org/puget-sound.htm, accessed October 19, 2016.

102 Dailey, "Coast Salish People."

103 Ibid.

104 Tom Dailey estimates 15,000 people inhabited the Puget Sound region prior to first contact, based on an estimate of 300 villages with an average of 50 people in each. *Native American Tribes of Washington*, http://www.native-languages.org/puget-sound.htm, accessed October 19, 2016.

105 Christopher L. Miller, *Prophetic Worlds: Indians and Whites on the Columbia Plateau* (Seattle, WA: University of Washington Press, 1985, 2003), 3.

106 Elliott West, *The Last Indian War: The Nez Perce Story* (New York: Oxford University Press, 2009), 17.

107 Sue Armitage, *Shaping the Public Good: Women Making History in the Pacific Northwest* (Corvallis, OR: Oregon State University Press, 2015), 29.

108 Miller, *Prophetic Worlds*, 13.

109 Confederated Tribes of the Umatilla Indian Reservation, ctuir.org.

110 Miller, *Prophetic Worlds*, 15.

111 Augustus Blanchet to Ignace Bourget, Feb., 1850, in *Selected Letters of A.M.A. Blanchet: Bishop of Walla Walla & Nesqualy, 1846–1879*, Roberta Stringham Brown and Patricia O'Connell Killen, eds., 76.

112 Kenneth (Greg) Watson, "Arthur Ballard and the Mythology of Southern Puget Sound," *White River Journal*, http://www.wrvmuseum.org/journal/journal_0799.htm, accessed February 15, 2016.

113 Allen P Slickpoo, Sr. and Dward E. Walker, Jr., *Noon Nee-Me-Poo (We, the Nez Perces) Culture and History of the Nez Perces*, Vol. 1 (Nez Perce Tribe of Idaho, 1973), 4.

114 Donald Hines, *Tales of the Nez Perce* (Fairfield, WA: Ye Galleon press, 1984), 43.

115 Slickpoo and Walker, 23.

116 Ibid., 1.

117 Miller, *Prophetic Worlds*, 3.

118 Roberta Conner and William L. Lang, "Early Contact and Incursion, 1700–1850," in Slickpoo and Walker, *Noon Nee-Me-Poo*, 23–24.

119 Eva Emery Dye, *The Conquest: The True Story of Lewis and Clark* (Chicago, IL: A.C. McClurg & Company, 1902), 290.

120 Ibid.

121 James P. Ronda, *Lewis and Clark among the Indians*, 256.

122 Ibid., 256–459.

123 Bernard DeVoto, *The Journals of Lewis and Clark*, 77n.

124 Ibid., 92.

125 Ibid., 120.

126 Ibid., 110.

127 Ibid., 111.

128 Ibid., 113.

129 Ibid., 77n.

130 Ronda, *Lewis and Clark Among the Indians*, 146–147.

131 Ibid., 258.

2

Trade Among Equals

Natives, British, and Americans jockey for control over
land and resources

*Emerging trade into the early decades of the nineteenth century brought Europeans
and Americans in long-term contact with Native Peoples for the first time. But contrary to popular belief, Natives were far from passive victims of greedy traders. As
all parties competed for control over diverse resources, Native Peoples entered trade
grounds as equals, and for a time, resisted the boundaries that came with trade.*

Chinook leader Comcomly brought alarming news to Fort Astoria, a Pacific Fur
Company outpost near the mouth of the Columbia River, on February 13, 1813. He
reported Kalapuyan Natives killed a party of trappers working the Willamette River
Valley. Comcomly claimed no first-hand knowledge of the attack, but expressed sympathy for the company's loss. A concerned Duncan McDougall, leader at Fort Astoria,
sent an agent to investigate, who concluded the report was simply "a fabrication of some
of the Indians."[1] Two weeks later, Comcomly returned with a new tale. This time, the
Kalapuyans supposedly raided the party's post at Wallace House.[2] Again, an investigation found the story to be "without foundation."[3]

Comcomly's actions should not surprise given his people's concerns. Residing along
the north bank of the Columbia across from Astoria, the Lower Chinook used their location to control trade. But as trade with Europeans and Americans evolved, it began to
undermine their position as middlemen. With permanent posts throughout the interior, traders like the Pacific Fur Company began to bypass the Chinook. Comcomly's
tales were arguably meant to drive a wedge between them and the Kalapuyans, thus
protecting the Chinook's pivotal role in trade.[4]

This episode reveals much about the dynamics of a fur trade focused on obtaining
wealth and power through commerce. This chapter will argue that the back-and-forth
struggle for control between Native Peoples and British, American, and Russian
traders defines the fur trade story. In essence, this era saw the rise of intensely guarded
economic boundaries. All parties wanted to derive the most benefit from trade and
Euro-American traders fought bitterly to drive competing nations from the field.
Additionally, trading companies held political goals. In the Pacific Northwest, a contested region for much of its early history, trade allowed nations like Great Britain and
the United States to enhance their claims. Importantly, trade expanded beyond furs,

Contested Boundaries: A New Pacific Northwest History, First Edition. David J. Jepsen and David J. Norberg.
© 2017 John Wiley & Sons, Ltd. Published 2017 by John Wiley & Sons, Ltd.

especially after the British Hudson's Bay Company (HBC) entered the region in 1821. By the 1840s, the company engaged in logging, fishing, and commercial agriculture, strengthening British dominance in the region. Ironically, diversification, especially in farming, actually hurt Britain's long-term interests and allowed Americans to challenge British claims. The bounty of their fields showcased the region's potential and, combined with the company's policy of buying food from local farmers, actively encouraged American settlement, undermining both trade and British power. Finally, trade led to the first sustained interactions between Native Peoples and Euro-Americans. Both sides recognized trade's benefits, motivating them to negotiate and compromise. They forged complicated, mutually beneficial relationships in which neither side maintained complete control.

Slow beginning for fur trade

The North American fur trade was well established before arriving in the Pacific Northwest. To put it in perspective, when regional trade opened in the 1780s, HBC had operated in North America for more than 110 years.[5] As with other aspects of the region's past, its remoteness caused the fur trade to develop later than elsewhere on the continent.

Russians opened the Northwest fur trade after the Vitus Bering and Aleksei Chirikov expedition of 1741 found a lucrative market for sea otter furs in China.[6] Independent traders opened the business, and the founding of the Russian-American Company in 1799 formalized the trade.[7] While Russians occasionally plied waters off Washington, Oregon, and California, they hunted mostly near Alaska. Rumors suggested the company considered building a post near the Columbia River in 1810, and it did establish an agricultural settlement in northern California in 1812.[8] Overall, however, Russian traders remained on the fringes of the Pacific Northwest, leaving opportunities for other nations.[9]

Spanish explorers dabbled in the Northwest fur trade but did not develop a significant presence, as they focused on keeping rivals out of a region they claimed for themselves. Russian traders, in particular posed a threat.[10] To counter them, Spain dispatched Juan José Pérez in 1774 to explore the coast from Mexico to Alaska, assess colonization, and take formal possession.[11] In the Queen Charlotte Islands in British Columbia, Pérez purchased sea otter furs and other goods from the Haida.[12] At Nootka Sound on Vancouver Island, Pérez noted in his journal how Natives traded "furs for shells which our men brought from Monterey." The crew also received "various sea otter skins and many sardines."[13] Aware of the Chinese market for fur, the Spanish developed a minor trade on the coast of California, but did not pursue it aggressively.[14]

An "astronomical" tale

The third voyage of famed British navigator James Cook raised the Northwest fur trade to a new level. Cook left Britain in 1776 in search of the Northwest Passage, arriving at the Oregon coast in March 1778.[15] From there, he sailed north, anchoring in Nootka Sound. His crew traded extensively with the Nuu-chah-nulth people, amassing roughly

1,500 furs.[16] After further coastal exploration, Cook sailed to Hawaii, where he died in conflict with native Hawaiians. From there, the expedition made one last excursion to the Northwest Coast before returning to Britain with a stop in Guangzhou (Canton) China. There, otter pelts sold for astronomical prices, often registering a 1,800% profit. Desperate to return to Nootka and profit further, crew members nearly mutinied. The expedition returned to Britain in 1780, where news of the windfall spread rapidly. The race to exploit the Northwest fur trade was on.[17]

'Single-minded' pursuit of otter skins

> "I am sorry we was oblidged [*sic*] to kill the poor Devils, but it cou'd [*sic*] not with safety be avoided."
>
> – *John Boit*[18]

On September 28, 1790, 16-year-old John Boit, the fifth-mate on Robert Gray's ship, the *Columbia*, set sail for the Northwest Coast and made the first entry in his richly detailed journal. This American expedition ventured forth with one goal: to turn a profit in the fur trade. The Northwest trade presented a golden opportunity for American merchants and sailors like Boit. The new nation had a sizable debt from the American Revolution, a depressed economy, and a damaged trade relationship with Great Britain. Hungry for opportunity, Gray's crew laid in supplies for "a four years cruise," and left the safety of Boston harbor.[19]

Gray's ventures highlight the maritime fur trade. British trader James Hanna opened this era in 1785 when he arrived on board the *Sea Otter*. Unlike Cook, who focused on exploration, Hanna single-mindedly pursued otter skins. Over five weeks at Nootka Sound, he acquired 560 pelts, which he sold in China for a healthy profit.[20] Six more British ships followed in 1786, and Gray paid his first visit to the Northwest Coast in 1788 under the command of John Kendrick.[21] That venture failed commercially, but Gray remained undeterred, leading to the 1790 voyage.

According to Boit, the first seven months of Gray's second voyage passed with few concerns, though mundane entries reveal his doubts. "Crew are all in health," he recorded in November, but "regulation of the ship as respects cleanliness" lacked attention. Three weeks later he lamented how the crew failed to air "out their beds and cloathing" and seemed to overlook "fumigating their berths."[22] Shortly thereafter he recorded their first tragedy, the death of "our dear friend Nancy the Goat." A veteran of Gray's first voyage, Nancy provided much desired milk. One can only imagine the smell of the ship given the presence of a goat and dirty linen.

Boit and his fellow sailors faced more serious problems in the spring when poor nutrition led to scurvy. Boit remained in good health, but the "mouths and legs" of several others grew "very bad." By late May, their "quite putrid" gums and swollen legs made work impossible. Miserable, to say the least, they landed on Vancouver Island on June 4, more than 8 months after leaving Boston. Fresh greens and spruce tea provided the Vitamin C the sick needed, and all hands were "once again on duty" in two weeks.[23]

Boit spent the next four months "beating to and fro" along the coast in search of Natives with fur. They bartered copper, blue cloth, and iron until they had "drain'd" each locale. Due to high demand and stiff competition among traders, Natives largely controlled the pace and terms of trade. Boit peppered his notes with phrases like "Copper was not in demand" and "*Iron* very dull sale."[24] Traders without sufficient trade items sailed away empty-handed and frustrated. Natives additionally swapped salmon, halibut, greens, game and other foodstuffs for fish hooks and nails.[25]

Near Cape Flattery, Boit casually noted a "Chief" offered "to sell us some young Children" captured in war.[26] He did not record the crew's response, but other American vessels seized the opportunity. Native Peoples throughout the Northwest dealt in slaves, haiqua (dentalium shells), candlefish oil, clamons (elk hide armor), and other goods long before Europeans and Americans arrived. Before long, the native economy and fur trade merged. Traders used strands of haiqua as currency, while the crew of the American ship, *Lydia*, "continually engaged in the slave trade." With a low demand for trade goods, a Captain Roberts exchanged chisels for clamons near the Columbia River in order to resell them to the Haida for sea otter skins.[27]

Gray established winter quarters in late September. More fortunate crews wintered in Hawaii or simply returned home after a season, but Gray put his crew to work building a sloop they christened *Adventure*. At first, the nearby Tla-o-qui-aht people, led by Wickanininsh, welcomed them, "made frequent visits," and "brought a good supply of fish and some Sea Otter Skins." Boit found them "enquisitive" and expressed bemusement when Natives "cou'd not understand why the Ship's and houses was decorated with spruce bows" on Christmas.[28]

Good relations, however, ended in mid-January. "Severall chiefs" visited and Boit observed one "busily employ'd talking with our Sandwich Island lad." That evening, the Hawaiian "made a confession." Wickananish, he explained, planned to attack and wanted him to sabotage their weapons. Alarmed, the men set a "strong guard" and waited. Near midnight, "we heard a most hideous hooping of *Indians*" and "every man immediately took his arms." Frustrated in their attempt to catch the crew by surprise, Wickananish's people retreated after an hour. They "did not seem so cheerful" afterwards, Boit noted, and only "old women and young girls" visited to trade and, he felt, spy on them.[29]

The expedition returned to sea in late March and spent the next six months gathering yet more fur. This period was especially productive, as they sailed into uncharted waters where Natives, unaccustomed to the trade and the high value of their goods, held "a great many furs which we purchas'd cheap."[30] Low prices did not last. Natives quickly recognized the high demand and value of their goods. Furthermore, they shrewdly understood the limited nature of the commodity, and used scarcity and competition to drive up prices. Many years later, a British trader on the coast of British Columbia recounted a price war between his ship and an American rival. "The Indians glory in having … opposition," he remarked "and know well how to take advantage of it."[31]

Gray clashed with Natives on several occasions throughout the summer of 1792. In May, Boit recounted how he "heard the hooting of Indians" and observed "canoes approaching the Ship" in the "bright moonlight." Warning shots deterred them at first, but a canoe "with at least 20 Men in her" got too close. The crew opened fire, "dash'd her all to pieces, and no doubt kill'd every soul in her."[32] Natives came on board the *Columbia* the next day to trade. Observing their behavior, Boit concluded "they had no Knowledge of fire arms previous to our coming" and expressed regret. I am sorry we was oblidged [*sic*] to kill the poor Devils," he wrote, "but it cou'd not with safety be avoided."[33] Boit recorded a number of such incidents. In some cases, offensive behavior from fur traders spurred attacks. In others, Native Peoples tried to raid trading parties when the benefits seemed to outweigh the risks. We should not exaggerate the prevalence of violence, however. Both sides eagerly engaged in and benefited from trade, and seldom resorted to violence.[34]

On May 11, Gray accomplished something that would put him in history books. He was the first non-native to locate the entrance to the Columbia River, the "Great River of the West," which would significantly strengthen American claims in the region[35] (for more on Gray's encounter at the Columbia River, see Chapter 1, Early Encounters).

In October, Gray set sail for Canton (Guangzhou), China, stopping in Hawaii for "Hogs and fowls … Tropical fruits in abundance" to sustain them on the journey. December found them in Canton alongside six American ships and 47 European vessels. They spent two months selling their fur and loading the ship "with a full Cargo of Teas … a small proportion of Sugar and China Porcelain" for sale in Boston. Chinese merchants, according to Boit, "*will* cheat you, if they can," and he warned readers to carefully inspect goods received.[36]

Conditions on the *Columbia* deteriorated during the six-month return home. By the end they ate "maggotty bread" and desperately sought out fresh food from passing ships. They landed in Boston on July 25, 1793, nearly three years after setting out, and an exhausted Boit concluded, "Tis impossible to express our feelings at again meeting with our friends."[37] He must have enjoyed the experience or been lured by the idea of greater profit, because he did not rest long. In 1794 he left for another multi-year voyage to the Pacific Northwest.[38]

Like the *Columbia*, numerous British and American expeditions vied for control of the Pacific Northwest. Great Britain controlled the early years of the maritime fur trade, but Americans quickly caught up. Four ships from each nation traded along the coast in 1789, and Americans gradually pulled ahead over the next decade. By 1800, Americans clearly dominated this contested region. From 1800 through 1810, American ships entered Northwest waters at least 120 times, compared to 13 British vessels.[39]

The maritime trade declined after 1813 due largely to overhunting.[40] Nootka Sound, the starting point of conflict between Spain and Britain, illustrates the point. By 1825, with the sea otter mostly hunted out, Nootka Sound "was seldom visited by traders," one British writer noted, because "of the … poverty of the place, yielding very few furs."[41] The situation was the same all along the coast. A pre-trade population of up to 300,000 sea otter was nearly extinct by the late 1820s.[42] By 1911, fewer than 2,000 remained, leaving the species threatened into the twenty-first century. Some American maritime traders continued to operate, trading sandalwood in Hawaii, moving into the beaver trade, and supplying the Russian-American Company in Alaska. While these endeavors showed profit, traders faced a new obstacle: the rise of the continental fur trade and the powerful British Hudson's Bay Company.[43]

Traders establish permanent presence in interior

> The Hudson's Bay Company virtually eliminated American competition in the interior and gave Britain a strong claim to ownership of the Pacific Northwest.

The continental fur trade, distinct from the maritime trade, opened in 1810. Where maritime traders came by ship and stayed for only a few months, continental traders traveled overland across North America, establishing permanent outposts throughout the interior and coast. While focused on beaver furs, they also accepted sea otter pelts and a variety of land animals like marten, wolverine, and land otter.[44] The nature of the business differed as well. Maritime traders bought nearly all of their furs from local Natives. Continental traders certainly purchased furs, but they also hired Natives from outside the region, including the Cree and Iroquois, to hunt beaver directly and sometimes joined the hunt themselves.[45] Importantly, the race for power in the region swung dramatically in this period, as Britain reasserted power lost in the maritime trade. By the 1830s, the Hudson's Bay Company virtually eliminated American competition in the interior and gave Britain a strong claim to ownership of the Pacific Northwest.

The British North West Company, formed in 1783–1784 by Montreal merchants, sent explorers west in search of new opportunities and first developed the continental trade in the Pacific Northwest.[46] Alexander Mackenzie, a North West Company founder, was the first. He led expeditions to the Arctic Ocean in 1789 and the British Columbia coast in 1793, but neither proved suitable.[47] Undeterred, he called on the company to form "regular establishments through the interior" and expand trade in "the markets of the four quarters of the globe."[48] His account influenced the Lewis and Clark expedition, and spurred the North West Company to send out Simon Fraser and David Thompson.[49] Between 1805 and 1808, Fraser established multiple posts in British Columbia. Thompson scoured the region from 1807–1812 and successfully charted the Columbia River, a major prize as they deemed the river to be an invaluable transportation route.[50] Along the way he established fur trade posts, including Kullyspel House and Spokane House in present-day Idaho and Washington.[51] He did not, however, establish a post at the mouth of the Columbia because Americans got there first.

Figure 2.1 Alexander Mackenzie looks a bit more like a gentleman than an explorer in this portrait printed in his "Voyages from Montreal on the River St. Lawrence through the Continent of North America to the Frozen and Pacific Oceans in the years 1789 and 1793." His exploits paved the way for later expeditions and the rise of the Northwest fur trade. Reprinted with permission from the Washington State Historical Society.

ALEXANDER MACKENZIE Esq.

The Pacific Fur Company, organized by American businessman John Jacob Astor in 1810, established Fort Astoria near the mouth of the Columbia just months prior to Thompson's arrival.[52] Astor sent one expedition by sea and one overland, but neither fared well. The overland party barely survived. His ship, the *Tonquin* landed a party at Astoria and left to trade, but Natives in the vicinity of Nootka Sound, angered by his arrogance, destroyed the ship.[53] When supply ships failed to arrive, and with the onset of the War of 1812, the Astorians feared capture by the British, and sold their holdings to the North West Company.[54] Soon thereafter, the British took possession of Fort Astoria and renamed it Fort George.[55]

Despite concerted efforts to profit from the region, North West Company operations along the Columbia routinely lost money and failed, due mainly to unsustainable transportation costs. The roughly 2,600 mile trip between Montreal and the Northwest sapped company returns. The trade produced "a very considerable loss to the Company," one leader commented, "as the furs did not pay the transport to Montreal."[56] Furthermore, the British government granted an exclusive monopoly on trade in China to the East India Company, shutting out the North West Company. In response, they contracted with Americans for shipping, but that required the payment of "heavy Charges & large Commissions."[57] Lastly, competition between the two British companies turned ruinous and shockingly violent.[58] Ultimately, the British government forced the companies to merge in 1821, enhancing HBC control in the Pacific Northwest.[59]

Hudson's Bay Company takes charge

While trade in British Columbia showed promise, a skeptical HBC nearly gave up on the southern "Oregon Country." In addition to facing competing claims from Russia and the United States, HBC understood the warmer climate produced a lower-quality fur.[60] Over the first two-plus decades of the nineteenth century, competition in the region thinned. Spain gave up claims north of California in the Adams-Onís Treaty of 1819, while Russia relinquished its claims south of Alaska to both the United States and Great Britain in 1824 and 1825.[61] Britain and the United States, however, failed to settle their differences and agreed to "joint occupancy" in 1818, keeping travel and trade open "to the vessels, citizens, and subjects of the two powers."[62] This posed two problems. First, the American presence would likely drive up fur prices. Second, HBC worried over the risk of developing operations in what could become U.S. territory.[63] Given the profit potential, company leaders were not going to simply hand over the Pacific Northwest to the United States. For now, British territory would remain in British hands.[64]

In 1824, HBC sent George Simpson to tour the region, implement reforms, and make the region profitable. Simpson, a pragmatic and arrogant, yet highly successful administrator, quickly proposed cutting the local work force nearly in half.[65] He then railed about money spent importing food and luxuries from Europe. Employees "may be said to have been eating Gold," he said, insisting it must be "discontinued."[66] Why import food when there were potatoes, game, and an "abundance of the finest Salmon in the World ... in short everything that is good or necessary for an Indian trader."[67]

Simpson went beyond cost-cutting and forced reluctant traders to farm, ignoring predictions that it would "drive off and extinguish the wild animals that furnish their commerce."[68] Farming required additional outposts on suitable land, and Fort George

Figure 2.2 Colville chief See-pay, the "Salmon Chief" or "Chief of the Waters," launched and organized his tribe's salmon harvest each season. He speared the first fish, directed placement of traps and oversaw construction of fishing platforms. Paul Kane oil on canvas. Image provided with permission from the Royal Ontario Museum.

did not fit the bill. Accordingly, Simpson ordered the construction of Fort Vancouver in 1824 on the northern bank of the Columbia. The company's new regional headquarters flourished, producing "10,000 pounds of cured pork in 1828" and 1,500 bushels of wheat and up to 5,000 bushels of potatoes the following year.[69] Fort Colvile, opened in 1825 near Kettle Falls in northeastern Washington, proved equally productive. Simpson next turned his eye towards eliminating foreign competition that chased after the same limited supply of furs and drove up prices. American traders posed the greatest threat, especially the St. Louis-based Rocky Mountain Fur Company, which dispatched the romanticized "mountain men" to trap fur on the southern and eastern flanks of HBC territory.[70] Additionally, Boston-based traders still dominated coastal trade, buying beaver shipped from the interior along native trade routes.[71]

Aggressive tactics create "fur deserts"

Larger and better financed than American competitors, HBC used aggressive business tactics to drive them from the region, as the case of Nathaniel Wyeth illustrates. Wyeth, a successful Boston businessman, felt he could challenge HBC. After an unsuccessful expedition to the region in 1832, he returned to establish Fort Hall in Idaho and Fort William in Oregon in 1834.[72] Unwilling to tolerate this encroachment, HBC rapidly moved to drive him out of business. They established Fort Boise in Idaho to siphon business away from Fort Hall and raised fur prices to ruinous levels. As one of Wyeth's companions wrote, "The fur trade was their business, and if an American vessel came up the river, or coast, they would bid up the price on furs, and if necessary a price ten to one above their usual prices."[73] It was all too much for Wyeth, who sold out to HBC in 1837. The company maintained Fort Hall but razed Fort William.[74] Wyeth relayed his experiences, warning that "the entire weight of the company" would fall on any who dared challenge HBC.[75] Clearly, Americans, relegated to working on the margins, recognized HBC's power.[76]

Nationalism, memory, and the Hudson's Bay Company

Historians recognize the Hudson's Bay Company's central role in the Northwest's early history, yet it has been frequently forgotten or marginalized in the region's collective American-centric memory.

In 1931, the community in Spanaway, Washington, celebrated the Longmire Party, the first Americans to cross Naches Pass in 1853.[77] Yet speeches that day failed to acknowledge HBC traders had been trotting that path a decade before the Longmires, to say nothing of the centuries-long use among Natives.[78]

The past was distorted further in a stamp in the U.S. Postal Service "Americana" series in 1978. It shows a Fort Nisqually bastion inscribed with, "Remote Outpost – New Nation Building Westward," clearly misleading users to believe Nisqually was an American fort.

These presentations of the past suggest that, until recently, Americans wanted to erase the former colonizing power from their collective memory.[79] In short, nationalism inspired Northwesterners to construct a narrative emphasizing American pioneers, while downplaying the prior presence of Native Peoples and the British HBC.

With competition continuing along the region's borders, HBC adopted a more aggressive policy hunting fur-bearing animals to extinction and turning the borderlands into "fur deserts," as historian Carlos Schwantes calls them.[80] American traders mostly trapped in the Rocky Mountains and rarely made the costly journey to the Columbia. They did, however, encroach on HBC territory in Idaho, notably along the Snake River. Simpson described the Snake Country as, "a rich preserve of Beaver" that the company "should endeavour [*sic*] to destroy as fast as possible" since an "exhausted frontier" would be "the best protection we have against the encroachments of rival traders."[81] Two large HBC hunting parties, named the Snake Brigade and the Southern Party, put this policy into effect.[82] A diverse mix of British traders and Natives from many cultures collected as much fur as possible, significantly reducing populations. In 1826, for instance, the Snake Brigade brought in 2,099 skins, but returns dropped to 800 furs by 1836.[83] They even encroached on American territory in the Rockies, actively disrupting operations. American mountain men held an annual "rendezvous" in the Rocky Mountains to exchange furs and obtain supplies. Starting in 1833, the Snake Brigade invaded the rendezvous, exchanging goods at prices Americans could not match. At the last rendezvous in 1841, HBC left triumphant.[84]

George Simpson employed similar methods against American competition on the coast. First, between 1831 and 1840, the company established a string of forts in British Columbia, including Forts Simpson, McLoughlin, Stikine, and Taku. Second, they deployed their own fleet including the SS *Beaver*, the first steamship to work the Northwest.[85] Simpson ordered his traders to outbid all American competition,

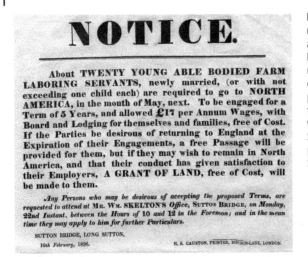

NOTICE.

About **TWENTY YOUNG ABLE BODIED FARM LABORING SERVANTS,** newly married, (or with not exceeding one child each) are required to go to **NORTH AMERICA,** in the month of May, next. To be engaged for a Term of 5 Years, and allowed **£17** per Annum Wages, with Board and Lodging for themselves and families, free of Cost. If the Parties be desirous of returning to England at the Expiration of their Engagements, a free Passage will be provided for them, but if they may wish to remain in North America, and that their conduct has given satisfaction to their Employers, **A GRANT OF LAND,** free of Cost, will be made to them.

Any Persons who may be desirous of accepting the proposed Terms, are requested to attend at Mr. Wm. SKELTON'S *Office,* Sutton Bridge, *on Monday,* 22nd Instant, *between the Hours of* 10 and 12 *in the Forenoon; and in the mean time they may apply to him for further Particulars.*

SUTTON BRIDGE, LONG SUTTON,
10th *February*, 1836.

H. K. CAUSTON, PRINTER, BIRCHIN-LANE, LONDON.

Figure 2.3 Hudson's Bay Company recruitment flyers attracted a diverse, and at times motley, lot to the Pacific Northwest. The terms of the position reflect the hierarchical nature of the company. Workers had to accept a place as "servants" and bind themselves to a five-year contract working for aristocratic leaders like Sir George Simpson. Reprinted with permission from the Washington State Historical Society.

commenting, "we can afford to undersell them by carrying on this business in conjunction with an Extensive Inland Trade."[86] To further undercut the Americans, HBC wooed away their largest buyer, the Russian-American Company, securing a contract in 1839.[87] As in the interior, HBC's aggressive tactics paid off, and American voyages fell to a trickle by the mid-1830s.[88]

British diversify beyond furs

The Pacific Northwest differed from other HBC lands in that its resources enabled the company to branch into logging, milling, salmon-packing, and commercial agriculture.[89] John McLoughlin, the Chief Factor at Fort Vancouver, explained the fur trade was soon to be "knocked up," and he felt raising cattle for tallow and hides would amount to more "than that of the furs collected west of the Rocky Mountains."[90]

Early British explorers and fur traders, who needed spars for repairs, developed a market for timber in Hawaii, where many wintered.[91] The HBC, however, established a large-scale, sustained logging business. They opened operations at Fort Vancouver in the late 1820s, and within a few years, 28 laborers operated 12 saws. The HBC marketed lumber successfully in Hawaii and, with somewhat disappointing results, in California and Valparaiso, Chile.[92]

Beyond timber, HBC traders quickly recognized the value of both fresh and dried salmon, which quickly became staples in Northwest trade by the 1820s.[93] Fur and traders did not actually fish themselves, however. They purchased it from Natives, or hired them to pickle the product and pack it into barrels for shipping.[94] The HBC processed salmon at several company posts, including the prominent Fort Langley, built in British Columbia in 1827. While fur production at Langley disappointed, Simpson expressed little concern.[95] "The returns in furs are gradually falling off," he admitted in 1841, "but the increasing marketable produce of the fisheries makes up for that deficiency."[96] Indeed, salmon-packing flourished, as production jumped to 605 barrels by 1835 and peaked at 2,610 by 1849, although tariffs and other fees shaved profits.[97] Commercial

Figure 2.4 Eager to trade with Britain's Hudson's Bay Company, Natives often gathered outside Fort Nisqually near what is now DuPont, Washington. The British artist Henry James Warre created this and other oil paintings while on a mission to spy on American interests in the region in 1845. Image provided with permission from the Royal Ontario Museum.

farming and ranching also developed into a major HBC business. As with fishing, they first farmed to feed employees and then sold surplus.[98] Production expanded through the 1830s thanks to the Russian-American Company contract in 1839.[99] Farming continued at established posts like Fort Vancouver and Fort Colvile, while the HBC's newly formed Puget Sound Agriculture Company (PSAC) operated at Cowlitz Farms in southwest Washington and Fort Nisqually between present-day Olympia and Tacoma.[100] Yields at Cowlitz Farms were significant. In 1846, it produced 9,000 bushels of grain, 2,000 bushels of peas, and 1,000 bushels of potatoes.[101] Fort Nisqually's poor soil led to modest harvests, but ranching prospered, providing tallow, leather, horns and wool for sale in Britain. By 1846, herds of 8,000 sheep and 3,000 cows roamed the outstations around the fort.[102]

The PSAC produced mixed results. From a business standpoint, the company achieved a remarkable scale of exports. In 1843, the company sent 9,314 bushels of wheat, 41,200 pounds of flour, 17,584 bushels of peas, 33,456 pounds of beef, and 5,448 pounds of butter to the Russians in Sitka and 6,263 pounds of wool to London.[103] Yet, while PSAC turned a steady profit, its policies discouraged British settlement. Officials had hoped to promote settlement to counter the growing number of Americans. Unfortunately, Russian demands forced PSAC to purchase food from retired fur traders and American settlers in the Willamette Valley, which facilitated American migration.[104] Furthermore, efforts to recruit British settlers mostly failed. The company offered Brits financial support and access to company land for a share of the produce, but it refused to give up control and sell land outright.[105]

Environmental history and the fur trade

Environmental history examines the interrelationships between humans and the environment. On one level, the environment has shaped and constrained human societies. Emigrants from the American Southeast, for example, could not establish tobacco plantations in the rainy Northwest, but they could hunt fur-bearing animals.[106]

Conversely, human activities shaped the environment. Long before the arrival of Euro-Americans, Native Peoples set fires on the prairies to keep the forests at bay and encourage the growth of edible plants such as camas and chocolate lilies.[107]

To the Hudson's Bay Company, the prairies around Fort Nisqually proved unsuitable for raising sheep, so they burned and reseeded them with clover and other desirable grasses.[108] Like the Natives before them, HBC employees altered the natural environment, but in doing so they disrupted the native economy. Obviously, trapping and trading the region's fur-bearing animals to the point of near extinction impacted the environment dramatically, but logging, fishing, and farming led to even more significant changes in the years ahead.

The diverse labor force at Nisqually and Cowlitz, as at all HBC establishments, deserves attention. The 17 employees at Nisqually in 1841, for instance, included a diverse mix of French Canadian, Scottish, English, Coastal Salish, and Hawaiian, among others.[109] Hawaiians, known as Kanakas ("human" in Hawaiian), accounted for over half the workforce in Fort Vancouver's sawmills and Fort Langley's packing plants.[110] Pay rates at Nisqually reveal the racial hierarchy within this labor force. British employees earned £35.00 a year, Hawaiians up to £17.00 and Natives between £4.00 to £8.00, a racially based pay scale that persisted into the twentieth century.[111]

HBC–Native relations – the ties that bind trade

It's difficult to imagine a flourishing fur trade without Natives hunting and processing most of the furs. But the relationship between traders and Natives, a source of controversy in historical works, deserves a closer look. Earlier histories claimed Euro-American traders took advantage of and manipulated Natives, often portrayed as passive victims.[112] That view, however, presents problems. Natives hunted fur-bearing animals and traded extensively with each other long before non-native fur traders arrived.[113] Additionally, amassing and giving away wealth increased prestige and power in many Northwest cultures.[114] Given that, it is not surprising Native Peoples actively sought trade on their own terms.[115] Traders like Simpson complained they did little to satisfy the company. Natives near Kettle Falls, would "pick up a few Skins to enable them to purchase the triffling [*sic*] articles of British Manufacture …"[116] Later he bemoaned that "if the Natives would but apply themselves to Hunting during the Winter Months the Trade would be greatly increased." But he wielded limited power, and Natives worked when it best fit their cultural patterns and personal desires.[117] If nothing else, keep in mind that Natives vastly outnumbered traders.

Although capable of destroying brigades and outposts, especially in the early years, Natives rarely exhibited violence because they recognized trade's potential. In other words, the growing fur trade did not immediately change or threaten native cultures.[118] Instead, it built upon existing practices and provided opportunities Natives readily seized.

Native attempts to control trade matched HBC's, and for the same reasons: profit and power. According to Simpson, nothing changed with the arrival of the HBC. He described the Chinook as "keen traders" who jealously guarded their monopoly on trade, going so far as to portray HBC as "Cannibals and every thing that is bad" to keep "other tribes on the Coast" at bay.[119]

Similarly, Natives living near HBC forts attempted to dominate access to other tribes. When the company began building Fort Victoria on Vancouver Island in 1843, it "appeared to please" the Songhee people, who "immediately offered their services in procuring pickets for the establishment."[120] The Songhee soon moved their village closer to the new fort in order to better control trade.[121] At Fort Nisqually, visiting Natives paid tribute to local tribes before trading, as described by William Fraser Tolmie, a HBC official in 1833. "Scetlam the Kaatchet chief having made peace with Chiatzasan by a present of two guns," he reported, "was permitted to visit us & says he has 27 beaver."[122] His comments are telling. Those around the fort held power and required appeasement before outsiders gained access. Neither the HBC nor Natives challenged the point.

The Chinook and failed Fort Winship

In 1810, Americans Jonathan Winship, Nathaniel Winship, Abiel Winship, and Benjamin Homer set out to establish a permanent fort on the banks of the Columbia River. William Gale, the captain's assistant recorded that as they worked on the post "Chinook and Cheheelees" arrived "all armed with bows and arrows, or muskets." While Natives claimed they intended to launch a retaliatory attack on another tribe, Americans remained skeptical.

Gale explained, "the Chinooks are strongly set against our coming up the river … as they are in the habit of purchasing skins of the upper tribes, and reselling them to the ships which occasionally arrive at the river." Fort Winship posed a real threat to Chinook control of local trade, and Gale feared they would attack.

After two increasingly tense days, the Winships concluded it was "impossible to prosecute the business" as planned and gave up. They informed the Chinook who appeared "quite satisfied" and sold furs before the Winships left.[123]

Cultural differences threatened to drive a wedge between traders and Natives. Traders typically viewed them with contempt and complained they were lazy, prone to stealing, deceitful, and generally immoral. They wrote disapprovingly of the common practice of polygamy, and disparaged native gender norms.[124] Women's labor in many native societies often provided up to half or even the majority of a family's diet, and they generally held more status than Euro-American women. British and American traders, misinterpreted the division of labor of course. Men who let women do the work were deemed lazy.[125] Not surprisingly, Natives similarly viewed traders with a mixture of disgust and contempt. The historian Alexandra Harmon points out they were put off by the pale, bad-mannered, unshaven traders ignorant of the country. For instance, the "important men often appeared lazy, bossing dependents instead of working alongside them.

They did not employ proper, self-deprecating expressions when addressing eminent outsiders" or "keep their tempers in check, as well-bred men and women did."[126] Despite these feelings, both sides put aside their dislikes to reap trade's benefits.

Native Peoples and fur traders interacted on what the historian Richard White calls a "middle ground," a contested space where neither party held complete control and both accommodated.[127] The practice of gift-giving provides a good example. Trade among Northwest Natives included a social element in addition to an exchange of commodities. Although they often chafed at doing so, traders learned to present gifts to establish relationships and smooth trade.[128] As historian Elizabeth Vibert put it, "If there was no gift, there was no such relationship; without a social relationship, there could be no trade."[129] She also points out cases where Native Peoples clearly saw "gifts" as payment for the use of their land and willingness to accept the presence of traders.[130] The HBC's tolerance of slavery provides another example. While common among Northwest Natives, Great Britain outlawed slavery in 1833, and HBC officials deplored the practice.[131] Regardless, employees often married Natives who owned slaves and brought them into HBC establishments. Leaders could not end slavery without harming relations and hurting their business, so they reluctantly accepted it.[132] This highlights a critical point: HBC generally maintained good relations with Natives because it served their interests. As HBC's McLoughlin put it, "We are traders, and apart from more exalted motives, all traders are desirous of gain. Is it not self-evident that we will manage our business with more economy by being on good terms with the Indians than if at variance."[133] In other words, it was about money, not morality.

HBC officials, like George Simpson, policed their employees to maintain good relations. While traveling, Simpson observed how brigades leaving Fort Okanagan passed through an area with "scarcely a Tree or Shrub" for firewood. Needing fuel, they removed wood from "the pallisades that surround the Graves of the Natives." "This is a most unwarrantable liberty and would on the other side of the mountain be considered the grossest insult," Simpson reported.[134] Similarly Simpson instructed Snake Brigade employees to keep away from the powerful Nez Perce. The brigade was a "motley crew" made up of the "very scum of the country," while the Nez Perce controlled the region. Fearing "quarrels," he concluded, "the less intercourse we have with the Nez Perces beyond what is absolutely necessary the better."[135] The case of Francis Ermatinger is even more telling. Ermatinger, put in charge of Fort Okanagan in 1826, formed a relationship with Cleo, a Shuswap woman. Although he professed little love for her, he hired someone to cut off the ears of a competing lover. HBC quickly transferred the jealous Ermatinger to Fort Colvile, choosing once again, profit over principle.[136]

The HBC demonstrated as much firmness with Natives as it did employees.[137] Attempts to "pillage the Brigades when the Country was first established," quickly ceased, according to George Simpson, because of "the example made of them at the time and subsequent conciliatory yet firm and judicious conduct of the traders."[138] More dramatic events unfolded in the northern waters of Puget Sound in 1828. Clallam on Lummi Island killed five members of a HBC party traveling to Fort Vancouver, and kidnapped the Native wife of one of the men. In response, HBC dispatched an attack force of HBC employees and Natives hostile to the Clallam. After talks failed, HBC fired on the village, set it ablaze and destroyed a second Clallam village. Sources give varying numbers, but between 17 and 29 Clallam were killed to "deter them & their countrymen from committing any acts of violence towards us."[139] The attack's effectiveness remains

Figure 2.5 Colville salmon fishing at Kettle Falls near Colville in what is now northeast Washington. This oil on canvas is one of dozens by Canadian painter Paul Kane, who traveled throughout Oregon Territory from 1845 to 1848 to create a lasting record of Native Peoples. Image provided with permission from the Royal Ontario Museum.

debatable given the cultural differences between both sides. Did the Clallam view it as an act of vengeance, an accepted practice at the time, or as a deterrent to future violence?[140] Regardless, attacks on HBC stopped as their name apparently held clout. When artist Paul Kane traveled the same route in 1843, a Nisqually leader traveling with him let passing Natives believe a piece of newspaper he carried was a letter from HBC. They left them alone.[141] Importantly, these moments of conflict should not be overemphasized. The company wanted to maintain good relations and conflict was the exception, not the norm.[142]

Interracial relationships, exceptionally common in trade, strengthened relations between traders and Native Peoples. North West Company and HBC employees spent long periods in a region where few Euro-American women lived prior to the 1840s. As such, intermarriage was desirable for personal and economic reasons and not generally stigmatized.[143] They established union "à la façon du pays" or "in the custom of the country" in which men first obtained permission from the woman's family and provided gifts. Traders and early historians described this as "buying" a wife, but that portrayal remains problematic. Gift-giving, a standard part of forming marriages, helped to establish and maintain relationships, what Simpson called a "useful link."[144] The labor of Native women proved beneficial as well. They made shoes, produced food, trapped small fur-bearing animals, processed furs, worked in various HBC industries, and generally filled the role of "helpmate."[145] For them, marriage enhanced their access to trade and traders and paved an avenue to prestige.[146]

Differing gender norms often created tension within country marriages. Women who had power in native societies, not surprisingly, expected to maintain it in marriages to Europeans or Americans, causing Simpson to complain, "When married or allied to the Whites they are under little restraint and in most cases gain such an ascendency that they give law to their Lords."[147] Similarly, a manager at Fort Colvile allowed "himself to be entirely governed & dictated to in his own house by his Old Squaw & Sons."[148] Their husbands, however, often pressured wives to adopt British values. Daughters of the fur trade faced even greater pressure. The daughter of a Fort Nisqually employee learned to quilt, can, bake, weave, wash and practice Christianity in Scottish tradition.[149] It should be noted, however, that fur trade marriages gradually fell out of favor, and the families pushed to the margins of society, as racial lines hardened and trade gave way to settlement.[150]

As Natives sought to manage trade, one thing proved beyond their control: the spread of catastrophic disease. The appearance of smallpox, measles, and influenza, among others, arrived with explorers in the late eighteenth century and then spread along intertribal trade routes.[151] Ongoing contact with traders furthered this process with devastating consequences, as on the Lower Columbia where the Native population fell by roughly 90% between 1830 and 1841.[152] While the spread of disease accompanied all encounters with Euro-Americans and was not a function of trade itself, it devastated native societies.[153] Nonetheless, trade brought prosperity and spurred development of art and material culture.[154] Importantly, however, Northwest Natives did not abandon cultural norms to take part in the fur trade. Rather, they built trade into their preexisting seasonal economies and used it to enhance cultural traditions and improve the quality of their lives.[155]

From 'bad to worse' and the end of an era

> The Americans are scattered all over the Country, from Fort George to the Cascades, and, as we may expect the emigration to increase, the fur trade must fall to nothing.
>
> – *Francis Ermatinger*[156]

The Northwest fur trade declined in the 1840s. In 1846, HBC's Columbia Department produced only 12,958 skins, compared to a peak of 21,746 in 1831.[157] Overhunting finally took its toll, combined with waning demand for beaver as silk hats came into vogue.[158] Finally, the rise of the Oregon Trail in the 1840s and the growing stream of American settlers turned things from "bad to worse," according to Francis Ermatinger. "The Americans are scattered all over the Country, from Fort George to the Cascades, and, as we may expect the emigration to increase, the fur trade must fall to nothing," he wrote.[159] John McLoughlin echoed Ermatinger's sentiments. "Every One Knows who is acquainted with the Fur trade that as the country becomes settled the Fur trade Must Diminish."[160]

Simpson recognized the United States might gain control of western Washington and moved HBC headquarters from Fort Vancouver to the newly established Fort Victoria

Figure 2.6 Spokane Garry's life transcended profoundly different historical eras. Born in the era of the fur trade, he came of age when the Spokane Tribe worked with traders on a middle ground. Everything changed as American settlers moved into the region. Ultimately forced off his land by trespassing Americans, he died destitute. A monument to Garry can be found in Spokane's Chief Garry Park. Reprinted with permission from the Washington State Historical Society.

CHIEF GARRY IN OLD AGE

in 1843.[161] His concerns were well founded, as the United States gained control of the Northwest below the forty-ninth parallel, including the Puget Sound region and Lower Columbia, in the Oregon Treaty of 1846.[162] The HBC retained its holdings in U.S. territory, where they continued operating until 1869, when the United States paid $650,000 for all HBC and PSAC possessions.[163]

The fur trade era profoundly affected the Pacific Northwest. It spurred significant migration, paved the way for permanent settlement, and brought Native Peoples into sustained relationships with non-natives. It also stimulated a diverse array of industries and connected the region to global markets. Interestingly, trade's success planted the seeds of its undoing. Hudson's Bay Company forts offered critical way-stations along the Oregon Trail greatly enabling American settlement in the 1840s and 1850s.

Explore more

Books

This chapter's overview of the fur trade draws heavily from the works of James Gibson, Richard Somerset Mackie, Alexandra Harmon, and Elizabeth Vibert. Gibson's *Otter Skins, Boston Ships, and China Goods* covers the maritime fur trade and *Farming the Frontier: The Agricultural Opening of the Oregon Country, 1786–1846* provides a detailed account of the Hudson's Bay Company's efforts to diversify. Mackie's *Trading Beyond the Mountains: The British Fur Trade on the Pacific 1793–1843* gives an excellent account of the rise, success, and decline of the Hudson's Bay Company operations in the Pacific Northwest. Nuanced discussions of trader-Native relations can be found in Harmon's *Indians in the Making: Ethnic Relations and Indian Identities around Puget Sound*, 1998 and Vibert's *Traders' Tales: Narratives of Cultural Encounters in the Columbia Plateau, 1807–1846.*

Online

Historylink.org (http://historylink.org/), the Oregon Encyclopedia (http://www.orego nencyclopedia.org/), and the Oregon History Project (http://oregonhistoryproject.org/) have many good, short entries on the fur trade. The Hudson's Bay Company (http://www3.hbc.com/) has a worthwhile section on the company's history. The Internet Archive (https://archive.org/) has free copies of fur trader journals and books from that era. HBC Archives can be searched online at https://www.gov.mb.ca/chc/archives/hbca/. While documents cannot be viewed directly, the archives do offer copy services.

Museums

Several fur trade forts, Fort Vancouver in Vancouver, Washington (http://www.nps.gov/fova/index.htm), Fort Nisqually Living History Museum (http://www.metroparksta coma.org/fort-nisqually-living-history-museum), and Fort Hall (http://www.forthall.net/) have been rebuilt and are well worth visiting. The Confederated Tribes of the Colville Reservation maintain the Fort Okanogan Interpretive Center (http://www.colvilletribes.com/fort_okanogan_interpretive_center.php).

What do you think?

Historians argue that Native Americans and Euro-American fur traders interacted on a "middle ground" and had to respect the interests of the other side whether they wanted to or not. Do you agree with the assessment? Why or why not?

Analyze the fur trade experience from the Native point of view. Why did they engage in the fur trade? Could individual cultures have realistically refrained from trading once neighboring peoples became involved? What were the short- and long-term benefits and drawbacks to trade?

Notes

1 Melinda Marie Jetté, "'Beaver are Numerous, but the Natives … Will Not Hunt Them':
Native-Fur Trader Relations in the Willamette Valley, 1812–1814," *Pacific Northwest
Quarterly* 98, no. 1 (Winter 2006/2007): 8.

2 Ibid., 8.

3 Ibid.

4 Ibid.," 9; Robert H. Ruby, John A. Brown, and Cary C. Collins, *A Guide to the Indian
Tribes of the Pacific Northwest,* 3rd ed. (Norman, OK: University of Oklahoma Press,
2010), 29–31.

5 Eric Jay Dolin, *Fur, Fortune, and Empire: The Epic History of the Fur Trade in America*
(New York: W.W. Norton & Company, 2010), 9; Carlos A. Schwantes, *The Pacific
Northwest: An Interpretive History,* 2nd ed. (Lincoln, NE: University of Nebraska Press,
1996), 63.

6 Schwantes, *The Pacific Northwest,* 43–44; James R. Gibson, *Otter Skins, Boston Ships,
and China Goods* (Seattle, WA: University of Washington Press, 1992), 12.

7 Gibson, *Otter Skins,* 13.

8 Robert H. Ruby and John A. Brown, *The Chinook Indians* (Norman, OK: University of
Oklahoma Press, 1976), 120; "Outpost of an Empire," Fort Ross Conservancy, accessed
February 27, 2016, http://www.fortross.org/russian-american-company.htm.

9 Gibson, *Otter Skins,* 18.

10 David J. Weber, "The Spanish Moment in the Pacific Northwest," in *Terra Pacifica: People and Place in the Northwest States and Western Canada,* ed. Paul Hirt (Pullman,
WA: Washington State University Press, 1998), 8; Dorothy O. Johansen and Charles M.
Gates, *Empire of the Columbia: A History of the Pacific Northwest* (New York: Harper
and Brothers, 1957), 29; Schwantes, *The Pacific Northwest,* 44.

11 Johansen, *Empire of the Columbia,* 29; Antonio Sanchez, "Spanish Exploration: Juan
Pérez Expedition of 1774 – First European Discovery and Exploration of Washington
State Coast and Nueva Galicia (the Pacific Northwest)," *HistoryLink,* accessed
September 28, 2014, http://www.historylink.org/.

12 Robin Fisher, *Contact and Conflict: Indian-European Relations in British Columbia,
1774–1890,* 2nd. ed. (Vancouver: University of British Columbia Press, 1992), 1–2.

13 Sanchez, "Spanish Exploration"; Juan José Pérez Hernández, *Juan Pérez on the Northwest Coast: Six Documents of His Expedition in 1774,* translated by Herbert K. Beals
(Portland, OR: Oregon Historical Society Press, 1989), 89.

14 Gibson, *Otter Skins* 18; Weber, "The Spanish Moment," 6–8.

15 Johansen, *Empire of the Columbia,* 32; Jean Barman, *The West Beyond the West: A History of British Columbia,* revised ed. (Toronto: University of Toronto Press, 1996), 22.

16 Dolin, *Fur, Fortune, and Empire,* 134–135.

17 Johansen, *Empire of the Columbia,* 36–37; Barman, *The West Beyond the West,* 22–23;
Gibson, *Otter Skins,* 22–23.

18 John Boit, "John Boit's Log of the Columbia, 1790–1793," ed. F.W. Howay, T.C. Elliott,
and F.G. Young, *The Quarterly of the Oregon Historical Society* 22, no. 4 (December
1921): 308.

19 Ibid., 265.

20 Gibson, *Otter Skins,* 23.

21 Ibid., 299.

22 Boit, "John Boit's Log," 266–267, 274.

23 Ibid., 275–278.

24 Ibid., 281, 317.

25 Ibid., 279–288; 317.

26 Ibid., 280.

27 Gibson, *Otter Skins*, 228–238.

28 Boit, "John Boit's Log," 291–296.

29 Ibid., 299–301.

30 Ibid., 307.

31 Quoted in Johansen, *Empire of the Columbia*, 158–159.

32 Boit, "John Boit's Log," 307–308; Dolin, *Fur, Fortune, and Empire*, 153.

33 Boit, "John Boit's Log," 308.

34 Fisher, *Contact and Conflict*, 12–17.

35 Center for the Study of the Pacific Northwest, *European and American Exploration of the 18th-Century Pacific Northwest*, accessed June 19, 2014, http://www.washington.edu.

36 Boit, "John Boit's Log," 333–338.

37 Ibid., 347, 349.

38 See John Boit, Edmund Hayes, and Hewitt R. Jackson, *Log of the Union: John Boit's Remarkable Voyage to the Northwest Coast and Around the World, 1794–1796* (Portland, OR: Oregon Historical Society, 1981).

39 Gibson, *Otter Skins*, 299–303.

40 Johansen, *Empire of the Columbia*, 74; Earl Pomeroy, *The Pacific Slope: A History of California, Oregon, Washington, Idaho, Utah, and Nevada* (Lincoln, NE: University of Nebraska Press), 19.

41 Quoted in Richard Somerset Mackie, *Trading Beyond the Mountains: The British Fur Trade on the Pacific 1793–1843* (Vancouver: University of British Columbia Press, 1997), 57.

42 Gibson, *Otter Skins*, 7; Mackie, *Trading Beyond the Mountains*, 79; Marianne L. Riedman and James A. Estes, "The Sea Otter (*Enhydra lutris*): Behavior, Ecology, and Natural History," *Biological Report* 90, no. 14 (September 1990): 73.

43 Gibson, *Otter Skins*, 256–261.

44 Mackie, *Trading Beyond the Mountains*, 88, 102, 246; Fisher, *Contact and Conflict*, 27.

45 Laura Peers, "Trade and Change on the Columbia Plateau, 1750–1840," *Columbia* 10, no. 4 (Winter 1996/1997): 8–9.

46 Johansen, *Empire of the Columbia*, 82–83; Mackie, *Trading Beyond the Mountains*, xvii, 8–9.

47 Johansen, *Empire of the Columbia*, 83–85; Barman, *The West Beyond the West*, 35.

48 Mackie, *Trading Beyond the Mountains*, 10; Johansen, *Empire of the Columbia*, 86; Alexander Mackenzie, *Voyages from Montreal Through the Continent of North America to the Frozen and Pacific Oceans in 1789 and 1793 with an Account of the Rise and State of the Fur Trade* (Toronto: The Courier Press, 1911), 358; David L. Nicandri, "Lewis and Clark: Exploring the Influence of Alexander Mackenzie," *Pacific Northwest Quarterly* 95, no. 4 (Fall 2004): 172.

49 Nicandri, "Lewis and Clark," 172; Barman, *The West Beyond the West*, 36; Pomeroy, *The Pacific Slope*, 15–16.

50 Barman, *The West Beyond the West*, 37; Johansen, *Empire of the Columbia*, 112–113; Mackie, *Trading Beyond the Mountains*,12–13.

51 Johansen, *Empire of the Columbia*, 115.

52 Ibid., 125–133.

53 Ibid., 126–131; Fisher, *Contact and Conflict* 17; Pomeroy, *The Pacific Slope*, 17.

54 Johansen, *Empire of the Columbia*, 124–125, 135–139; Mackie, *Trading Beyond the Mountains*, 14–17.

55 Johansen, *Empire of the Columbia*, 136–139.

56 Quoted in Mackie, *Trading Beyond the Mountains*, 24.

57 Quoted in Gibson, *Otter Skins*, 26.

58 Barman, *The West Beyond the West*, 39; James R. Gibson, *Farming the Frontier: The Agricultural Opening of the Oregon Country, 1786–1846* (Vancouver: University of British Columbia Press, 1985), 11.

59 Gibson, *Farming the Frontier*, 11; Johansen, 142–143; Barman 39; George Simpson, *George Simpson's Journal*, Frederick Merk, ed. (Cambridge, MA: Harvard University Press, 1968), xi–xiii.

60 Mackie, *Trading Beyond the Mountains*, 35, 82, 246.

61 Pomeroy, *The Pacific Slope*, 57; Johansen, *Empire of the Columbia*, 192; Mackie, *Trading Beyond the Mountains*, 126; Hubert Howe Bancroft, *History of the Northwest Coast* (San Francisco, CA: A.L. Bancroft & Company, 1884), 340–341, 348–351.

62 Johansen, *Empire of the Columbia*, 191.

63 Mackie, *Trading Beyond the Mountains*, 35–36.

64 Ibid., 36–38.

65 Simpson, *George Simpson's Journal*, 66.

66 Ibid., 47–48.

67 Ibid., 48.

68 Gibson, *Farming the Frontier*, 17.

69 Mackie, *Trading Beyond the Mountains*, 48; Gibson, *Farming the Frontier*, 29, 38; Murray Morgan, *Puget's Sound: A Narrative of Early Tacoma and the Southern Sound* (Seattle, WA: University of Washington Press, 2003), 28.

70 Carlos A. Schwantes, *In Mountain Shadows: A History of Idaho* (Lincoln, NE: University of Nebraska Press, 1996), 31.

71 Mackie, *Trading Beyond the Mountains*, 124.

72 Johansen, *Empire of the Columbia*, 175–179; Schwantes, *In Mountain Shadows*, 32–33; Mackie, *Trading Beyond the Mountains*, 99–100.

73 Quoted in ibid., 100.

74 Ibid., 99–107; Schwantes, *In Mountain Shadows*, 32–33; Johansen, *Empire of the Columbia*, 180–181.

75 Mackie, *Trading Beyond the Mountains*, 111.

76 Ibid., 100.

77 Steven A. Anderson, "The Forgetting of John Montgomery: Spanaway's First White Settler, 1845–1885," *Pacific Northwest Quarterly* 101, no. 2 (Spring 2010), 71; Kit Oldham, "First Emigrant Train Crosses Naches Pass through the Cascade Mountains in the Fall of 1853," *Historylink*, accessed February 27, 2016, http://www.historylink.org/index.cfm?DisplayPage=output.cfm&file_id=5053.

78 Anderson, "The Forgetting of John Montgomery," 71–72.

79 Jean Barman and Bruce M. Watson, "Fort Colvile's Fur Families," 147.

80 Schwantes, *The Pacific Northwest*, 74.

81 Mackie, *Trading Beyond the Mountains*, 47, 64.

82 Schwantes, *In Mountain Shadows*, 28–30; Mackie, *Trading Beyond the Mountains*, 102.

83 Ibid., 33, 107.

84 Ibid., 108–110.

85 Ibid., 125–141; Johansen, *Empire of the Columbia*, 155–160.

86 Mackie, *Trading Beyond the Mountains*, 57.

87 Ibid., 140; Barman, *The West Beyond the West*, 42.

88 Mackie, *Trading Beyond the Mountains*, 147–148.

89 Ibid., 244.

90 Ibid., 235.

91 Ibid., 204.

92 Ibid., 205–209.

93 Johansen, *Empire of the Columbia*, 154–155.

94 Morgan, *Puget's Sound*, 50; Mackie, *Trading Beyond the Mountains*, 189, 192.

95 Ibid., 219–220.

96 Ibid., 221.

97 Ibid., 222; Tom Koppel, *Kanaka: The Untold Story of Hawaiian Pioneers in British Columbia and the Pacific Northwest* (Vancouver: Whitecap Books, 1995), 44.

98 Mackie, *Trading Beyond the Mountains*, 151–153.

99 Morgan, *Puget's Sound*, 39; Johansen, *Empire of the Columbia*, 161–162; Gibson, *Farming the Frontier*, 85; Barman, *The West Beyond the West*, 42–43.

100 Gibson, *Farming the Frontier*, 86–87; Johansen, *Empire of the Columbia*, 162–163.

101 Gibson, *Farming the Frontier*, 94.

102 Ibid., 97, 102–103.

103 Ibid., 95, 103.

104 Ibid., 104, 109; Mackie, *Trading Beyond the Mountains*, 239–240.

105 Gibson, *Farming the Frontier*, 110–137, 139–142.

106 Carolyn Merchant, *The Columbia Guide to American Environmental History* (New York: Columbia University Press, 2005), xiii–xv.

107 Tom Schroeder, "Rediscovering a Coastal Prairie Near Friday Harbor," *Pacific Northwest Quarterly* 98, no. 2 (Spring 2007): 61–62; Richard White, *Land Use, Environment, and Social Change: The Shaping of Island County, Washington* (Seattle, WA: University of Washington Press, 1992), 20–23.

108 Carolyn Merchant, *The Columbia Guide to American Environmental History* (New York: Columbia University Press, 2005), xiii–xv.

109 Steven A. Anderson, "The Forgetting of John Montgomery: Spanaway's First White Settler, 1845–1885," *Pacific Northwest Quarterly* 101, no. 2 (Spring 2010): 73; Drew Crooks, "A Place Full of Life and Activity: Fort Nisqually, 1843–1870," DuPont Museum, accessed September 28, 2014, http://www.dupontmuseum.com/; Koppel, *Kanaka*, 48.

110 Koppel, *Kanaka*, 1, 21, 44.

111 Ibid., 49.

112 Fisher, *Contact and Conflict*, 1.

113 Gibson, *Otter Skins*, 5–9.

114 Elizabeth Vibert, *Traders' Tales: Narratives of Cultural Encounters in the Columbia Plateau, 1807–1846* (Norman, OK: University of Oklahoma Press, 1997), 142;

Alexandra Harmon, *Indians in the Making: Ethnic Relations and Indian Identities around Puget Sound* (Berkeley, CA: University of California Press, 1998), 27, 40.

115 Fisher, *Contact and Conflict*, 1; Dolin, *Fur Trade, Fortune, and Empire*, 135.

116 Simpson, *George Simpson's Journal*, 42.

117 Ibid., 95.

118 Fisher, *Contact and Conflict*, 39; Mackie, *Trading Beyond the Mountains*, 309.

119 Simpson, *George Simpson's Journal*, 98.

120 Mackie, *Trading Beyond the Mountains*, 277.

121 Fisher, *Contact and Conflict*, 29–30; Mackie, *Trading Beyond the Mountains*, 276–277.

122 William F. Tolmie, *Physician and Fur Trader: The Journals of William Fraser Tolmie* (Vancouver: Mitchell Press Limited, 1963), 220; Harmon, *Indians in the Making*, 37, 264.

123 Quoted in Hubert Howe Bancroft, *History of the Northwest Coast* (San Francisco: A.L. Bancroft & Company, 1884), 133–134.

124 Vibert, *Trader's Tales*, 120–127; David Peterson del Mar, "Intermarriage and Agency: A Chinookan Case Study," *Ethnohistory* 42, no. 1 (Winter 1995): 4.

125 Vibert, *Trader's Tales*, 127–131.

126 Harmon, *Indians in the Making*, 15, 40.

127 Ibid., 17, 31; Richard White, *The Middle Ground: Indians, Empires, and Republics in the Great Lakes Region, 1650–1815* (Cambridge: Cambridge University Press, 1991).

128 Vibert, *Trader's Tales*, 146–160; Harmon, *Indians in the Making*, 26–27.

129 Vibert, *Trader's Tales*, 145.

130 Ibid., 157–158.

131 Mackie, *Trading Beyond the Mountain*, 301–308.

132 Ibid., 306.

133 Quoted in Fisher, *Contact and Conflict*, 24.

134 Simpson, *George Simpson's Journal*, 53.

135 Ibid., 44, 55–56.

136 Lloyd H. Keith, "'A Place So Dull and Dreary': The Hudson's Bay Company at Fort Okanagon, 1821–1860," *Pacific Northwest Quarterly* 98, no. 2 (Spring 2007): 83, 87; Jean Barman and Bruce M. Watson, "Fort Colvile's Fur Trade Families and the Dynamics of Race in the Pacific Northwest," *Pacific Northwest Quarterly* 90, no. 2 (Summer 1999): 142.

137 Simpson, *George Simpson's Journal*, 48.

138 Ibid., 95.

139 Morgan, *Puget's Sound*, 26–28; Koppel, *Kanaka*, 45; Harmon, *Indians in the Making*, 18–19; Bancroft, *History of the Northwest Coast*, 483–484.

140 Harmon, *Indians in the Making*, 20–24.

141 Mackie, *Trading Beyond the Mountains*, 299; Morgan, *Puget's Sound*, 28; Harmon, *Indians in the Making*, 24.

142 Fisher, 38.

143 Sylvia Van Kirk, "The Role of Native Women in the Fur Trade Society of Western Canada, 1670–1830," *Frontiers: A Journal of Women Studies* 7, no. 3 (1984): 10; Emma Milliken, "Choosing Between Corsets and Freedom: Native, Mixed-Blood, and White Wives of Laborers at Fort Nisqually, 1833–1860," *Pacific Northwest Quarterly* 96, no. 2 (Spring 2005): 74.

144 Anderson, "The Forgetting of John Montgomery," 73; Vibert, *Trader's Tales*, 133; Van Kirk, "The Role of Native Women in the Fur Trade Society of Western Canada," 10.

145 Van Kirk, "The Role of Native Women in the Fur Trade Society of Western Canada," 10–11; Milliken, "Choosing Between Corsets and Freedom," 96–97; Barman, "Fort Colvile's Families," 149.

146 Harmon, *Indians in the Making*, 30–31.

147 Simpson, *George Simpson's Journal*, 99.

148 Barman, "Fort Colvile's Families," 149.

149 Milliken, "Choosing Between Corsets and Freedom," 97; Van Kirk, "The Role of Native Women in the Fur Trade Society of Western Canada," 11–12.

150 Barman, "Fort Colvile's Families," 145; Van Kirk, "The Role of Native Women in the Fur Trade Society of Western Canada," 11–12.

151 Peers, "Trade and Change on the Columbia Plateau," 7.

152 Larry Cebula, *Plateau Indians and the Quest for Spiritual Power: 1700–1850* (Lincoln, NE: University of Nebraska Press, 2003), 73; Joseph E. Taylor III, *Making Salmon: An Environmental History of the Northwest Fisheries Crisis* (Seattle, WA: University of Washington Press, 1999), 41.

153 Fisher, *Contact and Conflict*, 21–23, 44–45; Harmon, *Indians in the Making*, 38.

154 Fisher, *Contact and Conflict*, 20–21, 45–46.

155 Harmon, *Indians in the Making*, 40–41; Gibson, *Otter Skins*, 42–43; Fisher, *Contact and Conflict*, 47.

156 Mackie, *Trading Beyond the Mountains*, 245.

157 Ibid.

158 Ibid., 246.

159 Quoted in Ibid., 256.

160 Gibson, *Farming the Frontier*, 130–131.

161 Mackie, *Trading Beyond the Mountains*, 276–277; Johansen, *Empire of the Columbia*, 265.

162 Johansen, *Empire of the Columbia*, 267.

163 Keith, "'A Place So Dull and Dreary,'" 92; Johansen, *Empire of the Columbia*, 268.

3

Making a Christian Farmer

Native Peoples, missionaries, and saving souls in "Oregon Country"

Caught up in a frenetic religious revival known as the Second Great Awakening, American missionaries turned their sights west in the 1830s and 1840s. They saw it as their duty to teach Christian doctrine to Pacific Northwest Native Peoples believed eager to accept the Holy Gospel. But the spiritual and physical boundaries that came with a "civilized life" often led to unintended and sometimes tragic consequences.

On a rainy day in November 1841, a group of Cayuse rode into the Protestant mission at Waiilatpu along the Walla Walla River in "Oregon Country." Their leader, *Tiloukaikt*, was angry because earlier that day a mission employee escorted another Cayuse off mission grounds for attempting to steal a horse. *Tiloukaikt* irritation grew when he discovered yet another mission building under construction on Cayuse land.[1]

Things had changed since the Cayuse welcomed the missionaries five years earlier. The mission, now consisting of five buildings, a gristmill, millpond and several acres of planted crops, had grown well beyond expectations. The Cayuse wanted payment for the land and the timber used to construct the buildings. More worrisome, the mission, situated along a popular route to western Oregon, served as a magnet for settlers. A growing number of Cayuse now wanted the mission closed and the whites off their land.

What happened next is detailed in a letter from the missionary Narcissa Whitman to her father, Stephen Prentiss in New York. *Tiloukaikt* and Narcissa argued about the building. At one point, he struck Narcissa twice on the breast and pulled on her ear: Native sign, "You do not listen." To show how Christians turn the other cheek, Narcissa proffered the second ear to the Cayuse, who promptly pulled it. Back and forth they went, the Cayuse pulling one ear then the other. Finally, in exasperation, he snatched Narcissa's bonnet off her head and tossed it in the mud.[2]

By this time, a crowd of Natives and mission guests gathered to watch this strange confrontation between the white woman and the Cayuse. Someone from the crowd picked up the bonnet and handed it back to Narcissa, who put it on. Again, hat thrown in mud, hat placed on head. When Narcissa returned the muddy bonnet to her head the third time, it dripped "plentifully" down her hair and cheeks. Notoriously stubborn but trying to defuse the situation, she said "You must be playing." *Tiloukaikt* stormed off, clearly

Contested Boundaries: A New Pacific Northwest History, First Edition. David J. Jepsen and David J. Norberg.
© 2017 John Wiley & Sons, Ltd. Published 2017 by John Wiley & Sons, Ltd.

not playing and undoubtedly frustrated with this strange white woman and her apparent disregard for his concerns about the growing mission.[3]

This seemingly comical yet dangerous moment in Pacific Northwest history was one of many between the Cayuse and missionaries Marcus and Narcissa Whitman, who opened the religious outpost in 1836. While primary documents like Narcissa's correspondence often prove unreliable, it's well documented that tensions ebbed and waned throughout the Whitmans' 11 years at Waiilatpu. They quarreled frequently with the Cayuse over control of the land and its resources, the growing number of white settlers, and the heart-sickening rate at which Cayuse and other Native Peoples died from diseases for which they held no immunity.

Yet beyond disputes over land and settlement lies a much broader story – an epic drama about people from multiple cultures converging in a land without boundaries. The actors include Evangelical Protestants, swept up in a religious movement of historic proportions, and committed to spreading the word of God. Competing with them were Roman Catholics from British Canada, whose church had been converting the indigenous peoples of the Americas for two centuries. In the early decades of the nineteenth century, they had turned their sights on the continent's last religious frontier, the Pacific Northwest. Caught in the middle were Native Peoples themselves, struggling to maintain control of their land and their way of life. In many cases, Native Peoples eager to acquire the riches of the industrial economy, first opened their lands to traders. Later, equally piqued by the promise of spiritual riches, some opened their ears and hearts to the teachings of Jesus Christ. As the curtain fell on the drama, both promises had been crushed under the weight of incurable disease, unbridled settlement and the steamroller known as Manifest Destiny.

In search of a holy life

Conversion efforts in America can be traced back to the Puritans in the early seventeenth century. Beyond turning Native Peoples into Christians, they wanted them to join "civilized," society, or as the historian Francis Prucha put it, transform them into "copies of their white neighbors."[4] As Narcissa wrote in her first year at Waiilatpu, she believed she had a Christian duty to teach "savages" the path to "salvation through Jesus Christ, and the beauties of a well ordered life and godly conversion."[5]

Pacific Northwest Native's first exposure to Christianity began with Spanish explorers in the late eighteenth century. On his second voyage to the region in 1789, Esteban Jose Martinez brought six Catholic priests to Vancouver Island, where the "black robes," as Native Peoples called them, opened a mission at Nootka Sound. Little record exists of their work.[6]

More records exist of the proselytizing efforts of British and French-Canadian traders who worked the region in the first four decades of the nineteenth century. The British-owned Hudson's Bay Company (HBC) and its rival, the North West Company, deployed businessmen west to trade with Native People for furs and other goods. The Iroquois, an eastern Canadian tribe that largely converted to Catholicism during the Colonial era, traveled west with the traders, lived with Native Peoples and taught from the Bible.[7]

> Missionary goals for Native Peoples: "salvation through Jesus Christ, and the beauties of a well ordered life and godly conversion."[8]

In 1824, at the direction of the British Government, HBC stepped up conversion efforts in order to boost trade. Believing Native Peoples were more likely to respond to the Christian word from other Natives, the company began sending potential converts to their Red River settlement in central Canada. Two men, Kootenai Pelly and Spokane Garry, named after their tribes, agreed to go to learn about HBC as much as about Christianity. They lived with Anglican clergy, studied the Bible, and learned English. In 1829, they returned to the Pacific Northwest to share knowledge with their tribes.[9]

Seeking the "book of heaven"

The missionary era picked up steam in 1831 when a small delegation of Nez Perce and others journeyed to St. Louis presumably to learn more about "the white man's Book of Heaven."[10] They met with William Clark, of Lewis and Clark fame, now a general and superintendent of Indian Affairs. Clark introduced them to Catholic priests, who promptly baptized the converts. At least three similar delegations visited St. Louis over the next six years, although varying historical reports make it difficult to separate fact from myth. One group of Flatheads ventured east after a trader said Native spiritual beliefs were "wrong and displeasing to the Great Spirit."[11] A Nez Perce visit in 1833 triggered extensive publicity in the Christian press. A letter from a Methodist minister in March 1833 published in the *Christian Advocate*, proclaimed "How deeply touching is the circumstance of the four natives traveling on foot 3,000 miles … sincere searchers after truth! Let the Church awake from her slumbers and go forth to the salvation of these wandering sons of our native forests."[12]

American churches hardly slumbered in the 1830s. Between 1790 and 1840, America experienced what historians call the Second Great Awakening. Seen as a repeat of a similar event in the early eighteenth century, the second awakening was fueled in part by the spirit of independence following the Revolution. Americans deserted the ranks of brick-and-mortar institutions like the Church of England, turning instead to a form of evangelicalism that emphasized a personal relationship with God, a demonstrative "born-again" conversion experience, and what historian Daniel Walker Howe called a "once-and-for-all decision for Christ."[13] Few things were more important to Evangelicals than "saving lost sinners, reproducing the new birth, and promoting the life of holiness."[14]

Americans erected church buildings at the rate of 1,000 a year, and membership increased faster than the general population. By 1850, one-third of Americans identified with a specific denomination, twice the percentage of 1776. Church membership would continue to grow well into the twentieth century, especially in small towns and rural areas.[15]

Signs of this awakening emerged throughout society, especially in politics, education, social reforms, and in the family.[16] Importantly, it espoused the belief all peoples – men, women, African Americans and Native Peoples – were equal in the eyes of the Christian God.[17]

No group benefited more from the religious revival than women. With the expansion of the market economy in the first half of the nineteenth century, men increasingly worked in the factory or office, and immersed themselves in business and politics. These activities, mostly closed to women, left them confined in what historians call a "cult of domesticity." Society expected them to stay home, bear and nurture children, direct their children's education and manners, and make the home a "haven to which the husband returned from work each day to find love and warmth at the hearth."[18]

Historian James McPherson identifies an upside to such restrictions. Women leveraged their role as moral guardians into greater influence outside the home. More and more women learned to read and write and attended primary school and college. Throughout the nineteenth century and well into the twentieth, they fought their way into careers in medicine, law, publishing, and business – all of which laid the foundation for the early women's rights movement.[19]

Yet professional careers were mostly closed to women like young Narcissa Prentiss in the 1830s. Their best opportunities for meaningful work outside the home were found in teaching, religion and involvement in benevolent associations. Hundreds of single-issue, voluntary associations, collectively known as the Benevolent Empire, sprang up in America in the early decades of the nineteenth century. The majority were run by women, which helped to raise women's public profile and got them "out of the house and into the world."[20] More and more women spoke and prayed in public, gained leadership training and developed organizational and business skills previously out of their reach. Importantly, those working to address social ills helped to put women on equal footing with men. The American Board of Commissioners of Foreign Missions (ABCFM), American Home Missionary Society, Bible Society, Peace Society and the Sunday School Union were just a few. These groups fought against the twin evils of alcohol and tobacco, championed prison and educational reform, and campaigned against slavery.[21]

A young Narcissa Prentiss was a product of this religious and social awakening. Like her mother and father, she engaged in benevolent work, joined religious societies, led Bible studies for the Sabbath School Association, and distributed Bibles to poor families in and around her hometown, Prattsburg, New York.[22]

With this background, we can appreciate why the story of Native Peoples seeking knowledge about the white man's God struck an emotional chord among Christians. Aspiring missionary Dr. Marcus Whitman, an MD, and Narcissa likely saw advertisements in the *Christian Advocate* calling for Christians to take up the call to bring Natives to Christ. "Here! Here!," proclaimed one ad. "Who will respond to the call from beyond the Rocky Mountains? … All we want is men. Who will go? Who?"[23] Another referred specifically to the pliability of Pacific Northwest Native People. "Probably no heathen nations entertain less definite prejudice against the Gospel, or the arts of civilized life."[24] It convinced Christian leadership organizations that all of them hungered for "the truth."

Over the next five years Catholic, Methodist and other Protestant organizations sent young men and women on the long trek west with the ardent belief Native People could and should be saved.[25] Formed in 1810, the interdenominational ABCFM received federal funds to "gradually transform Indians into church going citizens of a new nation."[26] But Narcissa's hope of becoming a missionary would likely go unfulfilled unless she married. Twenty-five years old and living with her parents, she didn't fit the missionary profile. The ABCFM hesitated sending white women west, especially single ones. Coincidently, Dr. Whitman was lobbying ABCFM for a missionary post, and believed his best hope was to find a wife willing and capable of enduring the rigors of missionary life. With marriage on his mind, Whitman traveled to Prattsburg in February 1834 and met with Narcissa, whom he barely knew. According to Narcissa's biographer, the couple agreed to marry, not with romantic notions of true love, but to clear the way for both young people to achieve a life's dream.[27]

Figure 3.1 British artist Paul Kane drew these sketches of Protestant missionaries Narcissa and Marcus Whitman just a few months before they were killed at their mission at Waiilatpu near Walla Walla in 1847. Image reprinted with permission from the National Park Service and the Whitman Mission National Historical Site.

While the newlyweds lobbied for a post, Methodist Jason Lee established the first Protestant mission in the Pacific Northwest. Lee and his nephew Daniel arrived at Fort Vancouver in September 1834. He'd planned to proselytize among the Nez Perce and neighboring tribes in the region's interior until he heard about their "warlike and wandering" culture. Instead he settled in the Willamette Valley near Salem, a curious choice given the severely diminished Native population following smallpox and influenza epidemics in the 1770s.[28]

After the American Board gave Dr. Whitman his post, he traveled west with fellow missionary Samuel Parker to evaluate potential locations and meet with tribes. He returned to New York convinced Native Peoples eagerly awaited a Christian education. In March 1836, the newlyweds Marcus and Narcissa embarked on their nearly 3,000-mile journey. Henry and Eliza Spalding, missionaries stationed in Kansas who agreed to a transfer to Oregon, joined the Whitmans in Cincinnati. Life on the trail invigorated Narcissa, who wrote to her brother she "never was so contented and happy before. Neither have I enjoyed such health for years."[29]

In June, Narcissa saw Natives up close for the first time, likely Pawnee traveling with fur traders in Wyoming. "They are a noble Indian – large, athletic frames, dignified countenances, bespeaking an immortale exhistance [*sic*] within," she wrote.[30] Pawnee likely found the pale-skinned Narcissa equally curious. On July 4, the party summited the Rocky Mountains at South Pass in Wyoming, making Narcissa and Eliza the first white women known to cross the continental divide.[31] They arrived at Fort Walla Walla on September 1 and began to scout locations for their missions. The ABCFM, hoping to counter the mostly Catholic Hudson's Bay Company traders, chose to concentrate near HBC's Fort Walla Walla. They ordered Whitman to set up at Waiilatpu along the Walla

Walla River on Cayuse land, while Spalding located more than 100 miles east at Lapwai in Nez Perce territory. Whitman expressed satisfaction with site selection. "The soil and natives very favorable," he wrote. "We shall be able to cultivate quite extensively next summer."[32] It's likely Marcus was expressing his hope to start a successful farm, but he also planned on cultivating Native souls as well. Both goals would prove elusive.

Promising start in God's work

Missionary life at Waiilatpu started well enough when the Whitmans saw Cayuse attending services led by Catholic traders from Canada. They joined in hymns with Catholic traders, prayed daily, and discussed the Bible. While profoundly anti-Catholic, the Whitmans wisely did not interfere. Instead they supplemented the devotional activity with their version of prayer meetings and worship services. By January 1837, 12 to 14 boys and men regularly participated in Protestant prayer sessions and appeared "delighted with it."[33] A year later, 60 to 80 "scholars," regularly attended religious instruction.[34] To Narcissa's surprise, services resembled the many revivals she'd attended at home. Native People "manifested much deep feeling," while others expressed an "anxious and solemn countenance."[35] Again, it's important to view the Whitman letters with a healthy degree of skepticism, especially claims about Native conversions and attraction to Christianity. In this case, Narcissa's claims may or may not be accurate because they're directed to an ABCFM commissioner expecting to see results as measured by conversions.

Given the Native Peoples' world view of creation, their apparent interest in Christianity is understandable. According to historian Alexandra Harmon, writing about Puget Sound Native Peoples, they believed a man's success depended on his connection to the spiritual world. A productive hunt, victorious raid, or acquisition of wealth were byproducts of religious fulfillment. When Europeans and Americans started appearing in Oregon displaying the wonders of the industrial revolution, Native Peoples naturally wanted to hear about the "supernaturals" from whom the newcomers "obtained their extraordinary wealth and skills." That may explain why a Native boasted to French-Canadian priests that he won a battle because his "enemies did not know God, sang no canticle, and did not make the sign of the cross."[36]

The disruption of tribal life due to European diseases also helps to explain Christianity's appeal. Native Peoples suspected most whites survived an illness because of their relationship with their God.[37] Additionally, like the white man's guns and knives, new or unusual things naturally interested Natives. In 1834, a large group of Nez Perce and Cayuse traveled to Fort Hall in what is now southeastern Idaho to hear Jason Lee speak about a "strange new thing" that promised wealth and eternal life.[38]

> "What kind of God would condemn a man for doing what his people had done since the days of Coyote?"

The first three years at Waiilatpu were as uneven as the plateau plains. On one hand, growing crowds at daily prayer meetings and Sunday services encouraged the Whitmans.[39] Narcissa wrote to her mother that she believed Natives who attended services felt "the force of divine truth upon their minds."[40] But beyond attending services, singing and praying, the Whitmans reported little evidence of outright conversion.

Narcissa blamed language barriers because "nothing is more difficult" than conveying "religious truth in their language."[41] They tried to translate scripture into Cayuse, but it wasn't widely distributed.

The Whitman letters suggest that, for all the outward signs of conversion, most Native Peoples did not measure up to the expectations of these Evangelicals. Singing and praying alone did not make one a Christian. True Christians obeyed the Ten Commandments. Worshiping false gods, stealing, committing adultery or murder violated these laws and invited eternal damnation, the missionaries believed. But the concept of sin must have puzzled Natives. How could taking in a second wife, or killing the enemy be sinful? What kind of God would condemn a man for doing what his people had done since the days of Coyote? Were all Native Peoples then damned?

Cayuse Girl and God's will

On Narcissa Whitman's twenty-ninth birthday, March 14, 1837, the Protestant missionary gave birth to a daughter, Alice Clarissa, likely the first white child born in Oregon Country. A minor sensation among the Cayuse, men and women "thronged the house continually" to visit the "Little Stranger." One visitor called her "Cayuse-temi," or Cayuse Girl, because she was born on his land. He wondered why the baby wore a dress and remained in bed with her mother, instead of strapped to a cradleboard in a maternity lodge, the custom in most tribes.[42]

Alice offered a reprieve from a missionary life besieged with tension and disappointment. To the Native People's delight, she picked up a few words of Cayuse and enjoyed the run of the mission. On a Sunday in June 1839, while the Whitmans sat reading in the mission house, Alice wandered outside towards the river carrying two cups. When her parents realized she was missing, they began searching mission grounds. A Cayuse found the two cups and an unconscious Alice in the river. Revival efforts proved unsuccessful. Cayuse-temi, who apparently had gone to the river to fetch water, drowned.[43] Like most events in their lives, the grieving parents attributed the tragedy to God's will. "The Lord gave and the Lord hath taken away," Narcissa wrote to a friend.[44]

Perhaps no commandment proved more troublesome than the first, "Thou shalt have no other gods before me."[45] But try as they did, missionaries could not erase like chalk from a blackboard the spiritual past from Native consciousness. The legend of Coyote, for example, provided the framework for a "broad moral code ranging from the grossest misbehavior to the most exemplary heroism," according to anthropologist and linguist Phillip E. Cash. Children grew up hearing Coyote stories and committed them to memory, then passed them along to their children.[46] Marcus's response reflects the attitudes of the day about native spiritual practices. "They say they do not worship Idols but still I think many of their traditions are evidences of Idolitrous [*sic*] worship of some Animals & Birds."[47]

While perceived idolatry disturbed missionaries, stealing made them livid. Throughout their stay at Waiilatpu, they accused Native People of pilfering everything from horses and livestock to knives and household goods. Marcus called the Plateau people a "low, pilfering race."[48] More than once, accusations of theft erupted into dangerous confrontations. In February 1842, about a dozen Cayuse stormed into the Whitman kitchen armed with knives, clubs, and ropes concealed under blankets. Marcus, writing to ABCFM, said he had reprimanded a Cayuse earlier that day for stealing horses. The thief was a "bad man," he claimed he told them, and would "go to hell" for his sins. The Cayuse motive for storming into the mission is not clear, but there's no question about their mood. At one point, the intruders brandished their weapons, but after a few tense moments, tensions eased and the Cayuse left. While the region's early history is replete with stories about explorers, traders, missionaries and settlers accusing Natives of stealing their property, it would be inaccurate to label them as thieves.

Confrontations over killing, a violation of the sixth commandment, flared over the practice of extracting revenge on a healer, sometimes known as shaman, unable to save the lives of sick family members. Dr. Whitman, who frequently attended to the sick, lived under the same threat. In April 1845 a Cayuse chief stricken with "apoplexy," a type of stroke, died under his care. According to Marcus, the chief's grieving son accused him of killing his father and threatened retribution. A shaken Marcus later wrote, "I do not think I could be induced to come to such a people" again.[49]

If killing horrified missionaries, polygamy, a violation of the seventh commandment, appalled them, Narcissa believed women in a polygamous marriage were "slaves to their Husbands."[50] But the Catholic Missionary Bishop Augustin Magloire Alexandre (A.M.A.) Blanchet, while not approving of polygamy, understood it as a "custom deeply rooted in time immemorial," tied to survival on the plains.[51] Native Peoples believed coupling with multiple women benefited all parties, underscoring their value and stature in native society. Two wives could accomplish more work, gather more berries and dry more salmon. Explaining why Native Peoples had multiple wives, Blanchet wrote, "the more they have, the more work gets done and the more food there is."[52] Nor did Native Peoples accept the Christian concept of a holy vow and a promise before God. Men and women living together was not about marriage as Christians defined it, but rather nurturing a mutually beneficial relationship. Finally, men often brought in a second or third wife as an act of kindness, especially a sister of the first wife. In a culture built around family connections and clan networks, unattached women remained vulnerable.[53]

By 1844, several religious denominations had established a presence in Oregon Territory. Methodists proselytized from six missions, mostly west of the Cascade Mountains. Various Protestant groups concentrated their efforts east of the Cascades. In addition to the Presbyterians at Waiilatpu and Lapwai, two other missions opened in 1838 and 1839. Presbyterians Elkanah and Mary Walker and Congregationalists Cushing and Myra Eells ministered to the Spokane in the northeast corner of the region, while Asa and Sarah Smith worked with the Nez Perce in the southeast.

Protestants and Catholics compete for converts

Catholics enjoyed the strongest presence with missions on both sides of the Cascades. While Protestant Evangelicalism emerged mostly in the nineteenth century, Catholics had been ministering to settlers and Native Peoples in North America since the early seventeenth century. It's easy to overlook the fact that much of North America was claimed, explored, evangelized and partially settled by the French. Throughout the seventeenth and eighteenth centuries, French-Canadian Catholics built a strong presence

Figure 3.2 The St. Mary's Mission on the Bitterroot River near the current Idaho-Montana border drew thousands of potential converts. The tee-pees on the left in this Nicholas Point sketch show that many Flathead, Coeur d'Alene, and other Salish peoples set up semi-permanent residence on mission grounds. Image reprinted with permission from the Jesuit Archives Central United States.

from the St. Lawrence River in Canada to the Gulf of Mexico. They established missions in Quebec, Ontario, upper New York, around the Great Lakes and in the future states of Wisconsin, Michigan and Illinois. They traveled down the Mississippi, working with the indigenous peoples of Ohio, Indiana, Kentucky, Tennessee, Alabama and into Louisiana.

To French Canadians Fr. Francois Norbert Blanchet and Fr. Modeste Demers, Oregon Country was the Catholic's last religious frontier. They opened a mission on the Cowlitz River in 1838, and within a few years, Catholic priests had spread their version of the Gospel throughout the territory. With multiple denominations now operating in Oregon Country, HBC Chief Factor Dr. John McLoughlin worried the competition for souls would "bewilder our poor Indians already perplexed beyond measure by the number and variety of their instructors."[54]

Protestants and Catholics not only practiced contrasting styles of Christianity, they reviled and worked against one another. In America, the rivalry can be traced to the earliest days of the Republic when the Puritans carried a "deep seated English tradition of anti-Catholicism" into the New World. American Catholics were few in number until the nineteenth century when millions from Europe and elsewhere immigrated to the United States, giving rise to a nativist or anti-immigrant movement. Between 1830 and 1860 the number of Catholics jumped from 318,000 to 3,103,000, mostly Irish and Germans who settled in over-crowded tenements in the northeastern cities like New York and Philadelphia.[55]

Protestants called Catholicism "Romanism" and the priests were "papists," heretics, and idolaters under the control of the Pope. When Blanchet and Demers opened missions along the lower Columbia, Narcissa felt threatened. Revealing her profound anti-Catholic views, she expressed worry that Catholics would fill the minds of Native Peoples "with distraction about truths we teach."[56] Nothing less than the "interests of the Oregon Country hung in the balance." Three years later, after Catholic missions opened near Waiilatpu and Lapwai, she wrote "Romanism stalks abroad on our right hand and our left." Invoking images of beasts and false idols described in Revelation 13, she complained the "zeal and energy of her priests are without a parallel, and many, both white men and Indians, wander after the beasts."[57]

Narcissa was right about one thing. Catholic missionaries attacked their work with impressive energy. First, they attended to the spiritual needs of the British traders, most of whom were Catholic. Yet, they found time for extensive missionary work. For more than two decades they out-worked and out-traveled their competitors, and as a result won more converts. But historians attribute their relative success to factors beyond hard work. They point to a combination of "adaptation, creativity, compromise and resilience" that left a lasting impression on thousands of Pacific Northwest Natives.[58]

The Catholics' flexible approach to conversion contrasted sharply with Protestants. Focusing on the Holy Sacraments as a route to salvation, Catholics tried to let Natives be themselves and generally accommodated long-held traditions. Protestants, on the other hand, insisted Native Peoples abandon their culture and transform themselves into the image of a white Christian. Native languages, spiritual beliefs, social structure and marriage habits blocked the path to salvation, Protestants proclaimed.[59] By contrast, Catholic priests looked to Native People for evidence of "inner faith, not external conformity."[60] In the spirit of accommodation, priests stood by at the 1844 midnight Christmas Mass when some Flatheads and Coeur d'Alene's celebrated Jesus's birth with gunfire.[61] While all missionaries disapproved of nudity, priests said little when bare-breasted women and men covered only in loincloth attended Mass in the oppressive heat of mid-summer.[62]

Willingness to bear the drudgery and danger of travel enhanced the priests' credibility and ultimately their relative success. To show their respect for native ways, they presented gifts to chiefs when entering a village, and requested permission to stay. Over several weeks, they celebrated Mass, held religious instruction, administered sacraments like baptism and marriage and handed out rosaries and religious medals. By contrast, the Whitmans seldom traveled much beyond the immediate region. For example, Marcus could not have engaged in ministerial work of any kind when he returned east in 1842–1843 to shore up support for his mission and lobby an ABCFM disappointed with a scarcity of conversions. Even when at Waiilatpu, Marcus and Narcissa frequently fell sick, likely with dysentery or flu, and were unfit for travel.

Few things slowed Pierre Jean De Smet, a Belgian priest educated in Missouri. During the first of two tours of the region, he spent six weeks on the trail in late 1841, ministering to Native Peoples along the Clark and Ford rivers, Camas Prairie, Lake Pend Oreille and Fort Colville, oftentimes close to Protestant missions. He reportedly baptized 190, many sick with the flu or smallpox. On Christmas day he celebrated Mass before hundreds of Flatheads. Afterwards, they told De Smet the Virgin Mary appeared before an elderly woman, meriting them "the glorious title of true children of God."[63] At Tshimakain, a hundred or more Spokane traveled 30 miles to see De Smet and attend Mass. They rode

Figure 3.3 Many Salish and other Native Peoples eagerly accepted the Holy Sacraments including communion. Here, artist Nicholas Point captures the solemnity of communion inside St. Mary's Church. The fact Salish helped decorate the mission, including weaving the mats on the floor and ceiling, underscores their emotional commitment to Christianity. Image reprinted with permission from the Jesuit Archives Central United States.

on Saturday, camped at the mission, attended Sunday Mass and departed on Monday. Some stayed for a week or more.[64] De Smet moved freely among the villages and fishing grounds. In 1845, during his second tour, he visited Kettle Falls on the Columbia, where nearly a "thousand savages" fished for salmon. He constructed a "little chapel of boughs" and offered religious instruction three times a day, baptizing any eager man, woman, or child.[65]

While Protestants preferred Natives learn English, Catholics tackled the difficult native languages. At the Dalles mission, Father Louis-Pierre Rousseau translated Bible lessons, prayers, and children's songs into Chinook jargon, a hybrid of English, French, Chinook, and hand signs developed to conduct trade. Native Peoples memorized the Our Father, Hail Mary, the lengthy Apostles' Creed, and the Ten Commandments.[66]

"The Ladder," a teaching tool Native People called the "stick from heaven," taught Christian history.[67] Introduced in 1838 by Fr. Francois Blanchet, this 2-foot long paper scroll pasted to cloth contained dozens of images depicting Biblical history. Pictures of the Great Flood, Tower of Babel, Twelve Apostles, the Crucifixion, and Ten Commandments helped missionaries bring Christianity to life for curious converts.[68]

Not to be outdone, the Protestant missionary Eliza Spalding created a 5-foot version of the Ladder. The two versions illustrate the competition and animosity between the denominations. The Protestants displayed the pope "falling into the fires of hell on

Judgment Day," while the Catholic edition pictured Protestants "marooned" at a dead end on the road to heaven.[69] When a Native handed him a copy of the Catholic ladder, an enraged Marcus Whitman "smeared it in the blood of a steer."[70]

Priests surmised correctly that the colorful pageantry of the Mass and Catholic rituals fascinated Native Peoples in part because it mirrored many of their traditions. Holy Communion, singing, Latin chants, candles, incense, the rosary, and colorful vestments made for a multi-sensory and inspiring spectacle that seemed familiar to them.[71] Similar to Catholic veneration of saints, Native Peoples depended on the "mediating power of guardian spirits" to guide them in their present life and afterlife.[72]

> "[While] we point them with one hand to the Lamb of God ... we believe it to be equally our duty to point with the other to the hoe."

Baptism appealed to Native Peoples and further illustrates the Catholic-Protestant rivalry. Because Catholics believed baptism a requirement for salvation, they administered the sacrament to infants, children, and adults who professed their faith. American Evangelicals on the other hand restricted baptism to adults who completed extensive instruction and committed to a Christian life. Given the contrasting styles, we can appreciate why Marcus erupted when he learned Catholics baptized the son of a Cayuse chief under his tutelage.[73]

Bitter rivalries notwithstanding, it's important to remember Protestants and Catholics shared similar goals – bringing Native Peoples to Christ and preparing them to survive in Christian society. Both viewed Native Peoples as savages in the wild, barred from entering heaven unless they embraced Christian values.[74]

Protestant efforts to "civilize" Native Peoples involved more than baptism and prayer. Euro-American society expected people to work for a living, in a culturally specific way, which in the early industrial era meant farming. Interest in teaching Native Peoples agriculture dates to the earliest days of the republic. Leaders encouraged missionaries to teach Natives farming so they might embrace the value of private property, labor, and a civilized lifestyle as they saw it. Speaking before a House committee debating the creation of a "Civilization Fund" in 1819, a U.S. Congressman said Native People must pick up both "the primer and the hoe," so they will "grow up in habits of morality and industry."[75]

Marcus Whitman believed conversion and farming went hand in hand. "[While] we point them with one hand to the Lamb of God ... we believe it to be equally our duty to point with the other to the hoe."[76] He repeatedly requested American Board funds to purchase farming equipment, arguing farming would "save this starving multitude from an untimely grave."[77] To supplement the native diet with grain, Whitman helped them build and operate a gristmill, fueling hope "a spirit of independence is manifesting itself among them ..."[78]

Marcus's hope seemed well founded at first. Similar to their initial interest in Christianity, Cayuse viewed farming as potentially promising. They watched as Marcus taught them to turn up the prairie and plant corn, wheat, potatoes, and peas. In a letter requesting additional farming equipment, Marcus reported in 1843 that 50 Cayuse worked individual plots, some as large as three or four acres. Due to better soil at Lapwai, the Nez Perce enjoyed even more success, Marcus claimed. To supplement their harvest, people from both tribes tended small herds of cattle and sheep acquired from traders.[79]

The many trappings of farm life – cultivated land, tools, grist mills and livestock – suggest Native Peoples joining America as God-fearing farmers, except it didn't work out that way. Too much about native culture precluded a stationary existence tied to a single plot of land. Some Native Peoples ultimately gave up on agriculture because it interfered with hunting and gathering. Nomadic people who roamed the region up to nine months a year found it difficult to attend to wheat fields or vegetable gardens. Just as adopting Christianity meant forgoing spiritual traditions, farming disrupted the seasonal cycle of hunting and gathering.[80]

Disputes often occurred between Native Peoples struggling to maintain control of the land and missionaries who assumed ownership. When Cayuse horses wandered onto mission gardens in 1841, trampling vegetables and eating corn, Narcissa reminded the Cayuse the field was the mission's "plantation" and not a "horse pen." According to Narcissa's account, the indignant Cayuse denied having given away the land in the first place, and his horses did only what horses do, eat "the growth of the soil."[81] Narcissa's attitude reflects the widespread belief among Americans that, because Native Peoples had not worked or improved the land, they relinquished title to it.

Native American historian Allen P. Slickpoo, Sr., a Nez Perce, argues hunting and fishing skills underscored Native manhood and status. But missionaries interpreted reticence to farm as "laziness," which, according to Slickpoo, could "hardly have been further from the truth." Putting a hoe in the hands of Native men was "asking us to become like women."[82]

In February 1843, the Whitman grist mill burned, and with it hundreds of bushels of wheat, flour, and corn. Whether deliberate, or the result of an accident or carelessness, nearly everyone suspected the Cayuse. At the time, Marcus was back east while Narcissa visited missionaries in Salem. Although she had no evidence the Cayuse were responsible, the deeply frustrated Narcissa called them "proud domineering arrogant and ferocious." She promised to redouble her efforts for the Cayuse "salvation," yet the incident appears to have sapped her will. Work would continue, she wrote, "not from any good" in the Cayuse, but from a "firm reliance on the promises of God."[83]

Domestic life for the missionaries turned for the better the following year when the Whitmans adopted seven children whose parents, Henry and Naomi Sager, died on the Oregon Trail. The children, aged six months to 13 years, filled a void created in Narcissa's life following the death of her daughter, Alice, five years earlier. She especially adored the baby, Henrietta, born in a wagon in May 1844.[84] The presence of families with children signaled a shift in the makeup of newcomers to the territory. Native Peoples living along the Oregon Trail watched helplessly as more and more families in overloaded ox-drawn wagons plodded steadily west.

In May 1840, Narcissa wrote a "tide of immigration appears to be moving this way rapidly."[85] Situated on the route to the Willamette Valley, Waiilatpu became a stopping off point for immigrants seeking rest and supplies. As settlers arrived in growing numbers, Narcissa sensed the beginning of a "great change."[86] While earlier data is spotty, the non-native population in Oregon surpassed 13,000 by 1850 and 52,000 a decade later, turning the trickle of newcomers into veritable river by 1860.[87]

Cayuse who initially welcomed missionaries to Waiilatpu did not anticipate throngs of settlers in their wake. With increasing frequency, Native Peoples confronted emigrants, "openly" robbing their wagons. Sometimes the confrontations led to violence, as in September 1847, when, according to Marcus, an argument over stolen horses led to

Figure 3.4 Catholic priests, whom the Natives called "Black Robes," traveled throughout Oregon Country evangelizing at villages. Many set up temporary altars outdoors, administering communion and baptism to all willing people. Nicholas Point drawing reprinted with permission from the Jesuit Archives Central United States.

gunfire that killed a chief named Equator and an immigrant, and wounded three others."[88] The Whitmans felt the tension at Waiilatpu, frequently arguing with the Cayuse over payment for work, resources, and land. What once seemed like an opportunity to learn about the white man's God and obtain his goods had evolved into a threat to Cayuse land and their very existence.

Settlement also reordered missionary priorities. Initially focused on conversions, the Whitmans increasingly turned their attentions to emigrants. In May 1844, Marcus pledged to continue instructing Natives, but his "greatest work" lay in aiding "white settlement" and building the territory's "religious institutions."[89] Native Peoples, he wrote, failed "to multiply and replenish the Earth," and therefore they "cannot Stand in the way of others doing so."[90] Missionaries who once dreamed of salvation for Natives now saw them as obstacles to the success of others.

In 1846–1847, dysentery and measles worked their havoc on lower Columbia tribes. Narcissa wrote about the deaths of "most important Indians"[91] and "influential chiefs," many long-time mission supporters.[92] Living on continents geographically isolated from the remainder of the world, Native Peoples held no defense against diseases to which Europeans had developed resistance over the centuries. Dangerous pathogens like smallpox, measles, influenza, bubonic plague, and dysentery spread through South and Central America in the sixteenth and seventeenth centuries, and the eastern portions of North America in the seventeenth and eighteenth. Due to the remoteness of the Great Plains and Pacific Northwest, most diseases didn't arrive until the late eighteenth and early nineteenth centuries. Their paths to the Northwest trace back to Spanish explorers who touched land several times in the 1770s. Historian Robert Boyd argues the most likely origin coincided with Spain's 1775 expedition under the command of Bruno de Hezeta (Heceta) and Juan Francisco de la Bodega y Quadra.[93] Other possible sources include Russian colonists in present-day northwest British Columbia, or Native Peoples on the Great Plains who traded with tribes on the Columbia Plateau. Whatever their place of origin, diseases came in waves, one after the other, with deadly results. Smallpox, the most lethal, killed up to 90% of infected peoples during epidemics in the 1770s, 1800–1801, 1838 and 1862–1803.[94] Malaria took a comparable death toll along the lower Columbia and Willamette Valley in 1830–1833, followed by outbreaks of measles, flu, and dysentery.[95] While precise mortality rates on the Plateau are difficult to determine, historians can compare them to outbreaks elsewhere. Reliable data show smallpox killed over 13,000 or 92% of the Kalapuyan and Chinookan populations in western Oregon in the 1830s, and another 20,000 in northern British Columbia.[96] Second-hand reports from traders and missionaries hint at the cultural devastation decades earlier. Native Peoples recounted how "Immense numbers" had been "swept off by a dreadful visitation of the smallpox …"[97] Nez Perce told Congregational missionary Aza Smith a story about those hunting buffalo on the Great Plains returning in spring to find "their lodges standing in order, & the people almost to an individual dead."[98]

For centuries, Native Peoples turned to healers, who derived their power from the spiritual world, to cure everything from battle wounds to arthritis. They often placed the patient in a sweat box for hours and then plunged him or her in cold water.[99] Writing about the Nez Perce, historian Donald Hines attributes a healer's success to the "power of suggestion," rather than spiritual power, "that a cure had really occurred."[100]

But no suggestion could stop smallpox or convince someone he was cured. When their condition worsened, Native Peoples often turned to missionaries for help. Throughout the Whitman's stay in the territory, peaking in 1845 and 1846, a steady stream of desperately sick people stumbled into Waiilatpu seeking help from the doctor and his powerful God. Beyond prayer and making them comfortable, Whitman had little to offer.

In native cultures, healers who failed to save their patients sometimes faced vengeance from a grieving family, as Marcus learned in 1845 when his stroke patient died. But threats from Cayuse in 1847 seemed far more ominous. Rumors had spread that the doctor was "poisoning" Cayuse with his medicine and should be killed.[101] The danger prompted Marcus to consider relocating to the Willamette Valley, where he could evangelize to a growing white settlement, but his pride and stubbornness would not allow him to give up on Waiilatpu.[102]

That same year, problems over disease and settlement spiraled out of control at the Spalding Mission at Lapwai. Some Nez Perce shattered meetinghouse windows, tore down fences, and damaged the gristmill and dam. Darkening the mood, measles killed more than 30 Cayuse and Walla Walla men who apparently contracted the disease in California while on a quest to avenge the murder of a Walla Walla headman's son.[103]

Eleven years after arriving at Waiilatpu, the Whitmans found themselves increasingly isolated. Many Natives who earlier had supported their presence were dead, while survivors looked to lay blame. Narcissa's biographer, Julie Roy Jeffrey, concludes the 1846–1847 epidemics "tipped the balance of tribal power in favor of the anti-missionary faction" among the Cayuse.[104] In other words, the Whitmans were running out of supporters.

A day of reckoning at Waiilatpu

On a gloomy Monday afternoon, November 29, 1847, the rocky saga between the Whitmans and Native People reached its tragic conclusion. A group of Cayuse and Nez Perce entered the mission house armed with tomahawks and guns. Natives routinely came and went so their presence raised no immediate alarms. Accounts of what came next vary, but two men approached Marcus from behind. One delivered two tomahawk blows to the head while the other slashed his face with a knife. The men then shot two of the adopted Sager boys as they went for their guns. Narcissa took a bullet in the shoulder while attending to her stricken husband.[105]

The attackers left the house and stormed a barracks housing emigrants, killing several. Some managed to escape but the wounded Narcissa and others remained trapped in the house. By this time, men inside were armed so the attackers decided to wait them out. In the morning, they set fire to the house and shot Narcissa and others as they ran outside. A man lifted the dying Narcissa by the hair and mutilated her face with a leather quirt, or riding whip. In total, 14 people lay dead: Marcus, Narcissa, school headmaster Cornelius Rogers, two of the Sager boys, age 15 and 7, and nine men who had emigrated to the region with their families. Natives took more than 40 captives, mostly women and children, including Henry Spalding's young daughter, Eliza.[106]

The Natives held their captives for more than a month, during which time the women cooked and sewed for their captors. One was raped and three others were forced to become "wives." The vigil ended peacefully thanks to the intervention of Bishop A.M.A. Blanchet and the Hudson's Bay Company's Peter Ogden, both of whom met frequently with the hostage takers to negotiate a release. The release took place December 28 in exchange for blankets, clothing, guns, ammunition, and $500 cash.[107]

But no peaceful exchange satisfied angry settlers and the local militia. A volunteer force pursued the perpetrators for weeks, skirmishing with them more than once, but the elusive fugitives slipped away each time. Two years later, a Cayuse chief under tremendous pressure from the U.S. Army agreed to hand over the fugitives. Five men turned themselves in, including *Tiloukaikt*, a Cayuse whom the Whitmans had earlier baptized. While it's uncertain whether they all participated in the crime, five men were tried, found guilty and executed within a month. At his execution, *Tiloukaikt's* supposed last words derided Christian teachings. "Did not your missionaries tell us that Christ died to save his people?," he asked. "So die we, to save our people."[108]

How should students of history assess the early missionary era and all its players? If we judge missionaries by the number of conversions, their own self-imposed standard, they clearly failed. Under heavy criticism from fellow Methodists for lack of success, Jason Lee left the territory permanently in 1843 after nine years. An embittered Henry Spalding and family, who'd narrowly escaped a planned attack at Lapwai, relocated to the safe Willamette Valley where they ministered mostly to settlers. That temporarily left only the Catholics with any notable influence on Native Peoples. Their brand of Christianity, combined with flexibility and sure doggedness, helped them to prevail to some degree, yet they too expressed dissatisfaction with results. In 1850, Bishop A.M.A. Blanchet conveyed his disappointment with his results after two years in the region. Writing to his friend and mentor, the Bishop of Montreal, Ignace Bourget, he lamented that none of the first four missions had made "great progress." If Native Peoples agreed to live at or near the mission, it could "keep a missionary occupied," Blanchet lamented, but they "insist on remaining on their own land. ..." Quoting the parable of the Kingdom of Heaven growing out of a mustard seed, he asked the Bishop, "So there, Monsigneur [*sic*] is our grain of mustard?"[109] The Catholic seed did grow to some extent. They continued to minister to Native Peoples well into the twentieth century, and today several Northwest tribes, including the Coeur d'Alene's and Nez Perce in North and Central Idaho, practice Catholicism. In the United States, a majority of Native Peoples who identify themselves as Christian are Catholic.[110]

The disastrous outcome at Waiilatpu should not totally color our perceptions of the missionary era. Nearly two centuries removed from early regional history, we try to organize complicated events into an orderly parade of explorers, traders, missionaries and settlers marching in succession onto Native People's land. But history is neither orderly nor organized. The historian Prucha called the plethora of newcomers to the region "a complex web of relationships that is almost impossible, in this later day, to disentangle."[111]

The Whitmans and other Protestant missionaries entered that web naively and unaware of its complexity and dangers. They received no training as missionaries. The sole requirements were being Christian, married and willing, none of which prepared them for the hardships, loneliness, and hazards of life among indigenous people in a strange land. And neither Native nor missionary were equipped to cope with unforeseen tumults that swept over them in the form of repeated epidemics and unrelenting settlement.

Granted, missionaries like the Whitmans and Spaldings brought some of their troubles upon themselves. Both Marcus and Narcissa nearly broke under the strain of mission life. Inflexible regarding many of their Christian principles, and possessed of volatile personalities, haughty arrogance and condescending behavior, the Whitmans eventually wore out their welcome, and for that paid the ultimate price. Marcus, the first at Waiilatpu to die, and Narcissa the only woman killed, were obviously primary targets. The fact attackers mutilated Narcissa's face suggests built-up hatred and frustration with the white woman who didn't listen.[112]

Counter-productive behavior aside, the Whitmans and other missionaries traveled west with what Narcissa's biographer called "noble intentions."[113] While it's impossible to determine Narcissa's true motives, it's reasonable to assume she believed it her God-given duty to bring indigenous people to what she perceived as the their one avenue to salvation. Under the lens of the Second Great Awakening, women like Narcissa believed "the gospel must be preached to every creature," and they mourned for the millions of innocents around the world without access to the Christian message.[114]

We can also appreciate Narcissa's motives through the lens of restrictions placed on women. Missionary work "liberated women" and "encouraged unusually egalitarian marriages for the period."[115] In other words, women like Narcissa and Eliza Spalding partnered with their husbands in noble work, a rarity for the day.

For the better part of 170 years, the killings at Waiilatpu have been known as the "Whitman Massacre" and the Whitmans treated as martyrs in a noble cause. But such emotionally charged labels demonize Native Peoples and sanctify victims. Neither label is accurate or fair. Like the Whitmans, Native Peoples were products of their times. Tangled in a net not of their making, and faced with threats to their control, they followed the way of their ancestors. However wrong it may seem today, killing was an accepted way for Native Peoples to defend themselves against an enemy. It's also important to

Figure 3.5 This 27-foot marble monument, erected in 1897 to celebrate the fiftieth anniversary of the Whitman tragedy, overlooks the 97-acre Whitman Mission National Historic Site, near Walla Walla, Washington. Reprinted with permission from David J. Jepsen.

recognize that people commit crimes, not tribes or cultures. Blame should not lie with the Cayuse or Nez Perce. In this case a "handful of malcontents" who expected "bold magic" but found only "bad medicine" took matters into their own hands.[116] The official website for the Whitman Mission National Historic Park near Walla Walla asks whether the slayings were "justified legal retribution or an act of revenge."[117] It's reasonable to argue neither is fully accurate, but rather an act of self-defense in the Native People's struggle to retain control of their land, its resources, and their way of life.

However rationalized, no slayings could halt the twin intruders of disease and settlement. American missionaries represented a small, early wave in an unstoppable tsunami known as Manifest Destiny and America's desire for land. Catholics, on the other hand, were closely associated with British traders who needed Native cooperation in acquiring fur and other resources. Both missionary groups believed Christianity prepared Native Peoples for membership in society but nothing prepared them for what lay ahead.

In 1836, when Christian hopes for converting Native Peoples ran high, the famous Presbyterian minister Lyman Beecher met some missionaries in Cincinnati. Beecher believed America's grand destiny would be fulfilled in the West. But like most leaders of his day, he drew America in the narrowest terms, leaving no room for foreigners and Catholics and certainly not Native Peoples. "Go on and do the present generation of Indians all the good you can," he told the missionaries. "And get as many to heaven as possible for you will be the means of sending the next generation all to hell."[118]

During the eight years following the Whitman tragedy, events unfolded that left the United States clearly in control of the territory and underscored Beecher's prophetic vision. Congress granted Oregon Territory status in 1848, opening the door to runaway settlement and statehood in 1859. The Donation Land Claim Act of 1850 offered 320 acres of free land to single men and an additional 320 to his wife, if married prior to December 1851, igniting one of the biggest land rushes in U.S. history.[119] Attracted to the fertile soil, settlers filed claims for 3 million acres in western Oregon, although far fewer on the arid Columbia Plateau.[120] With increased settlement came more conflict as the Army engaged tribes in several territorial wars, including the Cayuse War (1848) and the Yakima War (1855–1858). Following the discovery of gold on the Rogue River in Southern Oregon in 1855, local Native People battled in vain to defend their land.

With American-Native relations spinning out of control, the territorial government negotiated more than 20 treaties between 1850–1855, designed to move them to reservations and clear the way for more settlement. Preparing Native Peoples for "civilization" would now take place on government reservations under the dictates of U.S. Indian Policy and stringent assimilation programs. Instead of salvation in afterlife, people from many tribes entered a hell on earth. Rather than gaining entry into society, they found themselves removed from society. Native Peoples who didn't embrace American culture were nearly stripped of their own, perhaps the biggest loss of all.

The centuries-long story of Native Peoples' struggles for equality, self-determination, and control over land is best left for later chapters, but one high point is worth noting here. On November 21, 1987, religious leaders issued a formal apology to the Natives of the Pacific Northwest and Alaska. Leaders from multiple denominations, including Catholics and Protestants, asked for forgiveness for "their long-standing participation in the destruction of traditional Native American spiritual practices." They called for protection of "sacred places and ceremonial objects," and confessed to contributing to the "rampant racism and prejudice" of the past.[121] Nearly a century and a half after Narcissa called native spiritual beliefs the "thick darkness of heathenism," Christian leaders made nothing less than a complete reversal of views.[122] The "ancient wisdom" of indigenous religions, they wrote, could be "great gifts to the Christian churches."[123]

Indian Removal Act of 1830 – a portent of trouble for Northwest natives

> It was then the depths of winter, and that year the cold was exceptionally severe; the snow was hard on the ground, and huge masses of ice drifted on the river. The Indians brought their families with them; there were among them the wounded, the sick, newborn babies, and the old men on the point of death.
>
> *Alexis de Tocqueville, Democracy in America*[124]

The French writer Alexis de Tocqueville, who wrote extensively about American government and society, happened to be in Memphis, Tennessee, in late 1831 when he saw a large group of Choctaw attempting to cross the Mississippi River.

Under the Indian Removal Act of 1830, nearly all Native Peoples east of the Mississippi were forced to give up their land and move to Indian Territory in what is now Oklahoma – an event notoriously known as the "Trail of Tears." While not the first incidence of removal in the United States, the 1830 Act entrenched the practice of removal into American Indian policy, and provided precedence for territorial governments west of the Mississippi in the coming decades.

The Indian Removal Act affected all Native Peoples in the east, especially Cherokee, Creek, Choctaw, Chickasaw and Seminole, known as the Five Civilized Tribes. Spread throughout much of the deep South, these people made significant strides in living side-by-side with their white neighbors. They practiced agriculture and kept livestock, and otherwise had taken on many of the trappings of "civilized" society. Unfortunately, that did not endear them to non-natives who objected to native presence. Native Peoples lived on valuable land deemed ideal for growing cotton and other crops, so were considered obstacles to progress.[125] The discovery of gold increased pressure for removal.

For over a century, settlers and local governments had justified taking Native lands because they were seen as not fully utilizing them. But with the Five Civilized Tribes increasingly taking up the hoe and plow, that rationalization did not hold water.

Civilized or not, President Andrew Jackson believed removal was in the best interests of everyone, including the Natives. In the face of heavy opposition from religious groups, Jackson signed the Indian Removal Bill on May 28, 1830. The famous frontiersmen David "Davy" Crockett then Congressman from Tennessee, called the legislation "oppression with a vengeance."[126]

Over the next eight years, nearly 100,000 Natives were dispossessed of their land, lawfully theirs under previous treaties, and force-marched west to Indian Territory. Nearly a third, mostly women, children and elderly, died on the trail.

Removal resulted in the transfer of more than 100 million acres of prime farmland throughout the South. In exchange, Native Peoples received about 30 million acres in Oklahoma and Kansas, plus a promise of $70 million, most of which never reached their hands.

Historian Daniel Walker Howe argues that beyond racism and white supremacy, removal was driven by American "imperialism," or a "determination to expand geographically and economically, imposing an alien will upon subject peoples and commandeering their resources."[127] Pacific Northwest Natives would feel the force of imperialism soon enough.

Beyond the written word – the drawings of Father Nicolas Point

Primary sources can tell absorbing tales of the past. The journal of a runaway slave, transcripts of a celebrated trial or the audio recordings of frightened soldiers excite our senses as well as our brains. And so it is with the power of art.

For anyone interested in early Pacific Northwest history, few sources can match the evocative power of the drawings and paintings of Fr. Nicholas Point, the Jesuit missionary who lived among the Native Peoples of the Northwest from 1841 to 1847. Hundreds of pencil sketches and colored paintings of Flathead, Coeur d'Alene and Blackfeet tell us much about Native life not easily detected through the written word. More than 600 drawings have been preserved, with many more lost or given away.[128] With pencil and pad, Point captured the vagaries of village society, the dangers of the hunt and battle, and importantly, the Natives' tenuous connection to Christianity.

Point was born in 1799 in Rocroi, France, during the tail end of that country's revolution. At age 12, he so impressed a local attorney with his immaculate penmanship that he gave the boy a job in his office. The product of a devout Catholic home, Point joined the Society of Jesus in 1822, was ordained in 1831 and taught at Jesuit schools in Switzerland, Spain, and later in the United States in Louisiana.[129]

In 1841 he pursued the opportunity to fulfill his long-time dream of teaching Christianity to Native Peoples. Fr. Pierre Jean De Smet invited Point to join him and four other priests on a mission to the Rocky Mountains. Over the next five years, Point created a pictorial history of Native lives and culture. Through his drawings we can see the vibrancy of village life: people

Figure 3.6 Titled the "Return of the Hunter," this Nicholas Point sketch illustrates the excitement of a Salish family who will soon have meat on the table. While the Northern reaches of what are now Idaho and Western Montana were rich in game, winters could be lean. Image reprinted with permission from the Jesuit Archives Central United States.

erecting tee-pees, building fires and dressing newly killed game. We see children playing at a riverbank and men gambling on stick games.[130]

The dangers of close-up hunting are evident in a series of drawings of men on foot, armed only with knives and spears, attacking a corralled buffalo. In another, a man uses his horse to shield himself from a pack of angry wolves.

Multiple drawings demonstrate the ferocity of warfare between the Flatheads, Blackfeet, and other Natives. In one, men mounted on horses charge each other, arrows drawn. In another, two men wrestle on the ground, one caught in a desperate stranglehold. Several drawings regale the exploits of Victor, a Flathead chief who singlehandedly went up against a dozen or more Blackfeet.

The prominence of women in Point's drawings clarifies their importance in tribal life beyond their traditional domestic duties. Women are shown fighting alongside men in combat and helping to kill buffalo.

Native Peoples engaging in Christian activities dominate Point's drawings: gathering for prayer, attending Mass, and erecting a cross at the gravesite of a chief. Point included Christian symbols in many of his drawings, including the letters IHS, which stand for Jesus, or a heart with a band of thorns, denoting the "sacred heart of Jesus."[131] Numerous portraits of Native People with Christian names like Michel, Pauline, and Pierre pose with a crucifix hung around their necks. Point had no formal artistic training and his portraits are a bit amateurish, yet they reveal a level of emotion and Native connection with Christian doctrine detectable only through the visual arts.

Two decades later, Gustav Sohon followed in Point's footsteps, leaving another pictorial record of many Native leaders who participated in the Northwest treaty talks conducted by Isaac Stephens.

Explore more

Books

Julie Roy Jeffrey's. *Converting the West: A Biography of Narcissa Whitman,* offers a balanced appraisal of the missionary's strengths and failings. Two excellent volumes detail the efforts of Roman Catholic missionaries: the *Selected Letters of A.M.A. Blanchet, Bishop of Walla Walla & Nesqualy, 1846–1879,* edited by Roberta Stringham Brown, and Patricia O'Connell Killen; and *Sacred Encounters: Father De Smet and the Indians of the Rocky Mountain West* by Jacqueline Peterson and Laura Peers. To better understand the impact of missionary presence and the broader settlement era read Alexandra Harmon's *Indians in the Making: Ethnic Relations and Indian Identities Around Puget Sound,* and finally, explore the thorough and provocative *Indians of the Pacific Northwest* by Robert H. Ruby and John A Brown.

Online

To read first-hand accounts of Protestant missionaries visit the National Park Service's website, Whitman Mission National Historic Site, at http://www.nps.gov/whmi/index.htm. The selected letters of Marcus and Narcissa Whitman, and other missionaries, posted on the site, illustrate the joys and hardships of missionary life.

Museums

The Whitman Mission National Historic Site (http://www.nps.gov/whmi/index.htm) near Walla Walla, Washington, has preserved mission grounds. The museum gallery probes the question: Was killing the Whitmans justified legal retribution, an act of revenge, or some combination of both?

Questions for further discussion

How would you assess the missionary efforts to convert Native People to Christianity? Despite their good intentions, did they do more harm than good? What initially attracted Natives to the Christian word and why was it rejected by many? How do you explain the rivalry between Roman Catholics and Protestants? What role did it play in the challenges both groups faced with conversions?

Notes

1 Narcissa Whitman to Stephen Prentiss, Nov. 18, 1841 (unpublished collection). Note: The letters of Marcus and Narcissa Whitman, Henry and Eliza Spalding, and other Protestant missionaries quoted in this chapter were provided by the National Park Service's Whitman Mission National Historic Site.
2 Ibid.
3 Ibid.
4 Francis Paul Prucha, "Two Roads to Conversion: Protestant and Catholic Missionaries in the Pacific Northwest." *The Pacific Northwest Quarterly* 79, no. 4 (October 1988): 131.

 5 Narcissa Whitman to Stephen Prentiss, Oct. 25, 1836.

 6 Gordon B. Dodds, *The American Northwest, A History of Oregon and Washington* (Wheeling: Forum Press, Inc., 1986), 48.

 7 Dodds, *The American Northwest*, 49.

 8 Narcissa Whitman to Stephen Prentiss, Oct. 25, 1836.

 9 Dodds, *The American Northwest*, 49.

 10 Robert H. Ruby and John A. Brown, *Indians of the Pacific Northwest* (Norman, OK: University of Oklahoma Press, 1981), 70.

 11 Julie Roy Jeffrey, *Converting the West: A Biography of Narcissa Whitman* (Norman, OK: University of Oklahoma Press, 1991), 39.

 12 Ibid.

 13 Daniel Walker Howe, *What Hath God Wrought: The Transformation of America, 1815 to 1848* (New York: Oxford University Press, 2007), 171–172.

 14 Leonard I. Sweet, "Nineteenth Century Evangelicalism," in the *Encyclopedia of the American Religious Experience: Studies of Traditions and Movements*, Vol. 2, Charles H. Lippy and Peter W. Williams, eds. (New York: Charles Scribner's Sons, 1988), 876.

 15 Howe, *What Hath God Wrought*, 186–187.

 16 Ibid., 174.

 17 Ibid., 187–178.

 18 James McPherson, *Battle Cry of Freedom: The Civil War Era* (New York: Oxford University Press, 1988), 34–36.

 19 Ibid.

 20 Howe, *What Hath God Wrought*, 191–192.

 21 Ibid.

 22 Jeffrey, *Converting the West*, 21–22.

 23 Ibid.

 24 Jeffrey, Converting the West, 44.

 25 Jacqueline Peterson and Laura Peers, *Sacred Encounters: Father De Smet and the Native People of the Rocky Mountain West* (Norman, OK: University of Oklahoma Press, 1993), 23.

 26 Henry Warner Bowden, "North American Native People Missions," in *Encyclopedia of the American Religious Experience: Studies of Traditions and Movements*, Vol. 3. Charles H. Lippy and Peter W. Williams, eds. (New York: Charles Scribner's Sons, 1988), 1,678.

 27 Peterson and Peers, *Sacred Encounters*, 53.

 28 Dodds, *The American Northwest*, 51–52.

 29 Narcissa Whitman to Edward Prentiss and Harriet Prentiss, June 3, 1836.

 30 Narcissa Whitman to Augustus and Julia Whitman, June 27, 1836.

 31 Clifford M Drury, *Marcus and Narcissa Whitman and the Opening of Old Oregon* Vol. 1 (Seattle: Northwest Interpretive Association, 1986, 1994, 2005),193, accessed October 23, 2016, http://www.nps.gov/whmi/historyculture/drury-book.htm.

 32 Marcus Whitman to Samuel Parker, Oct. 8, 1836.

 33 Narcissa Whitman to Clarissa Prentiss, Dec. 5, 1836.

 34 Marcus Whitman to David Greene, Oct. 22, 1839.

 35 Narcissa Whitman to Jane Prentiss, May 17, 1839.

 36 Alexandra Harmon, *Indians in the Making: Ethnic Relations and Indian Identities Around Puget Sound* (Berkeley, CA: University of California Press, 1998), 33.

 37 Harman, *Indians in the Making*, 39.

38 Ruby and Brown, *Native People of the Pacific Northwest*, 71.

39 Marcus and Narcissa Whitman to Clarissa Prentiss, Oct. 9, 1839.

40 Narcissa Whitman to Clarissa Prentiss, April 11, 1838.

41 Narcissa Whitman to Clarissa Prentiss, July 4, 1838.

42 Ruby and Brown, *Indians of the Pacific Northwest*, 77.

43 Jeffrey, *Converting the West*, 143–146.

44 Narcissa Whitman to Elvira Perkins, June 25, 1839.

45 Exodus 20:3.

46 Phillip E. Cash, "Oral Traditions of the Natitaytma," in *As Days Go By: Our History, Our Land, and Our People The Cayuse, Umatilla, and Walla Walla*, Jennifer Karson, ed. (Portland, OR: Oregon Historical Society Press, 2006), 15.

47 Marcus Whitman to Rev. David Greene, March 12, 1838.

48 Marcus Whitman to Rev. David Greene, Aug. 3, 1847.

49 Marcus Whitman to Stephen Prentiss, April 8, 1845.

50 Narcissa Whitman to Stephen Prentiss, May, 2, 1837.

51 A.M.A. Blanchet, 79n.

52 A.M.A. Blanchet to Ignace Bourget, Bishop of Montreal, Feb., 1850.

53 Ibid.

54 Ruby and Brown, *Indians of the Pacific Northwest*, 81.

55 Debra Campbell, "Catholicism From Independence to World War I" in the *Encyclopedia of the American Religious Experience*, Vol. 2, 357–361.

56 Narcissa Whitman to Clarissa Prentiss, Oct. 9, 1839.

57 Narcissa Whitman to the Reverend Allen, Aug. 23, 1842.

58 Brown and Killen, *Selected Letters of A.M.A. Blanchet*, 4.

59 Prucha, *Two Roads to Conversion*, 134.

60 Ibid.

61 Edwin V. O'Hara, "De Smet in Oregon Country" (Unpublished Manuscript, December 1909).

62 Ruby and Brown, *Indians of the Pacific Northwest*, 84.

63 Ibid., 86.

64 Ibid., 77–79.

65 O'Hara, *DeSmet in Oregon Country*, 16.

66 A.M.A. Blanchet to Jean-Charles Prince, January 27, 1849.

67 Brown and Killen, *Selected Letters of A.M.A. Blanchet*, 23n.

68 Ruby and Brown, *Indians of the Pacific Northwest*, 82.

69 Peterson and Peers, *Sacred Encounters*, 110–111.

70 Ruby and Brown, *Indians of the Pacific Northwest*, 82.

71 Ibid., 83.

72 Peterson and Peers, *Sacred Encounters*, 23–24.

73 Ruby and Brown, *Indians of the Pacific Northwest*, 81.

74 Ibid., 76.

75 R. Douglas Hurt, *Indian Agriculture in America: Prehistory to the Present* (Lawrence, KS: University Press of Kansas, 1987), 99–100.

76 Marcus Whitman to David Greene, April 21, 1838.

77 Ibid.

78 Marcus Whitman to David Green, March 23, 1840.

79 Marcus Whitman to David Greene, April 7, 1843.

80 Robert H. Ruby and John A Brown, *The Cayuse Indians: Imperial Tribesmen of Old Oregon* (Norman, OK: University of Oklahoma Press, 1972, 1975, 1989), 77.

81 Narcissa Whitman to Stephen Prentiss, Nov. 18, 1841.

82 Allen P. Slickpoo Sr. and Dward E. Walker, Jr. Noon Nee-Me-Poo (We, the Nez Perces) Culture and History of the Nez Perces, Vol. 2. (Lapwai, ID: Nez Perce Tribe of Idaho, 1973), 72.

83 Narcissa Whitman to Stephen Prentiss, Feb. 7, 1843.

84 Jeffrey, *Converting the West*, 184–187.

85 Narcissa Whitman to Clarissa Prentiss, May 2, 1840.

86 Ibid.

87 The Seventh Census of the United States: 1850 (Washington, DC, 1853); Statistics of the United States in 1860.

88 Marcus Whitman to David Greene, Sept. 13, 1847.

89 Marcus Whitman to Clarissa Prentiss, May 16, 1844.

90 Ibid.

91 Narcissa Whitman to Laura Brewer, July 17, 1846.

92 Narcissa Whitman to Abigail Smith, Feb. 8, 1847.

93 Robert Boyd, "Smallpox in the Pacific Northwest: The First Epidemics," *The British Columbia Quarterly*, Spring 1994, 101, 23.

94 Todd A. Graham, "The Dalles Before the Dalles: Native People, Missionaries and the Military, 1800–1860," (Unpublished manuscript, June 3, 1988).

95 "Natives and the Maritime Fur Trade," Center for the Study of the Pacific Northwest, Lesson 5, http://www.washington.edu/uwired/outreach/cspn/html.

96 Boyd, *Smallpox in the Pacific Northwest*, 28.

97 Ibid., 13.

98 Ibid., 13–14.

99 Brown and Killen, *Selected Letters of A.M.A. Blanchet*, 76

100 Hines, *Tales of the Nez Perce*, 19.

101 Jeffrey, *Converting the West*, 208.

102 Ibid., 215–216.

103 Ibid., 213.

104 Ibid.

105 Jeffrey, *Converting the West*, 217–220. See also Henry Spalding to Clarissa Prentiss, April 6, 1848.

106 Ibid.

107 Ibid.; and Selected Letters of A.M.A. Blanchet, 42n10.

108 Jeffrey, 220.

109 A.M.A. Blanchett to Ignace Bourget, Feb. 6, 1850. The parable of the mustard seed is from the World English Bible, Luke 13:18–19.

110 U.S. Conference of Catholic Bishops, accessed Oct. 9, 2014, http://www.uspapalvisit.org/backgrounders/native_american.htm.

111 Prucha, *Two Roads to Conversion*, 130.

112 Jeffrey, *Converting the West*, 221.

113 Ibid., xiii–xiv.

114 Ibid., 35.

115 Ibid., xiv.

116 Ruby and Brown, *Indians of the Pacific Northwest*," 102.

117 "Retribution or Revenge," Whitman Mission National Historic Site, accessed November 21, 2014, http://www.nps.gov/whmi/index.htm.

118 Ruby and Brown, *Indians of the Pacific Northwest*, 106.

119 Carlos Schwantes, *The Pacific Northwest: An Interpretive History* (Lincoln, University of Nebraska Press, 1996), 121.

120 Ibid.

121 Peterson and Peers, *Sacred Encounters*, 170.

122 Narcissa Whitman to Clarissa Prentiss, Dec. 5, 1836.

123 Peterson and Peers, *Sacred Encounters*, 170.

124 J.P. Mayer, ed. and George Lawrence, trans. Alexis de Tocqueville, *Democracy In America* (New York: Harper Collins Publishers, 1966), 324.

125 Daniel Walker Howe, *What Hath God Wrought* (New York: Oxford University Press, 2007), 342–357.

126 Ibid., 352.

127 Ibid., 421.

128 Thomas M. Rockford, "Father Nicholas Point: Missionary and Artist," *Oregon Historical Quarterly*, Spring 1996, 97, no. 1, 47.

129 Rockford, "Nicolas Point," 48–53.

130 A selected number of Point's drawings can be found at the Jesuit Archives of the Central United States, accessed October 19, 2016, http://jesuitarchives.org/nicolas-point-gallery/.

131 Rockford, "Nicolas Point," 55.

4

Building an American Northwest

To make it their own, American settlers redraw region's physical and cultural boundaries

Americans' initial perception of the Pacific Northwest as a vast wasteland soon gave way to a more promising image. As reports from explorers and traders spread east, more and more people believed the region offered great opportunity for anyone willing to brave the challenges of traveling overland and building new communities. As settlers arrived, drawing new lines on the land, Native Peoples pushed back, taking conflict to new heights.

On July 5, 1841, American missionary Dr. John Richmond spoke to a crowd of Americans, British traders and Natives to celebrate the nation's independence and outline his vision for the Pacific Northwest. Speaking outside the Nisqually Methodist Mission, Richmond suggested "this magnificent region," blessed with the "bounties of nature," would become a key part of the United States. Inhabited "by our free and enterprising countrymen," it would be the site of "magnificent cities, fertile farms, and smoking manufactures."[1]

Many Americans shared his vision and turned their gaze to the Northwest in the first half of the nineteenth century. They beheld a land of endless possibilities, and began to move west over the long, arduous Oregon Trail. On arrival, they started to redraw the region's physical and social boundaries and make it the exclusive domain of white Americans, remove or marginalize the British and Native Peoples, and transform the natural environment from an imagined wilderness into productive, orderly farms. Over time, they largely succeeded, but the region's political, cultural, and natural boundaries did not give easily.[2]

Americans look West

Americans developed an interest in the Pacific Northwest as reports from explorers and traders drifted east. As early as 1813, the *Missouri Gazette* called for American expansion, claiming emigrants would not have to worry about anything a "person would dare call a mountain" and, most likely, "would not meet with an Indian to interrupt their progress."[3] Those far-fetched claims did not inspire land-hungry Americans to venture into land dominated by Britain.

Contested Boundaries: A New Pacific Northwest History, First Edition. David J. Jepsen and David J. Norberg.
© 2017 John Wiley & Sons, Ltd. Published 2017 by John Wiley & Sons, Ltd.

Interest jumped after Britain and the United States established the Convention of 1818, which gave citizens of both nations the right to settle in the Pacific Northwest, spurring Congressional action. Virginia representative John Floyd urged the federal government to build a string of forts to "Oregon Country," grant land to settlers, and secure American claims. His bold plan raised the specter of war with Britain, and Congress quickly rejected it.[4]

Debating terminology

Contemporary historians contest the very words we use to describe the people who moved west on the Oregon Trail. Americans have often referred to them as "pioneers" or "settlers," but both words are problematic. "Pioneers" suggests they were the first people to enter the region, while "settlers" indicates that no one established settlements or otherwise developed the region before they arrived. Native Peoples, of course, lived in the Pacific Northwest for many thousands of years before the Oregon Trail period in well-established communities. From their point of view, the arrival of Americans began a process of invasion and conquest, not an era of settlement. While terms like "invaders" and "conquerors" may not be the norm in American culture, they more accurately describe the reality of the Northwest's past.[5]

Calls for action grew in the 1830s, led in part by Boston schoolteacher Hall Kelley. Inspired by the journals of Lewis and Clark, Kelley zealously promoted Oregon. In his mind, the "position of that country," its "physical appearance," and "qualities of soil and climate" made the benefits of colonization obvious. He felt a mere "three thousand of the active sons of American freedom" could win Oregon from Britain. Increased trade with Native Peoples and Asia would fuel economic growth, while those "cast out of employment, into idleness and poverty" could go to Oregon and "pursue usely occupations." Surely, he argued, "the most enlightened nation on earth" could not forego this "best means of national prosperity."[6]

Famed fur trader Jedediah Smith echoed Kelley's sentiments. Travel posed no problem as his wagons "could easily have crossed the Rocky Mountains," and he found abundant game and plenty of grass "for the support of the horses and mules." The Hudson's Bay Company's success convinced him the "convention with Great Britain in 1818 ... is a great and manifest injury to the United States." He urged Secretary of War John Eaton to terminate the convention and establish clear boundaries between American and British possessions.[7]

Kelley and Smith faced significant opposition, as naysayers predicted disaster for anyone daring to go west. Emigrants, they predicted, would starve or get trapped by mountain snow. Natives posed a great danger and the U.S. Army could sooner march "to the moon" than protect overland travelers. Risking the lives of children to suit "the mad ambition of their parents" seemed criminal, and even Horace Greeley, editor of the New York *Daily Tribune* and ardent promoter of western settlement, opposed migration.[8] Going to Oregon, in his opinion, contained an "aspect of insanity."[9] He relented by 1845, as the steady stream of migrants successfully crossing the plains made his position untenable, but he remained hostile to the idea. Samuel Thurston, Oregon's first representative in Congress, visited Greeley in 1849. "Oregon has nothing to expect from him," he wrote. He "will be both small, and mean, and stinted in all his views towards Oregon."[10] Predictions of doom, however, did not stop migration. Roughly 53,000 Americans risked life and limb to cross over the Oregon Trail between 1840 and 1860.[11]

Experiencing the Oregon Trail

"…Wagons, cattle, and horses" jammed "the road as far as the eye could see" turning the plains into a "living, moving mass, struggling toward Oregon."
– *Abigail Scott Duniway*[12]

Historical accounts typically cite Joel Walker and his family as the first Americans to travel to Oregon with the intent to settle. Guided by fur traders and missionaries, they made the 2,000-mile journey in 1840.[13] The missionary Marcus Whitman, on his second continental trek, led a mass migration in 1843. That year, roughly 875 emigrants and 5,000 head of cattle made the trek.[14] Migration west built through the 1840s and exploded after the discovery of gold in California in 1848. After that, "wagons, cattle, and horses" jammed "the road as far as the eye could see," turning the plains into a "living, moving mass, struggling toward Oregon."[15] Migration continued until the completion of transcontinental railroads in the 1880s and 1890s. The ease, speed and affordability of rail travel pulled migrants away from the trails, bringing the era to a close.[16]

Pioneers moved for a variety of reasons, but mostly for economic opportunities. Peter Burnett, for example, followed Whitman in 1843 because he struggled with debt. He saw no relief in sight until a senator from Missouri proposed a bill giving free land to migrants. Its provisions entitled Burnett "to sixteen hundred acres," and he hoped the "land would ultimately enable me to pay up."[17] The bill failed, but Burnett went anyway. Another migrant had plenty of land for himself but worried about his sons as land "was hard to get" in Missouri. He moved to a "new country" so his "boys could shift for themselves" as adults.[18]

Acquisition of land and farming promised more than economic opportunity, but freedom from the chains of wage work and controlling bosses.[19] Homesteaders attempted to fulfill Thomas Jefferson's vision of an America built by "yeoman farmers," who acquired wealth free from the dependency that came with debt and big business. They were hostile to land speculators, large corporations, and banks, and believed farming, "the first and most important occupation of man," led to wealth, happiness and solid communities.[20] Big business and city life, in contrast, created a few "proud millionaires" but more "sharpers, thieves, rowdys [*sic*], bullies, and vagabonds."[21] The seemingly open lands of the Pacific Northwest proved to be a powerful lure for settlers in search of personal independence.

More than a few migrants hoped to find a healthier climate. Peter Burnett's wife suffered through Missouri's cold winters. The trip, her physician suggested, would "either kill or cure her."[22] Michael Luark, who emigrated in 1853, felt the move "might benefit my general health,"[23] while another writer remembered an "Old Mr Enna" who went to "the mountains for his health" but died en route.[24]

Patriotism fired the hearts of some migrants, or at least they claimed such in their memoirs. Burnett, for instance, felt "a great American community would grow up … upon the shores of the distant Pacific." He went to "aid in this most important enterprise," and "settle the conflicting and doubtful claims of the two governments."[25] Other writers argued "the United States has the best right to that country" and sought to "keep the country from British rule."[26] Claims of nationalism faded from emigrant journals after the Oregon Treaty of 1846 established the border between the United States and Canada, settling the dispute for good.

Laying the foundation for new territories

Settlement of Pacific Northwest states and territories in the nineteenth century was made possible in part under the Northwest Ordinance, passed by the U.S. Congress on July 13, 1787, under the authority of the Articles of Confederation. Also known as the Ordinance of 1787, it is considered one of the most significant accomplishments to come out of the Confederation era because it created the country's first territory, and outlined a three-step process by which territories could grow into states.

The Northwest Territory, or "Old Northwest," included the lands west of the Appalachian Mountains between British Canada and the Great Lakes to the North, and the Ohio River to the south. The Mississippi River made up the western boundary. Congress authorized the creation of not less than three and no more than five new states. Over the next 45 years, five states from that region joined the union: Ohio, Indiana, Illinois, Michigan and Wisconsin.

The creation of the Oregon, Washington, and Idaho territories, and later those states, employed the same process. Importantly, the Ordinance of 1787 allowed new states to enter the union "on an equal footing with the original states in all respects whatsoever." This was a major departure from the way things had long been done by the monarchies of Europe, which considered newly conquered territories "permanently peripheral and inferior to the metropolitan center of the realm."[27]

Lastly, some migrants, like African Americans George Bush and George Washington, emigrated from Missouri to escape the onerous laws of the antebellum South. Missouri, a slave state, made it illegal for any "free negro or mulatto" to settle there and threatened to whip any free African American who failed to leave the state.[28] The state granted exceptions to Bush and Washington, but both sought better conditions elsewhere. Bush went to Oregon in 1844 and Washington followed in 1850, although they would not escape exclusionary laws by resettling in Oregon.[29]

Migrants faced many dangers on the Oregon Trail, but disease took the greatest toll. Abigail Scott Duniway, like Catherine Sager, lost her mother to the "camp cholera." Shortly thereafter, "the trail took" her four-year-old brother.[30] Mary Louisa Black suffered with illness throughout her journey in 1865. She took "Calomel and laudanum" to settle her stomach but then caught "the flux" – dysentery. "The flux is not so frequent," she wrote after a few days of misery, "but when I have actions I am puped out." [31] Death haunted Peter Burnett's party as well. "Mr. Paine died of fever," he recorded on August 4, 1843. Five days later, "Stevenson died of fever" and the party stopped to bury him on the banks of a stream.[32] Graves lined the trail. "We stopped remarking on them," one migrant remembered, "when we began to see them laid out in rows of fifties and in groups of seventies."[33] Another woman became so "numbed to the sight" that not even the spectacle of a dug-up grave with a women's "head ... just lying there" phased her much.[34]

Countless animals died en route, and their corpses made some sections of the trail intolerable. Duniway "saw a great many abandoned, lame, and worn out cattle" along stretches of the trail where the "air was literally filled with the stench of dead oxen." In the Blue Mountains, Catherine Sager saw worn out cattle on the side of the road. "The sight was pitiful," she exclaimed, "and the stench was awful." In one extreme case, a man entered a river on the Nebraska plains with 30,000 sheep. Only 5,000 survived, looking like "drowned rats."[35]

Emigrants suffered from countless accidents. Helen Stewart's mother fell under a moving wagon and it nearly "crushed her leg to pieces." She escaped without serious injury, however, as they were on sandy ground.[36] In a striking case, Duniway watched several Natives grieve for and bury a man "who had been thrown from his horse and had broken his neck."[37] Drowning claimed lives from the Missouri River to the Columbia River. Routinely heavily armed travelers accidently shot themselves and others. Others died from lightning, falling trees or disappeared on the prairie.[38] Natives rescued a few lost, but fortunate, travelers, like a William Lee Scroggs, and guided them back to their wagons.[39]

Pioneers, like Scroggs, typically benefited from their interactions with Native Peoples. Most commonly, they bought desperately needed goods: moccasins, bison robes, horses, and food.[40] Emigrants tired of salted bacon and other trail staples or simply ran short on food as they crossed the "sandy sage plains" of Idaho. Joel Palmer and his companions happily traded for fish at Salmon Falls where Natives had "an abundance of them" to trade in exchange for "hooks, powder, balls, clothing, calico and knives."[41] Several weeks later, he stopped in a Cayuse village with "a few cultivated fields." In "a brisk traffic that continued until dark," the Cayuse traded vegetables for highly desired western clothing.[42] Additionally, Natives guided emigrants to sources of water and grass, piloted travelers down the Columbia, carried mail, and generally facilitated travel.[43]

Settlers chafed, however, when Natives sought payment for use of their lands and resources. Helen Stewart recalled some demanding tolls to cross a bridge, and when the travelers refused to pay, they followed and "stole some of their horses and cattle in payment, a not uncommon occurrence on the trail."[44] Some emigrants, like Peter Burnett, intentionally gave food to prevent theft, but one party responded by shooting "at every Indian we saw" to deter it.[45] Many claimed a sense of entitlement to the land and its resources. They believed "the country we were traveling over belonged to the United States" and insisted "these red men had no right to stop us."[46] Not surprisingly, tensions mounted as emigrants with little regard for native rights grew in number.

Many emigrants lived in fear of attack and some loathed Natives. Duniway, for instance, denounced those living along the Umatilla River as "filthy-looking creatures" she deemed "too lazy to accomplish anything worth notice."[47] Helen Stewart captured a dramatic near-tragedy in her journal. Fearing rumors of an attack, a frightened "old bachelor" exhorted the men in the train to "kill every Indian man, woman, and child – even suckling babes." Calmer heads prevailed and the "great Indian army ... proved to be very friendly."[48] After trading peacefully, the party continued on its way.

In reality, Native Peoples rarely attacked wagon trains. Roughly 362 emigrants died in attacks between 1840 and 1860, according to the historian John Unruh, and accounted

Figure 4.1 A leading figure in Oregon's early history, Joel Palmer moved west in 1845. Palmer was appointed Superintendent of Indian Affairs and negotiated treaties in the 1850s. Perhaps a reflection of his Quaker roots, Palmer expressed sympathy for Natives, irritating settlers who eventually drove him from office. Image reprinted with permission from the Oregon Historical Society Research Library (Catalog No. OrHi 27903).

for just 4% of all emigrant deaths.[49] Settlers actually killed more Natives. Typically, Natives attacked in small numbers and rarely killed more than a few emigrants when violence erupted. They launched large-scale attacks, deemed "massacres," on just a few occasions between 1840 and 1870. In 1850, for example, one of the bloodiest attacks on settlers occurred on the Oregon Trail when Modocs killed over 90 men, women, and children in a surprise attack. Nineteen more perished near Fort Boise in the Ward Massacre a few years later.[50] These exceptions notwithstanding, it is perhaps striking that Natives did not attack more frequently, as pioneers brought disease and depleted native resources: bison, antelope, grass, and firewood.[51]

Exhausted emigrants commonly sought the assistance of American missionaries and the British when arriving in Oregon. Some in Joel Palmer's party broke off to the Whitman Mission in search of food in 1845.[52] Peter Burnett greatly appreciated "the generous kindness" provided by the "gentlemen in charge of the business of the Hudson's Bay Company." Astoundingly, the company provided "provisions, clothing, seed, and other necessaries on credit" even to those unlikely to pay their debts.[53] The work of missionaries and fur traders facilitated migration over the trail, allowing pioneers to establish new lives and American institutions in Oregon.

> "To the honor of the country, Peter H. Burnett's negro-whipping law was never enforced in a single instance."
>
> – *W.H. Gray*[54]

Figure 4.2 For decades, the men in this photograph were mistakenly identified as members of the Cowlitz Tribe. In fact, they hailed from the Warm Springs Reservation in Southern Oregon and served as scouts to the U.S. military during the Modoc War of 1872–1873 in Northern California. Conflict between Native Peoples existed long before the arrival of American settlers. As wars broke out, the United States actively sought to pit peoples against each other, as they sought to gain advantages over age-old enemies. Reprinted with permission from the Washington State Historical Society.

Forging American institutions in Oregon

The Hudson's Bay Company governed British citizens in Oregon, but Americans refused to accept its authority. Prior to the United States making Oregon a territory in 1848, the first emigrants formed their own government. It started in 1841 when Ewing Young, a wealthy settler with "a large band of cattle and horses," died with "no will" or "heirs in the country." Settlers called a committee to settle the estate, "form a constitution, and draft a code of laws" but failed to establish a permanent government. Pioneers, including W.H. Gray, the author of *A History of Oregon,* blamed opposition from the Hudson's Bay Company and missionaries for their failure.[55]

Two years later, in 1843, American settlers made another attempt. Expecting opposition, they decided to "get up a circulating library" as the first step. Realizing "almost every settler, the missions, the Hudson's Bay Company, and some Indians" owned cattle, they proposed collaboration to eradicate "wolves, bears, and panthers" that threatened livestock. In reality, the "wolf meeting" of February 2 simply masked their true intent: the creation of an American government. The ruse apparently worked as few attendees suspected "that more than protection for animals was meant." Most contributed funds to the project "till they saw the real object" of the committee. On May 2, settlers narrowly approved a measure to create a provisional government even though HBC officials "drilled and trained their voters" to always say "No." Delegates elected a sheriff, treasurer, judges, and a committee of nine to draft laws.[56]

Joined by Peter Burnett in 1844, the committee worked to fulfill American visions for the Northwest. As Burnett put it, he anxiously wanted to found a "State superior in several respects to those east of the Rocky Mountains." Accordingly, he backed laws outlawing alcohol, banning slavery, and barring free African Americans from settling in Oregon. The law gave slave owners three years to leave, send their slaves out of the country, or else they would be freed. It also called for the arrest of any "free negro or mulatto" remaining in Oregon. Men had two years to go, women three. Convicts faced "no less than twenty nor more than thirty-nine stripes" upon "his or her bare back."[57]

Burnett's "Lash Law" provoked immediate controversy. W.H. Gray, in his history of Oregon, commented "To the honor of the country, Peter H. Burnett's negro-whipping law was never enforced in a single instance."[58] Under pressure, Burnett quickly revised the law. The new code called for African Americans to be hired out to the person willing to remove them from Oregon in exchange for the least amount of work. Gray's criticism clearly troubled Burnett. In his memoir, written many years later, Burnett countered that "no sensible man would censure" another "for mistakes *he himself has corrected*." He insisted that he replaced the provision on whipping before it could have been enforced, and only wrote the exclusion law to keep African Americans from settling a place where they would find rampant discrimination and "conditions so humiliating." He concluded that, had he "foreseen the civil war, and the changes it produced," he would never have supported the measure.[59]

Oregon settlers opposed slavery for a variety of reasons. Abigail Scott Duniway and Samuel Thurston both felt it hurt economic growth. As Duniway crossed the Mississippi River, she reflected on the "contrast in the conditions between the different sides of the river." In the free state of Illinois, she saw hardworking farmers "contentedly following the plough." In Missouri, a slave state, "we often saw slaves at work" who "didn't seem to care how any part of their labor was performed." The difference between the "enterprising farming of Illinois and the dull, careless work of the negroes" made a tremendous impression on her.[60] Thurston, debating the issue in 1850 with a pro-slavery congressman from Maryland, asked "whether free territory did not flourish better than slave territory?" and maintained Oregon would best prosper as a free territory.[61]

Racist fears also motivated Thurston and the Provisional Government. A month before the exclusion law passed, James D. Sauls, "a man of color" married to a Native woman, "said he would stand for the Indians' rights" and would incite them to burn the house of another settler.[62] Remembering the case years later, Thurston defended exclusion as a matter of "life and death to us in Oregon." He believed that a "comingling of the races" would make Natives more "formidable than they otherwise would" be and lead to "long and bloody wars." Self-preservation, he concluded, rendered the law necessary.[63]

Oregon settlers held fast to the Provisional Government's anti-slavery and exclusionary laws. They debated both laws passionately after Oregon voted for statehood in 1857, but support for the laws trounced the opposition. More than 74% of the people backed

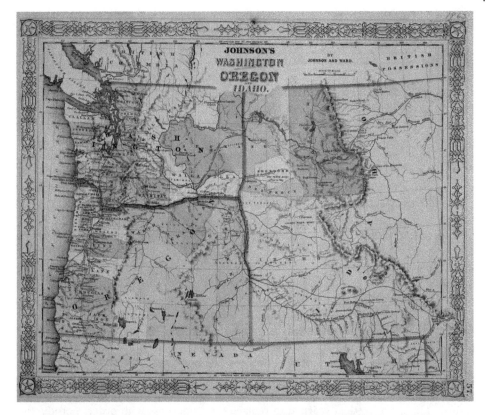

Figure 4.3 The borders of the American Northwest had largely solidified by the time this map appeared in Johnson's Atlas in 1863, and it suggests that the dreams of American settlers were largely coming to fruition. Importantly, the formative nature of the era can still be seen here, as the final borders of Idaho had yet to be drawn in. Reprinted with permission from the Washington State Historical Society.

the measure to keep slavery out of Oregon, while nearly 89% voted to keep free African Americans out of the state. They intended to make and keep Oregon a land of opportunity for whites only. Passage of the Fourteenth Amendment to the Constitution in 1868 made Oregon's exclusionary law unenforceable although it remained on the books until 1926.[64]

Taming a 'wilderness'

Settlers viewed the Northwest as a pristine wilderness rich in endless resources. Joseph Lane, Oregon's first territorial governor, described it as a place "untouched by the hand of cultivation" with "inexhaustible forests of the finest fir and cedar," streams that would never fail, "natural meadows" large enough for "innumerable herds of cattle," and "extraordinarily productive" for the production of "grain, vegetables and grapes."[65] Peter Burnett similarly extolled Oregon as one of the "loveliest and most fertile spots of earth" where "copious rains" kept fields "fresh and productive." He had no doubt that Oregon, in time, would be "densely populated and finely cultivated."[66]

In reality, settlers moved into an environment extensively altered by Native Peoples. While Natives did not establish farms in the European sense, they actively manipulated the environment to produce food and other resources. The "natural meadows" inspired settlers, but Natives periodically set fires to create and maintain them, helping to keep the forest at bay and create niches for desirable plants like the bracken fern with its edible roots. Similarly, fires facilitated the spread of camas, another staple that thrived on the prairies.[67]

American settlers, however, did not recognize native impact on the land. They argued Natives failed to engage in agriculture or otherwise improve the land and, accordingly, gave up rights to any "tracts, portions, or parcels of land, not actually occupied or used by them."[68] In their minds, boundless opportunities left by divine providence awaited ambitious pioneers in a wilderness unspoiled by human hands.[69]

Wilderness needed improvement. As one pioneer on Washington's Whidbey Island put it, they wanted to "get the land subdued and wilde nature out of it." Doing so would "increase our crops" and "make the cultivation of the soil a very profitable business."[70] Former U.S. President and Massachusetts Representative John Quincy Adams echoed those sentiments. "We claim that country – for what?," he asked, then answered, "To make the wilderness blossom as the rose, to establish laws, to increase, multiply, and subdue the earth, which we are commanded to do by the first behest of God Almighty."[71] Joseph Lane felt the "proper development" of Oregon's "agricultural resources" and "improvement of her immense water power" could supply the needs of the Pacific Coast. Even the harsh desert of Idaho's Snake River region seemed ripe for improvement to Peter Burnett, as "plentiful irrigation" might redeem those "wilderness plains."[72] In short, settlers yearned to replace the wilderness with orderly, productive farms.

Settlers started their work by carving the landscape into homesteads. In 1843, the Oregon Provisional Government allowed individuals to claim up to 640 acres of unoccupied land for free.[73] When Oregon became a territory, Congress continued to offer free land under the Donation Land Claim Act of 1850, which offered 320 acres to "every white settler" and "American half-breed Indians" who were American citizens or intended to apply for citizenship and filed claims by December 1, 1850.[74] Wives could claim an additional 320 acres, if they married by December 1, 1851. After that date, only whites could claim land and late-comers received half those amounts. All told, 8,455 settlers staked out roughly 2,800,000 acres in Oregon and Washington by the time the act expired in 1855.[75]

Both laws required settlers to improve the land and demonstrate their commitment to the territory. The 1843 law stipulated settlers should make "permanent improvements" within six months, and take up residence on the land within one year, while the Donation Land Claim Act required four years of cultivation.[76] To meet these requirements, settlers built houses and outbuildings, erected fences, and planted crops.

Farming profoundly changed the natural environment. To avoid intense tree and stump removal, most settlers staked claims on prairies and grasslands.[77] To make room for crops, they set fires and plowed up native plants like the bracken fern and camas bulb.[78] They introduced new species like wheat, oats, barley, tomatoes, cabbage, lettuce, onions, and countless others.[79] Unintentionally, they also added stubborn weeds like Scotch broom, tansy ragwort and Canadian thistle.[80] Similarly, they displaced deer and elk and introduced herds of sheep, pigs, and cattle.[81] Settlers feared predation by bears, wolves, and cougars, so they poisoned and hunted them to great effect.[82] Despite their best efforts, they improved relatively little land. On Washington's Whidbey Island, for instance, settlers only converted about 13% of the land they claimed land into pastures and fields by 1860.[83] Regardless, their labor steadily altered more and more acres, forever changed Northwest ecosystems, and steadily eroded the economy of Native Peoples.

Nothing settled – Indian reservations and war

Settler land use set the stage for conflict with Natives. Once established on prairies, settlers demanded Natives stop setting fires limiting their access to bracken and camas. Additionally, their livestock became a nuisance. Pigs feasted on camas fields and stray cows on Whidbey Island destroyed native owned potato fields. One settler, Rebecca Ebey, attributed the problem to "their own neglect in not fencing or guarding them," but her community took up a collection and paid $300 in damages to keep tensions from escalating.[84]

Settlers, to some degree, recognized native ownership of the land. In 1843, the Oregon Provisional Government proclaimed native "lands and property shall never be taken from them without their consent" and promised to create laws, "founded in justice and humanity," to prevent wrongdoing and preserve "peace and friendship."[85] Such idealistic pronouncements, however, did not stop settlers from claiming native lands. Rebecca Ebey's diary hints at this uncomfortable state of affairs when some "Klalm Indians [*sic*]" returned "to their old camping ground … in the lower part of our garden."[86] Uncomfortable with relations that grew "every year more embarrassing," settlers desperately wanted the federal government to establish treaties and give Natives "a home remote from the settlements."[87] To justify their actions, they self-servingly claimed removal would save Natives from poverty, crime, and disease.[88]

To their relief, Congress passed legislation in June 1850 authorizing the President to appoint commissioners and "negotiate treaties with the several Indian tribes" in Oregon. Additional provisions called for Natives to give up all their lands west of the Cascade Mountains and relocate to east of the Cascades if agents deemed it "expedient and practicable."[89] Various officials explored the idea but decided it would not work.[90] In part, they made their decision due to Native resistance. Not surprisingly, the idea filled those living in Western Oregon and Washington with an "indescribable dread," and those living east of the mountains objected as well.[91] Perhaps more surprisingly, settlers also voiced strong opposition and helped to squelch the idea.[92]

Relations with Native Peoples presented settlers with a dilemma. While they wanted to marginalize and remove Natives from the region, they lived with them, in the words of historian Alexandra Harmon, as intertwined peoples. Some sought trade and saw Natives as a profitable market for American products, while others lived off of berries, roots, fish and game birds until their farms could sustain them. Second, because men outnumbered women, more than a few married Native women.[93] Lastly, settlers needed laborers. Because pioneers preferred to work for themselves on their own land, labor was in short supply and Native communities filled a need. Rebecca Ebey's diary contains

Figure 4.4 This 1895 photograph of hop pickers in the Yakima region reveals the complex relationships that existed between Native Peoples and Americans who first established farms in the Oregon Trail period. Farmers needed laborers, and Natives relied on wage work to supplement their seasonal economy developed over thousands of years. Reprinted with permission from the Yakima Valley Museum.

many examples: she routinely employed Natives "to weed our onions," cut wood, "work our potatoes," carry letters, wash clothes, and scrub the floors.[94] Washington's first territorial governor, Isaac Stevens, recognized how Natives made "themselves useful" in a "variety of ways" and decided that "little objection … would be made by the whites" if Natives were "confined on reservations" in close proximity to American settlements.[95]

Stevens negotiated treaties with tribes throughout Washington with his first coming at Medicine Creek near Olympia after several cold, rainy days of meetings in December 1854.[96] He intended the treaty, drafted before negotiations even began, to set the stage for future treaty councils and presented it to the assembled "Nisqually, Puyallup, Steila-coom, Squawskin, S'Homamish, Stehchass, T'Peeksin, Squi-aitl, and Sa-heh-wamish tribes and bands," whom the treaty "regarded as one nation."[97]

Articles 1 and 2 of the treaty focused on land. Specifically, it required the "said tribes and bands" to "cede, relinquish, and convey to the United States" some 2.5 million acres – more than 99.8% of their lands. In exchange, they received three small tracts of land totaling less than 4,000 acres in size. Listed tribes had one year "to remove to and settle upon" these reservations. Additionally, the treaty maintained that no "white man" would be permitted to settle on reservations "without permission from the tribe and the super-intendent or agent," although the federal government did retain the right to build roads across reservations if necessary.[98]

Article 3 addressed the economic needs of the listed peoples. It guaranteed their "right of taking fish, at all usual and accustomed grounds and stations" and insisted they could fish "in common with all citizens of the Territory." Furthermore, it allowed peoples to engage in "hunting, gathering roots and berries, and pasturing their horses on open and unclaimed lands."[99] Seemingly straightforward, these passages on fishing rights played a central role in heated legal battles throughout the twentieth century (see chapters 9 and 12 for more on this issue).

Articles 4 and 5 provided financial compensation. First the government pledged $32,500 in goods and supplies to be paid out over 20 years. Additionally, it offered $3,250 to assist "the said Indians to remove and settle" on their lands and "clear, fence, and break up" land for farming.[100]

Stunningly, Article 6 undermined nearly everything preceding it. It allowed the President to "remove them from either or all of said reservations to such other suitable place or places," consolidate them with other "friendly tribes or bands" or divide the reservations into individual lots when the needs of the territory or "the welfare of the said Indians" called for action. In the same vein, later articles required the listed peoples to "acknowledge their dependence on the Government of the United States," "promise to be friendly," outlawed "the use of ardent spirits," prohibited trading with the British on Vancouver Island, and made them "free all slaves." The larger point could not have been clearer. The treaty expected Native Peoples to renounce their autonomy and completely accept that where and how they lived now rested with the federal government.[101]

Numerous problems marred treaty making. Native Peoples living in the Puget Sound region did not live in clearly defined tribes with centralized leaders. To get the treaties

Figure 4.5 Former Washington Territorial Governor Isaac Ingalls Stevens stands proudly in uniform in this 1861 lithograph. A West Point graduate, Stevens's controversial dealings with Native Americans plagued his career in the Pacific Northwest. He leapt to the Union's cause in the Civil War and died in 1862 in the Battle of Chantilly. Reprinted with permission from the Washington State Historical Society.

signed quickly, officials, in essence, created tribes and appointed leaders, like Quiemuth and Leschi as chief and sub-chief for the Nisqually. [102] Treating the Nisqually as one people, however, fueled frustration. Some lived on the coast, traveled by canoe, and mostly fished. Others lived inland, traveled mostly by horse, and preferred hunting to fishing. Steven's decision to give them one reservation satisfied some but angered others. [103]

Language posed more problems. Stevens' interpreter, Frank Shaw, presented the treaty in Chinook jargon. Developed for trade, jargon blended English, French, and several native words into a language too simple for legal transactions. [104] Native interpreters translated Chinook to their own languages, compounding opportunities for misunderstandings. Despite language barriers and the fact Puget Sound Natives had no tradition of buying or selling land, "the Indians comprehended every sentence" Steven's son later insisted. [105]

Such claims are open to dispute. Minutes from the Medicine Creek Treaty no longer exist, and multiple other accounts of negotiations contradict each other. Perhaps the greatest controversy surrounds the treaty signing. Years later, Frank Shaw claimed they used "no compulsion or persuasion" as those assembled "seemed anxious to sign it."[106] Several Nisqually men, however, maintained Leschi and Quiemuth never signed. One dramatic account describes how Leschi tore the certificate of leadership in Steven's face, "stamped on the pieces, and left the treaty ground, and never came back to it again."[107] Shaw insisted Leschi signed and "acted like a gentleman the whole time the treaty was being made."[108] Debate continues to the present, but somebody placed a signature-mark next to "Lesh-high" and "Qui-ee-metl" on the treaty.

Without question, Stevens encountered further resistance as he moved through a series of treaty councils throughout Washington. Talks at the Chehalis River Treaty Council broke down completely and Stevens left empty-handed. Negotiations with the Cayuse, Walla Walla, Umatilla, Nez Perce, and Yakama stalled too, infuriating Stevens. According to some accounts, he resorted to threats, telling them to sign or "walk in blood knee deep." Yakama chief Kamiakin signed but bit his lips so hard "they bled profusely."[109] Tensions mounted and broke into open conflict as white miners, in search of gold, trespassed on Yakama land and raped Yakama women. [110]

As war spread from Eastern Washington and engulfed the Puget Sound region, some settlers blamed Stevens. George Gibbs, a participant in the treaty making process, charged that "the reservations allowed them were insufficient" and had "a great deal to do in fomenting this war."[111] Under pressure, Stevens revisited the Medicine Creek Treaty. He provided better, larger, reservations for the Nisqually and Puyallup and created the Muckleshoot reservation between the White and Green rivers. [112] For the Medicine Creek tribes, resistance worked.

Naming controversies

Many places in the Pacific Northwest bear the names of influential figures from the exploration, fur trade, and settlement eras like Lewis and Clark, Isaac Stevens, Samuel Thurston, and President Franklin Pierce.

In the current era, social activists have challenged some of them. Locals initially named King County in Washington in honor of Vice President William Rufus King, a Southern planter and slave owner. Uncomfortable with the association, the King County Council voted to rename the county after civil rights leader Dr. Martin Luther King in 1986, and the state government made the change official in 2005.[113]

Some locals also question the name of Washington's tallest mountain, Mount Rainier. British explorer George Vancouver named it after a fellow officer when he toured the region in 1792, and critics feel it should be changed back to Tacoma, Tahoma, or one of its other Native American names. President Obama's decision to change Alaska's Mount McKinley back to the native name Denali in 2015 makes it entirely possible that Rainier's name could change in the future.[114]

Frustration permeated the Northwest even after the wars ended. Many American settlers came to the Pacific Northwest with high hopes of creating farming communities for American whites only. They saw progress in the exclusionary laws created by their local governments and treaties established by the federal government. But, their vision did not come to fruition as they expected as African Americans like George Bush and Native Americans like Kamiakin contested the boundaries settlers tried to draw around the region. Over time, settlers gained more and more power in the region, but the

Figure 4.6 Some 1,000 Nez Perce on horses thundered into the Walla Walla treaty council in 1855 and circled Isaac Stevens and other American dignitaries in this Gustavus Sohon watercolor. Clearly they hoped the dramatic entrance would intimidate Stevens and set the tone for negotiations. Reprinted with permission from the Washington State Historical Society.

Figure 4.7 Superintendent of Indian Affairs Joel Palmer and Isaac Stevens, Washington's territorial governor (foreground) serve dinner to leaders of multiple tribes at the 1855 Walla Walla treaty council. It is doubtful this show of goodwill assuaged them as control of their lands lay at the heart of negotiations. Reprinted with permission from the Washington State Historical Society.

battles fought over regional control continued to roil through the twentieth century as non-whites and Native Peoples fought for equal footing in the Pacific Northwest.

"Seeing the Elephant" – the Catherine Sager story

In late April 1844, ten-year-old Catherine Sager, her parents, Henry and Naomi, and six siblings joined thousands of Americans on the path to Oregon. She described her father as "a rolling stone" who "was never content to stay in one place long." He heard missionary Marcus Whitman make Oregon "sound almost like a heaven on earth" with a healthy climate, and off they went.[115]

The Sager saga illustrates the trials and hardships that greeted most migrants to Oregon. Roughly 1,475 people migrated to Oregon that year, and "it seemed to us we were living within a traveling circus."[116] She saw "long lines of wagons" lined up "as far as we could see in front and as far as we could see behind." Some emigrants painted their wagons with pictures of animals and slogans like the popular expression, "Goin' to See The Elephant!" They organized themselves into a wagon train, elected a captain, and amid "a great fluttering of handkerchiefs and gruff farewells" left Missouri.[117]

The journey started enthusiastically, but soon turned to drudgery. Her father hired a young man to drive the wagons while he hunted bison and antelope. Her brothers spent their days playing hide-and-seek in the grass, hunting, and "even helped drive the teams!" Catherine, however, cared for her younger siblings, including new-born Henrietta, and helped with cooking, sewing and washing. "I think the boys had more fun," she lamented, "It didn't seem fair. But I didn't dare complain."[118]

Drudgery turned to tragedy as the summer wore on. Catherine caught her dress while climbing into the wagon and fell under the wheel. It ran over her leg "and crushed it. Badly." She slowly recovered but rode in the wagon for the rest of the crossing. Not long afterwards, her father fell ill with typhoid and died. The family hired a young man to drive the team, but he borrowed the family's gun to hunt "and we never saw him again." Then, her mother's health failed. She passed from "lucid moments" that "lapsed back into delirium" for several days before she too died. "It occurred to me then," Catherine recalled "in the deepest grief and shock, that I was an orphan. … How would we ever get to Oregon?"[119]

Willis Shaw, wagon train captain, and a physician, Dr. Dagon, assumed care of the family, but accidents plagued them for the rest of the journey. One night, her sister got too close to the fire and "She went up like a candle." Dr. Dagon "beat the flames out with his bare hands" and saved her life, but Catherine felt tremendous guilt. "The girls were my responsibility," she explained. "No one blamed me for my carelessness, but I blamed myself." Shortly thereafter, her younger sister crawled out of bed, "wandered off into the cold night," and nearly froze to death. Finally, her brother tried to stoke a fire by "holding his powder horn over the small blaze." The gunpowder "exploded in his face," burning him badly. Short on food, sick, and weary with grief, the Sager children arrived in Umatilla, Oregon, on October 15 – nearly six months after leaving home.[120]

Catherine and her siblings found refuge at the Whitman Mission near Walla Walla. "The Whitmans were good to us," Catherine recalled, and she embraced her new life there. It did not last long, however. Two of her brothers died when a small group of renegade Cayuse and Nez Perce attacked the mission in 1847, killing 14 including Marcus and Narcissa Whitman. The rest of the family broke apart, and Catherine moved to Oregon's Willamette Valley. She later settled in Spokane and lived out the rest of her life in the Northwest.[121]

Mother Joseph – a Northwest builder

Cloaked in long black habits, members of the Sisters of Providence of Montreal stepped off a steamer on the north shore of the Columbia River at Fort Vancouver on December 8, 1856. Recruited by the Bishop of Walla Walla and Nesqualy, A.M.A. Blanchet, the nuns committed to serving the rapidly growing hoard of settlers arriving in Washington Territory almost daily.

Historians debate the impact of missionaries who proselytized to Natives throughout the Pacific Northwest at midcentury, yet few question the degree to which Sisters of Providence improved the quality of life in the region.

Under the tireless leadership of Sister Joseph, born Esther Pariseau, later made Mother Joseph, the group wasted no time in establishing a boarding school, orphanage, and the territory's first hospital, St. Joseph's. Over the next 46 years, Mother Joseph guided the construction of 30 schools, hospitals and homes for the poor. Sometimes her leadership extended to design and construction. The daughter of a respected coach maker in Quebec, Mother Joseph was known as "the Builder." She did not hesitate to climb scaffolding or stand on roofs to inspect work, sometimes tearing it apart and redoing it herself.[122]

To fund construction, Mother Joseph and other sisters conducted "begging tours." They would travel on horseback to mining camps throughout the region, begging miners for a few gold nuggets or pieces of silver and appealing to their conscience to help the unfortunate.[123]

In a 1875 letter to the Bishop of Montreal, Blanchet wrote he was pleased with Mother Joseph's work because "if there is any chance of [fund raising] success, it is she who has the qualities to make it happen."[124]

In 1878, the sisters opened Seattle's first hospital, converted from an existing house at Fifth Avenue and Madison Street. It quickly proved too small for the growing city and Mother

Figure 4.8 Settlers often viewed Catholic missionaries with suspicion since many came from Canada or Europe and sometimes seemed too sympathetic towards Native Americans. Mother Joseph's tireless efforts to help the poor and promote social services endeared her to many and made her an icon in the region's history. Image reprinted with permission from the Archives of the Sisters of the Holy Names of Jesus and Mary, U.S.-Ontario Province.

Joseph oversaw construction of a three-story, wood-framed hospital at Fifth and Spring, where today's federal courthouse now stands.

Mother Joseph died of cancer on January 19, 1902, at age 79. In 1980, the U.S. Senate accepted a statute of Mother Joseph, a gift from Washington State, honoring her "monumental contributions to health care, education, and social work throughout the Northwest."[125] Today, Providence Health & Services is a not-for-profit Catholic health care provider that operates hospitals, physician clinics and senior services in five western states.

Federal boarding schools challenge cultural boundaries

Americans wanted to go beyond establishing physical boundaries between themselves and Native Peoples through the creation of reservations in the second half of the nineteenth century. They demanded Native Peoples give up their cultures, adopt American values, and fully assimilate into the general population.

To that aim, American policy makers established federal Indian boarding schools on and off reservations following the model set by the Carlisle Industrial School. Founded in Pennsylvania in 1879 by Richard Henry Pratt, Carlisle separated native children from their families and communities to minimize contact with native influences and transform them into his idea of model citizens.[126] Students had to speak English, dress and wear their hair according to American fashion, practice Christianity, and generally conform to the norms of American society. Initially, government officials admitted students on a voluntary basis, but increasingly pressured families to send their children and, by the 1890s, withheld "rations and annuities from parents and guardians" to force compliance.[127]

Government funded boarding schools in the Northwest grew out of the treaties signed in the 1850s. The Medicine Creek Treaty of 1854, for instance, provided for the creation of "an agricultural and industrial school," leading to the founding of the Puyallup Indian School in 1860.[128] Initially it served just a handful of students as a day school but over time grew into the Cushman Indian School and ultimately served students from the entire Northwest and Alaska.[129]

The Chemawa Indian School, founded in 1880 in Oregon, became the largest boarding school in the region. Like Carlisle, Chemawa aimed to separate students "from the influence of the idle and vicious," and place them in an environment where the "teaching of the schoolmaster" could take hold.[130] Students split their time between the classroom and industrial training. Following contemporary ideas about gender roles, boys worked in the fields, orchards, and machine shops, while girls learned to sew, cook, and clean. Chemawa's first class of 25 students graduated in 1885 with a fifth-grade education. By 1920, the school went through tenth grade and oversaw more than 900 students from 90 tribes. By 1930, 8,000 students had passed through Chemawa, many earning a high school diploma.[131] Chemawa remains open, and continues to serve a diverse body of Native Peoples, albeit with a dramatically different mission. Instead of pushing assimilation, the school promotes cultural pride and provides students with a "safe and affirmative learning environment."[132]

A century ago, students often found terrible conditions. Henry Sicade, who attended the Puyallup school and eventually served as a director in the Fife Public Schools, recalled a monotonous diet of cornmeal mush, bread, and molasses, and the occasional potato stew. Students "never saw the apples or corn" grown at the school unless they dared "crawl under the fence and pick the windfalls."[133] Disease spread rapidly and students often received little medical care. "An epidemic of itch and measles," spread through Sicade's school, and left pupils "rotting with no care of any sort."[134]

Students who broke rules often faced severe punishment. Sicade described some teachers in glowing terms but remembered others who administered frequent whippings or sent pupils to the school jail shackled "with iron balls and chains" for even "minor offenses."[135] When school employees needed firewood, he bitterly recalled, they simply found excuses "to jail a few to cut wood."[136] Not surprisingly, students routinely fought back, ran away, or otherwise resisted imperious administrators.[137]

Federal boarding schools mostly closed in the 1920s and 1930s as federal policies changed (see Chapter 9), leaving a mixed legacy. Ripped from their cultures and forced into new lives, many students experienced intense trauma. On the other hand, the schools trained future leaders like Sicade and brought together peoples from various cultures. This in turn helped to break down the historic, cultural barriers that long divided tribes, fostering cooperation that may have strengthened efforts to resist assimilation policies and defend sovereignty.[138]

Explore more

Books

Robert Bunting's article "Michael Luark and Settler Culture in the Western Pacific Northwest, 1853–1899" (*Pacific Northwest Quarterly*, Fall 2005) inspired the general outline of this chapter and provides an excellent introduction to the era. While many works cover the Oregon Trail, John Unruh's *The Plains Across*, Will Bagley's *So Rugged and Mountainous: Blazing the Trails to Oregon and California, 1812–1848*, and Michael Tate's *Indians and Emigrants: Encounters on the Overland Trail* are good places to start with this important and complex topic. Alexandra Harmon's *Indians in the Making: Ethnic Relations and Indian Identities around Puget Sound* and Gray Whaley's *Oregon and the Collapse of Illahee: U.S. Empire and the Transformation of an Indigenous World, 1729–1859* are outstanding works on relations between settlers and Native Americans, while Richard Kugler's *The Bitter Waters of Medicine Creek: A Tragic Clash between White and Native America* gives a clear and highly readable account of the Medicine Creek Treaty proceedings and aftermath. For more on environmental history, see Richard White's *Land Use, Environment, and Social Change: The Shaping of Island County, Washington* along with articles by Robert Bunting and William Robbins. Lastly, Patricia Limerick's *The Legacy of Conquest: The Unbroken Past of the American West* is an essential piece on the history of the American West and explores many of the themes covered in this book.

Online

The Internet Archive (https://archive.org/) has many Oregon Trail journals and books written by early settlers available for download. Many documents can be found at the Washington Historical Records Project (http://www.sos.wa.gov/archives/hrp/default.aspx) and Oregon's Governor's Records Guides (http://sos.oregon.gov/archives/Pages/records/governors_guides.aspx). Additionally, the Washington State Library's Digital Collections have many excellent sources in the "Classics in Washington History" section (https://www.sos.wa.gov/library/publications.aspx). Be sure to check Historylink.org (http://historylink.org/) for essays on the settlement era in Washington State.

Museums

A number of museums capture the Oregon Trail Experience. To start, visit the End of the Oregon Trail (http://www.historicoregoncity.org/) center in Oregon City or the National Oregon/California Trail Center (http://www.historicoregoncity.org/) in Montpelier, Idaho. Pioneer Farm (http://www.pioneerfarmmuseum.org/) in Eatonville, Washington, Pioneer Village (http://history.idaho.gov/pioneer-village) in Boise, Idaho both give further insight into the lives of American settlers.

What do you think?

Relations between American settlers and Native America differed dramatically from those between fur traders and Native Americans. Why? American settlers and

Euro-American fur traders generally viewed native cultures with contempt, but their relations with Natives differed greatly. Explain why.

Notes

1 Herbert Hunt and Floyd C. Kaylor, *Washington West of the Cascades*, Vol. 1 (Chicago: S.J. Clarke Publishing Company, 1917), 97–99; Murray Morgan, *Puget's Sound: A Narrative of Early Tacoma and the Southern Sound* (Seattle, WA: University of Washington Press, 1979), 59–60; Alexandra Harmon, *Indians in the Making: Ethnic Relations and Indian Identities around Puget Sound* (Berkeley, CA: University of California Press, 1998), 45–46; Drew W. Crooks, "The Wilkes Expedition and Southern Puget Sound: An 1841 Encounter With Lasting Effects," DuPont Museum & Historical Society, accessed April 15, 2015, http://www.dupontmuseum.com/.

2 Morgan, *Puget's Sound*, 58–59; Crooks, "The Wilkes Expedition."

3 John David Unruh, *The Plains Across: The Overland Emigrants and the Trans-Mississippi West, 1840–1860* (Urbana, IL: University of Illinois Press, 1979), 1.

4 Walt Crowley, "Great Britain and the United States sign the Treaty of Joint Occupation of Oregon on October 20, 1818," *HistoryLink*, accessed February 23, 2016, http://www.historylink.org/; Gordon Dodds, *The American Northwest: A History of Oregon and Washington* (Arlington Heights, IL: The Forum Press, Inc., 1986), 64–65.

5 For more on this idea, see Patricia Nelson Limerick, *The Legacy of Conquest: The Unbroken Past of the American West* (New York: W.W. Norton & Company, 1987) and Francis Jennings, *The Invasion of North America: Indians, Colonialism, and the Cant of Conquest* (Chapel Hill, NC: University of North Carolina Press, 1975).

6 James D. Torr, ed. *Westward Expansion: Interesting Primary Documents* (San Diego, CA: Greenhaven Press, 2003), 41–44; Fred Wilbur Powell, "Hall Jackson Kelley – Prophet of Oregon," *The Quarterly of the Oregon Historical Society* 43, no. 1 (March 1917): 11–12.

7 Jedediah S. Smith, David E. Jackson, and W. L. Sublette, "Letter of Smith, Sublette, and Jackson," *The Quarterly of the Oregon Historical Society* 4, no. 4 (December 1903): 395–398.

8 Unruh, *The Plains Across*, 10–13.

9 Robert Chadwell Williams, *Horace Greeley: Champion of American Freedom* (New York: New York University, 2006), 43; Unruh, *The Plains Across*, 10.

10 Samuel Royal Thurston, "Diary of Samuel Royal Thurston," *The Quarterly of the Oregon Historical Society* 15, no. 3 (September 1914): 159.

11 Unruh, *The Plains Across*, 84–85.

12 Joyce Badgley Hunsaker, *Seeing the Elephant: Voices from the Oregon Trail* (Lubbock, TX: Texas Tech University Press, 2003), 134–135.

13 David Dary, *The Oregon Trail: An American Saga* (New York: Alfred A. Knopf, 2004), 63–64.

14 Unruh, 84; "Basic Facts about the Oregon Trail," U.S. Department of the Interior, Bureau of Land Management, National Historic Oregon Trail Interpretive Center, accessed February 23, 2016, http://www.blm.gov/.

15 Joyce Badgley Hunsaker, *Seeing the Elephant*, 134–135.

16 Carlos A. Schwantes, *The Pacific Northwest: An Interpretive History*, 2nd ed. (Lincoln, NE: University of Nebraska Press, 1996), 187–193.

17 Peter Burnett, *Recollections and Opinions of an Old Pioneer* (New York: D. Appleton and Company, 1880), 97–98.

18 Quoted in Robert Bunting, "Michael Luark and Settler Culture in the Western Pacific Northwest, 1853–1899," *Pacific Northwest Quarterly* 96, no. 4 (Fall 2005): 198.

19 Gregory H. Nobles, *American Frontiers: Cultural Encounters and Continental Conquest* (New York: Hill and Wang, 1997), 163–164.

20 George Abernathy, "Governor George Abernathy's Administration, Legislative Messages, 1845," Oregon Secretary of State, accessed June 25, 2015, http://arcweb.sos .state.or.us/; Bunting, "Michael Luark and Settler Culture," 200, 203; Gray H. Whaley, *Oregon and the Collapse of Illahee: U.S. Empire and the Transformation of an Indigenous World, 1729–1859* (Chapel Hill, NC: University of North Carolina Press, 2010), 165–171.

21 Robert W. Johannsen, *Frontier Politics and the Sectional Conflict: The Pacific Northwest on the Eve of the Civil* War (Seattle, WA: University of Washington Press, 1955), 9.

22 Burnett, *Recollections and Opinions of an Old Pioneer*, 98.

23 Quoted in Bunting, "Michael Luark and Settler Culture," 199.

24 Kenneth L. Holmes, ed., *Covered Wagon Women: Diaries and Letters From the Western Trails, 1864–1868*, Vol. 9 (Lincoln, NE: University of Nebraska Press, 1990), 70; Will Bagley, *So Rugged and Mountainous: Blazing the Oregon and California Trails, 1812–1848* (Norman, OK: University of Oklahoma Press, 2010), 124.

25 Burnett, *Recollections and Opinions of an Old Pioneer*, 97.

26 Quoted in Bagley, *So Rugged and Mountainous*, 123.

27 Gordon S. Wood, *Empire of Liberty: A History of the Early Republic, 1789–1815* (New York: Oxford University Press, 2009), 122.

28 "Missouri's Early Slave Laws: A History in Documents," Missouri Digital Heritage, accessed May 24, 2015, https://www.sos.mo.gov/.

29 Schwantes, *The Pacific Northwest;* 153, William Loren Katz, *The Black West* (New York: Doubleday, 1971), 72–77; Kit Oldham, "George and Mary Jane Washington found the town of Centerville (now Centralia) on January 8, 1875," *HistoryLink*, accessed February 23, 2016, http://www.historylink.org/.

30 Hunsaker, *Seeing the Elephant*, 136, 141.

31 Holmes, *Covered Wagon Women*, 63, 68.

32 Burnett, *Recollections and Opinions of an Old Pioneer*, 115.

33 Hunsaker, *Seeing the Elephant*, 160.

34 Ibid., 180.

35 Ibid., 117, 137, 181–187.

36 Ibid., 181.

37 Ibid., 139.

38 Unruh, *The Plains Across*, 346–349.

39 Michael L. Tate, *Indians and Emigrants: Encounters on the Overland Trails* (Norman, OK: University of Oklahoma Press, 2006), 77–78.

40 Ibid., 42–59.

41 Joel Palmer, *Palmer's Journal of Travels over the Rocky Mountains, 1845–1846,* Early Western Travels 1748–1846, ed. Reuben Gold Thwaites (Cleveland, OH: Arthur H. Clark Company, 1906), 93–94.

42 Palmer, *Palmer's Journal*, 111.

43 Hunsaker, *Seeing the Elephant*, 144; Burnett, *Recollections and Opinions of an Old Pioneer*, 128–129; Tate, *Indians and Emigrants*, 12, 75–81.

44 Hunsaker, *Seeing the Elephant*, 179.

45 Burnett, *Recollections and Opinions of an Old Pioneer*, 103, quoted in Unruh, *The Plains Across*, 146.

46 Quoted in ibid., 129.

47 Hunsaker, *Seeing the Elephant*, 144.

48 Ibid., 184.

49 Unruh, *The Plains Across*, 144, 345.

50 Tate, *Indians and Emigrants*, 178–179.

51 Ibid., 73–75.

52 Palmer, *Palmer's Journal*, 109.

53 Burnett, *Recollections and Opinions of an Old Pioneer*, 142.

54 Ibid., 213–222.

55 W.H. Gray, *A History of Oregon: 1792–1842, Drawn from Personal Observation and Authentic Information* (Portland: Harris and Holman, 1870), 199–204.

56 Ibid., 260–280.

57 Burnett, *Recollections and Opinions of an Old Pioneer*, 213–222.

58 Ibid.; Gray, *A History of Oregon*, 383.

59 Burnett, *Recollections and Opinions of an Old Pioneer*, 215–222.

60 Hunsaker, *Seeing the Elephant*, 132.

61 Thurston, "Diary of Samuel Royal Thurston," 163.

62 Gray, *A History of Oregon*, 395–396.

63 Patricia Nelson Limerick, *The Legacy of Conquest: The Unbroken Past of the American West* (New York: W.W. Norton & Company, 1987), 278.

64 Johannsen, *Frontier Politics and the Sectional Conflict*, 33–46; Schwantes, *The Pacific Northwest*, 377.

65 "Governor's Message," *Oregon Spectator*, Oct. 4, 1849.

66 Burnett, *Recollections and Opinions of an Old Pioneer*, 140–141.

67 Richard White, *Land Use, Environment, and Social Change: The Shaping of Island County, Washington* (Seattle, WA: University of Washington, 1992), 20–23.

68 Burnett, *Recollections and Opinions of an Old Pioneer*, 172.

69 White, *Land Use, Environment, and Social Change* 23, 25.

70 Ibid., 35.

71 Quoted in William Robbins, "Landscape and Environment: Ecological Change in the Intermontane Northwest," *Pacific Northwest Quarterly* 84, no. 4 (October 1993): 148.

72 Burnett, *Recollections and Opinions of an Old Pioneer*, 119.

73 J. Henry Brown, *Brown's Political History of Oregon*, Vol. 1 (Portland: Wiley B. Allen, 1892), 167.

74 "Donation Land Claim Act, 1850," Center for Columbia River History, accessed April 15, 2015, http://www.ccrh.org/; Dorothy O. Johansen and Charles M. Gates, *Empire of the Columbia: A History of the Pacific Northwest* (New York: Harper and Brothers, 1957), 290–292.

75 Johansen, *Empire of the Columbia*, 291–292; "Donation Land Claim Act."

76 Brown, *Brown's Political History of Oregon*, 167; "Donation Land Claim Act."

77 White, *Land Use, Environment, and Social Change*, 37; Robert Bunting, "The Environment and Settler Society in Western Oregon," *Pacific Historical Review* 64, no. 3 (August 1995): 417–418.

78 White, *Land Use, Environment, and Social Change*, 16–23, 36, 42; Tom Schroeder, "Rediscovering a Coastal Prairie near Friday Harbor," *Pacific Historical Review* 98, no. 2 (Spring 2007): 62; Peter G. Boag, "Overlanders and the Snake River Region: A Case Study of Popular Landscape Perception in the Early West," *Pacific Historical Quarterly* 84, no. 4 (October 1993): 148; Bunting, "Michael Luark and Settler Culture," 201.

79 Bunting, "The Environment and Settler Society," 418; Victor Farrar, ed., "Diary of Colonel and Mrs. I.N. Ebey," *The Washington Historical Quarterly* 8, no. 2 (April 1917): 135, 136, 143.

80 Bunting, "The Environment and Settler Society," 424; White, *Land Use, Environment, and Social Change*, 46–48.

81 Bunting, "The Environment and Settler Society," 426.

82 White, *Land Use, Environment, and Social Change*, 48–49; Bunting, "The Environment and Settler Society," 428–429; Bunting, "Michael Luark and Settler Culture," 202.

83 White, *Land Use, Environment, and Social Change*, 40; Bunting, "The Environment and Settler Culture," 414.

84 Farrar, "Diary of of Colonel and Mrs. I.N. Ebey," 135.

85 Quoted in Ronald Spores, "Too Small a Place: The Removal of the Willamette Valley Indians," *American Indian Quarterly* 17, no. 2 (Spring 1993): 173.

86 Farrar, "Diary of Colonel and Mrs. I. N. Ebey," 134.

87 George Abernathy, "Governor George Abernathy's Administration, Legislative Message, 1847," Oregon Secretary of State, accessed June 25, 2015, http://arcweb.sos.state.or.us/; William G. Robbins, "The Indian Question in Western Oregon: The Making of a Colonial People," in *Experiences in a Promised Land* ed. G. Thomas Edwards and Carlos A. Schwantes (Seattle, WA: University of Washington Press, 1986), 59.

88 "Governor's Message," *Oregon Spectator,* October 4, 1849; Robbins, "The Indian Question," 59.

89 Francis Paul Prucha, ed. *Documents of United States Indian Policy*, 3rd ed. (Lincoln, NE: University of Nebraska Press, 2000), 80.

90 Spores, "Too Small a Place," 175–176; Anson Dart, "Letter from Anson Dart to the Bureau of Indian Affairs in 1851," Center for Columbia River History, accessed June 30, 2015, http://www.ccrh.org/; Richard Kluger, *The Bitter Waters of Medicine Creek: A Tragic Clash between White and Native America* (New York: Alfred A. Knopf, 2011), 76; Harmon, *Indians in the Making,* 78.

91 Quoted in Spores, "Too Small a Place," 176.

92 Spores, "Too Small a Place," 176; Harmon, *Indians in the Making,* 78.

93 Harmon, *Indians in the Making,* 60–63.

94 Farrar, "Diary of Colonel and Mrs. I.N. Ebey," 126, 144–145; Victor Farrar, ed., "Diary of Colonel and Mrs. I. N. Ebey," *The Washington Historical Quarterly* 7, no. 3 (July 1916): 245; Victor Farrar, ed., "Diary of Colonel and Mrs. I.N. Ebey," *The Washington Historical Quarterly* 7, no. 4 (October 1916): 311; Victor Farrar, ed., "Diary of Colonel and Mrs. I.N. Ebey," *The Washington Historical Quarterly* 8, no. 1 (January 1917): 54, 61; Harmon, *Indians in the Making,* 58.

95 Quoted in SuAnn M. Reddick and Cary C. Collins, "Medicine Creek to Fox Island: Cadastral Scams and Contested Domains," *Oregon Historical Society* 106, no. 3 (Fall 2005): 378.

96 Morgan, *Puget's Sound*, 90–97.

97 Colin G. Galloway, *Pen and Ink Witchcraft: Treaties and Treaty Making in American Indian History* (New York: Oxford University Press, 2013), 177; Reddick, "Medicine Creek to Fox Island," 382; "Treaty of Medicine Creek, 1854," *HistoryLink*, accessed May 19, 2015, http://www.historylink.org/.

98 "Treaty of Medicine Creek, 1854."

99 Ibid.

100 Ibid.

101 Ibid.

102 Harmon, *Indians in the Making*, 79, 85; Kluger, *The Bitter Waters of Medicine Creek*, 74; Reddick, "Medicine Creek to Fox Island," 378–381.

103 Reddick, "Medicine Creek to Fox Island," 379.

104 Reddick, "Medicine Creek to Fox Island," 379; Kugler, *The Bitter Waters of Medicine Creek*, 78–79; Morgan, *Puget's Sound*, 95.

105 Quoted in Kugler, *The Bitter Waters of Medicine Creek*, 83.

106 Quoted in Ibid., 101.

107 Quoted in Reddick, "Medicine Creek to Fox Island," 383.

108 Quoted in Kugler, *The Bitter Waters of Medicine Creek*, 101.

109 Jo N. Miles, "Kamiakin's Impact on Early Washington Territory," *Pacific Northwest Quarterly* 99, no. 4 (Fall 2008): 166–167.

110 Ibid., 167.

111 Quoted in Sherburne F. Cook, Jr., "The Little Napoleon: The Short and Turbulent Career of Isaac I. Stevens," *Columbia* 14, no. 4 (Winter 2000–2001): 19.

112 Harmon, *Indians in the Making*, 91; Reddick, "Medicine Creek to Fox Island," 393.

113 Patrick McRoberts, "King County Council names county after Dr. Martin Luther King Jr. on February 24, 1986," *Historylink*, accessed February 27, 2016, http://www.historylink.org/index.cfm?DisplayPage=output.cfm&file_id=678.

114 Patrick McRoberts, "King County Council names county after Dr. Martin Luther King Jr. on February 24, 1986," *Historylink*, accessed February 27, 2016, http://www.historylink.org/index.cfm?DisplayPage=output.cfm&file_id=678.

115 Joyce Badgley Hunsaker, *Seeing the Elephant*, 110.

116 John David Unruh, *The Plains Across*, 84; Hunsaker, *Seeing the Elephant*, 111.

117 Ibid.

118 Ibid., 113.

119 Ibid., 113–121.

120 Ibid., 116–117.

121 Ibid., 121.

122 Mildred Andrews, Mother Joseph of the Sisters of Providence (Esther Pariseau) (1823–1902); http://www.historylink.org/

123 Ibid.

124 A.M.A. Blanchet to Ignace Bourget, Bishop of Montreal, June 17, 1875. *The Selected Letters of A.M.A. Blanchet, Bishop of Walla Walla & Nesqualy, 1846–1879*, Roberta Stringham Brown and Patricia O'Connell Killen, eds (Seattle, WA, University of Washington Press, 2013), 232.

125 Ibid.

126 Tabatha Toney Booth, "Cheaper than Bullets: American Indian Boarding Schools and Assimilation Policy, 1890–1930," in *Images, Imaginations, and Beyond: Proceedings of the Eighth Native American Symposium, November 4–6, 2009*, Mark B. Spencer, ed. (Durant, OK: Southeastern Oklahoma State University, 2010), 47; Cary C. Collins, "Oregon's Carlisle: Teaching 'America' at Chemawa Indian School," *Columbia* 12, no. 2 (Summer 1998), 7.

127 Quoted in Collins, "Oregon's Carlisle," 9.

128 "Treaty of Medicine Creek, 1854," *HistoryLink*, accessed May 19, 2015, http://www.historylink.org/.

129 Cary C. Collins, "Hard Lessons in America: Henry Sicade's History of Puyallup Indian School, 1860 to 1920," *Columbia* 14, no. 4 (Winter 2000-1): 6–11; Carolyn J. Marr, "Assimilation Through Education: Indian Boarding Schools in the Pacific Northwest," University of Washington Libraries Digital Collections, accessed July 18, 2016, http://content.lib.washington.edu/aipnw/marr.html.

130 Quoted in Collins, "Oregon's Carlisle," 6.

131 Ibid., 7–9.

132 SuAnn M. Reddick, "Chemawa Indian Boarding School," The Oregon Encyclopedia, accessed July 18, 2016, http://www.oregonencyclopedia.org; Melissa D. Parkhurst, "In Forest Grove, Echoes of Chemawa Indian School," Oregon State University Press, accessed July 18, 2016, http://osupress.oregonstate.edu/.

133 Collins, "Hard Lessons," 10.

134 Ibid.

135 Quoted in Ibid., 7.

136 Quoted in Ibid., 9.

137 Collins, "Hard Lessons," 9; Collins, "Oregon's Carlisle," 10; SuAnn M. Reddick, "Chemawa Indian Boarding School."

138 Marr, "Assimilation Through Education"; Collins, "Oregon's Carlisle"; Reddick, "Chemawa Indian Boarding School."

Important Dates and Events

1774	Juan José Pérez Hernández explored the north Pacific, and traded with Native Peoples.
1775	Bruno de Heceta and Juan Francisco de la Bodega y Quadra claimed for Spain parts of the Washington and British Columbia coastlines.
1776–1783	American Revolution and independence from Great Britain
1776–1780	British explorer James Cook led his third voyage to the Pacific Ocean, this time making landfall at Nootka Sound on Vancouver Island.
1789	Spain's Esteban José Martínez arrived at Nootka Sound to strengthen Spain's claims and seized British vessels and crews, touching off the Nootka Sound Affair. The dispute was settled in 1790 with the Nootka Sound Convention.
1792	George Vancouver, sent to the region to implement the Nootka Sound agreement with Spain, explored much of the coast, including Puget Sound. On his second voyage to the North Pacific, American Robert Gray found the entrance to the Columbia River, helping to strengthen American claims on the region.
1803	America purchased French-owned Louisiana, a vast region between the Mississippi River and Rocky Mountains, more than doubling the size of U.S. territory and clearing the way for further exploration.
1804–1806	The Corps of Discovery, headed by Meriwether Lewis and William Clark, explored the region by land, further strengthening American claims.
1810	Encouraged by the journals of Lewis and Clark, New York entrepreneur John Jacob Astor launched his fur trading venture in Oregon Country, including construction of Fort Astoria in 1811 and Fort Spokane in 1812.
1812	When the United States declared war on Great Britain (War of 1812) it strained already tense relations between traders of both countries. The British seized Fort Astoria in 1813 and renamed it Fort George.
1815	America retook possession following the signing of the Treaty of Ghent, establishing a "peaceful coexistence in the Pacific Northwest."
1818	Great Britain and the United States signed a "joint occupancy agreement," whereby the two nations would co-manage the Pacific Northwest, helping to ease tensions among settlers and traders.
1819	The United States and Spain signed the Adams-Onis Treaty. In addition to ceding Florida, Spain gave over its territory north of the forty-second parallel.
1821	Hudson's Bay Company began operations in Pacific Northwest. Its aggressive tactics heightened the trade of furs and other natural resources along the Pacific coast.
1846	The United States and Great Britain signed the Oregon Treaty, setting the boundary between the two countries along the forty-ninth parallel.
1848	In January, James Marshall discovered gold at Sutter's Mill in California, leading to a global gold rush. Thousands of Oregon farmers would exchange hoes for gold pans and head south to strike it rich. On February 2, the United States and Mexico signed the Treaty of Guadalupe Hidalgo, where for $15 million the United States gained possession of 525,000 square miles of new territory. On August 14, Congress created Oregon Territory, a vast stretch of western America that included all or portions of five future states, Oregon, Washington, Idaho and parts of Montana and Wyoming.
1850	To promote settlement, Congress passed the Donation Land Claim Act, gifting 320 acres to single men. Married men could also claim 320 acres, and their wives an additional 320. Claimants were required to settle and work the land for at least four years.

1853	On March 2, President Millard Fillmore signed a bill creating the Washington Territory out of Oregon Territory, which also encompassed parts of the future states of Idaho and Montana.
1854–1855	Washington Territorial Governor Isaac Stevens signed the first of several treaties with Western Washington tribes at Medicine Creek. In exchange for ceding their lands, tribes were promised $32,500, reservation land, and permanent access to hunting and fishing grounds. The following year, Columbia Plateau tribes received similar promises.
1859	February 14, President James Buchanan signed an act making Oregon the thirty-third state.

Part II

People and Place

Figure II.1 "This log will cut 40,000 shingles," boasted the photographer who snapped this shot of families standing on logs near Sedro-Woolley, Washington, in 1899. The photographer, Darius Kinsey, spent much of his career chronicling Washington's logging industry. Image reprinted with permission from the Washington State Historical Society.

Contested Boundaries: A New Pacific Northwest History, First Edition. David J. Jepsen and David J. Norberg.
© 2017 John Wiley & Sons, Ltd. Published 2017 by John Wiley & Sons, Ltd.

5

Riding the Railroad Rollercoaster

"Magician's rod" connected east with west, transforming everything it touched

Living in a remote corner of North America and desperate for rail connections to regional and national markets, Northwesterners entered a "Faustian bargain" with the railroads. Few boundaries are more literal than tracks laid on the land. In exchange for the growth and profits that came with affordable and reliable transportation, they partially sacrificed their independence, lost control of their destiny, and contributed to the degradation of the region's natural resources.

On December 16, 1873, a large crowd gathered just outside the small town of Tacoma, Washington, to drive the last spike in the just-completed western leg of Northern Pacific's transcontinental railroad. The 100-mile spur ran from Kalama on the Columbia River to Commencement Bay in Tacoma. With expectant town residents looking on, railroad and city officials took turns hammering down the last spike. From the other side of the tracks, a cluster of Irish and Chinese tracklayers watched the festivities disdainfully. Mostly hard-scrabble miners and veteran rail workers, they hadn't been paid in weeks. "Where's our money?" they yelled. "Where's our money?"[1]

The raucous workers threatened to spoil an event years in the making. Cities up and down Puget Sound competed for the western terminus even before Northern Pacific began constructing the eastern leg in Duluth, Minnesota, in 1870. Seattle, the largest city on Puget Sound, wooed the railroad with free land, tax breaks, and other incentives, and appeared to be the leading contender, with Tacoma running a distant second. But on July 14, 1873, Northern Pacific surprised everyone when they sent a telegram to officials in both cities: "We have located the terminus at Commencement Bay."[2]

City celebration was short-lived. In September, the Panic of 1873 sent the U.S. economy into a tailspin. Within weeks, dozens of banks failed and hundreds of businesses closed. Northern Pacific President Jay Cooke of Philadelphia, who pledged his personal fortune to build his railroad, was seriously over-extended. He had sold $30 million in bonds to fund construction as well as to purchase the Oregon Steam Navigation Company (OSNC), which owned the valuable right of way on the Columbia River. The railroad was so closely associated with Cooke that the public referred to it as "Jay Cooke's Banana Belt."[3] But like many of the railroad magnates of his day, he underestimated the costs and over-estimated his ability to manage them. When the bottom fell out of the

Contested Boundaries: A New Pacific Northwest History, First Edition. David J. Jepsen and David J. Norberg.
© 2017 John Wiley & Sons, Ltd. Published 2017 by John Wiley & Sons, Ltd.

market, Cooke was left holding the bag on runaway construction costs. When his bank closed on September 18, locking out desperate depositors, construction screeched to a halt. Cooke was ruined, and the celebrated Northern Pacific owned little more than a few hundred miles of deteriorating track.[4]

The astronomical costs of construction required financial support from the federal government in addition to traditional financing like bonds sales. The first transcontinental railroad, the Central Pacific, received federal subsidies for each mile of track laid. Swallowed in debt during the Civil War, the government took a different route with the Northern Pacific. In 1864, it issued the largest land grant in U.S. history, 60-million acres between St. Paul, Minnesota, and Puget Sound. The grants created a checkerboard pattern of alternating patches of government land and railroad land that decorates the land today. Income from land sales funded construction, but when the Northern Pacific missed a 1876 completion deadline, it forfeited 39 million acres.[5]

To avoid losing more, the railroad sold lots near the Tacoma terminus to fund completion of the Kalama line. With a December 19 contractual deadline looming, Chinese track layers hurried to finish the last leg of the route, grading 14 miles in 18 days. But the white spike drivers fumed over having not been paid in weeks. In November, a few miles south of Tacoma, 50 workers "put down their sledges and picked up guns" and stopped work.[6] They blockaded the track with rail ties, halted the construction train headed north, and took the engineer hostage. With workers holding all the cards, the territorial governor had little choice but to intervene and arrange for partial payment of back wages and a promise to pay the balance when passenger service began.[7]

> Farmers and businessmen were willing to sacrifice anything to satisfy their desire for rail connections, including the wholesale degradation of the region's natural resources.

The last spike was pounded down at the Tacoma terminus with three days to spare. The ceremony held little resemblance to the one commemorating the first transcontinental in Utah in 1869. No presidential speeches; no telegraph connection with eager Wall Street investors, and the spike was made of iron, not gold. It was a modest affair where the cacophony of protests from unhappy workers clashed with the clang of sledges on iron. Tracks now connected Kalama with Tacoma in the west, and Duluth with Bismarck in the east. Only one vast problem remained – the 1,500-mile gap in between. It would be a decade before tracks connected east with west.

Tacoma's last-spike ceremony encapsulates many elements of a broader story about the boundaries and barriers created by railroads in the Pacific Northwest. It's a story about people who lived in a remote corner of the country desperate for the touch of what writer Ralph Waldo Emerson called a "magician's rod" that would magically connect the region with the nation and the world.[8] It's about entrepreneurs and farmers cut off from profitable markets, railroads who gambled everything, and fledgling cities who wooed them like eager brides after indifferent husbands. But railroad magic also revealed a dark side, a "devilish Iron Horse" with the power to control the land and its natural resources.[9] What the nineteenth-century economist, Henry George, called "The Law of Compensation," demanded a hefty price from people desperate for progress.[10] They entered a Faustian bargain, willing to sacrifice anything to satisfy their desire for rail connections, including the wholesale degradation of the region's natural resources.

Unlimited opportunity, limited markets

By the 1870s, the once remote 2,000-mile Oregon Trail had been pounded into a deeply rutted dirt highway over which thousands of settlers annually plodded west on ox-drawn wagons. The day of the pioneer had given way to rapid population growth, emerging cities, and industrialization. Economic opportunity abounded, especially in the extraction industries – Puget Sound lumber, Columbia River salmon, Palouse wheat, Columbia Plateau cattle and sheep, and Idaho gold and silver. What a U.S. Senator once called a "vast and worthless area" full of "savages and wild beasts" was by 1880 home to a quarter of a million people and growing.[11]

Yet, while products moved, profits waned. The remote Pacific Northwest, so rich in resources, floundered under a grossly inadequate transportation system. The rocky, cascading Columbia River and its tributaries made movement of freight by steamboat slow and treacherous, requiring multiple, time-consuming portages. The falls at Oregon City on the Willamette, the 2-mile-long Cascades at the Columbia Gorge, and the multiple waterfalls at the Dalles and Celilo Falls all required men to unload freight, haul it with horse-drawn wagons to beyond the falls and reload it on a waiting steamer. Goods moving from Lewiston, Idaho, to Portland, for example, required three separate steamboats.[12]

The Oregon Steam Navigation Company, organized in 1860, managed most of the Columbia River traffic. Gold and silver from Idaho, wheat and other products from the Columbia Plateau and Willamette Valley and timber from throughout the region helped the OSNC earn a fortune in freight charges. The line of freight wagons at its Portland docks "appeared to be unbroken day and night, seven days a week," wrote transportation historian Carlos Schwantes.[13]

The OSNC operated a fleet of 30 passenger and freight steamboats, 13 schooners and four barges on the Columbia alone. Steamships from other operators dotted the region's many rivers and lakes. Boats hauled freight on Coeur d'Alene and Pend Oreille lakes in northern Idaho, the Clearwater and Snake rivers in central Idaho, and on Lake Chelan above Wenatchee, Washington.[14]

But steamboat travel proved slow and expensive. According to Schwantes, it cost as much to haul a crop as it did to raise it.[15] In 1879, the *Idaho Tri-Weekly Statesmen* in Boise counted the absurd amount of handling required to transport a load of wheat from Walla Walla to Portland. Workers transferred it no less than 16 times from the time it left the fields until it reached the steamer in Portland.[16] Freighters and owners throughout the extraction industries exhibited impressive creativity and innovation in getting their products to market. To reduce handling in Idaho mines, freighters improvised "saddle trains" along the Snake River. Up to 100 horses, each carrying 250–400 pounds, took up to two weeks to deliver gold or silver to Portland docks.[17] But the overland journeys were just the beginning. From Portland, goods were shipped worldwide. Wheat destined for England, for example, traveled down the Pacific to the Strait of Magellan (around Cape Horn) and up the Atlantic to England, a 16,000-mile journey.[18]

Timber harvested along the Columbia and shipped via the Pacific proved just as problematic. Steamboats struggled with the fast-moving river, sometimes waiting weeks to cross the treacherous bar where the river spilled into the ocean. For products shipped east, navigating upstream against the current also proved slow, cumbersome and risky.[19] Loggers demonstrated no less ingenuity. They built skids to move fallen timber to navigable water. Workers cleared a wide path, laid down greased log crossways, and then up to ten oxen hauled a string of logs up to two miles. Another innovation involved building a splash dam that created a large pool upstream that held the logs. When a crew released the water, the logs were literally flushed down stream. Such innovations proved manageable when logging relatively close to Puget Sound beaches or large lakes and rivers. But as the land near water was logged out, loggers moved deeper and deeper into the forest where skids and flash dams didn't work.[20]

Wheat growers on the Columbia Plateau east of the Cascades experienced a similar dilemma. By 1880, it had gained a national reputation as prime wheat growing country. Farmers reported average yields of 35–40 bushels per acre, far exceeding other regions.[21] So, while the region reportedly grew wheat "cheaper than in any other place in the United States," the length and cost of transport was greater "than any other wheat grown in the world."[22] The discovery turned the tide of emigration within the territory. The Willamette Valley, long the destination of choice for farmers, offered little affordable farmland by 1880. Descendants of the first settlers began to turn east for their livelihood, joining those from the Midwest.[23] Each new wave of settlement popped up farther and farther from waterways, leading to grain transports as harrowing as they were long. From farms sitting 2,000 feet above the river, plateau farmers guided horse-drawn wagons laden with wheat on trails that wound steeply down the sides of canyons. Their troubles weren't over when the goods reached the river. Backups at the docks often meant waiting in line for days to load their harvest on the steamer. Sometimes operators shut down their operations totally when water levels on the Snake and Columbia rivers dropped in the fall during the busy harvest season.[24] The Walla Walla-Wallula railroad, a short-line opened in 1875, erased troublesome portages on the Columbia, but it too led to increased traffic and long lines.[25]

In 1879, farmers let gravity power their wheat to market. They built a chute, a wooden pipe four-inches square and 3,200 feet long, that ran from the rim of the canyon to the river. Unfortunately the grain dropped so fast it ground into a "coarse flour and wore through the pipe." To slow the fall, the builders added switchbacks every few hundred feet. It worked well enough, and soon several grain chutes snaked into that section of the Snake River.[26]

Passenger traffic presented similar challenges. Stagecoaches ran from Portland to Sacramento and San Francisco over poorly maintained dirt roads, a trip that took weeks. The deep potholes and muddy ruts made going so tough a driver was once reported to have barked out orders to his passengers: "First class passengers keep your seats. Second class passengers get out and walk. Third class passengers get behind and push."[27]

Frenzy of railroad construction

Most people believed railroads would eventually solve transportation problems, but the Panic of 1873 brought the industry to its knees for nearly a decade. When good times returned in the 1880s, a frenzy of railroad construction set off the region's first major economic boom, created tens of thousands of jobs, turned villages into cities and linked businesses and people with national and global markets. Between 1880 and 1890 the total railroad trackage in Washington, Oregon, Idaho, and Montana increased six fold, from 1,124 miles to 6,090 miles.[28] The Northern Pacific resumed construction

Figure 5.1 This image fails to reveal the extravagance of the Northern Pacific last spike ceremony near Helena, Montana Territory, on September 8, 1883. To celebrate "east meeting west," the railroad paid travel costs for three hundred European guests, including members of British royalty, and former President Ulysses S. Grant, who spoke. Image reprinted with permission from the Washington State Historical Society.

of its transcontinental line in 1881, finally connecting St. Paul, Minnesota, and Puget Sound in 1883. Additionally, the company added regional lines, benefiting cities on both sides of the Cascade Mountains. On the eastern side, goods began to move speedily on the Northern Pacific and connecting railroads to Portland from burgeoning cities like Spokane, Colfax, Pullman, Moscow, Walla Walla, Cheney and Big Bend. The Northern Pacific also contracted with the Oregon Railway and Navigation Company in 1881 to operate a line between Wallula, on the Columbia, and Portland. With the help of a ferry that carried train cars across the Columbia, goods also moved north from Kalama to Tacoma. Later, the Northern Pacific's Cascade Division linked the Tri-Cities and Yakima with Puget Sound. In 1884, the Union Pacific, which built the western leg of the first transcontinental in 1869, added lines linking Puget Sound and Portland with Omaha and Kansas City in the Midwest. To connect those markets with the Pacific Northwest, it partnered with the Northern Pacific to complete a line across the Blue Mountains connecting Pendleton, Oregon, to the Snake River on the Oregon-Idaho border, tracing the route of the original Oregon Trail. According to historian D.W. Meinig, this steam-driven vehicle could travel more miles in an hour than an ox-drawn wagon could cover in a day.[29]

But it didn't stop there. Eventually, other national carriers entered the market. In 1887, the Southern Pacific connected farmers, lumbermen and fish canneries in Oregon with the rapidly growing markets in California and distant New Orleans. By the end of the century, the system had evolved from a haphazard scramble of unconnected lines into a coherent network upon which passengers and freight could travel throughout the region and to most anywhere in the United States and Canada.[30] Schwantes accurately points out that the region's first major lines had one thing in common. As their names implied, they all provided connections between the continent's interior with the Pacific Ocean.[31]

Big ideas from flawed men

The story of the railroad in the American West, so triumphant on one level, conceals a more sordid and murky saga on another. It's an all-too-familiar nineteenth-century tale of corruption, greed and financial mismanagement. No one epitomizes the fast-and-loose railroad era more than Henry Villard. Born in Bavaria in 1835, Villard's given name was Ferdinand Heinrich Gustav Hilgard. At the age of 18, he immigrated to the United States, changed his name to Villard, and landed a job as a journalist for German-language newspapers. A competent writer, he eventually covered the Civil War for the *New York Tribune*. He married Fanny Garrison, the daughter of the zealous abolitionist, William Lloyd Garrison, which placed him at the center of New England society. His reputation grew after the war when he was appointed secretary of the Social Science Association in Boston.[32]

Ill health took Villard to Europe in 1873, where he hobnobbed with the moneyed crowd and leveraged his German heritage to win the confidence of a group of German investors. In the wake of the Panic of 1873, they worried about their bond holdings in an American company that owned stagecoaches, steamships, and railroads in Oregon.[33] Bonds are a type of loan in which the issuer or borrower promises to make regular interest payments over the term of the loan and repay the principal at maturity. If the issuing company goes bankrupt, the bond loses value and the lender could lose the original investment. The nervous investors asked Villard to return to America to investigate. The company was run by Ben Holladay, a 53-year-old Kentuckian who built a stagecoach empire during the California Gold Rush in the 1850s. According to the historian Schwantes, the "Stagecoach King," was an "energetic and unscrupulous financial adventurer" who reportedly paid a $35,000 bribe to ensure passage of legislation that transferred federal land grants into his firm.[34] But like many industrialists of his day, he wanted too much too fast and when the bottom fell out of the market, his debt-ridden transportation company collapsed under its own weight. Things did not go well when Villard and Holladay met to discuss business in New York City in 1874. Holladay, reportedly loud, outgoing and crude, offended the formal, dignified Villard. A bit self-righteous and proud, he openly questioned Holladay's character, and labeled Holladay with an impressive string of adjectives, including "illiterate, coarse, pretentious, boastful, false and cunning."[35]

> The "triumphant" story of the railroad, "conceals a more sordid and murky saga on another. It's an all-too-familiar nineteenth century tale of corruption, greed and financial mismanagement."

Within two years, Villard had wrestled control of Holladay's companies, including the Oregon and California Railroad, the Oregon Central Railroad, and the two Oregon

Steamship companies. Determined to monopolize all aspects of regional transportation, he purchased Holladay's wharfs and warehouses in Portland. He negotiated with officials in Seattle to purchase the unfinished Seattle & Walla Walla railroad as well as the lucrative coal mines in Newcastle.[36]

To tap the Portland and Puget Sound markets, Villard entered a lease agreement with Northern Pacific to use their tracks along the Columbia River. But like a true monopolist – why share something you can own – he started quietly buying Northern Pacific shares. Short of the capital needed to take control, Villard generated $8 million in new financing through a financial maneuver called a blind pool, considered daring even by the freewheeling standards of the nineteenth century. Investors pooled their money based solely on Villard's reputation with little knowledge of the fund's actual purpose. By July 1881, Villard owned controlling interest in Northern Pacific and its subsidiary, the Oregon Railroad and Navigation Company. "Though he lived in New York," wrote historian Murray Morgan, "Henry Villard was now the most important man in the Pacific Northwest."[37]

Eventually, Villard's buying spree caught up with him. Desperate to complete the last legs of the Northern Pacific, Villard, who the historian Richard White called the "superhero of bad management," burned up capital like the coal that powered his trains.[38] With nearly 25,000 workers, three-fifths of whom were Chinese track layers, the company spent $4 million a month, eventually exceeding construction estimates by $14 million.[39]

The extravagance of the last-spike ceremony on September 8, 1883, at Gold Creek, west of Helena in Montana Territory, illustrates Villard's preference for pomp over profit. He spared no expense announcing to the world the once remote Northwest, and its supposed limitless resources, were just a short train ride away. Villard paid travel costs for 300 European guests including members of the British royal family. They held parades, speeches and dinners in St. Paul, Bismarck, North Dakota, and Portland. Former President Ulysses S. Grant spoke at the Gold Creek ceremony to dignitaries, the governors of several states and territories and thousands of eager Montanans.[40] But the event was more charade than celebration. The tracks had actually been laid a few days earlier, but were removed to stage a track laying demonstration. Opposing crews raced towards each other, laying down all but the last spike, a symbol of east meeting west.[41]

While Villard played big spender, his company fell deeper into debt, and eastern bankers and investors grew increasingly nervous. Before they'd advance further funding, they forced Villard to pledge his personal assets and resign as Northern Pacific's president in 1884.[42] The man who finally succeeded in uniting the Midwest and the Pacific Northwest with the nation had been forced out.

Marketing the "wasteland" as a "friendly place"

An up-and-running Northern Pacific heightened an already competitive landscape. The problem was cost versus revenue. In essence, the transcontinentals carried too few passengers over too great a distance. The only path to profitability was to sell the government-granted land. Cheap acreage would attract farmers, ranchers, businessmen, and tradesmen to fill the trains and build communities, which in turn would draw more settlers and eventually tourists. The challenge: the public's perception of the West as a "wasteland" of barren deserts, lonely prairies, inhospitable mountains, and hostile

Native Peoples. To paint a picture of a welcoming, hospitable Pacific Northwest, the railroads engaged in aggressive public relations campaigns. They discounted fares for "homeseekers" and immigrants, reduced acreage rates, and made mortgage loans with low down payments and generous terms. Railroad agents targeted European immigrants. They greeted Germans, Scandinavians, Russians, and others as they disembarked from their ships on New York docks. The message was clear: The opportunity immigrants sought in America awaited them in the Pacific Northwest.[43]

> Tacoma, was experiencing "marvelously rapid growth, with an immense commercial movement in wheat, coal, and lumber."
>
> – *Railroad promotion brochure*

An 1890 Northern Pacific publication typifies railroad promotion, starting with the "varied and striking scenery" and "cultivated country." With several railroads competing for a fixed number of passengers, the Northern Pacific claimed the cities on its route, offered "better opportunities" for settlement and business.[44] For example, Tacoma, the terminus city, was experiencing "marvelously rapid growth, with an immense commercial movement in wheat, coal, and lumber." Portland, "the rich and handsome commercial capital of the Columbia and Willamette Valleys" stood just a few hours south. To the north, the "prosperous commercial center" of Seattle on Puget Sound offered easy access to California and Asian markets.[45] Inland, the "rolling prairies" of the Columbia Plateau produced record levels of wheat that "never had a failure of crop." The "great gold and silver region" of Northern Idaho "is in the infancy of its development."[46]

The region's natural resources, were "practically inexhaustible," the railroad promised. Puget Sound's "immense forests" held the "finest body of timber in the world." By the railroad's calculation, 160 billion board feet of timber just waited to be felled and shipped around the world. Salmon fishing on the Columbia River promised a "business of such great dimensions." All in all, the land from the Great Lakes to the Pacific Ocean was "by far the best money making country in America."[47] Come to the "Golden West," urged one pamphlet, "Where money grows on trees."[48] Repeated references to "inexhaustible" resources, "immense" forests, and "marvelous" growth perpetuated the "myth of inexhaustibility," the idea that the well of the region's riches was virtually bottomless. The fallacy of that thinking would become apparent well into the twentieth century.

Railroad promotions hit the mark in at least one respect – the Pacific Northwest now seemed tantalizingly close. Credited with "annihilating" time and space, the railroad reduced a six-month odyssey into a leisurely six-day trip.[49] Instead of trudging along the Oregon Trail in a wagon, passengers could watch the West go by through the window in their sleeping or dining car, protected from the persistent winds, harsh climate, and endless dust. First-class passengers enjoyed their meals in "elegant dining cars" described as "marvels of luxury."[50] Served almost exclusively by African Americans, first-class passengers feasted on a "bountiful spread comprising all the delicacies of the season on both the Atlantic and Pacific Coasts."[51] They enjoyed the privacy of well-appointed sleeping cars, while those in second class furnished their own bedding or purchased an "outfit of mattresses, blankets, pillows, and curtains" for $3."[52] Few details were overlooked to convert the "inhospitable terrain into friendly space."[53]

But the railroad connection created something more fundamental than easy travel and cheap land. Newcomers seeking jobs, land, and business opportunities poured

Figure 5.2 To fill seats, railroads often promoted the region's "limitless" resources. The cover of this Oregon Railway and Navigation prospectus shows off the "three women of bounty." Notice how each state is associated with the tools of their dominant industry. Image reprinted with permission from the Washington State Historical Society.

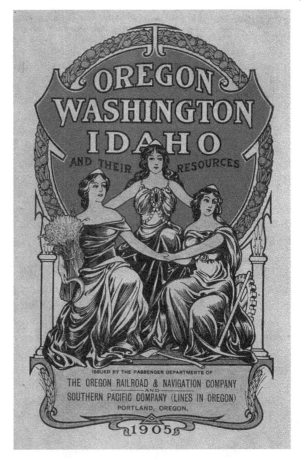

into the region in unprecedented numbers. The pioneer days receded and the once backwater towns blossomed into vibrant cities. The farms, villages, and cities along the rail line found themselves "enmeshed in a vast new market" stretching from Puget Sound to New York Harbor, from New Orleans to London, from San Francisco to Singapore.[54]

Life at home changed as much as business. Men and women enjoyed ordering goods from the Sears Roebuck and Montgomery Ward catalogs. Mother could purchase dinnerware, dresses, jewelry, and clothing for the children, while father ordered guns, tools, work clothes, and scores of other items previously unavailable. Thanks to the railroad, a shopper in Coeur d'Alene could now buy anything that a shopper in New York City or Philadelphia purchased. The transcontinental railroad democratized consumer spending for the people of the Pacific Northwest.[55]

> "The imagination of man can scarcely set bounds to the future grandeur of our Pacific empire …"
>
> – *Isaac Stevens, Washington's first territorial governor in 1858*

	1860	1870	1880	1890	1900	1910	1920
Washington	11,594	23,955	75,116	357,232	518,103	1,141,990	1,356,621
Oregon	52,465	90,923	174,768	317,704	413,536	672,765	783,389
Idaho	NA	14,999	32,610	88,548	161,772	325,594	431,866

Population growth among Pacific Northwest states and territories illustrates the impact of railroad construction after 1880. Notice the rapid growth in Washington relative to Oregon between 1880 and 1890, a period in which the total miles of railroad track increased 400%. While Idaho remained the smallest of the three states, it too experienced healthy growth. Source: United States Resident Population by State: 1860–1920. http://www.census.gov.

Figure 5.3 Pacific Northwest resident populations 1860–1920.

With railroads running, the "future" had arrived. Washington, Oregon, and Idaho's combined population nearly tripled between 1880 and 1890, and tripled again by 1920. Washington's population more than quadrupled between 1880 and 1890 from 75,116 to 357,232, more than a third of which settled east of the Cascades. Oregon grew at a more modest rate, although its population doubled during the same period from 174,768 to 317,704, while Idaho jumped from 32,610 to 88,548.[56]

A good number of the newcomers hailed from across the Atlantic. In addition to those who arrived directly from the old world, many were what historian Jorgen Dahlie called "second-stage" emigrants.[57] These Scandinavians, Germans, Irish, and Russians first built a life in America as farmers in Midwestern states like Minnesota, Wisconsin, Iowa, and the Dakotas. Drawn by the explosion in jobs and affordable land, they moved west in great numbers. Nearly a quarter of the half million foreign-born Americans living in Washington in 1900 originally hailed from Denmark, Sweden, and Norway.[58]

Making and breaking cities

As the region's population ballooned, so did its cities. For decades, life and commerce in the Pacific Northwest centered in and around Portland. Its proximity to the Columbia and Willamette rivers offered a strategic advantage in an era of wagon trains, stage coaches, and steamboats. From Portland, goods moved through the port to markets on both sides of the Pacific. When the Northern Pacific planned its route through Washington Territory to Puget Sound, it chose distance over gravity. It cost less to reach Puget Sound by going south around the mountains than through them, even after adding the cost of ferrying cars across the Columbia to the Kalama-Tacoma link. Portland grew with the flood of goods and people, and by 1880, it was by far the largest city in the region with a population of 17,577.

While Portland grew, Seattle floundered. When Northern Pacific selected Tacoma for its terminus in 1873, Seattle civic leaders felt rejected like a bride jilted at the altar. If it couldn't lure a railroad, the city decided to build its own. Using local capital and labor, they started construction of the Seattle & Walla Walla Railroad, to market local coal and create a link to grain and other markets. The tracks reached the Newcastle coal mines in eastern King County when the Panic of 1873 dried up funding.

Seattle's fortunes turned around when the Northern Pacific, using new pneumatic drilling technology, punched a 1.8-mile-long tunnel through Stampede Pass in the Cascade Mountains. With gravity defied, distance mattered. When the tunnel opened in 1888, Northern Pacific trains no longer had to divert south through Portland and north to Tacoma. They could steam over the pass about 40 miles east of Tacoma and north into Seattle.[59] Seattle was now back in the game for economic dominance, and by 1910 (with the help of the Klondike Gold Rush in the 1890s), surpassed Portland in population.

A similar south-to-north power shift occurred east of the mountains. Beginning with the fur traders and missionaries in the 1820s and 1830s, Walla Walla slowly emerged as a regional hub on the Columbia Plateau. East of the portages at Celilo Falls at the Dalles, Walla Walla experienced a "great flood of emigration" in the 1860s and 1870s. A "Motley throng of traders, land-hunters, cowboys, speculators, saloonkeepers, Indians, Chinamen and cayuse ponies" found their way into the city. By 1880, it was the largest on the plateau with a population of 3,588.[60] The arrival of the Northern Pacific spurred further growth to the point outsiders began to refer to the entire plateau as Walla Walla Country.

Its dominance began to wane following a flurry of mineral strikes in the northern reaches of Washington and Idaho territories in the 1880s. Following the strikes on the Coeur d'Alene River, an enterprising Northern Pacific official published a circular that grossly exaggerated the value of the claims. An "intense excitement has sprung up," the circular claimed. The "great amount of free gold ... fairly glistens" in the river. Supplies were "inexhaustible."[61] The circular resulted in a "virtual stampede" of feverish miners working the Coeur d'Alene. Three years later, prospectors discovered silver and lead deposits on the South Fork of the Coeur d'Alene, followed by similar strikes on the Indian reservation at Colville, and in the Okanagan region just to the west. Collectively they turned the northern reaches of the territory into a humming anthill of miners and suppliers.[62]

Spokane (then named Spokan Falls) benefited mostly as a stopping-off point for miners who arrived on the Northern Pacific, although a lack of regional rail connections impeded growth. Those headed to Lake Coeur d'Alene, for example, rode stagecoach or wagon from Spokane to the lake, where they boarded a steamer bound for the mines. Exporting minerals, most of which bypassed Spokane, proved equally tedious. Once again, a promising industry lay trapped behind an inadequate transportation system.

Beginning in 1885, a group of Montana businessmen under the leadership of Daniel Chase Corbin, a New York businessman living in Helena, explored building railroads to serve the Coeur d'Alene mines. The first connected the newly incorporated Coeur d'Alene with the Northern Pacific in Spokane. The second linked the Coeur d'Alene Railway and Navigation Company with the mining district at Burke, Idaho. But that was just the start. By 1905, Corbin's companies, the Northern Pacific and Great Northern had collectively built nine short-line railroads in the region to transport ore to smelters in Helena, Great Falls, Omaha, and Denver.[63]

While much of the minerals didn't actually enter Spokane, substantial ancillary business did. The city evolved into the dominant supply center for mining companies, many of which opened headquarters there. The Spokane Falls *Review* claimed that everything "from a horse to a frying pan" could be bought in Spokane.[64] The city, which in 1880 was home to fewer than four hundred farmers and shopkeepers, exploded. By 1890, it

Figure 5.4 Seattle real estate broker Eshelman-Llewellyn Investment Company used Washington statehood in November 1889 to promote investment in Seattle. The list of more than 30 commodities available from the state underscores the theme of abundance. The umbrella under Uncle Sam's arm suggests Seattle was already known for its rain. Image reprinted with permission from the Washington State Historical Society.

boasted a population of nearly 20,000, nearly four times as many as Walla Walla, and emerged as the principal distribution point for Idaho and Eastern Washington.[65]

Seattle, Tacoma, and Spokane are among dozens of Pacific Northwest cities that blossomed after the railroad blessed them with their presence. Many more were not so lucky and often withered away on the prairie. Yakima City, a small farming community incorporated in 1883 in Eastern Washington, illustrates the consequences of standing up to the railroad. Yakima was desperate for transportation links. In addition to a commercial farming center, the city became a favored layover for Eastern Washington cattlemen driving their herds over Snoqualmie Pass to Seattle. The sight of thousands of cattle trampling through Yakima headed over the pass prompted the editor of the *Yakima Signal* to suggest "the folks over at Seattle and down at Portland must be doing some tall eating to get away with so many of our bovines."[66] In winter, when snow and rain prevented mountain travel, drovers pushed their herds south to the Dalles for shipment to Portland or Puget Sound.[67]

In spite of the obvious need for a railway, Yakima landowners played hardball on the acquisition of land needed to build a right-of-way station. In an act of apparent corporate bullying, the Northern Pacific located the station four miles to the north, bypassing the city altogether. Message received. Within months Yakima City businesses began relocating to "North Yakima." More than 100 buildings were literally lifted out of the ground, placed on rolling logs and hauled by horse to the "new" Yakima, while the "old" Yakima reverted to a "barren sage-brush plain …"[68] The state legislature rechristened the city "Yakima" in 1918.

Extraction industry finally on wheels

These stories of Pacific Northwest cities explain why Henry George, a San Francisco newspaper editor, called the locomotive a "great centralizer." A keen observer of the railroad's impact on the West, he wrote how the railroad "kills little towns and builds up great cities, and in the same way kills little businesses and builds up great ones."[69] The region's extraction industries were no exception. Between 1880 and 1893, growth in lumber, wheat, livestock, and fish production exploded to unprecedented levels. In the 1860s and 1870s cattle ranchers thrived on supplying the Inland Empire's gold and silver mines. Later they turned to the burgeoning population centers of the Willamette Valley and Puget Sound. They drove herds of cattle, horses, and sheep over the mountains, or down along the Columbia for loading on steamboats. Later, even larger herds were driven south to Nevada, Utah, and California.[70]

Railroads not only sped up livestock delivery, they allowed for year-round shipment to markets previously out of reach. In addition to steady shipments west, stockmen leveraged railroad connections with San Francisco, Chicago, Omaha, Kansas City and much of the Midwest.[71] Eventually, Northwest cattle gained a reputation for being "superior to Texas cattle." Bred to withstand harsh winters, regional cattle drew high prices as the "prime favorites" from buyers.[72] Supplementing income from cattle, ranchers raised and shipped horses and sheep. In 1882, an Oregon rancher delivered 18,000 cattle, 10,000 sheep, and 1,500 horses to Kansas City.[73] Railroads did pose one problem for cattlemen, or the cattle themselves. Trains often killed cattle that wandered onto the tracks. In 1883, the territorial legislature in Washington enacted a law making the railroads potentially liable for livestock injured or killed by trains. By 1887, Oregon and Idaho had passed similar legislation.[74]

The cattle rancher's domain shrank as the farmer's expanded. In 1889 alone the railroad sold more than 416,000 acres to 2,279 purchasers at an average price of $3.68 per acre. By 1890, the amount of farmland shot up like corn stocks in summer. More than 5.6 million acres, much of it wheat, fell under the plow, slowly crowding out cattle ranchers.[75] By the mid-1880s, the reputation of Northwest wheat had grown. In its typical hyperbolic manner, the Northern Pacific extolled the virility of the region's soil. It's a "well-known fact that wheat will grow and mature wherever the 'bunchgrass' grow … the synonym for things good, strong, rich and great."[76]

The fishing industry matched the explosive growth in ranching and farming. For millennia, people had survived on the bounty of the region's rivers and Puget Sound. By mid-nineteenth century, commercial fishermen caught and canned salmon and scores of other fish. Cleaned, butchered, and packed in 1-pound cans – almost exclusively by Chinese laborers – the fish was sold mostly to local and regional markets, including San Francisco. The 5,000 cases shipped from Puget Sound in 1877 speak to the industry's modest beginnings. But by 1895 the number of cases shipped jumped to 100,000, and by 1901 to over 1 million. Columbia River activity offers a sense of the ferocity of the business in the last decades of the century. Hundreds of small, independent fishermen, collectively known as the "mosquito fleet," stretched for hundreds of miles along the lower Columbia during the peak harvest in mid-summer. In 1881, 35 canneries operated on the Columbia, employing as many as 4,000 Chinese.[77]

But the work was slow. The process of butchering and canning salmon required several men. Once unloaded from the boat, fish were hand carried to a "splitter's table." The splitter made ten cuts on the fish, one for each of the seven fins and three more to cut off the head, tail, and to clean the fish. Two more cuts divided the fish into pieces that fit in the can. Other workers then covered the fish with brine and a piece of salt.[78] That system was made obsolete in 1903 when Edmund A. Smith of Seattle brought efficiency to canning. He patented a machine that required just one operator to butcher, clean, and can the fish. Smith called his invention the "Iron Chink," a racial slur on the Chinese workers it replaced. One machine could perform the work of 20 workers. Smith's invention, as well as improvements in canning technology that created a tighter seal, allowed for safe export to distant markets, spurring ever more growth. Soon consumers on the East Coast, and distant markets like Great Britain and Australia developed a hefty appetite for Pacific Northwest salmon. In 1913, the world consumed more than 2.5 million cases of salmon from Puget Sound alone.

The most visible and far reaching impact of the railroad occurred in the region's forests. The timber industry had grown steadily since its days supplying the gold rush in California in the 1850s. By the 1880s, it was dominated by a handful of large firms whose owners "stood with one foot in San Francisco and the other at the point of production."[79] Pope and Talbot opened a mill at Port Gamble on Puget Sound in 1853 to supply California.[80] The Washington Mill Company shipped Puget Sound logs to Europe and throughout the Pacific Rim. The Tacoma Mill Company shipped out nearly 40,000 board feet per day, earning the reputation as "the best worked" plant in the region in the 1870s.[81] Numerous other operators dotted the shorelines of Bellingham, Everett, Seattle, Port Townsend, Port Ludlow, Port Orchard, Steilacoom, and Olympia. Mills operated along the Washington and Oregon coasts as well as on the Columbia River. Cities like Hoquiam, Aberdeen, Vancouver, North Bend, and Coos Bay owed their presence to timber. So did cities like Salem and Roseburg along the Willamette Valley.[82]

Nevertheless, in 1880, Washington still ranked thirty-first among all states and territories in timber production.[83] The railroads, which consumed massive amounts of wood for ties, bridges, and stations, started to change that, and the market grew as railroads spread across the region, connecting with regional and national lines. The addition of railroad spurs allowed penetration deeper into the forests, cutting the cost of transport. Nor was logging limited to the west. Large stands of hemlock, fir, and cedar, much of it railroad owned, attracted logging companies to Eastern Washington, Idaho, and Montana.[84]

Pacific Northwest operators initially struggled to compete nationally due to higher shipping costs. Mills in the California Sierras, Utah, Colorado, and the states surrounding the Great Lakes held a geographic advantage due to lower shipping rates. When the Central Pacific slashed its rates nearly in half for freight hauled from California to Denver, the Oregon Rail and Navigation Company (OR&N) was forced to follow suit, opening opportunities for Oregon operators, but slashing profits.[85]

By the late 1880s, new market entrants made for hefty competition. To compete with Oregon operators, mills in Vancouver, Washington, loaded railcars and barged them across the Columbia to the OR&N lines. Shingles from around Puget Sound soon covered the roofs of buildings in Pennsylvania, New York, and other eastern markets. The St. Paul and Tacoma Lumber Company sold bridge timbers in Iowa.[86] In addition to local, regional, and national markets, operators ventured around the Pacific Rim. Economic growth in Southern California, Mexico, Central America, Chile, Peru, New Zealand, Australia, China and the rest of Asia generated a demand for raw logs and lumber. China remained a strong market for Northwest logs well into the twentieth century.[87]

Cost reductions eventually positioned operators to compete with the large firms in the Great Lake states and the American South. Between 1879 and 1889, Washington's output increased six fold, and then doubled every five years between 1889 and 1909. In 1909 lumbermen cut down 4 billion board feet of timber, making Washington the nation's top producer.[88]

By contrast wood supplies around the Great Lakes, which had been logged for decades, began to dwindle, prompting millmen to look elsewhere. Well-capitalized operators soon muscled their way into the region, buying large tracks of land and opening mills. The Michigan Mill Company opened an operation in Vancouver, Washington, in the mid-1880s. In 1888, Charles Stimson moved from Minnesota to open the St. Paul and Tacoma Lumber Company.[89] In 1900, an aspiring Frederick Weyerhaeuser and a group of 15 investors purchased 900,000 acres of forestland from the Northern Pacific, in what the historian Norman Clark called "one of the largest land transactions – and most fantastic bargains – in American history."[90]

Demand drove innovation. Historically, loggers employed skids to harvest trees deep in the forest and miles from water. They greased logs and laid them crossways along cleared paths. A team of up ten oxen hauled the string of logs to the water where they could be floated down stream or loaded on to a steamer. But once land near the shore was logged out, skids became unworkable. The "steam donkey" provided a solution. A giant power-driven spool with a long line attached literally pulled the logs out of the forest to waiting steamers eventually cutting transport costs in half. By 1900, 328 steam donkeys were in use in Washington and Oregon.[91] An additional advantage of steam power over animal power: "you don't have to feed it when it is not earning anything."[92]

Not all is rosy in rail town

By 1892, the region's economy was running at full steam. Locomotives "huffed and puffed like powerful beasts of burden," hauling wheat, salmon, and timber – and a hundred other products – at levels unimaginable a decade earlier. Families reveled in the availability of affordable household goods and personal luxuries. Yet all was not perfect in rail town. Increased reliance on the railroad led to resentment. The "new freedom coupled with new dependency," observed Carlos Schwantes, spurred a "love-hate relationship" with the railroads.[93] The philosopher Henry David Thoreau put even more succinctly. "We do not ride on the railroad; it rides on us."[94]

Railroads proved to be heavy-handed masters. Essentially unregulated monopolies, they controlled everything from routes and schedules to ticket prices and worker wages. They became the region's largest landowner outside of the federal government. Yet "unjust, unreasonable, and extortionate" freight rates topped the list of complaints and greatest angst.[95] The rates for shipping goods from the Midwest to Spokane underscores the system's inequities. For goods hauled from Chicago or St. Paul, Spokane wholesalers paid higher rates than those in Portland, Tacoma, and Seattle even though those

Figure 5.5 An African American waiter serves apples to two passengers in a Chicago, Milwaukee, and St. Paul Railroad dining car. The railroad greatly contributed to the region's diversity as thousands of African Americans and other minorities found jobs on the road. Image reprinted with permission from the Washington State Historical Society.

cities were hundreds of miles farther away. Charging more for shorter routes than longer ones, a practice called "long-short" hauling, was prohibited by the Interstate Commerce Commission.[96] Unfortunately for inland cities, the federal government made exceptions in "terminal cities" on the coast that faced competition from ocean freighters.

The disparity in rates was meaningful. For industrial goods like metal plates or mining-car wheels, Spokane wholesalers paid about $1.25 per 100 pounds, while coastal cities paid 75 cents, a 40% difference. For consumer goods like baking powder, canned corn, and coffee, the Spokane rate was 30% higher than those charged to coastal cities. Distributors, of course, passed the increased costs on to the consumer.[97]

In addition to raising the cost of goods, steep rates literally cut Spokane out of the supply chain and put suppliers there at a competitive disadvantage with other cities. This was unacceptable for a city positioning itself as the distribution center for hinterland cities like Cheney, Colfax, and Pullman. For example, a farmer in Colfax ordering equipment from Chicago could save money by ordering through distant Portland rather than from nearby Spokane. According to testimony before the Interstate Commerce Commission in 1892, the rate disparity was so great that "Portland dealers can lay down merchandise in the territory immediately surrounding Spokane at prices which Spokane wholesalers can not profitably meet."[98]

The railroads' monopolistic power played out in other ways. Its mere presence endangered the very resources upon which those jobs depended. By the time the Northern

Pacific arrived in 1883, the Columbia River was already in danger of being overfished. In 1883, 1,700 commercial fishing boats supplied 39 canneries on the river. That year, 629,400 cases of salmon found their way to world markets. Between 1889 and 1920, the annual catch of Chinook averaged 2.5 million pounds.[99] When yields of Chinook ran low, the fishery pursued sockeye, steelhead, Coho, and chum. They began fishing during the fall run in addition to the traditional spring run, which further steepened declines. By the beginning of the twentieth century, the salmon runs on the upper Columbia had declined sharply due to over fishing on the lower Columbia.

Beyond overfishing, other industries threatened the river's ecosystem. Farming diverted water for irrigation, while mining and logging created siltation, polluting spawning streams. To mitigate the problems associated with overfishing and habitat destruction, salmon harvest managers in Washington and Oregon promoted developing hatcheries, but they could not reverse the decline.[100] In 1894, an Oregon fish and game official sounded the alarm. "It does not require a study of the statistics to convince one that the salmon industry has suffered a great decline during the past decade, and that it is only a matter of a few years under present conditions when the Chinook of the Columbia will be as scarce as the beaver that once was so plentiful in our streams."[101]

Loggers and millmen exhibited no more discipline than fisherman. Like the fishery, low entrance requirements allowed hundreds of small operators to join the big firms in hauling billions of board feet from the region's forests, leading to a breakdown in the system of supply and demand. When prices dropped precipitously, as they often did, small operators responded with equally steep increases in production. The historian Norman Clark called it a "mad world" in which hundreds of small operators milled timber around the clock until a "glutted market refused to take another stick or shingle."[102] Gifford Pinchot, the nation's first director of the U.S. Forest Service, predicted in 1900 that the U.S. would face a "timber famine by 1940."[103]

Fortunately, government proved more effective in preserving forests than it did the fishery. Rapid growth in the 1880s laid bare the myth of inexhaustibility, raising fears timber companies would deplete the supply of wood. But the forests faced a second threat from logging – fire. Hot, dry summers, combined with careless prevention made fire a constant worry. The Yacolt Burn, one of the largest fires in state history, killed 38 people in 1902 and destroyed nearly 240,000 acres in Clark, Cowlitz and Skamania counties alone.[104] The twin threats of deforestation and fire prompted the private and public sectors to act. Large firms like Weyerhaeuser began fire prevention programs and invested in sustainable yield research. The federal government instituted measures to conserve the nation's forests in 1891 with passage of the Forest Reserves Act. Under the leadership of President Grover Cleveland and later President Theodore Roosevelt, the federal government set aside 12.5 million acres in forest reserves in Washington, more than 25% of its total land mass.

Panic exposes poor management

The tangle of railroads that crisscrossed through the Northwest landscape collapsed almost as quickly as it rose up. The panic of 1893 mushroomed into a decade-long recession during which 15,000 businesses, 600 banks, and 74 railroads failed. It was the second meltdown in 20 years. One in five American workers found themselves out of a job. In the Pacific Northwest, the unemployed fled from cities like Seattle, Tacoma, and Spokane, many riding the flatbed cars on which they rode in earlier years.

> Railroaders "laid hands on a technology they did not fully understand, initiated sweeping changes, and saw these changes often take on purposes they did not intend."[105]

Of the six transcontinentals built between 1869 and 1893, only two survived, the Great Northern and Southern Pacific. Unlike other transcontinentals, which borrowed heavily to fund expansion, those two grew on a slower, more cautious track, filling seats, managing costs, and paying their bills along the way.[106] Their survival speaks to the failures of the others. Innovators like Holladay, Villard, and Cooke deserve credit for turning their visions into reality. But managing an enterprise requires a different skill set than envisioning one. By and large, their innovations were limited to the world of finance. They showed great creativity in raising funds, selling stock, and issuing bonds. They incurred heretofore unheard of levels of debt, gambling everything to hear the train whistle blow across the West. Brash, confident, and persuasive, they convinced thousands of investors to blindly hand over millions based mostly on their reputations. Unfortunately, these men lost more than investor fortunes. Financial mismanagement contributed to both the 1873 and 1893 panics and subsequent recessions. Northern Pacific's bankruptcy ignited the spark in 1873, while the failure of the Philadelphia and Reading Railroad frightened investors and helped to trigger the 1893 panic. The historian Richard White likens the railroad tycoons to the "Sorcerer's Apprentice," an eighteenth-century poem written by the German Johann Wolfgang von Goethe and popularized in Disney's 1940 animated classic film *Fantasia*. In the film, the apprentice Mickey brings near disaster upon himself when toying with a power he could not control. Likewise, the railroaders "laid hands on a technology they did not fully understand, initiated sweeping changes, and saw these changes often take on purposes they did not intend."[107]

White argues the transcontinentals weren't necessarily a bad idea, just ahead of their time – built before they were needed. There weren't enough people in the West in the last decades of the nineteenth century to justify one transcontinental, let alone six. While many of the regional lines proved essential to the region, too much was built too soon at too great a cost. "Their costs over the long term, and the short term, exceeded their benefits," White argues.[108] Granted, the railroads brought hundreds of thousands of people into the region, but it was a case of the tail wagging the dog. The railroads' endless promotions and cheap land sales created astounding growth, but at too high a cost and with an unworkable business model. In the words of the railroad baron Cornelius Vanderbilt, "Building railroads from nowhere to nowhere is not a legitimate business."[109] In fairness, the railroads contributed greatly to settling the American West, although the experience was haphazard and reckless to say the least. White points out that it took two and a half centuries for America to settle most of the land east of the Mississippi River, yet with help from the railroad, the nation settled the remainder of the continent within a generation.[110]

For the better part of three centuries, explorers sought the Northwest Passage, the mythical waterway that connected the Atlantic and Pacific oceans. But ultimately the passage was not a waterway carved from the relentless force of shifting glaciers, but one cut from the equally unyielding power of Manifest Destiny. As the nation's center

THROUGH THE

American Wonderland

THE PACIFIC NORTHWEST

Figure 5.6 Jobs and land were not the only reasons people were drawn to the Pacific Northwest. This 1923 booklet promotes the region's many tourist attractions. Image reprinted with permission from the Washington State Historical Society.

of gravity shifted from the Atlantic to the Pacific, people rode the "steel Nile" west well into the second half of the twentieth century.[111] But rail travel eventually lost favor in the 1950s and 1960s as Americans fell in love with a more modern form of transportation – the automobile. Like the railroad, it too connected east with west, transforming everything it touched and redrew the economic and cultural boundaries of the Pacific Northwest.

James J. Hill: from empire builder to noxious weed

When a Japanese steamer loaded with silk and tea pulled into Elliott Bay on August 31, 1896, Seattleites crowded the waterfront to watch her tie up. The city council declared it a holiday, and saluted the man who'd convinced the Japanese steamship line to choose Seattle over San Diego for its port of entry. Nearly everyone sang the praises of the man who connected Seattle with Asia, Great Northern President James J. Hill.[112]

A decade later the tune had changed. Children from Montana to Oregon were jumping rope to the rhyme, "Twix Hill and Hell there's just one letter. Were Hill in Hell we'd feel much better."[113] Hill had become an object of derision in farming communities where he had sold hundreds of aspiring farmers unworkable land.

Thus is the legacy of the railroad titan – adored and admired one year but reviled the next. Giants like Leland Stanford, Jay Cooke, Henry Villard, and E.H. Harriman made as many enemies as miles of track, but few generated more controversy than Hill. He was known as the "empire builder" to admirers, or "the barbed-wired, shaggy-headed, one-eyed old son-of-a-bitch of western railroading" to others.[114]

Born in Ontario, Canada, Hill began his railroad career as a shipping clerk in St. Paul, Minnesota, eventually starting his own freight business. In 1878, he recruited investors to acquire his first rail line, the bankrupt St. Paul & Pacific. Over the next 20 years, Hill cobbled together a sizable transportation empire. He acquired the Northern Steamship Company to carry freight on the Red River. He started an alliance with the Burlington Northern to connect with Chicago markets. In 1889, he gained controlling interest of the struggling Great Northern

Figure 5.7 Undated portrait of Great Northern President James Hill, who like many railroad tycoons, built a transportation empire but left in its wake a trail of financial mismanagement and unscrupulous business practices. Image reprinted with permission from the Washington State Historical Society.

Railway, with plans to build a competing line running parallel with the Northern Pacific from St. Paul to Puget Sound.[115]

In 1894, Hill controlled both the Great Northern and the Northern Pacific, the latter captured in a fight that drove up the share price from $87 to almost $1,000. Later he turned his sights onto the Union Pacific. Following a battle for control, Hill and Union Pacific President E.H. Harriman formed a joint venture, essentially monopolizing transcontinental service. But like most tycoons, Hill had reached too far. The courts ruled the partnership a violation of the Sherman Anti-Trust Act of 1890.[116]

The Great Northern business model made it the most profitable transcontinental. The Northern Pacific, for example, raised capital through the stock and bond markets, as well as the sale of land granted by the federal government. But that model proved unsustainable, especially during recessionary times and strings of empty railcars.[117] Instead of accepting grants, Hill purchased government land and resold it to settlers. Some flourished while others struggled on draught-prone prairies. He sold land cheaply to timber companies who in turn supplied the Great Northern with a steady supply of freight at competitive rates.[118]

Importantly, the Great Northern route to Puget Sound was shorter than the Northern Pacific's, with softer curves and fewer steep grades. Hill's engineer, John F. Stevens, chose a route long used by Native Peoples over the Cascades that now carries his name.[119] Importantly, profits also came from laying off workers and slashing wages during hard times. He notoriously inflated shipping rates on routes where farmers had no other freight options.[120] Plains farmers became so embittered they named a weed after Hill. The yellow mustard plant (*Sisymbrium altissimum*) that grew along the Great Northern tracks is known today as Jim Hill Mustard.[121]

Hill was a member of an elite club of nineteenth-century tycoons whose "bigger than life" images disguised a far less flattering portrait. The historian David H. Bain tabbed them "the heedless royalty of the developing republic, crushing enemies, exploiting the powerless, building empires."[122] The Empire Builder, the man, died May 29, 1916, at age 77. The Empire Builder, the train, still offers daily passenger service to the Pacific Northwest.

Cashing in on the Klondike Gold Rush

Harry L. Kepner, a bookkeeper at the North American Transportation and Trading Company in Yukon Territory, wrote a letter to his boss in August 1897 explaining why he was quitting his $40-a-month job. He planned on joining the thousands who had recently swarmed into the territory following the discovery of gold on the Klondike River. "Everything is excitement up here," he wrote, "the people that are coming up are wild, to hear them talk you would think that they can just pick up the gold." Claiming he "didn't have the fever yet," he said "the best thing I could do was go to the mines … I tell you I am going to make a mark up here yet and it won't be at bookkeeping."[123]

News of the discovery had spread up and down the Pacific Coast earlier that summer. The steamship *Excelsior* arrived in San Francisco on July 15 filled with Alaska passengers carrying more than $400,000 in Yukon gold. Two days later, the steamer *Portland* arrived at Elliot Bay with a similar haul. A feverish *Seattle Post-Intelligencer* quickly published its first "gold rush" edition. "There has never been," the paper proclaimed, "anything like the strike in the Klondike since the famous days of California nearly fifty years ago."[124] As get-rich stories spread across the country, an eastern journalist declared Seattle "has gone stark, staring mad on gold."[125]

The excitement energized a city caught in the throes of depression since 1893. Within weeks, Seattle boosters began organizing a campaign to capture the potentially huge market of supplying gold seekers and transporting them to the Yukon. The Seattle Chamber of Commerce formed a Bureau of Information to promote Seattle as the natural supply center and gateway to the Klondike. Erastus Brainerd an eastern newspaperman, headed the campaign designed to take away the supply business from competitors like Tacoma, Portland, San Francisco, and Vancouver, BC. Brainerd lobbied the railroads to open an assay office in Seattle where miners could value their gold and exchange it for cash. He encouraged the state legislature to promote Seattle's best qualities, and he placed ads in papers around the country extolling the city's virtues.[126]

One ad used the city's name like a hammer. "SEATTLE offers every advantage possessed by any Pacific Coast city … SEATTLE is the most progressive and best governed city on the Pacific Coast … SEATTLE merchants are alert, able and honorable … SEATTLE has outfitted nine-tenths of the persons who have gone to the Yukon."[127] Another ad proclaimed Seattle "is to the Pacific Northwest as New York is to the Atlantic Coast. All railroads in United States connect with three great transcontinental lines running to Seattle."[128] At one point, the competition between Seattle and Tacoma turned so heated an undated newspaper article scolded the two cities about the "petty jealousies" over the outfitting trade. "It is all so very childish," the paper claimed. Attempts of each city to "belittle" the other "is a contemptible business for two so called progressive cities to indulge in …"[129]

Located closer to the Yukon, Seattle enjoyed a geographical advantage over its southern competitors. Vancouver and Victoria were closer still, but the nascent cities lacked the resources to compete for the business. Moreover, Seattle benefited from its rail connections with the Northern Pacific and the Great Northern. By 1898, more than 100,000 gold seekers had chosen Seattle as its jumping off point for the Yukon.[130] Three years later, the annual volume of the gold trade in Seattle topped $50 million.[131]

For years, Seattle's streets and wharfs teemed with men and women purchasing supplies and booking passages on northbound steamers. Alfred McMichael, a would-be prospector, wrote "Seattle. This is a busy town. Vancouver and Victoria are like country villages in comparison."[132] William B. Ballou wrote that he liked Seattle, but shied from scams of the "different fakirs." Hustlers tried to sell him a "gold washer," a "K [Klondike] stove," and a "dog team with one lame dog which would get well by tomorrow."[133]

Among the hype and hustle, some warned of the risks and uncertainties of prospecting. In December 1897, the *Seattle Argus* published "A Klondiker's Advice," which asked the gold hungry visitors "to pause a moment and not go mad over that magical word, Klondyke [*sic*]." The gold "is not picked up at random," the paper advised. "It is not located in a moment, neither must one expect to get it easily … Every man in the Klondyke [*sic*] is not a mine owner, neither is he a millionaire, and the man who goes there expecting to become both in a few short months, or even years, will be sorely disappointed."[134]

Few people likely heeded the cautionary advice as news of strikes reached Seattle every few months. Among the larger strikes, deposits were found at Anvil Creek near Nome in July 1898, on the beaches of Nome in the summer of 1899 and in the Tanana Valley near Fairbanks in 1902. Between April and May 1900, more than 20,000 gold seekers boarded steamers in Seattle, headed for the gold fields.[135]

Most would come home with their fever broken and pockets empty. Like strikes throughout the American West, most of the individuals who profited in the Klondike and Yukon did so selling supplies and services to miners. The bulk of the real wealth went to large corporations with the capital and equipment required for large-scale extraction.

Seattle's success in capturing the gold trade propelled the city to new economic heights. Between 1900 and 1910, its population tripled to 237,174, bypassing Portland as the region's largest city. Energized city leaders embarked on civic improvements. In 1898, they undertook the massive regrade of downtown to expand the commercial district. Using his wealth from Alaska gold, Jafet Lindeberg, helped finance construction of the 15-story Alaska Building, the city's first steel-frame skyscraper in 1903, which housed the Alaska Club. In 1909, Seattle hosted a world's fair, the Alaska-Yukon Pacific Exposition, permanently linking its fate with Alaska, the "last frontier." Five years later, the 42-story L.C. Smith Building, later named the Smith Tower, opened, making Seattle the home of America's tallest building outside of New York City. Beyond its grandeur, the tower symbolized Seattle's emergence as a vital metropolis and permanent force in global trade.

Explore more

Books

A voluminous body of literature details the development and impact of railroads on the American West. Two beautifully illustrated volumes by Carlos Schwantes provide keen insights on the cultural impact of the railroads. The first is *Railroad Signatures Across the Pacific Northwest*. The more recent, *The West the Railroads Made*, was coauthored with James P. Ronda. Richard White's, *Railroaded: The Transcontinentals and the Making of Modern America*, tracks the rise of large corporations with western settlement. Finally, for an insightful look at the role railroads played in South Puget Sound, read *Puget's Sound: A Narrative of Early Tacoma and the Southern Sound*, Murray C Morgan.

Online

An online presentation of Schwantes and Ronda's *The West the Railroads Made* can be found at the Washington State Historical Society's website "Washington Stories" (http://washingtonhistoryonline.org/).

What do you think?

How can you explain the extraordinary measures residents took to overcome the lack of transportation prior to the arrival of the railroads? How would you characterize the business practices of railroad companies? Given the enormity and importance of their missions to America, did the ends justify the means? Do the railroad magnates deserve their villainous reputations, or should they be credited for having improved the lives of people in the West? How did industrialization affect the lives of Chinese, African Americans and other people of color?

Notes

1 Murray Morgan, *Puget's Sound: A Narrative of Early Tacoma and the Southern Sound* (Seattle, WA: University of Washington Press, 1979) 162–166.
2 Archie Binns, *Northwest Gateway, The Story of the Port of Seattle* (Portland, OR: Bindords & Mort, Publishers, 1941), 203, 210–211.
3 Carlos A. Schwantes, *Railroad Signature Across the Pacific Northwest* (Seattle, WA: University of Washington Press, 1993), 52.
4 Morgan, *Puget's Sound*, 165–166.
5 Carlos A. Schwantes, *Railroad Signatures*, 52.
6 Morgan, *Puget's Sound*, 166.
7 Ibid.
8 Ralph Waldo Emerson, "The Young American," in *Ralph Waldo Emerson: Essays and Lectures*. Joel Porte, ed. (New York: Library of America, 1983), 213. (As quoted in Carlos A. Schwantes and James P. Ronda, *The West the Railroads Made*.)
9 Ibid.
10 Henry George, "What the Railroad Will Bring Us," *Overland Monthly*, I (October 1868): 297–306.

11 Carlos A. Schwantes and James P. Ronda, *The West the Railroads Made* (Seattle, WA: University of Washington Press and the Washington State Historical Society, 2008), 123.

12 Schwantes, *Railroad Signatures*, 39–40.

13 Ibid., 41–42.

14 Ibid.

15 Ibid., 43.

16 Ibid., 46.

17 Ibid., 47.

18 Ibid., 35.

19 Thomas R. Cox, *Mills and Markets: A History of the Pacific Coast Lumber Industry to 1900* (Seattle, WA: University of Washington Press, 1974), 56–57.

20 Cox, *Mills and Markets*, 228–229.

21 D.W. Meinig, *The Great Columbia Plain: A Historical Geography, 1805–1910* (Seattle, WA: University of Washington Press, 1968, 1995), 250.

22 Meinig, *The Great Columbia Plain*, 254.

23 Ibid., 249–250.

24 Ibid., 251–253.

25 Ibid.

26 Ibid., 253.

27 Schwantes, *Railroad Signatures*, 49.

28 Ibid., 96.

29 Meinig, *The Great Columbia Plain*, 260–261.

30 Ibid.

31 Schwantes, *Railroad Signatures*, 17–18.

32 Richard White, *Railroaded: The Transcontinentals and the Making of Modern America* (New York: W.W. Norton and Company, 2011), 216–217.

33 White, *Railroaded*, 217.

34 Schwantes, *Railroad Signatures*, 54.

35 Ibid.

36 Morgan, *Puget's Sound*, 185.

37 Ibid.

38 White, *Railroaded*, 217.

39 Morgan, *Puget's Sound*, 191.

40 White, *Railroaded*, 220.

41 Schwantes, *Railroad Signatures*, 77–78.

42 White, *Railroaded*, 222.

43 Schwantes, *The West the Railroads Made*, 88.

44 *The Official Northern Pacific Railroad Guide for the Use of Tourists and Travelers.* St. Paul, MN: W.C. Riley, 1892.

45 Ibid.

46 Ibid.

47 Ibid.

48 William H. Maher, "The Golden West," railroad promotional brochure, 1911.

49 Schwantes and Ronda, *The West the Railroads Made*, 7.

50 *The Official Northern Pacific Railroad Guide.*

51 Ibid.

52 Ibid.

53 Schwantes, *Railroad Signatures*, 96.

54 Ibid., 60.

55 Schwantes and Ronda, *The West the Railroads Made*, 105–106.

56 J. Orin Oliphant, *On the Cattle Ranges of the Oregon Country* (Seattle, WA: University of Washington Press, 1968), 344.

57 Jorgen Dahlie, "Old World Paths in the New: Scandinavians Find A Familiar Home in Washington," in *Experiences in a Promised Land*, G. Thomas Edwards and Carlos A. Schwantes, eds. (Seattle: University of Washington Press, 1986), 100.

58 Ibid.

59 Schwantes, *Railroad Signatures*, 70.

60 Meinig, *The Great Columbia Plain*, 248.

61 W. Hudson Kensel, "Inland Empire Mining and the Growth of Spokane, 1883, 1905," *Pacific Northwest Quarterly* 81, no. 2 (April 1969): 84.

62 Kensel, "Inland Empire," 84–85.

63 Ibid.

64 Ibid.

65 Schwantes, *Railroad Signatures*, 100.

66 Oliphant, *On the Cattle Ranges*, 125.

67 Ibid., 129–130.

68 Schwantes, *The West the Railroads Made*, 114.

69 Henry George, "What the Railroad Will Bring Us, *Overland Monthly*, I (October 1868), 297–306; Schwantes and Ronda, *The West the Railroads Made*, 29–31.

70 Oliphant, *On the Cattle Ranges*, 115.

71 Ibid., 166.

72 Ibid.

73 Ibid., 175.

74 Ibid., 241.

75 Ibid., 343–344.

76 Meinig, *The Great Columbia Plain*, 264.

77 Richard White, *The Organic Machine, The Remaking of the Columbia River* (New York: Hill and Wang, 1995), 38.

78 Gordon B. Dodds, *The Salmon King of Oregon: R.D. Hume and the Pacific Fisheries* (Chapel Hill, NC: The University of North Carolina Press, 1959), 24.

79 Cox, *Mills and Markets*, 137.

80 Ibid., 61–62.

81 Ibid., 124–125.

82 Ibid., 106.

83 Center for the Study of the Pacific Northwest, Lesson Fourteen: "Industrialization, Technology, and Environment in Washington," accessed April 24, 2015, http://www.washington.edu/html.

84 John Fahey, "Big Lumber in the Inland Empire," *Pacific Northwest Quarterly* 76, no. 3 (July 1985): 96.

85 Cox, *Mills and Markets*, 202–203.

86 Ibid., 205.

87 Ibid., 215–221.

88 Ibid.

89 Ibid., 59.

90 Ibid., 239–240.

91 Ibid., 232–233.

92 Ibid.

93 Schwantes, *Railroad Signatures.* 97.

94 Henry D. Thoreau, *Walden*, Jeffrey S. Cramer, ed. (New Haven, CT: Yale University Press, 2004), 90, 186. Schwantes and Ronda, The *West the Railroads Made*, 4.

95 Annual Report of the Board of Railroad Commissioners, Topeka, Kansas, 1893, 22.

96 Douglas Smart, "Spokane's Battle for Freight Rates," *Pacific Northwest Quarterly* 45, no. 1 (January 1954): 19.

97 Ibid., 23.

98 Ibid., 20.

99 "Canneries," The Northwest Power and Conservation Council, accessed May 8, 2015, https://www.nwcouncil.org/history/Canneries.

100 Ibid.

101 Ibid.

102 Clark, *A Social History of Everett, Washington*, 68.

103 Joni Sensel, *Traditions Through The Trees: Weyerhaeuser's First 100 Years* (Seattle, WA: Documentary Book Publishers, 1999), 117–126.

104 Yacolt and the Fire Demon (1902), Clark County Washington, http://www.clark.wa.gov/.

105 White, *Railroaded*.

106 Schwantes, *Railroad Signatures.* 77–78.

107 White, *Railroaded*, xxxii.

108 Ibid., xxiv.

109 Morgan, *Puget's Sound*, 165–166.

110 White, *Railroaded*, xxiii.

111 The phrase belongs to Craig Miner as the title for chapter 3 in his *West of Wichita: Settling the High Plains of Kansas, 1865–1890* (Lawrence, KS: University Press of Kansas, 1986).

112 Murray Morgan, *Puget's Sound*, 298.

113 "Empire Builder," James J. Hill and David Wilma, ed., historylink.org. The article, written by Joel E. Ferris, originally appeared the Winter 1959 edition of *The Pacific Northwesterner*.

114 Morgan, *Puget's Sound*, 298.

115 "Empire Builder," James J. Hill and David Wilma, ed.

116 Morgan, *Puget's Sound*, 310.

117 Richard White, *It's Your Misfortune and None of My Own: A New History of the American West* (Norman, OK: University of Oklahoma Press, 1991), 256.

118 Morgan, *Puget's Sound*, 298.

119 "Empire Builder," James J. Hill and David Wilma, ed.

120 White, "It's Your Misfortune and None of My Own," 256.

121 "Empire Builder," James J. Hill, David Wilma, ed.

122 David Howard Bain, *Empire Express: Building the First Transcontinental Railroad* (New York: Viking, 1999), 711.

123 Harry L. Kepner to P.B. Weare, Kepner/Crane microfiche collection, Folder 8, Archives, University of Alaska Fairbanks.

124 Robert E. Ficken, *Washington State: The Inaugural Decade 1889–1899* (Pullman, WA: Washington, State University Press, 2007), 219.

125 Ficken, *Washington State*, 220.

126 *The Klondike Gold Rush*, Curriculum Materials for Washington Schools, Center for the Study of the Pacific Northwest, http://www.washington.edu/., accessed May 15, 2015.

127 University of Washington Libraries, Manuscript Division, Erastus Brainerd Scrapbook, Vol. 1, 39.

128 Ibid.

129 Ibid.

130 Carlos A. Schwantes, *The Pacific Northwest, An Interpretive History* (Lincoln, NE: University of Nebraska Press, 1996), 270.

131 The Klondike Gold Rush, Curriculum Materials for Washington Schools.

132 Diary and Letters of Alfred McMichael, Juliette Reinicker Papers, Yukon Archives, Whitehorse, Yukon Territory, Canada.

133 William B. Ballou Papers, Letters, 1898–1918, Archives, University of Alaska, Fairbanks.

134 "A Klondiker's Advice," in *Seattle Argus*, December 18, 1897.

135 *The Klondike Gold Rush*, Curriculum Materials for Washington Schools.

6

Seeking Dignity in Labor

Entangled in class warfare, "Wobblies" struggle for First Amendment rights and equities in the workplace

With railroad transportation in place, job growth accelerated with the power of a locomotive. In the early decades of the twentieth century, tens of thousands of unskilled workers migrated to the region for jobs in the region's extractive industries. But many found their willingness to work did not buy them entry into in a society that needed the labor but deplored the laborer.

On a cold day in Minneapolis in November 1909, an itinerant worker from Ashton, Idaho, climbed onto the roof of a Pullman railcar bound for Spokane. He likely couldn't afford to buy a ticket, but he claimed he rode outdoors through North Dakota and Montana in winter because he "didn't like to breathe the foul air inside the Pullman."[1]

S. Sorenson (first name unknown) braved freezing temperatures to support his fellow workers in a dispute between Spokane and the Industrial Workers of the World (IWW), a radical labor union with a strong foothold in the Pacific Northwest. Writing about events five years later, Sorenson detailed how soon after arriving in Spokane he joined in union activities: handing out flyers, picketing, recruiting, and making public speeches downtown. On November 23, he was one of scores of workers arrested for violating a city ordinance that prohibited public meetings on "streets, sidewalks or alleys" in downtown Spokane.[2] Sorenson climbed onto a platform, usually a wooden crate called a soapbox, and began to speak. He barely issued the standard opening, "Fellow workers," before the "bulls" pulled him off the soapbox, delivered "several jabs in the ribs," and hauled him to jail. Another speaker quickly took Sorenson's place and was also immediately arrested.[3]

After he spent 17 hours with six other men in an eight-by-ten-foot "sweatbox," Sorenson was moved to an "ice-cold cell" jammed with fellow Wobblies. Later, all prisoners arrested for violating the public-speaking ordinance were transferred to a nearby schoolhouse, where they survived on "2 ounces of bread twice a day" until police released the men on December 16.[4]

Contested Boundaries: A New Pacific Northwest History, First Edition. David J. Jepsen and David J. Norberg.
© 2017 John Wiley & Sons, Ltd. Published 2017 by John Wiley & Sons, Ltd.

Songs of the workers

The International Workers of the World, or Wobblies, mastered the art of publicity even when it cast them in a negative light. They published radical newsletters and pamphlets, blocked city streets with angry crowds, and stood on soapboxes to loudly decry injustices. But few public demonstrations rang louder than a chorus of men and women belting out Wobbly ballads from *The Little Red Songbook*.

The idea for a songbook originated in Spokane around 1908 when J.T. Walsh and other Wobblies found themselves competing for the public's attention with the Salvation Army, the Christian organization whose soldiers sang Christian songs on city streets. Wobbly songs often mimicked the Salvation Army's religious tunes. For example, if they struck up "Onward Christian Soldiers," Wobblies would burst in with their parody, "Christians at War": "Onward Christian soldiers! Duty's way is plain; Slay your Christian brothers, or by them be slain."[5]

Many Wobbly songs were written by Joe Hill, a Swedish-born radical labor activist executed for murder in Utah in 1915. Hill believed in the staying power of song. "A pamphlet, no matter how good, is never read more than once," he claimed, "but a song is learned by heart and repeated over and over ..."

Hill's "Where the Fraser River Flows," was sung to the Irish ballad "Where the River Shannon Flows," and celebrates the struggles of railroad workers in British Columbia.

Where the Fraser River flows

> Fellow workers pay attention to what I'm going to mention,
> For it is the fixed intention of the Workers of the World.
> And I hope you'll all be ready, true-hearted, brave and steady,
> To gather 'round our standard when the Red Flag is un-furled.

> Chorus:
> Where the Fraser River flows, each fellow worker knows,
> They have bullied and oppressed us, but still our Union grows.
> And we're going to find a way, boys, for shorter hours and better pay, boys;
> And we're going to win the day, boys; where the Fraser River flows.

> For these gunny-sack contractors have all been dirty actors,
> And they're not our benefactors, each fellow worker knows.
> So we've got to stick together in fine or dirty weather,
> And we will show no white feather, where the Fraser River flows.[6]

The hundreds of workers who converged on Spokane in the second half of 1909 were known as Wobblies, a tiny fraction of an American labor force that in 1900 totaled 36 million men, women, and children working in America's factories, mills and mines.[7] Their story is one of America coming to grips with the inequities wrought from the Industrial Revolution. Just a few generations earlier most families had worked for themselves in small shops and on farms in a subsistence economy. During the first three decades of the twentieth century, small shops gave way to modern factories and family farms to corporate enterprises.

Figure 6.1 As the cover of this IWW songbook shows, Wobblies used music to "fan the flames of discontent." According to songwriter Joe Hill, a pamphlet "is never read more than once," but a song is "learned by heart and repeated over and over ..." Image reprinted with permission from the Washington State Historical Society.

The Pacific Northwest also struggled with industrialization, population growth, and tapping the wealth from seemingly limitless resources. The region was coming of age, joining the rest of the American economy. The question we'll explore here, is where did the wage earner fit in this story? They were needed, that's certain, but not necessarily wanted. They were welcome to come and labor, wage workers were told, provided they stayed inside the social, political, and economic boundaries set by those in control. The Wobblies not only pushed against those boundaries, but sought to tear down and rebuild them in their favor.

Making sense of the Progressive Era

Any assessment of the events and players must be conducted in the context of the broader Progressive Movement during which the United States was far from united. Deep schisms existed along class lines, religion, race and ethnicity throughout the nineteenth century.[8] The Progressive Era, generally the period between 1890 and 1920, was in part a response to the inequities, abuses, and corruption born out of the Industrial Revolution. One historian called Progressivism "an extraordinary explosion of middle-class activism" where the middle and lower classes pushed against the boundaries that separated wealth and poverty in America.[9]

Examining the spectrum of American wealth and the attitudes of the wealthy in the late nineteenth century puts American labor in perspective. On one end of the wealth spectrum sat what historian Michael McGerr identified as the "upper ten" percent. On the other end stood the laborers. The gap was huge, and the upper ten was actually more like the upper 2%. They were America's richest: manufacturers, merchants, landowners, financiers, and other professionals who controlled a majority of the nation's resources. More than 4,000 families nationwide counted themselves as millionaires, extraordinary wealth for the times. Their wealth and values isolated them from and made them unsympathetic with America's wage earners and farmers.[10]

> The "failures which a man makes in his life are due almost always to some defect in his personality, some weakness of body, or mind, or character, will or temperament."
>
> – *John D. Rockefeller.*

America's wealthy believed in the power of the "individual," grounded in the sociological theory known as "Individualism." It held that individuals free to act on their instincts and abilities created wealth and advanced society. Individualism, according to steel baron Andrew Carnegie, was the "foundation" of an advancing society. In America, it's "the leaders who do the new things that count, all these have been Individualistic to a degree beyond ordinary men and worked in perfect freedom …"[11] The laboring class suffered not from class divisions and lack of opportunity, but from their individual shortcomings, according to the theory. The "failures which a man makes in his life are due almost always to some defect in his personality, some weakness of body, or mind, or character, will or temperament," wrote oil baron John D. Rockefeller.[12]

It's difficult to overstate the gulf between the wealthy and the working class in the early twentieth century. Uncertainty plagued the working class. Low wages, long hours, frequent layoffs, and workplace accidents were facts of life. Bound by these constraints, the laboring class had little faith in the power of individualism. They contended that power came not from the individual but from the group. "Realizing that they had to depend on one another to survive," McGerr writes, "workers developed a culture of mutualism and reciprocity."[13]

To illustrate mutualism, McGerr draws upon the American saloon, in which "a man bought a round of drinks for his mates, and they bought drinks for him."[14] Wage earners took care of each other; they understood that as individuals they held sway over nothing. Only as a group – comrades with a cause – did they yield any meaningful power. Wage earners developed what McGerr called a "strong sense of confederation." The typical American worker, said one progressive journalist, "has no respect for the traditional American individualism. … His own personality is merged in that of the union."[15]

Divided union struggles for power

The failure of mainstream unions to push management from their hard line on worker organization triggered the birth of the IWW. The exclusionary membership policies of the American Federation of Labor (AFL), where only white craftsmen need apply, hopelessly divided labor. Mainstream unions, called "labor aristocrats," looked down on the less-skilled workers and refused to support their cause.[16] The AFL also excluded minorities and to some degree women. African Americans, AFL leaders feared, were "dangerous competitors, scabs who threatened white jobs and white unions."[17]

The IWW was born to fill the void. At its organizational convention in Chicago in June 1905, the future Wobbly William D. "Big Bill" Haywood spoke forcefully to the conventioneers. "Fellow Workers," he proclaimed, "This is the Continental Congress of the Working Class." Over the next several days, delegates crafted a "Preamble" that directly challenged the AFL and the capitalist system. "The working class and the employer class have nothing in common," it said. "There can be no peace so long as hunger and want are found among millions of working people and the few, who make up the employing class, have all the good things of life."[18]

The "good things" were out of reach for most wage earners who toiled in the region's extraction industries and on the railroads. They cast nets across rivers, canned fish, loaded railcars, cleared forests, sawed lumber, harvested wheat, and drove cattle and sheep to stock pens. Women dominated the domestic trades, working in other people's homes, restaurants, and laundries. By any measure most wage workers lived an arduous, demanding, and oftentimes dangerous working life. "All of them, even the best-paid skilled workers, lived circumscribed, vulnerable lives, constrained by low pay and limited opportunity, and menaced by unemployment, ill health, and premature death," wrote the historian McGerr.[19]

Wages for unskilled workers, which ranged $2 to $6 a day, were as uncertain as the jobs themselves. There were no guarantees and few union contracts to protect them. Frequent economic recessions in the nineteenth and early twentieth centuries, such as the prolonged contraction that started in 1893, generally resulted in massive layoffs and steep wage cuts.[20] Workers in the extraction industries were further plagued by the very real threat of on-the-job injuries.

The only certainty for most wage workers was the permanency of their economic status. Skilled or unskilled, the wage earner held little hope he or she would someday land a high-paying job or join management. It was broadly accepted, "that working-men do not evolve into capitalists as boys evolve into men or as caterpillars evolve into butterflies…"[21]

The IWW recruited workers in most Pacific Northwest industries but focused their protests where they saw the greatest abuses – timber. The IWW confronted mill owners over wages, hours, safety and living conditions in logging camps. But what began as a typical conflict between employee and employer, evolved into a clash over a far more fundamental issue – freedom of speech. The Free Speech Fight, as it became known, spread across the region between 1909 and 1919. Municipal officials in Seattle, Everett, Aberdeen, Centralia, Wenatchee, Portland and other cities struggled to cope with legions of Wobblies who invaded their towns, opened up meeting halls, and railed in public against the injustices heaped on the working class.

At the mercy of predatory "job sharks"

The Free Speech Fight erupted in Spokane in 1909 when Wobblies began speaking out against "job sharks," disreputable employment agencies that represented mostly timbermen and farming companies. These agencies provided a steady supply of

Figure 6.2 The cry for "One Big Union," framed the IWW's Socialist-leaning platform whereby the common laborer, not managers or owners, would unite to control the workplace and American capitalism. Image reprinted with permission from the Washington State Historical Society.

workers when thousands of jobs opened up during peak hiring years in the first decade of the twentieth century. Working from shops along the city's skid road, they'd release the location of a job for a fee, usually $2 to $3, depending on the job. After paying, the worker often arrived at the site to find the job taken, or learned that it lasted for only a single shift. Because employers and the sharks split fees, both were incented to "keep the men coming and going to and from the camps …"[22] Workers who made trouble faced a gun-toting "boss with a badge."[23]

To combat the sharks, the IWW launched a "Don't Buy Jobs" campaign in Spokane. On October 25, police arrested IWW leader James P. Thompson for publicly criticizing the employment agencies. Even though he was eventually acquitted, the union vowed to take up the free-speech cause. A week later, the union's newspaper, the *Industrial Worker*, issued a nationwide distress call. "Big free speech fight in Spokane," the paper claimed, "come yourself if possible, and bring the boys with you!"[24] It especially irked the IWW that the city exempted the ministerial religious group, the Salvation Army, from the restrictions.

The campaign soon picked up speed as hundreds of men and women poured into Spokane to wave red flags, sing in the streets, and hand out flyers condemning the sharks. Day after day, the IWW organized groups of five or more Wobblies into "fighting committees" placed strategically around the city. On a pre-arranged signal, a "hobo orator" from each committee mounted the soapbox before crowds that sometimes numbered in the thousands, blocking traffic and disrupting business. The orators usually greeted their "fellow workers," and maybe got in a few words about the sharks or the abuses heaped on "wage slaves," before police hustled them off to jail. Another orator would immediately step up to take his place, who was then also arrested. By the end of November, Spokane police had made nearly 800 arrests, and as the IWW intended, completely disrupted law enforcement, city administration, and the courts. But unlike in other Northwest cities such as Everett and Centralia, events in Spokane ended peacefully. Beleaguered officials eased up on the speaking ban and with the state's help cracked down on the shady employment agencies.

A rough and tumble lumber business

A review of the competitive and volatile lumber industry helps to explain logging and milling companies' obsession with controlling costs, especially wages, as well as their general disregard for workers. The region's timber industry had grown steadily since its days supplying the California Gold Rush in the 1850s. Lumber companies dotted the shores of Puget Sound from Bellingham to Olympia, along the Washington and Oregon coasts, and throughout the Willamette Valley from Portland to Roseburg. Logging also thrived in portions of land east of the Cascade Mountains.[25]

Beginning in the 1880s, major operators in the Great Lake States of Michigan and Wisconsin, whose timber supplies had been running thin for years, began buying large tracts of forestland and opening mills in the Pacific Northwest. The Michigan Mill Company opened an operation in Vancouver, Washington. J.W. McDonnell erected a mill north of Seattle, which they sold to another Michigan operator, Charles Stimson. Everett Griggs spurred growth in South Puget Sound when he opened the St. Paul and Tacoma Lumber Company in 1888.[26] In 1900 a group of investors led by Frederick Weyerhaeuser purchased 900,000 acres of timberland from the Northern Pacific Railroad.[27] California millmen also looked to the region for logs, including Asa Simpson, who saw promise in the small harbor at Coos Bay, Oregon. They joined a host of established firms like Pope and Talbot, as well as dozens of small outfits who scrambled to capture their share of the already crowded timber market.[28]

Railroad expansion in the 1880s and 1890s opened even more of the region to affordable logging. In addition to Northwest markets, operators expanded throughout the Pacific Rim. Population growth in Southern California, Mexico, Central America, Chile, Peru, New Zealand, Australia, China and much of Asia all generated strong demand for logs and finished lumber.[29]

Improved cutting methods, especially power saws, further increased efficiency and production.[30] Healthy capital investment, access to railroad technology, and greater efficiency, transformed the logging industry "from the relatively simple sort of resource exploitation" to a "more complex world of modern industry."[31] As a result, regional mill owners harvested 11 billion board feet of timber in the 15 years between 1904 and 1919.[32]

Life for the owners could be as rocky as that of the wage workers. Lumber was an unstable, unregulated industry with too many competitors and not enough rules. Lumber demand often waned in the see-saw economy, depressing prices and forcing smaller, less efficient operators out of business. To create a semblance of order, mills throughout the region began forming cooperatives. Operators on Puget Sound joined forces with their Oregon competitors to create the Pacific Pine Manufacturers' Association. Collectively these co-ops conspired to bring some order to their industry by fixing prices, suppressing wages, and controlling supply.[33]

Price controls proved difficult in an industry with modest entrance requirements. For a few hundred dollars an entrepreneur could rent a small patch of land, build a shack, purchase saws, acquire logs, and hire men to cut them.[34] Small firms began underselling their larger competitors, suppressing prices even further. Mill owner Charles Stimson complained he had to "actually to give away the lumber and pay the freight on it from Seattle to Oakland."[35] The "condition of the Coastwide Lumber market is simply disgusting," said another observer.[36]

Over-production and extraction persisted for decades as more and more entrepreneurs found the capital to open mills, while larger firms expanded existing ones, unsettling supply and demand. The historian Robert Clark called it a "mad world" in which hundreds of small mills ran themselves into closure as they milled timber around the clock until a "glutted market refused to take another stick or shingle."[37]

Owners functioned in an American financial system that the historian Kevin Boyle argues was "underdeveloped, unpredictable and unstable." Strict adherence to the gold standard constrained capital and limited the amount of money in circulation. Moreover, manufacturers were better at delivering products to market than understanding that market's limits. Over-production presented a constant challenge, creating backlogs, and brutal price drops. When supply over-stripped demand, inventories piled up, forcing companies to cut production, which inevitably led to layoffs and wage cuts. In total, these factors lead to frequent economic downturns, what Boyle called the "the scourge of late-nineteenth-century American capitalism."[38] Eventually capital triumphed as more efficient firms used technology to manage costs. With large Midwestern producers steadily moving west, inefficient operators both large and small were pushed aside in what the historian Thomas R. Cox called a "Social Darwinist world from which there was no escape."[39]

Wage earners were pawns in this boom-or-bust, go-for-broke world. Hired when needed and dismissed when not, they were taken off the board with no apologies. Logging camps were "crowded and vermin-infested places," populated by young, single men, including many immigrants from throughout Europe who drifted from camp to camp. Unskilled, uneducated, and under-valued, they worked 12- to 14-hour days for as little as 20 cents an hour.[40] A Wobbly working in Aberdeen wrote that he was paid "$2.50 to $6.00 per day." The "Grub is fair," he claimed, but the men in the bunk houses were "packed like sardines." He especially resented a $2.50 weekly boarding fee and a 75-cent monthly "hospital fee."[41] Strict rules governed camp life. Weyerhaeuser, for example, prohibited liquor in camp and forbade the men to talk at meals.[42]

> "Sooner or later [the shingle weaver] reaches over a little too far, the whirling blade tosses drops of deep red into the air, and a finger, a hand or part of an arm comes sliding down the slick chute."

Logging was fraught with danger. Broken bones, severed fingers, and crushed feet were almost a daily occurrence. Fatal injuries were less common but an accepted part of the job. In 1917, the *Bend* (Oregon) *Bulletin* reported several accounts of workers killed from falling trees or limbs. Another met his fate "when a log rolling from a flat car struck him in the head."[43]

The introduction of power saws increased the hazards, especially in shingle making, which according to the historian Clark, were "conceived by a mind that worshipped efficiency more than humanity." They "quite suddenly made shingle sawing a mercilessly bloody vocation."[44] It took three men to turn a red cedar log into a stack of finished shingles. The first pushed the log into a large circular saw that cut it into manageable pieces. The shingle-saw operator then made 50 to 60 shingles a minute, running his hands back and forth over the whirling blades once every second or two. A third trimmed the shingles, eliminating rough edges and knotholes before throwing them down a chute for packing. The men who "wove" the shingles into bundles were called "shingle weavers," a label eventually bestowed upon all shingle workers. A typical mill could produce up to 30,000 shingles in a ten-hour shift.

Injuries were a fact of life. "Sooner or later he reaches over a little too far, the whirling blade tosses drops of deep red into the air, and a finger, a hand or part of an arm comes sliding down the slick chute."[45] With missing arms and digits (sometimes as many as eight) weavers were easy to spot.

While the blades cut flesh, clouds of cedar dust cut into the worker's lungs, leading to a condition known as "cedar asthma." A State Bureau of Labor Survey in 1909 showed that more than half of all shingle sawyers were victims of accidents. Of the 224 people who died in Everett in 1909, 36 were killed in mills.[46] For their perilous labors, shingle weavers earned $4 to $5 per day.

The depredation in the camps and mills made the lumber industry a prime target for unionization. The IWW, with about 30,000 members nationwide, established a presence in the Pacific Northwest when it opened an office in Portland to support a mill strike in 1907.[47] Over the next several years, the organization opened more than a dozen local chapters throughout the region. Their presence would lead to suspicion, resentment, hostility and violence wherever it landed.

Unlike established unions like the AFL and the Knights of Labor, the IWW recruited the tens of thousands of unskilled and semi-skilled who toiled for wages in the region's forests, mills, mines, and farms. The IWW's socialist-leaning messages resonated like a cowbell at chow time with the men and women unwanted in mainstream unions. The capitalistic "master class" and the worker had nothing in common, they were told. Where the older unions represented workers within an established labor-relations framework, the IWW sought to tear that framework down and build a new one. They would unite under "One Big Union," and replace their masters at the head of the table.

In the first two decades of the twentieth century, the IWW organized workers and led strikes throughout the region. They recruited lumber workers and fruit pickers in Idaho; construction workers, cooks, and waiters in Spokane; farm workers in Walla Walla; smeltermen in Tacoma and seamen in Seattle. Between 1907 and 1919 dozens of IWW led strikes disrupted production region-wide. But no industry felt the IWW charge more than lumber. Like throwing fuel on the fire, the free-speech confrontation in Spokane spread to more than a dozen cities throughout the three states and British Columbia.

Arrest and expulsion in Aberdeen

Events blew up in Aberdeen in the summer of 1911 when IWW organizers decided to take advantage of the presence of the U.S. naval fleet docked in Grays Harbor. The Grays

Harbor area had grown into a thriving center of lumber production by the first decade of the twentieth century. A.J. West operated three mills at the confluence of the Wishkah and Chehalis rivers. James M. Weatherwax ran the Anderson-Middleton Mill and Peter M. Emery, Gilbert F. Mack, and A.D. Wood started the American Mill. These and other operators crafted their lumber from trees cut in the dozens of logging camps that permeated the region's hillsides. A variety of businesses supported the industry. The Lamb Machine Company turned out machinery for the mills, while the Grays Harbor shipyards constructed vessels to haul finished lumber to California and around the Pacific Rim.[48]

As sailors and dock workers crowded city streets that summer, Wobblies handed out propaganda, waving their ever-present red flags, while their leader, William A. Thorne, denounced the injustices in the camps and mills. As the crowd gathered, Wobblies exchanged taunts with unsympathetic townspeople. When police arrived, they ordered Thorne to cease his verbal assault on mill owners. When he refused, they arrested him and another IWW organizer immediately stepped up on the soapbox.[49]

Like their counterparts in Spokane, Aberdeen city councilmen quickly passed an ordinance prohibiting speechmaking on many downtown streets. Violators were subject to arrest and a $100 fine. Also like Spokane, it exempted Salvation Army members who proselytized on the streets, prompting a protest of unfairness from the IWW. One labor sympathizer called the law a "grave mistake ... depriving us the rights of American citizens."[50]

After weeks of heated exchanges and numerous arrests, city officials weighed their options, hoping to avoid the chaos that overran Spokane. Instead of overcrowding the jails, they would expel their prisoners from town. On a rainy November night, more than 40 men were ushered into cars under heavy guard and driven east to the city limits. Some deputies threatened to tar and feather or horsewhip their charges, while others passed out loaves of bread. All were warned to never return. "What we have done we did by taking the law in our own hands," shouted I.G. Humbarger, former president of the Chamber of Commerce. "You men go and never return. God bless you if you remain away, but God help you if you ever return."[51] The vanquished Wobblies stormed away, some throwing the bread on the muddy roadside. Confrontations between the IWW and city officials continued into the new year, but seldom equaled the disorder exhibited in Spokane and in cities where trouble was about to visit.

Over the next four years, conflict arose wherever the IWW dared to open a union hall or stage a protest. In Wenatchee, Washington, 25 Wobblies were arrested for vagrancy in September 1911 but released without charges by a judge. In July 1916, police closed the IWW offices in Yakima, arrested 100 Wobblies and then released them.[52]

Running the gauntlet in Everett

Those confrontations pale in comparison to the 1916 tragedy known as the Everett Massacre. Over the previous decade, the "City of Smokestacks" had grown into one of the nation's leading lumber producers. In 1910, 95 manufacturing plants operated in and around the city, including 44 mills that produced lumber or shingles or both. An iron factory, paper mill, several machinists, shipyards, arsenic plant, and multiple specialist companies contributed to the "sawdust economy."[53] A majority of the 35,000 people in and around Everett owed their living directly to lumber.[54] But, typical for timber, prosperity didn't last as frequent contractions led to layoffs and wage cuts, inflaming already heated labor relations, especially in the shingle mills. During peak years, when mills cut up to 6 million red cedar shingles daily, more than any city in the world, Everett had emerged as a "regional nerve center of union consciousness" and a prime battleground for the IWW.[55] Like Spokane, the city instituted a public-speaking ban, leading to the now-familiar routine of arrests, fines, and expulsions. Sheriff Donald McRae, although a former lumber worker, showed little sympathy for Wobbly complaints. He considered Everett his town and could not allow "boxcar revolutionaries" to disrupt it.[56]

In late September, about 20 Wobblies traveled north from Seattle to challenge Everett's speaking ban. They set up operations at Hewitt and Wetmore avenues, where the ordinance expressly prohibited public protest. Hundreds of pro-labor citizens gathered to hear speeches, protest and stage rallies.[57] For two months, downtown streets roiled in a cauldron of discontent, protest, and violence as police and special deputies delivered justice with rifle butts and ax handles. Anyone attempting to speak was roughed up and sent packing. By the end of October, police had arrested and expelled from town up to 500 Wobblies and sympathizers.[58]

> On October 30, 1916, more than two hundred deputies, or more accurately vigilantes, formed two parallel lines, and forced the Wobblies to run a "gauntlet," clubbing them with saps, ax handles and rifle butts.

Events turned ugly on October 30, when 41 Wobblies rode the ferry from Seattle to stage a rally and presumably get arrested. When passengers disembarked at the docks that evening, police took all suspected Wobblies into custody and drove them to a remote site south of Everett. At that point, more than 200 deputies, or more accurately vigilantes, formed two parallel lines, and forced the Wobblies to run a "gauntlet," clubbing them with saps, ax handles, and rifle butts. Miraculously, no one was killed although many suffered serious injury. They were left to find their way back to Seattle. Most walked the 25 miles.[59]

The attack served only to embolden the IWW. Determined to exercise their constitutional rights and raise awareness of the gauntlet incident, more than 300 men steamed towards Everett on two ferries, the *Verona* and *Calista*, on November 5. The group included devoted Wobblies and Socialists, but most were simply down-on-their-luck laborers who wanted to support the union cause. Although some carried weapons, there is little evidence they intended violence.[60]

When McRae learned of the advancing party, he deputized some 200 businessmen and other citizens and positioned them around the Everett city docks. Set on preventing the agitators from entering town, he positioned his men around the harbor. Some lined the docks, others hid in sheds waiting for a signal, others still rode in tugboats around the harbor. Hundreds of onlookers gathered on the surrounding hillside.[61] As deckhands roped the *Verona* to the dock, McRae yelled "You can't land here."

"The hell we can't," someone retorted.

What happened next remains in dispute. According to court testimony, a shot rang out from McRae's right, followed by another, then another, as a hellish gunfight ensued, with bullets flying in all directions. McRae went down first, shot in the foot.

Panicked Wobblies rushed away from the fire, nearly capsizing the ship and flinging men overboard. Only the rope tied to the dock kept it from going over. But the line that saved the vessel now kept it from fleeing danger. With bullets raining from both sides, the *Verona*'s pilot struggled desperately to free his ship, eventually giving the engines a heavy thrust, snapping the rope. As the *Verona* pulled away, five men lay on the deck dead or dying. Twenty-seven suffered gunshot wounds, many critical. At least 12 more were missing, presumed washed overboard when the steamer nearly capsized. Things weren't much better on the docks, with two dead deputies and 20 wounded, some seriously.[62] On the return to Seattle, the *Verona* met the *Calista* and warned the pilot to turn around. When the *Verona* docked in Seattle, waiting police arrested 74 men and transported them back to Everett.

Prosecutors decided to try the IWW leader Thomas Tracy first. Held in Seattle, the trial included a visit to Everett, where judge and jury reviewed the scenes of the gauntlet and at the docks. They even tied up the *Verona* and positioned men around the wharfs and on the steamer to simulate the shootout.[63] All investigations failed to reveal who shot first or who was responsible for the bloodbath. According to the historian Norman Clark, examination of firsthand accounts, reports, and "impressive heaps of contradictory evidence" allow for no definitive conclusions and "conceal or distort more than they reveal."[64] No one shooting from the docks on that bloody Sunday was ever indicted.

After 13 hours of deliberation and numerous ballots, a jury acquitted Tracy, requiring prosecutors to drop the charges against the 73 others. Not surprisingly, reactions were mixed. Sympathizers with the defendants believed justice prevailed in a case of self-defense where far more Wobblies died than police. Most others believed Wobblies got away with murdering police officers while "fighting a defense action in what amounted to a war."[65] An editorial in the *Douglas County Hammer* in Wenatchee typifies the conservative response. It called for citizens of Everett to "take a lesson from frontier history when a well-executed lynch law made short work of an outlaw class."[66]

A parade of violence in Centralia

Events in Centralia, Washington, in 1919 would turn out much differently, when a gunfight between locals and Wobblies led to six deaths, a "well-executed" lynching, and lengthy prison sentences for seven Wobblies.

Centralia, with a population of about 8,000 thrived on farming and logging. Located along the tracks of the Northern Pacific Railroad, the city functioned as a commercial hub. Claimed one town booster: opportunity in Centralia does more than knock once, "here she keeps up a constant clatter. She is fairly screaming to attract the attention of the capitalist and the homeseeker ..."[67]

A strong union town with a Central Trades Council boasting 3,000 members, Centralia nevertheless wanted no part of its more radical brethren. Conversely, Wobblies felt they should not be "pariahs" in a town otherwise so "hospitable to organized labor."[68] In May 1918, locals sacked the IWW hall and ran its members out of town. The following June, vigilantes attacked a blind newspaper vendor named Tom Lassiter who hawked the *Seattle Union Record* and the *IWW Industrial Worker* on the streets. They beat him up, threw him in a ditch outside of town, and warned him never to return.[69]

Figure 6.3 Labor activist William H. Collins, whom police suspected of having shot at the Legionnaires on November 11, 1919, was not among the men eventually indicted and convicted for their role in the Armistice Day killings. Image reprinted with permission from the Washington State Historical Society.

WANTED

Information Concerning Whereabouts of

Wm. H. COLLINS

Description: Height, 5 Feet 8 Inches; Age 42.

Notify Sheriff of Lewis County; Chief of Police, Centralia, or American Legion, Centralia, Washington

Chronicle Print Centralia, Wn.

Determined to stand their ground, the IWW rented rooms on the ground floor of the Roderick Hotel on Tower Avenue in September 1919 and began publicly recruiting on the street. Livid about the union's return, businessmen met "secretly" at the Elks Hall to "combat IWW activities" and see "law and order maintained." According to the Centralia *Chronicle*, most attendees called for vigilante justice and applauded when someone yelled "Clean" em up, burn "em out."[70]

A poorly kept secret, the meeting prompted the IWW to circulate a flyer appealing to the "Law-Abiding citizens of Centralia." They accused the "profiteering class" of waving the American flag in order to "incite the town" and inviting veterans "to do their bidding." IWW's only crime, the flyer claimed, was "loyalty to the working class, and justice to the oppressed."[71]

Their fears proved well founded on November 11, when Centralia and cities nationwide celebrated the first Armistice Day commemorating the first anniversary of the end of World War I. Centralia's parade got underway around two o'clock, moving north along Tower Avenue. Hundreds of spectators lined both sides of the street.[72] Boy Scouts, uniformed American Legionnaires bearing the colors, Elks, veterans, and Red Cross volunteers paraded through town, waving flags as they passed buildings adorned with red, white, and blue bunting and American flags. But this quintessential American scene in a small American town was suddenly interrupted when several Legionnaires and veterans broke ranks and veered towards the Roderick Hotel.

To the Legionnaires, the scene about to unfold likely felt routine. The second raid on IWW offices in Centralia in two years, as well as numerous raids throughout the Pacific Northwest, fell into a familiar pattern: bang down the door, force the occupants outside, smash, burn or steal anything of value, and then run the "bums" out of town.[73] But it didn't go that way this time. Committed to defending their property, the Wobblies had sought legal counsel earlier that week. Centralia attorney Elmer Smith advised them of their right to protect their lives and property with force in the absence of protection from law enforcement.[74] So when the Legionnaires veered towards the Roderick, Wobblies were watching from the window. They had also positioned guards armed with rifles in the Avalon Hotel across the street and on Seminary Hill to the rear.[75]

The shooting started when the attackers smashed in the door and broke windows. Wobblies positioned at the windows, including Wesley Everest, reportedly shot into the mob with pistols and rifles. Hearing the gunfire, the men stationed across the street and on Seminary Hill joined in the gunfire. Three of the raiders fell immediately and died at the scene: Warren Grimm, commander of the Centralia American Legion and parade leader, and Arthur McElfresh and Ben Cassagranda. Several others suffered nonfatal gunshot wounds.[76]

More Legionnaires and veterans quickly joined the fray, overpowered the Wobblies and took control of the building. Police arrested about a dozen Wobblies, including five found hiding in an unused freezer locker in the rear of the building. Everest fled out the back door towards the Skookumchuck River with deputies in pursuit. They managed to capture Everest, but not before he shot deputy Dale Hubbard. The pursuers beat Everest severely, looped a belt around his neck, and dragged him to jail. A gathering mob jeered, threw stones, and punched the hapless Wobbly. The Legionnaires, "in a state of excited fury," cleared the Roderick's ground floor and then thoroughly ransacked IWW offices, throwing all files, furniture, and anything movable into the street and built a bonfire.[77]

As night fell, Centralia began to rage. Grimm, McElfresh, and Cassagranda were dead. Hubbard was taken to the hospital but died that night. John Watt suffered serious gunshot wounds but would survive. A call went out for 50 deputies to round up the remaining Wobblies, and more than 200 showed up. Worried events were getting out of hand, Centralia Mayor T.C. Rogers requested help from the National Guard.[78]

It arrived too late to help Everest. Vigilantes cut off power to the jail and then stormed in, demanding that the lone deputy on duty hand over Everest. They hustled him outside, forced him into to the backseat of a waiting car, and drove him to a bridge over the Chehalis River. A crowd of several hundred had gathered in time to watch the Legionnaires slip a rope around Everest's neck, sling the other end over a beam and push him over the side. The crowd roared as the enraged men repeatedly shot into the swinging corpse.[79] Participants in the lynching were never questioned or prosecuted.[80] A final death occurred on November 15, when a posse surrounding a suspected Wobbly hideout near Centralia mistakenly shot deputy sheriff John M. Haney.

As news of the Centralia "massacre" spread, vigilantes raided IWW halls and camps in several cities. Near Walla Walla, Legionnaires assaulted two construction camps and forced 120 men to line up with heads bared and swear their allegiance to America. Wobblies saw their halls trashed in Aberdeen, Astoria, and Portland.[81]

Most Centralians saw the shootings as ruthless slaughter of innocent men guilty of nothing other than honoring those who had sacrificed in World War I. The fact they intended to destroy private property was beside the point. Nothing justified murder; the IWW was a "prime evil," and "evil will thrive" when left unchecked.[82] Within days, prosecutors indicted 11 men: Michael Sheehan, Eugene Barnett, Loren Roberts, John Lamb, Britt Smith, brothers O.C. and Bert Bland, Ray Becker, James C. McInerney, Bret Faulkner, and Elmer Smith, the attorney who had earlier advised the IWW. The trial was moved to nearby Montesano where presumably the defense could secure a less biased jury. Charges against Faulkner were dismissed. Following 47 days of conflicting testimony and sensational news coverage, the jury took two days to acquit Smith and Sheehan and find Roberts guilty but "insane." Found guilty of second-degree murder were Smith, McInerney, Bland and Becker, while Barnett and Lamb were deemed guilty of "murder in the third degree." Judge John Wilson informed the jury there was no such charge, so they changed it to second degree, and recommended light sentences. Wilson, in no mood for leniency, sentenced the seven Wobblies to prison for 25 to 40 years.[83]

No one was happy with this verdict either. The defense argued the accused had a right to defend their property. The prosecution, which had filed first-degree murder charges, believed second-degree murder was inappropriate for an alleged "premeditated" crime. Due to the tireless campaigning of their attorney Smith, and the support of a sympathetic public, none of the defendants served the full sentence. McInerney died in prison in 1930 from tuberculosis, while O.C. Roberts, who had been found insane, was freed after a retrial. Bland and Barnett received pardons in 1932. Lamb, Britt Smith and Bert Bland were paroled the following year.[84] Becker was offered parole, but refused to accept the conditions. Stubbornly sticking to his principles and the IWW cause, he served more than 18 years before his release in 1939.[85]

Looking for answers in a violent past

How should we view the free-speech fight and the broader labor conflicts of a century ago? How can we explain the fear and loathing the IWW generated among business owners, mainstream labor, and society? Were cities like Everett and Centralia justified in their severe reaction to IWW protests? Were Wobblies mere victims of greed and ignorance, or were they partly responsible for their fate? Granted, they make for sympathetic characters: riding railcars from job to job, working for pauper's wages in dangerous conditions, gallant troubadours fighting for the oppressed is the stuff of Hollywood. The historian's job is to probe beyond superficialities to draw a balanced picture of what happened and why.

Disdain for Wobblies reflects American attitudes about Socialism and Communism following the Bolshevik atrocities during the Russian Revolution in 1917. Not all Wobblies were Socialists, but all were painted with the same brush. By 1911, Socialist Party offices dotted Puget Sound mill towns, including three in Everett. The IWW, argues Pacific Northwest historian John Findlay, transformed the dense Marxist theory into an accessible doctrine for uneducated, mobile workers. IWW members addressed each other as "comrade," joined "Karl Klubs," and socialized at IWW halls – a place where members could meet their human and social needs as well as the financial ones. In 1912, socialist Eugene V. Debs spoke in Everett to a packed crowd.[86] His messages about one

Figure 6.4 Seated front/left in this 1915 portrait is Ralph Chaplin, an IWW newspaper editor and songwriter. Chaplin wrote "Solidarity Forever," a pro-labor ballad that became the Wobbly theme song. Seated to Chaplin's left are his son Vonnie and wife Ruby. At center is IWW general secretary "Big Bill" Haywood. The Wobblies in the rear are unidentified. Image reprinted with permission from the Washington State Historical Society.

big union reigning over greedy capitalists and turning the capitalist system upside down proved heady stuff for the common laborer.

> From the owner's perspective, giving in to a union meant giving up control of your business, your property, the fruits of an individual's exercise of freedom.

Emboldened by events in Russia, the IWW wanted nothing less than class warfare, beginning with the release of Wobbly leaders or "class-war prisoners."[87] More material demands included a minimum wage of $5 a day and reasonable charges for living expenses and room and board in the lumber camps. They campaigned for collective bargaining and closed shops, which threatened to undermine owner control. But IWW strikes seldom produced meaningful change. Their strident tone during negotiations and dismissal of labor contracts as "a subtle form of entrapment," suggests they were more interested in political agitation than relieving wage earner oppression, argues the historian Robert Tyler.[88] They were less change-agents than fervent missionaries spreading the gospel of industrial unionism.

Conditions in the forests and mills eventually improved, but credit for most of those gains goes to the War Department. Desperate to prevent labor unrest from interfering with war production, it employed soldiers in the forest and organized all loggers into a new union, the Loyal Legion of Loggers and Lumbermen, or "4-L." They deployed soldiers, called the Spruce Divisions, and forced reforms for the benefit of enlisted man. But in the early twentieth century, "the union movement was still more a promise than a power."[89] Resistance to organization resounded from all corners. The employers, government, and unsympathetic courts handcuffed efforts to organize the working class. From the owner's perspective, giving in to a union meant giving up control of your business, your property, the fruits of an individual's exercise of freedom.

The beginning of the end

America's entry into World War I led to stronger suppression of free speech and became the "death knell" for the labor and progressive movements.[90] The wage earner's cause was no match for a war in which America intended to make the world "safe for democracy," especially when most Wobblies publicly opposed the war.[91] Americans generally came to accept the fact that war's heavy demands required sacrifice and loyalty, not strikes and sit-ins. Progressives and labor dissidents who disrupted the flow of commerce were labeled disloyal, acting in their self-interest, hurting the war effort, and even aiding the enemy. Victory demanded nothing less than a "loyal patriotic populace," in full support of the war. "It was a fight for the *minds* of men, for the 'conquest of their convictions,' and the battle-line ran through every home in every country," wrote progressive journalist George Creel.[92]

The Woodrow Wilson administration vigorously fought antiwar ideas and people. "Woe be to the man or group of men that seeks to stand in our way ... ," Wilson declared in June 1917. An eager Congress supported the President with a series of legislative acts to deter disloyalty and root out potential traitors. The Alien Act, the Alien Enemies Act, the Espionage Act, the Sedition Act, and the Trading with the Enemy Act "gave the federal government sweeping powers to fine and jail anyone obstructing the war effort in any way."[93] The Sedition Act prohibited "uttering, printing, writing, or publishing any disloyal, profane, scurrilous, or abusive language" about the United States government and military.[94]

The government used the repressive laws to pursue Socialists across the country, beginning with Congressman Victor Berger of Milwaukee. He was a journalist and the first Socialist elected to the House of Representatives, although later sentenced to 20 years for his public opposition to the war. More than 200 IWW members in Chicago, Kansas City, and Sacramento served time for one loyalty-related offense or another. Labor leader and then Socialist Party presidential candidate Debs was sentenced to ten years for sedition for speaking out against the draft.

In 1918, the Washington state legislature made it a felony to "advocate, teach, print, publish, or display anything" that advocated sedition or violence as a means of "effecting industrial, economic, social, or political change." Such laws gave police a means to suppress Wobbly demonstrations and raid their halls with impunity. It was also a felony

Figure 6.5 Traffic comes to a halt during the Seattle streetcar strike in November 1903. The local unit of the Amalgamated Association of Street and Electric Railway Employees of America demanded overtime pay and other concessions from the privately held Seattle Electric Company. Image reprinted with permission from the Washington State Historical Society.

to "be a member or associate with any group of persons" who advocated sedition."[95] To Centralia Sheriff Jeff Bartell, Wobblies were nothing less than anarchists "capable of terroristic activity..."[96]

Forcing Wobblies to take a loyalty oath became common practice during and after the war. Like the incident in Walla Walla following the Centralia tragedy, anyone suspected of disloyalty was forced to kiss the flag, buy Liberty Bonds, or swear allegiance to America. The Pacific Northwest held no monopoly on aggression against the IWW. In Bisbee, Arizona, vigilantes rounded up more than 1,000 Wobblies and left them in the desert without food or water. Incidences of beatings, tarring and feathering, and lynching were reported around the country.[97]

We can see the tragedy in Centralia and others more clearly through the lens of war hysteria. In many ways, the case against the Wobblies was more than a murder trial; the very legality of the IWW was at stake. If the union was a legitimate organization, then it had the right to defend its property under the stand-your-ground laws in Washington. But if the IWW was really the "abomination the law now declared it to be," if it were illegal even to be a Wobbly, then that defense posture was invalid.[98]

The Centralia incident hastened an IWW downfall that began with the Seattle General Strike in February 1919. The first such strike in U.S. history began when 35,000 shipyard

Figure 6.6 The General Strike that shut down Seattle for five days in February 1919 began at the city's shipyards a month earlier. Here, thousands of striking workers jam the Skinner and Eddy yards. Among other grievances, they demanded a living wage and safer workplace. Image reprinted with permission from the Washington State Historical Society.

workers walked off the docks on January 21. Their numbers swelled to 60,000 when the Seattle Central Labor Council and the AFL convinced multiple local unions to stage sympathy strikes. Streetcar workers, waiters, barbers, department store clerks, newsboys, warehousemen, and scores of other workers put down their tools and walked off the job on February 6. For five days, Seattle came to a standstill with all but the basic services shut down. The IWW appears to have played only a peripheral role in spearheading the strike, nevertheless it took the brunt of the blame. Like most IWW protests it generated few meaningful results, yet the union paid a heavy price. Looking for someone to blame, authorities raided the union's Seattle headquarters, arresting 39 Wobblies.[99]

The IWW did not die after 1919 so much as fade into irrelevancy. By 1930 most of their founders were dead or imprisoned. "Big Bill" Haywood was arrested in Chicago in 1918, along with scores of other Wobblies accused of treason and sabotage. A jury sentenced him to 20 years in prison, but in 1921, while out on bail during an appeal, he fled to Russia, where he lived until his death in 1928.

More and more workers began to turn to the AFL and other trade unions for support. The birth of the CIO (Committee of Industrial Organization) in 1935, which would merge with the AFL in 1955, created something approaching IWW's one big union. Moreover, the IWW's radical messages, never accepted by the broader labor community, began to wear thin among a membership frustrated by the absence of results. The historian Norman Clark argues the Progressive Era in general taught the working class an important lesson: Education was an "easier route toward middle-class securities than union militancy or class war."[100]

The deck was stacked against radicalism of any kind during the formative decades of the Industrial Revolution. The IWW ran through a gauntlet of heavy resistance: a political system in which the sanctity of private property and freedom to make contracts were valued over human rights; an upper class that held a general disregard for the working class; and a deep-seated suspicion of leftist political ideologies. Collectively these sentiments pounded the Wobblies as much as ax handles, rifle butts and bullets. It would take an economic calamity a generation later to bring the plight of the poor back into the national spotlight.

R.D. Hume, "pygmy monopolist" on the economic frontier

Draining from Crater Lake in the Cascade Mountains, the Rogue River meanders through southwestern Oregon, dropping 5,000 feet in 215 miles until it empties into the Pacific Ocean. For thousands of years, Native Peoples of the Tututni language group of tribes lived along the Rogue and dieted on its plentiful salmon. But beginning in the 1870s, much of the Rogue and its tidelands belonged not to Natives or even government, but to a private commercial fishing enterprise.

On any given day, its president, Robert Deniston Hume, known as R.D., could have stood above the river and surveyed his fiefdom. The Tututni were long gone, dead from disease, or sent inland to the Siletz Indian Reservation following the Rogue River War in 1855–1856. Hume owned everything in sight: the tidelands on both sides of the river, the cannery, bunkhouse, mess hall, and the steamships anchored offshore. If he looked upriver, he could see Wedderburn, his company town, including the Hume-owned general store, post office, hotel, and newspaper.[101]

A self-described "pygmy monopolist," Hume controlled all aspects of the commercial fishing business, and related economy of Southwest Oregon.[102] Although on a much smaller scale, he compares to the great monopolists of the nineteenth century who used vertical integration schemes (meaning a company owns or controls all aspects of production and distribution) in the railroad, oil, steel, and finance industries.

In the second half of the nineteenth century, much of the region's land not owned by the federal government was in the hands of private companies. Hume's business ventures on the Rogue sheds light on the debate over private-versus-public ownership of the region's rivers, timberland, and other natural resources.

Unlike most monopolists, Hume came from modest means. Born in Augusta, Maine, in 1845, Hume moved to San Francisco at age 18 to join his two brothers in the cannery business. Four years later, the three men moved to Oregon and opened a cannery in Astoria. Hume prospered over the next ten years, purchasing several Columbia River canneries. He married Celia Bryant in 1869 and the couple had two children. Their first, a daughter, died in infancy and their son died at age four in 1875. When Celia died a few months later, a despondent Hume sold his holdings and returned to San Francisco.

Within a year, he was back in business, purchasing the Rogue River tidelands and upstream almost 12 miles. He married Mary A. Duncan, age 19, in 1877, and the couple became known in Wedderburn as "King Bob and Queen Mary." Over the next 20 years, R.D. Hume and Company caught, processed, and shipped hundreds of thousands of cases of salmon to San Francisco, New York, Great Britain, and Australia.

Owning the tidelands awarded Hume control over fish that migrated between the spawning beds and ocean. Chinook, coho, sockeye, chum, and steelhead traveled through Hume property and into Hume nets. Men in small boats stretched a dragnet weighted at the bottom, called a seine, and literally dragged the fish to shore. Gillnetting involved trapping fish whose gills got caught in finely woven nets. From the shore, the fish were carried to the cannery, where Chinese workers cleaned and butchered the salmon, and canned them in brine for preservation. They were then shipped in wooden crates that held 48 1-pound cans.

Hume employed hundreds of laborers who worked in a two-tiered labor system. Literally all fishermen were white, mostly local farmers working under contract who could net up to

$90 a month.[103] Supervisors, ship captains, and clerical staff were also white. Many lived in the bunkhouse and ate in the mess hall, while better paid employees rented a house from Hume in Wedderburn for $6 to $8 a month.

Canning and other unskilled jobs were the province of the Chinese, experienced butchers recruited from San Francisco earning less than fishermen.[104] Chinese working for Hume apparently had it better than those under contract with the larger fisheries on the Columbia River, who often failed to provide the promised food, clothing, and shelter. Hume appears to have dealt honestly with Chinese, stocking his stores with tea, rice, and opium. They lived in a Chinatown outside Wedderburn, creating tensions between Hume and white residents who resented the Chinese presence.

But Hume was no benevolent employer. He opposed reform movements of the Knights of Labor and the American Federation of Labor, or anyone who threatened to challenge his control and dent profits. During the 1906 strike on the Southern Pacific, Hume wrote his nephew that he "would like to see the strike leaders shot."

Innovations in canning technology and refrigeration opened new markets for the region's fishery. Hume won several patents for machines that automated cutting and assembling cans, work that previously required a crew of 12. Realizing frozen fish offered more potential than canned, Hume installed refrigeration units on his schooners in 1906.

Canned or frozen, Northwest salmon became a staple of the industrial working class on the East Coast, Great Britain, and Australia. On average, Hume's cannery annually shipped about 15,000 cases, much of them overseas. In 1897, 75% of the 19,613 cases of salmon ended up on store shelves in Great Britain. Related industries flourished along with the fishery. The cans were manufactured on the Rogue and then packed in wooden boxes made by millmen in Coos Bay and Portland.

Hume spent much of his time fighting to maintain control of "his" river. Treating politics as an "arm of industry" Hume served two terms in the Oregon State Legislature as a Republican.[105] The ongoing debate: Did Hume's ownership of the tidelands entitle him to exclusive ownership of the fish? How far upriver did those rights extend? Were others entitled to a share of the catch? Who owned the other river resources like minerals and timber? Hume successfully lobbied for legislation that "entitled" the tidelands owner to the "exclusive right and privilege of fishing for salmon." He also claimed a share of the gold, coal, and copper found in abundance on the Rogue, even though most mines were located 100 miles or more upstream.

Witness to the over-fishing and abuses that earlier damaged the Sacramento and Columbia rivers, Hume emerged as a leading proponent of conservation and invested in research in propagation and hatchery development. Following a disappointing season in 1877, he built his first hatchery. He also attempted to control harvests by restricting river access through the assertion of his "riparian" rights, especially upriver where fisherman illegally dropped nets at the base of the dams. In 1908, he persuaded the legislature to regulate fishing near dams, appropriating funds for wardens to patrol the river and prohibit fishing within 600 feet of a dam. To promote his conservationist ideas, every case of Hume salmon contained a pamphlet warning consumers of the dangers to the resource.

Hume's conservation methods and hatchery practices initially won acclaim, but his "idiosyncratic biological theories and sloppy hatchery practices" were ultimately rejected by the fishery's scientific community.[106] And while his motives were as much about profit as preservation, they represent early efforts to conserve the region's natural resources.

In spite of efforts by Hume and others to promote conservation in the Pacific Northwest, they couldn't offset persistent over-fishing and destruction of the habitat from logging, mining and hydroelectric plants. On the Columbia, for example, the fishery began to decline in the 1880s, surged during World War I, and then fell into permanent decline.[107] In 1883, as many as 55 canneries operated on the Columbia River. Nearly a century later there was one. It shut down in 1980.

Hume's monopoly on the Rogue illustrates the power industrialists exercised over their domain on the "undeveloped economic frontier." Like the railroad baron who controlled his right away or the millmen who ruled over a timber town, Hume reigned through intimidation and force. When those failed, he turned to the law. He monopolized a river against all odds with the "intelligence and persistence to create new ways of maintaining the supply of natural wealth." Eventually state courts nullified many of Hume's ownership rights.

In November 1908, Hume suffered from over exposure during a heavy storm at sea and fell ill. Coping with complications from kidney ailments most of his adult life, he never fully recovered. He died in the town he built, Wedderburn, on November 25, 1908.

Explore more

Books

A number of excellent works bring life to the tumultuous labor radicalism in the early twentieth century. For historical tour of the boom-and-bust years, as well as the Everett tragedy itself, see Norman H. Clark, *Mill Town: A Social History of Everett, Washington*. John Jr McCelland's *Wobbly War: The Centralia Story*, delivers a vivid recount of the violence that fell upon that city. For a broader look at the Progressive Movement in America, see Michael McGerr, *A Fierce Discontent: The Rise and Fall of the Progressive Movement in America*.

Online

The University of Washington maintains several excellent websites on regional history. The oral histories of labor and civil rights leaders at the Seattle Civil Rights and Labor History Project at http://depts.washington.edu/civilr/ help bring the labor conflicts to life. For a look at the Seattle General Strike of 1919, see http://depts.washington.edu/labhist/strike/index.shtml.

Museums

The permanent exhibit at the Museum of History and Industry (http://www.mohai.org/exhibits) in Seattle details the emergence of that city during the booming industrial years.

What do you think?

Where would you come down on the "individualism" versus "mutualism" debate? Can you explain why those grouped in the "ten percent" believed a person's failure was a product of his own inadequacies? A century after the fact, how can we make sense of labor-related violence? Why were owners and employers so adamant against worker organization? Why did law enforcement, the courts, and a majority of citizens support employers instead of workers?

Notes

1 Gregory R. Woirol, ed., "Two Letters on the Spokane Free Speech Fight," *Pacific Northwest Quarterly* 77, no. 2 (April 1986): 68–71.
2 Ibid.
3 Ibid.
4 Ibid.
5 "Joe Hill, IWW Songs," Center for the Study of the Pacific Northwest, accessed January 25, 2016; http://www.washington.edu/uwired/outreach/cspn/Website/Classroom%20Materials/Reading%20the%20Region/Writing%20Home/Commentary/11.html.
6 *Songs of the Workers: On the Road, In the Jungles, And in the Shops*, 8th ed. (Cleveland, OH: I.W.W. Publishing Bureau, 1914), 39.

7 Michael McGerr, *A Fierce Discontent: The Rise and Fall of the Progressive Movement in America* (Oxford: Oxford University Press, 2003), 15.

8 Ibid., 4.

9 Ibid., 7.

10 Ibid., 6–7.

11 Ibid., 8.

12 Ibid.

13 Ibid., 13.

14 Ibid., 21.

15 Ibid.

16 Ibid., 33.

17 Ibid., 130.

18 Ibid., 140–141.

19 Ibid., 16.

20 Ibid.

21 Ibid., 17.

22 John McCelland Jr., *Wobbly War: The Centralia Story* (Tacoma, WA: Washington State Historical Society, 1987), 6–7.

23 Matthew S. May, "Hobo Orator Union: The Free Speech Fights of the Industrial Workers of the World, 1909–1916," unpublished PhD diss., University of Minnesota, 2009), 2.

24 May, "Hobo Orator Union," 33.

25 Thomas R. Cox, *Mills and Markets: A History of the Pacific Coast Lumber Industry to 1900* (Seattle, WA: University of Washington Press, 1974), 106.

26 Cox, *Mills and Markets*, 239–240.

27 Ibid., 213.

28 Ibid., xi.

29 Cox, *Mills and Markets*, 215–221.

30 Ibid., 227.

31 Ibid., 254.

32 "Industrialization, Technology and Environment in Washington," in Lesson 14 in the Center for the Study of the Pacific Northwest, accessed October 19, 2016, www .washington.edu.

33 Cox, *Mills and Markets*, 257–258.

34 Ibid., 71.

35 Ibid., 265.

36 Ibid.

37 Clark, *Mill Town*, 68.

38 Kevin Boyle, "Work Places: The Economy and the Changing Landscape of Labor, 1900–2000," in perspectives on *Modern America: Making Sense of the Twentieth Century*, Harvard Sitkoff, ed. (New York: Oxford University Press, 2001), 104.

39 Cox, *Mills and Markets*, 283.

40 Charles Pierce Lewarne, "The Aberdeen, Washington, Free Speech Fight of 1911–1912," *Pacific Northwest Quarterly* 66, no. 1 (January 1975): 1.

41 Lewarne, *Free Speech Fight*, 2.

42 Clark, *Mill Town*, 65.

43 Ronald L. Gregory, "Life in Railroad Logging Camps of the Shevlin-Hixon Company. 1916–1950," unpublished master's thesis, June 6, 1997, 34–36, Oregon State University.

44 Clark, *Mill Town*, 91.

45 May, "Hobo Orator Union," 148.

46 Ibid.

47 McGerr, *A Fierce Discontent*, 142.

48 Lewarne, *Free Speech Fight*, 1.

49 Ibid., 3.

50 Ibid.

51 Lewarne, *Free Speech Fight*, 5.

52 Chris Canterbury, "The International Union of Timberworkers, 1911–1923, Seattle Civil Rights and Labor History Project," accessed February 21, 2015, http://depts.washington.edu/civilr/.

53 Clark, *Mill Town*, 78.

54 Ibid.

55 Ibid., 91.

56 Ibid., 193.

57 Ibid., 188.

58 Ibid., 190.

59 Ibid., 195–197.

60 Ibid., 201–202.

61 Ibid., 203–204.

62 Ibid., 203–207.

63 McClelland, *Wobbly War*, 13.

64 Clark, *Mill Town*, 208.

65 Ibid.

66 McCelland, *Wobbly War*, 14.

67 Ibid., 4.

68 Ibid., 56.

69 Ibid., 52.

70 Ibid., 59.

71 Robert L. Tyler, *Rebels of the Woods: The I.W.W. in the Pacific Northwest* (Eugene, OR: University of Oregon Press, 1967), 158–159.

72 McCelland, *Wobbly War*, 66.

73 Ibid., 66.

74 Tyler, *Rebels in the Woods*, 159.

75 McCelland, *Wobbly War*, 72.

76 Tyler, *Rebels of the Woods*, 160.

77 McClelland, *Wobbly War*, 76–77.

78 Ibid., 80.

79 Ibid., 80–81.

80 Ibid., 86.

81 Ibid., 95.

82 Ibid., 239.

83 Tyler, *Rebels of the Woods*, 163–167.

84 Ibid., 221–224

85 Ibid., 231.

86 Clark, *Mill Town*, 116.

87 McClelland, *The Wobbly War*, 54.

88 Tyler, *Rebels in the Woods*, 53.

89 McGerr, *A Fierce Discontent*, 32.

90 Ibid., 281.

91 Ibid., 279.

92 Ibid., 288.

93 Ibid., 289.

94 Ibid.

95 McCelland, *Wobbly War*, 47.

96 Ibid., 55.

97 McGerr, *A Fierce Discontent*, 290

98 McClelland, *The Wobbly War*, 124.

99 "Seattle General Strike begins on February 6, 1919," from historylink.org, accessed July 25, 2015; http://www.historylink.org/

100 Clark, *Mill Town*, 236–237.

101 This sidebar article draws heavily from Gordon B. Dobbs, *The Salmon King of Oregon: R.D. Hume and the Pacific Fisheries* (Chapel Hill, NC: University of North Carolina Press, 1959).

102 Robert Deniston Hume (1845–1908), Oregon Encyclopedia.org, accessed May 20, 2015, http://www.oregonencyclopedia.org/articles/.

103 Dobbs, *The Salmon King of Oregon*, 22.

104 Ibid., 26.

105 Ibid., 229.

106 Oregon, Encyclopedia.org.

107 Dobbs, *The Salmon King of Oregon*, 147.

7

Dismantling a Racial Hierarchy

Minorities fight for equality in a region grappling with diversity

From the earliest days of settlement, the Pacific Northwest was defined by its racial diversity. The magnetic forces of natural resources and abundant land drew a steady stream of minorities who, like their white counterparts, had dreams of their own. In moving west, they faced a society often divided over race but determined to maintain its dominance. Yet minorities, especially Chinese and African Americans, eventually dismantled many racial barricades and carved out a permanent place in which they could live and work.

Ruby Chapin was nine years old in 1885 when the dark tide of racial oppression swept through Tacoma, Washington. Two years earlier, she had traveled from New York by train with her older sister to live with an uncle who operated a hotel on Tacoma's waterfront. At the time, Tacoma was locked in a cultural conflict between white residents and a growing population of Chinese immigrants. On November 3, Ruby watched in horror as "committees" of armed white men paraded through town, forcing more than 200 Chinese residents from their homes and businesses. They were herded to the train depot in nearby Lake View and put on the southbound Northern Pacific Railroad. Decades later, Ruby wrote the event "was the most unpleasant experience of my childhood."[1]

The "Tacoma Expulsion," as it would come to be known, is one of countless examples of the racial tensions that permeated the Pacific Northwest in the second half of the nineteenth century. This chapter contextualizes those tensions: Chinese who immigrated to America seeking new wealth and refuge from famine and war in China; African Americans, many former slaves or children of slaves, who migrated west in the hopes of finding work or owning land and to escape racial oppression; and Euro-Americans deeply divided over race and how to adjust to the steady influx of people of different color and cultures. And cope they certainly had to. By the second decade of the twentieth century, the region's cities housed a cultural milieu of African Americans, as well as immigrants from throughout Asia, the South Pacific, Mexico and Central and South America.

White settlers in the Pacific Northwest brought their racial attitudes with them from the East. Most Americans viewed the world in racial terms. Consistent with attitudes and scientific beliefs of the time, they accepted white superiority as a matter of course and viewed other races as genetically inferior. "Racialist" theories, distinct from racist,

Contested Boundaries: A New Pacific Northwest History, First Edition. David J. Jepsen and David J. Norberg.
© 2017 John Wiley & Sons, Ltd. Published 2017 by John Wiley & Sons, Ltd.

Figure 7.1 This 1892 handbill is similar to those posted throughout Tacoma prior to the Chinese expulsion in 1885. The 1892 meeting whereby citizens could express their opinion on the "Chinese question" was poorly attended. Apparently Tacoma's anti-Chinese sentiment had fizzled following the forced removal of hundreds of Chinese seven years earlier. Image reprinted with permission from the Washington State Historical Society.

held that "God created a superior Anglo-Saxon race destined to conquer and control all others."[2]

Racial inferiority was a permanent condition, according to racialist theory. Nonwhites were grouped into four races: Indians, Mexicans, "Mongoloids" (Asians) and blacks. As proof of their superiority, whites pointed to their centuries-long history of success conquering Native Peoples, enslaving blacks and marginalizing Mexicans. This was the natural order of things, they believed.

While most nineteenth-century whites believed in white superiority, not all held to racialist ideas. Some believed in the power of assimilation. Assimilationists held that proper education and exposure to white culture could eventually earn people of color a status equivalent to whites over time. Assimilation theories drove the government's policies towards Native Peoples throughout the nineteenth century.

Regardless of racialist attitudes, many whites believed the region's land and natural resources were the sole provenance of whites. They went to extraordinary measures to control the vast forests and farmlands. They created special taxes and exclusionary laws to keep nonwhites from harvesting the gold and silver in the region's mines. They enlisted the federal government to negotiate treaties to squelch immigration. When all that failed, they resorted to intimidation, violence, and forced expulsion.

Any examination of the history of racial minorities in the Pacific Northwest must be viewed through the twin lenses of racial attitudes and economic instability.

Yet this is not a simple story of one group excluding another. Whites were dependent on minority labor, especially during labor strikes, wartime, and economic booms. Further, the people of the Pacific Northwest, like much of America were divided over racial issues, especially slavery. There is ample evidence to show many whites were willing to make room for racial minorities, support their business enterprises, and come to their aid when facing trouble.

Economic issues exacerbated racial ones. Employment opportunities came and went as the burgeoning American economy cycled through frequent periods of boom and bust. In strong economies, like during the railroad boom of 1879–1882, jobs were plentiful. Railroads and mine operators needed workers, regardless of skin color, to stay on schedule or to replace white workers on strike, not an uncommon occurrence.

But economic good times were hard to sustain in the early industrial era. Corruption, lack of government oversight, indebtedness and heedless speculation propelled the economy through a roller coaster of booms, panics, deep troughs, and prolonged contraction. In the last three decades of the nineteenth century, there were seven economic recessions. Most lasted a year or two, but the Panic of 1873 and the resulting "Long Depression," persisted for five years. As the economy faltered, demand for raw materials like wood, coal, and wheat dropped sharply, paralyzing the Pacific Northwest's extraction-based economy.

For these reasons, any examination of the history of racial minorities in the Pacific Northwest must be viewed through the twin lenses of racial attitudes and economic instability. It's a complex picture of a racial hierarchy with whites sitting on top and in control. Writing about the settlement of the larger American West, historian Patricia Nelson Limerick called it a "legacy of conquest," where the power elite used all necessary means to monopolize the region's resources, preserve white superiority, and shape society and culture to match their vision of the future.[3] As a result, nonwhites worked within a binary labor system. Skilled or white-collar jobs were open to whites only, while nonwhites were relegated to menial labor, denied their civil rights, and economically marginalized. A closer look at the African American experience, followed by the Chinese, will help to clarify.

African Americans – seeking haven from racial oppression

Fear of discrimination did not discourage African Americans from venturing west. Some of the first worked for the U.S. Army. Natives called them "buffalo soldiers" because their dark, curly hair reminded them of buffalo hide. The name stuck. Others braved the six-month trek along the Oregon Trail with the thousands of other settlers at mid-nineteenth century. Others still rode sailing ships around Cape Horn at the southern tip of South America and north up the Pacific Coast.

Many African Americans moved west to escape racial injustices in the South or East. The Pacific Northwest gained a reputation for its tolerance of people of color. Upon arrival many would learn such a reputation was mostly unfounded. Like the rest of the country, the region was deeply divided over slavery. The exception was Oregon's black exclusion laws. In 1844, the provisional government outlawed slavery as a tactic to preclude settlers from bringing their slaves into the territory. Later the exclusion law was written into the state constitution, which was to be submitted to the U.S. Congress in

1857. The Senate approved Oregon's constitution, but the question of statehood stalled in the House over the exclusion clause. Ohio Representative John Bingham called this clause "injustice and oppression incarnate," while Massachusetts Representative Henry L. Dawes charged that Oregon's constitution "makes odious distinctions among classes of men and among individuals of the same class. It ruthlessly tramples the rights of the citizen in the dust."[4]

Early black settlers ran head first into the exclusion law. Their resistance and subsequent support from a significant number of white settlers illustrates the deep divisions in America over slavery and racial injustice. George Bush, one of the first settlers of any race in the south Puget Sound, exemplifies the challenges facing African Americans settling in the Pacific Northwest. The Bushes traversed the Oregon Trail from Missouri in 1844 intending to settle in the Rogue River Valley in Oregon Territory. Like many free blacks prior to the Civil War, the Bushes saw the American West as an opportunity for a fresh start, free from the oppressive racism in the South. But for Bush such freedom proved elusive in the face of Oregon exclusion laws.

Bush and several black families moved north of the Columbia River on land under the influence of the British-owned Hudson's Bay Company, which didn't enforce the exclusion law. In 1845, they built a homestead near what is now Tumwater, Washington, and opened a grist mill and saw mill. However, the Donation Land Act of 1850 soon threatened their place in this thriving community. To promote settlement in the Oregon Territory, the federal government gave 320 acres to single men and another 320 acres to his wife, provided they settled and worked the land for at least four years. Blacks were not eligible.

In a not uncommon show of interracial solidarity in the region, 55 members of the first Washington Territorial Legislature successfully petitioned the federal government to allow the Bushes to keep their land.[5] Whether their motives were humanitarian or driven by economic necessity (mills were in high demand), white settlers set aside racial attitudes for the sake of community.

Examples abound of white settlers defending the rights of African Americans. Richard Bogle, the son of a Jamaican slave, moved to the Oregon Territory in 1850 after having struck out in the California goldfields. In Salem, he met and married America Waldo, the free daughter of a slave who migrated west with her master, Daniel Waldo. The newlyweds now faced trouble on two fronts. Not only were they breaking the law remaining in the territory, but marriage between African Americans was not recognized. Salem's newspaper, the *Statesmen Journal*, called the union a "nigger wedding." In a sign of loyalty to his black charges, Daniel Waldo lavished the married couple with gifts and helped them relocate in Walla Walla, north of the Columbia River. There, Bogle opened a barbershop, one of the few skilled services available to African Americans. He later purchased a 200-acre farm and co-founded the Walla Walla Savings and Loan Association.[6]

The case of O.B. Francis and his brother Abner further illustrates the division over exclusionary practices in the region. Abner Hunt Francis and his wife Lynda moved from New York to Portland in 1851 to open a boarding house. Upon his arrival, he learned O.B. had been arrested for violating the Black Exclusion Law and was given six months to leave the territory. Abner, active in the abolitionist movement in the East, wrote a letter to his friend, Frederick Douglass, the famous abolitionist and publisher of the anti-slavery publication, *The North Star*. Francis called the Oregon law "unjust and devilish" and a violation of Article IV of the Constitution that guarantees citizens of one state the same "Privileges and Immunities" of citizens in other states. In an 1851 letter Francis wrote:

> Thus you see, my dear sir [Douglass] that even in the so-called free territory of Oregon, the colored American citizen, though he may possess all of the qualities and qualifications which make a man a good citizen, is driven out like a beast in the forest, made to sacrifice every interest dear to him, and forbidden the privilege to take the portion of the soil which the government says every citizen shall enjoy. Ah![7]

The Francis brothers were far from alone in their opposition to the exclusion law. In another sign of white-black solidarity, more than 200 people, including two territorial officials and the editor of the *Portland Oregonian*, signed a 1851 petition requesting repeal of the law. They wanted to "call attention to the severity of the law and the injustice often resulting from the enforcement of it." Oregon's "negroes" had "proved themselves to be industrious and civil" and simply wanted to "gain an honest living." They requested the repeal so that "all class of honest and industrious men may have an equal chance."[8]

While the Francis brothers lived in Portland for several more years, the exclusionary law was never repealed. In 1868 the U.S. Congress adopted the Fourteenth Amendment to the Constitution, which prohibited states from depriving any person of "life, liberty, or property" or the "equal protection of the laws." The amendment made the exclusionary law unenforceable, although it remained on Oregon's books until 1927.

The trickle of black migration swelled in 1883 when the Northern Pacific Railroad connected the Pacific Northwest with the rest of America. Soon, hundreds of African Americans working service jobs on the railroads and in the coal mines and shipyards called the region home. According to census figures, the black population in Washington, Oregon, and Idaho increased from about 900 in 1880 to about 3,900 by 1900, with most living in Seattle and Portland.[9]

Early industrialization and demand for substitute labor

Labor disputes drew many African Americans to the region in the 1880s. Railroads, which ran on coal, again played a central role. The Northern Pacific operated a coal mine in Roslyn east of Seattle, while the Oregon Improvement Company (OIC) maintained mines in Gilman (now Issaquah), Newcastle and Franklin in King County. Due to the hard, dangerous nature of the work, conflicts between owners and miners (exclusively white) flared up from the start. Working hundreds of feet below ground, they dealt with abominable conditions: poor ventilation, explosive gas, floods, and cave-ins. Mine operators, pressed to curtail costs in a competitive industry, paid meager wages and appeared insensitive to worker issues.

More than 1,000 miners in Roslyn, organized by the Knights of Labor, walked out on the job in 1888, refusing to return until the mine operators met their demands for increased wages and improved safety conditions. Unwilling to adhere to worker demands, owners adopted a well-established strikebreaking tactic – hiring substitute labor. For decades, increased industrialization in Eastern states led to labor conflict in most industries, especially mining, railroads, and steel. Management relied on "scab"

Figure 7.2 Miners stop to pose for a photo in a Wilkeson coal mine in Pierce County, Washington, in 1913. In high demand to fuel the region's railroads, coal also fueled tensions between miners and owners over wages, work safety, and hiring African Americans during strikes.

labor, as it was known, to break strikes. When white workers walked out, unemployed African Americans and European immigrants filled the gap. With the onset of coal strikes, substitute labor, a hallmark of American industry throughout the nineteenth century and much of the twentieth, had come to the Pacific Northwest.

Desperate for workers, Northern Pacific recruited miners in Virginia, Kentucky, and North Carolina to break the strike. By 1889, an estimated 300 black miners were working in Roslyn, while their white counterparts stood by, enraged, bitter, and helpless. In a report to the Territorial Governor, the Kittitas County Sheriff wrote, "There is a bitter feeling against the Negroes and U.S. marshals among the miners, and I fear there will be bloodshed over the matter."[10]

In the exception that proves the rule, little blood was shed in this labor dispute. Within months, most white miners had begrudgingly returned to work. More telling was the community-building and interracial cooperation that took place over the following decade. Blacks and whites worked together to build a school. Black men organized a Masonic Lodge and other fraternal organizations, while their wives joined organizations like the Eastern Star and Daughters of Tabernacle. The Baptist Church in Roslyn and the African Methodist Episcopal Church were centerpieces of a vibrant social life.

There was no happy ending to the coal mining strikes in Newcastle and Franklin. In 1891, the miners unanimously rejected a contract offer from OIC and walked out. Witness to the favorable results in Roslyn, management immediately began recruiting substitute labor. Ads in Midwest newspapers called for "500 colored coal miners and laborers for inside and outside work ... Steady work for three years ... The best country on earth." The ad included one outright fabrication: "No strike or trouble of any kind."[11]

On May 13, 500 African Americans, including women and children, arrived in Franklin under heavy guard. The *Seattle Post-Intelligencer* labeled the procession "THE BLACK TRAIN," and accused OIC of "colonizing its mining camps with non-union labor."[12] Fearing trouble, OIC surrounded the buildings and living quarters in Franklin with barbed-wire and posted Pinkerton guards to stand watch.

White miners responded immediately, calling sympathy strikes in the nearby Black Diamond and Cedar Mountain mines. Miners in Wilkeson in Pierce County declared in a statement, they "cannot and will not recognize the negro as worthy of association with us."[13] A joint resolution from miners in King and Pierce counties protested the "inhuman action of the Oregon Improvement Company in importing cheap colored labor to take the place of honest white labor."[14] The striking miners saw their black replacements as naïve pawns of management recruited from the slums of American cities. In truth, most Franklin and Newcastle replacements were experienced miners from Iowa, Illinois, Indiana, and Missouri. Although deceived about the potential for trouble, they must have suspected the truth, given the standing practices of management at many mining companies.

Black miners defended their decision to break the strike. In a letter to the editor of the *Post-Intelligencer*, one miner wrote, "We are aware that prejudice is against us here; but where can we go? ... Let them call us scabs if they want to. We have concluded that half a loaf is better than none."[15] In support of the replacement workers, a group of black ministers declared they "expect to enjoy all the rights and immunities guaranteed to all true patriotic Americans, and as such we deem it our right and privilege to remain not only in Franklin but in any other locality within the jurisdiction of the United States."[16]

On June 8, the exchange of words erupted into an exchange of bullets. By this time, many striking miners had returned to work, but soon tensions led to gunfire. According to reports, armed miners exchanged more than 1,000 rounds, killing two miners and seriously wounding four. Washington Governor Elisha Ferry called in the National Guard to restore order. Although the *Post-Intelligencer* warned of trouble from African Americans "who regard any white man as an enemy," there was little conflict after 1891.[17] Blacks and whites worked side by side until the mining industry in Washington collapsed in the Panic of 1893. Triggered in part by overbuilding in the railroads, the subsequent recession forced many operators to shut down.

How should we assess the parties involved in the strikes? It would be easy to label mine operators as greedy capitalists intent on slashing costs and retaining control over workers. What about those white workers? Were they guilty of abandoning their jobs and worse, failing to find common ground with their black replacements? Were the replacements themselves nothing more than innocent victims, manipulated by capitalists?

Such explanations are not wholly inaccurate, but strike students of history as far too simple. If we look more closely, it's evident all parties faced extreme pressure in a complex set of events. Coal mining was a highly speculative and competitive industry with volatile prices and narrow profit margins. Northern Pacific and OIC faced stiff competition from other operators in Washington and British Columbia. Success in selling a commodity like coal is based almost exclusively on price. Inflated labor costs could price them out of business.

Closer examination of the white miners reveals a workforce largely powerless in the face of employers. More to the point, they were dependent on them. After a 10- or 12-hour day working in company mines, they returned home to company-owned housing. They bought goods in the company store and relaxed over a beer in the company saloon. Much of what they consumed was purchased on credit, leading to debts subtracted from the paycheck. Facing intolerable conditions and intractable ownership, miners used the only leverage they possessed – their feet, to walk off the job. When the replacement miners arrived, they took their frustrations out on this new threat.

The black miners were caught in the middle of this struggle. It's inaccurate to label them solely as innocents manipulated by owners and harassed by whites. Most were experienced miners in an industry with a long history of worker strife and a track record of employing substitute labor to break strikes. On the other hand it's clear they had few good choices. When most jobs were unavailable to them, they took what was offered. Responding to an advertisement that promised steady work in "the finest country on earth" must have been an easy decision.

Chinese – the travails of life on "gold mountain"

Chinese began arriving in the United States in the early 1850s when word about the California Gold Rush spread around the globe. The opportunity for riches in California, known as the land of "*gum saan*," or "gold mountain," offered a way out of China, where famine and war ripped through the southern provinces. By 1880, an estimated 105,000 Chinese lived in the United States, with more than 16,000 in Washington, Oregon, and Idaho.[18] Many immigrants were "freemen" who could afford the cost of a ticket to America ($40 to $50). The majority, however, entered into a labor contract with a broker. In exchange for the cost of passage and job placement, immigrating Chinese pledged a percentage of their wages.[19]

Like African Americans, opportunities were limited for Chinese immigrants who faced discrimination and hostility in almost all areas of life. They mostly worked jobs white men scoffed at. On the railroads, they performed both the most menial and most dangerous tasks. The Northern Pacific Railroad recruited more than 21,000 Chinese in 1882 to build its line through Montana, Idaho, and Washington territory.[20] To blast tunnels, the railroad used Chinese for the extremely hazardous job of setting charges. Later those same crews cleared away the rubble in wheelbarrows. Life was much the same for Chinese working in the gold and coal mines in Idaho and Washington and the forests of Oregon. In towns and cities, they were relegated to the backbreaking, repetitive work at the lumber mills, canneries, and waterfront. They became a growing presence in service jobs such as cooks, domestic help, and laundrymen. In spite of racial tensions, they offered an attractive source of labor for cost-conscious employers consistently coping with labor shortages. White workers tended to tolerate them, especially during the high points in the frequent economic cycles. Such tolerance disappeared, however, during downturns like those in 1873 and 1893, when jobs were scarce for everyone.

Also like African Americans, the Chinese presented a competitive threat to white labor. They worked for lower wages and crossed picket lines during strikes. They frequently attempted to break out on their own. In the gold fields, they worked the

Figure 7.3 The region's salmon industry, including this Kingfisher cannery in Bellingham, Washington, photographed in 1899, depended on Chinese labor. Thanks to improvements in handling and canning, Northwest salmon became a staple of the working class on the East Coast, Great Britain and Australia in early twentieth century. Image reprinted with permission from the Washington State Historical Society.

less-profitable sites abandoned by whites. They ventured into fishing and farming, selling their goods at below-market prices.

But the Chinese presented a threat beyond economic competition. Unlike other racial minorities, they threatened the dominance of white culture. African slaves were forced to adopt Western norms in the eighteenth century. Within a few generations they created a singular culture that was mostly Western yet uniquely African American. In the nineteenth century, government assimilation policies pressured Native Peoples into abandoning their language, religions, dress, and traditional rituals. So by the latter decades of the nineteenth century, the people of the Pacific Northwest largely displayed an all-American sameness in dress, language, and even religion – except the Chinese. Because many anticipated returning to China after accumulating sufficient savings to support their families at home, they stubbornly clung to their ways. They stood out in the territories, an irritating reminder to whites. Young Ruby Chapin in Tacoma commented on their appearance. She said Native men "dressed like the white men," but the Chinese "looked very queer, with a pigtail that hung down their backs."[21]

With anti-Chinese activity erupting throughout the region, territorial governments and the unions representing white workers began pressuring the federal government to do something about the "Chinese problem." In May 1882, President Chester A. Arthur signed into law the Chinese Exclusion Act. This treaty with the Chinese Government severely restricted Chinese from entering America and required the deportation of any who arrived after 1880. The act stated that, "in the opinion of the Government of the United States the coming of Chinese laborers to this country endangers the good order of certain localities within the territory ..."[22]

The treaty appears to have spurred rather than deterred violence. In 1885, the American West roiled in anti-Chinese violence. In September, in an incident beyond the pale, 28 Chinese were murdered and 15 injured in Rock Springs, Wyoming. Gangs of white miners angered because management assigned Chinese to the richer areas of the mine, raged through town, burning homes and shooting residents. Five days later, near what is now Issaquah, Washington, people from two races conspired against a third. A gang of white and Native hop pickers attacked a Chinese camp, killing three and wounding three others. The following week, in Pierce City, Idaho, white vigilantes lynched five Chinese accused of murdering a white merchant, D.M. Fraser. While frontier attitudes often condoned quick justice for the guilty, there was little or no evidence against the accused.[23]

The Tacoma Method – organized vigilantism at gunpoint

The Tacoma expulsion is noteworthy, not due to the body count, but because of how it went down. Following months of agitation, town meetings, and threats, city officials took action. In November, on prearranged signals, "committees" of men, led by Tacoma Mayor Jacob Robert Weisbach and the Tacoma Police, stormed through town, busting down doors and rousting Chinese from their homes and businesses. It's not clear how young Ms. Chapman immediately reacted. More than likely she stood by helplessly as family servants or hotel employees were forcefully removed from the premises. All told, armed vigilantes ushered more than 200 Chinese to the Northern Pacific Railroad depot, where they boarded the southbound train the following morning. Two Chinese died from exposure during the night. Later, the small "Chinatown" on Tacoma's waterfront mysteriously burned.

Many alcohol-fueled incidences of anti-Chinese violence ignited spontaneously. The Tacoma expulsion stands out because it was planned and organized; not a spur-of-the-moment tragedy, but a well-thought-out eviction. It became known as the "Tacoma Method." While the term was meant derogatorily by citizens who found the expulsion distasteful, it fits. The Tacoma incident was organized and timed from the beginning. As early as September, posters screaming, "The Chinese Must Go!," or "Chinese? No! No! No!" invited residents to town meetings to "consider the Chinese question."[24] The leaders were not intoxicated union workers, but community leaders, elected officials, and union organizers intent on purging their town of the foreign presence.

Other cities, including Seattle, employed aspects of the Tacoma Method. On February 7, 1886, armed men ushered about 350 Chinese to the Seattle waterfront, where 200 were loaded onto a San Francisco bound steamer, with the remainder spending the night on the docks. When police attempted to restore order and escort the Chinese back to their homes the following morning, a riot broke out among whites in which five were wounded and one died.

Later in February, members of the local Knights of Labor and Anti-Coolie League marched to a boarding house in Oregon City where 40 to 50 Chinese millworkers slept.

The armed men rousted the Chinese from their beds and hustled them down to the Willamette River and the steamboat *Latona*, which ferried them to Portland. Police arrested the mob's leaders but charges were later dismissed.

Caroline Leighton – observing Washington Territory

The writer, Caroline C. Leighton, who moved from Boston to Washington Territory with her husband in 1865, found much to admire in the Chinese. *Life At Puget Sound*, published in 1884, is replete with anecdotes of the people and landscape of the Pacific Northwest. Their "China boy," Ah Sing, a servant was "very impulsive and enthusiastic" and "almost too zealous to learn." The Leightons gave Sing English lessons and he repeated words "over and over to himself, with great emphasis while he is washing the clothes." Leighton was equally struck with how "The Chinese stand in great awe of their grandmothers." Where Western culture values youth, Leighton observed, the Chinese "woman increases in value" as she ages. "The young girl who is a slave to her mother can look forward to the prospect of being a goddess to her grandchildren." (Caroline C. Leighton, *Life At Puget Sound* (Boston: Lee and Shepard Publishers, 1884), 168.

But Tacoma's methodical approach to expelling Chinese remains a notorious standard for this nineteenth-century version of ethnic cleansing. Ringleaders who led the purge were prosecuted but not convicted. The Chinese presence was effectively wiped out in Tacoma in a span of two months. They did not begin returning to the city in any great numbers until after World War II.

Clashing with "mongoloid races" in Idaho's goldfields

Tensions enveloped the Idaho goldfields. Chinese first appeared in the territory in 1860 following a gold strike on the North Fork of the Clearwater River, the first of many over the next decade. By 1870, more than 4,200 Chinese resided in Idaho, mostly working mines from Coeur d'Alene to Boise.[25] In a pattern repeated throughout the West, the Chinese – unwelcome in mining camps except as labor – oftentimes struck out on their own. Patient, painstakingly thorough and willing to accept the smallest of profits, they worked areas abandoned or ignored by white miners or mining companies. In placer mines, where gold was panned in streambeds, the Chinese picked through every pebble and sandbar. They muscled rock and boulders for a payoff too small to interest mining companies using expensive removal equipment.

When it proved impossible to stop wildcat digs, local governments copied tactics employed during the California Gold Rush decades earlier. They enacted "foreign miners" taxes or required licenses, potentially wiping out the miniscule profits. A law passed by the Idaho territorial legislature in 1864 targeted all Chinese, not just miners. It said "all Mongolians, whether male or female, and of whatever occupation, shall be considered foreigners and shall pay a license tax of four dollars for each and every month they reside in the territory."[26]

Explaining the enmity against Chinese remains a challenge. Historians agree that class, racial and cultural issues coupled with fierce economic competition, spurred a level of violence extreme even by Western standards.

Tensions and jealousies peaked in May 1887 when a group of white men entered a Chinese camp at night on the Oregon side of the Snake River and murdered as many as 34 Chinese miners. The victims were shot, their bodies stripped and mutilated, and thrown into the river. The invaders stole gold dust valued at about $5,000, a sizable load in the late nineteenth century. The crime went undiscovered until bodies were found floating 60 miles north near Lewiston, Idaho.[27] The savagery heaped on the victims suggests this was more hate crime than robbery. James H. Slater, a U.S. Senator from Oregon, urged the Oregon Attorney General to investigate "a most daring outrage on a camp of unoffending Chinamen …"[28]

For modern readers, explaining the enmity against Chinese remains a challenge. Historians agree that class, racial, and cultural issues coupled with fierce economic competition, spurred a level of violence extreme by Western standards. Whites tended to tolerate Chinese as long as they confined their presence to jobs few white men wanted. But when they sought better jobs or ventured into more lucrative industries trouble brewed, especially during hard times. Whites believed employers deliberately hired Chinese to drive down labor costs. The possibility of whites working for the same pay as the "mongoloid races" was reprehensible.

White paranoia is evident in a letter written by a former Tacoma city official who participated in the expulsion. James Wickersham, a delegate for the Alaskan Territory in 1916, attempted to justify his actions in Tacoma 31 years earlier. According to Wickersham, whites in the Pacific Northwest feared "being confronted by millions of industrious hard-working" Chinese, who would outdo their white neighbors and "gain possession of the Pacific coast of America."[29]

While such fears proved unfounded, it's important to view the Chinese as more than victims. While there is no question the Chinese were exploited and victimized, such events tell only part of the story. We should not ignore the many accomplishments of the Chinese and their successful efforts to resist exclusion. They challenged discriminatory taxes in court, skirted immigration restrictions, refused to obey court-ordered evictions and armed themselves with Colt revolvers and Bowie knives. An editor at the *Idaho World* wrote, "A Chinaman is slow to deeds of desperation, but when he starts in he generally means business."[30]

The Pacific Northwest offered economic opportunity for the ambitious, and the Chinese were certainly that. It's also worth noting that Chinese who migrated to the United States in the nineteenth century were better off than most of those who remained in their home provinces. While Chinese were fighting for their rightful place in the Idaho economy, millions were dying in a civil war known as the Taiping Rebellion and other conflicts (1851–1864).[31]

Cultural differences and stereotypes help to explain white fears. In addition to retaining traditional dress and hairstyles, Chinese carried over other cultural practices. They loved games of chance and operated gambling houses in Boise, Idaho City, as well as in Oregon and Washington. They viewed gambling as a social activity, whereas white residents saw it as a source of crime and violence. Opium often spurred white angst as much as dice or playing cards. While most Chinese were only casual users, it disgusted most whites and reinforced the stereotype that all Chinese were opium addicts.[32]

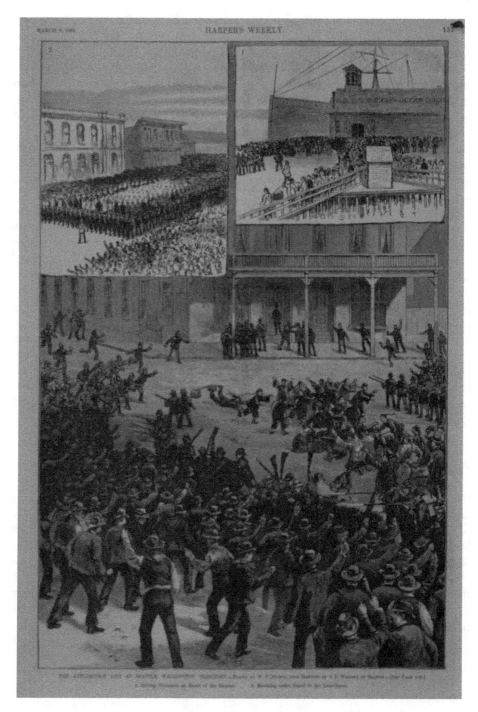

Figure 7.4 On February 7, 1886, armed men ushered about 350 Chinese to the Seattle waterfront, where 200 were loaded onto a San Francisco bound steamer, with the remainder spending the night on the docks. When police attempted to escort the Chinese back to their homes, a riot broke out in which a man was killed and five wounded. Image reprinted with permission from the Washington State Historical Society.

Whites held no monopoly on aggressive behavior. Chinese often met violence with violence, especially to settle disputes among themselves. Much of the Chinese population in the Boise Basin belonged to one of two clans: the See Yup and the Yung Wah. Economic competition created tensions that often erupted into clan violence. In October 1872, a shooting in an Idaho City meat market between opposing gang members erupted into open warfare. Gun battles in the streets during the day and sniper shootings at night went on for days. The conflict subsided only after a committee of whites led by Sheriff Samuel Stewart brought the warring clans together.[33] Chinese also resorted to violence to settle disputes with whites. In 1870, white and Chinese miners argued over water usage at Mores Creek near Idaho City. Three Chinese men, Hen Lee, Ah Teung, and Sam Sing, were arrested for shooting Edward Cahill through the neck. They were later acquitted for a lack of evidence.[34]

Although the Chinese faced hostility, fear, and misunderstanding, they enjoyed a measure of success in Idaho. The Chinese and white communities eventually learned to peacefully coexist. Many returned to China, although their meager pickings in the mines made that difficult. Most carved out a livable wage, living in the minefields for years, while others moved into the cities. Importantly, many Chinese in Idaho adopted aspects of Western culture while whites grew more tolerant and understanding. Some Chinese converted to Christianity while others opened businesses that catered to all. Ah Fong Chuck, a herbalist, acupuncturist, and medical practitioner, immigrated to the United States in the 1860s and attended to Chinese in the camps. Later he opened a clinic and apothecary in Boise, treating Asians and whites alike.[35] In 1901, Ah Fong won the legal right to practice medicine, making him one of the first licensed acupuncturists to practice in America. In another example of racial intermingling, people from the Chinese community participated in Red Cross activities during World War I, suggesting support for both local and national values.[36]

A century and a half of change

Racial tensions in the Pacific Northwest did not end so much as fade away with changing laws and attitudes. It took a Civil War and the death of more than 600,000 Americans to resolve the slavery question. However, racialist attitudes and white supremacy persisted long afterward. African American struggles for equality continue today, but climaxed with the Civil Rights Movement in the 1950s and 1960s. The Chinese Exclusion Law effectively arrested Chinese immigration for nearly a half century. In 1920, 38 years after the law's enactment, there were about 6,000 Chinese in the region, two-thirds fewer than the peak year of 1880.[37] Immigrants from China would not return in any measurable numbers until after World War II and the relaxation of U.S. immigration laws.

European immigration – overlooked stories of the American West

Racial and ethnic minorities played leading roles in the saga of the Pacific Northwest. But sometimes lost in that great drama are the contributions of European immigrants. In the late nineteenth and early twentieth centuries, tens of thousands of newcomers from throughout Europe sought new homes and jobs in the region. For many it was Part Two in their American journey, having previously settled and farmed in Midwestern states like Wisconsin, Minnesota, and North and South Dakota.

Most settled near Puget Sound, where they became a permanent fixture in the fisheries and other industries. Logging drew thousands to the mills and forests from Bellingham to Centralia. In 1900, more than 10,000 Scandinavians worked in Washington's wood industry. East of the mountains, Scandinavian farmers found the wheat growing regions near Spokane and the Palouse irresistible for its affordable land and rich soil.[38] By the first decade of the twentieth century, European immigrants had carved out a life in the region's extractive industries.

"European immigrants are the forgotten people of the American West," whose stories do not fit well in to the accepted narrative of Western history, wrote historian Frederick Luebke.[39] According to Luebke, recent historical work has focused on the conflicts between whites and Native Peoples, Mexicans, Asians and African Americans. Historians have paid less attention to the stories of European immigrant groups, such as the "Irish laborer, Slavic minors, Scandinavian loggers, Italian truck farmers, Basque shepherds, Jewish peddlers, or German farmers," according to Luebke. They too faced discrimination and warrant the researcher's attention.[40]

Country of Origin	Idaho	%	Wash.	%	Oregon	%
England	7,290	7.9	25,519	4.9	16,394	4
Germany	8,579	5.3	43,555	8.4	36,547	8.8
Ireland	5,643	3.5	23,548	4.6	14,058	3.4
Norway	2,766	1.7	18,814	3.6	5,566	1.4
Scotland	3,044	1.9	10,013	1.9	6,542	1.6
Sweden	5,522	3.4	21,361	4.1	8,270	2
Totals	**32,843**	**23.7**	**142,810**	**27.5**	**87,377**	**21.2**

Figure 7.5 By 1900 European immigrants made up nearly a quarter of the Pacific Northwest population. Many were on their second stop in America, having initially settled in the Midwest. The availability of affordable farmland, and strong job growth in the extraction industries drew them even further west. *Source*: Data courtesy Washington State Historical Society. U.S. Bureau of the Census, *Census Reports, vol. 1 Twelfth Census of the United States, 1900*.

Doc Hay and generous medicine – a prescription for cultural acceptance

With the history of violence against Asians and other minority groups, it's easy to overlook immigrant success stories. Thousands of foreign born made a good life in the Pacific Northwest, building a business, starting a family, and in some cases, leaving a legacy.

That's the case with Ing "Doc" Hay, a medical practitioner who treated the people of John Day and much of Southeastern Oregon – Chinese and American alike – for six decades. Doc Hay practiced "pulsology," which involves treating ailments based on "pulse signals," and distributed herbal remedies.[41]

Figure 7.6 Ing "Doc" Hay practiced "pulsology" to treat the medical needs of the people of John Day and much of Southeastern Oregon. Image reprinted with permission from the Kam Wah Chung State Heritage Site.

Born in Guangdong Province China, Hay immigrated to Washington in the 1880s, leaving behind a wife and two children. In 1887, he relocated to John Day and joined the Kam Wah Chung Company, a general store and trading post. With that as a home base, Hay and his partner Lung On attended the medical needs of Chinese working in the gold mines. When the mines were played out and most Chinese had moved on, his practice broadened to Americans who visited him for everything from frostbite to infertility. According to the Kam Wah Chung & Co. Museum, Hay's herbal concoctions – sometimes known as "Doc Hay's sacks of bitter weeds" – were steeped in broth or water, pulverized, or coated with oil or honey.[42]

Hay's popularity with local residents didn't always forestall trouble. In 1905, a mob raided the Kam Wah Chung store upon rumors it was selling opium. Lung On and two other Chinese were ordered to leave town, but On remained and pleaded not guilty. He was acquitted. Local medical doctors, whose businesses were threatened by Hay and On, frequently complained to local law enforcement. Hay was charged three times with practicing medicine without a license, although those charges were also dismissed.[43]

Hay's generosity may have helped him find favor in the courts. In addition to funneling much of his earnings to his family in China, Hay was also generous with his patients. After his death, friends found over $23,000 in uncashed checks from his patients, some written during the Great Depression. Hay retired in 1948 and died in Portland four years later. Upon his request the Kam Wah Chung building was deeded to the City of John Day to be used as an interpretive center and museum. The Kam Wah Chung State Heritage Site in John Day is open May through October.[44]

Explore more

With a growing consensus that "race matters," Pacific Northwest historians have produced an impressive body of research on the minority experience over the last 30 years.

Books

Two outstanding works detailing the struggles facing Chinese immigrants are *Strangers From a Different Shore, A History of Asian Americans* by Ronald Takaki; and Liping Zhu's *A Chinaman's Chance: The Chinese on the Rocky Mountain Mining Frontier*. For a perspective on how white society in the West conspired to marginalize all people of color see *The Legacy of Conquest* by Patricia Nelson Limerick.

Online

Blackpast.org (http://www.blackpast.org/),the online reference guide to African American history, was started in 2004 by University of Washington Professor Quintard Taylor. Initially focused on the Pacific Northwest, the site now serves as an online reference guide to African American history throughout the nation and the world.

Museums

Two Seattle museums, located close enough to be visited on the same day, reveal the rich histories of the region's minority groups: the Wing Luke Museum (http://www.wingluke.org/); and the Northwest African American Museum (http://www.naamnw.org/).

What do you think?

How would you explain the antipathy towards racial minorities in the West in the nineteenth and twentieth centuries? How did the African American experience differ from that of other minorities? What drove the fear and violence towards Chinese? Did all anti-Chinese incidences fall into the same pattern? If not, how was the 1885 Tacoma expulsion different? How would you characterize racial conflict of the past versus that in American cities in the twenty-first century? How did the experiences of European immigrants differ from that of people of color?

Notes

1 Ruby Chapin Blackwell, *A Girl in Washington Territory* (Tacoma, WA: Washington State Historical Society, 1972), 21.
2 Richard White, *It's Your Misfortune and None of My Own, A New History of the American West* (Norman, OK: University of Oklahoma Press, 1991), 320.
3 Patricia Nelson Limerick, *The Legacy of Conquest* (New York: W.W. Norton & Company, 1988) 19.
4 "Oregon's Exclusion Laws, Race Was Central to the Debate over Oregon Statehood," Oregon Historical Society, History Minutes, accessed October 19, 2016, http://www.ohs.org/.

5 Darrell Millner, "George Bush of Tumwater: Founder of the First American Colony on Puget Sound," *Columbia Magazine*, Winter 1994/95, 14–19.

6 Abe Proctor, "Bogle Family Brings Barbershops to City," *The Skanner*, 2005.

7 C. Peter Ripley, ed., *The Black Abolitionist Papers Volume 4, The United States, 1847–1858* (Chapel Hill, NC: University of North Carolina Press, 1991), 103–104. Quoted in Quintard Taylor, *The History of African Americans in the West*, accessed November 8, 2016, http://faculty.washington.edu/qtaylor/Courses/313.

8 Archives of the Oregon Historical Society, quoted in Quintard Taylor, *The History of African Americans in the West*, accessed November 8, 2016 http://www.quintardtaylor. com.

9 U.S. Census Bureau. For a more detailed review of African Americans in the West see Lee Billington and Roger D. Hardaway, eds., *African Americans on the Western Frontier* (Boulder, CO: University Press of Colorado, 1998)

10 Quintard Taylor, "A History of Blacks in the Pacific Northwest, 1788–1970," unpublished Ph.D. diss., University of Minnesota, 1977. Quoted from *Through Open Eyes (Ninety-Five Years of Black History in Roslyn, Washington)*, accessed February 2, 2014, http://www. blackpast.org.

11 Robert A. Campbell, "Blacks and The Coal Mines of Western Washington," in *African Americans on the Western Frontier*, Monroe Lee Billington and Roger D. Hardaway, eds (Niwot, CO: University Press Colorado, 1998), 98.

12 Ibid.

13 Campbell, "Blacks and the Coal Mines of Western Washington," 99.

14 Ibid., 100.

15 Ibid., 101.

16 Ibid., 102.

17 Ibid., 104.

18 "Industrialization, Class, and Race; Chinese and the Anti-Chinese Movement in the Late 19th-Century Northwest," Center for the Study of the Pacific Northwest, accessed October 19, 2016, http://www.washington.edu/uwired/outreach/cspn/Website/index.html.

19 Liping Zhu, *A Chinaman's Chance: The Chinese on the Rocky Mountain Mining Frontier* (Boulder, CO: University Press of Colorado, 1997), 22.

20 White, *It's Your Misfortune and None of My Own*, 283.

21 Blackwell, *A Girl in Washington Territory*, 20–21

22 "Chinese Exclusion Act; May 6, 1882," The Avalon Project at Yale Law School, accessed October 19, 2016, http://avalon.law.yale.edu/.

23 Zhu, *A Chinaman's Chance*, 171.

24 Washington State History Museum Collections Online, accessed October 19, 2016, http://www.washingtonhistory.org/, Two broadsides dated 1885 and 1892.

25 Center for the Study of the Pacific Northwest, accessed October 19, 2016, http://www. washington.edu/uwired/outreach/cspn/Website/index.html.

26 Zhu, *A Chinaman's Chance*, 133.

27 "The Chinese Massacre at Douglas Bar, Snake River," Idaho State Historical Society Reference Series, No. 441, 1967.

28 Gregory, R. Nokes, "A Most Daring Outrage," Murder at Chinese Massacre Cove, "1887," *Oregon Historical Quarterly*, 107, No. 3 (2006), 344.

29 James Wickersham to Herbert Hunt, April 21, 1916, 2.

30 Zhu, *A Chinaman's Chance*, 150.

31 Ibid., 4.

32 Ibid., 81–82.

33 Ibid., 149–150.

34 Ibid., 151.

35 "C.K. Ah Fong – 1845–1927," Idaho State Historical Society Reference Series, No. 1130, 1996, accessed March 14, 2015, https://history.idaho.gov.

36 "Changing Perceptions of Idaho's Chinese Population," Idaho State Historical Society Reference Series, No. 896, 1988, accessed March 14, 2015, https://history.idaho.gov/.

37 "Class, and Race; Chinese and the Anti-Chinese Movement in the Late 19th-Century Northwest," Center for the Study of the Pacific Northwest, accessed August 3, 2013, http://www.washington.edu.

38 Jorgen Dahlie, "Old World Paths in the New: Scandinavians Find A Familiar Home in Washington," in *Experiences in a Promised Land*, G. Thomas Edwards, Carlos A. Schwantes, eds. (Seattle, WA: University of Washington Press, 1986), 101.

39 Frederick Luebke, ed, *European Immigrants: American West Community Histories*, (Albuquerque, NM: University of New Mexico Press, 1998), xii.

40 Ibid., vii–viii.

41 Jodi, Varon, "Ing Hay ('Doc Hay') (1862–1952)," Kam Wah Chung & Co. Museum, accessed October 19, 2016, http://oregonencyclopedia.org/articles/ing_doc_hay_1862_1952_/".VqpZL1J8Eec.

42 Ibid.

43 Ibid.

44 Ibid.

8

Liberation in the West

In a society as unsettled as the land, women gain newfound recognition and rights

> *The pioneer spirit was about more than gritty settlers coping with hardship, heartache, and hard work. It also required an openness to new ideas and ways of doing things. Everyone was needed to pitch in and do their part in building homesteads and permanent communities. Working side by side with the men in their lives, Pacific Northwest women managed to achieve an unprecedented level of independence and break through the cultural, economic, and political boundaries that impeded most women in the East.*

Like most Americans, Dr. Katherine Manion of Portland found herself enveloped in a storm of patriotic fever when the United States entered World War I in April 1917. She wanted to serve her country and bring her medical skills to the battlefields of Europe. The following spring, Manion and three other female physicians, Drs. Mae Cardwell, Mary MacLachlan, and Emily Balcom visited the Army's medical training center in Vancouver, Washington, to apply for a military commission. By the second decade of the twentieth century, women had made notable inroads into traditional male bastions like higher education, law, and medicine. About 6% of the country's doctors were female.[1]

Eager to serve, the four women presented themselves to the major in charge at the training center. Anticipating resistance, they displayed impressive credentials: diplomas from reputable universities, licenses, references, and testimonials from patients – by all measures, qualified physicians capable saving lives in battle. They had reviewed the military's requirements, which made no mention of gender, and believed they met all conditions.[2] Unfortunately, the nonplused Army major didn't see it that way. He knew no precedent for enlisting women doctors. "It hasn't been done," he declared, which led to a "long debate." As a compromise, he invited the women to enlist as nurses, a non-commissioned position, but they refused. "Would you?" one asked.[3]

To end the stalemate, the major passed the buck to the Surgeon General in Washington, D.C., William Crawford Gorgas, who telegraphed back the following day. He would not permit women doctors to enter the U.S. Army as commissioned officers. A disappointed, nevertheless proud Manion later told a reporter she considered it a distinction to have challenged the Army's restrictive policies.[4]

Contested Boundaries: A New Pacific Northwest History, First Edition. David J. Jepsen and David J. Norberg.
© 2017 John Wiley & Sons, Ltd. Published 2017 by John Wiley & Sons, Ltd.

A World War I story is appropriate here because the doctors were four of countless women who challenged the barriers that repressed women for most of recorded history. This essay will show that the history of the Pacific Northwest is in part a triumphant tale of women who fought for and found liberties denied to women elsewhere in America: pioneer women who exerted their moral authority in the male-dominated West; working-class women who demanded equal pay and fair treatment on the job; European immigrants intent on building stable communities in mining and fishing towns; and middle-class women who exercised their emerging independence if only to exercise their constitutional rights. Add to their stories those of minority women who faced dual challenges: African Americans battling racialist attitudes and exclusionary policies; Native Peoples resisting government assimilation policies; and Chinese immigrants building lives in a strange land where they were not wanted.

Despite these challenges, why did women in the Pacific Northwest appear to win rights ahead of those in other parts of America? What cultural and economic factors contributed to their success? The historian Richard Etulain asked whether the frontier experience was "liberating." Did life in the West encourage pioneers to break with the traditions and culture of Eastern society? Finally, how should we assess the men of the West? What role did they play in improving women's lives? Were husbands, fathers, and brothers also liberated by the Western experience?[5]

Historians agree women played a critical role in the West from the earliest presence of Euro-Americans. The first white women known to cross the Rocky Mountains, Protestant missionaries Narcissa Whitman, Eliza Spalding, and Mary Richardson Walker, arrived in Oregon Territory in the 1830s intent on, as they saw it, civilizing and Christianizing Native Peoples. While their prejudices and contempt for their potential converts often proved counter-productive (see Chapter 3), they set the course of future generations of missionaries for over a century.[6]

Women ventured West in greater numbers following passage of the Donation Land Claim Act of 1850. To promote settlement, the government offered single men 320 acres free, and if they were married, their wives could claim an additional 320 acres. The great land giveaway prompted tens of thousands of men and women to migrate West over the Oregon Trail. While young single men sought the riches of California gold mines, families looking to farm, start a homestead, and build a community mostly ventured to Oregon.

Thanks to novels, movies, and television, women in the West suffer from multiple stereotypes. The first, what historian Glenda Riley called the "Saint in the Sunbonnet," sat passively on the buckboard of the covered wagon while her husband blazed trails and fought natives. The second, the Annie Oakley wannabe, dressed and acted like men, smoked, spat, and could shoot a bear from 200 yards. The third worked in the saloon, a hard-nosed madam ruling over a den of fallen women practicing the "world's oldest profession."[7] Mary Josephine Welch, known as Chicago Joe, was just such a woman. She moved from Chicago in the 1860s and opened a dance hall in Helena, Montana. She imported young women, known as "hurdy-gurdy girls," to dance with men for a dollar.[8]

In reality, most female pioneers were wives and mothers overwhelmed by the excessive violence and immorality in western towns. Historians offer conflicting views of women pioneers. Some describe them as unwilling victims in their husbands' quest for a new life, land, or riches. Dragged grudgingly into a harsh land, she lived in a lonely, dreary place, permanently removed from friends and family. Others paint a more positive picture of women who sought their own opportunities, free from the shackles of Eastern communities.[9]

The historian Catherine Clinton offers insightful questions. Did the advantages of western migration outweigh the hardships? Did the fact women had to frequently take on men's work open new opportunities? Did the scarcity of women in the West clear a path to equal rights, including the right of exercising their franchise?[10]

Clinton argues the pioneer experience gave women confidence and abilities mostly unavailable in the East. Men expected their wives to contribute as a partner in building a homestead. It's reasonable to suggest that their daughters – a second generation of pioneering women – carried the same spirit of freedom and accomplishment, unbound by Eastern social conventions.[11]

Women serve as the moral authority

Mining and logging towns were overwhelmingly male, although women worked in the camps as cooks and dining hall staff. Few churches and schools could be found, but there was no shortage of saloons, bordellos, and opium dens. The only constant was crime. Mining towns, declared one Idaho school teacher, were "the hardest place to live upon principle I ever saw, and the young are almost sure to be led away."[12] According to the western historian Richard White, women pioneers looked to Victorian values and the Protestant Church "to stabilize a rootless and dangerous social world" of the American West.

> Women and merchants both sought the protection of a Christian home and became allies in civilizing the West. The merchant counted his return in profits, the woman in morality.

What western towns needed most was permanency. The restless men inhabiting mining and logging towns showed no interest in putting down roots. They shifted aimlessly from one job to another, spending hard-won earnings on satisfying base needs. White argues that brothels and saloons were profitable businesses, but destructive to a stable community because they violated American standards of morality and decency.[13] Merchants, whose long-term profits depended on a viable community, welcomed the female influence. Women and merchants both sought the protection of a Christian home and became allies in shaping the West in their own image. The merchant counted his return in profits, the woman in morality.[14]

The answer lay not in eliminating vice, but in controlling it, and the presence of women provided a means for control. Shaped by Eastern standards, what the historian Barbara Welter called the "cult of true womanhood," women began to reshape Western communities in their own image.[15] In her examination of nineteenth-century women's literature, Welter uncovered four virtues by which society judged women – "piety, purity, submissiveness, and domesticity." Perceived as naturally religious, women supposedly found strength and direction in worship. Men were advised to look first for piety in choosing a woman. Purity was the byproduct of a woman's piety. She was expected to resist carnal urges until her wedding night, "the single great event of a woman's life." Once married, the woman was expected to give up control of her life and submit to her husband's wishes. Women may be the guiding moral light in the family, but the man was

Figure 8.1 Two women carry picket signs to support workers striking over minimum wages near Multnomah County, Oregon, in 1913. The state legislature was considering a minimum wage bill to protect "the lives, health and morals of women and minor workers." Image reprinted with permission from the Washington State Historical Society.

the doer. Her role was in the domestic sphere, tending to children and home, while the husband boldly made a place for himself in the world.[16]

As the Industrial Revolution unfolded, man's place was found more and more in the cities and factories, allowing women to slowly strengthen their grip on the home. Increasingly the "guardians" of hearth and home raised the bar on building a moral community, and brought that mentality with them to the West.[17] As women and children came West, the Protestant Church soon followed. Ministers intent on serving white settlers emerged as a driving force in bringing morality to a community. Women and their ministers sat at the center of the growing circle of community members intent on taking the wild out of the Wild West.[18] As a community's moral leaders, women asked the obvious question: Should they not exercise moral authority outside the home as much as within? Should not the standard bearers of decency in the parlor dictate the standards in the political hall?[19] That profound idea would take root and grow like wheat on the prairie over the succeeding decades.

Working-class labor in farm yard and factory

While middle-class women sought morality, the working class needed and found jobs in Western cities that were bursting at the seams. With extraction industry jobs not open to them, women worked in restaurants, hotels, stores, laundries and private homes. The first female workers cannot be found in labor statistics – the countless mothers and daughters who worked on the farm to supplement family income. They labored over "put out" or piecework, selling butter, eggs, vegetables, and other farm products. Others leveraged their skills weaving, dying, and sewing garments.[20]

Increasingly, women in the West took city jobs to escape the grind of the working farm. The never-ending work, limited opportunities of rural life, and a stifling patriarchal environment could choke the life out of many young women. The complaints of a young newlywed in Hamlin Garland's autobiographical novel, *Main-Traveled Roads*, illustrate the point. "I have a farm-life ... It's nothing but fret, fret, and work the whole time, never going any place, never seeing anybody but a lot of neighbors just as big fools as you are. I spend my time fighting flies and washing dishes and churning. I'm sick of it."[21]

Abigail Scott Duniway, Oregon's famous suffragist and newspaper publisher, wrote about her life as a frontier farmer's wife in Oregon in the 1850s. She recalled "washing, scrubbing, churning, or nursing the baby" while preparing meals in a "lean-to kitchen." "To bear two children in two and a half years from my marriage day, to make thousands of pounds of butter every year for market ... to sew and cook, and wash and iron; to bake and clean and stew and fry; to be, in short, a general pioneer drudge, with never a penny of my own, was not pleasant business for an erstwhile school teacher ..." Duniway would spend half of her life raising awareness of the hardships of womanhood.[22]

Men weren't the only ones moving to the city. In the last decades of the nineteenth century, women left the farm in equivalent numbers to men. For over a half century beginning in 1880, the female population in Western cities rose steadily. According to the 1920 census, for every 20 farm boys, as many as 30 farm girls moved from rural to urban settings, leading to a dramatic turnaround in the gender makeup of male-dominated Western towns. "The farmer's daughter is more likely to leave the farm and go to the city than is the farmer's son," read the Census Bureau report.[23]

Certainly the profound poverty of the rural Northwest drove young women to the city, but many were rejecting something more fundamental. The very meaning of womanhood was in question. They sought independence and denounced "separate spheres and the self-sacrificing wife," as well the stifling protection of the men in her life.[24]

A 1913 Department of Agriculture survey confirmed women's rejection of the Jeffersonian vision of "Republican Motherhood." Women complained about being overworked, the limits placed on their lives, the lack of educational and vocational opportunities and "old fashioned" male attitudes about a woman's place in the world. "Isolation, stagnation, ignorance, loss of ambition, the incessant grind of labor," one woman wrote, "are all working against the farm woman's happiness."[25]

Many women found escape in the classroom. A Washington State mandate to provide all children with an eighth-grade education created a demand for teachers and job opportunities for young women. To meet its mandate, the state opened teacher colleges, called normal schools, in Cheney in 1890, Ellensburg in 1891, and Bellingham in 1904. Initially, they offered free tuition to students who committed to teach for two years. Most teachers were young, white, Protestant women from farming families. Because state law required teachers to remain single, they had to delay marriage. Most quit after two years to pursue a family, but many stayed on, dependent on the steady but paltry pay.[26]

Teaching offered intellectual and social opportunities not available in the home. Normal schools required student teachers to participate in women's clubs and literary societies. Once on the job they led afterschool opportunities for students, volunteered at the Young Women's Christian Association (YWCA), and tackled social issues like temperance and homeless children. Teachers relished in the intellectual challenges and lifelong friendships that came with public life.[27] Participation in clubs and other institutions, wrote historian Karen J. Blair, "created an impressive force for educational improvement in the Pacific Northwest."[28]

Some resented the expectations placed on women once they finished high school – marry or teach. For example, Doris Elder Butler of Oregon, with no marriage prospects, complained that "it seemed that everyone remotely concerned took it for granted that I would follow that custom."[29]

Women in urban areas often sought a different route. In Portland, where only about half the women over age 15 were married, more and more lived independently or in chaperoned boarding homes. Increasingly, young women chafed under the restrictions that came with supervised living. Claimed one young woman who refused to live in the Portland Women's Union home, "the very fact of having to live under restrictions makes it appear as if we are in need of surveillance and incapable of taking care of ourselves, and no girl likes to admit that."[30] Portland's Protestant ministers rebuffed this trend, insisting men needed women at home, as "companions of great & good men, the mothers of the more glorious men of the future."[31]

Beyond a job, the city offered something the countryside could not – the opportunity to determine their own affairs, earn income they didn't have to share with the family, and the chance to be a consumer in the industrial era. With a steady paycheck, women in Western cities were able to spend money, albeit modestly, on clothes, jewelry and makeup. They could dine out and go to the movies. According to the historian Mary Murphy, young women relished in the independence of city life. "Their dress, their assertive presence on the sidewalk, and their flirtatious manners proclaimed their right to share the street" on their own terms.[32]

Therein lies a story within a story. In addition to middle-class women breaking the bonds of "true womanhood," lies a less-told tale of working-class women thriving on independence. The historians Robert V. Hine and John Mack Faragher called them "urban pioneers." "These young women should be given their appropriate place as urban pioneers, side by side with the forty-niners and migrating families in the drama of the moving American."[33]

The rise in female labor was nothing short of astonishing. Between 1900 and 1920, the number of women who held jobs in Seattle, for example, jumped nearly 700% to more than 33,000, nearly double the city's population growth. Even more notable was a 900% jump in working married women, from 881 to 8,203.[34] Such growth can be mostly explained by World War I, when women took jobs vacated by men at war. Mobilizing for war, states the historian Maurine Weiner Greenwald, "conferred new dignity on women's wage work, as businessmen and politicians congratulated women for outstanding contributions to the nation's wartime economic welfare."[35]

Replacing men, of course, meant doing men's work, or jobs exclusively within the male domain. Women occupied semi-skilled jobs in canneries, lumber mills, and machine shops. They drove taxi cabs, assisted electricians, and operated drill presses. Men found all of this more than a little threatening, especially in the tight postwar job market. When owners used women to break strikes, lower wages, and fill jobs deskilled with new technologies, it shined a harsh spotlight on female labor.[36]

Married women further stretched the boundaries of social norms. They too sought independence working outside the home, challenging the fundamental tenants of "civilized society," and the male's role as breadwinner. Society grudgingly accepted widowed, divorced, or even married women who needed income to survive, but not those who simply exercised their individual right to work, regardless of need. In challenging the

Figure 8.2 Women packing salmon at the Pacific American Fisheries cannery in Bellingham, Washington, around 1905. Washington and Oregon eventually passed laws limiting the hours women could work on their feet. A "woman's physical structure" and "maternal functions," the courts ruled, endangered her ability to produce "vigorous offspring." Image reprinted with permission from the Washington State Historical Society.

husband's "exclusive role" as provider, they were rewriting the narrow definition of a woman's role, and shattering the "family ideal." Women began seeing such ideas as out of date and paternalistic.[37] Women wanted the right to choose, to direct their own lives, and to become productive members of society – regardless of their marital status or financial need.[38]

Greenwald researched the *Seattle Union Record*, the official paper of the Washington State Federation of Labor. For two years, during and after World War I, debate raged over whether married women should work. Opponents defended the institution of marriage and "true womanhood" while proponents argued working for wages met a real economic need, fostered independence, and ended social isolation.[39]

Letters to the *Union Record* reveal the veracity of debate. One Seattle woman likened her home to a "mausoleum." "Why should getting married banish women to the kitchen forever after when she is supposed to be free and equal to men?" she asked.[40] Another claimed technology eased the burdens of managing a home. Manufactured clothing, refrigeration, electric appliances, and processed foods freed women's time at unprecedented levels.[41] Others still questioned the very institution of marriage. "There are too many square pegs in round holes," one woman wrote, "and if women enter industry in large numbers, I believe, it will force a reorganization, not only of industries, but of the home – to the advantage of both."[42] Beneath these arguments about equality and economic opportunity lay a more fundamental issue – women's desire to be treated as human beings, for their "individual potential, abilities, talents, intelligence, interests, and achievements ..."[43]

Challenging long hours and low pay

Few women felt more strongly about working rights than Alice Lord, who founded the Seattle Waitresses Union Local 240 in 1900. Waitresses worked 10 to 15 hours a day, seven days a week, for $3 to $6 dollars a week. To draw attention to the woes of waitressing, Lord walked from Seattle to Olympia in 1900 to testify before the state legislature. "You give even your horses one day's rest in seven," she later told the legislators.[44] The next year, Washington enacted a ten-hour day for working women. Lord also pressed for a six-day week, but that did not become law until 1920. She continued to lobby for better wages and working hours, until legislators passed the "Waitresses' Bill," in 1911, making Washington one of the first states to mandate an eight-hour day for women. Two years later, lawmakers approved a $10-per-week minimum wage for women, excluding domestic and agricultural workers.[45]

Washington was not alone in seeking protection for working women. In 1908, the U.S. Supreme Court, in *Muller v. Oregon*, upheld a 1903 Oregon law mandating a ten-hour work day for women. On the grounds that working long hours on her feet jeopardized a woman's ability to procreate, the court ruled unanimously in Oregon's favor. According to the unanimous opinion, "healthy mothers are essential to healthy offspring."[46] In essence the court suggested that women were "different" and warranted protections from their government not available to men. The idea that women were different from, versus equal to, men drove even more maternalistic legislation, but raised the ire of feminists who had long argued for absolute equality.[47]

The idea that women needed protection at work was a logical extension of the cultural norm that women needed protection. Women spent most of their lives under the security of one man or another, first their fathers and then their husbands. Outside the home, women were denied the ballot in part to shield them from the distastefulness of politics and juries. Women should not work, the argument went, but if they must, government owed them safeguards from unhealthy and unsafe working conditions and low pay.[48] For example, in 1913, the Oregon State Legislature considered a bill to establish a female minimum wage, part of a platform of progressive reform that blossomed in Oregon at the turn of the century. The "Oregon System," as it was called, transformed

Oregon's political landscape over three decades, spurring a spate of similar legislation. In the 1912 election, for example, Oregon voters cast ballots on more than 30 state and local initiatives, including women's suffrage. Caroline Gleason, a researcher working for the Consumer League of Oregon, compiled data that proved working women were overworked and underpaid, and lived near poverty (see "Caroline Gleason: Debunking the Myths of Women's Work").

The dual challenge – female and minority

Not all working-class women benefited from progressive legislation, nor fitted the model of true womanhood. Native American, African American, Asian, and other foreign-born women carried multiple burdens. In addition to being female, they struggled with what historians called "otherness" – other than white, other than Christian and other than native born.

Government programs to assimilate Native Peoples in the late nineteenth and early twentieth centuries included an attempted wholesale remaking of women's gender and acceptance of the power they held in Native societies. Men were encouraged to give up hunting and pick up a plow, while well-intended middle-class white women, or "field matrons," pressured native women and girls to embrace the value of true womanhood. The goal: transform women into "chaste, submissive, and nurturing housewives prescribed by the ideology of Victorian womanhood."[49]

Assimilation started with taking control of the woman's offspring. The Bureau of Indian Affairs (BIA) established boarding, mission, and day schools on reservations throughout the Pacific Northwest, including Spokane, Coeur d'Alene, and Salem. The Chemewa Indian School near Salem is the only such school still operating in the region. But our story about Native women exercising their agency is best told though Wendy Hall's examination of records at the Round Valley Reservation 150 miles north of San Francisco. Her study shows that reservation women did not go quietly into home life. Granted, they adopted western dress codes, worked in the service economy, and placed their children in reservation schools – all in an effort to survive – yet some intrusions proved to be out of bounds. From the BIA's viewpoint, the road to civilization was paved with legal marriage, sexual purity, and the separate spheres. Divorce and polygamy, accepted traditions in many tribes, breached Victorian standards.

So too did female ownership of property, made possible under the 1887 Dawes Act, or General Allotment Act, whereby the government divided reservations into individual tracts of land. Families lived on the property but the government held title in trust for 25 years, after which the owner took possession. In Round Valley, married men and single women were allotted ten acres, while married women received only five. Government officials, literally all men, assumed the wife could do with less because she could rely on his support. They did not consider the higher rate of divorce on reservations. More problematic was how officials defined "wife." The law did not recognize unions made under tribal custom. The BIA insisted couples apply for a marriage license and formalize their nuptials in a church or court.[50]

The government expected Native women and girls to become "chaste, submissive, and nurturing housewives prescribed by the ideology of Victorian womanhood."[51]

The reservation superintendent at Round Valley in 1912, Thomas B. Wilson, vigorously enforced government marital policy, pressuring dozens of couples into "legal" marriages. The case of Belle Wilsey, a 41-year-old widow living with a 21-year-old man, illustrates how Native women often broke through the rigid confines of government policy. When directed to marry her live-in boyfriend, Wilsey refused. Beyond stubbornly defying a meddling Indian agent, Wilsey understood inheritance law. As a widow, her allotment passed to her children upon her death, but if she remarried it passed to her husband. The county prosecutor refused to take action, informing Superintendent Wilson that Wilsey committed no crime living with a boyfriend. The law could not compel Wilsey to marry and neither was fornication outside of marriage a crime in California. Wilsey would keep her allotment and her boyfriend.[52]

Reservation boarding schools created another source of friction. In the belief that "the only good Indian is an educated Indian," schools inserted a wedge between mothers and their children. Disapproving of divorce, causal living arrangements, and alcohol consumption, the BIA favored boarding schools over day schools. Only by removing children from the home could they be "sufficiently isolated from the contaminating influence of their home environments."[53]

In addition to reading, writing, and basic math, students took part in programs intended to instill a "love of labor and a habit of working." Instructors drilled the boys in farming and semi-skilled crafts like carpentry and blacksmithing. They served apprenticeships under the gardener, carpenter, stockman, and stablemen. Girls received training in homemaking, sewing, and cooking. Teachers lectured frequently on the importance of moral standards and avoiding premarital sex. Boys and girls were housed and taught separately and seldom allowed to even play together. Educating the "mothers of tomorrow," reformers believed, help to "prepare the ground for the education of generations to come."[54]

In 1891, the BIA enlisted support from the Women's National Indian Association, a reform group. They assigned "field matrons," or "domestic missionaries," to visit the homes and "help put Indian women on "the right basis, which is the home basis." They taught kitting, sewing, ironing, gardening, and bread making. Instructors lectured on temperance, the necessity of attending church and the pitfalls of adultery and divorce.[55]

Minnie Card offers further evidence of female resistance to governmental interference in the home. When Card's daughter failed to return to school following a Sunday visit at home, a school official came knocking. Card refused to let her daughter go because she needed her help at home. Two days later the school official returned with police, and a scene erupted in the front yard. According to one account, policemen pushed Card to the ground, choked her, forced the girl into a car and returned her to the school. In a separate incident, Card, whose husband was serving a 40-year prison sentence, butted heads with the superintendent because she was living with another man before her divorce was final. Wilson ordered Card to move out of her boyfriend's home until the divorce was finalized, at which point they should marry, but Card refused and the couple stayed together.[56]

The stories of Belle Wilsey and Minnie Card illustrate how Native women with little leverage and less power, maintained autonomy over their families and futures. The conflicts at Round Valley came to a head in 1914 when two boys set fire to the schoolhouse, destroying it and several nearby buildings, the third arson incident at the school in four years. The BIA gradually moved away from mandatory education, and by 1923, most Native children nationwide attended public schools.[57]

Figure 8.3 Native American women, like these picking hops near the White River Valley, Washington, around 1905, found work as pickers and other unskilled jobs throughout the Pacific Northwest. Image reprinted with permission from the Washington State Historical Society.

Chinese build a presence in a strange land

The challenge of uncovering the history of Chinese women, or people in all ethnic groups, involves digging beyond the stereotypes. Women who ventured from China *east* to the United States and settled in the Pacific Northwest have been cast mostly as "passive, simplistic stereotypes of prostitutes and imported wives ..."[58] But students of history willing to explore further will find a more complex story. The historian Annette White-Parks points out that Chinese women, mostly the wives or daughters of middle-class wage earners, traded one set of restrictions for another upon entering the United States. Ancient traditions and Confucian laws bound them to obey first their father, then their husband, and finally their eldest son.[59]

According to the 1910 census, 66,855 Chinese men and 4,676 Chinese women lived in the United States, the most skewed male-female ratio among all ethnic groups. Of the 2,700 Chinese living in Washington in 1910, only about 5% were women. Chinese immigration dried up following the 1882 Exclusion Act, which not only limited Chinese from entering America but required the deportation of any who arrived after 1880. The ban included most women, and "permanently stunted" the growth of Chinese American communities in Washington.[60]

In San Francisco, prior to the Exclusion Act, most Chinese women served as slaves or prostitutes. In the Pacific Northwest, however, Chinese "were neither helpless nor immoral," according to Chuimei Ho, who studied the records of Chinese who entered the United States prior to 1910. Unlike the stereotype of "helpless victims," they "overcame enormous personal obstacles," and "contributed greatly" to the region's Chinese community.[61] The stories of Chinese women who built lives in Seattle reveal the challenges they faced immigrating to the Pacific Northwest.

Fourteen-year-old Lee See How married a 23-year-old Chinese merchant from Seattle in 1878. Merchants frequently traveled to China to marry and then returned, leaving their brides behind, sometimes for years, or until he could afford to raise a family. Like How, a significant percentage of Chinese women married men ten or more years older and lived in such a "split-household" arrangement. Although exclusion laws were in place after 1882, they permitted the families of merchants to enter the country.[62]

How immigrated shortly after her marriage. When she disembarked the steamer in Seattle she was, like many Chinese women, hobbled by bound feet, illiterate, and ignorant about America. Teenage brides coped with the conflicting values and customs of China and the United States, to say nothing of anti-Chinese sentiment. While she had little family support, she likely took comfort in living among her own people in Seattle's Chinatown. According to Ho, women like How "must have had huge adjustment issues when they jumped from being a sheltered daughter to be a stranger's wife." But How was far from a helpless Chinese girl lost in the Pacific Northwest. Her marriage lasted for 26 years until her husband died in 1904. They raised six children, ran successful businesses in Seattle and Olympia, and by all accounts lived productive, happy lives in America.[63]

Dong Oy, an American citizen, was born in San Francisco but moved to China with her parents when she was a young teen. At age 17, she married Chin Lem, also an American citizen and successful Seattle merchant. The couple had a daughter, Margaret, in 1896, after which Lem returned to Seattle. Oy would not see her husband again until she moved to Seattle with Margaret sometime around 1901. After living with Lem for five years, she and Margaret returned to China. Her difficulty reentering the United States in 1909 underscores the challenges facing Chinese immigrants. Although American citizens, Dong and Margaret could not produce their passports, and were delayed at customs. Apparently, Dong had lost favor with her husband's parents, who had written "slandering letters" to the Immigration Bureau, accusing their daughter-in-law of being a prostitute, an accusation sure to bar Dong's entry. Only after 12-year-old Margaret impressed customs agents with her fluent English, did they accept the fact the girl and her mother were American citizens. Although Dong's marriage to Lem didn't work out, her life in America did. She supported Margaret, and a niece working as a nanny and dressmaker. Margaret graduated from the University of Washington in 1919 and married a Seattle architect.[64]

The Irish – moving beyond the domestic

A significant percentage of Pacific Northwest immigrants originally hailed from Northern Europe. Norwegians, Swedes, Germans, and Irish came with families, formed their own communities and made a living in the extractive industries. The story of an Irish community in Anaconda in western Montana, demonstrates how Irish women broke Old-World boundaries in newfound ways. Unlike Chinese, Irish faced fewer obstacles entering the country, although they faced Irish stereotypes. The demand for domestic workers, combined with the potato famine in Ireland, made America look attractive, especially to young Irish women. The United States, wrote historian Laurie Mercier, "offered female immigrants economic and personal opportunities – a chance to earn wages, find a suitable husband and escape the watchful eyes of parents, priests and neighbors."[65]

Between 1885 and 1920, more than 600,000 young women immigrated from Ireland. Many found their way to the Pacific Northwest. Drawing upon newspaper articles and advertisements, and oral history interviews, Mercier paints a colorful portrait of Irish women in Anaconda, a copper mining town, in the early twentieth century.[66]

By 1900, 25% of Anaconda's 9,000 residents were first- or second-generation Irish immigrants. The women, not allowed to work in the copper smelters, met the town's domestic needs. During boom years, Anaconda suffered labor shortages, especially in the hotels, restaurants, laundries, and private homes. Most Irish women worked for wages, while the more entrepreneurial started their own business, especially boarding houses. The *Anaconda Standard* carried numerous ads for boarding houses that catered to the itinerant smelter worker. "Good Board and Lodging at the Very Lowest Rates," read an ad for Ann Walsh's Girton House. A reputation for "kindliness, efficiency, and cleanliness," helped to separate Margaret O'Connor's Vendome House from the competition.[67]

In immigrating to America, women struggled to shed the ties that bound them in Ireland. They were expected to marry, quit work, and to tend to home, husband, and children. That said, hard times often meant hard work. Frequent and often steep declines in copper prices invariably led to layoffs and pay cuts, requiring the wives and children to join the father in the job market. Women often took in laundry or boarders, while those with large families often functioned as "general contractors," hiring out their daughters to babysit, clean, and cook, and the sons to collect bottles, deliver papers, and clean schools and churches.[68]

Frequently, women managed the tight household budgets. Delia Vaughan taught herself to read and do math in order to set up her family's budget. Her husband handed over his paycheck from the smelter and got an allowance in return. Many women actually picked up their husband's paycheck from the Anaconda Company "to assert their control over family wages and acquisitions."[69]

Irish traditions constrained a woman's choice of husband as they were expected to marry Irish men. The desire to build a core Irish community outweighed matters of the heart. But the frequency of fatal accidents in the mines often shattered traditions. Widows, especially those with many children, were highly vulnerable. Unable to work outside the home, they took in laundry, sewing, and boarders. Mary McNelis was widowed twice, losing her first husband in a mining accident and the second to emphysema, a chronic lung ailment for miners. McNelis eked out a living as a midwife, often leaving her children in a local orphanage for days at a time.[70] Like the women who crossed the prairies or those who defied social boundaries in the region's city, the "Women Irish" forged a life and a community on their own terms.[71]

African Americans – finding confidence and self-worth

The story of Beatrice Morrow Cannady, civil rights activist and newspaper editor in Portland, helps us appreciate the success of some African American women in breaking through both racial and gender barriers.

Figure 8.4 Beatrice Morrow Cannady of Portland, editor of the black-owned newspaper, *The Advocate*, devoted her life to building understanding and acceptance among the city's black and white communities. Image reprinted with permission from the *Oregonian*.

As Oregon's first black woman to graduate from the Northwest College of Law (later merged with Lewis & Clark College), Cannady sat proudly at the graduation ceremonies at the swank Multnomah Hotel in Portland on May 24, 1922. In addition to receiving her diploma, Cannady, a talented vocalist who once aspired to an operatic career, sang two solos at the event. Afterwards, her pride turned to shame when the law school dean asked Cannady and her family to leave the whites-only hotel. Being "publicly insulted and humiliated" and countless other encounters served to energize Cannady's determination to fight prejudice and racial discrimination wherever she met it.[72]

Born into a large family in Texas on January 9, 1889, Beatrice Morrow graduated from the all-black Wiley College in Marshall Texas in 1908. She moved to Portland in 1912 to marry Edward D. Cannady, and soon afterwards took the job as associate editor and manager of the *Advocate*, a black-owned weekly newspaper founded by her husband and others. Beatrice Cannady ran the *Advocate* and became the voice, champion, and guardian of Portland's black community for the next 26 years.

Cannady became Portland's most visible African American, and "ambassador of good will," to whom city officials could go to for counsel on issues "affecting the harmony of relations between the races."[73] Historian Kimberly Mangun called Cannady a "force for change." As a founding member and stalwart leader of the Portland branch of the NAACP, she used her position and prestige to foster understanding between Portland's white and "Negro" communities. She battled segregation and Jim Crow, championed individual successes in the African American community, and counseled young people, especially women, to rise above the degrading stereotypes that prevailed in a nearly all-white city.

> Portland could be a lonely place for African Americans, as one long-time resident complained that she "could walk around for hours" without encountering another black person.[74]

The Pacific Northwest in the 1920s experienced a rise in ultra-conservative movements. Anti-immigration groups (called Nativists) and a reemerging Ku Klux Klan rode roughshod over any resident not native born, white, or Protestant. Race relations appeared to have reverted to the territorial years when exclusion laws banned "free Negroes in Oregon."[75] There were just 16 African Americans living in Portland in 1860, 775 in 1900 and 2,244 in 1920, less than 1% of the city's population.[76] Seattle, with 2,900 African Americans in 1920, and Idaho with 920, were similarly mostly white.

As the *Advocate's* editor, Cannady understood the need to help build a sense of "real" community among Oregon's "socially or physically isolated" African Americans. Portland could be a lonely place, as one long-time black resident complained that she "could walk around for hours" without encountering another black person. Longing to connect with others, she sometimes went to the train depot just to watch black porters at work.[77]

Much of the space in the *Advocate* addressed discrimination, what Cannady called "the root of all evils, for when people do not know one another they are suspicious and distrustful of one another."[78] Often a victim of such segregation, Cannady filed suit against the Portland School Board in 1916 for denying her entry to the public swimming pool, which was closed to African Americans on all but Saturday nights. She demanded to be placed "on an equal basis with other women ..." A circuit court judge dismissed the case, ruling the district "was within its constitutional rights in segregating white and colored races" in the use of school district facilities.[79]

Among her many lectures on interracial relations and black history, Cannady stressed educating whites about African Americans. In "The Negro's Contribution to Civilization," Cannady stressed that prejudice lay in the misconception that the "Negro has never contributed anything to the progress of mankind." These lectures not only helped to change white perceptions, but worked to "validate the student's existence in an overwhelmingly white environment."[80]

Canady accused the white press of ignoring or downplaying the accomplishments of Portland African Americans, rendering them "invisible at the group level and nameless and faceless on the individual level."[81] To that end, news about graduations, business startups, and homes purchases littered the *Advocate* pages. She saluted those who, "worked hard to put down roots despite racial antipathy."[82] "Honesty, civic pride and home buying," she stressed, "are three things that will command the respect and consideration of people in all walks of life."[83]

When she hosted "interracial teas" in her home in Northeast Portland, Cannady confronted racial ignorance in the most personal way. Prominent white, Jewish and black women gathered to discuss public issues, listen to guest lectures, and learn about black culture. White women found themselves listening to Negro spirituals, readings of black literature, or lectures on black culture – all in an effort to "stimulate the interest of white people in the Negro."[84]

Portland's black women, most of whom toiled in domestic and service work, were all but invisible to the broader community. Cannady tried to instill pride and self-worth. In a speech at the NAACP national convention in Los Angeles in 1928, she challenged African American women to stand up for themselves in a "white man's world." To serve others, "the Negro woman must first learn to believe in herself and her race – ridding herself always of any false notions of racial or self-inferiority." She encouraged women to join the NAACP in order to serve others and educate whites. "Paradoxical as it may seem, the Negro women of America must become the teachers of the white race," she lectured.[85]

Cannady moved to Los Angeles in 1938, where she continued her civil rights work. She died on August 19, 1974 at age 85.

Winning the franchise

Beatrice Cannady wasn't the first woman to use the press to address social injustices in her community. More than 40 years before the first issue of the *Advocate* hit Portland streets, Abigail Scott Duniway's *New Northwest* pecked away at the political barricades confronting women in the Pacific Northwest.

When Duniway launched the *New Northwest* in 1871, the Fifteenth Amendment to the Constitution, which broadened suffrage rights for men, both black and white, was less than a year old. Nearly all American men could vote "including former slaves, immigrants, illiterates and criminals."[86] It was widely assumed the franchise would soon be extended to women. Yet Duniway was 78 years old when she became the first woman in Oregon to cast a ballot in 1912, and it would take passage of the Nineteenth Amendment in 1920 before all women could exercise their constitutional rights.[87] But in many Western states, women had been voting for several years. Literally all states that gave women the franchise prior to 1920 were in the West: Wyoming (1869), Utah (1870), Colorado (1893), Idaho (1896), Washington (1910), California (1911), Arizona, Kansas, and Oregon (all in 1912), and Montana and Nevada (1914).[88]

Few women did more for the suffrage cause in the Pacific Northwest than Duniway. In a speech before the Idaho Constitutional Convention in 1889, which was considering a suffrage amendment, Duniway equated women's demand for equal suffrage with the American Revolution. The country's founders, Duniway argued, "formed newer and broader conceptions of the fundamental principles of a true democracy," beyond those "dreamed of by their ancestors across the Atlantic seas." Similarly, the people of the West formed "broader conceptions of the glorious heritage in store for them and their children" than established society in the East. Like the colonists who rebelled against British authoritarian rule, women were treated as "servants without wages, taxed without representation and governed without consent …"[89] The suffrage amendment failed but Idaho became the fourth state to permanently grant women the vote in 1896.

Oregon put women's suffrage on the ballot six times in 28 years: 1884, 1900, 1906, 1908, 1910, and 1912, more than any other state. In the heart of the 1884 campaign, a reader asked Duniway to counter the many objections to women voting. The justifications strike us a bizarre today, but reflect the attitudes of many men and some women of

Figure 8.5 This political cartoon graced the front page of *Votes for Women*, the Washington Equal Suffrage Association newspaper in 1910. Note the respectability and determination of the women in contrast to the men, portrayed as drunk and corrupt. Image reprinted with permission from the Washington State Historical Society.

the day, beginning with the belief women "don't want to vote." So be it, Duniway retorted. "There will be no law to compel them to vote ..."[90]

Many held fast to the true womanhood ideal that a woman's place or "sphere" was in the home, and participation in politics would distract from her responsibilities. Duniway merely pointed to the growing number of working women. How do you explain, she asked, the "thousands of women who have no sphere ... unless they go out and earn them?" Further, why assume women would neglect their homes? "Are all the *men* who vote vagabonds?"[91]

Suggestions that politics was too "filthy for women to dabble in," said more about politics than men's need to protect their women, Duniway reasoned. "How come the political pool is so filthy?" Isn't that proof "a change is necessary"?[92] She showed no patience for the belief women should be shielded from serving on juries. Women should sit on juries in which the defendant was female, she believed, and "not to be allowed to do so is an outrage before God and ought to be before man."[93]

But rather than cast a strident tone, Duniway and others learned from the struggles of Eastern suffragists whose aggressive approach did not play well in the West. Duniway, Emma Smith DeVoe, May Arkwright Hutton, and others gave men, the only ones who could vote, what they expected to see. Framing their campaign around the theme of "domestic housekeeping," leaders employed a strategy known as the "still hunt," which called for a demure, ladylike approach. Women privately lobbied their husbands, fathers, brothers, and uncles, who were in turn encouraged to lobby their friends, neighbors, and fellow workers.[94]

Duniway advised women not to argue with the anti-suffragists, because "reasonable and reasoning men who have given the measure mature deliberation will vote for the Amendment," while unreasonable men "would better be let alone." Encourage men to vote for suffrage, she counseled, "in the same sweet winning way that you long ago learned to use when asking for a new bonnet for yourself, or new shoes for the children, or new furniture for the parlor. 'You will make me very happy to-day, dear, if you will vote for Woman Suffrage.'"[95]

Emma Smith DeVoe, a suffragist from Illinois, joined the National American Woman Suffrage Association (NAWSA) to recruit women in Idaho. Her personal beauty, stylish dress, and feminine air fit the still hunt approach perfectly. Acting on the principle of "Always be good natured and cheerful," DeVoe charmed men into supporting the cause.[96] Aware that men saw female public speaking as unwomanly, she put them at ease with a simple message: Women's suffrage would benefit men. Women, who she believed abhorred violence, would counterbalance men's naturally aggressive tendencies, helping to avoid warfare. "Give [women] the ballot," she proclaimed, "and their influence would be cast on the side of peaceful solution of the difficulties which lead to war and carnage." She often concluded her talks with patriotic or romantic songs written by her husband. DeVoe successfully organized 23 suffrage clubs in Idaho and continued contributing energy, organization, and national support for the Oregon and Washington associations.[97]

While the still hunt produced results, other suffragists championed a more direct approach. In Washington, they published a newspaper, hung banners, held rallies and paraded down Main Street. Women initially won the vote in Washington Territory in 1883, but the courts rescinded it five years later due to the controversy around women on juries. When the Washington Constitutional Convention opened on July 4, 1889, women's suffrage petitions "flooded the convention." Delegate Edward Eldridge moved to strike the word "male" from the voting section. A territory-wide vote ratified the Constitution on October 1, 1889, admitting Washington as the forty-second state on November 11, but a separate women's suffrage proposal lost by 19,000 votes. Suffragists resumed their skirmish in 1898, lobbying to put a constitutional amendment to voters. Results were closer this time, but the amendment still lost by nearly one-thousand votes. Some blamed saloon interests who feared a female electorate would strengthen an active temperance movement.[98]

> Like the colonists who rebelled against British authoritarian rule, women were treated as "servants without wages, taxed without representation and governed without consent …"
>
> – *Abigail Scott Duniway*

In February 1909, Washington's legislature again placed a constitutional amendment on the ballot, scheduled for vote in November 1910. Working the theme "It's a matter of justice," organizers assembled a statewide grassroots organization, built coalitions with voter groups, and engaged in aggressive media tactics.[99] The monthly newspaper *Votes for Women,* the campaign centerpiece, informed readers of suffragist activities

Figure 8.6 Members of the Waitresses Association of Seattle participate in the 1912 Labor Day parade in Seattle. Arguing for a six-day work week in 1901, waitress union founder Alice Lord chided legislators, "You give even your horses one day's rest in seven." Image reprinted with permission from the Washington State Historical Society.

worldwide, posted progress reports, recognized volunteers, and most of all editorialized on the rightness of their cause. In its inaugural issue, the paper served notice: "Women of Washington – 'Our business is to work.'"[100]

Campaigners recruited women of all social classes and ethnicities. They trained housewives, farmer's wives, shopkeepers, secretaries, and teachers to canvass their towns and raise funds. "Cake sales, apron showers, sewing bees, and nickels and dimes saved out of the grocery and millinery bills of a thousand women – that's how the money came," said Dr. Cora Smith Eaton of Seattle. Volunteers hung thousands of posters on telegraph poles and in every possible shop or business. One featured a photo and quotation from Abraham Lincoln. "I go for all sharing the privileges of government who assist in bearing its burdens, by no means excluding women."[101]

They paid special attention to women's clubs. Because men excluded women from their fraternal organizations and other institutions, middle- and upper-class women created their own institutions, which "allowed them to extend their activities and interests" into the public world of politics and economics.[102] In cities throughout the Pacific Northwest, women organized clubs to address a dizzying number of causes: health care, homelessness, orphans, civic reform, temperance, hospitals, libraries, city parks and above all, suffrage. The historian Susan Armitage credits the eventual success of women's suffrage in the West to these organizations. In the nascent Pacific Northwest women engaged in institution-building that "eastern women, in longer-established regions, did not have."[103] The clubs sold cookbooks, baked goods, aprons, and chocolate. They staged shows and led parades at county fairs. At one event, "a marching club of young ladies in uniform, accompanied by a ladies' drum corps," marched down Main Street.[104] The Washington State Federation of Colored Women (WSFCW), with 120 clubs underscores how suffrage crossed racial and social class lines.

During her term as president of the Washington Equal Suffrage Association, DeVoe convinced the Northern Pacific Railway to run a train called the "Suffrage Special," to transport delegates to the NAWSA national convention in Seattle in 1909. Later, she garnered even more publicity when the Suffrage Special carried suffragists from Spokane to the 1909 Alaska Yukon-Pacific Exposition in Seattle, arriving on "Suffrage Day."[105]

Washington became the fifth state to enact women's suffrage when the amendment passed by a hefty margin – 52,299 to 29,676. Every Washington county and nearly all demographic groups voted for approval with the strongest support west of the Cascades.[106] At a post-election banquet, May Arkwright Hutton from Spokane gave partial credit to "the broad-minded ideas of the men of Washington, who stand for a square deal in all things."[107]

Washington's victory helped to energize the national campaign, but there would be no still hunt in Washington DC. The National Women's Party, under the leadership of Alice Paul, employed more aggressive tactics. In 1917, ten women were arrested while picketing the White House. When the prisoners refused to eat, guards beat and force-fed them. Under intense pressure from rights groups, Congress finally took action, passing the Nineteenth Amendment on June 4, 1919. It stated that the "right of citizens of the United States to vote shall not be denied or abridged by the United States or by any State on account of sex." The amendment was ratified on August 18, 1920, following approval by the required 36 states.[108]

Answering the "why" question

How do we explain women of the Pacific Northwest acquiring rights and recognition ahead of women in most other states? According to the historian Daniel Walker Howe, opportunities for higher education, especially in religious based colleges, helps to explain the rise of the broader women's rights movement at mid-nineteenth century. America became the first country in which the literacy rate for women equaled that of men, as women attended coeducational Methodist, Calvinist, and other colleges pioneering higher education for women. By 1880, one-third of all college students were female, far more than any western country. Historians argue that female access to education exemplifies American exceptionalism, and its influence over many other countries.[109]

In addition to educational opportunities, multiple other factors opened avenues for women during the Industrial Revolution. Advances in transportation and communications helped to eliminate isolation. A rapidly growing market economy offered jobs and importantly personal income. Husbands working in the city or factory solidified the separate spheres for men and women. The home became the sole domain of an increasingly confident and independent woman. Participation in her local church, human rights issues like abolitionism, and multiple benevolent causes provided avenues to public life that did not violate social norms nor threaten male authority.[110]

But those explanations fail to address the accelerated pace of change in the Pacific Northwest. Was the Western experience truly "liberating" for both men and women? Did it make women more confident and independent? Or did the West act as a magnet for people already disposed to independence and breaking social norms? It's reasonable to argue that people who eagerly transplanted their lives from the relative safety

Figure 8.7 This 1920 James Griswold cartoon satirizes how women's suffrage turned men into hapless domestic slaves responsible for housekeeping and child care. Image reprinted with permission from the Washington State Historical Society.

of Eastern society to an unknown West were by nature independent and accepting of change.

It's important to note that women were "full and vigorous participants" in building Western communities. Women partly or wholly owned many homesteads and "acted as genuine partners … contributing equal labor and taking part in decisions." While the stereotype of the "passive, suffering female pioneer" plays well in books and film, it doesn't match reality. Women kept too busy inside and outside the home to sit by passively while the men did all the work.[111]

In a 1900 speech, in Washington, DC, Duniway gave partial credit to the men of the West, who appreciated the "inalienable rights of women." They saw women "not as the parasitic woman who inherits wealth," or the equally selfish woman who lives in idleness upon her husband's toil, but as their helpmates, companions, counsellors, and fellow-homemakers …"[112]

Richard White argues the cut-and-dried political arena in the West smoothed the road to full suffrage. Eastern politics, roiled in conflicts over immigration and race, muddled suffrage messages when most Democratic voters feared enactment of prohibition and other restrictive laws.[113]

When writing her biography long after she retired from public view, Duniway recalled an event when she was a young teen and her mother gave birth to a daughter, the last of 12 children. "Poor baby!," her mother cried. "She'll be a woman some day! Poor baby! A woman's lot is so hard!"[114] The story of the Pacific Northwest is about countless women and men who led the way in improving the lot of women everywhere, paving the way for more profound changes in the decades ahead.

Muller v. Oregon

Did women need government protection?

When Emma Gotcher arrived at work at the Grand Laundry in Portland early on September 4, 1905, little did she know she was about to make history. Sometime during that ten-hour shift, Gotcher's supervisor ordered her to work overtime, knowingly violating Oregon's law requiring employers at laundries and factories to limit the workday for women to ten hours.[115]

Two weeks later, the state of Oregon pressed criminal charges against Grand Laundry owner Hans Curt Muller. The charge set in motion a three-year legal tussle that would work its way to the U.S. Supreme Court and trigger a series of reforms protecting workers of both sexes and shifting the boundaries governing employer and employee alike.[116]

Oregon passed the protective legislation in 1903, mimicking similar statutes in Washington and Nebraska. Oregon legislators initially hoped to apply the law to nearly all jobs requiring women to spend long hours on their feet: stores, hotels, and restaurants, as well as laundries and factories. Heavy opposition, however, compelled the authors to limit the restrictions to "a mechanical establishment, or factory or laundry." It also required employers to provide women "suitable seating."[117]

Oregon intended to address the needs of a growing but small audience. In 1903, fewer than 1 in 11 women worked outside the home, and only one in five of those were covered under the law. Nevertheless, the toils of women working on their feet for up to 14 hours a day were well known. The Shirtwaist and Laundry Workers Union, Local 90 in Portland, walked off the job in 1902, demanding shorter hours and better pay. In retaliation the following year, the Laundry-men's Association locked out more than 500 female employees in laundries across the state. Nothing less than the control of their business was at stake. "We don't want the union to tell us how to run our business," declared one laundry owner. The association won the standoff, and the crippled union all but dissolved. That's when the Laundrymen's Association decided to contest the law, and selected the Grand Laundry and Muller to create a test case. Forcing Gotcher to work overtime was a calculated move to bring the issue to the courts.[118]

The legal question surrounded Muller's rights under the Fourteenth Amendment versus the state's right to make laws to protect women. Courts had long come down on the side of business, prohibiting states from interfering in the rights of employers and employees to contract privately for jobs and set wages. Specifically the Fourteenth Amendment prohibits states from denying any person "life, liberty or property, without due process of law" or to "deny to any person ... equal protection of the laws." As recently as 1905, the Supreme Court had struck down a New York law that capped the work day of bakery employees, nearly all of whom were men.

Muller's case quickly wound its way through the courts. The circuit court in Multnomah County found Muller guilty of a misdemeanor in 1906 and fined him $10. He then appealed to the state Supreme Court, which also sided with the state, setting the stage for an appearance before the Supreme Court.

The state hired Attorney Louis D. Brandeis, a future Supreme Court justice, to defend the law before the Supreme Court in *Muller v. Oregon* of 1908. Brandeis, a noted supporter of reforms to protect workers, overwhelmed the court with volumes of scientific evidence showing a causal relationship between long hours of work and women's health. Known as the *Brandeis Brief*, the evidence argued that Oregon's self-interest in protecting women's health superseded an employer's right to freely make contracts.[119]

In a unanimous decision the court upheld *Muller v. Oregon*, ruling that "healthy mothers are essential to healthy offspring." Writing for the court, Associate Justice David Brewer declared that a "woman's physical structure" and "maternal functions" justify legislation restricting "the conditions under which she should be permitted to toil." Having to spend long hours on her feet "day after day," the justice wrote, presented a threat to "vigorous offspring ..." He concluded that protecting a woman's wellbeing was in the public's interest "in order to preserve the strength and vigor of the race."[120]

Interestingly, the brief accomplished more than convincing the court on the constitutionality of Oregon's law. Brandeis's uninhibited use of data compelled the court for the first time to look beyond strict interpretation of the constitution and consider the social and economic conditions of the class in question, a common practice today.[121]

Like many progressive reforms, the decision led to unintended consequences. Writing at the one-hundredth anniversary of *Muller v. Oregon*, Associate Justice Ruth Bader Ginsburg argued that placing the working woman "in a class by herself," amounted to a double-edged sword. While progressive legislation protected against exploitation, it also "contributed to the confinement of women to a subordinate place in the paid labor force." This proved true immediately after the ruling when many women lost their jobs to men, especially Chinese, who made no demands on working hours.[122]

Regardless of the negative consequences, *Muller vs. Oregon* spearheaded numerous new laws protecting women. Employers in more and more states found themselves constrained by laws to regulate maximum hours, minimum wage, and health and safety. Other laws barred women from night work, required mandatory break time, and limited what they could lift or carry. In 1913, Oregon took its law to the next level, calling for a ten-hour limit for all "persons" employed in mills and factories.[123]

Fueled by the raft of legislation, the Labor department introduced the Fair Labor Standards Act of 1938, prescribing a national minimum wage for male and female workers, and overtime pay for work exceeding eight hours in a day. In 1941, the Supreme Court unanimously upheld FLSA, fully empowering states to legislate the workforce with little risk of violating the due process and equal protection clauses of the Fourteenth Amendment.[124]

Caroline Gleason – debunking the myths of women's work

Caroline Gleason, a University of Minnesota graduate who moved to Portland in 1908, was the driving force behind Oregon's groundbreaking minimum wage bill. Working for the Consumer League of Oregon, a social reform organization, Gleason compiled data that supported the widespread belief women were overworked and underpaid. They conducted several surveys of working women that quantified down to the penny the "Female Wage Earner's" expenses, income, and living conditions.

Gleason's work concluded that working women lived on the precipice of poverty. Even if they managed their money well, they still earned enough only for the "bare necessities of life." The research debunked the perception that women's wages went for personal treats or luxuries, known as "pin-money." The data showed that many working women were heads of households whose wages supported a family. Wages were "miserably inadequate ... and gravely detrimental to their health; and since most women wage earners are potential mothers, the future health of the race is menaced by these unsanitary conditions," Gleason wrote in her report. Ten dollars a week, she concluded, was the "very least on which the average self-supporting woman can live decently and keep herself in health."[125] Introduced at the opening of the 1913 state legislative session, the minimum wage bill called for protecting "the lives, health and morals of women and minor workers." It established minimum wage and maximum hours, set up penalties for violations, and established the Industrial Welfare Commission (IWC) to enforce compliance.[126]

Like most legislation, the minimum wage created as many questions as answers. The IWC grappled with determining what constituted a reasonable minimum wage. How many hours should women be allowed to work in a day or week? Should office workers, who adhered to a dress code and therefore incurred higher clothing expenses, earn more than women in laundries or packing houses? In an era when it was unseemly and presumably unsafe for women to be in public after dark, should women work the night shift? Interestingly, restrictions to night work drew the most criticism from the workers themselves, who resented interference in their personal lives and needed the higher pay that accompanied late shifts.[127]

Like the maximum hour case, it didn't take long for the minimum wage law to face a court challenge. Frank C. Stettler, who owned a Portland box manufacturing plant, filed a lawsuit contesting the IWC's mandates for a $8.84 minimum weekly wage, nine-hour work day, and a 54-hour week in manufacturing jobs. A second suit, filed by Stettler employee Elmira Simpson, claimed the limits "would deprive her of the right to work." Not surprisingly, the Oregon court upheld the IWC rulings and Stettler appealed to the U.S. Supreme Court. It upheld the constitutionality of the Oregon laws by a curious 4-4 vote in 1917, in part because sentiment for the "women are different" opinion began to lose public favor.

It's difficult to assess the effectiveness of the spate of protective legislation for women. On one hand, "minimum wage seems to have succeeded more as a cause than in practice," according to the historian Janice Dilg. Yet Oregon's leadership inspired similar progressiveness across the United States and other industrial economies. More important, it cleared the way for the Fair Labor and Standards Act in 1938, which set compulsory minimum wage and hours for all workers regardless of gender.[128]

Figure 8.8 Caroline Gleason of Portland devoted her life to social work, especially the needs of working women. Her research led to the Oregon Legislature passing a bill in 1913 to provide women a minimum wage and limit their working day. Image reprinted with permission from the Archives of the Sisters of the Holy Names of Jesus and Mary, U.S.-Ontario Province.

Following her victory over the minimum wage law, Gleason decided to devote her considerable energies to God, joining the Sisters of Holy Names of Jesus and Mary in Portland as Sister Miriam Theresa. She continued her social work and teaching until her death in 1962.

Explore more

Many of women's countless contributions to the Pacific Northwest are detailed in books, websites, and museums listed below.

Books

Women in Pacific Northwest History, edited by Karen J. Blair, recounts the experiences of women from all social classes and ethnicities. Abigail Scott Duniway's *Path Breaking: An Autobiographical History of the Equal Suffrage Movement in Pacific Coast States* reprints many of Duniway's columns written for her suffrage newspaper, the *New Northwest*. Kimberly Jensen, *Mobilizing Minerva: American Women in the First World War* and Sue Armitage, *Shaping the Public Good: Women Making History in the Pacific Northwest* further highlights women's critical roles in shaping history.

Online

HistoryLink.org, the free online encyclopedia of Washington State history (http://www.historylink.org/), and the Oregon Encyclopedia (http://www.oregonencyclopedia.org/), a project of the Oregon Historical Society, are replete with excellent stories of women of the Pacific Northwest.

Museums

The Oregon Historical Society Museum (http://www.ohs.org/) in Portland has made the state's rich history accessible to all for more than a century.

What do you think?

What historical events led women to break out of their traditional roles as wife, mother, and care giver? What role did women play in settling the Pacific Northwest, and how did that impact their status and civil rights? How did World War I and World War II affect job opportunities for women? Were there any long-term impacts beyond getting a job?

Notes

1 Kimberley Jensen, *Mobilizing Minerva: American Women in the First World War* (Urbana, IL: University of Illinois Press, 2008), 89–90.
2 Ibid.
3 Ibid.
4 Ibid.
5 Richard W. Etulain, *Beyond the Missouri: The Story of the American West* (Albuquerque, NM: University of New Mexico Press, 2006), 263.
6 Susan Armitage, "Tied To Other Lives: Women in Pacific Northwest History," in *Women in Pacific Northwest History*, Karen J. Blair, ed. (Seattle, WA: University of Washington Press, 1988), 11.

7 Catherine Clinton, *The Other Civil War: American Women in the Nineteenth Century* (New York: Hill and Wang, 1984), 103. Also see Glenda Riley, "Images of the Frontier-swoman: Iowa as a Case Study," in *The Western Historical Quarterly* 8, no. 2. (April 1977): 189–202.

8 Clinton, *The Other Civil War*, 102.

9 Ibid, 103.

10 Ibid.

11 Ibid, 106.

12 Richard, White, *It's Your Misfortune and None of My Own, A New History of the American West* (Norman, OK: University of Oklahoma Press, 1991), 307.

13 White, *It's Your Misfortune and None of My Own*, 307–308.

14 Ibid.

15 Barbara Welter, "The Cult of True Womanhood: 1820–1860," accessed January 17, 2016, at www.colorado.edu/.

16 Welter, "The Cult of True Womanhood," 2–5.

17 White, *It's Your Misfortune and None of My Own*, 307–308.

18 Ibid.

19 Ibid.

20 Daniel Walker Howe, *What Hath God Wrought: The Transformation of America, 1815–1848* (New York: Oxford University Press, 2005), 555–556.

21 Robert V. Hine and, John Mack Faragher, eds., *The American West: A New Interpretive History* (New Haven, CT: Yale University Press, 2000), 418.

22 Abigail Scott Duniway, *Path Breaking An Autobiographical History of the Equal Suffrage Movement in Pacific Coast States*(Portland: James, Kerns &Abbott Co. 1919), 10.

23 Ibid.

24 David Peterson Del Mar, "His Face Is Weak and Sensual': Portland and the Whipping Post Law," in *Women in Pacific Northwest History*, Karen J. Blair, ed. (Seattle, WA: University of Washington Press, 1988), 60–61.

25 Hine and Faragher, *The American West*, 419.

26 Karen J. Blair, "Normal Schools of the Pacific Northwest: The Lifelong Impact of Extracurricular Club Activities on Women Students at Teacher Training Institutions, 1890–1917," *Pacific Northwest Quarterly* 101, no. 1 (Winter 2009/2010): 3–5.

27 Blair, "Normal Schools of the Pacific Northwest", 6.

28 Ibid., 14.

29 Kathleen Underwood, "Schoolmarms on the Upper Missouri," *Great Plains Quarterly* 11 (1991): 228.

30 Peterson Del Mar, "'His Face Is Weak and Sensual," 61.

31 Ibid.

32 Hine and Faragher, *The American West*, 420.

33 Ibid.

34 Maurine Weiner Greenwald, "Working-Class Feminism and the Family Wage Ideal: The Seattle Debate on Married Women's Right to Work, 1914–1920," *Women in Pacific Northwest History*, 100.

35 Greenwald, "Working-Class Feminism, 101.

36 Ibid.

37 Ibid., 96.

38 Ibid., 102–103.

39 Ibid., 95.

40 Ibid., 109.

41 Ibid., 108.

42 Ibid., 109.

43 Ibid., 115.

44 "Alice Lord, 1877–1940," HistoryLink.org, accessed September 30, 2015, at http://www.historylink.org/.

45 Ibid.

46 Barbara Welke, "The Fourteenth Amendment and the Rights Revolution," University of Minnesota, accessed July 25, 2015, at http://www.hist.umn.edu/.

47 Janice Dilg, "'For Working Women in Oregon': Caroline Gleason/Sister Miriam Theresa and Oregon's Minimum Wage Law," *Oregon Historical Quarterly*, 110, no. 1 (Spring, 2009): 96–129.

48 Ibid., 106.

49 Wendy Wall, "Gender and the "'Citizen Indian'", in *Writing the Range: Race, Class, and Culture in the Women's West*, Elizabeth Jameson and Susan Armitage, eds. (Norman, OK: University of Oklahoma Press, 1997), 203–204.

50 Ibid., 207–208.

51 Ibid., 203–204.

52 Ibid., 217.

53 Ibid.

54 Ibid., 209.

55 Ibid., 212.

56 Ibid., 217–218.

57 Carolyn J. Marr, "Assimilation Through Education: Indian Boarding Schools in the Pacific Northwest," accessed April 17, 2014, https://content.lib.washington.edu/.

58 Annette White-Parks, "Beyond the Stereotypes: Chinese Pioneer Women in the American West," in *Writing the Range: Race, Class, and Culture in the Women's West*, Elizabeth Jameson and Susan Armitage, eds. (Norman, OK: University of Oklahoma Press, 1997), 258–259.

59 Ibid.

60 Chuimei Ho, "Housewives or Prostitutes? Chinese Women in Washington and other Northwestern States before 1910," presented at the Pacific Northwest History Conference, 2010. Ho studied the immigration records of women who settled in the Pacific Northwest prior to 1910, as well as a variety of other primary sources detailing the lives of 73 Chinese couples married in Washington.

61 Chuimei Ho "Housewives or Prostitutes."

62 Ibid.

63 Ibid.

64 Ibid.

65 Laurie Mercier, "'We Are Women Irish', Gender, Class, Religious, and Ethnic Identity in Anaconda, Montana," in *Writing the Range: Race, Class, and Culture in the Women's West*, Elizabeth Jameson and Susan Armitage, eds. (Norman, OK: University of Oklahoma Press, 1997), 313.

66 Ibid.

67 Ibid., 313–314.

68 Ibid., 315.

69 Ibid., 316.

70 Ibid.

71 Mercier coined the term "Women Irish" in "We Are Women Irish."

72 Kimberly Mangun, *A Force for Change: Beatrice Morrow Cannady and the Struggle for Civil Rights in Oregon, 1912–1936* (Corvallis, OR: Oregon State. University Press, 2010), 29.

73 Ibid.,27.

74 Ibid., 39.

75 Ibid., 17.

76 Ibid., 39.

77 Ibid.

78 Ibid., 97

79 Ibid., 26.

80 Ibid., 11.

81 Ibid., 43.

82 Ibid., 17.

83 Ibid., 83.

84 Ibid., 102.

85 Ibid., 94.

86 Ruth Barnes Moynihan, "Of Women's Rights and Freedom: Abigail Scott Duniway," in *Women in Pacific Northwest History*, Karen J. Blair, ed. (Seattle: University of Washington Press, 1988), 28.

87 Ibid.

88 White, *It's Your Misfortune and None of My Own*, 356–357.

89 Abigail Scott Duniway, *Path Breaking*, 127–129.

90 Jean M. Ward and Elaine A. Maveety, eds., *"Yours for Liberty": Selections from Abigail Scott Duniway's Suffrage Newspaper* (Corvallis, OR: Oregon State University Press, 2000), 226–227.

91 Ibid.

92 Ibid.

93 Ibid.

94 Blair, *Women in Pacific Northwest History*, 26.

95 Ward and Maveety, *"Yours for Liberty,"* 242,

96 Jennifer Ross-Nazzal, "Emma Smith DeVoe: Practicing Pragmatic Politics in the Pacific Northwest," *Pacific Northwest Quarterly* 99, no. 2 (Spring 2005): 76.

97 Ross-Nazzal, "Emma Smith DeVoe," 77.

98 Women's Voices, Women's Votes, Washington State Historical Society, accessed September 23, 2015, at http://washingtonhistoryonline.org.

99 Ibid.

100 Ibid.

101 Ibid.

102 Dilg, "For Working Women in Oregon," 103.

103 Armitage, "Tied To Other Lives," 15.

104 *Votes for Women*, November 1909, accessed September 23, 2015, at http://washingtonhistoryonline.org.

105 Ross-Nazzal, Jennifer, "Emma Smith DeVoe," 78.

106 Marte Jo Sheeran, "The Woman Suffrage Issue in Washington, 1890–1910," unpublished master's thesis, University of Washington, 1977, 144–150

107 "Women's Voices, Women's Votes."

108 "Women's Voices, Women's Votes."

109 Howe, *What Hath God Wrought*, 464.

110 Ibid., 605.

111 Patricia Nelson Limerick, *The Legacy of Conquest: The Unbroken Past of the American West* (New York: W.W. Norton & Company, 1987), 53.

112 Abigail Scott Duniway, *Path Breaking*, 165.

113 White, *It's Your Misfortune and None of My Own*, 358.

114 Abigail Scott Duniway, *Path Breaking*, 8.

115 Nancy Woloch, *A Class by Herself: Protective Laws for Women Workers, 1890s to 1990s* (Princeton, NJ: Princeton University Press, 2015), 58.

116 Ibid., 58–60.

117 Ibid.

118 Ibid, 57.

119 Lawrence Lipin, "*Muller v. Oregon*" (1908), accessed July 25, 2015, http://www .oregonencyclopedia.org.

120 Barbara Welke, "The Fourteenth Amendment and the Rights Revolution," University of Minnesota, accessed July 25, 2015, http://www.hist.umn.edu/.

121 Key Supreme Court Cases, *Muller v. Oregon* (20 U.S. 412, 1908), American Bar Association, accessed July 27, 2015, http://www.americanbar.org/.

122 Ruth Bader Ginsburg, "*Muller v. Oregon*: One Hundred Years Later," 369, presented at the Willamette University College of Law, Atkinson Lecture, in Salem, Oregon, on September 12, 2008. A pdf file can be found at http://www.willamette.edu/, accessed October 24, 2016.

123 Ginsburg, *Muller v. Oregon*, 366.

124 Ibid., 369.

125 Dilg, "For Working Women in Oregon," 113.

126 Ibid., 114.

127 Ibid., 119.

128 Ibid., 123–124.

Important Dates and Events

1862	On July 1, Congress passed the Pacific Railway Act of 1862, providing Federal subsidies in land and loans for the construction of a transcontinental railroad.
1869	On May 10, the Central Pacific and Union Pacific railroads met at Promontory Point, Utah, completing the nation's first transcontinental railroad.
1873	The failure of the Northern Pacific triggered a financial panic, and a deep depression, putting hundreds of thousands out of work. Railroad construction halted nationwide, with half of the companies filing for bankruptcy.
1883	On September 8, the Northern Pacific began daily passenger service between St. Paul, Minnesota and Puget Sound, following a decade-long delay. The Washington Territorial Women's Suffrage Act passes both houses of the legislature.
1885	On November 3, months of tension between Tacoma's white and Chinese residents boiled over when "committees" of armed white men forced the Chinese from their homes and businesses, and put on the southbound Northern Pacific. The Tacoma Expulsion all but eliminated the city's Chinese population.
1887	In May, a group of white men entered a Chinese camp at night on the Oregon side of the Snake River and murdered as many as 34 Chinese miners. In a stunning reversal, women of Washington lost the right to vote when the Territorial Supreme Court ruled that women sitting on juries violated the intent of the earlier law.
1889	On October, 2, Washington voters overwhelmingly approved the new state constitution, clearing the way for statehood. Washington officially joined the Union as the forty-second state on November 11.
1890	On July 3, Idaho is granted statehood, making it the forty-third state in the union.
1891	Congress passed the Forest Reserve Act of 1891, allowing the president to set aside forest reserves on public land. Today, more than 45.5 million acres are designated national forests in Washington, Oregon and Idaho.
1893	For the second time in twenty years, the nation succumbed to a financial panic and depression, one that wreaked havoc on the Pacific Northwest's extraction economy.
1898	On May 1, Commodore George Dewey defeated the Spanish fleet at Manila Harbor in the Philippines, America's opening salvo in the Spanish-American War. Victory in the "Splendid Little War," boosted America's commercial interests in the Pacific, clearing the way for increased trade.
1900	The combined population of Washington, Oregon and Idaho exceeded one million, a symbolic milestone as the era of settlement gave way to rapid growth, commerce and urbanization. The population would double in ten years.
1909	Between June 1 and October 16, Seattle hosted the Alaska-Yukon-Pacific Exposition, introducing itself as the gateway to Alaska, the Yukon and Asia. More than three million visitors strolled the ornately manicured grounds on the University of Washington campus, viewed hundreds of educational exhibits, and enjoyed the games and rides on the Pay Streak.
1910	On November 8, the Fifth Amendment to the Washington State Constitution is passed, giving women the right to vote in all state and local elections.
1914	One August 15, the Panama Canal opened, cutting the journey from New York to the Pacific Northwest from thirteen thousand to less than six thousand nautical miles, lowering shipping costs and opening new markets for the region's extractive industries.
1916	On November 5, an estimated twenty men died and nearly fifty injured in the Everett Massacre, a shootout between labor radicals and police at the Everett docks.
1917	On April 2, President Woodrow Wilson reverses his campaign pledge of neutrality, and asked Congress to declare war on the Central Powers. America's entry into World War I proved a boon for the Pacific Northwest extraction industries.
1918	On May 16, the Sedition Act of 1918, intended to squelch dissent during World War I, broadened the definition of treason. Washington state and several of the region's cities used similar laws to prosecute labor radicals who opposed the war.

1919	On January 21, 35,000 shipyard workers in Seattle and fourteen thousand in Tacoma go on strike. The shipyard strike is the spark that ignites the five-day Seattle General Strike on February 6. Working life in Seattle came to a halt when another 25,000 union members joined dock workers. On Nov. 11, Armistice Day, five Centralia men were shot and killed in a raid on the local headquarters of the International Workers of the World (IWW). One Wobbly was lynched and seven others served lengthy prison sentences for second-degree murder.
1920	On August 18, 1920, the 19th Amendment to the United States Constitution, which grants women the right to vote, is ratified. Washington women had won the vote in 1910, after which Washington suffragists had helped with the national campaign to amend the constitution so that all American women could vote.

Part III

Crisis and Opportunity

Figure III.1 President Franklin Roosevelt visits the Grand Coulee Dam construction site, one of his more impactful New Deal projects on October 2, 1937. While the "Eighth Wonder of the World" created jobs, generated affordable electricity, and contributed to America's victory in World War II, it took a heavy toll in damage to the salmon habitat and Native American culture. Image reprinted with permission from the Washington State Historical Society.

Contested Boundaries: A New Pacific Northwest History, First Edition. David J. Jepsen and David J. Norberg.
© 2017 John Wiley & Sons, Ltd. Published 2017 by John Wiley & Sons, Ltd.

9

Beyond Breadlines

The Great Depression, New Deal and the making of the "Federal West"

Mired in an economic slowdown following World War I, the Pacific Northwest remained highly vulnerable to the devastating effects of the Great Depression. Extraction industries ground to a halt as the cost of production exceeded depressed prices for food, fish and lumber. With unemployment exceeding 20% in most areas, the region gladly accepted the government's helping hand in the form of the New Deal, transforming the economy and creating a powerful federal presence in the region.

On his nineteenth birthday on January 23, 1938, Edwin Hill stepped off a Civilian Conservation Corp (CCC) "troop train" near Vancouver, Washington, and began a new life in the Pacific Northwest.[1] Born into a poor farming family in Georgia, Hill, like countless other Americans, faced dire prospects. The American economy collapsed in 1929, plunging the nation into the Great Depression. For more than ten years, Americans wrestled with hardship and economic uncertainty. Ten years old at the start of the Depression, Hill recounted that he "always seemed to be hungry" and his insatiable hunger earned him the nickname "Lick Skillet." Life for Hill got even harder in 1935 when his mother died following a prolonged illness. The loss of a stable home and need for work led Hill to join the CCC, where he "hoped to find companionship and security as well as a means of support."[2] Established in 1933 as a relief measure, the CCC put young men into camps supervised by the U.S. Military and gave them a place to live and work, an education, and a sense of hope.

Hill first spent a year at Camp Hard Labor Creek in Georgia building dams to fight erosion and reclaim farmland. For the first time in his life, he delighted in the "the variety and amount" of plentiful food. He felt "great pride and satisfaction at the work accomplished," but he left the camp for a truck-driving job that didn't last. Unemployed and missing the CCC, Hill re-enlisted.[3]

This time, the CCC allowed him to choose a camp. He asked the officer in charge, "Where is the farthest camp you can send me to from here?" That happened to be Camp Sunset near Vancouver, Washington. There, and at Camp Skamania on the Columbia River, he drove trucks supporting CCC construction and firefighting operations.[4]

Contested Boundaries: A New Pacific Northwest History, First Edition. David J. Jepsen and David J. Norberg.
© 2017 John Wiley & Sons, Ltd. Published 2017 by John Wiley & Sons, Ltd.

Hill's experience of the Great Depression personifies that of the Pacific Northwest as a whole. Without question, the region suffered through a prolonged period of economic misery, homelessness, exceptional levels of unemployment, and political radicalism. Hard times, however, eventually led to the rise of a new, stronger Pacific Northwest. More than anything else, unprecedented levels of federal aid broke down economic barriers and laid a foundation for future growth. The now "Federal West" spurred development of new industries and propelled the region towards prosperity and national prominence.

Returning to the not so "Roaring '20s"

The Northwest economy fluctuated dramatically prior to the Great Depression. The region boomed during World War I, as wartime industries needed raw materials, spurring coal and lumber industries to new heights. Meanwhile, American troops and their European allies needed food, increasing wheat prices nearly 250%. Farmers enjoyed good times and, hoping to take advantage of wartime opportunities, borrowed to expand their fields.[5] Similarly, the fishing industry prospered by selling much of its output to the federal government, while shipbuilding exploded.[6] Forty-one shipyards in Washington and Oregon produced nearly 300 ships for the war effort.[7] The Boeing Airplane Company similarly expanded during this era of growth.[8]

Good times, however, did not last. The war's end ushered in a deep, nationwide recession as wartime spending ground to a halt. The sudden decline in demand caused mine operators, logging companies, and manufacturers to lay off workers.[9] Fifteen thousand lumber workers in Washington and 7,000 in Oregon lost their jobs.[10] Shipbuilding, the region's number two war industry, fell by 90%.[11] Nationwide, unemployment skyrocketed to 11.7% in 1921, while food prices plummeted.[12] Wheat prices fell to less than half their wartime highs, and farmers who borrowed in good times now struggled to meet obligations, leading to the closure of more than 20 banks in Idaho in the early 1920s.[13]

The U.S. economy quickly recovered, ushering in the "Roaring '20s." Personal income rose by an astonishing 38% between 1921 and 1929, while rising wages and advances in industry fueled an emerging consumer culture. The automobile, perhaps as much as anything, demonstrates the growth of the 1920s, as Americans purchased some 17 million cars and entire industries rose up to support them. By 1926, unemployment fell to 1.8% and prosperity rose to the point that Herbert Hoover, Republican presidential candidate in 1928, promised Americans "a chicken in every pot and a car in every back yard."[14] Not everyone fared well in the 1920s, however. Economic inequality grew significantly as minorities, unskilled workers, farmers, and the Pacific Northwest as a whole did not fully share in the nation's prosperity.[15]

Parts of the Northwest did recover during the 1920s. Manufacturing grew beyond World War I output by the mid-1920s. In Seattle, the furniture industry nearly tripled in size and value and employed 792 people in 1929, up from 270 in 1919. Similarly, the printing industry expanded from 1,871 workers in 1919 to 2,471 in 1929.[16] Not surprisingly, growth in those industries spurred construction in cities like Seattle and Portland, where building peaked in 1925 and 1928 respectively. Lumber exports also increased significantly, making logging even more prominent in the Washington and Oregon economies.[17]

Figure 9.1 The Second Ku Klux Klan rose to prominence throughout the nation in the 1920s and advocated a virulent mixture of racism, nativism, and anti-Catholic sentiments. Members of the Oregon Klan, pictured here, successfully backed a measure requiring all students to attend public school in 1922. Meant to shutter Catholic schools, the move backfired as the U.S. Supreme Court ultimately struck the law down in a precedent-setting decision three years later. Image reprinted with permission from the Oregon Historical Society Research Library. (Catalog No. OEHI51012).

Most historians argue, however, that the economy of the Pacific Northwest limped through the 1920s and failed to keep pace with national trends.[18] In particular, resource industries fared badly. Logging output may have increased but prices fell after 1924 due to overproduction.[19] Farmers were hit severely, as food prices remained low. In Washington, wheat farmers left 750,000 acres fallow, while desperate farmers sought federal relief. Answering their call, Senator Charles McNary from Oregon worked with Representative Gilbert Haugen from Iowa to push two relief measures through Congress, but President Calvin Coolidge, a conservative who opposed federal intervention in the economy, vetoed both.[20] Economic stagnation cast a pall over the region, causing a decline in the region's population growth. Roughly 50,000 people left Oregon, while a similar number migrated out of Idaho to search for better opportunities elsewhere.[21]

Going from bad to worse

"The fundamental business of the country … is on a sound and prosperous basis."
– *The Bend (Oregon) Bulletin*

Things worsened for Northwesterners in 1929. On October 24, the stock market crashed sending an already faltering economy into the Great Depression. Two important points need to be made here. First, the crash triggered, but did not directly cause, the Great

Depression, and historians continue to debate root causes.[22] Second, Americans did not recognize the magnitude of the crisis or immediately feel its effects. On the day of the crash, one leading banker saw "nothing to worry about."[23] A few days later, President Herbert Hoover, in a speech reprinted in *The Bend* (Oregon) *Bulletin*, maintained "The fundamental business of the country ... is on a sound and prosperous basis."[24] Year-by-year, however, the economy worsened until the federal government stepped up efforts to fight the Depression in 1933.

The Great Depression hit the resource-dominant Pacific Northwest harder than most other parts of the nation.[25] Markets for coal, metals, lumber, and other materials dried up as manufacturing and homebuilding declined. Exports declined too, as the Depression spread around the globe. Farmers already facing tough times watched prices plunge ever lower. Not surprisingly, Idaho, where resource extraction dominated the economy, suffered through the sixth highest decline in income in the nation.[26] Workers in Oregon and Washington who depended on the same industries struggled along with Idahoans.

Data illustrates the depths of the Great Depression. Estimates on unemployment vary significantly, but roughly 25% of the nation's workers lost their jobs.[27] In Seattle, unemployment hovered around 30% on average but may have exceeded 50% in some parts of the city.[28] Logging, the region's leading industry, simply collapsed. Output in Washington declined by two-thirds, and roughly 80% of Washington and Oregon mills closed.[29] In Idaho, white pine production dropped 62% between 1929 and 1933. Other commodity prices fell just as dramatically. Wool plummeted from $0.36 a pound in 1929, to $0.09 in 1933, while wheat declined from $0.72 a bushel in the difficult 1920s to a mere $0.26 in the 1930s.[30] Prices fell so badly that the cost of production often exceeded prices, prompting some farmers to leave food in the field to rot, while some apple growers cut and burned their orchards to avoid maintenance costs.[31] Other major resource industries suffered as well. Over that same four-year period, output from Idaho mines dropped 70%, from $32 million to $9.5 million, while the Northwest's salmon pack fell by an astonishing 120 million pounds.[32]

Early on, President Hoover called for local communities and cooperative efforts to handle relief. He opposed federal intervention in the economy, arguing federal aid "weakens the sturdiness of our national character." Mobilizing the "infinite agencies of self-help in the community," he felt would best address many problems facing the nation.[33] Without much in the way of federal assistance, Northwesterners looked to each other for help.

The mounting crisis soon overwhelmed relief efforts of local charities and community funds. In Portland, the Public Welfare Bureau, YMCA, Salvation Army, and other organizations effectively aided the needy throughout the first years of the Depression.[34] By the early 1930s, however, donations to the community chest fell well short of goals, and increasingly desperate citizens demanded tax relief. Strapped for cash, Portland simply could not provide enough assistance as the number of people needing relief swelled to extremes by 1933.[35]

"Let's call this place Hooverville"

As local efforts failed, desperate men and women, like Seattle's Jesse Jackson, took matters into their own hands. A lumberjack, Jackson "made fairly good wages" and "spent

Figure 9.2 Officials at the Family Welfare Office in Tacoma staged this photograph in 1931, presumably, to tug at heartstrings and encourage aid to those facing dire straits. In the end, local services and charities simply could not keep up, and weary voters increasingly looked to the federal government for action. Reprinted with permission from the Washington State Historical Society.

most of these wages freely" before the Depression set in. He exhausted his "small savings account" by October 1931 and felt "compelled to seek help from a community fund agency." At a soup kitchen, he received dinner "that resembled pig swill more than it did human food," while the shelter had no beds or blankets, forcing him "to sleep upon the hard floor" with "a few newspapers that I had picked up during the day for a bed." After a week of this "abuse," he set out on his own.[36]

Jackson joined 20 other men to build shacks on vacant land owned by the Seattle Port Commission.[37] Others quickly joined, prompting a backlash from city officials. "They considered us a bunch of ne'er-do-well undesirables and wanted to get rid of us," Jackson explained. Authorities ordered the men to leave and, seven days later, "swooped down upon us, with cans of kerosene and applied the torch."[38] With few options, the men quickly rebuilt their shelters using fire-proof corrugated tin when possible. Eventually, municipal elections brought new, more sympathetic leaders to power, and they allowed the camp to exist as long as residents maintained order. The city refused, however, to allow women or children to live in the camp. Needing a name for the camp, one man commented, "This is the era of Hoover prosperity; let's call this place 'Hooverville,'" and the name stuck.[39]

At peak, Seattle's Hooverville housed about 1,200 residents at any given time, with another 7,000 passing through during the Depression.[40] As the effective leader, or

Figure 9.3 Shared poverty during the Great Depression broke down racial barriers in Seattle's Hooverville, which was far more diverse than the larger region. More than 97% of Washingtonians were white in 1930, but some 29% of Hooverville's residents were minorities. They managed the camps cooperatively. Reprinted with permission from the Washington State Historical Society.

"mayor" of Hooverville, Jackson oversaw enforcement of camp rules. Most people, he explained, tried to "do the right thing" but they dealt with their "share of undesirables." And sometimes "a party of Hooverville residents" were evicted.[41]

Hooverville residents did what they could to eke out a living. Some fished, others collected driftwood and sold firewood, or performed services for other residents. "None of them realize very much," Jackson explained, but he and others took great pride in caring for themselves. They could "hold their heads up and say, 'I am not on relief.'"[42]

Similar Hoovervilles sprang up across the Pacific Northwest. The poor first established Tacoma's camp, known as "Hollywood-on-the-Tideflats," in the 1920s, and some 1,200 squatted there by 1937.[43] In contrast to Seattle, women and children lived in Tacoma's Hooverville, prompting concern in the surrounding community. Only 15% to 20% of the children attended school and a survey maintained the "health and moral conditions are distressingly bad. There are no playfields, churches, or schools in the area" contributing to "the highest murder, suicide, and crime rate."[44] Tacoma's authorities voiced mixed feelings about the camp. Mayor Harry Cain expressed sympathy for "those who are dispossessed," while the chief of police wanted to drive out "undesirables," proclaiming, "If they're not good enough for other cities in this state, they're not good enough for us."[45] In contrast, authorities responded more positively to the leaders of Klamath Falls' Hooverville in Oregon. *The Klamath News* reported favorably on "mayor" Richard McHurin (later spelled McHern) in 1931, noting that the chief of police and city leaders had "the highest regard" for him and his cooperation in "keeping order."[46] Police continued to work with his successor, William "Mike" Reed, providing 40 jackrabbits and 20 loaves of bread for Sunday dinner in January 1932.[47]

Hard times in the Pacific Northwest didn't deter people from other regions from look-ing west and adding to the region's woes. Many came from the Midwest where drought and over-farming dried out the soil, contributing to massive dust storms that buried farms and displaced over 1 million farmers.[48] Many of them headed for the coast. The majority went to California, but more than 100,000 ventured to the Northwest.[49] For nearly all of its history, Northwesterners actively promoted the region and encouraged growth, but now they viewed newcomers with skepticism. As historian Gordon Dodds explained, "old residents were afraid" newcomers "would steal a job ... would require higher taxes to pay for relief measures" or even "become riotous or radical."[50] Regard-less, new arrivals did their best to make it and some adjusted quite well. Wheat farmers Lloyd and Mary Dewing struggled in North Dakota and moved to Washington in 1936. After spending a year near Spokane, they moved to Olympia. Through hard work and self-reliance, they made a living, established good relations within the community, and assimilated into the region.[51]

Out with the old, and in with the New Deal

Although national in scope, the New Deal provided more aid and had a greater effect on the Pacific Northwest than many other parts of the country.

In 1932, the nation reached a point of absolute desperation. President Hoover's limited response to the economic crisis angered Americans, and radicalism reared its head. In Seattle, radicals took control of the Unemployed Citizens' League, a self-help organiza-tion formed in 1931. Founded by socialists, the League pursued a moderate course of action and worked effectively with city leaders. Members cut wood on donated land, gleaned surplus food from farms, fished, and distributed food and supplies to the needy. As radical labor leaders, and later communists, took control, the League led hunger marches to Olympia, faced increasing hostility, and lost influence in the city.[52] In Idaho, desperate people set forest fires in an attempt to get jobs fighting them. It didn't work. An incredulous Governor Ben Ross declared martial law and called out the National Guard in those counties.[53] In Oregon, the growing Communist Party held meetings and faced intense opposition. Portland authorities arrested 12 members under a state "criminal syndicalism" law and sentenced one activist, Dirk DeJonge, to seven years in prison. Eventually the Supreme Court overturned his conviction, citing the First Amendment, but his case clearly illustrates the fear of radicalism.[54]

Given these events, it isn't surprising the Pacific Northwest political landscape shifted sharply left. At the start of the Great Depression, Oregon, Washington, and Idaho all had Republican governors, and Republicans dominated the region. In Washington, Gover-nor Roland Hartley held to staunchly conservative values, opposing unions, taxes, and government interference in the workplace.[55] Federal elections in Oregon underscore Republican dominance. Democrats failed to win a single county in the presidential elec-tions of 1920, 1924, and 1928.[56]

The Depression changed everything. Republicans increasingly fell out of favor with people like Mike Reed, the "mayor" of Klamath Falls' Hooverville. He identified him-self as a Republican and voted for Hoover in 1928, but stated "I don't think I'll do it again."[57] Such sentiments swept Democrats into power in 1932 when Franklin Delano

OREGON CITY , OREGON . FREIGHT TRAIN ON SIDING . UNEMPLOYED ROBBING
APPLE ORCHARD . 1934 . THE GREAT DEPRESSION .

Figure 9.4 Raised by socialists, the artist Ronald Ginther took an active role in radical political movements and captured the spirit of the times in numerous watercolor paintings like this one of desperate men riding the rails and helping themselves to apples as they passed an orchard outside Oregon City, Oregon. Reprinted with permission from the Washington State Historical Society.

Roosevelt, a Democrat, ran for the presidency. Calling for a "New Deal," he promised the federal government would do more to help the people. At a campaign rally in Portland, he announced "the next great hydroelectric development to be undertaken by the federal government must be that on the Columbia River," and large crowds cheered his additional statements on the plight of farmers and the need for more jobs.[58] A measure of "justice," he argued, could "come only through the revival of industry and employment. Not charity, but a chance to earn a living."[59] His message resonated, and he easily won, carrying numerous Democrats into state and local offices with him.[60]

Once inaugurated, Roosevelt (known as FDR) immediately launched the New Deal, creating numerous programs in his first hundred days. Waves of legislation, sometimes called the Second and Third New Deals, followed through the 1930s and dramatically increased the role of the federal government in American life.[61] Although national in scope, the New Deal provided more aid and had a greater effect on the Pacific Northwest than many other parts of the country.[62] It provided relief, created jobs, promoted conservation of natural resources, restored hope, and advanced fundamental changes in the region's economy.

While not necessarily more significant than other New Deal programs, a detailed look at the CCC allows us to see how the New Deal affected everyday people in the Pacific Northwest. Created shortly after Roosevelt took office, the CCC enrolled young, single men eligible for relief, and put them to work on conservation programs.[63] FDR, in the words of Secretary of Labor Frances Perkins "loved trees and hated to see them cut and not replaced ... He thought any man or boy would rejoice to leave the city and work in the woods."[64] With the president's support, the program grew rapidly.

Given the frequency of camp movements and men rotating in and out of the program, exact numbers are unavailable, but some 2.5 to 3 million men served in over 45,000 camps nationwide before the program closed in 1942.[65] As early as August 1933, the CCC ran 96 camps in Idaho, 64 in Oregon, and 57 in Washington.[66] Each camp provided about 200 men with food, shelter, clothing, and medical care. According to one report, enlistees who entered the camps malnourished gained, on average, more than eight pounds from exercise and proper nutrition.[67] Enlisted men earned $30 a month, but all except $5 was sent to their families to broaden the program's beneficiaries. Educational programs introduced by the late 1930s taught some 50,000 men to read and write, while another 400,000 took high school and college courses.[68]

CCC members like Edwin Hill built hiking trails, campgrounds, roads, and recreational facilities in National Forests and Parks, replanted trees on logged-over land,

Figure 9.5 Young men in the newly created Civilian Conservation Corps pose for the camera. While they may seem ambivalent in this photo, many readily embraced the opportunities found in the Corps and formed life-long friendships. Reprinted with permission from the Washington State Historical Society.

erected dams, cleared rivers, served as fire lookouts, and fought forest fires.[69] To give a sense of the CCC's reach, the federal government spent $57 million in Idaho alone, building 187 fire lookouts, stringing 15,000 miles of telephone lines, and planting 10 million trees, among other projects.[70]

On weekends, men patronized movie theaters, restaurants, bars, and dance halls, benefiting surrounding towns. Periodically, they washed all the equipment, scrubbed the barracks, dressed in their best clothes, and held dinners and dances for local residents. Doing so helped to build good relations with neighboring communities and more than a few men met their wives while in camp. Lastly, the newly built campgrounds, picnic shelters, and outdoor fireplaces provided inexpensive recreation for locals. Hill recalled how visitors at Mount Adams "set up tents for a weekend, for a week or two, or even for all summer." Campers often took advantage of the abundant supply of huckleberries and sold them to commercial buyers. "The opportunity to camp-out, and earn money," Hill thought, "was appreciated by visitors to the National Forest" in those tough times.[71]

Beyond his work accomplishments, Hill was most proud of getting an education in the CCC. "I completed high school," he remembered, "as well as correspondence courses in forestry, and in fire presuppression from the California State Department of Education, and also first aid and automobile mechanic classes taught at camp." He wanted to study "photography, welding, and woodworking," but simply did not have enough time in between work and his other classes.[72]

Towards the end of his stint in Washington's camps, Hill fell for a young woman staying at the nearby Smokey Creek Campground. CCC officers refused to let him leave the camp for a wedding during fire season, so he "did what any determined twenty-year-old, red-blooded American would do" and went AWOL "long enough to help make wedding plans, get married, and enjoy a short honeymoon."[73] A week later, the CCC generously offered to find a place for him to stay with his wife, and he returned to camp to finish out his enlistment. After leaving the CCC in 1939, Hill served in the U.S. Army in World War II and lived out his life in Washington.[74] He considered his time in the CCC to be "the most enjoyable and rewarding of my life" and revered the program as "one of the greatest things that ever happened in this country."[75]

The enduring legacy of the CCC

Work done by the Civilian Conservation Corps continues to benefit the Pacific Northwest and create jobs in outdoor recreation and tourism. Men in the CCC constructed popular hiking trails like the Timberline Trail around Mt. Hood in Oregon and the Flapjack Lakes Trail in Olympic National Park.[76] They also developed many parks like Ginkgo Petrified Forest and Twanoh State Parks in Washington, Silver Falls State Park in Oregon, and Heyburn State Park in Idaho.[77] The structures they built remain in use in many places, are often labeled, and are very much worth visiting when traveling the region.

Putting Americans to work in the city

The Works Progress Administration (WPA) stands out among the multiple New Deal work relief programs. Formed in 1935, the WPA put more than 8 million Americans to

Figure 9.6 United Air Lines and Works Progress Administration officials are all smiles as they prepare to board a flight celebrating ongoing work to expand the Snohomish County Airfield. Renamed Paine Field in 1941, this WPA project supported military efforts in World War II and the Korean War, and remains an important center for aviation. Reprinted with permission from the Washington State Historical Society.

work on an astonishingly wide array of small-scale projects.[78] They built roads, bridges, sidewalks, and city park structures throughout the nation, many of which remain in use.[79] The Federal Writers' Project interviewed elderly residents in Washington and published their stories in the three volume series, *Told by the Pioneers: Reminiscences of Pioneer Life in Washington*.[80] The Federal Theatre Project put actors to work, including Seattle's Negro Repertory Company, which employed some 200 African Americans, and staged 15 productions between 1936 and 1939.[81] Lastly, the Federal Art Project commissioned large public murals and smaller works by artists like Washington's Ernest Norling. His colorful, often disturbing portrayals of CCC and logging camps remain on display in public buildings and museums region-wide.[82]

The New Deal support for Northwest farmers improved the quality of life in rural communities. Since overproduction exacerbated low food prices, the 1933 Agricultural Adjustment Act (AAA) paid farmers to produce less and promoted soil conservation.[83] Idaho farmers accepted $2.5 million in aid and allowed 150 million acres to go fallow

Figure 9.7 Buoyed by New Deal legislation protecting the right of workers to organize and strike, timber workers throughout the region launched a major strike in 1935. Tensions erupted into violence in Tacoma as the National Guard came in to break the strike. Here, guardsmen aid an "innocent man" caught up in the turmoil. Reprinted with permission from the Washington State Historical Society.

in 1934, giving the land time to recover from years of over-farming.[84] The Farm Credit Administration and Farm Security Administration provided loans and other forms of assistance, while the Rural Electrification Program brought electricity to farming communities. In Idaho, 54% of all farms had electricity by 1939, up from 30% in 1934.[85]

The New Deal also reached Indian Reservations, where the Indian Civilian Conservation Corps enabled Natives to live at home while working on conservation and other small-scale projects.[86] More dramatically, the Indian Reorganization Act (Wheeler-Howard Act) dramatically reversed long-held federal assimilation policies. Promoted by Commissioner of Indian Affairs John Collier, the act supported efforts to restore native cultures, and allowed federally recognized tribes to establish independent governments.[87] Some tribes rejected the act, however, including Washington's Colville, Spokane, Shoalwater, Lummi, and Yakama tribes.[88] Already distrustful of the government due to past abuses, tribes feared the act gave too much power to the Secretary of the Interior.[89] For example, the Secretary would have held jurisdiction over all land sales, native forestry programs and grazing on range lands.[90]

On the labor front, the National Industrial Recovery Act gave workers the right to organize without interference from employers, triggering a resurgence in union membership.[91] The American Federation of Labor (AFL) and Industrial Workers of the World (IWW), whose memberships declined after World War I, found themselves back in the fight. Loggers, longshoreman, truck drivers, among many other workers, managed to organize and launched heated strikes in the mid-1930s.[92] Additionally, the 1938 Fair Labor Standards Act prohibited child labor, established a minimum wage, and created a 44-hour workweek. The act did not cover farm workers, but provided important protections for countless other laborers in the Northwest and the nation as a whole.[93]

Did the government create a "nation of softies"?

> "Personally, I feel that the whole relief program has drugged the soul of the nation."
> *– Letter from a minister to FDR*

The New Deal's expansion of the federal government and aid to the people spurred a mixed response. Some, like Oregon Governor Charles Martin likened the New Deal to "National Socialism sneaking in the back door as in Germany."[94] An Army veteran, Martin won election to the U.S. House of Representatives as a Democrat in 1930, but often sided with Republicans in the early days of the Great Depression.[95] Although he supported FDR in 1932, he sat out during the early months of the administration and simply did not vote on many New Deal programs. Two years later, seeing the New Deal's popularity, he won the Oregon gubernatorial election tying himself to Roosevelt.[96] Once in power, he made his true feelings known, condemning relief programs that, in his view, created a "nation of softies."[97] Instead, he wanted "our people to show the courage and fortitude of good soldiers," and warned the nation would lose its "moral force" by "pampering" the people.[98] He even endorsed a proposal to chloroform most of the 969 "hopelessly feeble-minded" children housed at the Fairview Home in Salem after a report suggested it would save the state $300,000 a year.[99]

Election results indicate, however, that most Northwesterners strongly disagreed with Governor Martin, as his failed bid for re-election suggests. Meanwhile, Washington, Oregon, and Idaho supported FDR's 1936 campaign and continued to vote for his unprecedented bids for a third and fourth term. A 1936 editorial in Salem's *Daily Capital Journal* forcefully defended the New Deal, reminding readers of "the shuffling breadlines, the soup kitchens every few blocks, ... the jungles of the Hoovervilles," and countless other problems the nation faced prior to FDR's inauguration. Arguing that Hoover's lack of aid "was the best way known to make communists," the writer lauded FDR's efforts to "put an end to the nightmare of the depression at any cost" and maintained he was "being damned ... by those who most benefited."[100] The president's continued success in the polls indicates voters agreed with those views to at least some extent.

Construction of the Grand Coulee Dam and the 12,000 jobs it generated certainly contributed to the president's popularity in the region. More than anything else, perhaps, the New Deal profoundly changed the region by building dams on its rivers, including Grand Coulee, the "Eighth Wonder of the World,"[101] Construction began in earnest in September 1933 and over the life of the project created a steady flow of good paying jobs and turned tiny Coulee City into a boomtown.[102] Completed in 1941, Grand Coulee

Dam continues to provide numerous benefits to the region: flood control, water for irrigation, and cheap, clean electricity for industries.[103] The dam did come with real costs, however. Most significantly, engineers built the dam without fish ladders, permanently blocking salmon from migrating and spawning above the dam.[104] Native Peoples who depended on the river's salmon for thousands of years faced tremendous financial and cultural hardship as Grand Coulee and other dams devastated their fisheries (for more on the dam see "The Eighth Wonder of the World" at the end of this chapter).

Without question, public works projects like dam building had tremendous support and, if anything, people in the region wanted more of them. In western Washington, for instance, citizens enthusiastically campaigned for a canal connecting Puget Sound to Grays Harbor with a secondary canal from Grays Harbor to the mouth of the Columbia River. Building on an idea developed since the late 1800s, advocates argued construction would create up to 20,000 jobs, make shipping safer, improve transit times from California to Seattle, and boost the local economy. Their calls to "Dig the Canal!" received support from Washington's governor and attracted federal attention, but the War Department rejected the canal as "not justified" in 1934. Disappointed Washingtonians continued to promote the scheme into the 1970s, but nothing ever came from their efforts.[105]

One last insightful look into opinions on the New Deal comes from a survey of clergy conducted by the Roosevelt Administration in 1935. The survey asked clergy to comment on "the conditions in your community" and for advice on how "our government can better serve our people."[106] Of the 165 respondents from Washington State, 54% expressed general support for the New Deal while 24% opposed – the rest expressed neutral views.[107] On specific issues, they tended to support work relief programs like the CCC and dam building. One minister, commenting on Grand Coulee Dam, praised its development "of manhood to those who are given employment" and ability to remake the "defeated and discouraged."[108] A notable majority of clergy, however, disapproved of relief programs, worrying relief would make people lazy and dependent on government. "Personally, I feel that the whole relief program has drugged the soul of the nation," one minister lamented, concluding "I do not expect the country to recover from its evil effects during my life." Some even criticized work programs as "just relief anyway."[109] Overall, their replies to the president's survey reveal the complex feelings of at least some Northwesterners. They had real reservations about specific aspects of the New Deal, but they supported it in general during the desperately hard times the country faced.

Pointing towards a new era

One particularly difficult question about the New Deal, "Did it work?," defies simple answers. On one hand the economy clearly improved. Personal income in 1937 approached levels seen in 1929, industrial output rebounded, people increasingly found jobs, and the mood of the region improved substantially.[110] The New Deal failed, however to restore the economy fully. People had jobs because of federal programs, but unemployment shot back up in 1937 as spending on works projects declined.[111]

Economists and historians continue to debate why the New Deal did not fully succeed, but more than a few suggest FDR simply did not spend enough to stimulate a complete economic recovery. American entry into World War II and the subsequent massive increase in federal spending fully ended the Great Depression. To put it in perspective, the federal government spent roughly $32 billion on the entire New Deal compared to a staggering $98 billion in 1945 alone.[112] The Northwest economy, powered by the new dams on the Columbia, roared to life to meet the manufacturing needs of the war and, for the first time in years, the region grappled with a labor shortage. Better times led city officials in Seattle and Tacoma to burn their Hoovervilles in 1941 and 1942, and the Great Depression slowly faded into memory.[113] The legacies of the New Deal live on, however, in the seemingly countless picnic shelters, sidewalks, public buildings, murals, bridges, state parks, and dams that can be seen throughout the Pacific Northwest.

Building the "Eighth Wonder of the World"

The federal government's New Deal during the Great Depression changed the course of the region's economy, but the "Eighth Wonder of the World," the Grand Coulee Dam, and other reclamation projects changed the course of its rivers.[114]

Northwesterners dreamed of building dams to "reclaim" (irrigate) land for farming long before the Great Depression hit. In particular, the Columbia Basin in central Washington stood out as a place ripe for development. The region, however, simply lacked sufficient resources for making dreams into reality.[115]

The drive to reclaim central Washington picked up steam during World War I.[116] Looking to grow more food for the war effort, civic leaders in Ephrata dreamed about building a dam at the head of Grand Coulee, an ancient canyon carved by massive floods during the Ice Age. Water pumped from the river into a reservoir in the coulee several hundred feet above could turn 1 to 2 million acres of desert into productive farms. An outlandish idea at the time, an engineering study in 1918 confirmed that the idea held merit.[117] Shortly thereafter Rufus Woods, owner of the *Wenatchee Daily World*, picked up the idea and promoted the dam as a source of water and electricity throughout the 1920s, calling it "The last, the newest, the most ambitious idea in the way of reclamation and the development of water power ever formulated."[118]

Proponents of Grand Coulee Dam faced stiff opposition. Private electric companies feared competition, some scoffed at the unprecedented size of the proposed dam, while Spokane business leaders forwarded a competing "gravity" plan. Instead of pumping water into Grand Coulee, they wanted to build a network of canals from Lake Pend Oreille in Idaho to the Columbia Basin. Although their proposal would not have produced electricity, it received a significant boost in 1922 when Major General George W. Goethals, a leader of the Panama Canal project, lent his support to the cause, calling power production "a question of the future."[119] Supporting the plan as a "national project," Goethals insisted that only the federal government possessed the resources to bring such an enormous project to fruition.[120] Ultimately, advocates of the dam won out in part because the sale of electricity would subsidize irrigation costs. Engineers estimated the gravity plan would cost farmers $400 dollars per acre, while water from the dam would only cost $85 an acre.[121]

In his first campaign for the presidency, Franklin D. Roosevelt pledged support for dam building in the Pacific Northwest and elsewhere, and he quickly acted once elected.[122] Initially, he allocated money for a low dam but expanded the project in 1935. The dam, 550 feet tall, provided abundant electricity and officials hoped to irrigate enough land to support 80,000 farm families displaced by the Dust Bowl.[123] To ensure that land went to family farmers and prevent speculation, FDR signed legislation in 1937 restricting farm sizes and required anyone owning excess land to sell the remainder.[124]

Creating more than 12,000 jobs throughout the life of the project caused nearby Coulee City to blow up into a rowdy Western outpost.[125] In 1936, Norman Goll, then a farm worker, hitched a ride as he "had to see" the dam and hoped to find work. The crowded town, situated in the middle of "this parched, deserted landscape," seemed "like a mirage," where he found "an attitude of utter freedom." The workers spent their money freely and "Their wants were few: food, drinks, dancing, gambling, a place to sleep, and women." The historian and journalist Murray Morgan similarly recalled how the project lured a fellow student at the University of Washington to the town. He did not care about getting a job or the money but

Figure 9.8 The historic Northwest meets the emerging Northwest in this photograph of sheep crossing Grand Coulee Dam. While the dam redirected the region's economy, farming, fishing, logging, and mining remained prominent for generations to come. Reprinted with permission from the Washington State Historical Society.

simply wanted "to be a part of it." He felt the dam would be his generation's contribution to the region's history and exclaimed, "Why, the thing is going to be completely useful. It's going to be a working pyramid. I just want to help build it."[126]

Completed in 1941, the dam came online just in time to power the region through World War II. Cheap electricity fueled the rise of aluminum factories, and Boeing turned aluminum into critically needed bombers. It also powered America's successful effort to develop the world's first atomic bomb[127] (for more on the bomb, see Chapter 10).

While few deny the prosperity, bountiful irrigation, and affordable electricity created by the dam, it's equally clear the region is paying unanticipated costs. Most significantly, engineers built the dam without fish ladders, permanently blocking salmon from migrating and spawning past the dam.[128] The Bureau of Reclamation tried to maintain the salmon population by improving spawning grounds below the site and by building fish hatcheries, but the dam undoubtedly contributed to declines in the salmon population.[129]

In addition to Grand Coulee, the federal government built many more dams on the Columbia during the New Deal and following decades, including Bonneville Dam, The Dalles Dam, McNary Dam, and Wanapum Dam. Collectively, the dams radically changed the very nature of the Columbia River, replacing a relatively narrow, cold, and free flowing river with a series of wide, warm, and slow moving lakes. Salmon thrived in the former habitat, but not in the latter. Instead, newly introduced species, like carp and shad thrived in this new ecosystem.[130]

The cost to Native American peoples is almost immeasurable. Lake Roosevelt, the reservoir that backed up behind Grand Coulee, inundated Kettle Falls, an ancient fishing site on the upper Columbia River. Bonneville Dam eliminated numerous fishing sites, and The Dalles

Dam submerged the productive fishery at Celilo Falls. Not surprisingly, Native Peoples contested and continue to challenge these developments. Treaties signed in the 1850s guaranteed tribes the right to fish "at all usual and accustomed places," and in a Washington State fishing case in 1905 the U.S. Supreme Court ruled that treaties were "not a grant of rights to the Indians, but a grant of rights from them."[131] In other words, the court argued the government could not infringe on native fishing rights. Clearly, dam construction violated treaty rights and required compensation. Recognizing the situation, federal officials building Bonneville Dam promised, in 1939, to build six new fishing sites on 400 acres of land to replace lost traditional sites. The federal government, however, failed to fulfill that promise in the twentieth century and controversy continues.[132] The Confederated Tribes of the Colville Reservation similarly challenged the effects of Grand Coulee and settled with the federal government in 1994, receiving a one-time payment of $53 million and yearly payments of at least $15.25 million. In contrast, the Spokane Tribe, also affected by the dam, received a trivial payment in 1940 and continue to fight for full compensation.[133]

Explore more

Books

Much of this chapter is drawn from articles in *Pacific Northwest Quarterly, Columbia* magazine, and *HistoryLink.org*. Edwin Hill's *In the Shadow of the Mountains: The Spirit of the CCC* gives a lively first-hand account of Hill's time in the Civilian Conservation Corps. For more on Grand Coulee Dam, see *The Dam* by Murray Morgan, *The Organic Machine: The Remaking of the Columbia River* by Richard White, and *Empty Nets: Indians, Dams, and the Columbia River* by Roberta Ulrich.

Online

The Great Depression in Washington State project (http://depts.washington.edu/depress/) is an exceptionally rich source of interpretive essays, primary source documents, and photographs from the era. The National Archives at Seattle (https://www.archives.gov/seattle/exhibit/picturing-the-century/great-depression.html) provides a brief overview along with photos. The Civilian Conservation Corp Legacy website (http://www.ccclegacy.org/home.php) covers the national history of the CCC. Be sure to look through the CCC History Center. Lastly, the Living New Deal (http://www.livingnewdeal.org/) has an interactive map of New Deal projects. Many of the sites listed remain extant and the website welcomes contributions from community members.

Museums

Regional museums generally have small, permanent displays on the Great Depression. Grand Coulee Dam (http://www.usbr.gov/pn/grandcoulee/) and Bonneville Dam (http://www.usbr.gov/pn/grandcoulee/visit/) both have visitor centers. Grand Coulee offers more regular tours along with laser light shows in the summer.

What do you think?

Evaluate the following statement. Who would agree or object with it and why? "Although the Great Depression was a period of abject financial misery, the rise of the 'federal West' ultimately created opportunities for people in the Northwest and made their lives better."

Notes

1 Edwin Hill, *In the Shadow of the Mountains: The Spirit of the CCC* (Pullman, WA: Washington State University Press, 1990), 40.
2 Ibid., 2, 11.
3 Ibid., 26–33.
4 Ibid., 36.
5 Leonard J. Arrington, *History of Idaho*, Vol. 2 (Moscow, ID: University of Idaho Press, 1994), 7–8; Tom G. Hall, "Wilson and the Food Crisis: Agricultural Price Control During World War I," *Agricultural History* 47, no. 1 (January 1973): 25; Gordon Dodds, *The American Northwest: A History of Oregon and Washington* (Arlington Heights, IL: The

Forum Press, Inc., 1986), 20; Carlos A. Schwantes, *The Pacific Northwest: An Interpretive History*, 2nd ed. (Lincoln, NE: University of Nebraska Press, 1996), 357–359, 364.

6 Dodds, *The American Northwest*, 202.

7 Dorothy O. Johansen and Charles M. Gates, *Empire of the Columbia: A History of the Pacific Northwest* (New York: Harper and Brothers, 1957), 547–548.

8 Dodds, *The American Northwest*, 201–202; Schwantes, *The Pacific Northwest*, 357–358; Johansen, *Empire of the Columbia*, 547–548.

9 Schwantes, *The Pacific Northwest*, 364.

10 Johansen, *Empire of the Columbia*, 552.

11 Ibid., 551–552; Schwantes, *The Pacific Northwest*, 357.

12 United States Bureau of the Census, *Historical Statistics of the United States: Colonial Times to 1970* Bicentennial Ed., Part 1 (Washington: U.S. Department of Commerce, 1975), 126.

13 Arrington, *History of Idaho*, 30, 33; Schwantes, *The Pacific Northwest*, 364.

14 United States Bureau of the Census, *Historical Statistics of the United States*, 126; Jennifer D. Keene, Saul Cornell, and Edward T. O'Donell, *Visions of America: A History of the United States* 2nd ed. (Boston: Pearson, 2013), 626; Eric Foner, *Give Me Liberty!: An American History* Brief, 3rd ed. (New York: W.W. Norton, 2012), 614; "'Shall Use Words to Convey Meaning, Not to Hide It,' Smith Declares in Boston; Names G.O.P Chiefs as 'Socialists,' Too," *Brooklyn Daily Eagle*, October 25, 1928.

15 Foner, *Give Me Liberty!*, 614–615.

16 Richard C. Berner, *Seattle 1921–1940: From Boom to Bust* (Seattle, WA: Charles Press, 1992) 169–170.

17 Johansen, *Empire of the Columbia*, 552–553.

18 Ibid., 554; Schwantes, *The Pacific Northwest*, 364–365; Arrington, *History of Idaho*, 33–37.

19 Connie Y. Chiang and Michael Reese, "Evergreen State: Exploring the History of Washington's Forests," Center for the Study of the Pacific Northwest, accessed August 25, 2015, http://www.washington.edu/.

20 Arrington, *History of Idaho*, 35.

21 Johansen, *Empire of Liberty*, 554; Arrington, *History of Idaho*, 36.

22 Foner, *Give Me Liberty!*, 635; Keene, *Visions of America*, 656–658.

23 Claude A. Jagger, "Most Tremendous Panic in Financial History is Recorded on Wall Street," *The Oregon Statesman*, October 25, 1929.

24 "Hoover Sees Sound Basis for Business," *The Bend Bulletin*, October 26, 1929.

25 Johansen, *Empire of the Columbia*, 555; Arrington, *History of Idaho*, 41–42.

26 Ibid., 41–42.

27 United States Bureau of the Census, *Historical Statistics of the United States*, 126.

28 Marc Horan Spatz, "The Unemployed Councils of the Communist Party in Washington State, 1930–1935," The Great Depression in Washington State Project, accessed August 1, 2015, http://depts.washington.edu/depress/; Ali Kamenz, "On to Olympia! The History Behind the Hunger Marches of 1932–1933," The Great Depression in Washington State Project, accessed August 1, 2015, http://depts.washington.edu/depress/.

29 Carlos A. Schwantes, "Uncle Sam's Response to the Great Depression," *Columbia* 11, no. 1 (Spring 1997): 14; Dodds, 226.

30 Arrington, *History of Idaho*, 33, 42.

31 Schwantes, "Uncle Sam's Response," 14; Johansen, *Empire of the Columbia*, 555.

32 Arrington, *History of Idaho*, 42–43, Johansen, *Empire of the Columbia*, 555.

33 William Mullins, "I'll Wreck This Town If It Will Give Me Employment: Portland in the Hoover Years of the Depression," *Pacific Northwest Quarterly* 79, no. 3 (July 1988), 109; William Mullins, "Self-Help in Seattle, 1931–1932: Herbert Hoover's Concept of Cooperative Individualism and the Unemployed Citizens League," in *Experiences in a Promised Land*, G. Thomas Edwards and Carlos A. Schwantes, eds. (Seattle, WA: University of Washington Press, 1986), 323–325; Herbert Hoover, "Statement on Public v. Private Financing of Relief Efforts," The American Presidency Project, accessed August 10, 2015, http://www.presidency.ucsb.edu/.

34 Mullins, "I'll Wreck this Town," 110.

35 Ibid., 111, 116–118.

36 Calvin F. Schmid, *Social Trends in* Seattle (Seattle, WA: University of Washington Press, 1944), 286.

37 Greg Lange, "Hooverville: Shantytown of Seattle's Great Depression," *HistoryLink*, accessed July 29, 2015, http://www.historylink.org/.

38 Schmid, *Social Trends in Seattle*, 287.

39 Ibid., 287, 289.

40 Ibid., 289, 291.

41 Quoted in Hilary Anderson, "A Tale of Two Shantytowns: Tracing the Similarities between Seattle's Hoover Town and Tacoma's Hollywood-on-the-Flats," *Columbia* 26, no. 2 (Summer 2012): 12.

42 Schmid, *Social Trends in Seattle*, 289.

43 Anderson, "A Tale of Two Shantytowns," 10, 12.

44 Quoted in ibid., 12.

45 Quoted in ibid., 13.

46 Bob Galloway, "Canned Heat Parties Not Thrown in Hooverville is Proud Assertion of Mayor," *The Klamath News*, December 3, 1931.

47 "Feast Promised at Hooverville," *The Klamath News*, January 11, 1932.

48 Keene, *Visions of American*, 670–671; Foner, *Give Me Liberty!*, 650.

49 Rolland Dewing, "The Great Depression: A Personal Memoir of a Dust Bowl Migrant to the Pacific Northwest," *Columbia* 10, no. 1 (Spring 1996): 29; Johansen, 555, Schwantes, "Uncle Sam's Response," 14.

50 Dodds, *The American Northwest*, 251.

51 Dewing, "The Great Depression: A Personal Memoir," 29–32.

52 Mullins, "Self-Help in Seattle," 323–338; Kamenz, "On to Olympia!"; David Wilma, "Hunger Marchers Demand Relief from the Washington State Legislature on January 17, 1933," *HistoryLink*, accessed August 1, 2015, http://www.historylink.org/.

53 Arrington, *History of Idaho*, 52; Carlos A. Schwantes, *In Mountain Shadows: A History of Idaho* (Lincoln, NE: University of Nebraska Press, 1996), 203.

54 Dodds, *The American Northwest*, 231.

55 Ibid., 212–213; Margaret Riddle, "Hartley, Governor Roland Hill (1864–1952)," *HistoryLink*, accessed August, 1, 2015, http://www.historylink.org/.

56 Dodds, *The American Northwest*, 220.

57 "Hooverville Owes Woman For New Mayor Chosen Friday," *The Klamath News*, December 12, 1931.

58 Quoted in Gary Murrell, "Democrats Disintegrate: Bonneville Dam, Public Power, the New Deal, and Governor Charles Henry Martin," *Columbia* 17, no. 3 (Fall 2003): 6.

59 "Roosevelt is Welcomed by Portlanders," *The Bend Bulletin*, September 21, 1932.

60 Dodds, *The American Northwest*, 228–236; Schwantes, *The Pacific Northwest*, 383–384; "Politics," The Great Depression in Washington State Project, accessed August 1, 2015, http://depts.washington.edu/depress/.

61 Foner, *Give Me Liberty!*, 644–663.

62 Johansen, *Empire of the Columbia*, 555.

63 Hill, *In the Shadow of the Mountains*, xv; Arrington, *History of Idaho*, 56.

64 Quoted in Hill, *In the Shadow of the Mountains*, ix.

65 Arrington, *History of Idaho*, 56; Foner, *Give Me Liberty!*, 648.

66 "CCC Camps Across America," American Experience, accessed August 25, 2015, http://www.pbs.org/.

67 Hill, *In the Shadow of the Mountains*, 32.

68 Ibid., xvi, 52; Arrington, *History of Idaho*, 56.

69 Hill, *In the Shadow of the Mountains*, 29–31, 42, 70–71; Arrington, *History of Idaho*, 56; Schwantes, *The Pacific Northwest*, 384–385.

70 Arrington, *History of Idaho*, 57.

71 Hill, *In the Shadow of the Mountains*, 50–51, 59, 71, 78.

72 Ibid., 52.

73 Ibid., 79, 84.

74 "Obituary," McCommons Funeral Home, accessed August 25, 2015, http://www.mccommonsfuneralhome.com/.

75 Hill, *In the Shadow of the Mountains*, ix, 12.

76 "Timberline National Historic Trail #600," U.S. Forest Service, accessed July 21, 2016, http://www.fs.usda.gov/; Gail H.E. Evans, "Historic Resource Study," Olympic National Park, accessed July 21, 2016, https://www.nps.gov/.

77 Zeb Larson, "Silver Falls State Park," The Oregon Encyclopedia, accessed July 21, 2016, http://www.oregonencyclopedia.org/; "Heyburn State Park," Idaho Parks & Recreation, accessed July 21, 2016, https://parksandrecreation.idaho.gov/; "Gingko Petrified Forest / Wanapum Recreational Area," Washington State Parks, accessed July 21, 2016, http://parks.state.wa.us/; "Twanoh State Park," National Park Service, accessed July 21, 2016, https://www.nps.gov/.

78 Keene, *Visions of America*, 668.

79 Foner, *Give Me Liberty!*, 656–657; Schwantes, "Uncle Sam's Response," 17–18; Arrington, *History of Idaho*, 65–66; Keene, *Visions of America*, 668–669.

80 Schwantes, *In Mountain Shadows*, 205.

81 Paula Becker, "Negro Repertory Company," *HistoryLink*, accessed July 29, 2015, http://www.historylink.org/.

82 Eleanor Mahoney, "The Public Works of Art Project in Washington State" The Great Depression in Washington State Project, accessed August 1, 2015, http://depts.washington.edu/depress/.

83 Foner, *Give Me Liberty!*, 50; Keene, *Visions of America*, 670.

84 Arrington, *History of Idaho*, 59.

85 Ibid., 60–62.

86 Arrington, *History of Idaho*, 58; Alexandra Harmon, *Indians in the Making: Ethnic Relations and Indian Identities around Puget Sound* (Berkeley, CA: University of California Press, 1998), 193.

87 Harmon, *Indians in the Making*, 193–205; David Wilma, "Wheeler-Howard Act (Indian Reorganization Act) Shifts U.S. Policy towards Native American Right to self-determination on June 18, 1934," *HistoryLink*, accessed August 10, 2015, http://www.historylink.org/.

88 Wilma, "Wheeler-Howard Act."

89 Robert H. Ruby, John A. Brown, and Cary C. Collins, *A Guide to the Indian Tribes of the Pacific Northwest* 3rd ed. (Lincoln, NE: University of Nebraska, 1996), 94.

90 Vine Deloria, Jr., ed. *The Indian Reorganization Act: Congresses and Bills*, 6th ed. (Norman, OK: University of Oklahoma Press, 2002), 20–23.

91 Dodds, *The American Northwest*, 237.

92 Ibid., 237–241.

93 Keene, *Visions of American*, 677.

94 Quoted in Murrell, "Democrats Disintegrate," 5.

95 Ibid., 6.

96 Ibid., 6–7.

97 Quoted in Dodds, *The American Northwest*, 230.

98 Quoted in Murrell, "Democrats Disintegrate," 9.

99 Ibid.,11; "Goldweiser Agrees With Dr. Laughlin on Feeble-Minded Deaths," *Daily Capital Journal*, March 13, 1936; "Euthanasia Commended By Governor," *Daily Capital Journal*, March 14, 1936.

100 "The Old Guard Way," *Daily Capital Journal*, October 6, 1936.

101 Cassandra Tate, "Grand Coulee Dam," *HistoryLink*, accessed July 29, 2015, http://www.historylink.org/.

102 Murray Morgan, *The Dam* (New York: Viking Press, 1954), 24; Tate, "Grand Coulee Dam".

103 Dodds, *The American Northwest*, 241; Tate, "Grand Coulee Dam".

104 Ibid.

105 Quoted in Shanna Stevenson, "Dig the Canal: The Proposed Grays Harbor to Puget Sound Canal," *Columbia* 20, no. 1 (Spring 2006), 10.

106 Quoted in Monroe Billington and Cal Clark, "Clergy Opinions and the New Deal: The State of Washington as a Case Study," *Pacific Northwest Quarterly* 81, no. 3 (July 1990), 96.

107 Ibid., 97.

108 Quoted in ibid., 98.

109 Quoted in ibid., 98–99.

110 Johansen, *Empire of the Columbia*, 556; Arrington, *History of Idaho*, 68.

111 Foner, *Give Me Liberty!*, 662–663.

112 Arrington, *History of Idaho*, 55; Steven M. Gillon, *The American Paradox: A History of the United States Since 1945* (Boston: Houghton Mifflin Company, 2003), 1–2.

113 Anderson, "A Tale of Two Shantytowns," 14.

114 Cassandra Tate, "Grand Coulee Dam."

115 Murry Morgan, *The Dam*, 18; Hugh T. Lovin, "Arid Reclamation in Eastern Oregon during the Twentieth Century," *Pacific Northwest Quarterly* 100, no. 4 (Fall 2009): 159–171.

116 Eric L. Flom, "The *Wenatchee Daily World*, first reports on the proposal to dam the Columbia River at Grand Coulee on July 18, 1918," *HistoryLink*, accessed August 23, 2015, http://www.historylink.org/.

117 Dorothy O. Johansen and Charles M. Gates, *Empire of the Columbia*, 593–594; Morgan, *The Dam* 19; Richard White, *The Organic Machine: The Remaking of the Columbia River* (New York: Hill and Wang, 1995), 3.

118 Quoted in Flom, "The *Wenatchee Daily World* first reports on the proposal to dam the Columbia River".

119 Morgan, *The Dam*, 20–23; "Great Engineer O.K.'s Irrigation Project," *Pullman Herald* April 21, 1922; Paul C. Pitzer, "The Mystique of Grand Coulee Dam and the Reality of the Columbia Basin Project," *Columbia* 4, no. 2 (Summer 1990): 30.

120 "Great Engineer O.K.'s Irrigation Project."

121 Johansen, *Empire of the Columbia*, 594–595; Tate, "Grand Coulee Dam."

122 Kerry E. Irish, "The Water Rises: Clarence C. Dill's Battle for Grand Coulee Dam," *Columbia* 15, no. 3 (Fall 2001): 6.

123 Ibid.; Dodds, *The American Northwest*, 241.

124 Johansen, *Empire of the Columbia*, 595; Pitzer, "The Mystique of Grand Coulee Dam," 36.

125 Morgan, *The Dam*, 24; Tate, "Grand Coulee Dam."

126 Norman W. Goll, "Grand Coulee: A Reminiscence," *Columbia* 11, no. 3 (Fall 1997): 3–5; Morgan, xviii.

127 Tate, "Grand Coulee Dam"; Pitzer, "The Mystique of Grand Coulee Dam," 32.

128 Tate, "Grand Coulee Dam".

129 Ibid.; White, *The Organic Machine*, 93–97; Pitzer, "The Mystique of Grand Coulee Dam," 32.

130 White, *The Organic Machine*, 90–97; Roberta Ulrich, *Empty Nets: Indians, Dams, and the Columbia River* 2nd ed. (Corvallis, OR: Oregon State University Press, 2007), 8, 15.

131 "Treaty with the Yakama, 1855," *HistoryLink*, accessed June 25, 2015, http://www.historylink.org/; quoted in Ulrich, *Empty Nets*, 14.

132 Ibid.,1–53, 230–241.

133 Jake Thomas, "The Price of Progress: Why the Spokane Tribe says it's still owed for Grand Coulee Dam," *Inlander*, accessed August 23, 2015, http://www.inlander.com/; Tate, "Grand Coulee Dam."

10

Marching through Global Conflict

Region's strategic locale brings explosive growth, while erasing barriers for some and fencing others

For the second time in a little more than two decades, America found itself pulled into another world war. The Pacific Northwest, strategically located on the Pacific Rim, and blessed with hydro-electric capacity and deep-water ports, benefited greatly from World War II and other conflicts with world powers. But this story is less about battles in foreign lands and more about people who found themselves thrust into battle on the home front.

On a bright, sunny day in September 1963, President John F. Kennedy addressed 30,000 people at Hanford, Washington, where nuclear reactors produced plutonium for some of the nation's first atomic bombs.[1] The President would speak at Cheney Stadium in Tacoma the following day as part of an 11-state tour. At Hanford to dedicate a ninth reactor, the first to produce electricity in addition to plutonium, Kennedy described the region as "an extraordinary place to visit" that "changed the entire history of the world."[2] After praising Hanford and Grand Coulee Dam, he asked, "how many people who are sitting here today were born in the State of Washington?" A show of hands quickly demonstrated a strong majority had migrated from elsewhere, and Kennedy emphasized that work benefiting one region provided rewards to the entire nation. "There is an old saying that a rising tide lifts all boats," he explained, "and as the Northwest United States rises, so does the entire country, so we are glad."[3]

Kennedy's observation hit upon a key aspect of regional history. For more than three decades starting in 1939, the Pacific Northwest made tremendous contributions to American efforts in World War II and the Cold War. Simultaneously, federal spending to fight those conflicts stimulated the rise of new industries and lifted the region to new prosperity. They created staggering economic growth, produced a labor shortage, and spurred the migration of tens of thousands of job seekers from all walks of life. Population growth and increased diversity forced the region to grapple with longstanding racist and sexist boundaries, while wartime hysteria pushed long-time residents behind barriers of barbed wire and guard towers.

Contested Boundaries: A New Pacific Northwest History, First Edition. David J. Jepsen and David J. Norberg.
© 2017 John Wiley & Sons, Ltd. Published 2017 by John Wiley & Sons, Ltd.

The winds of war sweep across the Pacific Northwest

Global tensions mounted in the 1930s as Nazi Germany and Imperial Japan expanded in Europe and Asia, and came to a head when Germany invaded Poland on September 1, 1939. Britain and France declared war on Germany in response, plunging the world into World War II. The United States responded to these events by declaring neutrality, just as it did at the start of World War I. In the days following Germany's invasion, President Franklin Delano Roosevelt (FDR) insisted "his administration would do everything in its power" to keep the United States out of the war, and promised to enforce laws against the sale of weapons to warring nations.[4]

Despite American neutrality, Northwesterners soon realized the war's potential impact on the region. On September 2, 1939, the *Oregon Statesman* ran an article titled "64 Plants in Oregon Ready on War Orders." The piece maintained local factories held "sealed orders for airplanes, ammunition, and other articles" that could be activated should the nation enter the fray. Additionally, the Northwest could "expect to supply much of the food – wheat, potatoes, sugar and fruit necessary to keep an army on the march" in addition to "lumber, metals, and other materials" vital to the war effort.[5] For a region still feeling the lingering effects of the Great Depression, the onset of war held out the promise of full economic recovery.

It didn't take long. Roosevelt, who strongly sympathized with Allied Forces Britain and France, made clear his opposition to the arms embargo, and took steps to prepare the country for war. Less than a week after the conflict started, the Associated Press reported on FDR's desire to give "all belligerents … access to American markets."[6] Roosevelt soon urged Congress to adopt a new policy known as "cash and carry." In theory, the policy maintained American neutrality since nations paid cash for weapons and supplies, and transported them on their own ships. In reality, it clearly favored the Allies. Britain had the naval power to access American markets. Germany did not. Opponents described the plan as "the road to war"; nevertheless it went into effect at year end.[7]

Congress approved substantial increases in defense spending in 1940. Motivated by "the light of world conditions," as Carl Vinson, the chair of the House Naval Committee put it, Congress committed more than $4 billion to expand the Navy's air force and build 200 new ships. Supporters felt this action, a step towards a two-ocean navy, would allow the nation "to make faces at Europe" and "tell the Japs where to get off."[8] Similarly, FDR called for spending to increase aircraft production. To make America's "defense invulnerable" and "security absolute," he set a goal of producing up to 50,000 planes per year.[9] For the Pacific Northwest, Congress's decisions meant jobs.

In September 1940, the *Oregon Statesmen* excitedly announced that the West Coast would build many of the Navy's new vessels. In Seattle, the federal government planned to spend 5 million dollars building a shipyard for destroyer construction on Elliot Bay, "where a hundred shanty dwellers now squat." Federal officials also planned to build destroyers, costing $42 million, at the existing Puget Sound Navy Yard in Bremerton.[10]

Oregonians received similar news in January 1941, as the federal government announced plans to build new shipyards in the Portland area for the construction of merchant ships, creating up to 7,000 new jobs.[11]

The 1941 Lend-Lease Act triggered another wave of spending through the nation and the Pacific Northwest. The measure allowed FDR to "lend, lease, or otherwise dispose of" weapons to Britain and other nations fighting the Axis powers.[12] While immediate aid came from existing stocks, FDR asked Congress for $7 billion for the production of "every gun, plane, and munition of war" possible.[13]

After more than two years of escalated involvement in the war, the U.S. found itself dragged into the conflict on December 7, 1941 when the United States was "suddenly and deliberately attacked by the naval and air forces of the empire of Japan."[14] Throughout the 1930s and early 1940s, the United States vigorously opposed Japanese expansion in Asia and retaliated with economic sanctions, culminating in a complete ban on trade in July 1941. Cut off from critical imports of American fuel and scrap metal, Japanese leaders decided to continue expansion in the hopes of capturing resource rich territories and, realizing the move would lead to war, launched a surprise attack against the American fleet at Pearl Harbor, Hawaii. The devastating attack sank or damaged 19 ships, destroyed close to 200 aircraft and killed over 2,400 Americans. "We are at war," the editors of the *Oregon Statesmen* announced. "We have been at war before and have acquitted ourselves honorably. We will do so again."[15]

Northwest industries rise to the challenge

> While the dawn of the nuclear age stunned the world, workers at Hanford planned a Labor Day celebration "that will pop almost as loud as the bomb that hit Hiroshima …"
>
> – *Oregon Statesman*

Northwest industries exploded as the nation shifted to a wartime economy, sweeping away the lingering effects of the Great Depression and fundamentally changing the regional economy. Extraction industries like farming, fishing, mining, and logging – long the stalwarts of the regional economy – enjoyed steady growth throughout the war. Yet their growth would pale in comparison to defense. Shipbuilding, especially, enjoyed a remarkable resurgence. The overwhelming demand for new combat ships and trade vessels led companies to establish new yards and refurbish facilities in Oregon and Washington that had been neglected following World War I.

The most significant wartime industry in Oregon, shipbuilding brought new opportunities in Portland, where five yards operated, including two new, large facilities built by Henry J. Kaiser. Kaiser, a New York industrialist who played prominent roles building Grand Coulee and Bonneville dams, introduced significant innovations to reduce building times. Instead of building vessels on shipways (or "ways") from start to finish, his company manufactured large sub-assemblies in outlying buildings and then quickly welded them together on the ways. At peak efficiency, his workers produced a 441-foot cargo ship, or "Liberty ship," in a record-breaking ten days.[16] With 60,000 workers at peak employment, the Portland yard put out more than 300 Liberty ships, and 100 other vessels for the Allied cause.[17]

In Washington, the yards in Bremerton, Seattle, Tacoma, and Vancouver buzzed with activity. The Bremerton facility, built in 1891, focused on repairs, first to the battleships that survived Pearl Harbor, as well as carriers, destroyers, cruisers, battleships, and smaller vessels. Bremerton also contributed more than 50 ships to the cause: aircraft carriers, destroyers, and various others.[18] Twenty-nine yards operated in Seattle, while the Seattle-Tacoma Shipbuilding Company built 37 escort carriers, freighters, tankers, and

Figure 10.1 Eleven shipways ("ways") are visible in this aerial view of the Henry J. Kaiser Shipyards in Portland, Oregon. The facility mostly produced cargo ships known as "Liberty" ships. By the war's end, Portland contributed more than 400 ships that supplied Allied soldiers fighting in Europe and Asia. Image reprinted with permission from the Oregon Historical Society Research Library. (OrHi 68758).

assorted other vessels on the Blair Waterway in Tacoma.[19] In Vancouver, Kaiser opened a yard with 12 ways to build landing craft for tanks (LSTs), troop transports, Liberty ships, and 50 escort carriers.[20] The overwhelming scale of production put an astounding number of men and women to work: up to 32,000 in Bremerton, 40,000 in Seattle, 33,000 in Tacoma, and 38,000 in Vancouver.[21]

Airplane manufacturing in Washington took off during the war, especially at the Boeing Company. William Boeing, a Michigan timber baron, founded the Pacific Aero Products Company in Seattle in 1916. After building wooden planes for the military during World War I, the company produced boats and furniture as demand fell at the end of the war.[22] During the Great Depression, the workforce fell to 600. Facing growing losses, Boeing's leaders gambled on an effort to design and build a new multi-engine bomber for the Army. The B-17 Flying Fortress debuted in 1935, and ultimately reversed the company's fortunes.[23] Sales to Britain fueled initial growth, but production soared once the

Figure 10.2 Workers, both men and women, at the Seattle Boeing plant celebrate completion of the 5,000th B-17 "Flying Fortress" in 1944, and many added their signatures to mark the occasion. While they obviously celebrated the milestone, the line of waiting aircraft stood as a reminder that their work remained unfinished as the war raged on. Reprinted with permission from the Washington State Historical Society.

United States joined the war. By the height of World War II, 50,000 workers at Boeing facilities in Washington produced 16 B-17s a day and one, larger, B-29 Super Fortress every five days.[24] By war's end in 1945, Northwesterners contributed 6,981 B-17s and 1,119 B-29s for the cause. The effect on the local economy can hardly be overstated, particularly in relation to the female and minority workforces. In 1939, all of Seattle's manufacturing plants produced goods worth $70 million dollars, whereas Boeing brought in nearly nine times as much by 1944.[25]

Numerous other facilities fueled the Northwest economy during war years. Pacific Car and Foundry (later named PACCAR) manufactured B-17 parts and Sherman tanks.[26] Reynolds Metal Company in Longview made aluminum for aircraft, as did the Aluminum Company of America (ALCOA) in Vancouver and Troutdale, and two federally funded plants near Spokane.[27] In Auburn, a massive Lend-Lease depot stored goods for shipment to the Soviet Union and other Allies.[28]

Perhaps the region's most significant, and controversial, work took place in Eastern Washington, where the federal government established the Hanford Engineer Works as part of the Manhattan Project. The top-secret effort to design and build atomic bombs required uranium-235 and plutonium-239. Facilities in Tennessee produced uranium, but project manager General Leslie Groves required plutonium. Although they had not yet located the production site, Groves contracted with DuPont Corporation to build the reactors. Fearful of accusations of war profiteering, DuPont refused to take any payment above $1.[29]

Late in 1942, the U.S. Army Corps of Engineers and DuPont began searching for a safe location. Risks posed from radiation to the 125,000 people in nearby Knoxville eliminated Tennessee, so officials looked west.[30] Lieutenant Colonel Franklin Matthias, plutonium project lead, and DuPont engineers surveyed remote areas of Oregon and Washington from the air.

The desert around the small farming communities of Hanford and White Bluffs near the Columbia River looked promising. The project required at least 560 acres of land, far removed from large populations, with access to copious amounts of clean water to cool the reactors. Grand Coulee Dam would provide electricity to run the water pumps and infrastructure supporting the reactors.[31] Construction began in March 1943 and some 2,000 residents were given 30 days to pack up and leave.[32]

Seemingly overnight the government turned the small town of Richland into a booming city. Constructing three reactors, two separation plants, and some 500 other structures required a workforce of 45,000.[33]

Project workers and residents in surrounding communities had no knowledge of the facility's purpose.[34] James Parker, a teenager from Idaho who moved to Hanford and worked on the project with his parents, heard the "whole plant was designed to make plastic tableware for the post-war world."[35] Some even quit Hanford out of a sense of patriotism because they wanted to work on projects critical to the war.[36] Louis Chesnut reminisced how undercover FBI agents sat at lunch counters while "workers who speculated out loud about the purpose of the project" received visits from agents.[37] The Wanapum, who held treaty rights to fish on the Hanford reach, complicated the understandably tight security. Wanting to avoid attention, Matthias permitted them to continue fishing, but under constant supervision.[38]

Hanford produced its first plutonium in February 1945, and all three reactors reached full capacity by March. Hanford plutonium fueled the first atomic bomb tested by the military at Alamogordo, New Mexico on July 16, 1945.[39] Hanford workers and the world learned about the Manhattan Project on August 6, 1945, when President Harry Truman announced the bombing of Hiroshima, Japan. That bomb used uranium from Tennessee, but the Fat Man bomb dropped on Nagasaki three days later used plutonium.[40] While the dawn of the nuclear age stunned the world, workers at Hanford planned a Labor Day celebration "that will pop almost as loud as the bomb that hit Hiroshima," as a local newspaper editor put it. "We've done nothing but keep quiet and hold secrets for two years and now we're going to yell to the world how happy we are."[41]

In addition to defense, the region met the nation's insatiable demand for resources. Construction of wartime housing, military installations, and numerous other applications, revitalized the logging industry. Idaho mills turned out more than 400 million board feet in 1942, more than doubling depression-era production. Similarly, Idaho and other Northwest mines raced to produce defense-related metals like tungsten and antimony. [42] Lastly, farms and fisheries expanded to meet the needs of hungry soldiers and wartime laborers. Recognizing the need for better food storage, Idaho's J.R. Simplot opened facilities to dehydrate potatoes and onions, shipping over 33 million pounds annually to the military. After the war, Simplot supplied the nation with Idaho potatoes, including the forerunner of the fast food industry, McDonald's restaurants.[43]

Figure 10.3 While the Northwest took great pride in the ships and planes it produced during both world wars, it also yielded much needed lumber from its forests. U.S. soldiers served as loggers during World War I and the government aggressively recruited labor in World War II. Reprinted with permission from the Washington State Historical Society.

While the war brought prosperity, it also ushered in divisions. Urban areas in Washington and Oregon received a disproportionate share of military contracts and steadily shifted away from dependence on resource industries and towards federal spending on shipping, aircraft, and nuclear weapons. Idaho, in contrast, stepped up resource extraction and watched in concern as more and more residents left the state for better opportunities in Washington and Oregon.[44]

Imperial Japan attacks Oregon

The Northwest's roaring economy made it an obvious enemy target, creating worries Japan might attack. Those fears turned to reality, sort of, but Japanese assaults ultimately had little effect on the region.

At the start of the war, Japanese submarines patrolled the waters off the coast and attacked three ships in late 1941 and 1942 and shelled Fort Stevens on the Columbia River but failed to cause significant damage. National Forests in Southwestern Oregon came under attack in September when Japanese pilot Nobuo Fujita took to the skies in a sub-based seaplane and dropped incendiary bombs.

Japanese officials hoped forest fires would sap away U.S. resources, but Forest Service lookouts quickly spotted the fires and called in firefighters to put them out. Fujita's sorties were the last direct attacks, but the Japanese military fixed bombs to small hot air balloons and allowed the winds to carry them across the Pacific in late 1944 and 1945. Northwesters found more than 100 remnants, but most had no effect. One, however, came shockingly close to success. It hit power lines in central Washington, disrupted the power grid, and caused Hanford's reactors to shut down completely. Although a meltdown was never imminent, the event captured the attention of federal officials and created genuine concern.[45]

A critical shortage of workers breaks down barriers

"Women took an awfully bad beating in Final Assembly," Hellen Nelson recalled. "There was harassment and sexism and that kind of thing ... Women were considered too stupid to know how to do anything."

– Female defense worker.

Explosive job growth created a constant, desperate need for labor. To put the crisis in perspective, the Vancouver shipyards employed 38,000 at the height of production in a city of just 18,000 in 1942.[46] The military draft and a patriotic rush to volunteer worsened the shortage. All told, 12.8% of the combined population of Washington, Oregon, and Idaho served in the armed forces during the war.[47] To fill critical jobs, regional employers and the federal government recruited laborers nationwide, and pushed aside existing discriminatory barriers barring women and minorities from the workforce.

Conditions in the shipyards offer insight into the experience of women. Men dominated the industry pre-war and ridiculed the idea of female shipbuilders.[48] Kaiser yards in Portland met heavy resistance when it started hiring women in April 1942. One woman recalled how a foreman "kicked up a storm when he found out he was going to have to hire women on the crew." He went on a tirade, threw his hat on the ground, "jumped up and down and just turned the air blue." Another's husband insisted, "You cannot work down there in the shipyards. They're too rough and the language is bad." Most of the men seemed "pretty nice," said one woman, but she encountered "a lot of hardheads" who felt women "were supposed to be pregnant and barefoot."[49]

Women, while battling stereotypes and sexual harassment, gained increasing acceptance as the war progressed and their numbers increased. By May 1943, recruiters went door-to-door encouraging women to apply, while Kaiser, the U.S. Employment Service, and the War Manpower Commission blanketed the media with advertisements. Apparently, their efforts paid off, as nearly 40,000 women worked in the Portland-Vancouver yards by 1944.[50]

In addition to their presence in the shipyards, women provided substantial labor at Boeing and Hanford. By 1943, women accounted for roughly 44% of Boeing's workers in the Seattle-Renton area.[51] Like their shipbuilding counterparts, they faced a good deal of pushback from men. "Women took an awfully bad beating in Final Assembly," Hellen Nelson recalled. "There was harassment and sexism and that kind of thing ... Women

Figure 10.4 Farmers in the Willamette River Valley, and throughout the region, found themselves desperately short of labor in 1943. Mrs. Mable Mack, pictured here, led the Women's Land Army in Oregon, where some 15,000 women helped to bring in the harvest and propel the Allies to victory. Image reprinted with permission from the *Oregonian*.

were considered too stupid to know how to do anything"[52] (for more on women's wartime experience, see "Women for the defense").

In addition to creating jobs, military spending broadened the Pacific Northwest's racial diversity. Between 1940 and 1950 the African American population of Washington, Oregon, and Idaho surged from just over 10,500 to more than 43,000.[53] Like women, African Americans were excluded from most defense industry jobs prior to the war. To deter discriminatory practices, President Roosevelt issued Executive Order 8802 barring discrimination in defense industries and established the Fair Employment Practices Committee to enforce it.[54] Boeing officials resisted the order, pointing to the worker's union, a branch of the International Association of Machinists that refused to accept non-white workers.[55] The stand-off attracted national attention from prominent civil rights leaders like Thurgood Marshall and A. Philip Randolph. Randolph called Boeing "One of the most conspicuous examples in the United States of race discrimination," which from the beginning of the war "refused to employ Negroes."[56] Under pressure, the union changed policies in April 1942, but resented how "the war situation" forced changes to "an old-established custom."[57] By 1943, 329 African Americans, mostly women, worked at Boeing, climbing to 1,600 by 1945.[58]

Racial tensions mounted as the black population grew. Strikingly, Washington Governor Arthur Langlie shared his concerns with Hanford officials. Expecting unemployment to rise once construction ended, he urged Hanford to "return most of the construction workmen back to their original centers of activity, particularly the negroes."[59] African Americans working in defense throughout the region lived in segregated housing and faced systematic discrimination in local establishments.[60] Frustration over inequality grew along with the white backlash to the rising black population, prompting

Figure 10.5 Volunteers with the American Red Cross pass out food and milk to African American soldiers in Washington State. For many, it was their first visit to the Pacific Northwest and more than a few decided to put down roots in the region once the war ended. Reprinted with permission from the Washington State Historical Society.

Seattle's Chief of Police to comment, "We're preparing for anything that might result from a crowded, mixed, and excited wartime population."[61]

Tensions erupted in August 1944 at Seattle's Fort Lawton, which housed Italian prisoners of war who volunteered to help the Allies through work in organizations known as Italian Service Units. Through their labor, they earned a monthly salary and incremental privileges.[62] African American soldiers resented the prisoners' preferential treatment and access to city services. Bars and restaurants that denied entry to African Americans served Italian POWs, while women made "a big fuss over the Italians" and found them "romantic."[63] A fight between a handful of Italians and African Americans following a night of drinking touched off a riot. African American soldiers stormed the Italian barracks, sent more than 30 Italians to the hospital, and hanged one POW, Guglielmo Olivotto, with a tent rope.[64] In response, the U.S. Army convicted 28 black soldiers of rioting and murder and sentenced them to a combined 200 years in prison, the largest, single court-martial during the war.[65] In 2007 and 2008, the Army reviewed the case and concluded the men did not receive a fair trial. Ultimately, Army officials overturned all 28 convictions, formally apologized, and granted honorable discharges with back pay to those involved.[66]

Native Peoples, too, found new opportunities in wartime industries. Ira Shawaway, a Yakama from Wapato in Eastern Washington, operated a rivet-making machine in Seattle for the Navy. Others took positions at Boeing and worked "steadily and efficiently to turn out Flying Fortresses." Others helped to build ships, cut trees, and haul in fish.[67] On the Swinomish Reservation north of Seattle, the Sagstad Shipyard leased land from the tribe and employed 30 Natives. Andrew Joe, a Swinomish leader, expressed pride when his daughter christened a newly finished barge built for the Army. Additionally, 30 men from the tribe served in the armed forces, while others bought war bonds to support the greater cause.[68]

Work opportunities off the reservations led to unanticipated consequences. Federal officials argued that "Indians, long dependent upon government guardianship, have demonstrated that they can assume the responsibilities that eventually will come with termination of federal trusteeship."[69] In the early 1950s, governmental termination policies promoted efforts to "emancipate" Natives from paternalistic policies and make them "subject to the same laws and entitled to the same privileges and responsibilities" as other American citizens. Critics argued that termination weakened the reservation system and protections established under the 1850s treaties, undermined tribal governments, eroded New Deal programs to restore native cultures, and ushered in significant new challenges for Native Peoples in the region.[70]

Defense contractors were not alone in their need for workers. As laborers left the farm for higher paying defense jobs, the agricultural industry turned to yet another minority to meet its labor shortage – Mexican citizens.[71] The seasonal nature of the work added to the problem. In the years before the war, fruit, hop, and vegetable farms in the Yakima Valley needed about 500 workers in the off-season, while the labor force swelled to more than 33,000 during harvest. By 1941, the industry faced extreme shortages and braced for severe losses if crops went unharvested.[72]

At first, communities in Oregon, Washington, and Idaho enacted a variety of emergency measures. In the spirit of wartime sacrifice, people from all corners were asked to step up: schools closed so children could work in the fields; police closed taverns and pool halls, and rounded up hobos; businesses closed and released their employees; and prison inmates were granted early release. Even the mentally ill in state institutions did their share of picking.[73] Efforts to organize women into a "Women's Land Army" achieved limited success. More than 18,000 answered the call in Oregon and Idaho in 1943, but overall they preferred defense jobs to agriculture.[74] Idahoans recruited "soldiers in overalls" from Jamaica and commented positively on their work, but, despite everything, agricultural labor remained in short supply.[75]

Under pressure from growers, the federal government established the Emergency Farm Labor Supply Program in 1942, better known as the Bracero Program, to recruit Mexican citizens for work in the United States.[76] Terms of the deal required the U.S. Government to give workers a contract written in both English and Spanish, ensure growers paid prevailing wages, and provide transportation and housing.[77] The first braceros arrived in the Northwest in October, and by 1947 nearly 47,000 worked in the region.[78] They harvested onions, peas, sweet corn, sugar beets, cucumbers, hops and other crops, and, in direct violation of the agreement, found themselves pressed into jobs in canneries and food processing plants. The U.S. Forest Service even employed braceros as fire fighters, where at least one died on the job.[79]

In spite of their considerable contributions to the war effort, braceros faced a mixed response in Northwest communities. Residents praised braceros as a "God-send to farmers," yet they routinely faced overt discrimination. [80] Bars and other public accommodations denied entry with signs reading "No Mexicans, White Trade Only" and "No Japs or Mexicans Allowed." A marshal in Stanwood, Washington, claimed his "town would be much better off without them."[81] In a particularly striking case, police in

Medford, Oregon, arrested a bracero for drunkenness when in actuality he was staggering after having been assaulted by a group of white men.[82] Importantly, some residents objected to racist behavior on moral grounds. "Something should be done about the Nazi minded element," exclaimed an Idaho woman. "Does not our Constitution demand liberty and justice for all?"[83] Expressing more pragmatic concerns, others worried racism would drive away workers and deliver "a blow" to the farmers desperate for labor.[84]

Bad working and living conditions added to frustrations. The growers typically assigned braceros the most physically demanding and lowest paying jobs.[85] In camp, six men usually shared a single tent. In Eastern Washington, Oregon, and Idaho, they roasted in the summer and froze in the winter. Kerosene stoves presented a constant fire danger. Worse, the food was terrible by almost any standard. Due to government rationing, camp managers rarely offered Mexican fare.[86] The contract with Mexico called for periodic camp inspections, but with only two inspectors for the region, including Utah and Montana, most abuses went unchecked.[87] Braceros occasionally found support among the region's small Mexican-American communities, yet life in the region took an emotional toll.[88] Not surprisingly, a mix of homesickness and culture shock, coupled with the hardships of life, fostered resentment and resistance.[89]

Braceros went on strike more often in Washington, Oregon, and Idaho than elsewhere, even though their contracts prohibited it.[90] In the Southwest, growers near the border had the power to deport and replace striking workers, yet those in the distant Northwest could not. Recognizing the situation, the Mexican consulate in Salt Lake City encouraged labor activism, prompting braceros to walk off the job for better pay and food.[91] Farmers broke most strikes, but some brought better treatment. The federal government stepped in and obtained permission from Mexico to employ braceros as camp cooks, cutting down on complaints and improving morale.[92]

Designed as a temporary measure to fill jobs during the war, the program continued at the national level until 1964, but effectively ended shortly after the war in the Pacific Northwest as Mexican-American migrant workers met the local demand for labor. Many braceros returned to Mexico following the war but large numbers eventually returned and settled permanently in the Northwest, further increasing the region's diversity.[93]

Japanese Americans challenge new boundaries

(No) "armed uprising of Japanese" would take place and no Japanese problem existed on the West Coast.
— *Government report on the threat Japanese residents posed to U.S. security.*

Fear gripped the West Coast in the days following the Japanese attack at Pearl Harbor. Civil defense officials in cities like Salem ordered blackouts as reports "of an enemy aircraft carrier off the Pacific coast" heightened concerns.[94] As worries built, Americans along the Pacific Coast increasingly looked upon Japanese with suspicion and demanded the federal government take action.

Political and military leaders worried about disloyalty well before the war started. In Hawaii, local officials argued "local Japanese" routinely met with Japanese sailors in port and posed a threat to security.[95] President Roosevelt, in a 1936 memo, maintained that "every Japanese citizen or non-citizen on the Island of Oahu" meeting with Japanese ships should be "identified … on a special list" and would be "placed in a concentration camp in the event of trouble."[96]

As tensions mounted, the federal government actively investigated the Japanese community in America to ascertain its loyalty. Conducted by Lieutenant Commander Kenneth Ringle of the Office of Naval Intelligence (ONI) and Curtis Munson, a businessman, the studies generally divided Japanese into two groups: Issei and Nisei.[97] The Issei, or first generation, immigrated to America. Under the Naturalization Act of 1790, only "free white" persons could become citizens, and Issei remained "aliens" no matter how long they lived in the country.[98] Their children, the Nisei, became citizens at birth, as called for in the Fourteenth Amendment.

Both Munson and Ringle concluded that Japanese in America posed no significant threat to national security. The Issei, in Munson's opinion held little loyalty to Japan, as "they have chosen to make this their home and have brought up their children here." Munson described the Nisei as "90 to 98% loyal" and "pathetically eager" to demonstrate it. He felt a few "fanatical" individuals might attempt sabotage but suggested they would likely fail "because of their easily recognized physical appearance."[99] In general he emphatically stated that "no armed uprising of Japanese" would take place and no Japanese problem existed on the West Coast. If anything, he worried more about the threat that angry white mobs posed to Japanese communities.[100]

Despite their conclusions, the federal government labeled the Issei "enemy aliens" and moved against them after Pearl Harbor.[101] FBI and ONI agents arrested some 2,000 Issei leaders in less than a week, while the Roosevelt Administration froze their assets and prohibited Japanese farmers from selling food.[102] Other restrictions limited travel and made it illegal to own cameras, weapons, or anything else that could be used for espionage or sabotage.[103] Monica Sone, a Nisei women in Seattle, recalled how at first those arrested "had been prominent in community affairs," while "it became less and less apparent why the others were included" over time.[104] Her family worried that her father would be arrested any day, and packed his suitcase just in case. To avoid suspicion, they burned Japanese books, newspapers, music, and anything else that might seem questionable. Doing so, however, did not remove their anxiety, and they waited to see what would come next.[105]

Their worst fears came to pass when President Roosevelt signed Executive Order 9066 on February 19, 1942. It allowed the military to create areas "from which any or all persons may be excluded" in order to protect "against espionage and against sabotage to national-defense material, national-defense premises and national-defense utilities."[106] Ten days later, Lieutenant General John L. DeWitt, responsible for West Coast security, established military zones covering Western Washington and Oregon, California, and parts of Arizona. His announcements made it clear that the approximate 112,000 Japanese aliens and citizens on the Pacific Coast would be moved inland.[107]

Military leaders justified internment on the basis of military necessity. Secretary of War Henry Stimson worried that Japanese Americans might support a potential invasion.[108] General DeWitt flatly stated, "The Japanese race is an enemy race."[109] It was only natural, he argued, for immigrants to remain loyal to their home country. Certainly, whites who moved to Japan would not "become loyal Japanese subjects" eager to take up arms "against the nation of their parents." In the end, nothing Japanese Americans

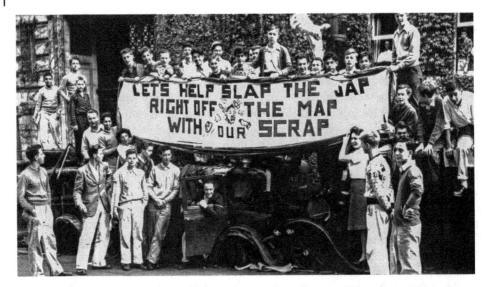

Figure 10.6 Everyone was expected to do their part during the war by purchasing war bonds, conserving resources, or, as captured here, gathering scrap metal for weapons production. Beaming with pride, these young people expressed both patriotism and deep-seated anti-Japanese sentiments. Image reprinted with permission from the *Oregonian*.

said or did could placate him. Even the absence of a single incident of sabotage, was a "disturbing and confirming indication that such action will be taken."[110]

In the end, the Roosevelt Administration largely decided on internment because the public demanded it. Importantly, their calls for action dovetailed with longstanding hostility towards Japanese on the West Coast.[111] As Monica Sone put it, "the professional guardians of the Golden West had wanted to rid their land of the Yellow Peril" for years. The war simply "provided an opportunity for them to push their program through."[112] FBI Director J. Edgar Hoover readily admitted that public pressure, not "factual data," fueled the drive for "mass evacuation." Lurid media accounts "resulted in a tremendous amount of pressure" on leaders, while local politicians and citizens launched "a widespread movement demanding complete evacuation of all Japanese, citizen and alien alike."[113]

A variety of motives led Americans in the West to lobby for internment. Fear and racism drove some, like a woman in Seattle who asked FDR to "Kindly give some thought to ridding our beloved Country of these Japs." In her view, they had no "love or loyalty to our God, our ideal or our traditions, or our Government" and "should *never* have been allowed here."[114] Economic interests fired the hearts of others. Many whites on the West Coast resented the power of Japanese farmers and businesses.[115] "We're charged with wanting to get rid of the Japs for selfish reasons," admitted the head of the Grower-Shipper Vegetable Association, "We might as well be honest. We do." He felt white farmers could "take over and produce everything the Jap grows" and did not want Japanese to return.[116] U.S. Attorney General Francis Biddle similarly commented that "special interests" wanted Japanese removed "from good farm land and the elimination of their competition."[117]

The forced removal of Japanese started on Bainbridge Island, Washington, in late March 1942 under the authority of the Wartime Civil Control Administration.[118] The agency ordered them to bring clothing, linens, toiletries, dishes and utensils, but no more than the family or individual could carry.[119] Once packed, they typically had just a few days to sell or store all other possessions. Many lost nearly everything: homes, pets, cars, businesses, and a lifetime of possessions.[120] In Washington, most Japanese went initially to "Camp Harmony" built on the Puyallup Fairgrounds near Tacoma. Monica Sone described how each family lived in a small room with one window, a wood stove, and a floor that "consisted of two-by-fours laid directly on the earth" with dandelions growing through the cracks.[121] In Oregon, the Portland Livestock Pavilion housed roughly 36,000 people in one large facility divided into small family units.[122] The 1,200 Japanese living in Idaho, which fell outside of the military zones, were not required to report to a camp.[123]

Internees spent a few months in the assembly centers, before federal authorities transferred them to one of ten camps run by the War Relocation Authority (WRA), where most would sit out the war.[124] Many Puget Sound and Portland area internees wound up at the Minidoka Relocation Center near Twin Falls, Idaho.[125] Located on a remote stretch of flat prairieland, Minidoka "sizzled on the average of 110 degrees" in the summer and froze in the winter.[126] At first, Monica Sone and her sister refused to wear winter WRA-issued clothing, because they would "rather freeze than lose our femininity." They changed their minds after a man "became lost one night in a snowstorm and died from exposure."[127]

Both the Issei and Nisei coped as best they could and worked to improve camp conditions. They planted gardens, built furniture from scrap materials, organized schools and church services, and fielded competitive baseball teams.[128] Others passed the time through labor. In April 1942, WRA head Milton Eisenhower met with local politicians to arrange for internees to pick sugar beets and other crops for fair wages.[129] Western governors initially opposed to the idea gave in as labor shortages mounted. Japanese began working in Oregon's Malheur County in May with the approval of Governor Charles Sprague.[130] Idaho Governor Chase Clark also accepted the plan, but that didn't stop his anti-Japanese rhetoric. "Japs live like rats, breed like rats and act like rats," he thundered. "We don't want them … permanently located in our state." Facing criticism, he later qualified his remarks, and praised those who helped with the "beet thinning emergency."[131] By war's end, roughly 33,000 Japanese worked outside the camps, and some settled permanently in Idaho and Oregon farming communities.[132]

Despite the gross violation of their rights, some Nisei men volunteered for Army service once policies allowed it, and far more served when later drafted. The all-Nisei 100th Infantry Battalion and 442nd Regimental Combat Team fought valiantly in Europe and earned more decorations than most other units in the war. Despite their service and sacrifice, they faced continued prejudice at home. In Hood River, Oregon, the American Legion tried to remove Nisei names from their honor roll, while the Disabled American Veterans in Hermiston excluded Nisei from their post.[133]

Internees gradually left camps as wartime policies eased. Many pursued education and jobs, provided they remained east of the exclusion zones. Meanwhile, several Nisei challenged government actions in court.[134] Gordon Hirabayashi, a University of Washington student, disobeyed curfews, while Fred Korematsu of California refused to evacuate.[135] Lawyers for Mitsuye Endo, also from California, argued the government held her

Figure 10.7 Japanese Americans interned at Minidoka did what they could to form communities and provide needed services for their fellow internees. The demeanor of these "hospital workers" suggests a tight bond existed between them. Reprinted with permission from the Washington State Historical Society.

without charge in clear violation of her rights. Ultimately, the U.S. Supreme Court ruled against both men, but sided with Endo in early 1945. The U.S. Army, aware of the impending decision, changed policies and allowed Nisei to return to the West Coast. The Issei, however, remained incarcerated until the war ended and camps closed.[136]

Following the war, Japanese Americans engaged in a long campaign for compensation. Their struggles culminated in the late 1980s when federal courts overturned the Korematsu and Hirabayashi decisions, and Congress passed a reparations bill.[137] Finally, in 1988, President Ronald Reagan signed a Civil Liberties Act granting $20,000 to all internees still living while proclaiming internment a "grave wrong" and a national "mistake."[138]

From a World War to a Cold War

During production, operators dumped more than four hundred billion gallons of (nuclear) waste into the ground, often in long, unlined trenches known as "cribs."

With the economy trending down in 1945 and 1946, Northwest residents worried the region would fall into a post-war recession, similar to the one following World War I. Boeing's B-29 orders fell sharply, leading to 20,000 lost jobs in the months after the war.[139] Eventually the workforce fell to 9,000, or 20% of the wartime peak.[140] The two Kaiser shipyards in Portland closed, while the Bremerton shipyard plummeted from 32,000 employees to less than 9,000 by late 1946.[141]

In sharp contrast to expectations, the region enjoyed continued economic growth due to a new conflict: the Cold War. Although the U.S.-Soviet alliance proved critical to defeating Nazi Germany, tensions quickly emerged after the war. On one hand, political ideology divided the nations. The United States promoted democracy, capitalism, and religious belief, in stark contrast to Soviet communism. On the other hand, Soviet leaders, concerned mostly with protecting their western borders, demanded a share of the power in the post-war world. U.S. leaders objected, and increasingly saw Soviet ambition as a threat to American interests. At the urging of American diplomat George Kennan, President Truman laid out bold, new policies to contain Soviet expansion.[142]

Global tensions translated to federal contracts for the region's defense industries, especially Boeing. The company built B-50 and B-52 bombers for the newly established U.S. Air Force, and later designed and manufactured intercontinental ballistic missiles like the Minuteman.[143] Thanks to a roaring commercial aircraft market, combined with a steady flow of new contracts during the Korean and Vietnam wars, Boeing's Seattle area employment jumped to 28,000 in 1951 and an astounding 101,000 by 1968.[144] Growth remained uneven, however. Military cutbacks following the drawdown in Vietnam in the early 1970s led to a 60% cutback in Boeing's local workforce. Famously, two men put up a billboard outside the city urging the last leaving to "Turn out the lights."[145] The joke was a tangible sign of the downside of the region's long-term dependence on federal dollars. As the federal budget went, so went the region's economy.

Hanford rode the Cold War money train as well, especially after the Soviet Union tested its first atom bomb in 1949.[146] Turning from fission to the more powerful fusion technology in the 1950s, both nations raced to out-produce each other.[147] Requiring more and more plutonium, the government steadily poured funds into Hanford, and by 1955, eight reactors churned out plutonium. It's not surprising citizens cheered Congress's decision to build a ninth, or "N" reactor, in 1962, the first to produce electricity and plutonium.[148]

Regional prospects seemingly dimmed just a few years later when the federal government cut plutonium production, and began closing the aging Hanford reactors.[149] By 1971, only the "N" reactor remained in operation, but it too closed in 1987, followed by the separation plants in 1990.

At first glance the pullout seemed like a devastating blow to the nearby Tri-Cities of Kennewick, Richland, and Pasco.[150] Yet cleaning up the almost unfathomable levels of nuclear waste continues to generate jobs and fuel the local economy. During production, operators dumped more than 400 billion gallons of waste into the ground, often in long, unlined trenches known as "cribs." According to the Washington State Department of Ecology, one crib alone, number "216-A-36B" for example, handled "up to 116,000 gallons of diluted nitric acid, ammonium nitrate, and ammonium fluoride per day" over 11 years.[151] High-level radioactive waste went into 177 underground storage tanks, nearly one-third of which leaked. All told, the tank farms contained 54 million gallons of high-level radioactive waste, posing an immense environmental risk. Additionally, Hanford released vast amounts of air pollution and generated copious volumes of solid waste.[152]

In 1989, Washington State, the Department of Energy, and the Environmental Protection Agency signed the Tri-Party Agreement to begin clean-up at "the most contaminated site in the nation."[153] Initially, they planned to spend $57 billion over 30 years, but costs soared over the following decades. In 2013, official estimates exceeded

$114 billion, but clean-up remains behind schedule and over budget.[154] A $13.4 billion vitrification plant, designed to encase radioactive waste in glass for long-term storage, is scheduled to begin operations in 2019 but may not meet that goal.[155] Given the enormous challenges of clean-up, Hanford will realistically produce jobs well into the future.

A changed Northwest?

President Kennedy's claim that Hanford "changed the entire history of the world" also describes the role of the larger Pacific Northwest. Beyond question, federal spending during World War II and the Cold War transformed the Pacific Northwest, but its central role in achieving victory justified every dollar. Its Pacific Coast location and proximity to Asia put the region, if not in the storm's eye, certainly within its sphere. Existing defense industries like Boeing, numerous deep-water ports, and military bases like Fort Lewis in Tacoma provided critical launch points for planes, ships, and personnel. The region not only equipped the military, it housed and fed it, thanks to vibrant logging, farming, and fishing industries. The unrelenting demand for workers throughout the war stimulated both population growth and racial diversity, and opened avenues for women and racial minorities.

But it's also clear that in certain respect the war's positive effects were remarkably limited in scope. Rather than finding doors opened to them, Japanese Americans found them closed and guarded with barbed wire. Moreover, for a balanced perspective on the war, it's important to view it through the eyes of residents living in the vast rural sections of Washington, Oregon, and Idaho. They will offer a more tempered review of the war's benefits. When the guns stopped firing, they remained deeply dependent on resource extraction and did not fully share in the economic fortunes realized in the Puget Sound and Portland regions.[156] The resulting economic disparity between the urban, industrialized Northwest and the rural, resource-based Northwest continued to deepen into the twenty-first century.

Women for the defense

World War II may have created job opportunities for women in the male-dominated defense industries, but they stepped into an environment of stereotyping, sexism, and even hostility in the workplace.

The vast majority of women at the Kaiser shipyards, for example, worked as clerks, general helpers, and welders. Only an exceptional few broke through the all-male bastions of crane operators, electricians, machinists, and other specialized trades.[157]

Similarly, they found few opportunities to advance. As one woman remembered it, they "were allowed to do the basic work but none of the boss jobs, none of the lead jobs."[158] In practice, some found themselves doing the work of lead men, but rarely received the commensurate title or pay.[159]

Patriotism fired the hearts of some women while others took jobs for pragmatic reasons. A majority had worked before the war, largely in lower-paying service and clerical jobs.[160] Work in the shipyards could pay up to four times more than other work. "It was an unbelievable amount of money," said one woman, and simply "too good to pass up."[161]

Whatever their motivations, women like Augusta Clawson, generally took immense pride in their work. Working for the U.S. Office of Education, Clawson went undercover in the shipyards to root out the causes of the high turnover rate among female employees. She eventually proposed numerous improvements to training and orientation to build confidence in new employees, but along the way came to identify with her jobs and fellow workers.[162] At the start, she felt self-conscious wearing her "working togs and working dirt" in public, but eventually became "proud of them." She "swelled with pride" as her ships slid into the water, and decided, "I must have a grandchild ... so that I can say, 'Darling, in the last war your grandmother built ships.'"[163]

Although Clawson felt at times "sick of men," she generally had "no complaints" about their behavior and built good relations with coworkers.[164] Many others, however, reported serious problems with sexual harassment and objectification. Men at the Todd Shipyard in Seattle hit on Mary Todd Doullard constantly. "They kept hanging around me and looking and trying to get me to go out with them," she recalled, worried she'd lose her job for ignoring their propositions.[165] Other women complained about men with "four hands" and found themselves welding in the rain, sometimes getting shocked, and suffering other retaliation for refusing advances from supervisors.[166] Portland shipyard worker Doris Ashalomov resented the beauty pageants held in her yard. "I was really embarrassed about the whole thing," she remembered, but Ashalomov's coworkers "were so proud" that she was chosen," she set her reservations aside.[167]

No break from domestic duties

Female workers often struggled to manage work and home life. Early in her training, Clawson returned home and exclaimed, "Jingle, Jangle, Jingle – thank God I'm single!"[168] While she cooked and did laundry only for herself, social expectations pressured married women and mothers to maintain their households despite the rigors of industrial labor.[169] Along the same lines, Clawson noted how women struggled with "the problem of looking after young children."[170] Kaiser responded by building two childcare facilities in Portland through

Figure 10.8 The wartime economy opened doors for African American women like Dorothy Williams, who trained on a belt sander at the Rainier Aircraft Training School in 1945. While the region welcomed additional labor, many resisted social change and African American women faced both racism and sexism on the job. Reprinted with permission from the Washington State Historical Society.

a national, federally funded program.[171] In addition to providing care around the clock, the centers mended clothing, administered vaccinations, led parent education, and sold boxed dinners to the overworked women.[172] The quality of care won over parents and earned Kaiser national acclaim from *Parents Magazine* and professional educators.[173]

Pervasive racism remained a significant barrier for African American women. Beatrice Marshall, an African American from Indiana, trained as a machinist and moved to Portland for a job in the shipyards. On arrival, she and other women were told "that they didn't have any openings as lathe or drill-press operators; and that we would have to either accept painter's helper or a sweeper." In reality, openings existed for whites, and Marshall soon left in frustration. "They was doing all this advertising … and here I am spending time and getting trained and qualified and couldn't get it," she fumed, "I was real mad."[174]

At Hanford, women filled some 13% of jobs. Most worked in the mess halls, as clerical staff, or in other occupations traditionally seen as appropriate for women.[175] A few worked as chemists but had their work derided by an Army engineer. He felt they did "satisfactory work" when following precise orders, but he maintained women "are by no means capable of carrying out tests or analysis without prior instructions."[176]

Women who wanted to keep their positions after the war faced the reemergence of old barriers as unions moved in to protect men's jobs. Just over half of the women working for Kaiser in the Portland shipyards answered "yes" to the question, "Do you intend to continue in an industrial job after the war?" That prompted a local publication to lament how "welding wives" might not "return to baking buns instead of building barges."[177] Similarly, a woman at Boeing insisted that, "most women did not want to leave work at the end of the war," since "A job was a job and the whole level of existence had changed."[178] Regardless, most women were laid-off from industrial jobs after the war. Edna Hopkins, a shipyard welder, poignantly recalled that when the American victory was announced over the radio, she went back to work instead of listening to the broadcasts. When questioned, she told her boss, "This is the last pipe I'll ever weld." Despite his assurances to the contrary, she was let go the next day.[179]

Hopkins may have welded her last pipe, but American industry had not heard the last of women. There would be no going back to pre-war America. A more confident, experienced female worker emerged in the decades following the war despite pressures to return to domestic duties. Discrimination would continue, and in some cases worsened, as men tried to recapture their pre-war dominance, but the course was set. Women had tasted the fruit of liberation and wanted to dine on the entire bowl, unleashing profound changes on the job and in the home.

Maggie, Scoop, and the Federal Northwest

Military spending drove the Pacific Northwest economy, especially Washington State, from before the Pearl Harbor bombing in 1941 until after the fall of the Berlin Wall in 1989. For over five decades, the federal government pumped billions of dollars into the "federal Northwest," creating tens of thousands of jobs and squashing unemployment.

Few people symbolize the region's federalism more than Washington's Democratic Senators Warren G. ("Maggie") Magnuson, and Henry M. "Scoop" Jackson. Collectively, Scoop and Maggie spent 87 years in the nation's capital representing the state's interests, becoming arguably the most powerful Senate duo in American history.

Magnuson, born in 1905, was raised in the Midwest and moved to Seattle to attend the University of Washington. After successful stints as a state legislator and King County Prosecutor, he won a seat in the U.S. House of Representatives in 1936, where he served for eight years. His energy, effectiveness, and easy-going style helped him get elected to the Senate in 1944, where he served six terms. Minnesota Senator Eugene McCarthy said, "Maggie is the most loved man in the Senate."[180]

Magnuson's political skills eventually landed him key committee assignments. He chaired the influential Appropriations Committee and the equally important Commerce Committee. He engineered passage of notable legislation in health care and research, consumer protection and environmental protection, especially issues related to marine mammals, fisheries, and Puget Sound. He lobbied to award Washington two world's fairs, Century 21 Exposition in 1962 and Spokane's Expo '74.[181]

Jackson experienced a similar trajectory to Senate leadership. Born in 1912 in Everett, Washington, he delivered newspapers in his youth, earning him the nickname Scoop. Like Magnuson, he served as a county prosecutor (Snohomish) before winning a seat in the House in 1940, representing the Second Congressional District. At age 32, he was the youngest member of Congress, where he served six terms. In 1952, Jackson joined Magnuson in the Senate, where they would double-team for Washington State constituents for the better part of three decades. He ran for President in 1972 and 1976, but the obstacles were insurmountable for a relatively unknown politician from a small Western state. In 1972 President Richard Nixon asked him to join his cabinet as Secretary of Defense, but Jackson turned him down.

Like the state they represented, both Senators sat front and center throughout Cold War tensions between the United States and the Soviet Union. With Jackson sitting on the Armed Forces Committee and Magnuson's leadership in Appropriations, the Evergreen State was on the receiving end of extraordinary federal largesse. Jackson earned the reputation as a "Cold Warrior," but both men helped to funnel defense dollars to military installations throughout the state, including the Naval Shipyard in Bremerton, the Trident submarine support base in Bangor, Whidbey Island Naval Air Station, the Yakima Training Center and Hanford.

With Jackson's doggedness, a string of contracts with the U.S. Air Force propelled the Boeing Aircraft Company to dramatic growth in the 1950s and 1960s, making it the state's largest employer. The design and assembly of the Boeing B-52 bomber, America's workhorse in the Korean and Vietnam wars, created many thousands of jobs, and paved the way for development of the Boeing-707, the company's first commercial jet.

The flow of military dollars into Washington amounted to an embarrassment of riches. Jackson became known as the "Senator from Boeing," a moniker he abhorred, while Magnuson earned a similar reputation for pork-barrel politics. "He is scrupulously fair with federal funds," claimed Minnesota Senator Walter Mondale, "one half for Washington state, one half for the rest of the country."[182]

The dynamic duo was split up in 1980 when Magnuson lost to Slade Gordon during the Ronald Reagan-led Republican sweep in 1980. "My constituents have put me out to pasture," the 75-year-old senator said in his concession speech. He died on May 20, 1989, at age 84. Reporting about his death, the *New York Times*, said Magnuson "defied ideological pigeon-holing; his liberal voting record dated from the New Deal, yet he considered himself a conservative guardian of the taxpayers' dollars."[183]

Jackson won reelection for a fifth term in 1982, but just ten months later, on September 1, 1983, died of a heart attack. He was 71. The cigar-smoking Magnuson, known in Washington, DC, as the "man about town," outlived the straight-arrowed Jackson by six years. Former Washington Governor Daniel Evans was appointed to Jackson's vacated Senate seat.

Jackson was awarded the Presidential Medal of Freedom in 1984. At the award ceremony, President Ronald Reagan called Jackson "one of the great Senators in our history and a great patriot who loved freedom first, last and always." His focus on national security, the President said, was based on an understanding that "there is great good in the world and great evil, too, that there are saints and sinners among us."[184] Thanks to Jackson and Magnuson, funds to fight the battle against the perceived evils of the Cold War were frequently spent in Washington.

Explore more

Books

Amy Kesselman's *Fleeting Opportunities: Women Shipyard Workers in Portland and Vancouver During World War II and Reconversion* dispels popular misconceptions about women workers and offers an excellent introduction to the topic. For a personal account of life in the yards, start with August Clawson's *Shipyard Diary of a Woman Welder* and also consult *A Mouthful of Rivets: Women at Work in World War II* by Nancy Baker Wise and Christy Wise. Quintard Taylor's books, *The Forging of a Black Community: Seattle's Central District from 1870 through the Civil Rights Era* and *In Search of the Racial Frontier: African Americans in the American West, 1528–1990*, give detailed coverage of the African American experience, and Erasmo Gamboa's *Mexican Labor and World War II: Braceros in the Pacific Northwest, 1942–1947* is a leading work on the subject. For more on internment, see Greg Robinson's *By Order of the President: FDR and the Internment of Japanese Americans*. Additionally, *Nisei Daughter* by Monica Sone is an autobiographical account of her life before, during, and after the war. Lastly, *Atomic Frontier Days: Hanford and the American West* by John Findlay and Bruce Hevly presents a thorough overview of the Hanford project, while Michele S. Gerber's *On the Homefront: The Cold War Legacy of the Hanford Nuclear Site* gives especially good information on pollution and clean-up efforts at Hanford.

Online

The Densho Project (http://www.densho.org/) is an incredibly rich resource on internment. Also see the Camp Harmony Exhibit (https://www.lib.washington.edu/exhibits/harmony/Exhibit/) at the University of Washington Libraries Site. The federal government provides much information on Hanford at http://www.hanford.gov/, while Black Past (http://www.blackpast.org/) has good information on the African American experience during the war.

Museums

The Boeing Museum of Flight (https://www.museumofflight.org/) in Seattle is a popular attraction and has numerous aircraft from the World War II era on display. The Puget Sound Navy museum in Bremerton also offers good displays on this period. The federal government has opened Hanford to tours (http://www.hanford.gov/page.cfm/HanfordSiteTours) and is developing the Minidoka internment camp in Idaho into a National Historic Site (http://www.nps.gov/miin/index.htm).

What do you think?

Some historians have argued that World War II transformed the Pacific Northwest. Do you agree with that characterization? How much did the region change? To what degree did it remain consistent with its past? Among the people of the region, who were the winners and losers in the war?

Notes

1 Cassandra Tate, "President Kennedy Participates in Ground-breaking Ceremonies for Construction of N Reactor at Hanford on September 26, 1963," *HistoryLink*, accessed November 29, 2015, http://www.historylink.org/; John Findlay and Bruce Hevly, *Atomic Frontier Days: Hanford and the American West* (Seattle, WA: University of Washington Press, 2011), 166.

2 Tate, "President Kennedy Participates in Ground-breaking Ceremonies"; John F. Kennedy, "Remarks at the Hanford, Washington, Electric Generating Plant," The American Presidency Project, accessed November 29, 2015, http://www.presidency.ucsb.edu/.

3 Kennedy, "Remarks."

4 "US Looks for Declarations Coming Today," *The Oregon Statesman*, September 2, 1939; Richard L. Turner "Neutrality of United States is Proclaimed," *The Oregon Statesman*, September 6, 1939.

5 "64 Plants in Oregon Ready on War Orders," *The Oregon Statesman*, September 2, 1939.

6 Turner, "Neutrality of United States is Proclaimed."

7 Turner, "Neutrality of United States is Proclaimed"; Richard L. Turner, "FDR Eloquent in Please for 'Cash-Carry,'" *The Oregon Statesman*, September 22, 1939; James A. Henretta, Rebecca Edwards, and Robert O. Self, *America's History* 7th ed. (Boston: Bedford / St. Martin's, 2011), 755.

8 "Navy Expansion to Cost Over Billion Dollars," *The Oregon Statesman*, November 5, 1939; "Fleet Expansion is Asked by Navy," *The Oregon Statesman*, January, 9 1940; "FDR Declares Overseas War Isn't for US," *The Oregon Statesman*, July 11, 1940; "Navy Increase Bill is Signed by Roosevelt," *The Bend Bulletin*, July 20, 1940.

9 "50,000 Planes Annually Goal Says President," *The Oregon Statesman*, May 17, 1940.

10 "West to Build Many Vessels, Navy Program," *The Oregon Statesman*, September 10, 1940.

11 "Oregon to Get Big Shipbuilding Program," *The Oregon Statesman*, January 12, 1941.

12 Henretta, *America's History*, 756; "Seven Billion Asked as War Bill is Signed," *The Bend Bulletin*, March 11, 1941.

13 "War Aid Fund Request Made by Roosevelt," *The Bend Bulletin*, March 12, 1941.

14 Franklin Delano Roosevelt, "'A Date Which Will Live in Infamy': FDR Asks for a Declaration of War," History Matters: The U.S. Survey Course on the Web, accessed October 4, 2015, http://historymatters.gmu.edu/.

15 Henretta, *America's History*, 756–766; Leonard J. Arrington, *History of Idaho*, Vol. 2 (Moscow, ID: University of Idaho Press, 1994), 77; "War Comes: We Face the Test," *The Oregon Statesman*, December 8, 1941.

16 Gordon Dodds, *The American Northwest: A History of Oregon and Washington* (Arlington Heights, IL: The Forum Press, Inc., 1986), 262–264; Amy Kesselman, *Fleeting Opportunities: Women Shipyard Workers in Portland and Vancouver During World War II and Reconversion* (Albany, NY: University of New York Press, 1990), 13.

17 Dodds, *The American Northwest*, 264; Kit Oldham, "Kaiser Shipyard in Vancouver Launches its First Escort Aircraft Carrier on April 5, 1943," *HistoryLink*, accessed October 4, 2015, http://www.historylink.org/; L.A. Sawyer and W. H. Mitchell, *The Liberty Ships* 2nd ed. (London: Lloyd's of London Press, 1985), 117; "Kaiser and Oregon Shipyards," The Oregon History Project, accessed October 24, 2015, http://oregonhistoryproject.org/.

18 Daryl C. McClary, "Puget Sound Naval Shipyard," *HistoryLink*, accessed October 4, 2015, http://www.historylink.org/.

19 Dodds, *The American Northwest*, 264; James R. Warren, "World War II Home Front on Puget Sound," *HistoryLink*, accessed October 4, 2015, http://www.historylink.org/; Julie Van Pelt, "Port of Tacoma Sees Launch of Todd Shipyards' Freighter *Cape Alava* on August 3, 1940," *HistoryLink*, accessed October 5, 2015, http://www.historylink.org/.

20 Dodds, *The American Northwest*, 264; Oldham, "Kaiser Shipyard in Vancouver Launches its First Escort Aircraft Carrier."

21 Dodds, *The American Northwest*, 264; McClary, "Puget Sound Naval Shipyard"; Oldham, Kaiser shipyard in Vancouver"; Van Pelt, "Port of Tacoma sees Launch of Todd Shipyards' freighter."

22 John Schultz and David Wilma, "Boeing, William Edward (1881–1956)," *HistoryLink*, accessed October 22, 2015, http://www.historylink.org/; Carlos A. Schwantes, *The Pacific Northwest: An Interpretive History*, 2nd ed. (Lincoln, NE: University of Nebraska Press, 1996), 358.

23 Alan J. Stein, "Boeing Flying Fortress B-17 Prototype Takes her Maiden Flight on July 28, 1935," *HistoryLink*, accessed October 25, 2016, http://www.historylink.org/.

24 Quintard Taylor, "Swing the Door Wide": The World War II Economy Opened the Job Market for Blacks in the Pacific Northwest," *Columbia* 9, no. 2 (Summer 1995), 26–27; Richard S. Kirkendall, "The Boeing Complex and the Military-Metropolitan-Industrial Complex, 1945–1953," *Pacific Northwest Quarterly* 85, no. 4 (Fall 1994), 138; Dodds, *The American Northwest*, 238.

25 Warren, "World War II Home Front on Puget Sound"; Schwantes, *The Pacific Northwest*, 411; Taylor, "Swing Wide the Door," 26.

26 Dorothy O. Johansen and Charles M. Gates, *Empire of the Columbia: A History of the Pacific Northwest* (New York: Harper and Brothers, 1957), 560; Warren, "World War II Home Front on Puget Sound"; Paula Becker, "PACCAR Inc." *HistoryLink*, accessed October 22, 2015, http://www.historylink.org/.

27 Kit Oldham, "Alcoa Plant at Vancouver Produces the First Aluminum in the West on September 23, 1940," *HistoryLink*, accessed October 25, 2016, http://www.historylink.org/; Dodds, *The American Northwest*, 265.

28 William E. Saxe, "Arming the Soviets: The Pacific Northwest Played an Important Role in Providing Our Russian Allies with Lend Lease Materiel During World War II," *Columbia* 20, no. 2 (Summer 2006).

29 Kit Oldham, "Construction of Massive Plutonium Production Complex at Hanford begins in March 1943," *HistoryLink*, accessed October 25, 2015, http://www.historylink.org/; Findlay, 16, 23–24.

30 Findlay, *Atomic Frontier Days*, 17.

31 Findlay, *Atomic Frontier Days*, 17–20; Louis C. Chesnut, "Siting the Hanford Engineering Works: I Was there, Leslie!" *HistoryLink*, accessed October 24, 2016, http://www.historylink.org/.

32 Findlay, *Atomic Frontier Days*, 20.

33 Findlay, *Atomic Frontier Days*, 22, 25; Oldham, "Construction of Massive Plutonium Production Complex."

34 "Atomic Bomb Super Secret," *The Post-Register* (Idaho Falls), August 7, 1945.

35 Quoted in Findlay, *Atomic Frontier Days*, 29–30.

36 Ibid., 26.

37 Chesnut, "Siting the Hanford Engineer Works."

38 Findlay, *Atomic Frontier Days*, 21.

39 Ibid., 35.

40 Findlay, *Atomic Frontier Days*, 36–37; Oldham, "Construction of Massive Plutonium Production Complex."

41 "Bomb Workers to Celebrate," *The Oregon Statesman*, August 9, 1945.

42 Arrington, *History of Idaho*, 42, 81; Carlos A. Schwantes, *In Mountain Shadows: A History of Idaho* (Lincoln, NE: University of Nebraska Press, 1996), 214.

43 Arrington, *History of Idaho*, 81; Schwantes, *In Mountain Shadows*, 221.

44 Arrington, *History of Idaho*, 82, 92; Schwantes, *In Mountain Shadows*, 214, 219.

45 Marc K. Blackburn, "Balloon Bombs and Submarines," *Columbia* 8, no. 4 (Winter 1994/95): 6–13.

46 Oldham, "Kaiser Shipyard in Vancouver."

47 John Caldbick, "1940 Census: The 16th Federal Census is First to use Statistical sampling; Confirms Continuing Slowdown in Washington State Population Growth; Migration from Rural to Urban Areas Tapers Off; Federal Employment Programs Skew Labor Statistics," *HistoryLink*, accessed October 20, 2016, http://www.historylink.org/; Dodds, *The American Northwest*, 262; Arrington, *History of Idaho*, 80; Schwantes, *In Mountain Shadows*, 214; Kessleman, *Fleeting Opportunities*, 13; Quintard Taylor, *In Search of the Racial Frontier* (New York: W.W. Norton, 1998), 253.

48 Kesselman, *Fleeting Opportunities*, 6, 14–15.

49 Quoted in Kesselman, *Fleeting Opportunities*, 15, 28, 49.

50 Kesselman, *Fleeting Opportunities*, 2, 6, 20–21; Karen Beck Skold, "The Job He Left Behind: Women in the Shipyards During World War II," in *Women in Pacific Northwest History: An Anthology*, ed. Karen J. Blair (Seattle, WA: University of Washington Press, 1988), 111.

51 Polly Reed Myers, "Boeing Aircraft Company's Manpower Campaign during World War II," *Pacific Northwest Quarterly* 98, no. 4 (Fall 2007): 185.

52 Quoted in ibid., 184.

53 Taylor, *In Search of the Racial Frontier*, 253.

54 Myers, "Boeing Aircraft Company's Manpower Campaign," 185; Kesselman, *Fleeting Opportunities*, 40.

55 Myers, "Boeing Aircraft Company's Manpower Campaign," 185; Quintard Taylor, *The Forging of a Black Community: Seattle's Central District from 1870 through the Civil Rights Era* (Seattle, WA, University of Washington Press, 1994), 163; Dodds, *The American Northwest*, 267.

56 Quoted in Myers, "Boeing Aircraft Company's Manpower Campaign," 187.

57 Quoted in ibid.

58 Myers, "Boeing Aircraft Company's Manpower Campaign," 187; Taylor, *The Forging of a Black Community*, 261.

59 Quoted in Findlay, *Atomic Frontier Days*, 145.

60 Dodds, *The American Northwest*, 266; Findlay, *Atomic Frontier Days*, 84.

61 Quoted in Taylor, *The Forging of a Black Community*, 167.

62 Jack Hamann, *On American Soil: How Justice Became a Casualty of World War II* (Chapel Hill, NC: Algonquin Books of Chapel Hill, 2005), 24.

63 Quoted in Heather MacIntosh, Priscilla Long, and David Wilma, "Riot Involving African American Soldiers Occurs at Fort Lawton and an Italian POW is Lynched on August 14, 1944," *HistoryLink*, accessed October 31, 2015, http://www.historylink.org/; Taylor, *The Forging of a Black Community*, 167; Taylor, *In Search of the Racial Frontier*, 264–265.

64 MacIntosh, "'Riot Involving African American Soldiers'; Taylor, *The Forging of a Black Community*, 167; "Rioting By Negro Soldiers, Hanging of Italian Is Told," *The News Palladium* (Benton Harbor, MI), November 25, 1944.

65 "27 Negro Soldiers Convicted of Rioting and Given Long Prison Sentences at Big Court Martial," *The New York Age*, December 23, 1944; "Convict 27 Soldiers on Riot Charges," *The Gazette and Daily* (York, PA), December 19, 1944; MacIntosh, "Riot involving African American soldiers."

66 Ibid.

67 M. Barrows, "Northwest Indians on the Warpath Again!" *The Seattle Times*, September 5, 1943; Alexandra Harmon, *Indians in the Making: Ethnic Relations and Indian Identities around Puget Sound* (Berkeley, CA: University of California Press, 1998), 205–206.

68 "Swinomish Tribe is Proud of Part it Plays in War," *The Seattle Times*, September 17, 1944.

69 "Self-Help Policy Outlined by Indian Bureau Director," *The Oregonian*, April 3, 1954.

70 "Program to Emancipate Indian Tribes Viewed as Premature Action by Bureau," *The Oregonian*, December 2, 1954; Harmon, *Indians in the Making*, 206–217; John Caldbick, "DeLaCruz, Joseph 'Joe' Burton (1937–2000)," *HistoryLink*, accessed October 25, 2015, http://www.historylink.org/.

71 Erasmo Gamboa, *Mexican Labor and World War II: Braceros in the Pacific Northwest, 1942–1947* (Seattle, WA: University of Washington Press, 2000), 23.

72 Ibid., 4, 23–24.

73 Gamboa, *Mexican Labor and World War II*, 24–29; "Harvest Labor Situation Critical Here," *The Post Register* (Idaho Falls), October 10, 1944.

74 Gamboa, *Mexican Labor and World War II*, 45–46.

75 "Jamaicans Prove Good Farmers," *The Post-Register* (Idaho Falls), July 12, 1943; "Harvest Labor Situation Critical Here."

76 Gonzalo Guzman, "Mexican Nationals Arrive in Washington State under the Bracero Program Beginning on October 5, 1942," *HistoryLink*, accessed October 25, 2016, http://www.historylink.org/; Dodds, *The American Northwest*, 269; Gamboa, *Mexican Labor and World War II*, 40.

77 Gamboa, *Mexican Labor and World War II*, 40–41.

78 Guzman, "Mexican Nationals Arrive"; Gamboa, *Mexican Labor and World War II*, viii, 41.

79 Gamboa, *Mexican Labor and World War II*, 55, 57, 58, 116.

80 Quoted in ibid., 63.

81 Quoted in ibid., 112–113.

82 Ibid., 113–114.

83 Quoted in ibid., 115.

84 Ibid., 113.

85 Ibid., 54.

86 Ibid., 99.

87 Ibid., 53.

88 Ibid., xix.

89 Ibid., 95.

90 Ibid., 74.

91 Ibid., 75–78.

92 Ibid., 82–88, 99–100.

93 Ibid., 131.

94 "Salem on Alert in Blackout," *The Oregon Statesman*, December 9, 1941.

95 Greg Robinson, *By Order of the President: FDR and the Internment of Japanese Americans* (Cambridge, MA: Harvard University Press, 2001), 54–58.

96 Quoted in ibid., 56.

97 Robinson, *By Order of the President*, 64–68, 78–85; Michi Weglyn, *Years of Infamy: The Untold Story of America's Concentration Camps* (New York: Morrow, 1976), 34–35.

98 "Naturalization Act of 1790," Densho Encyclopedia, accessed November 8, 2015, http://encyclopedia.densho.org/; Monica Sone, *Nisei Daughter* (Seattle: University of Washington Press, 1979), viii.

99 Quoted in Robinson, *By Order of the President*, 67; quoted in Weglyn, *Years of Infamy*, 45–46.

100 Robinson, *By Order of the President*, 66–68.

101 Roger Daniels, "The Exile and Return of Seattle's Japanese," *Pacific Northwest Quarterly* 88, no. 4 (Fall 1997): 167.

102 Daniels, "The Exile and Return of Seattle's Japanese," 167; Robinson, *By Order of the President*, 75.

103 Sone, *Nisei Daughter*, 150; Daniels, "The Exile and Return of Seattle's Japanese," 167; Robinson, *By Order of the President*, 75.

104 Sone, *Nisei Daughter*, 151.

105 Ibid., 151–156.

106 Quoted in Robinson, *By Order of the President*, 108; United States, *Personal Justice Denied: Report of the Commission on Wartime Relocation and Internment of Civilians* (Washington, DC: The Commission), 1983, 2.

107 Robinson, *By Order of the President*, 108, 128; "Military Areas 1 and 2," Densho Encyclopedia, accessed November 8, 2015, http://encyclopedia.densho.org/; *Personal Justice Denied* 6; Weglyn, *Years of Infamy*, 76–77.

108 Robinson, *By Order of the President*, 105.

109 Quoted in *Personal Justice Denied*, 6.

110 Quoted in ibid., 6.

111 Patricia Nelson Limerick, *The Legacy of Conquest: The Unbroken Past of the American West* (New York: W.W. Norton, 1987), 273–277.

112 Sone, *Nisei Daughter*, 157.

113 Quoted in *Personal Justice Denied*, 72–73.

114 Quoted in Robinson, *By Order of the President*, 91.

115 Ibid., 90.

116 Quoted in *Personal Justice Denied*, 69; Robinson, *By Order of the President*, 90.

117 Quoted in ibid., 83.

118 Robinson, *By Order of the President*, 129; Weglyn, *Years if Infamy*, 78–79.

119 "Round-Up to the Camp," Camp Harmony Exhibit, accessed November 8, 2015, https://www.lib.washington.edu/; Robinson, *By Order of the President*, 129.

120 *Personal Justice Denied*, 3; Weglyn, *Years of Infamy*, 76–77.

121 Sone, *Nisei Daughter*, 173–174; "Puyallup (detention facility)," Densho Encyclopedia, accessed November 8, 2015, http://encyclopedia.densho.org/.

122 "Portland (detention facility)." Densho Encyclopedia, accessed November 8, 2015, http://encyclopedia.densho.org/; Weglyn, *Years of Infamy*, 79.

123 Schwantes, *The Pacific Northwest*, 418.

124 Robinson, *By Order of the President*, 131.

125 Schwantes, *The Pacific Northwest*, 418; Dodds, *The American Northwest*, 270.

126 Sone, *Nisei Daughter*, 192–194.

127 Ibid., 196–197.

128 Sone, *Nisei Daughter*, 195; Schwantes, *The Pacific Northwest*, 418.

129 Louis Fiset, "Thinning, Topping, and Loading: Japanese Americans and Beet Sugar in World War II," *Pacific Northwest Quarterly* 90, no. 3 (Summer 1999), 125–126.

130 Ibid., 126.

131 Quoted in ibid., 127.

132 Ibid., 123, 136.

133 Michelle Marshman, "Go for Broke: The All Japanese American 442nd Infantry Regiment," *White River Journal* (January 2006), accessed November 8, 2015, http://www.wrvmuseum.org/; Dodds, *The American Northwest*, 272; David Takami, "World War II Japanese American Internment – Seattle / King County," *HistoryLink*, accessed November 8, 2015, http://www.historylink.org/; Arrington, *History of Idaho*, 90–91.

134 Daniels, "The Exile and Return of Seattle's Japanese," 170; Sone, *Nisei Daughter*, 216.

135 Daniels, "The Exile and Return of Seattle's Japanese," 170; Robinson, *By Order of the President*, 209; Dodds, *The American Northwest*, 271; Schwantes, *The Pacific Northwest*, 419.

136 Daniels, "The Exile and Return of Seattle's Japanese," 170.

137 Schwantes, *The Pacific Northwest*, 419; "Korematsu v. United States," Densho Encyclopedia, accessed November 8, 2015, http://encyclopedia.densho.org/; "Gordon Hirabayashi," Densho Encyclopedia, accessed November 8, 2015, http://encyclopedia.densho.org/.

138 "Redress Movement" Densho Encyclopedia, accessed November 8, 2015, http://encyclopedia.densho.org/; Schwantes, *The Pacific Northwest*, 419; Ronald Reagan, *Public Papers of the Presidents of the United States: Ronald Reagan, 1988–1989* (Washington, DC: U. S. G. P. O., 1991), 1054–1055.

139 Kirkendall, "The Boeing Complex and the Military-Metropolitan-Industrial Complex, 1945–1953," 138.

140 Ibid., 138–139.

141 McClary, "Puget Sound Naval Shipyard."

142 Eric Foner, *Give Me Liberty!: An American History* Brief 3rd ed. (New York: W.W. Norton, 2012), 710–713.

143 Kirkendall, "The Boeing Complex and the Military-Metropolitan-Industrial Complex, 1945–1953," 139–148; Walt Crowley, "Boeing Launches its First Minuteman Intercontinental Ballistic Missile (ICBM) from Cape Canaveral on February 1, 1961," *HistoryLink*, accessed November 9, 2015, http://www.historylink.org/.

144 Kirkendall, "The Boeing Complex and the Military-Metropolitan-Industrial Complex, 1945–1953," 147; James Wallace, "Boeing Layoffs – How Bad Will it Get?," *The Seattle Post Intelligencer*, accessed November 9, 2015, http://blog.seattlepi.com/.

145 Ibid.

146 Michele S. Gerber, *On the Homefront: The Cold War Legacy of the Hanford Nuclear Site* 3rd ed. (Lincoln, NE, University of Nebraska Press, 2007), 39–41.

147 Gerber, *On the Homefront*, 41.

148 Findlay, *Atomic Frontier Days*, 160–170; Michele S. Gerber, "Hanford's Historic Reactors: The Story of Hanford's Early Years is One of Constant Change," *Columbia* 9, no. 1 (Spring 1995), 31–32.

149 Findlay, *Atomic Frontier Days*, 167–168.

150 Findlay, *Atomic Frontier Days*, 168; R.E. Gephart, "A Short History of Hanford Waste Generation, Storage, and Release," Pacific Northwest National Laboratory, accessed November 11, 2015, http://www.pnl.gov/, 2.

151 Gerber, On the Homefront, 34; "216-A-36B Crib Closure Unit Group 12 (CUG-12)" Department of Ecology: State of Washington, accessed November 11, 2015, http://www.ecy.wa.gov/; Gephart, "A Short History of Hanford Waste Generation," 9; Findlay, *Atomic Frontier Days*, 201.

152 Gephart, "A Short History of Hanford Waste Generation," 6–10.

153 Quoted in Findlay, *Atomic Frontier Days* 201, 257.

154 Annette Cary, "Estimated Cost to finish Hanford Cleanup Now at $114.8B," *The Tri-City Herald*, accessed November 29, 2015, http://www.tri-cityherald.com/.

155 Hal Bernton, "Treatment Plant at Hanford May not be Done by 2019 Deadline," *The Seattle Times*, accessed November 29, 2015, http://www.seattletimes.com/.

156 Johansen, *Empire of the Columbia*, 562.

157 Amy Kesselman, *Fleeting Opportunities: Women Shipyard Workers in Portland and Vancouver During World War II and Reconversion* (Albany, NY: University of New York Press, 1990), 35.

158 Quoted in ibid., 39.

159 Ibid., 38–39.

160 Kesselman, *Fleeting Opportunities*, 2, 28–29; Augusta H. Clawson, *Shipyard Diary of a Woman Welder* (New York: Penguin Books, 1944), 139.

161 Quoted in Kessleman, *Fleeting Opportunities*, 29; Clawson, *Shipyard Diary*, 39.

162 Ibid., vii, 75, 96.

163 Ibid., 22, 41, 166.

164 Ibid., 144, 106.

165 Nancy Baker Wise and Christy Wise, *A Mouthful of Rivets: Women at Work in World War II* (San Francisco, CA: Jossey-Bass, 1994), 55.

166 Clawson, *Shipyard Diary*, 146–147; Kesselman, *Fleeting Opportunities*, 61.

167 Quoted in ibid, 55.

168 Clawson, *Shipyard Diary*, 15.

169 Kesselman, *Fleeting Opportunities*, 65–66.

170 Clawson, *Shipyard Diary*, 34.

171 Karen Beck Skold, "The Job He Left Behind: Women in the Shipyards During World War II," in *Women in Pacific Northwest History: An Anthology* Karen J. Blair, ed. (Seattle, WA: University of Washington Press, 1988), 111.

172 Ibid., 111; Kesselman, *Fleeting Opportunities*, 77–82.

173 Ibid., 82–83.

174 Quoted in ibid., 42.

175 Findlay and Hevly, *Atomic Frontier Days*, 27.

176 Quoted in ibid., 28–29.

177 Quoted in Kesselman, *Fleeting Opportunities*, 99–100.

178 Quoted in Myers, "Boeing Aircraft Company's Manpower Campaign during World War II," *Pacific Northwest Quarterly* 98, no. 4 (Fall 2007): 193.

179 Kessleman, *Fleeting Opportunities*, 110.

180 Shelby Scates, *Warren G. Magnuson and the Shaping of Twentieth-Century America* (Seattle, WA: University of Washington Press, 1997), 324.

181 Magnuson, Warren G. (1905–1989), HistorLink.org (by Kit Oldham), accessed January 4, 2016, http//.www.historylink.org.

182 Scates, *Warren G. Magnuson*, 217.

183 Wolfgang Saxon, "Warren G. Magnuson Dies at 84; Held Powerful Positions in Senate," accessed February 4, 2016, http://www.NewYorkTimes.com.

184 Ronald Reagan's tribute to Henry M. Jackson, *The Herald*, accessed February 4, 2016, http://www.heraldnet.com.

11

El Movimiento: Chicanos Unite to Improve Economic Standing

Rejecting second-class citizenship, Mexican Americans unite to improve economic standing and reclaim their identity

Inspired by the Civil Rights Movement in the American South in the 1960s, Mexican Americans throughout the West started to chip away at the barriers that blocked them from their constitutional rights and full participation in the American economy. Farmworkers demanded better pay, union representation, and humane working conditions in the fields. In the cities, as more and more Mexican Americans began aspiring for higher education, they pressured colleges and universities to recruit faculty and design curriculum programs that reflected their values and culture.

Mexican citizens Juan Díaz and his wife Tomasa Lara first crossed the border into the United States around 1918, the start of an American story that crisscrossed through the West for nearly three decades. The Jalisco-born Juan held a high school degree and trained as an engineer, but professional jobs were not available to him in America. He worked in the mines in Arizona, picked fruit in New Mexico, operated a bakery in Santa Monica, California, and toiled in the sugar beet fields in Lucerne, Wyoming. At each stop, the couple sought better jobs and greater security for their rapidly growing family. Tomasa would eventually bear 15 children, ten girls and five boys.[1]

In 1942, the Díaz family settled in Wapato, Washington, in the Yakima Valley, where they found steady work, security, and hospitable weather. They lived in a three-bedroom home with an outdoor toilet and water pump. Juan and his older sons worked in the sugar beet and hop fields and picked tomatoes, apples, and peaches. Mónica Díaz, the twelfth of the 15 Díaz children, remembers her father and brothers returning home after a long day in the peach orchards and scrubbing off the irritable peach fuzz.

Mónica began working the fields during summer months at age 13. Starting at four in the morning to pick potatoes and working through noon, she worked alongside her brothers, harvesting the bounty of the fertile Yakima Valley. She was relieved when the bosses moved her out of the blazing sun to pack cherries and plums indoors. Each fall Mónica returned to school while her older brothers worked to season's end in November.

Contested Boundaries: A New Pacific Northwest History, First Edition. David J. Jepsen and David J. Norberg.
© 2017 John Wiley & Sons, Ltd. Published 2017 by John Wiley & Sons, Ltd.

Mónica did not question the long hours and paltry pay, or complain about the lack of drinking water or the filthy outhouse that men and women shared. She did not worry about handling fruits or vegetables covered in pesticides. Ideas like union contracts and collective bargaining did not enter her mind. Young girls didn't think about such things, and they certainly didn't complain. "It was just life," Mónica said decades later. "It was the only thing I knew. You just did your job ..."[2]

The questioning would come later, followed by anger and eventually action, when Mónica and her husband, Ricardo García, joined what would be called *El Movimiento*, The Movement, in the mid-1960s. Inspired in part by the Civil Rights Movement in the American South, Mexican Americans throughout the West united under the "Chicano" banner to improve their economic and political standing. Farmworkers demanded higher pay, union contracts, better working conditions, and all the rights accorded other workers in America. College and university students campaigned for better representation on campus, more instructors of Hispanic descent and ethnically relevant study programs. *El Movimiento* unfolded in the region's fields, orchards, and colleges in the 1960s and 1970s as what is now America's largest minority rallied to dismantle the barriers that defined them as second-class citizens. They built coalitions, developed leadership and public relations skills, and challenged the powerful agriculture industry and academic institutions to permanently enhance their quality of life.

A rights movement that inspires others

Historians generally agree that the success of the Civil Rights Movement following World War II spawned other rights movements throughout the country. When the U.S. Supreme Court found segregation unconstitutional in *Brown v. the Board of Education* in 1954, activists in the West began demanding better schools. The year-long bus boycott in Birmingham, Alabama, in 1955 and 1956, the march on Washington, DC, in 1963 and on Selma in 1965, inspired marches, boycotts, and sit-ins throughout the West. More and more, Mexican Americans – as well as Native Peoples and other minority groups – stopped trying to win acceptance through assimilation into white society and demanded inclusion in white society on their own terms throughout the 1960s, 1970s, and into the 1980s. The notion of "a melting pot that melded diverse peoples into a single homogeneous America" gave way to groups of individual peoples held together in a patchwork quilt of American ethnicities.[3] Simultaneously, minority groups like Mexican Americans and Native Peoples increasingly embraced their identities while also shedding racial stereotypes – literally turning their identities inside out. Negros became blacks, Indians gave way to Native Americans, Mexicans or Mexican Americans became Chicanos.[4]

Few did more to unite Mexican American farm workers than the union organizer César Chávez, who devoted his life to improving their economic status and political power. His bold action, organization, savvy public relations skills, dedication to the movement and dogged determination inspired a generation of Mexican Americans, including the Garcías and scores of other future leaders in the heavily Hispanic regions of Eastern Washington and Oregon.

The diversity and history of the American West and the Pacific Northwest complicated race relations. In the nineteenth century, whites viewed nonwhites as foreigners, racially inferior and intruders in an orderly white society. Native Peoples, although their presence predated whites, were tabbed as separate nations within a larger nation. Chinese, Japanese, and other Asians, all immigrants at one point, seldom earned full citizenship status. Mexican Americans were slapped with "illegal status" even though many were citizens. "The western equation of colored skin with foreignness allowed even newly arrived white westerners to regard native-born westerners with dark skin as aliens although their ancestors had been in the West for generations," wrote the Western historian Richard White.[5]

The first Hispanic presence in the region dates back to Mexican vaqueros working for cattle ranchers who drove their herds from California to eastern Oregon in the mid-nineteenth century. When Peter French drove his herd of 1,200 head from California to Oregon, several vaqueros remained. Others worked for traders, lending their skills as mule-pack drivers prior to the arrival of the railroads. Unknown numbers of Mexicans were among the thousands who rushed north following gold and silver strikes in Oregon and Idaho. Later, thousands more traveled to the region when farmers needed laborers to provide wheat, corn, and other foods to the U.S. Army during World War I. To pave the way for workers, the United States eased previously strict entrance requirements under the 1917 Immigration Act. According to the historian Carlos S. Maldonado, Mexicans viewed their movement to the Pacific Northwest as a "Nuestro Viaje al Norte," or "Our Journey North."[6] But for much of the war, Mexican workers faced on-the-job hardships, for example a dispute broke out in 1918 when workers complained about conditions in sugar processing plants near Idaho Falls, Idaho.[7]

Braceros, a world war and a war on poverty

With the onset of World War II, the Pacific Northwest found itself again short of workers as tens of thousands of young men left their jobs to join the Armed Forces. African Americans from the South and Midwest moved into the region to take jobs in shipyards and at Boeing. Women, previously denied entry into America's factories, suddenly found themselves indispensable at defense plants and docks in Seattle and Portland. The acute need for farm workers led to some creative policy making under the Bracero Program, when tens of thousands of workers, called braceros (laborer), were literally bussed over the border to jobs from San Diego to Seattle. Additionally, Americans from Texas, Arizona, Colorado and California, ventured north on their own accord. By the time the Bracero Program was terminated in 1964, the number of contract workers in the United States, both legal and undocumented, had exploded to 4 million.[8]

The contract negotiated between the United States and Mexico in 1942 was meant to guarantee fair wages and working conditions. Housing, transportation, health care, food and reasonable working hours were all spelled out. Unfortunately, neither the Immigration and Naturalization Service, nor the Mexican consular monitored conditions in the fields or checked for compliance. The growers virtually ignored the agreements and conditions deteriorated into what one historian called "legalized slavery."[9] Few took notice of the immigrant workers, until they complained. Talk of unions, demands for better wages or complaints about living conditions brought reprisals and termination. Nevertheless, labor issues surfaced from the beginning. In 1946, braceros and transient workers from California tangled with potato growers in Klamath Falls, Oregon, over lower

Figure 11.1 These farmworkers, picking potatoes in Oregon in 1943, were among tens of thousands of "braceros" who emigrated from Mexico to the United States to address a labor shortage during World War II. Image reprinted with permission from the Oregon Historical Society Research Library. (Catalog No: ORHI73286).

wages. The following June, more than 1,000 braceros and other Hispanics went on strike at four plants in Idaho's Amalgamated Sugar Company.[10]

For two decades beginning in the late 1950s, the issue of poverty moved up on the agenda of American social ills, and Mexican Americans were among the poorest of the poor. Local, state and federal governments, as well as church organizations, each took turns addressing the plight of farmworkers. The intolerable working and living conditions eventually drew the attention of the Oregon Council of Churches, which petitioned the legislature to investigate the "serious problems" on the farms in 1956.[11]

In 1958, the Oregon Bureau of Labor investigated wages, housing, health sanitation, and education in the labor camps. The subsequent report, which *The Oregonian* called "shocking," revealed unbridled deceit and corruption among labor contractors who recruited and placed workers on the farms. The legislators heard testimony about contractors who exploited workers from the day they arrived in the state. Often transported north several weeks before harvest, they ran up sizable bills for room and board. These expenses, seldom itemized or explained, were docked from workers' pay at season's end, leaving the worker with little to live on.[12]

A 1968 American Civil Liberties Union (ACLU) study of living conditions among the Hispanic communities in Yakima County put a statistical face on poverty. Hispanics fell in the lowest two-fifths of rural populations of all counties in the United States, with 39% living below the poverty level as measured by income, education, housing, health and mortality.[13]

The causes of poverty remain a subject of debate among historians and social scientists. A study comparing Hispanics in Washington and Oregon with the whole population reveals notable differences in marriage age, family size, and education. It paints a portrait of Pacific Northwest Hispanics as a "young, urban mobile society composed of relatively large families, a society that suffers from educational, occupational, and income differences."[14]

Mexican American women, or Chicanas, were more likely to marry at an earlier age than Anglo women, give birth to more children, and drop out of school earlier, according to the study. In Washington, for example, one-quarter of Chicanas married between the ages of 14 and 17, versus 17% for all women. The differences were even more startling in Oregon, where nearly 30% of Chicanas 17 and under tied the knot. Early marriages generally led to more frequent pregnancies and more children, it was reported. In rural areas of Washington and Oregon, Chicano families reared on average one to two more children than Anglos. While the numbers are clear, the causes are less so. Some sociologists associate increased fertility with "machismo," a kind of masculine pride among Hispanic men. Others suggest such attitudes are more myth than reality, and point to the teachings of the Roman Catholic Church, which staunchly disavows birth control and abortion.[15]

Historians also disagree over the reasons behind lower education levels. About half of young Hispanic men in Washington and Oregon graduated from high school in 1970, versus more than 60% of the full population. The differences among women was even greater: 50% for Hispanics, versus 64% for all women.[16]

Some, less accepted, studies blame the shortcomings on the individual. Weak parental support, language differences, and cultural attitudes that disregard the importance of education were seen as root causes. More recent studies point to deficiencies in the schools as opposed to the individual. Cultural bias, racism, lack of bilingual education and a dearth of Hispanic instructors better explain the elevated dropout rate among students. Interestingly, the 1970 study revealed that while Hispanics in Washington and Oregon trailed the whole population in educational attainment and employment, they enjoyed "substantially higher levels of education and employment and a better standard of living than their counterparts elsewhere in the nation."[17]

The Yakima County Housing Authority's 20-year tussle with growers over the conditions of labor camps illustrates the point further. Most permanent workers rented two-bedroom homes or apartments with indoor plumbing, up-to-code electrical wiring, and equipped kitchens. But growers housed their seasonal farm workers in "minimum shelters," one-room cabins with no running water or indoor toilets, built in the 1940s for braceros. Workers generally labored from April through October, and those who didn't return to the Southwest lived in the shelters through the winter. Heat came from a wood cook stove, and a single bulb hanging from a cord provided the only lighting. During the day, light streamed in from gaps in the walls. The units were arranged in groups of four, as well as a separate building that housed a communal toilet and shower.

Children too young to work were often left unattended or taken into the fields with their parents. Neither the government nor the employers provided schools or childcare facilities for children of temporary workers. Frequent attempts to bring the living units up to code failed, and in 1968, the housing authority, under pressure from the state, finally shut down 180 shelters at the Ahtanum labor camp outside of Yakima and about 90 at Crewport near Granger. Some of the dislodged families moved temporarily to 74 two-bedroom apartments built for fulltime workers.[18]

Figure 11.2 Built for migrant farmworkers during World War II, these one-room "minimum shelters," in the Yakima Valley had no running water or indoor toilets. Under pressure from the state, hundreds of units like these were removed or destroyed in 1969 and 1970. Image reprinted courtesy of the *Yakima Herald Republic* Collection and the Yakima Valley Museum.

Federal government enters the war on poverty

The federal government inserted itself into the poverty dilemma in 1964 when Congress approved President Lyndon Johnson's Economic Opportunity Act, which established the Office of Economic Opportunity (OEO) and launched the "War on Poverty." In the Pacific Northwest, OEO community development grants helped establish a host of organizations to address employment, health, housing, education and various legal needs. Beginning in 1965, the Yakima Valley Council for Community Action YVCCA opened centers to meet the farmworkers' health and social service needs. A year later they expanded to educational and legal services, offering adult basic education, English as a second language, high school equivalency programs, vocational training, health clinics, and day care. Volunteer attorneys helped workers address conflicts with immigration authorities and social service agencies.

Washington Citizens for Migrant Affairs (WCMA), a fledgling operation that started in Pasco, Washington, in 1966, soon mushroomed into a statewide organization. By 1968, WCMA operated nine day-care centers in eight Washington counties, providing meals, clean clothing, health care and bilingual education. Another OEO-funded program, the Yakima Valley Farmworkers Clinic, provided medical care, and today is one of the largest health care providers in the region with more than 20 clinics throughout Eastern Washington.

Hyphenated Americans

On January 13, 1969, the *Yakima Herald-Republic* lamented how minority groups increasingly used hyphens to strengthen their identity, especially in the heavily Hispanic communities of Eastern Washington, Oregon and Idaho. This unsigned editorial illustrated how Americans of all ethnic origins struggled to crystalize their identities, especially during the tumultuous 1960s and 1970s.

"Increasingly, we found Negroes – or at least some militants among them – calling themselves Afro-Americans," the paper wrote. "Some of the Spanish descent singled themselves out as Mexican-Americans. And so on and on."

To other Americans, "the unhyphenated kind," the writer suggested, the practice was un-American because "it seemed like serving notice of having second thoughts on exactly how American the minorities wanted to be."

Seemingly blind to the racial exclusion that permeated the region, the paper reminded minorities that the "nation was founded on the arrival of outsiders ... where neither religious nor nationality factors would lessen the acceptance of the newcomers on these shores."

With tongue in cheek, the paper took hyphenation to the extreme. "Shall we encourage all descendants of Erin (Arron) to band together as Irish-Americans? Shall there be Italian-Americans, French-Americans, Swedish-Americans, Cuban-Americans and so on, endlessly on?"

Even the use of "Native Americans" seemed pointless because "even those early Americans are presumed to have come here from Asia on an ice bridge to become the first inhabitants. Should they then be called Asian-Indian-Americans?" (*Yakima-Herald Republic*, unsigned editorial, January 13, 1969, 6).

In Idaho, OEO Community Action Programs adopted a novel approach to organizing its schools for children of itinerant workers. Dissatisfied with results in Twin Falls, program leader Jesse S. Berain abandoned the traditional age-grade system. Rather than grouping students by age, he divided them into family groups regardless of age, resulting in improved performance. To bridge cultural gaps, organizers paired Hispanic and Anglo children in summer camps.[19]

The proliferation of federally funded programs, coupled with isolated incidences of mismanagement, racism, and fraud led to widespread criticism. "I do not understand why so much attention and services are extended to Mexicans," wrote a Sunnyside, Washington resident, in a letter to Governor Dan Evans in 1970. "I know a lot of pressure is on by Mexican radicals, but are we going to give them everything they ask for ...?"[20] Another critic asked, "Where and when are all these special programs going to come to an end?"[21]

While many OEO programs fostered change for the better, critics believed they provided little more than desk jobs for activists with no incentive to solve problems. For example, Jesus Lemos, a member of the United Farm Workers (UFW) Organizing

Committee, said finding solutions to address poverty "would put an end to their jobs." He accused "poverty warriors" of spending their time "filling out forms in triplicate, writing activity reports, attending workshops and conferences" in order to get their programs refunded.[22] The historian White observes that such programs were part of a pattern whereby "minority protest against federal policies had culminated in dependence on the federal government and unfulfilled expectations."[23]

> "We had to face the fact that in order to address social change, we had no other choice than to face controversy."
>
> – *Ricardo García*

Ricardo García argues that such criticisms miss the point. The OEO and other government programs created a "generation of Chicanos who learned to lead," he insists. César Chávez, who initiated his service at the Community Service Association in Los Angeles; Tomás Villanueva, who co-founded the United Farm Worker's Cooperative in Yakima; and Samuel Martínez, YVCCA's first executive director, all leveraged new-found management and organizational skills into leadership positions in the Chicano movement. García cut his teeth in the Cursillo Movement, a Catholic-based community leadership program with origins in Spain. In 1964 García and other church members attended a three-day retreat organized by Father Frederick O'Hearn, pastor at St. Peter Claver Catholic Church in Wapato. Under the direction of Father Finian, a Franciscan priest from California, they discussed effective, Christian-based community service strategies. On the last day, Cursillo leaders hammered home the "very strong message" that "now is the time to get involved in your community." It resonated with García and others. He could no longer in good conscience ignore the injustice perpetrated on his Chicano brothers, no matter the cost and sacrifice. "We had to face the fact that in order to address social change, we had no other choice than to face controversy," he said.[24] In a 1991 interview, García stressed the importance of "brotherhood." "You have to put into action the act of brotherhood, the act of helping one another, helping the church grow, becoming a stronger family."[25]

He left the retreat committed to acquiring the leadership skills necessary to help lead his fellow Chicanos. By this time, Ricardo and Mónica were married and had two of their three children. Mónica worked in a beauty salon and eventually earned a master's degree at Heritage University in 1989 and taught elementary school in Yakima for 30 years. Ricardo worked as an office clerk at a Yakima office of the National Cash Register Company while earning his bachelor's in social work at Central Washington University, leading to what would be a 40-year career in public service. He cut his teeth at YVCCA, became the Executive Director of the Northwest Rural Opportunities (NRO) organization in 1972, and eventually founded and managed for 22 years community KDNA Radio, the nation's first fulltime public Spanish-language station. In 1971, Washington Governor Dan Evans appointed Ricardo as the first executive secretary of what is now the Commission of Hispanic Affairs. He retired from KDNA in 2005.

California's rising star shines on Yakima Valley

Like many budding activists, the Garcías drew their inspiration from César Chávez, leader of the United Farm Workers Union in California, later shortened to UFW.

Chávez's star rose when he organized the Delano Farms strike on September 8, 1965, which would drag on for more than five years. Chávez and co-founder Dolores Huerta built the UFW into a viable political force to garner rights already available to most other workers under the National Labor Relations Act ("NLRA") of 1935. Under the NLRA, nonfarm workers were entitled to petition for union recognition, engage in collective bargaining, and address grievances with private employers. The NLRA did not cover farmworkers, domestic workers, and the self-employed. Rights had to be gained by other means. Using boycotts, strikes, and aggressive public relations as weapons, the UFW brought farm workers together under "La Causa," where a prideful people struggled to build a better life.[26] Its most potent weapon, the boycott, attacked growers where it hurt most – their pocketbooks. Over a tumultuous five years, the UFW effectively persuaded consumers nationwide – not just Chicanos – to stop purchasing nonunion grapes and lettuce. Radical elements within the Chicano movement, including the fringe group, the Brown Berets, advocated more aggressive means of change, namely violence, but Chávez would have none of it. Committed to non-violence, he fasted for 25 days in 1968 to "protest the increasing advocacy of violence within the union." While data on grape and lettuce consumption during the strike is unreliable, the true measure of their success is best gauged by grower capitulation. On July 29, 1970, 26 Delano growers signed contracts with the UFW, securing raises and improved conditions for farm workers throughout California. Over the next 20 years, despite conflicts with the Teamsters Union and never-ending legal entanglements, Chávez and a small army of fellow Chicanos helped to improve the quality of life and political standing of Mexican Americans throughout most Western States and Florida. Chávez died April 23, 1993, of unspecified causes at the age of 66.

The movement caught fire in the Yakima Valley in 1966 when two sons of farm workers, Tomás Villanueva and Guadalupe Gamboa, traveled to Delano to meet with Chávez. They returned resolute to fight for change and opened a United Farm Worker's Cooperative office in Toppenish. The two activists initially worked within the framework of the OEO and the War on Poverty, but chafed under the restrictive politics of a public agency and eventually turned to more direct action. Villanueva immersed himself in organizing farm workers and pressuring the Washington Legislature to pass protective legislation. Gamboa went on to study law and became a director of Evergreen Legal Services. Activist ranks grew as a large contingent of young and idealistic men and women joined the cause, including Roberto and Carlos Trevino. But rather than going after grape and lettuce growers, they immediately targeted one of the Yakima Valley's most lucrative crops – hops, a key ingredient in beer. Gamboa told *The Yakima Herald* that working conditions in the hop fields were the worse in the industry due to "bad facilities and seven-day work weeks without overtime pay." The first strike originated in Granger, and soon spread to as many as 15 ranches throughout the Yakima Valley.[27] They timed the strikes when the growers were "most vulnerable," in the spring "when the hop vines are hand-trained to climb on string," and during fall harvest when "there is no question we can hurt them."[28] While neither side reported violence on the picket lines, two Yakima Valley growers faced charges in January 1971 for brandishing weapons and threatening union organizers. The farm workers eventually brought charges against the growers.[29]

While some growers agreed to wage concessions, raising the minimum from $1.65 to $2 an hour, they refused to recognize a union. The following year, growers blacklisted the more active union participants.[30] While the goal of a recognized union remained

Figure 11.3 César Chávez (center) speaks to United Farmworkers supporters at a gathering in Yakima in December 1969. The California-based union organizer and labor activist helped farm workers throughout the Pacific Northwest address grievances with growers. Image reprinted courtesy of the *Yakima Herald Republic* Collection and the Yakima Valley Museum.

out of reach, their determination spurred future organizational efforts, leading to more permanent successes in the 1980s.

Workers fight the "slave bill" in Oregon

In 1971, Oregon growers pursued more direct action to prevent farmworkers from organizing, pressuring the legislature to pass Senate Bill 677. What became known as the "anti-farmworker bill," or the "slave bill," prohibited boycotts, outlawed strikes during harvest season and required union organizers to register with the state, among other restrictions.[31] The Idaho legislature passed a similar bill in 1972. When Chávez got word of the Oregon bill, he dispatched his chief lawyer and lobbyist, Jerry Cohen, to Oregon to pressure the moderate Republican Governor Tom McCall to veto the legislation. Cohen and the United Farmworkers of Oregon immediately rallied to the cause, organizing a prayer vigil at the Capitol steps in Salem and swamping the governor's office with letters and calls.[32] To keep the heat on Governor McCall, Chávez threatened to launch a national boycott of all Oregon products, not an insignificant threat given the diversity of Oregon exports, including timber and salmon. Chávez traveled to Salem and spoke at the Capitol. More than 5,000 people cheered as the famous union organizer denounced the bill "in the strongest terms."[33] On July 11, McCall reluctantly vetoed SB 677. However, Chávez's threat irked McCall, who had previously appeared sympathetic with farmworkers. Their strong-arming almost backfired as the governor said Chávez's threats "very nearly persuaded me to sign the bill." Two years later, the legislature passed a state collective bargaining law, which benefited public employees, but excluded farmworkers.[34]

> Short-term effects of exposure to pesticides include "skin rashes, systematic poisoning, and even death." Long-term exposure could result in "cancer, brain and nervous system damage, birth defects, and infertility."

Without the power of collective bargaining, unions lacked the leverage to address the farmworker's most pressing problem – exposure to pesticides. A review of pesticide usage among Oregon growers suggests the degree to which those throughout the region relied on chemicals to control pests and disease. According to the Oregon farmworkers union, PCUN, (Pineros y Campesinos Unidos del Noroeste, or Northwest Treeplanters and Farmworkers United) Oregon growers used on average 16 million pounds of pesticides annually in the 1960s and 1970s. Farmworkers were often "required to tolerate unsafe working conditions." Workers lacked safety equipment to administer pesticides, leading to "drift," exposing children "in their homes, yards, sandboxes, swing sets, wading pools and other play areas."[35] Short-term effects of exposure include "skin rashes, systematic poisoning, and even death."[36] Long-term exposure could result in "cancer, brain and nervous system damage, birth defects, and infertility."[37]

El Movimiento comes to campus

Throughout the five-year Delano strike, the UFW tightened its grip on consumer sentiment, putting more and more pressure on supermarket chains to stop selling nonunion grapes. In the Northwest, A&P and Quality Food Center (QFC) chains capitulated in 1968, but Safeway and Albertsons held fast to their opposition. In September, students turned the heat on the University of Washington, one of the state's largest food sellers.

The conflict picked up steam in September when the University of Washington (UW) chapters of the YMCA and YWCA issued a position paper urging the University to suspend grape sales, starting with dormitory cafeterias. But Food Service Director J. Arthur Pringle refused to act, calling the decision to boycott "an individual matter instead of an institutional one." The University took the position that, as a public institution dependent on state funding, it could not take sides in a "political dispute." "This would become the administration's position on the matter for the duration of

Figure 11.4 A group of unidentified migrant farmworkers make camp near Zillah, Washington, in 1970. During peak season, a housing shortage required many workers and their families to live in tents near the fields. Image reprinted courtesy of the *Yakima Herald Republic* Collection and the Yakima Valley Museum.

the grape struggle," according to Jeremy Simer, writing for the Seattle Civil Rights and Labor History Project.[38] In October, students living in the dorms voted their position on this "individual matter." Nearly 60% of the 6,090 students who voted supported the boycott.[39]

Buoyed by broad student support, some of the few Chicano students enrolled at the time organized the United Mexican American Students (UMAS). Under the leadership of Guadalupe Gamboa, his cousin Erasmo Gamboa, and Jesus Lemos, they condemned the sale of grapes on campus. "The time has come when the University should show more concern and responsibility toward poverty than merely studying it," read the UMAS statement. The fledgling organization demonstrated savvy leadership and public relations skills, generating favorable coverage in the press and building coalitions with other groups like the Black Student Union (BSU), the Associated Students of the University of Washington (ASUW), and the American Civil Liberties Union (ACLU).[40]

For the next month, the University waffled on whether to sell grapes. First they decided to offer them only if requested, but later, at the urging of the office of the state's attorney general, the administration reversed course. Grape sales at the University would continue.

Unwilling to accept "no" for an answer, UMAS organized a boycott in January 1969 of the five university restaurants and all sandwich and snack machines. More than 100 students began to picket outside the HUB. At night they made hundreds of peanut butter sandwiches and other snacks and passed them out to "hungry students" who honored the picket line. The "sandwich brigade" appeared effective until the Seattle Health Department shut it down because the picketers did not apply for a license to handle food. Whether they got sandwiches or not, students increasingly shunned university food services, and in the first week of the boycott, sales dropped by about 20%.

Not all students supported the boycott, of course, especially the UW chapter of the Young Republicans. To counter UMAS public relations, they invited growers from Delano to speak to students on January 10, which resulted in a shouting match with black and Chicano students. Tempers flared again a week later when boycott supporters threatened to "confiscate" the grapes in the HUB if Assistance Manager John Bickford didn't remove them immediately. To "play it cool," Bickford removed the grapes, deferring to the HUB Advisory Board for guidance. Livid over what the Young Republicans called "give in politics" to "screaming militants," they sent Governor Dan Evans a telegram asking him to intervene. Tensions escalated the following day when the Young Republicans set up an information table, handed out anti-boycott flyers, and disrupted the UMAS rally. A scuffle ensued and security was called in.[41]

On February 7, 1969, *The Daily*, the University of Washington newspaper, published a letter from University President Charles E. Odegaard. He reiterated the school's antiboycott position and blamed dissident students who used the grape issue "as an excuse to abuse the University when their basic goal is the wrecking of the very society which the Mexican Americans wish to join more fully." He then mysteriously compared the protest movement with the rise of the Nazi Party in Germany in the 1930s, where "[t]yranny easily takes over a people who have already let the safeguards of their individual freedoms be eroded by sloth or folly in a succession of individual cases."

"How a University president could get away with comparing the Third Reich with college students advocating on behalf of farmworkers is hard to fathom," Simer wrote.[42]

With food sales plummeting, eventually the University made an economic decision, if not a political one. On February 17, the administration announced that, for the remainder of the season at least, "California table grapes will not be sold" on campus. It was a limited victory, but a victory nonetheless. More to the point, it suggests a more telling story about the political rise of a minority group bounded by second-class status. UMAS, the Black Student Union and other minority groups developed leadership and public relations skills to press for change. According to Simer, it was the first instance in which students and faculty united to challenge a major university, "a collective effort that changed the way things worked."

Figure 11.5 Supporters of the United Farmworkers union picket outside the Safeway Store in Yakima in 1974. For more than five years, the union led boycotts against Safeway and other grocers who sold nonunion grapes. Image reprinted courtesy of the *Yakima Herald Republic* Collection and the Yakima Valley Museum.

Changing how a university serves its minority communities

Student demands didn't stop with labor issues – they pressed for a wholesale remaking of minority education. It started in Los Angeles in March 1968 when an estimated 20,000 middle school and high school students took to the streets of East Los Angeles protesting inferior education, discrimination, and racism among teachers.[43]

Later that year, black students at the University of Washington founded the Black Student Union, in order "to form a power base from which to present certain demands to the University administration." They began pressing for increasing minority enrollment, hiring minority faculty and coaches, and creating a black studies program.[44] Cries for ethnic specific study programs soon echoed across campuses throughout the Pacific Northwest. In the early 1970s, Chicano students at the UW, Washington State University and Yakima Valley Community College (YVCC), organized Mexican American Student Association (MASA) chapters and used new-found political clout to force public universities and colleges to rethink their role in addressing minority needs.[45]

In January 1973, illustrating the interracial alliances that marked the broader rights movements, black and Chicano students marched on the YVCC campus to protest the college's inaction in hiring Chicano faculty and developing a Chicano studies program. Ricardo García, then a 35-year-old student and recently appointed head of the Mexican American Affairs Commission, read a statement to the gathering crowd. School officials "are living in a fantasy of the nineteenth century, and it's time they face the reality of this community's human needs today," García declared. Students voiced their distaste over recent revelations from the state auditor that, in the face of budgetary woes, the college spent $1,500 on "fishing trips, alcoholic beverages and other items in connection with educational conferences."[46]

Tensions heightened on January 23 when students from the Black Student Union occupied an office in the YVCC administration building. At about 10 a.m. students stormed into an unoccupied office, slapped a paper "BSU office" sign above the door, pinned posters on the walls, and turned on their boom box. Within minutes a college security officer and Dean of Student Affairs Ken Burns arrived, and threatened to call the police if they didn't leave in 10 minutes. In response, the students, now joined by several Chicanos, sat down, requested to speak with YVCC President Thomas Deem and turned up the volume on the boom box.[47]

A crowd of 50 students filled the small office and spilled into the hall by the time Deem arrived on the scene. Students reiterated their demands to expand the fledgling minority studies programs and hire minority instructors and coaches. They also called for Deem and Burns to resign. Finally, they wanted a permanent BSU office on campus. The college had already provided an office off campus, but students rejected it. "It felt like we were in the back of the bus," said a black student. Soon, five Yakima city detectives and 30 uniformed officers – what must have been the entire Yakima police force – arrived. At Deem's request, they waited in a building across the street, while negotiations continued. Deem told the students he would take their complaints seriously. "Give me a chance," he said.[48]

> "You had a chance," retorted BSU President Claudell Young.
> "Give me another chance," Deem repeated.
> "So you can run over us again?" Young asked.

With negotiations at an impasse, the police rushed in and arrested Young and eight other students. They offered no resistance when handcuffed and taken to the Yakima city jail. They were charged with criminal trespass and released on their own recognizance.[49]

The next day school officials rejected student demands, issuing vague promises about enhancing minority studies programs. Student demands "were not new," the college claimed, and "improvements and advances have been made." Deem blamed the "crisis" on the "continuous and inflammatory and biased reporting and editorializing" by *The Herald-Republic*, which the paper later called a "cheap shot."[50]

For the next month, students continued to picket, stage rallies, and issue statements. "The response of the Administration is an insult to the intelligence and dignity of the community we represent," read a MASA statement. "They are saying that the problems are caused by the press, not by them … They are living in a fantasy of the nineteenth century and it's time they face the reality of their community's human needs today."[51]

The University of Washington fell under the same Chicano demands two years later. On April 29, 1975, a group of Chicano faculty and students paraded into the office of Dr. George M. Beckmann, Dean of the College of Arts and Sciences, to protest his apparent inaction in addressing concerns about the direction of the Chicano studies program and failure to interview minority candidates for an associate dean position. The search committee had ruled out three Chicanos deemed unqualified.[52] This was the third time in less than a year when Chicano groups had occupied university offices over hiring practices. The previous May students "sat in" at the offices of the Psychology Department, and two weeks later at the College of Arts and Sciences.

The most recent confrontation, while heated, ended peacefully, although Beckman felt threatened and promptly fired two members of the program and suspended a third, saying the "use or support of threats of violence to persons or property cannot be tolerated ..." Dismissed were Juan Sánchez, a 27-year-old supervisor in the Minority Affairs office, and Gary Padilla, age 25, acting director of the Chicano studies program. Rosa Morales, a program secretary, received a 15-day suspension. Sánchez said later he heard no threats against the Dean, nor did the incident turn violent. "I'm very upset," Padilla told reporters. "I feel the university has committed itself against the entire Chicano community."[53] Later he charged that the failure to hire a Chicano was an example of the "Poncho almost made it" syndrome. "It is always a case where Chicanos get second or third place – but we never make the finals."[54]

Faculty reaction to the dismissals was sharp and telling. Twenty Chicano faculty members, administrators, and staffers immediately resigned, including Theresa de Shepro, vice provost for special programs, and Roberto Garfias, professor of ethnomusicology, and the only fulltime Chicano professor. In a letter to UW President John R. Hogness, the group said they were "appalled" by the University's "insensitive behavior," and unwillingness to address "much needed changes."[55]

Tensions peaked on May 12 when about 600 Chicanos and supporters took to the streets, marching through the University District chanting, "Beckmann is a racist. He shall be removed."[56] The following day, 2,000 students converged on the UW's administration building, calling for a two-day boycott of classes.[57]

By late September, the Chicano faculty and staff carved out a compromise with the University. The school injected $90,000 in new funds to revamp the Chicano studies program and reinstated Padilla and Sánchez and rescinded Morales' suspension. Finally they committed to upgrading African American, Indian and Asian programs.[58]

A sluggish pace of change resulted in supporters continuing to demonstrate, occupy offices and file complaints with government agencies throughout the 1970s and 1980s. Thanks to an emerging social consciousness among America's younger generation, ethnic studies programs have become a staple of most institutions of higher learning. Moreover, 250 student-run chapters of MEChA (formerly MASA) operated on campuses nationwide in 2015, making it one of the largest organizations of its type.[59]

Radio KDNA links with itinerant audiences

In the Yakima Valley, *El Movimiento* needed a means for fast and reliable communications with farmworkers. Organizers feared they could not rely on "Anglo media" to get their messages out, which had demonstrated little interest in farmworker issues, and appeared more sympathetic with growers, according to García. A Spanish-language radio station offered the perfect medium for communicating with an audience that in the 1970s and 1980s was mostly itinerant, largely illiterate, and difficult to reach. The call letters, KDNA, short for *cadena*, means chain, a perfect metaphor for connecting with listeners.

We wanted them (migrant farm workers) to settle down, get active, register to vote and participate in the American dream. Radio was the perfect instrument to communicate that message.

– Ricardo García

Initially, KDNA used a Seattle public radio station, KRAB, to air its music, children's programming, and public service announcements. But that arrangement was an "unworkable situation," García said. The founders – Julio César Guerrero, Dan Robal, Rosa Ramón, and García – agreed that their listeners lived primarily in Eastern Washington. The group incorporated as the Northwest Chicano Radio Network, and applied to the Federal Communications Commission in 1976 for a permit to construct a public radio station. For the next three years, volunteers went about opening the first fulltime Spanish-only station in the United Sates (KBBF in Santa Rosa started broadcasting as a bilingual station in 1973). They leased property from the Yakima Indian Nation, built a studio, purchased used equipment, erected an 80-foot tower, and trained Chicano students in broadcasting skills. Radio KDNA (91.9 on the dial) first broadcast on December 19, 1979. Relying on public broadcasting grants and listener donations, *La voz del campesino*, the "voice of the farm worker," soon expanded programming to help farmworkers overcome barriers of literacy, language, discrimination, poverty, and illness. "Our goal was simple," García said, "mobilize, motivate, organize." The station hammered home the benefits of settling down to workers who migrated from Mexico and the American Southwest each season. "Going back and forth interrupted their children's education," García said. "We wanted them to settle down, get active, register to vote and participate in the American dream. Radio was the perfect instrument to communicate that message."

Among the multiple farmworker challenges, none disrupted daily life more than the INS (Immigration and Naturalization Service) raids. Beginning in the 1970s, the INS scrambled to contain the flood of undocumented workers that crossed the Rio Grande annually. Between 1970 and 1980, the number tripled from 760,000 to 2.2 million, about half of which were undocumented.[60] Without warning, Federal INS agents would sweep into towns throughout the region, arresting suspected undocumented immigrants and holding them for possible deportation. Acting on tips from listeners, the station would alert workers about an upcoming raid. They would play a song about *la migra*, an abbreviation of "immigration," and dedicated it to the town about to be raided. The 1986 Immigration Reform and Control Act under President Ronald Reagan, which offered amnesty to immigrants who entered the United States illegally before January 1, 1982, lifted the pale of illegal status for millions of Mexicans and stifled the raids.

Limited victories in Washington and Oregon

In 1986, farmworkers in Washington founded the United Farm Workers of Washington State to "bring a collective voice to farm workers attempting to combat workplace abuses …" While the UFW of Washington originally operated independently, it aligned with the AFL-CIO in 1994 increasing its power and influence. A year later, it secured a contract for Washington farmworkers, ending an eight-year strike against the Chateau

Ste. Michelle winery, the first such victory in farmworker organizing history in Washington.[61]

In 1998 in Oregon, PCUN and the UFW secured a similar first for farmworkers, winning contracts with four separate growers. The deal assured workers of more than a dozen rights including overtime pay, paid breaks, minimum wages, and grievance procedures. The breakthrough occurred when a major grower, Nature Fountain Farms, broke ranks with other growers. "It is my hope that in creating an example, a working model … labor and ownership can work together as one to open a window to change and growth," said Scott Frost, co-owner.

Farmworkers remain excluded from protection under the National Labor Relations Act, but life on the farms and orchards has improved substantially in recent decades. Farmworkers eventually heeded the call to settle down, and today a majority live permanently in the region. The journey north, *"Nuestro Viaje al Norte,"* evolved into *"Nuestro Hogar del Norte,"* our Northern Home.[62]

For example, most workers at Gilbert Orchards, a fruit grower in the Yakima Valley since the 1890s, reside permanently in the Valley, according to Cragg Gilbert, a fourth generation owner. The company does not offer housing, "preferring to provide good wages," which for cherry pickers averages about $19 an hour and as high as $30 for the faster workers. Hourly and salaried employees earn minimum wage or more and participate in Social Security, Medicare, unemployment insurance, and Labor and Industries coverage. Salaried employees working 1,560 hours per year are eligible for medical, dental and life insurance, paid vacation and the 401k plan. During peak apple harvest, Gilbert boosts its workforce by 25% "not unlike the need for seasonal workers in retail, ski resorts and tourism."

Pesticide use, while a lingering problem in Northwest orchards, is regulated by the departments of agriculture in Washington, Oregon, and Idaho. A growing consumer preference for organic fruits and vegetables, the employment of organic sprays, and integrated pest management techniques has helped to lessen, but not erase the dangers associated with pesticides. A review of enforcement actions in Washington from 2013 to 2015, shows growers, applicators, and others incurring $7,500 in fines for improper handling and spraying. Gilbert said his firm has reduced the use of man-made chemicals, while increasing organic production. "This is not just good for the planet, but it is good for all of us involved in farming."

Farmworker issues have evolved over the last two decades, and any in-depth discussion of recent events is best left to others. Labor and the agriculture industry struggled with issues surrounding collective bargaining, minimum wage, overtime pay, and benefits like breaks and vacations. On the immigration front, an issue as old as the Constitution itself, activist groups like PCUN lobbied against bills in Oregon and Washington, DC, to tighten residency requirements and reactivate the Bracero Program. In 1996 and 1997, anti-immigrant forces began gathering signatures on four separate initiatives to clamp down on undocumented immigration. Patterned after California's infamous Proposition 187, they would have forced public schools to verify the legal status of immigrant students, required documentation to obtain a driver's license, and denied public benefits and services to anyone undocumented. A coalition between PCUN and a Chicano group called CAUSA, prevented anti-immigration forces from collecting the required 97,000 signatures and kept the initiatives off the election ballot.

That victory, coupled with the earlier contracts in Washington and Oregon presented major stepping stones that are best summed up in the PCUN motto "Si se puede," or "yes we can." Coined by César Chávez, the motto symbolizes the emergence of a rights consciousness that energized a generation of men and women like Ricardo and Mónica García who proclaimed "yes," we can end the discrimination and racism that marred Americans society for most of its history.

Figure 11.6 Ricardo García during interview with *Yakima Herald Republic* reporter in 1971.

"Taking off the mask"

Gays and lesbians seek identity, acceptance, and equal rights

When Washington's marriage equality law took effect on December 6, 2012, hundreds of couples seeking marriage licenses lined the halls of the King County Administration Building in Seattle. Honored with the first license were octogenarians Jane Abbott Lighty and Pete-e Peterson, partners for over 35 years. "It's very humbling to be chosen first. We feel like we're representing a lot of people in the state who have wanted this for a long time," Petersen told a *Seattle Times* reporter.[63]

Lighty and Peterson were the first to receive a license but not the first to apply. Forty-one years earlier, Paul Barwick and John Singer walked into the King County auditor's office and "demanded" a license. Sympathetic with the couple's wishes but powerless to act, county auditor Lloyd Hara sought the advice of then Deputy Prosecutor, Norm Maleng. He told Hara to deny the request, a decision later upheld in the Washington State Court of Appeals.[64]

The four decades between the two events represent a transformative awakening for the Lesbian, Gay, Bisexual, and Transgender (LGBT) community in the Pacific Northwest. Like racial minorities struggling for inclusion in American society, the social and political landscape for LGBT shifted profoundly in the 1960s and 1970s. A life of denial and shame for many evolved into to one of self-acceptance; from hiding in the closet to taking to the streets; from legal persecution to equality before the law.

Sexual orientation crosses all classes

Historian Peter Boag has revealed that same-sex relationships surfaced into public view during the Pacific Northwest's early industrial years at the dawn of the twentieth century. Men open to same-sex companionship were often drawn to the region's extractive industries, where tens of thousands of young men wandered from job to job in the forests, farms, and mines.[65]

But homosexuality was not confined to the working class as many at the time believed. Sex scandals in Portland and elsewhere gave evidence of homosexuality among middle-class men living and working in the cities. While such scandals were hardly unprecedented, a 1912 event in Portland turned into a public spectacle. A frightened 19-year-old man arrested and questioned by police gave evidence of a "thriving male homosexual community" in Portland and other large West Coast cities. His public confession dispelled the notion that "sexual deviancy" was a problem of the lower classes, immigrants, and minorities, who reformers had long blamed for "imperiling white youths and therefore the middle-class family."[66]

Through the first several decades of the twentieth century, homosexuals were mostly invisible to broader society. Fearing harassment, persecution, and arrest, they maintained comparative secrecy.[67] They removed the mask of anonymity only in the privacy of a tight circle of friends or in bars and nightclubs that tolerated them in Portland's North End and Seattle's Pioneer Square, areas long known for their sexual permissiveness. The Casino in Pioneer Square, nicknamed "Madame Peabody's Dancing Academy for Young Ladies," allowed same-sex dancing. For stage entertainment, gays and lesbians took in acts of female impersonators at the nearby Spinning Wheel. Outside of bars, men could find companionship at Seattle's Greyhound Bus Depot, Volunteer Park, or in the University District. While authorities generally looked the other way, content to keep the "sexual deviants" quartered in a city's darker corners, raids and arrests were not uncommon.[68]

Out on liberty in World War II

World War II brought significant, some would argue transformative, change for sexual minorities. Just as the extraction industries brought single men together in an earlier era, now so did war. Nationwide, more than 12 million men and women joined the armed forces, working and living in segregated units.[69] The historian Boag explains that gay men mobilizing for war were thrust into an all-male environment where they "learned more about their own feelings, and forged lasting friendships with like-minded people ..."[70] The region's cities bulged with thousands of soldiers, sailors, and defense workers. Portland and Seattle lit up at night as gays and lesbians increasingly enjoyed liberty at a growing lineup of bars and clubs that exclusively catered to them. Historian John D'Emilio said World War II "created something of a nationwide coming out experience."[71]

Where war gave homosexuals space, peace brought prosperity. America emerged triumphantly from World War II brimming with confidence and a belief that anything was possible. What historian James Patterson called the "grand expectations" of the 1950s and 1960s remade most aspects of American life. Prolific advances in technology, Cold War military spending, and booming population growth drove economic prosperity for a generation. From 1950 to 1960, Gross National Product (GNP) increased 37%; family income 30%; and home ownership 20%. Millions of veterans enrolled in college under the GI Bill, married and built families. All told, 76.4 million babies were born between 1946 and 1964 – the Baby Boom Generation – representing two-fifths of the American population of 192 million, and helping to drive long-term economic health.[72] While economic data specific to gays and lesbians is not readily available, it's reasonable to assume they participated in America's post-war prosperity.

Prosperity came more easily than acceptance in post-war America, where victory had infused men with a sense of "manliness." They had overthrown Fascism, dropped the first atomic bomb, and returned home victorious. "Long after the war, many Americans tended to glorify the "manly" virtues of toughness. Those who were "soft" ran the risk of being defined as deviant," argues the historian Patterson.[73]

From a threat to middle-class morality, homosexuals emerged as a threat to national security during the Cold War hysteria over communism and the Red-baiting of Wisconsin Senator Joseph McCarthy. McCarthy called himself a "man's man," and mocked anyone who disagreed with him as "homos" and "pretty boys."[74] The historian and popular social commentator Arthur Schlesinger, Jr, wrote that communism was "something secret, sweaty, and furtive like nothing so much ... as homosexuals in a boys' school."[75] Homosexuals made easy targets when McCarthy made sensational headlines about communists infiltrating the state department, U.S. army, public universities, and Hollywood. And thus "5000 Homosexuals Pose D.C. Problem," claimed a headline in one Northwest newspaper. "Perverts Said Easy Market for Foreign Spies," reported another. In this way, explains the historian Boag, "homosexuality and communism became linked in the American consciousness."[76]

America finds sexual liberation

Where commie-hunters branded homosexuals as threats, the books of Dr. Alfred Kinsey spoke to their normalcy. Kinsey, an entomologist at Indiana University, published two books based on lengthy research into the sexual behaviors of men and women. *Sexual Behavior in the Human Male* (1948), and *Sexual Behavior in the Human Female* (1953), dismantled American perceptions about human sexuality. Data from 18,000 personal interviews revealed a previously unacknowledged sexual appetite among both genders. According to Kinsey research, up to 90% of American men and 50% of women engaged in premarital sex. Ninety-two percent of men and 62% of women had masturbated at least once. Just as shocking was the number of men (37%) and women (13%) who admitted to at least one same-sex experience in their lives. Another 10% reported being exclusively homosexual.[77]

While pundits from both the political left and right criticized Kinsey's research, few questioned the work's impact on social consciousness. It put sex on the front pages of daily newspapers and magazine covers. Like it or not, Americans were more sexually active and liberal than people had previously believed. Nor could they continue to dismiss homosexuality as aberrant behavior. It's no coincidence that as the Kinsey debate rumbled from coast to coast, homosexuals began to organize. The first such organization, the Mattachine Society, founded in Los Angeles in 1950, soon began to unify homosexuals isolated from their own kind as well as educate heterosexuals about a lifestyle they clearly didn't understand.

Book publishers and Hollywood studios soon cashed in on America's sudden fascination with all things sexual. The steamy novels of *Peyton Place* and *Lolita* made bestseller lists, while the movie versions appeared in American theaters. So did the 1959 film *Compulsion*, a crime thriller based on the 1924 murder trial of two homosexual students who murdered a young boy just to prove they could get away with it. The film portrayed one killer as a "sadistic, mother-dominated bully," while the other depicted a "submissive, introverted sissy." Both roles reframed the stereotypes of gay men.[78] Over the course of a half century, the homosexual identity swirled around a pool of negative stereotypes, from deviant to national security threat to mother coddled sadists.

It's helpful to evaluate evolving public perceptions and the rise of gay rights within the fractured state of American society in the late 1960s. The feel-good 1950s and early 1960s gave way to social unrest and division as young Americans raised and educated in secure, middle-class homes began demanding more from American institutions. Inspired by the Civil Rights Movement and increasingly intolerant of injustice everywhere, young people spawned broad social change and shook the foundations of government. To end America's involvement in Vietnam, activists shutdown college campuses, demonstrated on city streets, and disrupted the Democratic National Convention in Chicago in 1968. The previously nonviolent protest in the Civil Rights Movement succumbed to black militancy following the assassination of Martin Luther King, Jr. April 4, 1968. African Americans rioted in 130 cities charring the urban landscape from coast to coast. Native Americans, Mexican Americans. and feminists all began to noisily demand more from their government[79] (see Chapter 11).

The gay rights movement took root in this America. Like other minority groups, gays and lesbians began to resist the injustices flung at them. One of the best remembered, though certainly not the earliest example of resistance, is the Stonewall riots that began in the early morning hours of June 28, 1969, when police raided the New York gay bar of the same name. As authorities attempted to arrest Stonewall employees and club patrons dressed in drag, the crowd started throwing bottles, forcing the officers to take shelter inside the inn until reinforcements arrived. The incident touched off a string of protests in New York City and breathed life into a movement for social and political equality for gays and lesbians that had been forming for years.[80]

A broader definition of nontraditional families and greater equality for women encouraged a gradual acceptance of homosexuality. During the 1970s and 1980s, more and more Americans rejected the narrow view of family as portrayed by Ward and June Cleaver in the 1950s television show *Leave it to Beaver*. A more inclusive family emerged in which women worked outside the home, attended college, and enrolled in postgraduate programs. By 1980, one in three children were born to single mothers. Divorce rates climbed steadily, topping out at more than 40%. Unmarried couples lived together in monogamous relationships, while others postponed having children. By the mid-1980s, less than one-third of households consisted of the traditional two-parent family with children.[81]

Public acceptance of same-sex relationships moved in parallel with these trends. In 1973, the American Psychiatric Association removed homosexuality from its list of mental disorders. That same year, the National Organization of Women announced its support for gay rights.[82] Two years later, the U.S. Civil Service Commission lifted its ban on employing gays, and by 1980, 12 states scratched anti-sodomy laws from their books.[83] Such laws were repealed in Oregon in 1972 and Washington in 1976 as part of broader reforms to their criminal codes. The Supreme Court struck down sodomy laws in all states, including Idaho's, in 2003.

The formation of organized counseling and support services further normalized different sexual orientations. Seattle's groundbreaking Dorian Society began counseling gay and lesbian students at the University of Washington and the growing community on Capitol Hill as early as 1967. The Seattle Gay Alliance, Gay Liberation Front, and multiple other organizations opened Seattle's first gay community center in Pioneer Square in 1971. In Portland, counseling and support services, as well as a sustained activist culture, were slow to emerge in the post-Stonewall environment. Boag points to a lack of local leadership, a more furtive pre-Stonewall atmosphere, and a relative lack of police harassment to explain the slow growth of organization in that city.[84]

Beginning in the early 1970s, greater tolerance and support encouraged gays and lesbians to strip away the mask and publically proclaim their sexual orientation. What started with small crowds at neighborhood block parties soon ballooned into citywide gay-pride celebrations. In 1977, Seattle Mayor Charles Royer and Portland Mayor Neil Goldschmidt each issued "Gay Pride" proclamations. Mayor Royer noted the gay community's contributions to "neighborhood restoration, community life, business, government and the arts." In 1979, the first major gay-pride parade in the nation's capital attracted over 100,000 people who took pride in their sexual identity and demanded equal rights. By comparison, Seattle's 2015 parade and related events drew upwards of 400,000.[85]

As in physics, history shows that for every action there is an opposite reaction. The remarkable advances of women and racial and sexual minorities in the 1960s and 1970s, created a backlash from conservatives who felt America had lost its moral backbone and family values. The dawn of this cultural pushback was humorously illustrated in a 1971 episode of the popular television sitcom *All in the Family*. The lead character, Archie Bunker, played by Carroll O'Connor, was a blue-collar racist and sexist living with his wife Edith, daughter Gloria, and son-in-law Mike. The episode "Judging Books by Covers" parodied sexual stereotyping. In Archie's opinion, Mike's friend Roger was "queer as a four dollar bill," because of his flamboyant dress and "effeminate" and "sensitive" demeanor. On the other hand, Archie's long-time friend Steve, a former NFL linebacker, was a "man's man." Steve was a well-groomed and physically fit "bachelor" who had "always acted kind of privately." "Have you ever heard me mention a girl?" Steve asked the incredulous Archie.[86] Interestingly a real-life Steve played football at the University of Washington in the 1960s. Dave Kopay, an All-American running back, played in the NFL for eight years, retiring in 1972. Three years later, he "came out." One of the first professional athletes to publicly disclose his sexual orientation, Kopay is credited with inspiring other amateur and professional athletes.

Less humorous dramas were played out in the Pacific Northwest throughout the 1970s and 1980s, as Christian evangelicals and other conservatives lobbied to roll back what few laws there were protecting the rights of gays, lesbians, and transgendered people. Oregon conservatives consistently blocked proposed gay rights bills through much of the 1970s and again in 1987. In 1988, the Oregon Citizens Alliance (OCA) engineered the repeal of Oregon Governor Neil Goldschmidt's recent executive order prohibiting discrimination in state employment. From 1992 to 1994, voters in Oregon, Washington, and Idaho narrowly defeated repeated OCA-backed initiatives to undo all protections. Activists in Portland, Seattle, and even Eugene also found themselves embattled with Christian conservatives. The anti-gay forces succeeded in Eugene, managing to repeal a 1977 ordinance.

A similar struggle played out in Seattle in 1978, where Initiative 13 proposed repealing city ordinances protecting employment and housing rights as well as closing the city's Office of Women's Rights. Filed by Seattle Police Officer David Estes, Proposition 13 asked voters if they were concerned homosexuals were "teaching" and "recruiting" their children, while employers were "being forced to hire homosexuals."[87] Gay and lesbian activists hesitated to aggressively oppose the initiative fearing publicity would only enable Estes to collect the required signatures.

The low-key strategy failed and Proposition 13 was scheduled for a vote on November 7. The campaign exemplifies the startling misconceptions about homosexuality in the 1970s. The anti-gay forces used fear and religious themes to label homosexuals as immoral people who "engaged in abominable sex acts" and threatened American families. The anti-13 forces, in addition to mobilizing gays and lesbians, warned that anyone could be persecuted on the assumption they're gay. "All someone has to do is think or say you are gay," read one campaign add. "The burden of proof then rests on you, the accused, rather than on the accuser."[88]

Seattle voters soundly defeated the anti-gay initiative, 64,225 yes and 108,124 no, defining Seattle as a city that now embraced advances for sexual minorities and women. "We have proven that we can win an electoral battle; we have broken the charge of the bigots," reported the *Seattle Gay News*.[89]

Teeter-totter politics prompted some sexual minorities to flee rather than fight. In the 1970s, dozens of women determined "to live in a separatist lesbian world" initiated a back-to-the-land movement and set up communes in Southern Oregon and California. Like other minority activist groups of the era, "lesbian feminists" partly owed their existence to the Civil Rights Movement of earlier decades. Rather than breaking through old barriers, however, they chose to create their own communities, separating themselves "physically, emotionally, and sexually" from men.[90] It made for a challenging life that required women to maintain a "sustainable, earth-friendly" lifestyle, often without the conveniences of electricity and other modern amenities.[91]

The appearance of the deadly human immunodeficiency virus, or HIV, complicated the path to acceptance and tolerance. The virus, which originally appeared in Africa, led to acquired immune deficiency syndrome (AIDS) through the transfer of blood or semen. Between 1981 and 2004, nearly 1 million cases of HIV, predominately among gay men, were reported in the United States, according to the Foundation for AIDS Research. Of those, more than 56% died of AIDS.[92] Infection and death rates in the three Pacific Northwest States mirrored U.S. rates. Between 1981 and 2014, 14,338 cases of HIV and 6,206 AIDS related deaths were reported in Washington, and 9,685 cases and 4,042 deaths in Oregon. Idaho reported 569 cases of AIDS and an estimated 400 deaths from 1985 through 2005.[93]

With the new levels of prejudices threatening gay men as a result of the AIDS plague, state legislatures responded. Executive orders issued in Washington in 1985 and 1991 prohibited state agencies and public colleges and universities from discrimination based on sexual orientation. In 2006, the Washington legislature strengthened those prohibitions and added transgendered to the list of protected individuals. The 2007 Oregon Equality Act provided similar safeguards in that state. In 2011, an American Civil Liberties Union (ACLU) survey showed that 78% of Idaho voters favored some legal protections for gays and lesbians, yet by 2012 the Idaho State Legislature failed to amend the state's civil rights act.[94]

Redefining union

That brings us back to long-time partners Abbott Lighty and Pete-e Peterson and thousands of other same-sex couples who waited years and decades to legalize their relationships. The debate over gay marriage took center stage in the political arena with U.S. Congressional passage of the Defense of Marriage Act (DOMA) in 1996. The act defined marriage as a legal union between a man and a woman, and enabled states to refuse to recognize same-sex marriages from other states. Although activists argued vociferously that it violated the Fifth and Fourteenth amendments to the Constitution, the Republican-controlled Congress passed and Democratic President Bill Clinton signed DOMA on September 21.

Governor Gary Locke was less accommodating when he vetoed Washington's proposed DOMA law in 1997, stating his opposition to "any measure that would divide, disrespect or diminish our humanity." Undeterred, the legislature overrode Locke's veto of a similar bill in 1998. The marital tug-of-war played out similarly in Oregon where voters passed Ballot Measure 36, invalidating all same-sex marriages in 2004.

In 2012, Washington became one of the first of three states in which marriage equality was approved by voters on the same day. (Previously, the legislatures of a few other states had approved gay marriage, rather than by public vote.) The U.S. Supreme Court settled the issue in June 2015 when it ruled that state-level bans on same-sex marriage were unconstitutional under the due process and equal protection clauses of the Fourteenth Amendment.

While the court overturned DOMA, the 5-4 ruling did not fully guarantee a right to marriage equality. Rather, it declared that state and federal DOMA laws were unconstitutional and same-sex couples were entitled to the same federal benefits as heterosexual couples. In his majority opinion, Justice Anthony M. Kennedy, said DOMA "denies same-sex couples the dignity that the states intended them to have and sets them apart in a way that violates the due process and equal protection principles guaranteed under the Constitution."[95] U.S. Attorney General Eric Holder said the court's decision "gives real meaning to the Constitution's promise of equal protection to all members of our society, regardless of sexual orientation."[96]

Justice Antonin Scalia, who joined Chief Justice John G. Roberts Jr., in the dissenting opinion, argued the court's narrow decision impeded states' rights and promoted federalism. "Some will rejoice in today's decision, and some will despair at it," Scalia argued, but the court "cheated both sides, robbing the winners of an honest victory, and the losers of the peace that comes from a fair defeat."[97]

Paul Barwick, who'd been denied a marriage license in Seattle 1971, lived in San Francisco at the time of the ruling. His former partner, John Singer, who changed his name to Faygele benMiriam, died of cancer in 2000. In the four decades since his historic gesture, Barwick witnessed firsthand the many victories and losses of the gay rights movement, but few moved him more than marriage equality. He said he didn't believe he'd "ever live [to] see legal gay marriage" and watching couples finally getting legally married "brought tears to my eyes."[98]

Movin' on up ... and outside the Central District

Like any young family starting out, Robert L. Jones, a Seattle postal worker, and his wife Eda, were likely excited at the prospect of buying a new home. In 1959, the African American couple found one they liked outside the Central District on East 70th Street. It belonged to John O'Meara, a U.S. Coast Guard Commander who had been transferred to Washington, DC. After inspecting the home, Jones instructed his attorney to deliver a $1,000 down payment on the $18,000 home, to be financed through the Federal Housing Authority (FHA).[99]

The next day O'Meara returned the check to the attorney without explanation. Jones, convinced he'd been discriminated against on the basis of color, filed a complaint with the Washington State Board Against Discrimination (WSBAD), triggering one of the more momentous Civil Rights struggles in the city's history.

Like much of America in the second half of the twentieth century, the Civil Rights movement in the Pacific Northwest was fought on many fronts – in the workplace, at school, in the courts, and on the steps of capitol buildings. But few struggles can match the one waged for open housing in Seattle and other large cities. The historian Quintard Taylor called it the "most acrimonious and yet ultimately the most successful" Civil Rights struggle in Seattle's history.[100]

Discrimination in housing drew multiple boundaries: legal ones in the form of restrictive covenants, as well as unofficial ones laid down by the real estate industry. In the 1960s, when nearly 80% of Seattle's African Americans lived in the Central District, real estate agents would not show them a home in a white neighborhood.

Jones got as far as he did because he didn't use an agent. The WSBAD upheld his claim, leading to *O'Meara v. Washington State Board Against Discrimination*, in which the Washington State Supreme Court, in a five-to-four ruling, found for O'Meara. The state law prohibiting discrimination in housing financed through government loans did not apply with the FHA, the court ruled.

In 1961, the NAACP and several African American groups stepped up its pressure on the Seattle City Council to pass an ordinance prohibiting discrimination in housing. An advisory committee recommended such an ordinance but the city balked. By the summer of 1963, council members found themselves facing large crowds on the streets and in council chambers.

Following a crowded and contentious meeting on July 1, about 35 members of the Central District Youth Club marched out of council chambers and into Mayor Gordon Clinton's office and plopped themselves down. There they sat for 25 hours, when black religious leaders extracted concessions from the city on a potential ordinance. One of those leaders, the Rev. Mance Jackson, said "what the young people did was heard louder than all the speeches we made in presenting the Negro's cause for equality and representation."[101]

Rather than passing its own open housing ordinance, the city council put it on the general election ballot, scheduled for March 10, 1964. The real estate industry called it "forced housing legislation" intended to "control the thoughts and actions of individual citizens."[102]

The Congress for Racial Equality (CORE), the NAACP, other civil rights and religious groups led a restrained yet energetic campaign to build public support. They suspended picketing outside real estate companies for fear of losing voters, yet they were far from invisible. Large

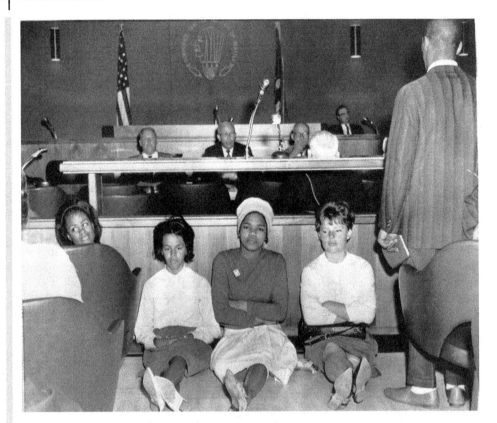

Figure 11.7 Protesters stage a sit-down at the Seattle City Council meeting on July 25, 1963. Activists had been pressuring the city to address discrimination in housing for several months. The protesters are, from left, Delores Hall, 18; Jackie Ellis, 11; Infanta Spence, 20; and Susan Van Dong, 20. The councilman on the left, Charles M. Carroll, was tripped by protesters as he left the meeting. Image reprinted with permission from the Washington State Historical Society.

crowds picketed the Seattle Real Estate Board's annual man-of-the-year award at the Olympic Hotel. On March 7, one group started out from the Seattle Center and another from the Federal Court House downtown. They met under the monorail at Westlake Mall, conducting a huge rally in the rain.[103]

The backlash gave evidence that Seattle wasn't as open to integration as some believed. White neighborhoods throughout the city fell under the industry's fear tactics. Yet the strongest reaction occurred in the suburbs, in neighborhoods outside the ordinance's jurisdiction. Crosses burned at night, incendiary devices blew up in front yards, and shotgun blasts shattered windows.[104] The King County Council soon passed its own ordinance, prohibiting discrimination in housing throughout all unincorporated areas.

Seattle voters indeed were not ready for open housing, as the ordinance went down to defeat two to one (112,448 to 53,453). A white supporter expressed his disappointment with his city. The resounding no-vote was "conclusive evidence that Seattle is not yet aware of the plight of its minority citizens and that only dramatic events will bring about recognition and determination to correct it."[105]

A most dramatic event came four years later with the assassination of Martin Luther King Jr., on April 4, 1968, an event that rocked America. Facing severe public pressure, the Seattle City Council finally acted. Under the leadership of its first African American member, Sam Smith, the council unanimously passed an open housing ordinance "prohibiting unfair housing practice" against racial minorities. In 1975 it was amended to protect sexual minorities and other groups.[106]

Explore more

Books

Recent printed scholarship on the Chicano Movement in the Pacific Northwest is pretty thin, but two volumes on César Chávez and the broader farm workers movement are worth checking out. See Matt Garcia's *From the Jaws of Victory: The Triumph and Tragedy of César Chávez and the Farm Worker Movement*, and *The Crusades of César Chávez, A Biography* by Miriam Pawel.

Online

HistoryLink.org and the Seattle Civil Rights and Labor History Project both offer solid overviews of the Chicano Movement and the broader civil rights struggles of the 1960s and 1970s. See the "Chicano Movement in Washington: Political Activism in the Puget Sound and Yakima Valley Regions, 1960s–1980s." at HistoryLink.org; and "La Raza Comes to Campus: The New Chicano Contingent and the Grape Boycott at the University of Washington, 1968–69," at http://depts.washington.edu.

What do you think?

How would you compare the civil rights struggles of Mexican Americans with those of African Americans, especially in light of the latter's conflicts with police in recent years? Given the substantial progress made in the second half of the twentieth century, what more can Americas do to address racial issues? If segregation is illegal and unconstitutional, how do you explain the existence of stark color lines in neighborhoods in many of America's largest cities? What other economic and cultural factors are at play?

Notes

1 Author interview with Mónica García, Nov. 19, 2015.
2 Ibid.
3 Richard White, *It's Your Misfortune and None of My Own, A New History of the American West* (Norman, OK: University of Oklahoma Press, 1991), 578.
4 White, *It's Your Misfortune and None of My Own*, 577.
5 Ibid.
6 Carlos S Maldonado and Gilberto García, eds. *The Chicano Experience in the Northwest* (Dubuque: Kendall/Hunt Publishing Company, 1995), 1–5.
7 Ibid., 6.
8 Lynn Stephen, "The Story of PCUN and the Farmworker Movement in Oregon," revised edition, Center for Latino/a and Latin American Studies, University of Oregon, PDF document, accessed November 3, 2015, www.http://uoregon.edu/pcunstory/html, 8–9.
9 Ibid.
10 "Timeline: Farmworker Organizing in Washington State," Seattle Civil Rights and Labor History Project," accessed December 16, 2015, http://depts.washington.edu/civilr/farmwk_timeline.htm.
11 Stephen, *The Story of PCUN*.

12 Ibid., 10.

13 Rosales Oscar Castaneda, "Chicano Movement in Washington: Political Activism in the Puget Sound and Yakima Valley Regions, 1960s–1980s," HistoryLink.org Essay 7922, accessed October 14, 2015 http://www.historyLink.org.

14 Richard W. Slatta, "Chicanos in the Pacific Northwest: A Demographic and Socioeconomic Portrait," Pacific Northwest Quarterly 70, no. 4 (October 1949): 161.

15 Slatta, "Chicanos in the Pacific Northwest," 158–159. Slatta sources two studies on Hispanic poverty: "The Social Science Myth of the Mexican American Family," *El Grito* 3 (Summer 1970): 56–63; and Rub W. Espinosa, Celestino Fernandez, and Sanford M. Dornbusch, "Factors Affecting Effort and Achievement in High School," *Atisbos* (Summer 1975): 9–30.

16 Ibid.

17 Slatta, "Chicanos in the Pacific Northwest," 159–160.

18 Yakima Valley Herald, "Minimum Shelters at Labor Camps 'Closed,'" January 4, 1969, 1.

19 "Hispanic Migrant Workers' Social and Educational Services in Idaho," Idaho State Historical Society Reference Series, no. 1092, February 1995. PDF file found online, accessed December 16, 2015, http://history.idaho.gov/search/google.

20 Alvin T. Knudtson to Daniel J. Evans, June 11, 1970. Agency Files 1970, Daniel J. Evans, Box 2S-2-481. Folder: Mexican American Task Force.

21 Mr. and Mrs. Leonard Houle to Daniel J. Evans, July 1970. Agency Files, 1970, Daniel J. Evans, Box 2S-2-481. Folder: Mexican American Task Force.

22 Jesus Lemos, "A History of the Chicano Political Involvement and the Organizational Efforts of the United Farm Workers Union in the Yakima Valley, Washington," 63.

23 White, *It's Your Misfortune*, 601.

24 Author interview with Ricardo García, Nov. 19, 2015.

25 Margaret Miller, "Community Action and Reaction: Chicanos and the War on Poverty in the Yakima Valley, Washington," unpublished MA thesis, University of Washington, 1991), accessed October 20, 2016, http://courses.washington.edu.

26 White, *It's Your Misfortune and None of My Own*, 593–594. *Yakima Valley Herald*, April 25, 1971.

27 Harris, "Hops Heads List of Chávez' Union."

28 Ibid.

29 Dixie Koening, "Growers Defendants: Hops-labor Trial under Way, *Yakima Valley Herald*, January 31, 1971, 1.

30 "Hop Ranch Workers Seek Farm Affiliate," *The Daily Chronicle*, September 9, 1970.

31 Stephen, *The Story of PCUN and the Farmworker Movement in Oregon*, 11.

32 Miriam Pawel, *The Crusades of César Chávez, A Biography* (New York: Bloomsbury Press, 2014), 244.

33 Galen Barnett, "César Chávez's mark on Oregon history," The Oregonian, March 4, 2009, accessed November 23, 2015.

34 Stephen, *The Story of PCUN and the Farmworker Movement in Oregon*, 11.

35 Ibid., 18.

36 Ibid.

37 History of PCUN, accessed November 27, 2015, http://www.pcun.org/about-pcun/history-of-pcun/.

38 Jeremy Simer, "La Raza Comes to Campus: The New Chicano Contingent and the Grape Boycott at the University of Washington, 1968–69," accessed November 23, 2015 at http://depts.washington.edu/civilr/la_raza2.htm.

39 Ibid.

40 Ibid.

41 Ibid.

42 Ibid.

43 White, *It's Your Misfortune and None of My Own*, 596.

44 Dave Doctor, "New Black Image Emerging." *The Daily*, February 15, 1968, 6–7

45 Maldonado and Gilberto, The Chicano Experience in the Northwest, 71–72.

46 Ron Kay, "Pickets March at YVC," *The Herald Republic*, January 28, 1973, 3.

47 Larry Burrough, "Arrest of 9 Ends YVC Occupation," *The Herald-Republic*, January 24, 1973, 1.

48 Ibid.

49 Ibid.

50 Kaye, Ron, "YVC Officials Reject Demands," *The Herald-Republic*, January 25, 1973, 1. The paper responded to the criticism in an editorial, "The fuss at YVC," *The Herald-Republic*, January 26, 1973, 2.

51 Kaye, Ron, "Chicanos Could Get Jail Terms," *The Herald-Republic*, January 27, 1973, 1.

52 Constantine Angelos, "Search for Dean Throws U.W. into Controversy Again," *The Seattle Times*, May 7, 1975.

53 Julie Emery, "U.W. Fires 2 Chicanos; 20 Others Quit in Protest," *The Seattle Times*, May 7, 1975, 1.

54 Angelos, "Search for Dean Throws U.W. into Controversy Again."

55 Emery, "U.W. Fires 2 Chicanos; 20 Others Quit in Protest."

56 Julie Emery, "Chicano Protesters at U.W. Take to the Streets," *Seattle Times*, May 13, 1975, A7.

57 Timeline: Farmworker History in Washington State, Seattle Civil Rights and Labor History Project, Accessed December 8, 2015, http://depts.washington.edu/civilr/farmwk_timeline.htm.

58 Angelos, "New Chicano Study center will be set up at U.W.," *Seattle Times*, September 19, 1975.

59 Like many Hispanic organizations accronyms represent Spanish names. In this case MEChA stands for *Movimiento Estudiantil Chican@ de Aztlán*,"Chican@ Student Movement of Aztlán."

60 Jeffrey S. Passel, D'Vera Cohn and Ana Gonzalez-Barrera, "Migration Between the U.S. and Mexico," Pew Research Center, found at http://www.pewhispanic.org/2012/04/23/ii-migration-between-the-u-s-and-mexico/. Accessed December 5, 2015.

61 Oscar, Rosales Castaneda, "The Creation of the Washington State UFW in the 1980s," Seattle Civil Rights and Labor History Project, accessed December 12, 2015, http://depts.washington.edu/civilr/farmwk_ch9.htm.

62 Maldonado and García, *The Chicano Experience in the Northwest*, 10.

63 Alexa Vaughn and Brian M. Rosenthal, "A license to marry: it's official," *Seattle Times*, December 6, 2012, accessed February 2, 2016, http://www.seattletimes.com/seattle-news/a-license-to-marry-its-official.

64 Casey McNerthney, "Gay marriage license given at site of Seattle rights struggle," *SeattlePI.com*, accessed January 21, 2016, http://www.seattlepi.com. Also Alan J. Stein,

"Marriage Equality and Gay Rights in Washington," HistoryLink.org, accessed November 10, 2015; http://www.historylink.org/.

65 Peter Boag, *Same-Sex Affairs: Constructing and Controlling Homosexuality in the Pacific Northwest* (Berkeley, CA: University of California Press, 2003), 3–4.

66 Ibid.

67 Chrystie Hill, "Queer History in Seattle, Part 1: to 1967," History Link File 4154, accessed January 29, 2016, http://www.historylink.org/.

68 Ibid.

69 National World War II Museum, accessed February 8, 2016, http://www.national ww2museum.org.

70 Peter Boag, "'Does Portland Need a Homophile Society?' Gay Culture and Activism in the Rose City Between World War II and Stonewall," *Oregon Historical Quarterly* 105, no. 1 (Spring, 2004): 10.

71 Ibid.

72 James T. Patterson, *Grand Expectations: The United States, 1945–1974* (New York: Oxford University Press, 1996), 77.

73 Ibid., 181.

74 Ibid., 197.

75 Arthur Schlesinger, Jr., *The Vital Center: The Politics of Freedom* (Boston: Houghton Mifflin Company, 1949), 151.

76 Boag, "Does Portland Need a Homophile Society?," 14.

77 Patterson, *Grand Expectations*, 356–357.

78 Ibid., 360, and the movie review website Rotten Tomatoes, accessed October 20, 2016, http://www.rottentomatoes.com/m/compulsion/.

79 Patterson, *Grand Expectations*, 448–9.

80 Chrystie Hill, "Queer History in Seattle, Part 2: After Stonewall," HistoryLink.org, accessed January 29, 2016, http://www.historylink.org/.

81 Michael Schaller, Robert Schulzinger, John Bezis-Selfa, Janette Thomas Greenwood, Andrew Kirk, Sarah J. Purcell, and Aaron Sheehan-Dean. *American Horizons, U.S. History in a Global Context, Vol II, Since 1865* (New York: Oxford University Press, 2015), 1029.

82 Patterson, *Grand Expectations*, 711.

83 Schaller et al., *American Horizons*, 1029.

84 Boag, "'Does Portland Need a Homophile Society?" 35.

85 Schaller et al., *American Horizons*, 1029; Hill, "Queer History in Seattle, Part 1. and "Looking Back at 40 Years of Portland Pride," *Portland Monthly*, accessed February 5, 2016, http://www.pdxmonthly.com/.

86 *All in the Family*, produced by Norman Lear and written by Burt Styler and Norman Lear, Tandem Licensing Corp, 1971.

87 Gary L. Atkins, *Gay Seattle: Stories of Exile and Belonging* (Seattle: University of Washington Press, 2003), 242–243.

88 Atkins, *Gay Seattle*, 248.

89 Ibid, 257.

90 Catherine Kleiner, "Nature's Lovers: The Erotics of Lesbian Land Communities in Oregon, 1974–1984," in *Seeing Nature Through Gender*, Virginia J. Scharff, ed. (Lawrence, KS: University Press of Kansas, 2003), 242–262.

91 Ibid.

92 The Foundation for AIDS Research, accessed February 4, 2016, http://www.amfar.org/.

93 Washington State HIV Surveillance Semiannual Report, December 2015, 15; Oregon Public Health Division, Oregon Cases of HIV infection by year of diagnosis and sex, 1981–2015; and the 2006 Idaho Epidemiologic Profile, "What is the scope of the HIV/AIDS epidemic in Idaho?"

94 Peter Boag, "Gay and Lesbian Rights Movement," *OregonEncyclopedia.org*, accessed October 10, 2015, http://oregonencyclopedia.org, Hill, "Queer History in Seattle"; Monica Hopkins, "Non-Discrimination Ordinances in Idaho," The American Civil Liberties Union of Idaho, accessed February 5, 2016, https://acluidaho.org/.

95 John Schwartz, "Between the Lines of the Defense of Marriage Act Opinion," *New York Times*, accessed February 8, 2016, http://www.nytimes.com/.

96 Eyder Peralta, "Court overturns DOMA, Sidesteps Broad Gay Marriage Ruling," National Public Radio, accessed February 9, 2016, http://www.npr.org.

97 Ibid.

98 Casey McNerthney, "Seattle Gay Fights Pioneer Recalls Struggle for Marriage £quality," Seattle-PI.com, accessed January 21, 2016, http://www.seattlepi.com.

99 Anne Frantilla, "The Seattle Open Housing Campaign, 1959–1968: Housing Segregation and Open Housing Legislation," accessed December 12, 2015, http://www.blackpast.org/.

100 Quintard Taylor, *The Forging of a Black Community: Seattle's Central District from 1870 through the Civil Rights Era* (Seattle: University of Washington Press, 1994), 201.

101 Joan Singler et al., *Seattle in Black and White: The Congress of Racial Equality and the Fight for Equal Opportunity* (Seattle: University of Washington Press, 2011), 119.

102 Frantilla, "Seattle Open Housing Campaign."

103 Singler, *Seattle in Black and White*, 121–125.

104 Taylor, *The Forging of a Black Community*, 205.

105 Ibid.

106 Frantilla, "Seattle Open Housing Campaign."

12

The Fractured Northwest

Pocketbook politics compete with environmental preservation
in a globalized economy

> *References to the "Pacific Northwest" evoke an image of a single, homogenous region
> in the far left-hand corner of America. But in many ways Washington, Oregon, and
> Idaho, as this text narrowly defines the region, are as different as its rolling plains
> and rugged mountains. The relevance of these mostly economic and political dif-
> ferences tend to ebb and flow with the blue-state, red-state dichotomy of the pres-
> idential election cycle. But in recent decades they've sparked a more fundamental
> debate over control of the region's future, one that extends well beyond jobs ver-
> sus the environment. Both sides promote jobs, whether in resource extraction, or
> tourism and recreation.*

In January 1998, Eddie Baker, Jr., a descendant of Idaho's early pioneers, mounted his
horse to inspect his cattle on the family's ranch edging the East Fork of the Salmon River.
When he came across the bloody remains of a cow, he looked up and spied a wolf. While
he found the animal "pretty to look at," the wolf's presence signaled a political debate as
sharp as its bite.[1]

Until recently, wolves presented no threat to ranchers because Oregon Trail settlers
a century and a half earlier launched a long, and successful eradication campaign. In
viewing nature, settlers sought to mold the environment to meet human needs. Wolves
threatened cattle and sheep ranchers, so they eliminated them. Similarly, they saw
unlimited potential in the region's resources and believed forests should be logged, rivers
fished, and coal and ore deposits mined.

A new philosophy of environmentalism developed, however, in the decades following
World War II, and activists began a campaign to restore the wolf population. Many farmers and ranchers responded with outrage and mounted a vigorous effort to block them.
After lengthy court battles, environmentalists prevailed and federal officials released
four gray wolves into Idaho's Frank Church-River of No Return Wilderness in January
1995.[2] Their numbers rapidly climbed and, as they spread across the range, reached the
Baker ranch three years later.

More wolves meant more attacks on livestock, alarming ranchers. Not only did predation hit them financially, it threatened their lifestyle. In Baker's case, U.S. Fish and
Wildlife officials intervened. Through a mixture of hunting and relocation they broke up

Contested Boundaries: A New Pacific Northwest History, First Edition. David J. Jepsen and David J. Norberg.
© 2017 John Wiley & Sons, Ltd. Published 2017 by John Wiley & Sons, Ltd.

the pack attacking his animals, but calm did not return.[3] Environmentalists pledged to redouble their "efforts to put the Bakers ... out of the ranching business permanently."[4]

Increasingly, ranchers longed to hunt wolves and reduce threatening packs, but federal protections blocked them even though the growing population far exceeded that necessary for removal from protection under the Endangered Species List. Finally in 2011, Idaho Representative Mike Simpson secured legislation placing management in state hands.[5]

This led to more, not less, controversy. The federal government required Idaho to maintain a population of at least 150 wolves, while an estimated 746 roamed the state in 2011. Seeing an opportunity to greatly thin the packs, hunters took more than 500 animals in two years.[6] In 2014, Idaho Governor Butch Otter signed legislation establishing a wolf management board and appropriated $400,000 to fund eradication. His stated goal? Kill just enough wolves so "the feds don't come in and take it over again."[7] Outraged environmentalists accused Otter of declaring "a war on wolves" and staged protests, including an incident where a Virginia woman chained herself to Otter's office door.[8] As of 2014, an estimated 770 wolves remained in Idaho, and the controversy raged on.[9]

The Idaho "wolf wars" offer insight into the political, economic, and cultural boundaries that mark the contemporary Northwest. An examination of them reveals stark divisions that appear to be widening well into the twenty-first century. Nowhere, perhaps, are the differences more stark than in the attitudes and practices involving the region's eclectic environments and diverse natural resources.

In the late twentieth and early twenty-first centuries, a new economy centered on high-technology, outdoor recreation, tourism, and commercial goods eclipsed traditional resource industries like logging, fishing, farming, and mining. Instead of seeing the environment as a source of raw materials, new-economy Northwesterners wanted to protect, conserve, and in the case of wolves, restore the region's natural environment. Their efforts repeatedly brought them into conflict with struggling rural communities, and land-use battles will likely divide the region into the foreseeable future.

A new Northwestern economy

With the emerging global economy, resource extraction and manufacturing operations declined or moved overseas while high-tech industries, finance, commerce, and service industries thrived. The Northwest found itself well positioned to capitalize on these developments. Deep-water ports and trade relations with Asia first developed during the fur trade two centuries earlier. These connections helped make the region a powerhouse in international trade. Additionally, the beauty of the area's natural environment facilitated the rise of tourism. Luck also played a role, as economic trendsetters like Microsoft's Bill Gates and Paul Allen hailed from the region by mere happenstance.

A 2009 study by the Milken Institute, an economic think tank, listed the greater Seattle area as the number two high-tech center in the nation, behind California's Silicon Valley, and the far-and-away leader in software publishing thanks to Microsoft. Founded in 1975, Microsoft initially built its headquarters in New Mexico to be near its primary client, Micro Instrumentation and Telemetry Systems.[10] Growth followed as the company developed products for other vendors. Sales quickly exceeded a million dollars per year, and the company moved its headquarters to Bellevue, Washington in 1978.[11]

Two years later, Microsoft won a contract to produce an operating system for IBM. The Windows system followed in the 1990s, and Microsoft emerged as a global leader in the software industry.[12] As of 2015, the company reported $93.58 billion in global net revenue and employed nearly 43,000 in the Puget Sound region alone.[13]

Microsoft's stunning success sent shockwaves throughout the region. In 2008, it contributed $9.16 billion to Washington's economy and the company's spending spurred local businesses to add jobs. One study estimated that Microsoft's presence sustained 8.4% of the state's workforce, and Microsoft alumni launched numerous start-ups in the region.[14] Rob Glaser left Microsoft to form the audio and video streaming company Real Networks in 1994, for instance, while Gabe Newell and Mike Harrington created the video game company Valve in 1996.[15]

Figure 12.1 Dressed in a clean suit, a worker oversees operations at a Micron Technology facility in Boise, Idaho. While it may not be as well-known as other Northwest technology companies, it is a global leader in semiconductor production and should be recognized alongside Microsoft, Amazon, and other regional icons. Image reprinted with permission from Micron.

Figure 12.2 While skyscrapers line the banks of the Willamette River in Portland, the abundance of trees reflect the efforts of Oregon's leaders, like former governor Tom McCall (1967–1975), to manage growth and preserve the natural environment, and it is fitting that this waterfront park bears McCall's name. Image reprinted with permission from David J. Jepsen.

Beyond Microsoft and its off-shoots, Amazon.com, founded by Jeff Bezos in a Bellevue area garage in 1995, started as an online bookseller and expanded into an international retailer and provider of web services. With $88 billion in revenue in 2014 the company grew into a prominent fixture in the region's economy.[16] Other notable companies with a Northwestern presence include Cray, PopCap Games, Adobe and Nintendo. Cray supercomputers and PopCap maintained their headquarters in Seattle, while San Jose based Adobe built offices in Seattle and Japan's video game company, Nintendo, employed roughly 650 at its North American headquarters in Redmond as of 2010.[17]

Tech's influence spread far beyond the Puget Sound region. Notably, the Milken Institute marked the Portland-Vancouver-Beaverton region in Oregon and the Boise City-Nampa area in Idaho as the nation's number two and three centers for "Semiconductor and other electronic component manufacturing."[18] Intel, which dominates Oregon's "Silicone Forest," is most known for its computer processors and is a leading employer with more than 19,000 workers in the state. Idaho's Micron Technology, Inc., with a local workforce of 5,000 in 2011, produces computer components like random access memory and solid state drives.[19]

The big business of outdoor recreation

The region's natural beauty lends itself to outdoor recreation. Hiking, camping, skiing, fishing, boating, hunting, and bird watching are big business. According to a 2013 study by the Outdoor Industry Association, outdoor enthusiasts spent $22 billion in Washington, $12.8 billion in Oregon, and $6.3 billion in Idaho in 2012. Such spending sustained more than 226,000 direct jobs in Washington, 141,000 in Oregon, and 76,000 in Idaho. The importance of the industry can hardly be overstated, given it employs nearly as many people as the tech industry in Washington and 13% of all workers in Idaho.[20]

Numerous outdoor and athletic companies, large and small, make their homes in the Pacific Northwest. Seattle's Recreational Equipment, Inc. (REI), maintains stores nationwide, retailing hiking, biking, skiing, and camping gear. Oregon Freeze Dry, established in the 1960s, supplied the U.S. military with preserved food during the Vietnam War. Today, its subsidiary, Mountain House, caters to hikers and campers and dominates the industry with a market share fluctuating between 60% and 80%. Bellevue's Eddie Bauer and Portland's Columbia Sportswear are both well known retailers that sell general purpose and outdoor clothing. Portland is also home to Nike, Inc., the globally recognized maker of shoes and athletic wear that brought in $30 billion in revenue in 2015.[21]

Tourism contributes significantly to the local economy. In 2014, over 19 million visitors to the greater Seattle region spent $6.4 billion, while the state as a whole brought in $19.5 billion.[22] The Port of Seattle has a significant role in this business. Where fishing and other industrial work flourished in the past, large cruise ships now bring tourists and consumer spending. In 2014, the port serviced 179 ships and is expanding

Figure 12.3 The REI flagship store near downtown Seattle is nearly as much a destination as retail store. Boasting a 65-foot tall climbing wall, the store offers classes in climbing and other outdoor pursuits that fuel this ever-growing industry. Image reprinted with permission from David J. Jepsen.

Figure 12.4 Seattle's soaring skyscrapers and bustling waterfront, as seen from the waters of Elliott Bay, make the city's eye-popping growth in the recent past self-evident. Rising above everything else, the 76-story Columbia Center opened in 1985 and stands taller than any other building in the region. Image reprinted with permission from David J. Jepsen.

operations. "We are proud to be the busiest cruise port on the U.S. West Coast," remarked Port Commissioner John Creighton, "and we are working with the cruise lines toward our goal of doubling the economic impact of the cruise business to Washington state in the next 25 years."[23] Oregon and Idaho also enjoy a thriving tourist business as well, with annual revenues of $10.3 billion and $3.4 billion respectively.[24]

Northwest ports, particularly those in Washington, also conduct business in international commerce. In 2014, the state's ports shipped goods worth $90.5 billion, 5.6% of all U.S. exports. The largest share went to China, and Washington captured nearly one-fourth of all U.S. trade to that nation. Oregon handled 1.3% of the nation's exports in 2014, but faced significant declines with the loss of key contracts in 2015. With only one ocean-going port in Lewiston, Idaho struggled to compete. In 2014, it managed a mere 0.3% of national exports, and diminished as the effects of declines in Oregon rippled up the Columbia River.[25]

As an emerging leader in trade, Washington hosted prominent, multinational economic conferences. In 1993, President Bill Clinton met with leaders of Pacific Rim nations in the successful Asia-Pacific Economic Cooperation conference in Seattle. Three years later, APEC designated Seattle as its U.S. headquarters. Similarly, in 1999, dignitaries from 135 nations met in Seattle for the World Trade Organization's conference, but, in sharp contrast to the APEC meetings, the WTO summit brought disastrous results and ultimately tarnished the city's rising image.[26]

Established in 1995, the WTO promotes free trade through the removal of tariffs and regulations on international trade. Strongly supported by Washington's corporate and political leaders, Democrats and Republicans alike, the WTO meetings aroused intense criticism from labor unions, environmentalists, and human rights activists. In a famous case, the United States ran afoul of the WTO in 1998 when it established regulations on shrimp imports to protect sea turtles. Importantly, the WTO objected because the U.S. enforced the laws unevenly, showing favoritism to certain nations, skirting protection. The WTO stressed member nations could "and should" create "measures to protect endangered species," and eventually approved the measure when it was implemented even-handedly. The finer points of the ruling were lost. Activists saw only that a cherished environmental effort had been thwarted by the WTO. As a result, puzzled television news viewers worldwide watched as protesters wearing sea turtle costumes swam among the tens of thousands of protesters on the streets of Seattle throughout the WTO event.[27] The ensuing melee vividly illustrates the diverging interests among the residents of the Pacific Northwest

The city found itself woefully unprepared to manage both the conference and the protests. Starting well before police anticipated, protesters packed city streets, blocking WTO delegates from attending the opening ceremony at the Washington State Convention Center. Using pepper spray and tear gas, authorities unsuccessfully tried to push protesters off the streets to clear a path for delegates. Organizers ultimately canceled that event.[28] Large protests continued throughout that day and night. While the vast majority of protesters used peaceful methods and engaged in non-violent civil disobedience, a small number, known as the "black bloc," smashed business windows and covered storefronts in graffiti.[29] Growing civil unrest led Seattle Mayor Paul Schell to crack down by declaring a state of emergency and imposing strict limits on protest activity. Law enforcement from around the area and the National Guard enforced the new policies with liberal use of tear gas and mass arrests. More than 500 arrests in three days jammed the municipal courts.[30]

The city's handling of the protests provoked sharp criticism. The Chief of Police, Norm Stamper, announced his retirement and left the position several months later, while Mayor Schell lost in the next election's primaries. Federal courts upheld the city's limits on protests, but concluded that some arrests violated civil rights. In the end, the city had to pay some $2 million in compensation to those harmed by its actions.[31]

Regional corporations, like Nike and Starbucks, found themselves in the spotlight as controversy over globalization and business practices became increasingly heated in the late 1990s and early 2000s. Exposés like Jeffrey Ballinger's 1992 article "The New Free-Trade Heel: Nike Profits Jump on the Backs of Asian Workers" described how Nike closed U.S. factories in the 1980s and moved operations to nations like Indonesia, Malaysia, and China. Sadisah, the Indonesian woman profiled in the piece, typically worked more than ten hours a day, earning a mere $1.03. Other accounts revealed child labor and harsh working conditions, including one notorious case in which "a manager slapped a worker with part of a shoe."[32] Coffee companies like Starbucks came under fire for both the treatment of workers and harm to the environment. Traditionally, farmers grew coffee in the shade, but rising demand led them to replace forests with large plantations in full sunlight. The change increased yields but led to the loss of 2.5 million acres of forest in Central America alone, and deforestation contributed to declines in migratory bird populations.[33]

It is important to recognize that both companies responded to criticism. Commenting that Nike shoes had "become synonymous with slave wages, forced overtime and

Figure 12.5 A Boeing P-8A Poseidon soars high over western Washington. While the region took a hit when Boeing moved its headquarters to Chicago in 2001, the aerospace industry remains a vital part of the region's economy. Image reprinted with permission from The Boeing Company.

arbitrary abuse," CEO Philip Knight promised reforms. In 1998 the company stopped hiring workers under the age of 18 and permitted labor advocates to join factory inspections.[34] Similarly, Starbucks established a partnership with Conservation International and announced in 2015 that 99% of its coffee beans came from ethical, environmentally friendly sources.[35] While their actions satisfied critics to a fair degree, larger controversies over globalization and the plight of workers and the environment remain a hot topic in the twenty-first century and suggest the labor battles that rocked the region in the late 1800s and early 1900s have not ended. They have simply moved overseas.

A region divided by uneven growth

> "It sure feels good to work up a good sweat for six hours and then go home and be tired. It feels good to … know you've done a good day's work. I don't know if another job would be as satisfying."
>
> *– Olympic Peninsula logger*

As the winds of the new economy swept across the region, a growing divide emerged. Urban centers like Seattle, Portland, and Boise enjoyed population growth and rising prosperity. The rural Northwest, however, found itself falling on hard times as it largely remained focused on traditional and often declining resource industries.

Farming and ranching remain the dominant industries in much of the rural Northwest and employ many. Labor statistics vary given the significant seasonal fluctuations in farm work, but, on average, some 160,000 worked on farms in Washington, 50,000 in Idaho, and nearly 29,000 in Oregon in 2012–2013. Washington led the nation in apple production and, overall, produced agricultural goods worth $9.1 billion in 2012. Idaho followed at $7.8 billion with its leading crop of potatoes and significant output of cattle, dairy, grains, and legumes. Oregon's relatively smaller industry yielded commodities valued at $4.8 billion,[36] led by "greenhouse and nursery products" followed by cattle, hay, milk, and wheat.[37]

While farming held its ground, the logging and mining industries plummeted from the strong positions of the past. To put it in perspective, timber sustained roughly 63% of all jobs in Washington State in 1910. As of 2015, however, mining and logging accounted for less than half of 1% of the civilian labor force in Washington, Oregon, and Idaho according to the U.S. Bureau of Labor Statistics.[38]

Mechanization and increased efficiency in logging contributed significantly to the decline. Between the late 1970s and 1980s, production from Northwest mills increased from 11 billion to 16.5 billion board feet per year, but 81 mills closed and 18% of workers lost their jobs. In an effort to cut transportation costs, companies often preserved mills closer to cities and closed those in more remote, rural communities.[39]

The woes of timber workers deepened as the federal government placed restrictions on logging in old growth forests in the 1990s. Implemented to protect the Northern Spotted Owl, new federal policies caused harvests to fall dramatically. Where loggers in Washington and Oregon cut 15.7 billion board feet in 1988, their output fell to just 8.3 billion in 1996. The largest declines came from logging in National Forests. In the 1980s, federal lands provided almost 40% of timber but that fell to just 10.5% by 1996.[40]

Despite dire predictions, the region weathered the transition away from logging remarkably well. Between labor cuts in the 1980s and growth in the overall economy, forestry employed just 4.3 percent of workers in Oregon and 1.6 percent in Washington by the late 1990s. Additionally, the majority of workers lived relatively close to urban areas, making it possible for them to move into new lines of work as logging faded.[41]

Those living in more remote areas fared much worse, and Oregon's Harney County in the southeast corner of the state provides a good case study. In the early 1970s, Harney boasted a strong economy and residents brought in wages well above the state average. Logging and milling at businesses like the Edward Hines Lumber Company fueled the local economy. As elsewhere, jobs faded in the 1980s and mills closed after the federal government restricted logging in the nearby Malheur National Forest. The last company in the industry closed in 2008, taking other businesses with it. As one resident put it, "You could have thrown a rock down main street and not hit anybody." Ranching and government jobs kept the remaining residents going, but income in the 2010s trailed the rest of the state and more than half of students received subsidized school lunches. Location, in the eyes of one county leader, posed "the biggest impediment to development" in the county. "We're a long way from nowhere," he remarked, making it "very difficult" to attract new industries.[42]

The decline of resource industries, even for those able to find new work, created tremendous social, cultural, and personal angst. Loggers, miners, ranchers, and farmers historically provided society with essential resources. They took pride in and built their personal identities around their work. As one logger on the Olympic Peninsula put it, "It sure feels good to work up a good sweat for six hours and then go home and be tired. It feels good to … know you've done a good day's work. I don't know if another job would be as satisfying."[43] In sharp contrast, a mill operator in Oregon's Harney County found work as a prison guard after the mills shut down. It paid the bills, but the experience left him feeling "sour as hell."[44] Many like him blame federal environmental policies for their plight, fueling discontent in a polarized political landscape.

Politics from left to right

Stark differences in the urban and rural economies parallel deep political divisions. Cities like Seattle, Tacoma, and Portland trend heavily towards liberalism, while conservatism dominates the rural Northwest. Perhaps no two people better illustrate the range of regional political views in the early twenty-first century as Seattle City Councilwoman Kshama Sawant and Idaho Governor Clement Leroy "Butch" Otter.

Born in India, Sawant immigrated to the United States in 1996, completed a Ph.D. in economics, and relocated to Seattle in 2006. A member of the Socialist Alternative party, she taught economics at Seattle Central Community College and first won election to the Seattle City Council in 2013. An advocate for the poor, immigrants, and organized labor, she called on Boeing employees to "take over the factories, and shut down Boeing's profit-making machine." Once in charge, she suggested workers might "re-tool the machines to produce mass transit like buses" instead of "war machines." Arrested in 2014 during protests for a $15 an hour minimum wage, Sawant won re-election in 2015 and symbolizes the deep vein of liberalism running through the city of Seattle.[45]

Figure 12.6 Kshama Sawant presents a $500 check from her Solidarity Fund to support the Seattle teacher's strike in September 2015. The Seattle Education Association's strike led to higher wages, and concessions on student testing, teacher evaluations, overtime pay, and efforts to address racially skewed discipline and other equity issues. Photo by Clay Showalter.

Butch Otter, the son of migrants who fled the Dust Bowl in the 1930s, grew up "on farms and ranches" and entered Idaho politics in the early 1970s. A Republican with a notable libertarian streak, Otter holds strongly conservative views on social and fiscal issues and won election to his third term as Idaho's governor in 2014.[46] While a member of the U.S. House of Representatives, he supported efforts to crack down on undocumented immigrants and build a fence along the border with Mexico.[47] As governor he worked to reduce taxes and create, in his words, a "competitive, business-friendly environment."[48] In contrast to Sawant's efforts to raise wages, Otter championed Idaho's low wages in a letter to gun manufactures, urging them to move to Idaho where "We balance our budget, we are investing in growth, and our taxes are going down!"[49] Along the same lines, he opposed expanding federal policies and called President Obama's healthcare reform plan "an unconstitutional abuse of power." To combat it, he signed an Idaho Health Freedom Act, and announced, "The citizens of our state won't be subject to another federal mandate or turn over another part of their life to government control."[50] His popularity and long, successful career undeniably reflect the strong conservative ideals underlying Idaho politics.

Washington State, with large urban populations in the Puget Sound region, is known for its liberal politics. Voters in the state chose Democratic governors in every election from 1984 through 2016, and last voted for a Republican presidential candidate in 1984 when Ronald Reagan soundly defeated Walter Mondale.[51] Additionally, votes on social issues reflect liberal leanings. In February 2012, the state government adopted legislation recognizing same-sex marriage.[52] Opponents placed a referendum to overturn the law on the ballot that fall, but voters chose to retain it. The same election saw Washington's voters, along with Colorado's, back an initiative legalizing recreational use of marijuana.[53]

A closer look at voting patterns, however, reveals the contested nature of Washington's politics. Democratic Governor Jay Inslee won the 2012 election with strong support in King County where Seattle holds sway, but lost in every single county in the more rural eastern half of the state. In Garfield County, he garnered a paltry 26.58 percent of the vote.[54] Even the more rural areas of King County, such as the town of Enumclaw, went to his Republican opponent.[55] Votes on same-sex marriage and marijuana followed the same pattern. More liberal voters in the cities strongly favored both measures, while conservatives in Eastern Washington tended to vote against them. Same-sex marriage proved to be especially polarizing, and more than 60% of voters in several eastern counties voted in opposition.[56]

Trends in Oregon mirror those in Washington. The Democratic Party won control of the governor's mansion in 1986 and had not given it up as of 2016. Voting patterns in Oregon are perhaps even more polarized than those in Washington. In 2014, John Kitzhaber narrowly won the gubernatorial election with just 49.8% of the vote and captured only seven of Oregon's 36 counties. Nearly 70% of voters in Multnomah County, including Portland, backed him, compared to 24.5% of voters in rural Harney County.[57] Oregon also legalized recreational use of marijuana with overwhelming support in the cities and vehement opposition from the countryside.[58]

It's not surprising that Idaho, with a noticeably smaller urban population and more resource based economy, is much more conservative than Washington and Oregon. Strikingly, Idaho's residents voted for Democratic President Lyndon B. Johnson in 1964 and then voted Republican in every single presidential election from 1968 through 2016.

A few Democrats served as governor in the 1970s and 1980s, but Republicans captured that office in the mid-1990s and continued to hold it through the 2014 election. In contrast to Washington and Oregon, Idaho retained strict laws on marijuana use and a 2015 poll suggested that 64% either strongly or somewhat opposed legalization.[59] Same-sex marriage also generated significant opposition in the state. A 2012 poll showed only 41% in favor of it, and Idaho's political leaders expressed dismay when the U.S. Supreme Court made same-sex marriage legal throughout the nation in 2015.[60] U.S. Representative Raul Labrador wanted Congress to "move quickly to protect the religious liberty" of businesses and individuals opposed to same-sex marriage, while Governor Otter described the decision as "truly disappointing for states, including Idaho, where the people chose to define marriage for themselves as between one man and one woman." In his mind, the states, and not the federal courts, should have decided "whether same-sex marriage is consistent with the values, character, and moral fabric" of the people.[61]

Terrorism and social strife in Idaho

Terrorist attacks in Paris and California in late 2015 triggered a debate over refugees in Idaho. The state originally created a refugee assistance program in the aftermath of the Vietnam War, and, in recent years, has taken in roughly 1,000 people a year from countries like Iraq, Syria, Somalia, Congo, and Burma.

The attacks, however, made some residents worry that dangerous radicals "wanting to do us harm" might enter the country in the guise of refugees. "You can't help but connect the dots," one state representative warned, "Terrorists are slipping in." That same sentiment led Governor Butch Otter to oppose President Obama's plan to bring more Syrian refugees into the nation.

While some Idahoans defended the refugee program on moral grounds, business leaders stressed the need for skilled workers in manufacturing, high-tech, and similar industries. As the director of Idaho's Department of Labor explained, the state had a "healthy economy" limited by "an aging workforce" with skills "that don't match employer needs." Refugees, who often come with significant education and work experience, provide "part of the solution" to the local economy's needs. Ultimately, state leaders found themselves torn between economic, moral, and security concerns with no easy solutions to satisfy their divided constituents.[62]

Environmental politics: resources vs. recreation

> "Mining and energy development proposals are popping up" around the edges of the Canyonlands … "The time to safeguard the Owyhee is now."
> – *Brent Fenty, executive director, Oregon Natural Desert Association*

Battles over the best use of the natural environment have been among the most contested political issues in the contemporary Pacific Northwest. On one side, loggers, miners, farmers, and ranchers wanted to develop natural resources and create much needed jobs in struggling rural communities. On the other side, environmental activists saw a different value in nature. Along with moral and aesthetic motives, they argued a

Figure 12.7 Two young hikers make their way along the Snow Lake Trail in Mount Rainier National Park. The park's extensive trail system draws tourists from around the world and is so popular that a permit is required for overnight camping to limit effects on the environment. Image reprinted with permission from David Norberg.

healthy environment enhances the region's livability, attracts new companies, and creates jobs in the rising tourism and outdoor recreation industries. As a spokesperson for the Washington Wildlife and Recreation Coalition put it, those parts of the "economic engine" depends on "conserving and opening" public lands.[63] Two efforts to protect sensitive environments, the Wild Olympics and Owyhee Canyonlands campaigns, provide insight into this controversy. In both cases, environmental activists wanted to place land under the care of the federal government to ensure it would remain protected from further industrial development, while rural communities favored resource use and feel local governments should retain control.

The Wild Olympics and Wild and Scenic Rivers Act, first introduced in 2012 by Senator Patty Murray and Representative Norm Dicks of Washington, called for the permanent protection of 126,554 acres in Olympic National Forest and classified 19 rivers as "Wild and Scenic." The law would have allowed recreation and further development of access points along those rivers, but prohibited dam construction and limited activity on government owned land within a quarter-mile of river banks.[64] Protecting these "amazing natural treasures" and "the crown jewels" of the state, in the eyes of Senator Murray would "build on the strong foundation of conservation" established "over generations" in Washington.[65]

Wild Olympics supporters emphasize the economic benefits of preservation. The bill itself maintained that "more than 12,000,000" people visit wilderness areas across the nation each year to "participate in recreation activities" that create jobs.[66] Those jobs only persisted, environmentalists argued, in a healthy environment. As the owner of a raft and kayak store in Port Angeles commented, "My livelihood depends on clean free-flowing rivers." He felt further federal protections seemed a smart "investment in our region's economic future" since companies like his "depend on access to the high quality natural resources the Olympic Peninsula is known for."[67] For similar reasons, REI and Patagonia, an outdoor clothing company, promoted the Wild Olympics campaign.[68]

Backers also suggested the bill would encourage indirect growth. As one business owner explained, "these spectacular public lands were the final determinant" when he

Figure 12.8 Signs expressing vehement opposition to the Wild Olympics Bill, like these affixed to the Quinault Rain Forest Visitor Information Center, can be found all around the Olympic Peninsula. Some of the largest evergreen trees in the world stand tall just a few miles from this building along with popular hiking trails to Enchanted Valley and Low Divide. Image reprinted with permission from David Norberg.

chose the Olympic Peninsula for his medical device manufacturing company.[69] Additionally, the bill's authors contended local companies benefit as "ancient forests, salmon streams, and unique scenery" provide "a competitive edge over other regions in attracting and retaining" talented employees.[70]

Wild Olympics proponents insisted that 99% of the land in question was already off-limits to logging due to federal policies, but representatives from timber companies and many Peninsula residents remain staunchly opposed.[71] Arguing that "timber harvests on the Olympic National Forest have fallen over ninety percent due to litigation, analysis paralysis, and broken federal policies," the American Forest Resource Council, objected to any new policy restricting "responsible timber management and other activities" in the Olympic National Forest.[72] Fears of adding "further burden to an already struggling economy" caused the Port Angeles Business Association to oppose the measure, and the idea that timber jobs would "be replaced by tourism related jobs" seemed utterly ridiculous to one Quinault Valley logger. He lamented that, "Olympic National Park, the spotted owl and the marbled murrelet have taken most of our jobs and homes." Now, he bristled at this new effort that threatened "the remaining few that we have."[73] As of January 2016, the Wild Olympics Bill had failed to pass through Congress but retained support from backers.

Conflict over the Owyhee Canyonlands Conservation Proposal mirrors that over the Olympic National Forest. Sponsored by the Oregon Natural Desert Association and Portland's Keen Footwear Company, the campaign aims to protect 2.5 million acres of public land and critical habitat "for over 200 species of wildlife, including the imperiled Greater Sage-grouse" in Southeast Oregon. Supporters of the plan feared resource industries would overrun the area unless action was taken quickly. "Mining and energy development proposals are popping up" around the edges of the canyonlands, warned Brent Fenty, ONDA executive director. "The time to safeguard the Owyhee is now."[74]

Proponents insisted conservation would not threaten industry. Since ranchers depended on the region, the proposal would "'grandfather in' grazing as it is permitted at the time of designation." If anything, supporters expected the move would improve the local economy thanks to "increased opportunities for rafting, hiking, backpacking, hunting, fishing," and similar pursuits. They estimated visitors spent more than $9 million in 2008 and emphasized that, "Tourism and recreation are one vital component of the economy, and a promising area for future growth."[75]

The vast majority of residents in the region, however, fervently opposed the plan. As Bob Skinner, a leading rancher put it, "Not only no, but hell no."[76] They saw any action by the federal government to lock up land for environmental reasons as a direct threat to their livelihoods and simply do not trust a grandfather clause protecting the interests of ranchers. "Don't believe that stuff," Skinner warned, "The proponents … are professional litigators. Once this gets to court, all bets are off."[77] In the end, the Malheur County Cattlemen's Association predicted the proposal would simply "have a devastating effect on the ranching community and agriculture in Malheur County."[78] Opponents also warned that preservation in the end, would curtail "rights to ranching, hunting, recreation, and more."[79]

To support their point, opponents contended the establishment of the Grand Staircase-Escalante National Monument in Utah in 1996 devastated that region's economy. As one Utah politician explained, environmentalists worked to "reduce grazing," shut down "our timber mill," and limited public access by "constantly" lobbying "to close roads" ever since the monument came into existence. Accordingly, the people of Malheur County wanted their land to remain as much as possible in local and state hands and resent any notion of turning management over to the federal government.[80]

We should take care to not over simplify this issue. Outdoor recreation is popular in both rural and urban communities. Both loggers and high-tech workers want to maintain access for recreation. The battle is over how much to preserve, the role of the federal government in shaping policy, and control over the decision-making process. Additionally, preservationists and recreation advocates periodically find themselves in conflict. Hordes of hikers on popular trails, among many other activities, pose real threats to the environment, and activists increasingly demand limits like the strict quota system placed on the Enchantments in Washington's Alpine Lakes Wilderness.[81] Outdoor enthusiasts also find themselves at odds quite regularly, as the diverse interests of hikers, hunters, off-roaders, birdwatchers, and the like often clash.

Intense battles compelled some environmentalists and proponents of industry to find common ground. In John Day, Oregon, and Randle, Washington, both sides wanted to thin forests. It meant work for loggers and better habitat and wildfire protection to environmentalists. These small-scale cases of cooperation suggest that while these boundaries remain fiercely contested, collaboration in the future is possible.[82]

An uncertain future

At this writing, it was impossible to say with any certainty where the debate over the region's future was headed, but development over the past two decades points unmistakably in a clear direction. Resource extraction defined the Pacific Northwest from the dawn of the fur trade well into the twentieth century, but that era faded into the past as the region took its place in the global economy. A commercial, high-tech, service-based economy prevailed throughout the region, and a growing majority placed environmental protection ahead of resource extraction. Rural communities have won delays but, despite their efforts, forests have been preserved, wolves roam and multiply across the plains, and rivers and wetlands thrive under federal protection.

While these battles might seem to be new developments coinciding with globalization, they are just the latest incarnation of battles over powers that have defined the region's past. Current residents vie for control just as the Chinook fought for command over trade on the Columbia River in the fur trade era, railroads companies sought to dominate the region's economy in the late 1800s, and labor unions battled with company bosses for influence in industry at the turn of the twentieth century. Constant struggles over political, economic, national, cultural, and ideological boundaries have shaped the Pacific Northwest as we know it, and that remains as true as ever in the early years of the twenty-first century.

From building to breaching dams

For most of the twentieth century, Pacific Northwesterners favored dam construction and the many benefits that came from them: power production, flood control, navigation, and water for municipal water systems and irrigation. If anything, they viewed free flowing rivers as a source of waste and longed to capture their potential with yet more dams.

In the recent past, however, environmentalists, concerned about falling salmon populations, launched campaigns to breach dams and restore river ecosystems. Some older dams lack fish ladders and block fish from reaching upstream spawning beds, and even those with ladders add to the problem. After hatching, salmon have to pass over or through dams on their return to the sea and many die in the process. One study by the U.S. Fish and Wildlife Service, published in 1988, found that 66% of Steelhead released into the Elwha River did not survive the journey past the Elwha and Glines Canyon Dams.[83]

Efforts to remove dams, like those on the Elwha, received a boost from federal courts, as Native Americans filed lawsuits challenging restrictions on their fishing rights. In 1974, district judge George H. Boldt ruled in favor of Natives since treaties signed in the 1850s guaranteed the right to fish "at all usual and accustomed grounds and stations."[84] Importantly, the right to fish is worthless if there are no fish to be had, and federal courts maintain that the treaties require habitat protection. District judge Ricardo S. Martínez reinforced that position in 2007 when he ruled that culverts built by the state of Washington blocked salmon migration and therefore violated treaty rights. While the case did not address dams directly, the implication of the ruling certainly calls their effect on salmon populations into question.[85]

In 1979, the Lower Elwha Klallam Tribe first proposed removal of the Elwha and Glines Canyon Dams to protect salmon along with the safety of their people. The dam experienced a significant failure when first completed, and tribal members warned that a rupture threatened their lives and land.[86]

Opposition from the community and powerful politicians like former Senator Slade Gorton of Washington delayed the effort, but, in the end, failed to stop removal. In 2011, the state of Washington shut down the turbines and started demolition. By late 2014, both dams had been removed and observers watched salmon swimming up the Elwha for the first time in over 100 years. While similar campaigns have brought down dams elsewhere in the country, the Elwha restoration is the largest yet completed, and its success is fueling efforts to remove larger dams on the lower Snake River in southeastern Washington.[87]

Built in the 1960s and 1970s, the Ice Harbor, Lower Monumental, Little Goose, and Lower Granite dams are "run-of-the-river" dams that produce electricity but do not store large amounts of water in reservoirs. As such, they produce significant amounts of power in the spring as snow in the mountains melts, but less as the year goes on. Environmentalists contend that the Northwest has a surplus of power in the spring and contend the region can afford to remove all four for the sake of healthier salmon runs. Furthermore, they maintain that more fish will attract tourists and offset the economic effects of removal.[88]

The clothing manufacturer Patagonia strongly supports the "Free the Snake" campaign, but communities in Eastern Washington and Idaho strenuously object to any idea of dam removal. A guest editorial in the *Tri-City Herald* in October 2015, railed against the plan and accused Patagonia of hypocrisy since the company "depends on fossil fuel and hydroelectric power" to operate its "35 factories in Asia." The same piece argued that the Snake River dams should not be compared to the Elwha Dams. Where the former produced relatively little power and had no fish ladders, those on the Snake have fish ladders and "provide $20 billion in annual economic impact." Farmers are among the most vocal opponents, as the dams provide water needed for irrigation and make it possible for ocean going barges to carry their produce to market.[89]

As of 2016, the fight over the Snake remains unresolved and the fate of the dams uncertain. Given the high financial and ecological stakes involved, we can expect that this battle will not end quietly.

Standoff at the Malheur National Wildlife Refuge

On January 2, 2016, heavily armed men broke into federal buildings on the Malheur National Wildlife Refuge in Oregon, established a fortified presence, and refused to leave until the government met their demands. While they did not explicitly threaten to use violence to achieve their ends, Ammon Bundy, one of the leaders, warned they "would defend" themselves if necessary. Ultimately, FBI officials moved in and, not wanting to make Bundy into a martyr, settled in for a long, protected standoff.[90]

Initially angered by a federal criminal case in which the government convicted two local ranchers of illegally setting fires on public lands, the militants claimed the federal government had no legal authority to own the land making up the refuge and insisted federal authorities pass control to local officials.[91] As Bundy explained, he wanted to "restore the land and resources to the people" and "jump start this economy" by putting "the logger back to logging, … the rancher back to ranching, … the miner back to mining, [and] the farmer back to farming."[92] To emphasize their point, they covered the refuge's welcome sign with a banner reading "Harney County Resource Center," encouraged locals to join their cause, and promoted their message at community meetings.

After more than three weeks, federal and state officials took Bundy and other extremist leaders into custody as they traveled from the refuge to one such meeting. While most surrendered peacefully, police fired on and killed one militant who reached towards his jacket while charging them. Most of those remaining at the refuge fled when news of the arrests reached them, but four remained until the FBI surrounded them and convinced them to surrender on February 11, more than 40 days after the standoff started.[93]

While many in the region surrounding the refuge wanted Bundy to "Get the hell out" of the county and rejected his extremist methods, his complaints about the federal government and restrictions on resource use found a receptive audience.[94] They too complained about an "overreaching" federal government and Greg Walden, U.S. Representative for the area, gave a blistering speech in Congress against "overzealous bureaucrats and agencies" and a federal government "that has gone too far for far too long." He emphasized he did not approve the standoff "in any way" but admitted "I understand and hear their anger."[95] Along the same lines, Matt Manweller, a state representative from rural Washington, described the occupation as "not right" but expressed sympathy for "strong men reduced to tears by the Dept of Fish and Wildlife" and "families driven to bankruptcy and despair by the Dept of Ecology."[96]

Ironically, while the armed occupation sought to improve economic opportunities for local ranchers, miners, and loggers, it actually threatened the livelihood of others. The Malheur Refuge is a key stopping point for migrating birds and is a popular place for birding, hunting, and fishing. All told, some 25,000 tourists visit each year and contribute $15 million to the local economy.[97] Those working in hospitality and outdoor recreation worried the prolonged crisis would jeopardize their jobs and expressed relief when the standoff ended before spring and the arrival of the tourist season.

To the surprise of many, Ammon Bundy and six supporters prevailed in court. Federal prosecutors charged Bundy with overly narrow charges, primarily conspiracy to prevent federal employees from carrying out their duties, and failed to make an effective case. Jurors indicated they did not condone Bundy's beliefs and might have convicted him of criminal trespass or other lesser charges. Regardless, the outcome seemed to empower Bundy and raised fears the acquittal will inspire similar acts. The conflict underscores the polarizing competition between job growth in resource industries versus tourism and environmental protection, as well as resentment of federal management of western lands. The trial's outcome ensures this battle will rage for years.[98]

Explore more

Books

William Dietrich's *The Final Forest: The Battle for the Last Great Trees of the Pacific Northwest* is an excellent, highly readable account of the battle over the Spotted Owl and is based heavily on conversations with those involved on both sides. William Robbins's and Katrine Barber's *Nature's Northwest: The North Pacific Slope in the Twentieth Century* has good sections on the recent past. Also, see Nancy Langston's *Where Land and Water Meet: A Western Landscape Transformed* for more on the Malheur National Wildlife Refuge and background on the armed standoff that erupted in early 2016.

Online

Websites run by the federal government provide excellent information on the contemporary Pacific Northwest. Look, for instance, to the Bureau of Labor Statistics (http://www.bls.gov/), United States Department of Agriculture (http://www.usda.gov/wps/portal/usda/usdahome), and the United States Census Bureau (http://www.census.gov/). State government websites also maintain good data on agriculture and employment. Companies like Microsoft (https://www.microsoft.com/) and Amazon (http://www.amazon.com/), often provide detailed overviews of their corporate histories. Lastly, advocacy sites like Wild Olympics (http://wildolympics.org/) and Citizens in Opposition to the Owyhee Canyonlands Monument (http://www.opposetheocm.com/), Owyhee Canyonlands (http://wildowyhee.org/), and the proponent site Owyhee Canyonlands (http://wildowyhee.org/), cover current political issues but must be used with caution as they are obviously one-sided.

What do you think?

Environmental politics tend to be divisive in the current era. What is at stake on both sides? What does each stand to lose or gain? To what degree would it be possible for opposing forces to find middle ground and compromise on environmental policies? What stands in the way of conciliation?

Notes

1 Greg Stahl, "Wolf Wars: Idaho Ranchers See their Livelihood at Stake," *Idaho Mountain Express*, accessed February 8, 2016, http://archives.mtexpress.com/.
2 "Wolves Ready, but Court Won't Let 'Em Out of Pens," *Standard-Speaker* (Hazelton, Pennsylvania), January 13, 1995.
3 Stahl, "Wolf Wars."
4 Quoted in ibid.
5 Brian Smith, "Conflicts Rise Between Idaho Ranchers, Gray Wolves," *MagicValley.com*, accessed February 9, 2016, http://magicvalley.com/; Rocky Barker, "20 Years Ago Today, 4 Wolves Were Released into Idaho. What If It Never Happened?," *Idaho State Journal*, accessed December 17, 2015, http://www.idahostatejournal.com/; Phil Taylor, "Budget's

Wolf Delisting Opens Pandora's Box of Species Attacks, Enviro Groups Warn," *New York Times*, April 13, 2011.

6 Smith; "2011 Idaho Wolf Monitoring Progress Report," Idaho Department of Fish and Game, accessed February 9, 2016, https://fishandgame.idaho.gov/.

7 Nicholas K. Geranios, "Idaho Governor Signs Wolf-control Bill," *Missoulian*, accessed December 17, 2015, http://missoulian.com/; Rocky Barker, "Wolf Lovers Meet with Otter at Idaho Capitol Protest," *Idaho State Journal*, accessed December 17, 2015, http://www.idahostatesman.com/.

8 Betsy Z. Russell, "Pro-wolf Activist Chains Self to Idaho Governor's Office Door," *The Spokesman-Review*, accessed December 17, 2015, http://www.spokesman.com/.

9 2014 Idaho Wolf Monitoring Progress Report," Idaho Department of Fish and Game, accessed February 9, 2016, https://fishandgame.idaho.gov/.

10 Cliff Saran, "Well Known Computer Firms of the Past – Where Are They Now?" *Computer Weekly*, accessed January 10, 2015, http://www.computerweekly.com/.

11 Cassandra Tate, "Microsoft Corporation" *HistoryLink*, accessed January 7, 2016, http://www.historylink.org/.

12 Ibid.

13 "Facts About Microsoft," Microsoft, accessed January 9, 2016, http://news.microsoft.com/.

14 "Microsoft Has 'Ripple' Effect on Washington State Economy," Microsoft, accessed January 9, 2016, http://news.microsoft.com/.

15 Matt Rosoff, "These Former Microsoft Employees are Worth Millions After They Did Their Own Startups," *Business Insider*, accessed January 9, 2016, http://www.businessinsider.com/.

16 "Amazon Media Room: Overview," Amazon, accessed January 9, 2016, http://phx.corporate-ir.net/; Alistair Blair and Ilaina Jones, "Amazon pays top dollar to buy Seattle HQ," *Reuters*, accessed January 9, 2016, http://www.reuters.com/; Natasha Chen, "Amazon Space Could Allow for Triple the Number of Employees in Seattle," *Kiro 7*, accessed January 11, 2016, http://www.kiro7.com/.

17 "About Adobe: Office Locations," Adobe, accessed January 11, 2016, http://www.adobe.com/; Katherine Long, "Nintendo Celebrates Opening of New Headquarters in Redmond," *The Seattle Times*, accessed January 11, 2016, http://www.seattletimes.com/; "Company Information," Cray, accessed January 11, 2016, http://www.cray.com/; "About Us," PopCap, accessed January 11, 2016, http://www.popcap.com/.

18 Ross C. DeVol, Kevin Klowden, Armen Bedroussian, and Benjamin Yeo "North America's High-Tech Economy: The Geography of Knowledge-Based Institutes," Milken Institute, accessed January 10, 2016, http://assets1c.milkeninstitute.org/.

19 "Intel in Oregon," Intel, accessed January 11, 2016, http://www.intel.com/; Mike Rogoway, "Intel's Soaring New Office Building is Huge, and Nearly Invisible," *Oregonian*, accessed January 11, 2016, http://www.oregonlive.com/; "Corporate Profile," Micron, accessed January 11, 2016, https://www.micron.com/; "Inside Boise-Based Micron Technology," *National Public Radio*, accessed January 11, 2016, https://stateimpact.npr.org/.

20 "Outdoor Recreation Economy," Outdoor Industry Association, accessed January 16, 2016, https://outdoorindustry.org/; "Outdoor Recreation in State Yields $22 Billion in Spending," *The Seattle Times*, accessed January 16, 2016, http://www.seattletimes.com/; Lora Shin, "Outdoor-recreation Jobs Abound in Washington State," *The Seattle Times*, accessed January 16, 2016, http://www.seattletimes.com/; Adam Behrman, "Outdoor

Recreation Drives Idaho Economy," *KBOI 2*, accessed January 16, 2016, http://kboi2. com/.

21 "REI Overview," REI, accessed January 11, 2016, http://www.rei.com/; "Our Founder," Eddie Bauer, accessed January 11, 2016, http://www.eddiebauer.com/; Allan Brettman, "Nike Hits $30 Billion in Revenue for Fiscal Year 2015," *Oregonian*, accessed January 11, 2015, http://www.oregonlive.com/; Allan Brettman, "King of the Hill in Freeze-dried Backpacking Food? It's Mountain House, in Oregon's backyard," *Oregonian*, accessed January 11, 2015, http://www.oregonlive.com/.

22 Jon Talton, "Tourists and Their Money are Welcome Here," *The Seattle Times*, accessed January 16, 2016, http://www.seattletimes.com/; "Snohomish County Tourism Bureau 2014 Annual Report," Snohomish County, accessed January 16, 2016, http://snohomish countywa.gov/.

23 Talton, "Tourists and Their Money Are Welcome Here."

24 "Welcome to Travel Oregon," Travel Oregon, accessed January 16, 2016, http://industry. traveloregon.com/; "Tourism Resources," Idaho Commerce, accessed January 16, 2016, http://commerce.idaho.gov/.

25 "State Exports from Washington," United States Census Bureau, accessed January 16, 2016, https://www.census.gov/; "State Exports from Idaho," United States Census Bureau, accessed January 16, 2016, https://www.census.gov/; "State Exports from Oregon," United States Census Bureau, accessed January 16, 2016, https://www.census.gov/; Molly Harbarger, "Container-terminal loss at Port of Portland felt deeply upriver," *Oregonian*, accessed January 16, 2016, http://www.oregonlive.com/.

26 Walt Crowley, "President Clinton convenes APEC summit on Blake Island on November 20, 1993," *HistoryLink*, accessed January 16, 2016, http://www.historylink.org/; Kit Oldham, "WTO Meeting and Protests in Seattle (1999) – Part 1," *HistoryLink*, accessed January 16, 2016, http://www.historylink.org/.

27 Oldham, "WTO – Part 1"; Kit Oldham, "WTO Meeting and Protests in Seattle (1999) – Part 2," *HistoryLink*, accessed January 16, 2016, http://www.historylink.org/; "India etc versus US: 'shrimp-turtle'," World Trade Organization, accessed January 16, 2016, https://www.wto.org/.

28 Oldham, "WTO – Part 2".

29 Ibid.

30 Ibid.

31 Oldham, "WTO – Part 2"; "Ministerial Conferences," World Trade Organization, accessed January 16, 2016, https://www.wto.org/.

32 Samantha Marshall, "Nike's Labor Woes Leave Soiled Footprint on Image," *Wall Street Journal*, accessed January 17, 2016, http://www.wsj.com/; Jeffrey Ballinger, "The New Free-Trade Heel: Nike's Profits Jump on the Backs of Asian Workers," *Harpers*, August 1992, 46–47.

33 George Blacksell, "How Green is Your Coffee?," *The Guardian*, accessed January 17, 2016, http://www.theguardian.com/; Jennifer Bingham Hull, "Can Coffee Drinkers Save the Rain Forest?," *The Atlantic*, accessed January 17, 2016, http://www.theatlantic.com/.

34 John Cushman, Jr., "Nike Pledges to End Child Labor and Apply U.S. Rules Abroad," *The New York Times*, accessed January 17, 2016, http://www.nytimes.com/.

35 "Ethical Sourcing: Coffee," Starbucks, accessed January 9, 2016, http://www.starbucks. com/; "Starbucks Verifies 99% of Coffee Ethically Sourced," Starbucks, accessed January 9, 2016, https://news.starbucks.com/.

36 *Environmental Issues in Pacific Northwest Forest Management* (Washington, DC: National Academy Press, 2000), 161–162.

37 "Agriculture: A Cornerstone of Washington's Economy," Washington State Department of Agriculture, accessed January 20, 2016, http://agr.wa.gov/; "Industry Statistics: An Overview of the U.S. Apple Industry," US Apple Association, accessed January 20, 2016, http://www.usapple.org/; Eric Mortenson, "Oregon Agricultural Production Sets Record; Top 10 Crops Include Nursery Plants, Cattle, and Hay," *Oregonian*, accessed January 20, 2016, http://www.oregonlive.com/; "2012 Census of Agriculture State Profile: Idaho," United States Department of Agriculture, accessed January 20, 2016, http://www.agcensus.usda.gov/; "2012 Census of Agriculture State Profile: Oregon," United States Department of Agriculture, accessed January 20, 2016, http://www. agcensus.usda.gov/; "2012 Census of Agriculture State Profile: Washington," United States Department of Agriculture, accessed January 20, 2016, http://www.agcensus.usda. gov/; "Farm Employment," Idaho Department of Labor, accessed January 20, 2016, https://lmi.idaho.gov/; "Oregon's Agricultural Sector," State of Oregon Employment Department, accessed January 20, 2016, https://www.qualityinfo.org/.

38 Connie Chiang and Michael Reese, "Evergreen State: Exploring the History of Washington's Forests," Center for the Study of the Pacific Northwest, accessed January 20, 2016, http://www.washington.edu/; "Oregon," Bureau of Labor Statistics, accessed January 20, 2016, http://www.bls.gov/; "Washington," Bureau of Labor Statistics, accessed January 20, 2016, http://www.bls.gov/; "Idaho," Bureau of Labor Statistics, accessed January 20, 2016, http://www.bls.gov/.

39 *Environmental Issues in Pacific Northwest Forest Management*, 161–162.

40 Ernie Niemi, Ed Whitelaw, and Andrew Johnson, *The Sky Did NOT Fall: The Pacific Northwest's Response to Logging Reductions* (ECONorthwest, 1999), 4.

41 Ibid., 26–27.

42 Molly Young, "Behind the Harney County Standoff, Decades of Economic Decline," *Oregonian*, accessed January 16, 2016, http://www.oregonlive.com/.

43 William Dietrich, *The Final Forest: The Battle for the Last Great Trees of the Pacific Northwest* (New York: Penguin Books, 1992), 39.

44 Kirk Johnson, "Rural Oregon's Lost Prosperity Gives Standoff a Distressed Backdrop," *The New York Times*, accessed January 18, 2016, http://www.nytimes.com/.

45 Lewis Kamb, "Growing Wealth Gap Spurs on Socialist in Seattle Council Race," *The Seattle Times*, accessed January 23, 2016, http://www.seattletimes.com/; Gary Horcher, "Seattle City Councilmember-elect Shares Radical Idea with Boeing Workers," *Kiro 7*, accessed January 24, 2016, http://www.kirotv.com/; Josh Eidelson, "Capitalism is a 'Dirty Word': America's New Socialist Council Member Talks to Salon," *Salon*, accessed January 23, 2016, http://www.salon.com/; George Howland, Jr., "Introverted Socialist," *Real Change*, accessed January 23, 2016, http://www.realchangenews.org/.

46 "What You Should Know about Governor C. L. 'Butch' Otter," Boise State Public Radio, accessed January 23, 2016, http://boisestatepublicradio.org/.

47 John Miller, "Idaho Candidates Weigh in on Bush Border Plan," *Moscow-Pullman Daily News*, May 16, 2006.

48 Emilie Ritter Saunders, "Idaho Gov. Butch Otter Works Toward Third-Straight Year of Tax Cuts," *National Public Radio*, accessed January 23, 2016, https://stateimpact.npr. org/; Butch Otter, "Letter," *The Spokesman-Review*, accessed January 23, 2016, http:// media.spokesman.com/.

49 Otter, "Letter"; Saunders, "Idaho Gov. Butch Otter Works Toward Third-Straight Year of Tax Cuts."

50 "Fighting Obamacare," Idaho.gov, accessed January 23, 2016, http://gov.idaho.gov/; "Governor Signs Idaho Health Freedom Act," Idaho.gov, accessed January 23, 2016, https://gov.idaho.gov/.

51 "November 1984 General," Washington Secretary of State, accessed July 17, 2016, http://www.sos.wa.gov/.

52 Lornet Turbull, "Gregoire Signs Gay Marriage into Law," *The Seattle Times*, accessed December 28, 2015, http://www.seattletimes.com/.

53 Jonathan Martin, "Voters approve I-502 legalizing marijuana," *The Seattle Times*, accessed February 27, 2016, http://www.seattletimes.com/.

54 "November 06, 2012 General Election Results," Washington Secretary of State, accessed January 23, 2016, http://results.vote.wa.gov/.

55 April Chan, "Looking Back: How Did Enumclaw Vote in November 2012 Elections?," *Enumclaw Patch*, accessed January 23, 2016, http://patch.com/.

56 "November 06, 2012 General Election Results," Washington Secretary of State, accessed January 23, 2016, http://results.vote.wa.gov/.

57 "Kitzhaber Wins Oregon Governor's Race," *Oregonian*, accessed January 23, 2016, http://gov.oregonlive.com/.

58 "2014 General Election," *Oregonian*, accessed January 23, 2016, http://gov.oregonlive.com/.

59 "Otter Vetoes Marijuana Extract Oil Bill," *Idaho Statesman*, accessed January 10, 2016, http://www.idahostatesman.com/.

60 Andrew R. Flores and Scott Barclay, "Public Support for Marriage for Same-sex Couples by State," The Williams Institute, accessed December 28, 2015, http://williams institute.law.ucla.edu/.

61 Jeff Selle, "Idaho Leaders Decry Supreme Court's Same-sex Ruling," *Coeur d'Alene*, accessed December 28, 2015, http://www.cdapress.com/.

62 Miriam Jordan, "In Aftermath of Terror Attacks, Tensions Rise in Idaho Over Refugee Workers," *Wall Street Journal*, accessed July 21, 2016, http://www.wsj.com/; "About Refugees in Idaho," *Idaho Office for Refugees*, accessed July 21, 2016, http://www.idaho refugees.org/.

63 Talton, "Tourists and Their Money Are Welcome Here."

64 Lynda V. Mapes, "126,554 Acres of Olympic Peninsula Would be Protected by New Bill," *The Seattle Times*, accessed January 29, 2016, http://www.seattletimes.com/.

65 Ibid.

66 "S. 1510 – Wild Olympics Wilderness and Wild and Scenic Rivers Act of 2015," Congress.gov, accessed January 29, 2016, https://www.congress.gov/.

67 "Peninsula Economic Leaders Announce New Partnership with REI, Patagonia, & Wild Olympics," Wild Olympics, accessed January 29, 2016, http://wildolympics.org/.

68 Ibid.

69 Ibid.

70 "S. 1510 – Wild Olympics Wilderness and Wild and Scenic Rivers Act of 2015."

71 Rob Ollikainen, "Forestry Group Opposes Wild Olympics Legislation Introduced by Lawmaker," *Peninsula Daily News*, accessed January 29, 2016, http://www.peninsuladaily news.com/.

72 "Press Release," American Forest Resource Council, accessed January 29, 2016, http://www.amforest.org/.

73 R.A. Pilling, "Letter," Port Angeles Business Association, accessed January 29, 2016, http://www.notac.org/; Keith Olson, "Letter," North Olympic Timber Action Committee, accessed January 29, 2016, http://www.notac.org/.

74 Terry Richard, "Owyhee Canyonlands Preservation Proposal Includes 2.5 Million Acres, *Oregonian*, accessed January 30, 2016, http://www.oregonlive.com/; "The Owyhee Canyonlands Campaign," Owyhee Canyonlands, accessed January 30, 2016, http://wildowyhee.org/.

75 "The Owyhee Canyonlands Campaign."

76 Eric Mortenson, "Oregon Ranchers Dead Set against Owyhee Canyonlands Wilderness Proposal," *The Register-Guard*, accessed January 30, 2016, http://registerguard.com/.

77 Sean Ellis, "Hundreds Pack Gym to Oppose Malheur County Monument Proposal," *Capital Press*, accessed January 30, 2015, http://www.capitalpress.com/.

78 Sean Ellis, "Ranchers Oppose Malheur County Monument Designation," *Capital Press*, accessed January 30, 2016, http://www.capitalpress.com/.

79 "Oppose the Owyhee Canyonlands Monument Proposal," Citizens in Opposition to the Owyhee Canyonlands Monument, accessed January 30, 2016, http://www.opposetheocm.com/.

80 Ibid.

81 "Enchantment Area Wilderness Permits," U.S. Forest Service, accessed July 17, 2016, http://www.fs.usda.gov/.

82 Jeff Barnard, "Conservationists, Loggers Team Up on Forest Health," *The Washington Times*, accessed July 17, 2016, http://www.washingtontimes.com/; Robert McClure, "Prospects Looking Up for Logging," *Seattle Post-Intelligencer*, accessed July 17, 2016, http://www.seattlepi.com/.

83 R.C. Wunderlich, D.A. Zajac, and J. H. Meyer, *Evaluation of Steelhead Smolt Survival through the Elwha Dams* (Olympia: U.S. Fish and Wildlife Service Fisheries Assistance Office, 1988), iii.

84 "Treaty of Medicine Creek, 1854," *HistoryLink*, accessed May 19, 2015, http://www.historylink.org/; Walt Crowley and David Wilma, "Federal Judge George Boldt Issues Historic Ruling Affirming Native American Treaty Fishing Rights on February 12, 1974," *HistoryLink*, accessed July 21, 2016, http://www.historylink.org/.

85 Michael C. Blumm and Jane G. Steadman, "Indian Treaty Fishing Rights and Habitat Protection: The *Martinez Decision* Supplies a Resounding Judicial Affirmation," *Natural Resources Journal* 49, no. 3/4 (Summer–Fall 2009): 653–706.

86 "Case Study – Restoration of the Elwha River Ecosystem," United States Department of Agriculture, accessed July 21, 2016, http://www.nrcs.usda.gov/; Kit Oldham, "Ceremony Marks Start of Demolition of Elwha River Hydroelectric Dams on September 17, 2011," *HistoryLink*, accessed July 21, 2016, http://www.historylink.org/.

87 Oldham, "Ceremony Marks Start of Demolition of Elwha River Hydroelectric Dams."

88 "Free the Snake: Restoring America's Greatest Salmon River," Patagonia Works, accessed July 21, 2016, http://www.patagoniaworks.com/; "Why Remove The 4 Lower Snake River Dams," Save Our Wild Salmon, accessed July 21, 2016, http://www.wildsalmon.org/.

89 Colin Hastings, "Guest Column: The Hypocrisy of Efforts to Remove Lower Snake River Dams," *Tri-City Herald*, accessed July 21, 2016, http://www.tri-cityherald.com/.

90 Holly Yan and Joe Sutton, "Armed Protesters Refuse to Leave Federal Building in Oregon," *CNN*, accessed July 21, 2016, http://www.cnn.com/.

91 Ibid.

92 Yan and Sutton, "Armed Protesters Refuse to Leave"; Kelly House, "Bundy: Militants 'Forwarding Our Plan' to Privatize Oregon Wildlife Refuge," *The Oregonian*, accessed July 21, 2016, http://www.oregonlive.com/.

93 Julie Turkewitz and Kirk Johnson, "Ammon Bundy and 7 Oregon Protesters held; Lavoy Finicum is Reported Dead," *New York Times*, accessed July 21, 2016, http://www.nytimes.com/; Les Taitz, "LaVoy Finicum Shot 3 Times as He Reached for Gun, Investigators Say," *The Oregonian*, accessed July 21, 2016, http://www.oregonlive.com/.

94 Les Taitz, "Oregon Standoff: Anger, Frustration Boil over at Community Meeting," *The Oregonian*, accessed July 21, 2016, http://www.oregonlive.com/.

95 Taitz, "Oregon Standoff: Anger, Frustration Boil Over"; Les Taitz, "Oregon Militants: Walden Takes BLM to Woodshed – Transcript," *The Oregonian*, accessed July 21, 2016, http://www.oregonlive.com/.

96 Matt Manweller, "Facebook Post from January 3, 2016," *Facebook*, accessed January 6, 2016, https://www.facebook.com/matt.manweller.

97 Laura Gunderson, "Militants' Choice of Wildlife Refuge Provided Isolation, Ready Compound," *The Oregonian*, accessed July 21, 2016, http://www.oregonlive.com/; Laura Gunderson, "Wildlife Enthusiasts Plan Protests over Oregon Occupation," *The Oregonian*, accessed July 21, 2016, http://www.oregonlive.com/.

98 Maxine Bernstein, "Oregon Standoff Prosecutors Failed to Prove 'Intent' to impede Federal Workers," *The Oregonian*, accessed November 3, 2016, http://www.oregonlive.com/.

Important Dates and Events

1924	On July 26, the Ku Klux Klan drew up to 13,000 people to a rally near Issaquah, Washington. In the early 1920s, this racist organization spread its anti-Semitic, anti-Catholic views throughout the Pacific Northwest.
1929	Pacific Northwest stock market investors watched in disbelief when the Dow Jones Industrials lost nearly 6% of its value on October 23, ending a five-year boom market and ushering in the Great Depression. By 1933, stocks bottomed out, down 80% from their highs in the late 1920s.
1933	In September, construction began in earnest on Grand Coulee Dam, bringing more than 12,000 jobs to the job-starved Northwest, and changing the course of the region's history. Over the next 20 years the federal government constructed eight more by 1984.
1934	On June 18 the Indian Reorganization Act, reversed long-held assimilation policies, and recognized Indian self-determination. Among other things, the law abolished the land allotment system, permitted tribes to establish governments and allowed the formation of corporations to manage tribal resources.
1935	Congress passed the National Labor Relations Act (NLRA), or Wagner Act, reversing years of federal opposition to organized labor. The statute guaranteed the right of employees to organize, form unions, and bargain collectively with their employers.
1942	On March 30, acting under the authority of President Franklin Roosevelt's Executive Order 9066, 275 Japanese American residents living on Bainbridge Island were removed from their homes and interned at Camp Harmony, a relocation facility set up on the fairgrounds in Puyallup, Washington. Eventually more than 110,000 Japanese Americans living on the West Coast will be transported to ten inland prison camps.
1943	In March, the U.S. Army Corps of Engineers began construction of a top secret project on the Columbia River near Richland, Washington. The massive Hanford facility produced fuel for the first ever atomic explosion (a test) at Alamogordo, New Mexico, and the atomic bomb dropped on Nagasaki, Japan.
1945	On August 6, the *Enola Gay*, the Boeing designed B-29 Superfortress, dropped an atomic bomb, named Little Boy, on Hiroshima, Japan. Three days later the Hanford-built bomb named Fat Man, was dropped on Nagasaki. Japan surrendered on August 15.
1948	Washington State Representative Albert F. Canwell (R-Spokane) presided over what will become known as the Canwell Hearings. Dozens of suspected communists were questioned about their alleged ties to the Communist Party. Although little evidence was produced, three University of Washington professors and others who refused to answer the committee's questions lost their jobs.
1950	On June 25, the Korean War began when North Korean troops invaded South Korea, heightening Cold War tension. Like in World War II, the strategically located Pacific Northwest benefited economically, contributing weapons, materiel, and troop transport.
1974	On February 12, Federal Judge George Boldt reaffirmed the rights of Washington Indian tribes to fish in "accustomed places," and allocateed 50% of the annual catch to treaty tribes, infuriating commercial and sports fishermen.
1973	On January 27, the United States agreed to withdraw its troops from Vietnam, although fighting between the North and Sound continued. On April 30, 1975 Saigon fell to Communist forces bringing a permanent end to the Republic of South Vietnam.
1980	On May 18, Mount St. Helens erupted, literally blowing away the volcano's north face, causing widespread destruction and killing 57 people, mostly from asphyxiation.
1990	On March 25, a longstanding dispute between Tacoma and the Puyallup Tribe was settled. In exchange for $162 million in cash, real estate, and economic development programs the tribe abandons claims to some 18,000 acres of land on Commencement Bay. On October 14, the U.S. government apologized to five Japanese Americans, all of whom were over age 100, who had been unjustly incarcerated during World War II. Eventually, 60,000 Japanese would be eligible for a payment of $20,000 in retribution.

Bibliography

Chapter 1

Allen, John Logan. "Summer of Decision: Lewis and Clark in Montana, 1805," *We Proceeded On*. Fall 1976.

Ambrose, Stephen, E. *Undaunted Courage, Meriwether Lewis, Thomas Jefferson, and the Opening of the American West*. New York: Touchstone, 1996.

Blumenthal, Richard W., ed. *With Vancouver in Inland Washington Waters, Journals of 12 Crewmen, April–June 1792*. Jefferson, OR: McFarland & Company, 2007.

Bragg, L.E. *More Than Petticoats, Remarkable Idaho Women*. Helena, MT: Morris Book Publishing, 2001.

Clayton, Daniel Wright. *Islands of Truth: The Imperial Fashioning of Vancouver Island*. Vancouver: University of British Columbia Press, 2000, 128–129.

DeVoto, Bernard, ed. *The Journals of Lewis and Clark*. Boston: Houghton Mifflin Company, 1981.

Gates, Charles Marvin, ed. *Readings in Pacific Northwest History: Washington 1790–1895*. Seattle, WA: University Bookstore, 1941.

Gough, Barry. "A Tangle of Rock and Moving Water," *Columbia: the Magazine of Northwest History*, Winter (2013–14): 20–25.

Harmon, Alexandra. *Indians in the Making: Ethnic Relations and Indian Identities Around Puget Sound*. Berkeley, CA: University of California Press, 1998.

Hine, Robert V. and John Mack Faragher. *The American West: A New Interpretive History*. New Haven, CT: Yale University Press, 2000.

Howay, Frederic W. *Voyages of the "Columbia" to the Northwest Coast: 1787–1790 and 1790–1793*. Portland, OR: Oregon Historical Society Press in cooperation with the Massachusetts Historical Society, 1990.

Johansen, Dorothy O. *Empire of the Columbia*. New York: Harper and Row, 1967.

Lamb, W. Kaye, ed. *The Voyage of George Vancouver, 1791–1795*, Vol. IV. London: The Hakluyt Society, 1984.

Manby, Thomas. *Journal of the Voyages of the H.M.S. Discovery and Chatham*, 1798.

Millner, Clyde A. II, O'Connor, Carol A., Sandweiss, Martha A. *The Oxford History of the American West*. New York: Oxford University Press, 1994.

Nash, Gary B. "The Image of the Indian in the Southern Colonial Mind," *The William and Mary Quarterly*, 3rd Ser., 29, no. 2 (April 1972): 197–230.

Contested Boundaries: A New Pacific Northwest History, First Edition. David J. Jepsen and David J. Norberg.
© 2017 John Wiley & Sons, Ltd. Published 2017 by John Wiley & Sons, Ltd.

Pinkham, Allen V., Sr. "We Ya Oo Yet Soyapo," in *Lewis and Clark through Indian Eyes*. Alvin M. Josephy, Jr., ed., with Marc Jaffe New York: Knopf, 2006.

Prosser, William Farrand. *History of the Puget Sound Country Its Resources, Its Commerce and Its People*. New York: The Lewis Publishing Company, 1903.

Ronda, James P. *Lewis & Clark Among the Indians*. Lincoln, NE: University of Nebraska Press, 1984.

Ruby, Robert H. and John A Brown. *Indians of the Pacific Northwest*. Norman, OK: University of Oklahoma Press, 1981.

Schwantes, Carlos, A. *The Pacific Northwest, An Interpretive History*. Lincoln, NE: University of Nebraska Press, 1996.

Speck, Gordon, *Northwest Exploration*. L.K. Phillips, ed. Portland, OR: Bindfords & Mort, 1970.

Vancouver, George. *A Voyage of Discovery to the North Pacific Ocean, and Round the World in Which the Coast of North-West America Has Been Carefully Examined and Accurately Surveyed*. London: Printed for G.G. and J. Robinson, Paternoster-Row and J. Edwards, Pall-Mall, 1798.

West, Elliott. *The Last Indian War: The Nez Perce Story*. New York: Oxford University Press, 2009.

Whitebrook, Robert. *Coastal Exploration of Washington*. Palo Alto, CA: Pacific Books Publishers, 1959.

Wilenz, Sean. *The Rise of American Democracy*. New York: W.W. Norton & Company, 2005.

Wood, Gordon S. *Empire of Liberty: A History of the Early Republic, 1789–1815*, New York: Oxford University Press, 2009.

Chapter 2

Anderson, Steven A. "The Forgetting of John Montgomery: Spanaway's First White Settler, 1845–1885." *Pacific Northwest Quarterly* 101, no. 2 (Spring 2010): 71–86.

Arrington, Leonard J. *History of Idaho*. Moscow, ID: University of Idaho Press, 1994.

Bancroft, Hubert Howe. *History of the Northwest Coast*. 2 vols. San Francisco, CA: A. L. Bancroft & Company, 1884.

Barman, Jean. *The West Beyond the West: A History of British Columbia*. Revised ed. Toronto: University of Toronto Press, 1996.

Barman, Jean and Bruce M. Watson. "Fort Colvile's Fur Trade Families and the Dynamics of Race in the Pacific Northwest," *Pacific Northwest Quarterly* 90, no. 3 (Summer 1999): 140–153.

Beals, Herbert K., trans. *Juan Pérez on the Northwest Coast: Six Documents of His Expedition in 1774*. Portland OR: Oregon Historical Society Press, 1989.

Boit, John, Young, F.W., Elliot, T.C., and Young, F.G. "John Boit's Log of the Columbia, 1790–1793." *The Quarterly of the Oregon Historical Society* 22, no. 4 (December 1921): 257–351.

Cebula, Larry. *Plateau Indians and the Quest for Spiritual Power; 1700–1850*. Lincoln, NE: University of Nebraska Press, 2003.

Crooks, Drew. "A Place Full of Life and Activity: Fort Nisqually, 1843–187." Accessed September 28, 2014. http://www.dupontmuseum.com/.

Dolin, Eric Jay. *Fur, Fortune, and Empire: The Epic History of the Fur Trade in America*, New York: W.W. Norton & Company, 2010.

Fisher, Robin. *Contact and Conflict: Indian-European Relations in British Columbia, 1774–1890.* 2nd ed. Vancouver: University of British Columbia Press, 1992.

Fort Ross Conservancy. "Russian Expansion to America (Russian American Company in California)." Accessed September 28, 2014. http://www.fortross.org/.

Gibson, James R. "A Diverse Economy: The Columbia Department of the Hudson's Bay Company, 1821–1846." *Columbia* (Summer 1991): 28–31.

Gibson, James R. *Farming the Frontier: The Agricultural Opening of the Oregon Country, 1786–1846.* Vancouver: University of British Columbia Press, 1985.

Gibson, James R. *Otter Skins, Boston Ships, and China Goods.* Seattle, WA: University of Washington Press, 1992.

Harmon, Alexandra. *Indians in the Making: Ethnic Relations and Indian Identities around Puget Sound.* Berkeley, CA: University of California Press, 1998.

Jetté, Melinda Marie. "'Beaver are Numerous, but the Native…Will Not Hunt Them': Native-Fur Trader Relations in the Willamette Valley, 1812–1814." *Pacific Northwest Quarterly* 98, no. 1 (Winter 2006/2007): 3–17.

Johansen, Dorothy O. and Charles M. Gates. *Empire of the Columbia: A History of the Pacific Northwest.* New York: Harper and Brothers, 1957.

Keith, H. Lloyd. "'A Place So Dull and Dreary': The Hudson's Bay Company at Fort Okanagan, 1821–1860." *Pacific Northwest Quarterly* 98, no. 2 (Spring 2007): 78–94.

Koppel, Tom, *Kanaka: The Untold Story of Hawaiian Pioneers in British Columbia and the Pacific Northwest,* Vancouver: Whitecap Books, 1995.

Mackenzie, Alexander. *Voyages from Montreal through the Continent of North America to the Frozen and Pacific Oceans in 1789 and 1793 with an Account of the Rise and State of the Fur Trade.* 2 vols, Toronto: The Courier Press, 1911.

Mackie, Richard Somerset. *Trading Beyond the Mountains: The British Fur Trade on the Pacific 1793–1843.* Vancouver: University of British Columbia Press, 1997.

Merchant, Carolyn. *The Columbia Guide to American Environmental History.* New York: Columbia University Press, 2005.

Merk, Frederick. *Fur Trade and Empire, George Simpson's Journal.* Cambridge, MA: Harvard University Press, 1968.

Milliken, Emma. "Choosing between Corsets and Freedom: Native, Mixed-Blood, and White Wives of Laborers at Fort Nisqually, 1833–1860." *Pacific Northwest Quarterly* 96, no. 2 (Spring 2005): 95–101.

Morgan, Murray. *Puget's Sound: A Narrative of Early Tacoma and the Southern Sound,* Seattle, WA: University of Washington Press, 2003.

Nicandri, David L. "Lewis and Clark: Exploring the Influence of Alexander Mackenzie," *Pacific Northwest Quarterly* 95, no. 4 (Fall 2004): 171–181.

Peers, Laura. "Trade and Change on the Columbia Plateau, 1750–1840." *Columbia* 10, no 4. (Winter 1996–1997): 6–12.

Peterson del Mar, David. "Intermarriage and Agency: A Chinookan Case Study." *Ethnohistory* 42, no. 1 (Winter 1995): 1–30.

Pomeroy, Earl. *The Pacific Slope: A History of California, Oregon, Washington, Idaho, Utah, and Nevada.* Lincoln, NE: University of Nebraska Press, 1965.

Riedman, Marianne L. and James A. Estes. "The Sea Otter (*Enhydra lutris*): Behavior, Ecology, and Natural History." *Biological Report* 90, no. 14 (September 1990): 1–136.

Ross, Alexander. *The Fur Hunters of the Far West: A Narrative of Adventures in the Oregon and Rocky Mountains.* 2 vols. London: Smith, Elder, and Co., 1855.

Ruby, Robert H., John A. Brown. and Cary C Collins. *The Chinook Indians*. Norman, OK: University of Oklahoma Press, 1976.

Ruby, Robert H., John A. Brown, and Cary C. Collins. *A Guide to the Indian Tribes of the Pacific Northwest*, 3rd ed. Norman, OK: University of Oklahoma Press, 2010.

Sánchez, Antonio, "Spanish Exploration: Juan Pérez Expedition of 1774 – First European Discovery and Exploration of Washington State Coast and Nueva Galicia (the Pacific Northwest)." *HistoryLink.org*. Accessed September 28, 2014. http://www.historylink.org/.

Schwantes, Carlos A. *In Mountain Shadows: A History of Idaho*. Lincoln, NE: University of Nebraska Press, 1996.

Schwantes, Carlos A. *The Pacific Northwest: An Interpretive History*. 2nd ed. Lincoln, NE: University of Nebraska Press, 1996.

Schroeder, Tom. "Rediscovering a Coastal Prairie Near Friday Harbor," *Pacific Northwest Quarterly* 98, no. 2 (Spring 2007): 55–63.

Taylor III, Joseph E. *Making Salmon: An Environmental History of the Northwest Fisheries Crisis*. Seattle, WA: University of Washington Press, 1999.

Tolmie, William Fraser. *Physician and Fur Trader: The Journals of William Fraser Tolmie*, Vancouver: Mitchell Press Limited, 1963.

Van Kirk, Sylvia. "The Role of Native Women in the Fur Trade Society of Western Canada, 1670–1830," *Frontiers: A Journal of Women Studies* 7, no. 3 (1984): 9–13.

Vibert, Elizabeth. *Traders' Tales: Narratives of Cultural Encounters in the Columbia Plateau, 1807–1846*, Norman, OK: University of Oklahoma Press, 1997.

Weber, David J. "The Spanish Moment in the Pacific Northwest." In *Terra Pacifica: People and Place in the Northwest States and Western Canada*, Paul Hirt, ed. Pullman, WA: Washington State University Press, 1998, 3–24.

White, Richard. *The Middle Ground: Indians, Empires, and Republics in the Great Lakes Region, 1650–1815*. Cambridge: Cambridge University Press, 1991.

White, Richard. *Land Use, Environment, and Social Change: The Shaping of Island County, Washington*. Seattle, WA: University of Washington Press, 1992.

Chapter 3

Boyd, Robert. "Smallpox in the Pacific Northwest: The First Epidemics." *The British Columbia Quarterly* (Spring1994): 101.

Brown, Roberta Stringham and Patricia O'Connell Killen, eds. *Selected Letters of A.M.A. Blanchet, Bishop of Walla Walla & Nesqualy, 1846–1879*. Seattle, WA: University of Washington Press, 2013.

Brown, Roberta Stringham and Patricia O'Connell Killen, eds. "Spiritual Boundaries in Flux: Making Sense of Religious Interaction in Mid–19th–Century Washington." *Columbia, the Magazine of Northwest History* (Winter 2013–14): 12–16.

Cash Phillip E. "Oral Traditions of the Natitaytma," in *As Days Go By: Our History, Our Land, and Our People The Cayuse, Umatilla, and Walla Walla*. Jennifer Karson, ed. Portland, OR: Oregon Historical Society Press, 2006.

Dippie, Brian W. *The Vanishing American: White Attitudes and U.S. Indian Policy*. Middletown, CT: Wesleyan University Press, 1982.

Dodds, Gordon B. *The American Northwest, A History of Oregon and Washington*. Wheeling: Forum Press, Inc., 1986.

Drury, Clifford M. *Marcus and Narcissa Whitman and the Opening of Old Oregon*. Seattle, WA: Northwest Interpretive Association, 2005.

Furtwangler, Albert. *Bringing Indians to the Book*. Seattle, WA: University of Washington Press, 2005.

Graham, Todd A. *The Dalles Before the Dalles: Indians, Missionaries and the Military, 1800–1860*. Unpublished manuscript, June 6, 1988.

Harmon, Alexandra. *Indians in the Making: Ethnic Relations and Indian Identities around Puget Sound*. Berkeley, CA: University of California Press, 1998.

Hines, Donald. *Tales of the Nez Perce*. Fairfield, WA: Ye Galleon Press, 1984.

Howe, Daniel Gordon. *What Hath God Wrought: The Transformation of America, 1815 to 1848*. New York: Oxford University Press, 2007.

Hoxie, Frederick E. *A Final Promise: The Campaign to Assimilate the Indians, 1880–1920*. Lincoln, NE: University of Nebraska Press, 1984.

Hurt, Douglas R. *Indian Agriculture in America: Prehistory to the Present*. Lawrence, KS: University Press of Kansas, 1987.

Jeffrey, Julie Roy. *Converting the West: A Biography of Narcissa Whitman*. Norman, OK: University of Oklahoma Press, 1991.

Karson, Jennifer, ed. *As Days Go By: Our History, Our Land, and Our People The Cayuse, Umatilla, and Walla Walla*. Portland, OR: Historical Society Press Pendleton, in association with the Tamastslikt Cultural Institute and the University of Washington Press, Seattle, 2006.

Meinig, D.W. *The Great Columbia Plain: A Historical Geography, 1805–1910*. Seattle, WA: University of Washington Press, 1968, 1995.

McPherson, James. *Battle Cry of Freedom: The Civil War Era*. New York: Oxford University Press, 1988.

Miller, Christopher L. *Prophetic Worlds: Indians and Whites on the Columbia Plateau*. Seattle, WA: University of Washington Press, 2003.

O'Hara, Edwin V. *De Smet in Oregon Country*. Unpublished manuscript, December, 1909.

Peterson, Jacqueline and Laura Peers. *Sacred Encounters: Father De Smet and the Indians of the Rocky Mountain West*. Norman, OK: University of Oklahoma Press, 1993.

Prucha, Francis Paul. "Two Roads to Conversion: Protestant and Catholic Missionaries in the Pacific Northwest." *The Pacific Northwest Quarterly* 79, no. 4 (October 1988): 130–137.

Ruby, Robert H. and John A. Brown. *Indians of the Pacific Northwest*. Norman, OK: University of Oklahoma Press, 1981.

Ruby, Robert H. and John A. Brown. *The Cayuse Indians: Imperial Tribesmen of Old Oregon*. Norman, OK: University of Oklahoma Press, 1989.

Schwantes Carlos A. *The Pacific Northwest: An Interpretive History*. Lincoln, NE: University of Nebraska Press, 1996.

Slickpoo, Allen P. Sr. and Dward E. Walker, Jr. *Noon Nee-Me-Poo (We, the Nez Perces) Culture and History of the Nez Perces*, Vol. 2. Lapwai, ID: Nez Perce Tribe of Idaho, 1973.

Swan, James G. *The Northwest Coast, Or Three Years' Residence in Washington Territory*. New York: Harper & Brothers, 1867.

West, Elliott. *The Last Indian War: The Nez Perce Story*. New York: Oxford University Press, 2009.

Whitman, Marcus. *The Letters of Dr. Marcus Whitman, 1834–1847*; National Park Service Transcripts, Whitman Mission National Historic Site, unpublished.

Whitman, Narcissa. *The Selected Letters of Narcissa Whitman, 1835–1847*; National Park Service Transcripts, Whitman Mission National Historic Site, unpublished.

Chapter 4

Arrington, Leonard J. *History of Idaho*. Moscow, ID: University of Idaho Press, 1994.

Bagley, Will. *So Rugged and Mountainous: Blazing the Oregon and California Trails, 1812–1848*. Norman, OK: University of Oklahoma Press, 2010.

Berwanger, Eugene H. *The Frontier Against Slavery: Western Anti-Negro Prejudice and the Slavery Extension Controversy*. Urbana, IL: University of Illinois Press, 1967.

Boag, Peter G. "Overlanders and the Snake River Region: A Case Study of Popular Landscape Perception in the Early West." *Pacific Northwest Quarterly* 84, no. 4 (October1993): 122–129.

Booth, Tabatha Toney. "Cheaper than Bullets: American Indian Boarding Schools and Assimilation Policy, 1890–1930," in *Images, Imaginations, and Beyond: Proceedings of the Eighth Native American Symposium*, November 4–6, 2009. Mark B. Spencer, ed. Durant, OK: Southeastern Oklahoma State University, 2010.

Brown, J. Henry. *Brown's Political History of Oregon*, Vol. 1. Portland, OR: Wiley B. Allen, 1892.

Bunting, Robert. "The Environment and Settler Society in Western Oregon." *Pacific Historical Review* 64, no. 3 (August 1995): 413–432.

Bunting, Robert. "Michael Luark and Settler Culture in the Western Pacific Northwest, 1853–1899." *Pacific Northwest Quarterly* 96, no. 4 (Fall 2005): 198–205.

Burnett, Peter H. *Recollections and Opinions of an Old Pioneer*. New York: D. Appleton and Company, 1880.

Calloway, Colin G. *Pen and Ink Witchcraft: Treaties and Treaty Making in American Indian History*. New York: Oxford University Press, 2013.

Collins, Cary C. "Oregon's Carlisle: Teaching 'America' at Chemawa Indian School." *Columbia* 12, no. 2 (Summer 1998): 6–10.

Collins, Cary C. "Hard Lessons in America: Henry Sicade's History of Puyallup Indian School, 1860 to 1920." *Columbia* 14, no. 4 (Winter 2000–01): 6–11.

Cook, Jr., Sherburne F. "The Little Napoleon: The Short and Turbulent Career of Isaac I. Stevens." *Columbia* 14, no. 4 (Winter 2000–2001): 17–20.

Dary, David. *The Oregon Trail: An American Saga*. New York: Alfred A. Knopf, 2004.

Dodds, Gordon B. *The American Northwest: A History of Oregon and Washington*. Arlington Heights, IL: The Forum Press, Inc., 1986.

Gray, W. H. *A History of Oregon: 1792–1842, Drawn from Personal Observation and Authentic Information*. Portland, OR: Harris and Holman, 1870.

Harmon, Alexandra. *Indians in the Making: Ethnic Relations and Indian Identities around Puget Sound*. Berkeley, CA: University of California Press, 1998.

Holmes, Kenneth L., ed. *Covered Wagon Women: Diaries & Letters From the Western Trails, 1864–1868*, Volume 9. Lincoln: University of Nebraska Press, 1990.

Hunsaker, Joyce Badgley. *Seeing the Elephant: The Many Voices of the Oregon Trail*. Lubbock, TX: Texas Tech University Press, 2003.

Johannsen, Robert W. *Frontier Politics and the Sectional Conflict: The Pacific Northwest on the Eve of the Civil War*. Seattle, WA: University of Washington Press, 1955.

Johansen, Dorothy O. and Charles M. Gates. *Empire of the Columbia: A History of the Pacific Northwest*. New York: Harper and Brothers, 1957.

Katz, William Loren. *The Black West*. New York: Doubleday, 1971.

Kluger, Richard. *The Bitter Waters of Medicine Creek: A Tragic Clash between White and Native America*. New York: Alfred A. Knopf, 2011.

Limerick, Patricia Nelson. *The Legacy of Conquest: The Unbroken Past of the American West*. New York: W.W. Norton, 1987.

Marr, Carolyn J. "Assimilation Through Education: Indian Boarding Schools in the Pacific Northwest." University of Washington Libraries Digital Collections. Accessed July 18, 2016. http://content.lib.washington.edu/.

Miles, Jo N. "Kamiakin's Impact on Early Washington Territory." *Pacific Northwest Quarterly* 99, no. 4 (Fall 2008): 159–172.

Morgan, Murray. *Puget's Sound: A Narrative of Early Tacoma and the Southern Sound*. Seattle, WA: University of Washington Press, 1979.

Nobles, Gregory H. *American Frontiers: Cultural Encounters and Continental Conquest*. New York: Hill and Wang, 1997.

Prucha, Francis Paul. *Documents of United States Indian Policy*. 3rd ed. Lincoln, NE: University of Nebraska Press, 2000.

Reddick, SuAnn M. and Cary C. Collins. "Medicine Creek to Fox Island: Cadastral Scams and Contested Domains." *Oregon Historical Society* 106, no. 3 (Fall 2005): 374–397.

Robbins, William G. "The Indian Question in Western Oregon: The Making of a Colonial People," in *Experiences in a Promised Land: Essays in Pacific Northwest History*. G. Thomas Edwards and Carlos A. Schwantes, ed. Seattle, WA: University of Washington Press, 1986.

Robbins, William G. "Landscape and Environment: Ecological Change in the Intermontane Northwest." *Pacific Northwest Quarterly* 84, no. 4 (October 1993): 140–149.

Ruby, Robert H., John A. Brown, and Cary C. Collins. *A Guide to the Indian Tribes of the Pacific Northwest*, 3rd ed. Norman, OK: University of Oklahoma Press, 2010.

Schwantes, Carlos A. *In Mountain Shadows: A History of Idaho*. Lincoln, NE: University of Nebraska Press, 1996.

Schwantes, Carlos A. *The Pacific Northwest: An Interpretive History*, 2nd ed. Lincoln, NE: University of Nebraska Press, 1996.

Schroeder, Tom. "Rediscovering a Coastal Prairie near Friday Harbor." *Pacific Northwest Quarterly* 98, no. 2 (Spring 2007): 55–63.

Smith, Jedediah S., David E. Jackson, and W. L. Sublette. "Letter of Smith, Sublette, and Jackson." *The Quarterly of the Oregon Historical Society* 4, no. 4 (December 1903): 395–398.

Spores, Ronald, "Too Small a Place: The Removal of the Willamette Valley Indians, 1850–1856." *American Indian Quarterly* 17, no. 2 (Spring 1993), 171–191.

Tate, Michael L. *Indians and Emigrants: Encounters on the Overland Trails*. Norman, OK: University of Oklahoma Press, 2006.

Thwaites, Reuben Gold, ed. *Early Western Travels: 1748–1846*, Vol. 30. Cleveland, OH: The Arthur H. Clark Company, 1906.

Thurston, Samuel Royal and George H. Himes. "Diary of Samuel Royal Thurston." *The Quarterly of the Oregon Historical Society* 15, no. 3 (September 1914): 153–205.

Torr, James D., ed. *Westward Expansion: Interesting Primary Documents*. San Diego, CA: Greenhaven Press, 2003.

Unruh, John David. *The Plains Across: The Overland Emigrants and the Trans-Mississippi West, 1840–1860*. Urbana, IL: University of Illinois Press, 1979.

Whaley, Gray H. *Oregon and the Collapse of Illahee: U.S. Empire and the Transformation of an Indigenous World, 1792–1859*. Chapel Hill, NC: University of North Carolina, 2010.

White, Richard. *Land Use, Environment, and Social Change: The Shaping of Island County, Washington*. Seattle, WA: University of Washington Press, 1992.

Williams, Robert Chadwell. *Horace Greeley: Champion of American Freedom*. New York: New York University Press, 2006.

Chapter 5

Bain, David Howard. *Empire Express: Building the First Transcontinental Railroad*. New York: Viking, 1999.

Binns, Archie. *Northwest Gateway, The Story of the Port of Seattle*. Portland, OR: Binfords & Mort, Publishers, 1941.

Clark, Norman H. *Mill Town: A Social History of Everett, Washington, from Its Earliest Beginnings on the Shores of Puget Sound to the Tragic and Infamous Event Known as the Everett Massacre*. Seattle, WA: University of Washington Press, 1970.

Cox, Thomas R. *Mills and Markets: A History of the Pacific Coast Lumber Industry to 1900*. Seattle, WA: University of Washington Press, 1974.

Dahlie, Jorgen, "Old World Paths in the New: Scandinavians Find A Familiar Home in Washington," in *Experiences in a Promised Land, Essays in Pacific Northwest History*. Thomas G. Edwards and Carlos A. Schwantes, ed. Seattle, WA: University of Washington Press, 1986.

Dodds, Gordon B. *The Salmon King of Oregon: R.D. Hume and the Pacific Fisheries*. Chapel Hill, NC: University of North Carolina Press, 1959.

Emerson, Ralph Waldo. "The Young American," in *Ralph Waldo Emerson: Essays and Lectures*. Joel Porte, ed. New York: Library of America, 1983.

Fahey, John. "Big Lumber in the Inland Empire," in *Pacific Northwest Quarterly* 76, no. 3 (July 1985), 96.

Ficken, Robert E. *Washington State: The Inaugural Decade 1889–1899*. Pullman, WA: Washington State University Press, 2007.

Henry, George, "What the Railroad Will Bring Us, *Overland Monthly* I (October 1868) 297–306 Found at umich.edu/moajrnl.

Hine, Robert V. and John Mack Faragher. *The American West: A New Interpretive History*. New Haven, CT: Yale University Press, 2000.

Kensel, Hudson W. "Inland Empire Mining and the Growth of Spokane, 1883,1905," *Pacific Northwest Quarterly* 81, no. 2 (April 1969):. 84–97.

Meinig, D.W. *The Great Columbia Plain: A Historical Geography, 1805–1910*. Seattle, WA: University of Washington Press, 1995.

Morgan, Murray C. *eSkid Road: An Informal Portrait of Seattle*. New York: Viking Press, 1951.

Morgan, Murray C. *Puget's Sound: A Narrative of Early Tacoma and the Southern Sound*. Seattle, WA: University of Washington Press, 1979.

Oliphant, J. Orin. *On the Cattle Ranges of the Oregon Country*. Seattle, WA: University of Washington Press, 1968.

Schwantes, Carlos A. *Railroad Signatures Across the Pacific Northwest*. Seattle, WA: University of Washington Press, 1993.

Schwantes, Carlos A. *The Pacific Northwest: An Interpretive History*. Lincoln, NE, University of Nebraska Press, 1996.

Schwantes, Carlos A. and James P. Ronda. *The West the Railroads Made.* Seattle, WA: University of Washington Press and the Washington State Historical Society, 2008.

Sensel, Joni, *Traditions Through The Trees: Weyerhaeuser's First 100 Years.* Seattle, WA: Documentary Book Publishers, 1999.

Smart, Douglas. "Spokane's Battle for Freight Rates," *Pacific Northwest Quarterly* 45, no. 1 (January 1954): .19–27,

White, Richard. *It's Your Misfortune and None of My Own, A New History of the American West.* Norman: University of Oklahoma Press, 1991.

White, Richard. *The Organic Machine, The Remaking of the Columbia River.* New York: Hill and Wang, 1995.

White, Richard. *Railroaded: The Transcontinentals and the Making of Modern America.* New York: W.W. Norton and Company, 2011.

Chapter 6

Boyle, Kevin. "Work Places: The Economy and the Changing Landscape of Labor, 1900–2000," in *Perspectives on Modern America: Making Sense of the Twentieth Century.* Harvard Sitkoff, ed. New York: Oxford University Press, 2001.

Clark, Norman H, *Mill Town: A Social History of Everett, Washington, from Its Earliest Beginnings on the Shores of Puget Sound to the Tragic and Infamous Event Known as the Everett Massacre.* Seattle, WA: University of Washington Press, 1970.

Cox, Thomas R. *Mills and Markets: A History of the Pacific Coast Lumber Industry to 1900.* Seattle, WA: University of Washington Press, 1974.

Dodds, Gordon B. *The Salmon King of Oregon: R.D. Hume and the Pacific Fisheries.* Chapel Hill, NC: University of North Carolina Press, 1959.

Edwards, Thomas G. and Carlos A. Schwantes. *Experiences in a Promised Land, Essays in Pacific Northwest History.* Seattle, WA: University of Washington Press, 1986.

Foner, Philip Sheldon. *The Industrial Workers of the World, 1905–1917, in History of the Labor Movement in the United States*, Vol. 4. New York: International Publishers, 1965.

Green, James. *Death in the Haymarket: A Story of Chicago, The First Labor Movement and the Bombing That Divided Gilded Age America.* New York: First Anchor Books, 2007.

Gregory, Ronald L. "Life in Railroad Logging Camps of the Shevlin-Hixon Company. 1916–1950," unpublished master's thesis, June 6, 1997, Oregon State University.

Lembcke, Jerry and William A. Tattam. *One Union in Wood: A Political History of the International Woodworkers of America.* New York: International Publishers, 1984.

Lewarne, Charles Pierce. "The Aberdeen, Washington, Free Speech Fight of 1911–1912." *Pacific Northwest Quarterly* 66, no. 1, (January 1975): 1–11.

May, Matthew S. "Hobo Orator Union: The Free Speech Fights of the Industrial Workers of the World, 1909–1916," unpublished PhD diss., University of Minnesota, 2009.

McCelland, John Jr. *Wobbly War: The Centralia Story.* Tacoma, WA: Washington State Historical Society, 1987.

McGerr, Michael. *A Fierce Discontent: The Rise and Fall of the Progressive Movement in America.* New York: Oxford University Press, 2003.

Morgan, Murray C. *Puget's Sound: A Narrative of Early Tacoma and the Southern Sound.* Seattle, WA: University of Washington Press, 1979.

Prouty, Andrew Mason. *More Deadly Than War! Pacific Coast Logging, 1827–1981*. New York: Garland Publishing, 1985.

Schwantes, Carlos A. *The Pacific Northwest: An Interpretive History*, Lincoln, NE: University of Nebraska Press, 1996.

Tyler, Robert L. *Rebels of the Woods: The I.W.W. in the Pacific Northwest*. Eugene, OR: University of Oregon Press, 1967.

Watkins, Marilyn P. *Rural Democracy: Family Farmers and Politics in Western Washington, 1890–1925*. Ithaca, NY: Cornell University Press, 1995.

Woirol, Gregory R. ed."Two Letters on the Spokane Free Speech Fight," *Pacific Northwest Quarterly* 77, no. 2, (April 1986): 68–71.

Chapter 7

Avalon Project at Yale Law School. "Chinese Exclusion Act: May 6, 1882." Accessed July 9, 2013. http://avalon.law.yale.edu/.

Black Past.org. "Through Open Eyes: Ninety-Five Years of Black History in Roslyn, Washington." Accessed July 13, 2013. http://www.blackpast.org/

Blackwell, Ruby Chapin. *A Girl in Washington Territory*. Tacoma, WA: Washington State Historical Society, 1972.

Billington, Lee and Roger D. Hardaway, eds. *African Americans on the Western Frontier*. Boulder, CO: University Press of Colorado, 1998.

Campbell, Robert A. "Blacks and The Coal Mines of Western Washington," in *African Americans on the Western Frontier*. Monroe Lee Billington and Roger D. Hardaway, eds. Niwot, CO: University Press Colorado, 1998.

Center for the Study of the Pacific Northwest. "Industrialization, Class, and Race; Chinese and the Anti-Chinese Movement in the Late 19th-Century Northwest." Accessed June 3, 2013. http://www.washington.edu/.

Dahlie, Jorgen. "Old World Paths in the New: Scandinavians Find A Familiar Home in Washington," in *Experiences in a Promised Land*. G. Thomas Edwards, Carlos A. Schwantes, eds. Seattle, WA: University of Washington Press, 1986.

Hine, Robert V. and John Mack Faragher. *The American West, A New Interpretive History*. New Haven, CT: Yale University Press, 2000.

Idaho State Historical Society. Reference Series. Accessed July 9, 2013. http://history.idaho.gov/.

Leighton, Caroline C. *Life At Puget Sound*. Boston: Lee and Shepard Publishers, 1884.

Limerick, Patricia Nelson. *The Legacy of Conquest*. New York: W.W. Norton & Company, 1988.

Luebke, Frederick, ed. *European Immigrants: American West Community Histories*. Albuquerque, NM: University of New Mexico Press, 1998.

Millner, Darrell. "George Bush of Tumwater: Founder of the First American Colony on Puget Sound." *Columbia Magazine*, Winter 1994/95.

Milner II, Clyde A, Carol A. O'Connor, and Martha A Sandweiss, eds. *The Oxford History of the American West*. New York: Oxford University Press, 1994.

Nokes, Gregory R. "A Most Daring Outrage, Murder at Chinese Massacre Cove, 1887." *Oregon Historical Quarterly* 107, no. 3 (Fall2006). 326–353.

Nokes, Gregory R. *Massacred For Gold, The Chinese in Hells Canyon.* Corvallis, OR: Oregon State University Press, 2009.

Oregon Historical Society. *History Minutes.* Accessed August 10, 2013. https://oregonencyclopedia.org

Ripley, Peter C., ed. *The Black Abolitionist Papers vol 4. The United States, 1847–1858.* Chapel Hill, NC: University of North Carolina Press, 1991.

Takaki, Ronald. *Strangers From a Different Shore: A History of Asian Americans.* New York: Little Brown and Company, 1998.

Taylor, Quintard. "A History of Blacks in the Pacific Northwest, 1788–1970," unpublished Ph.D. diss., University of Minnesota, 1977.

University of Washington. "The History of African Americans in the West." Accessed July 10, 2013. http://faculty.washington.edu/.

Washington State History Museum. Online Collections. Accessed July 6, 2013. http://www.washingtonhistory.org/.

White, Richard, *It's Your Misfortune and None of My Own, A New History of the American West.* Norman, OK: University of Oklahoma Press, 1991.

Zhu, Liping. *A Chinaman's Chance: The Chinese on the Rocky Mountain Mining Frontier.* Boulder, CO: University Press of Colorado, 1997.

Chapter 8

Armitage, Sue. *Shaping the Public Good: Women Making History in the Pacific Northwest.* Corvallis, OR: Oregon State University Press, 2015.

Blair, Karen J. "The Seattle Ladies Musical club, 1890–1930," in *Experiences in a Promised Land, Essays in Pacific Northwest History.* G. Thomas Edwards and Carlos A. Schwantes, eds. Seattle: University of Washington Press, 1986, 124–138.

Blair, Karen J. *Women in Pacific Northwest History.* Seattle, WA: University of Washington Press, 1988.

Blair, Karen J. "Normal Schools of the Pacific Northwest: The Lifelong Impact of Extracurricular Club Activities on Women Students at Teacher Training Institutions, 1890–1917." *Pacific Northwest Quarterly* 101, no. 1 (Winter 2009/2010): 3–16.

Bragg, L.E. *More Than Petticoats: Remarkable Idaho Women,* Helena, MT: Morris Book Publishing, 2001.

Clinton, Catherine. *The Other Civil War: American Women in the Nineteenth Century.* New York: Hill and Wang, 1984.

Dilg, Janice. "'For Working Women in Oregon': Caroline Gleason/Sister Miriam Theresa and Oregon's Minimum Wage Law," *Oregon Historical Quarterly,* vol. 110 No. 1 (Spring, 2009) 96–129.

Dinkin, Robert, J. *Before Equal Suffrage: Women in Partisan Politics from Colonial times to 1920.* Westport, CT: Greenwood Press, 1995.

Duniway, Abigail Scott. *Path Breaking: An Autobiographical History of the Equal Suffrage Movement in Pacific Coast States.* Portland, OR, James, Kerns & Abbott, 1919.

Etulain, Richard W. *Beyond the Missouri: The Story of the American West.* Albuquerque, NM: University of New Mexico Press, 2006.

Frank, Dana. *Purchasing Power: Consumer Organizing, Gender and the Seattle Labor Movement, 1919–1929.* New York: Cambridge University Press, 1994.

Hine, Robert V. and John Mack Faragher. *The American West: A New Interpretive History.* New Haven, CT: Yale University Press, 2000.

Howe, Daniel Walker. *What Hath God Wrought: The Transformation of America, 1815–1848.* New York: Oxford University Press, 2005.

Jameson, Elizabeth and Susan Armitage, eds. *Writing the Range: Race, Class, and Culture in the Women's West.* Norman, OK: University of Oklahoma Press, 1997.

Jensen, Kimberly. *Mobilizing Minerva: American Women in the First World War.* Urbana, IL: University of Illinois Press, 2008.

Limerick, Patricia Nelson. *The Legacy of Conquest: The Unbroken Past of the American West.* New York: W.W. Norton & Company, 1987.

Mangun, Kimberly. *A Force for Change: Beatrice Morrow Cannady and the Struggle for Civil Rights in Oregon, 1912–1936.* Corvallis, OR: Oregon St. University Press, 2010.

Pieroth, Doris H. "Bertha Knight Landes: The Women Who Was Mayor," in *Pacific Northwest Quarterly* 75, no. 3 (July 1984), 117–127.

Ross-Nazzal, Jennifer. "Emma Smith DeVoe: Practicing Pragmatic Politics in the Pacific Northwest." *Pacific Northwest Quarterly* 96, no. 2 (Spring 2005).

Sheeran, Marte Jo. "The Woman Suffrage Issue in Washington, 1890–1910," unpublished M.A. Thesis, University of Washington, 1977.

Stevenson, Shanna. *Women's Voices, Women's Votes: Washington State Women's Suffrage Centennial, 1910–2010.* Published by the Washington State Historical Society and distributed by the Washington State University Press, 2009.

Ward, Jean M. and Elaine A. Maveety, eds. *"Yours for Liberty: Selections from Abigail Scott Duniway's Suffrage Newspaper."* Corvallis, OR: Oregon State University Press, 2000.

White, Richard. *It's Your Misfortune and None of My Own, A New History of the American West.* Norman, OK: University of Oklahoma Press, 1991.

Wilentz, Sean. *The Rise of American Democracy.* New York: W.W. Norton & Co., 2005.

Woloch, Nancy. *A Class by Herself: Protective Laws for Women Workers, 1890s to 1990s.* Princeton, NJ: Princeton University Press, 2015.

Chapter 9

Anderson, Hilary. "A Tale of Two Shantytowns: Tracing the Similarities between Seattle's Hoover Town and Tacoma's Hollywood-on-the-Flats." *Columbia* 26, no. 2 (Summer 2012): 10–14.

Arrington, Leonard J. *History of Idaho.* Moscow, ID: University of Idaho Press, 1994.

Becker, Paula. "Negro Reperatory Company." *HistoryLink.org Online Encyclopedia of Washington State History.* Accessed August 25, 2015. http://www.historylink.org.

Berner, Richard C. *Seattle 1921–1940: From Boom to Bust.* Seattle, WA: Charles Press, 1992.

Billington, Monroe and Cal Clark. "Clergy Opinion and the New Deal: The State of Washington as a Case Study." *Pacific Northwest Quarterly* 81, no. 3 (July 1990): 96–100.

Dewing, Rolland. "The Great Depression: A Personal Memoir of a Dust Bowl Migrant to the Pacific Northwest." *Columbia* 10, no. 1 (Spring 1996): 29–32.

Dodds, Gordon B. *The American Northwest: A History of Oregon and Washington.* Arlington Heights, IL: The Forum Press, Inc., 1986.

Flom, Eric L. "The *Wenatchee Daily World*. First Reports on the Proposal to Dam the Columbia River at Grand Coulee on July 18, 1918." *HistoryLink.org Online Encyclopedia of Washington State History.* Accessed August 25, 2015. http://www.historylink.org/.

Foner, Eric. *Give Me Liberty! An American History.* Brief 3rd ed. New York: W.W. Norton, 2012.

Gillon, Steven M. *The American Paradox: A History of the United States Since 1945.* Boston: Houghton Mifflin Company, 2003.

Goll, Norman W. "Grand Coulee Dam: A Reminiscence." *Columbia* 11, no. 3 (Fall 1997): 3–5.

Hall, Tom G. "Wilson and the Food Crisis: Agricultural Price Control During World War I." *Agricultural History* 47, no. 1 (January 1973): 25–46.

Harmon, Alexandra. *Indians in the Making: Ethnic Relations and Indian Identities around Puget Sound.* Berkeley, CA: University of California Press, 1998.

Hill, Edwin G. *In the Shadow of the Mountain: The Spirit of the CCC.* Pullman, WA: Washington State University Press, 1990.

Irish, Kerry E. "The Water Rises: Clarence C. Dills Battle for Grand Coulee Dam." *Columbia* 15, no 3. (Fall 2001): 5–15.

Johansen, Dorothy O. and Charles M. Gates. *Empire of the Columbia: A History of the Pacific Northwest.* New York: Harper and Brothers, 1957.

Kamenz, Ali. "On to Olympia! The History Behind the Hunger Marches of 1932–1933." *The Great Depression in Washington State Project.* Accessed August 25, 2015. http://depts.washington.edu/.

Keene, Jennifer D., Saul Cornell, and Edward T. O'Donnell. *Visions of America: A History of the United States*, 2nd ed. Boston: Pearson, 2013.

Lange, Greg. "Hooverville: Shantytown of Seattle's Great Depression." *HistoryLink.org.* Accessed August 25, 2015. http://www.historylink.org/.

Lovin, Hugh T. "Arid Land Reclamation in Eastern Oregon during the Twentieth Century." *Pacific Northwest Quarterly* 100, no. 4 (Fall 2009): 169–180.

Mahoney, Eleanor. "The Public Works of Art Projects in Washington State." *The Great Depression in Washington State Project.* Accessed August 25, 2015. http://depts.washington.edu/depress/PWAP.shtml.

Morgan, Murray. *The Dam.* New York: Viking Press, 1954.

Mullins, William. "I'll Wreck the Town If It Will Give Me Employment: Portland in the Hoover Years of the Depression." *Pacific Northwest Quarterly* 79, no. 3 (July 1988): 109–118.

Mullins, William. "Self-Help in Seattle, 1931–1932: Herbert Hoover's Concept of Cooperative Individualism and the Unemployed Citizens League," in *Experiences in a Promised Land: Essays in Pacific Northwest History.* G. Thomas Edwards and Carlos A. Schwantes, ed. Seattle, WA: University of Washington Press, 1986.

Murrell, Gary. "Democrats Disintegrate: Bonneville Dam, Public Power, the New Deal, and Governor Charles Henry Martin, 1932–1939." *Columbia* 17, no. 3 (Fall 2003): 5–12.

Pitzer, Paul C. "Grand Coulee Dam and the Reality of the Columbia Basin Project." *Columbia* 4, no. 2 (Summer 1990): 28–38.

Pitzer, Paul C. "The Columbia Basin Project Farmers." *Columbia* 10, no. 1 (Spring 1996): 6–11.

Riddle, Margaret. "Hartley, Governor Roland Hill (1864–1952)," *HistoryLink.org Online Encyclopedia of Washington State History.* Accessed August 25, 2015. http://www.historylink.org/index.cfm?DisplayPage=output.cfm&file_id=8008.

Ruby, Robert H., John A. Brown, and Cary C. Collins. *A Guide to the Indian Tribes of the Pacific Northwest*, 3rd ed. Norman, OK: University of Oklahoma Press, 2010.

Schmid, Calvin. *Social Trends in Seattle*. Seattle, WA: University of Washington Press, 1944.

Schwantes, Carlos A. *In Mountain Shadows: A History of Idaho*. Lincoln, NE: University of Nebraska Press, 1996.

Schwantes, Carlos A. *The Pacific Northwest: An Interpretive History*, 2nd ed. Lincoln, NE: University of Nebraska Press, 1996.

Schwantes, Carlos A. "Uncle Sam's Response to the Great Depression." *Columbia* 11, no. 1 (Spring 1997): 14–19.

Spatz, Marc Horan. "The Unemployed Councils of the Communist Party in Washington State, 1930–1935." *The Great Depression in Washington State Project*. Accessed August 25, 2015. http://depts.washington.edu/.

Stevenson, Shanna. "Dig the Canal: The Proposed Grays Harbor to Puget Sound Canal." *Columbia* 20, no. 1 (Spring 2006): 6–11.

Tate, Cassandra. "Grand Coulee Dam." *HistoryLink.org*. Accessed August 25, 2015. http://www.historylink.org/

Ulrich, Roberta. *Empty Nets: Indians, Dams, and the Columbia River*, 2nd ed. Corvallis, OR: Oregon State University Press, 2007.

White, Richard. *The Organic Machine: The Remaking of the Columbia River*. New York: Hill and Wang, 1995.

Wilma, David. "Hunger Marchers Demand Relief from the Washington State Legislature on January 17, 1933." *HistoryLink.org*. Accessed August 25, 2015. http://www.historylink.org/.

Wilma, David. "Wheeler-Howard Act (Indian Reorganization Act) Shifts U.S. Policy Toward Native American Right to Self-Determination on June 18, 1934." *HistoryLink.org*. Accessed August 25, 2015. http://www.historylink.org/.

Chapter 10

Arrington, Leonard J. *History of Idaho*. Moscow, ID: University of Idaho Press, 1994.

Becker, Paula. "PACCAR Inc." *HistoryLink.org*. Accessed October 22, 2015. http://www.historylink.org/.

Caldbick, John. "DeLaCruz, Joseph 'Joe' Burton (1937–2000)." *HistoryLink.org*. Accessed October 25, 2015. http://www.historylink.org.

Chesnut, Louis C. "Siting the Hanford Engineering Works: I Was There, Leslie!" *HistoryLink.org*. Accessed October 24, 2015. http://www.historylink.org.

Clawson, Augusta H. *Shipyard Diary of a Woman Welder*. New York: Penguin Books, 1944.

Crowley, Walt. "Boeing Launches Its First Minuteman Intercontinental Ballistic Missile (ICBM) from Cape Canaveral on February 1, 1961." *HistoryLink.org*. Accessed November 9, 2015. http://www.historylink.org/

Daniels, Roger. "The Exile and Return of Seattle's Japanese." *Pacific Northwest Quarterly* 88, no. 4 (Fall 1997): 166–173.

Densho.org. "Gordon Hirabayashi." Accessed November 8, 2015. http://encyclopedia.densho.org/.

Densho.org. "Korematsu v. United States." Accessed November 8, 2015. http://encyclopedia.densho.org/.

Densho.org. "Military Areas 1 & 2." Accessed November 8, 2015. http://encyclopedia. densho.org/.

Densho.org. "Naturalization Act of 1790." Accessed November 8, 2015. http://encyclopedia. densho.org/.

Densho.org. "Portland (Detention Facility)." Accessed November 8, 2015. http:// encyclopedia.densho.org/.

Densho.org. "Puyallup (Detention Facility)." Accessed November 8, 2015. http:// encyclopedia.densho.org/.

Densho.org. "Redress Movement." Accessed November 8, 2015. http://encyclopedia. densho.org/.

Dodds, Gordon B. *The American Northwest: A History of Oregon and Washington.* Arlington Heights, IL: The Forum Press, Inc., 1986.

Findlay, John M. and Bruce Hevly. *Atomic Frontier Days: Hanford and the American West.* Seattle, WA: University of Washington Press, 2011.

Fiset, Louis. "Thinning, Topping, and Loading: Japanese Americans and Beet Sugar in World War II." *Pacific Northwest Quarterly* 90, no. 3 (Summer 1999): 123–139.

Foner, Eric. *Give Me Liberty!: An American History.* Brief 3rd ed. New York: W.W. Norton, 2012.

Gamboa, Erasmo. *Mexican Labor and World War II: Braceros in the Pacific Northwest, 1942– 1947.* Seattle, WA: University of Washington Press, 2000.

Gerber, Michele Stenehjem. "Hanford's Historic Reactors: The Story of Hanford's Early Years is One of Constant Change." *Columbia* 9, no. 1 (Spring 1995): 31–36.

Gerber, Michele Stenehjem. *On the Homefront: The Cold War Legacy of the Hanford Nuclear Site,* 3rd ed. Lincoln, NE: University of Nebraska Press, 2007.

Gillon, Steven M. *The American Paradox: A History of the United States Since 1945.* Boston: Houghton Mifflin Company, 2003.

Harmon, Alexandra. *Indians in the Making: Ethnic Relations and Indian Identities around Puget Sound.* Berkeley, CA: University of California Press, 1998.

Henretta, James A., Rebecca Edwards, and Robert O. Self. *America's History.* 7th ed. Boston: Bedford / St. Martin's, 2011.

Johansen, Dorothy O. and Charles M. Gates. *Empire of the Columbia: A History of the Pacific Northwest.* New York: Harper and Brothers, 1957.

Keene, Jennifer D., Saul Cornell, and Edward T. O'Donnell. *Visions of America: A History of the United States,* 2nd ed. Boston: Pearson, 2013.

Kennedy, John F. "Remarks at the Hanford, Washington, Electric Generating Plant." *The American Presidency Project.* Accessed November 29, 2015. http://www.presidency. ucsb.edu/.

Kesselman, Amy. *Fleeting Opportunities: Women Shipyard Workers in Portland and Vancouver During World War II and Reconversion.* Albany, NY: State University of New York Press, 1990.

Kirkendall, Richard S. "The Boeing Company and the Military-Metropolitan-Industrial Complex, 1945–1953." *Pacific Northwest Quarterly* 85, no. 4 (Fall 1994): 137–149.

Limerick, Patricia Nelson. *The Legacy of Conquest: The Unbroken Past of the American West.* New York: W.W. Norton, 1987.

MacIntosh, Heather, Priscilla Long, and David Wilma, "Riot Involving African American Soldiers Occurs at Fort Lawton and an Italian POW is Lynched on August 14, 1944." *HistoryLink.org.* Accessed October 31, 2015. http://www.historylink.org/.

364 Bibliography

Marshman, Michelle. "Go for Broke: The All Japanese American 442nd Infantry Regiment." *White River Journal*. Accessed November 8, 2015. http://www.wrvmuseum.org/.

McClary, Daryl C. "Puget Sound Naval Shipyard." *HistoryLink.org*. Accessed October 4, 2015. http://www.historylink.org/.

Myers, Polly Reed. "Boeing Aircraft Company's Manpower Campaign During World War II." *Pacific Northwest Quarterly* 98, no. 4 (Fall 2007): 183–195.

Oldham, Kit. "Alcoa Plant at Vancouver Produces the First Aluminum in the West on September 23, 1940." *HistoryLink.org*. Accessed October 25, 2015. http://www.historylink.org/.

Oldham, Kit. "Construction of Massive Plutonium Production Complex at Hanford Begins in March 1943" *HistoryLink.org*. Accessed October 25, 2015. http://www.historylink.org/.

Oldham, Kit. "Kaiser Shipyard in Vancouver Launches its First Escort Aircraft Carrier on April 5, 1943." *HistoryLink.org*. Accessed October 4, 2015. http://www.historylink.org/.

Robinson, Greg. *By Order of the President: FDR and the Internment of Japanese Americans*. Cambridge, MA: Harvard University Press, 2001.

Sawyer, L.A. and W.H. Mitchell. *The Liberty Ships*. 2nd ed. London: Lloyd's of London Press, 1985.

Saxe, William E. "Arming the Soviets: The Pacific Northwest Played an Important Role in Providing Our Russian Allies with Lend-Lease Materiel During World War II." *Columbia* 20, no. 2 (Summer 2006): 16–21.

Schwantes, Carlos A. *In Mountain Shadows: A History of Idaho*. Lincoln, NE: University of Nebraska Press, 1996.

Schwantes, Carlos A. *The Pacific Northwest: An Interpretive History*, 2nd ed. Lincoln, NE: University of Nebraska Press, 1996.

Schultz, John and David Wilma. "Boeing, William Edward (1881–1956)." *HistoryLink.org*. Accessed October 22, 2015. http://www.historylink.org/.

Skold, Karen Beck. "The Job He Left Behind: Women in the Shipyards During World War II," in *Women in Pacific Northwest History: An Anthology*. Karen J. Blair, ed. Seattle, WA: University of Washington Press, 1988.

Sone, Monica. *Nisei Daughter*. Seattle, WA: University of Washington Press, 1979.

Stein, Alan J. "Boeing Flying Fortress B-17 Prototype Takes Her Maiden Flight on July 28, 1935." *HistoryLink.org*. Accessed October 25, 2015. http://www.historylink.org/.

Takami, David. "World War II Japanese American Internment – Seattle / King County." *HistoryLink.org*. Accessed November 8, 2015. http://www.historylink.org/.

Tate, Cassandra. "President Kennedy Participates in Ground-Breaking Ceremonies for Construction of N Reactor at Hanford on September 26, 1963." *HistoryLink.org*. Accessed November 29, 2015. http://www.historylink.org.

Taylor, Quintard. *The Forging of a Black Community: Seattle's Central District from 1870 through the Civil Rights Era*. Seattle, WA: University of Washington Press, 1994.

Taylor, Quintard. "Swing the Door Wide" WWII Wrought a Profound Transformation in Seattle's Black Community." *Columbia* 9, no. 2 (Summer 1995): 26–32.

Taylor, Quintard. *In Search of the Racial Frontier: African Americans in the American West, 1528–1990*. New York: W.W. Norton, 1998.

Van Pelt, Julie. "Port of Tacoma Sees Launch of Todd Shipyards' Freighter *Cape Alava* on August 3, 1940." *HistoryLink.org*. Accessed October 5, 2015. http://www.historylink.org/.

Warren, James. R. "World War II Home Front on Puget Sound." *HistoryLink.org*. Accessed October 4, 2015. http://www.historylink.org/.

Weglyn, Michi. *Years of Infamy: The Untold Story of America's Concentration Camps*. New York: Morrow, 1976.

Wise, Nancy Baker and Christy Wise. *A Mouthful of Rivets: Women at Work in World War II*. San Francisco: Jossey-Bass, 1994.

Chapter 11

Boag, Peter. *Same-Sex Affairs: Constructing and Controlling Homosexuality in the Pacific Northwest*. Berkeley, CA: University of California Press, 2003.

Boag, Peter. "'Does Portland Need a Homophile Society?': Gay Culture and Activism in the Rose City Between World War II and Stonewall. *Oregon Historical Society* 105, no. 1 (Spring, 2004): 6–39.

Boag, Peter. *"Gay and Lesbian Rights Movement," HistoryLink.org*, accessed October 18, 2015, http://www.historylink.org/.

Brown, Jerald Barry. "The United Farm Workers Grape Strike and Boycott, 1965–1970: An Evaluation of the Culture of Poverty Theory," unpublished Ph.D. diss. Cornell University, 1972).

Castaneda, Oscar Rosales. "Chicano Movement in Washington: Political Activism in the Puget Sound and Yakima Valley Regions, 1960s–1980s." *HistoryLink.org*. Accessed October, 14, 2015. http://www.historyLink.org.

Garcia, Matt. *From the Jaws of Victory: The Triumph and Tragedy of Cesar Chavez and the Farm Worker Movement*. Berkeley, CA: University of California Press, 2012.

Hill, Chrystie. "Queer History in Seattle, Part 1: to 1967." *HistoryLink.org*. Accessed January 29, 2016. http://www.historylink.org/.

Hill, Chrystie. "Queer History in Seattle, Part 2: After Stonewall." *HistoryLink.org*. Accessed January 29, 2016. http://www.historylink.org/.

Hill, Chrystie. *"Marriage Equality and Gay Rights in Washington, HistoryLink.org*. Accessed January 20, 2016. http://www.historylink.org/.

Hine, Robert V. and John Mack Faragher. *The American West: A New Interpretive History*. New Haven, CT: Yale University Press, 2000.

Kleiner, Catherine. "Nature's Lovers: The Erotics of Lesbian Land Communities in Oregon, 1974–1984." *Seeing Nature Through Gender*, Virginia J. Scharff, ed. Lawrence, KS: University Press of Kansas, 2003. 242–462.

Maldonado, Carlos S. and Gilberto García, eds. *The Chicano Experience in the Northwest*. Dubuque: Kendall/Hunt Publishing Company, 1995.

Miller, Margaret. "Community Action and Reaction: Chicanos and the War on Poverty in the Yakima Valley Washington," unpublished master's thesis, University of Washington, 1991).

Patterson, James T. *Grand Expectations: The United States, 1945–1974*. New York: Oxford University Press, 1996.

Pawel, Miriam. *The Crusades of Cesar Chavez, A Biography*, New York: Bloomsbury Press, 2014.

Schaller, Michael, Robert Schulzinger, John Bezis-Selfa, Janette Thomas Greenwood, Andrew Kirk, Sarah J. Purcell, and Aaron Sheehan-Dean. *American Horizons, U.S. History in a Global Context*, Vol II, Since 1865. New York: Oxford University Press, 2015.

Schlesinger Arthur, Jr. *The Vital Center: The Politics of Freedom*. Boston: Houghton Mifflin Company, 1949.

Simer, Jerry. "La Raza Comes to Campus: The New Chicano Contingent and the Grape Boycott at the University of Washington, 1968–69." Seattle Civil Rights and Labor History Project. Accessed December 1, 2015. http://depts.washington.edu/

Singler, Joan, Jean Durning, Betty Lou Valentine, Maid Adams. *Seattle in Black and White: The Congress of Racial Equality and the Fight for Equal Opportunity*, Seattle, WA: University of Washington Press, 2011.

Slatta, Richard W. "Chicanos in the Pacific Northwest: A Demographic and Socioeconomic Portrait." *Pacific Northwest Quarterly* 70 no. 4) (October 1949): .155–162

Stavans, Ilan, ed. *Cesar Chavez: An Organizer's Tale*. London: Penguin Books, 2008.

Stephen, Lynn, "The Story of PCUN and the Farmworker Movement in Oregon." Revised ed. Center for Latino/a and Latin American Studies, University of Oregon. Accessed November 3, 2015.PDF document. www.http://uoregon.edu/.

Taylor, Quintard. *The Forging of a Black Community: Seattle's Central District from 1870 through the Civil Rights Era*. Seattle: University of Washington Press, 1994

White, Richard. *It's Your Misfortune and None of My Own, A New History of the American West*. Norman: University of Oklahoma Press, 1991.

Chapter 12

Blumm, Michael C. and Jane G. Steadman. "Indian Treaty Fishing Rights and Habitat Protection: The Martinez Decision Supplies a Resounding Judicial Affirmation." *Natural Resources Journal* 49, no. 3/4 (Summer–Fall 2009): 653–706.

Crowley, Walt and David Wilma. "Federal Judge George Boldt Issues Historic Ruling Affirming Native American Treaty Fishing Rights on February 12, 1974." *HistoryLink.org*. Accessed July 21, 2016. http://www.historylink.org/.

Dietrich, William. *The Final Forest: The Battle for the Last Great Trees of the Pacific Northwest*. New York: Penguin Books, 1992.

Environmental Issues in Pacific Northwest Forest Management. Washington, DC: National Academy Press, 2000.

Langston, Nancy. *Where Land and Water Meet: A Western Landscape Transformed*. Seattle, WA: University of Washington Press, 2003.

Niemi, Ernie, Ed Whitelaw, and Andrew Johnson. *The Sky Did NOT Fall: The Pacific Northwest's Response to Logging* Reductions. ECONorthwest, 1999.

Oldham, Kit. "Ceremony Marks Start of Demolition of Elwha River Hydroelectric Dams on September 17, 2011." *HistoryLink.org*. Accessed July 21, 2016. http://www.historylink.org/.

Oldham, Kit. "WTO Meeting and Protests in Seattle (1999) – Part 1." *HistoryLink.org*. Accessed January 17, 2016. http://www.historylink.org/.

Oldham, Kit. "WTO Meeting and Protests in Seattle (1999) – Part 2." *HistoryLink.org*. Accessed January 17, 2016. http://www.historylink.org/.

Robbins, William G. and Katrine Barber. *Nature's Northwest: The North Pacific Slope in the Twentieth Century*. Tucson, AZ: University of Arizona Press, 2011.

Wunderlich, R.C., D.A. Zajac, and J.H. Meyer. *Evaluation of Steelhead Smolt Survival through the Elwha Dams*. Olympia: U.S. Fish and Wildlife Service Fisheries Assistance Office, 1988.

Index

Page numbers with an *f* refer to a figure. Bolded page numbers refer to a page range for an entire chapter.

a

Adams, John Quincy   96
Adams-Onís Treaty (1819)   41
Adobe   324
Adventure (ship)   38
Advocate   210
AFL (American Federation of Labor). *See* American Federation of Labor
African Americans
  at Boeing   263
  Cannady's civil rights role   209–212
  court martial of   264
  discrimination against   179–184
  as emigrants   90
  exclusion laws. *See* exclusion laws/ practices impact
  Italian POW treatment comparisons   264
  job barriers for   274, *274f*
  railroad passenger service by   126, *134f*
  as scab labor   181–184, *182f*
Agricultural Adjustment Act (1933)   241–242
Agriculture. *See* farming/ranching
Ah Fong Chuck   190
Ah Sing   187
Ah Teung   190
AIDS   310–311
aircraft production
  during Cold War   271
  during World War II   256, 258–259, *259f*
  See also Boeing
Alaska-Yukon Pacific Exposition   142
ALCOA (Aluminum Company of America)   259
Alfred Kinsey
  Sexual Behavior in the Human Female (1953)   308
  Sexual Behavior in the Human Male (1948)   308
Alien Act   165
Alien Enemies Act   165
Allen, Paul   322
altercation fatalities
  in Clallam-Hudson's Bay Company conflict   48
  of Cook   4, 37
  on Gray's expedition   11, 12, 38
  in mining strike   183
  on Oregon Trail   71–72, 91–92
  See also massacres
Aluminum Company of America (ALCOA)   259
Amalgamated Association of Street and Electric Railway Employees of America   *166f*
Amalgamated Sugar Company   290
Amazon.com   324
American Board of Commissioners of Foreign Missions   62

Contested Boundaries: A New Pacific Northwest History, First Edition. David J. Jepsen and David J. Norberg.
© 2017 John Wiley & Sons, Ltd. Published 2017 by John Wiley & Sons, Ltd.

American Civil Liberties Union (ACLU)
290, 299, 311
American Federation of Labor (AFL)
about 167
CIO merger with 167
exclusionary policies of 152–153
IWW contrasted with 157
opposition to 170
resurgence of 243
UFW merger with 303–304
American Mill 158
American "neutrality" 256
American Pacific Fur Company 35
Anaconda (MT), Irish community in
208–209
Anderson-Middleton Mill 158
anti-Chinese violence 185–186
Anti-Coolie League 186–187
anti-farmworker bill 296–297
anti-government protesters. *See* protests
anti-immigrant sentiment 211, 304–305
anti-Japanese sentiment 266–268,
268f
anti-slavery laws 94–95
anti-sodomy laws 309
anti-war sentiments 165, 308
APEC (Asia-Pacific Economic Cooperation
conference) 326
armed forces
African Americans in 179, 264, *264f*
as labor drain 262, 289
logging by *261f*
Native Americans in 265
Nisei volunteers/draftees in 269
See also United States Army
Armistice Day killings 161–162
Armitage, Susan 215
art
Kane's paintings/sketches *24f, 25f, 42f,*
49f, 63f
Point's drawings *67f, 69f, 72f, 79f*
Socialist *238f*
as WPA projects 241
Arthur, Chester A. 185–186
Ashalomov, Doris 273
Asia-Pacific Economic Cooperation
conference (APEC) 326

assimilation
boarding schools role in 106, 107
of gender roles 205
as government policy driver 178
inclusion vs. 288
policy reversals 242
Associated Students of the University of
Washington (ASUW) 299
Astor, John Jacob 41
Astoria, Fort 41
atomic bombs 259–260
authority hierarchy, Chinese 207
automobiles
as railroad replacement 138
sales growth of 232

b

back-to-the-land communes 310
Bain, David H. 140
Bainbridge Island (WA), Japanese-
American removal from 269
Baker, Eddie, Jr. 321–322
Baker, Joseph 3, 7
Balcom, Emily 197–198
Ballinger, Jeffrey 327
Ballou, William B. 142
band/tribal factional politics 17–18
bank closures 232
Barnett, Eugene 163
Bartell, Jeff 166
Barwick, Paul 306, 312
Beaver (ship) 43
Becker, Ray 163
Beckmann, George M. 301–302
Beecher, Lyman 76–77
Benevolent Empire 62
Berger, Victor 165
Bering, Vitus 3, 36
Bezos, Jeff 324
BIA (Bureau of Indian Affairs) 205–206
Bickford, John 299
Biddle, Francis 268
Bingham, John 180
Black, Mary Louisa 90
Black Student Union (BSU) 299, 301
Blanchet, Augustin Magloire Alexandre
(A.M.A.) 66

Blanchet, Francois Norbert
Cowlitz River mission of 67
disappointment of 74–75
hostage intervention by 74
on Mother Joseph 104
on polygamy 66
teaching tools of 69
Bland, O.C. and Bert 163
blind pool investment strategy 125
Boag, Peter 306, 307, 309
boarding schools 106–107, 205, 206
Bodega y Quadra, Juan Francisco de la 4, 73
Boeing
airplanes built by *328f*
Cold War employment at 271
female employees at 262–263
Jackson as senator for 276–277
resistance to non-white workers 263
during World War I/II 232, 258–259, *259f*
Boeing, William 258
Bogle, Richard 180
Boise
Chinese in 190
gambling houses in 188
growth of 328
high-tech industries in *323f*, 324
Boise, Fort 42, 92
Boit, John 37–39
Boldt, George H. 337
Bonneville Dam 247
Bourget, Ignace 74–75
boycotts
prohibiting 296
against Safeway *300f*
by UFW 295, *300f*
by UW students 297–299
Boyd, Robert 73
Boyle, Kevin 156
Bracero Program (1942) 265–266, *290f*
braceros' war on poverty 289–292
Brainerd, Erastus 141
Brandeis, Louis D. 218–219
Bremerton shipyards 256, 257–258, 270, 276
Brewer, David 219

Britain
Convention of 1818 88
exploration/claims 3–10, 35–36
in fur trading 39
"joint occupancy" with United States 41
British North West Company 40, 41, 49
Broughton, William R. 5
Brown Berets 295
Brown v. the Board of Education 288
Bryant, Celia 169
BSU (Black Student Union) 299, 301
Bundy, Ammon 339
Bureau of Indian Affairs (BIA) 205–206
Burlington Northern Railroad 139
Burnett, Peter
on agricultural potential 95–96
on emigrant deaths 90–91
on emigration motivation 89–90
Native Americans' interaction with 91
negro-whipping law (lash law) 92, 94
Burns, Ken 301
Bush, George 101, 180
Butler, Doris Elder 202

C
Cain, Harry 236
Cameahwait (chief) 16, 29
Camp Hard Labor Creek (Georgia) 179
Camp Harmony (Puyallup) 269
Camp Skamania (Columbia Gorge) 179
Camp Sunset (Vancouver, WA) 179
Cannady, Beatrice Morrow 209–212, *210f*
canneries
in Bellingham *185f*, *203f*
closing of 171
Hume's production from 169–170
number of 132, 135
Card, Minnie 206
Cardwell, Mae 197–198
Carlisle Industrial School 106
Carnegie, Andrew 152
"cash and carry" policy 256
Cassagranda, Ben 162
Catholic missionary work
in 1800s 62
flexibility of 68–69
pageantry as appealing 70

Catholic missionary work (*Continued*)
  Protestant competition with   66–73
  sketches of. *See* Point, Nicholas
  during Spanish exploration   60
  teaching tools of   69–70
  travel by   *72f*
cattle, quality of   131
Cayuse, emigrants as threat to   71–72
Cayuse War (1848)   77
CCC (Civilian Conservation Corp)
      231–232, 239–240, *239f*
cedar asthma   157
Central District Youth Club   313
Centralia massacre   160–163
Central Pacific Railroad   120, 132
Central Trades Council   160
Chapin, Ruby   177, 185, 186
Chaplin, Ralph   *164f*
Charbonneau, Toussaint   15, 27–28
Chateau Ste. Michelle winery   303–304
Chatham (ship)   *1f*, 6, *11f*
Chávez, César   288, 294–297, *296f*
Chemawa Indian School   106, 205
Cherokee   78
Chesnut, Louis   260
Chickasaw   78
childcare   273–274, 291
child labor, prohibition of   243
China
  East India Company monopoly in   41
  fur prices
    in glutted market   11–12, 39
    in lucrative market   4, 37
Chinese
  as cannery labor   131–132, 169–170,
      185f
  clans of   190
  discrimination against   170, 177–178,
      178f, 184–190, *189f*
  expulsion of   177, 186–187
  labor broker contracts with   184
  as scab labor   184–185
  taxes directed at   187
  women's contributions   207–208
Chinese Exclusion Act (1882)   185–186,
      190, 207
Chin Lem   208

Chinook
  housing of   *25f*
  Lewis and Clark interaction with   19–20
  name origin   12
  smallpox impact on   73
  as traders   17, 35–36, 47
Chirikov, Aleksei   36
Choctaw   78
Christian conversion, history of   60
Chuimei Ho   208
church membership growth   61
CIO (Committee of Industrial
      Organization)   167
Civilian Conservation Corp (CCC)
      231–232, 239–240, *239f*
civilization, definition of   22
Civil Rights Movement   190, 288
Civil War debt   120
Clark, Chase   269
Clark, Norman H.   133, 135, 160, 167–168
Clark, Robert   156, 157
Clark, William   13–21
class warfare, as IWW goal   164
Clatsop, Fort   18–19
Clatsop people   18
Clawson, Augusta   273–274
Cleo (Shuswap woman)   48
Clerke, Charles   4
Cleveland, Grover   135
Clinton, Bill   311, 326
Clinton, Catherine   199
Clinton, Gordon   313
coal
  decline in   234
  mining of   181–183, *182f*
  price fluctuations of   183, 232
Coast Salish   22–23
Coeur d'Alene mining district   121, 129
Coeur d'Alene Railway and Navigation
      Company   129
Cold War
  employment during   270–272
  growth during   255
  homosexuality as a threat during   307
collective bargaining   297
Collier, John   242
Collins, William H.   *161f*

Columbia Center   *326f*
Columbian Plateau people   23–26
Columbia Rediviva (ship)   11, *11f*, 12, 37
Columbia River
  charting of   40
  ecosystem damage   135
  exploration of   5, 10–13, 38
  overfishing of   134–135, 171
  right of way   119
  transportation on   121
Columbia Sportswear   325
Colvile, Fort   42, 45
Colville, mineral strikes at   129
Colville Indians   *42f, 49f*, 248
Comcomly   35
Committee of Industrial Organization   167
Communism   163, 307
Communist Party First Amendment rights
  237
compensation for ceded land
  Japanese American reparations bill as
    270
  for Native Americans   99, 248
Congregational missionary work   66
Congress for Racial Equality   313
conservation
  federal programs for   135, 241–242
  habitat protection, as treaty requirement
    337
  Hume's attempts at   170–171
  Weyerhaeuser's sustainable yield research
    135
Consumer League of Oregon   220
consumer spending democratization, mail
    order shopping as   127
contemporary economy. *See* economy
contested boundaries
  discrimination
    against LGBT   **306–312**
    against minorities   **177–193**
    against women   **197–221**
  early exploration   **3–29**
  economy   **321–340**
  global conflict   **255–277**
  Great Depression   **231–248**
  IWW   **149–171**
  missionary work   **59–80**

El Movimiento   **287–315**
  Pacific Northwest settlement   **87–105**
  railroads   **119–140**
  trading   **35–51**
  women's roles   **197–221**
Convention of 1818   88
Cook, James   4, 36–37
Cooke, Jay   119–120, 139
Coolidge, Calvin   233
Corbin, Daniel Chase   129
Corps of Discovery   13–21, *14f*
Coulee City   243, 246
court-martial of African American soldiers
    264
Cowlitz Farms   45, 46
Cox, Thomas R.   156
Cray supercomputers   324
Creek people   78
Creel, George   165
Creighton, John   326
Crocket, David (Davy)   78
cruise ships   325–326
Cruzatte, Pierre   *14f*, 18
cultural clashes
  overcoming   192–193
  whites with Chinese   188–189
  whites with Native Americans   5–6,
    47–49
Cushman Indian School   106

d
Dagon, Dr.   103
Dahlie, Jorgen   128
The Dalles Dam   247
dams   247, 337–338
  See also Grand Coulee Dam; *specific*
    dams
Dawes, Henry L.   180
Dawes Act (1887)   205
Debs, Eugene   163–164, 165
Deem, Thomas   301
Defense of Marriage Act (1996)   311
deforestation/fire threats   135
DeJonge, Dirk   237
Delano Farms, strike at   295
Demers, Modeste   67, 68
D'Emilio, John   307

Democratic victory   237–238
De Smet, Pierre Jean   68–69, 79
DeVoe, Emma Smith   213, 214, 216
DeVoto, Bernard   29
Dewing, Lloyd and Mary   237
DeWitt, John L.   267
Díaz, Juan and Tomasa Lara   287
Dicks, Norm   333
Dilg, Janice   220
disabled, chloroforming   243
The Discovery (ship)   *1f*, 3, 6, *11f*
discrimination
   against minorities   **177–193**
     about   177–179
     African Americans   179–184
     Chinese   177–178, *178f*, 184–190
     European immigrants   191, *191f*
     Japanese-Americans   266–270
     Mexicans   265–266
   Cannady's role in combating   209–212
   economic cycles as factor in   179
   in employment   169–170
   against LGBT   306–312
   in Oregon Territory   94
   pay scales based on   46
   segregation
     overturning   315
     in Portland   211
     in Seattle   263, *314f*
   tensions stemming from   263–264
   against women. *See* women's roles
   World War II progress in   259, 263
   See also African Americans; Chinese
disease
   at boarding schools   106
   dysentery   72
   influenza   50, 63
   during Lewis and Clark expedition   19
   malaria   73
   measles   50, 72
   Native population decline from   6, 23,
     50, 60, 72–73
   on Oregon Trail   90–91, 103
   scurvy   37
   smallpox   6, 50, 63, 73
   venereal diseases   19
divorce   205

Dodds, Gordon   237
Donation Land Claim Act (1850)
   about   77, 96, 198
   African American exclusion policy   180
Dong Oy   208
Dorian Society   309
Douglas County Hammer, conservative
   editorial   160
Douglass, Frederick   180–181
Doullard, Mary Todd   273
dual-purpose reactor   255, 271
Duluth-Bismarck railroad link   120
Duncan, Mary A.   169
Duniway, Abigail Scott
   on men's view of women   217
   Oregon Trail experiences of   89, 90, 91
   on slavery   94
   as suffragist   201, 212–214
   on women's lot   217
DuPont Corporation   259–260
Dust Bowl, emigration from   237

e

early exploration   **3–29**
   background   3–5
   Columbia River exploration   5, 10–13,
     38
   cultural clashes   5–6
   European misconceptions   9–10
   explorers. *See specific explorers*
   Lewis and Clark expedition   5, 13–21,
     21f
   Puget Sound   xv, *4f*, 6–9
East India Company   41
Eaton, Cora Smith   215
Eaton, John   88
Ebey, Rebecca   97–98
Economic Opportunity Act (1964)   292
economic recessions
   about   179
   Great Depression. *See* Great Depression
   Panic of 1873   119–120, 122–123, 124,
     128, 136
   Panic of 1893   135–136, 183
   selective recovery from   232
economy
   after World War II   307

contemporary **321–340**
  dam demolition   337–338
  environmentalism in   321–322,
    333–336
  high-tech industries   322–324
  outdoor recreation   324–326,
    332–335
  politics in   330–335, 339–340
  uneven growth of   328–330
  wolf population restoration   321–322
  World Trade Organization conference
    326–328
Eddie Bauer   325
education
  CCC camps as source of   239, 240
  of Hispanics   291, 293
  Indian boarding schools   106–107, 205,
    206
  of minorities   300
  novel approaches to   293
  union militancy/class war vs.   168
  of women   62
Edward Hines Lumber Company   329
Eels, Cushing and Myra   66
eight-hour day   204
Eisenhower, Milton   269
Eldridge, Edward   214
electric companies, Grand Coulee Dam as
    competition for   246
Ellis, Jackie   *314f*
Elwha Dam, removal of   337
Emergency Farm Labor Supply Program.
    See Bracero Program
Emery, Peter M.   158
Empire Builder (train)   140
employment
  economic cycles of   179
  federal   xvii, 276–277
  job-shark agencies   153–155
  labor. *See* labor
  New Deal. *See* New Deal
  from railroad construction   123
Endangered Species Act   322
Endo, Mitsuye   269–270
"entitlement" of Europeans   10, 91
environmental impact
  of agriculture   96–97

  of fur trading   46
  humans and   46
  of Starbucks   327–328
environmentalism
  opponents of   334, *334f*
  wilderness preservation   332–334
  wolf population restoration   321–322
Equator, Chief   71–72
Ermatinger, Francis   48
Eshelman-Llewellyn Investment Company
    130f
Espionage Act   165
Estes, David   310
ethnic cleansing
  African American exclusion laws. *See*
    African Americans
  Chinese expulsion   177, 186–187
ethnic studies programs, as staples   302
Etulain, Richard   198
European immigrants
  discrimination against   191, *191f*
  as scab labor   181
European misconceptions   9–10
Evangelical Christians   61
Evans, Daniel   277, 293, 299
Everest, Wesley, lynching of   162
Everett Massacre   158–160
Evergreen Legal Services   295
exclusion laws/practices impact
  on African Americans   90, 94–95,
    101–102, 179–180
  Chinese Exclusion Act (1882)   185–186,
    190, 207
  on female physicians   197
  on women and children   234–235
  See also African Americans; Chinese;
    women's roles
expansionist outlook   87
extraction industries
  decline of   330
  during Great Depression   231, 234
  in Idaho   261
  Klondike gold rush   141–142
  same-sex relationships in   306
  transportation for
    difficulties of   121
    railroads role in   129, 131–133

extraction industries (*Continued*)
  wartime boom of   232
  after World War I   232–233
  during World War II   257, 260
  See also gold

f

Fair Employment Practices Committee
  263
Fair Labor Standards Act (1938)   219, 220,
  243
Fairview Home, chloroforming residents of
  243
Faragher, John Mack   202
Farm Credit Administration   242
farming/ranching
  dominance in rural areas   329
  environmental changes from   96–97
  federal aid to   241–242
  by Hudson's Bay Company   42, 45
  hunting and gathering lifestyle vs.
    70–71
  wartime harvesting   263, 265, 269
  women's role in   200–201
Farm Security Administration   242
farm-to-city migration   201
Faulkner, Bret   163
FDR (Roosevelt, Franklin Delano). *See*
    Roosevelt, Franklin Delano
Federal Art Project   241
federal government
  as region's largest employer/landowner
    xvii, 276–277
  relief measures. *See* relief measures
  war on poverty   292–294
  See also United States
Federal Theatre Project   241
Federal Writers' Project   241
female property ownership   205
Fenty, Brent   334
Ferry, Elisha   183
Fifteenth Amendment   212
Findlay, John   163
Finian, Father   294
Finicum, LaVoy   xv
fire fighters. *See* forest fires
First Amendment rights   237

fishing
  Chinese labor for   *185f*
  Grand Coulee Dam impact on   244, 247
  during Great Depression   234
  hatcheries for   135, 170
  overfishing   134–135, 170–171
  by R.D. Hume and Company   169–170
  volume of   131–132
  wartime price fluctuations   232
fishing rights   98–99, 260, 335
fish ladders, lack of   244, 247, 337
Five Civilized Tribes   78
food
  cattle   131
  dehydrated   260
  harvesting
    strikes. *See* strikes
    during wartime   *263f*, 265, 269
  Hudson's Bay Company production of
    41–42, 44–45
  price fluctuations of   232–233
  salmon. *See* salmon
  Washington State production of
    121–122, 131, 232
  wheat. *See* wheat
food services boycott   299
forest fires
  fire fighters   237, 265
  as Japanese act of war   261–262
  prevention of   135
Forest Reserves Act (1891)   135
forts. See *specific forts*
4-L (Loyal Legion of Loggers and
    Lumbermen)   165
Fourteenth Amendment   95, 181, 218
Francis, Abner Hunt and Lynda   180
Francis, O.B.   180
Frank Church-River of No Return
    Wilderness   321–322
Fraser, Simon   40
Free Speech Fight
  in Aberdeen   158
  in Everett   159
  region-wide   153, 157
  in Spokane   149, 153–155
  World War I as end of   165
French, Peter   289

French-Canadian Catholics   66–67
Frost, Scott   304
Fujita, Nobuo   261–262
fur trading
   American   5
   background   36
   British   4
   coastal   37–39
   environmental impact of   46
   fur deserts   42–44
   Hudson's Bay Company dominance
         39–40, 41–44
   interior   39–41
   Native control of   35, 37–38, 46–47
   posts   40–41
   prices
      in China   4, 11–12, 36, 37, 39
      from Natives   6, 38
      outbidding   42–44
   termination of   50–51
   See also trading

g
Gale, William   47
gambling houses   188
Gamboa, Ernesto   298
Gamboa, Guadalupe   295, 298
García, Mónica   287–288, 294
García, Ricardo   288, 294, 300–301,
      303
Garfias, Roberto   302
Garland, Hamlin
   Main-Traveled Roads   201
Garrison, Fanny (daughter)   124
Garrison, William Lloyd   124
Gates, Bill   322
Gay Liberation Front   309
gay rights movement   308–309
General Allotment Act   205
George, Fort. *See* Astoria, Fort
George, Henry   131
Gibbs, George   100
Gilbert, Cragg   304
Gilbert Orchards   304
Ginsburg, Ruth Bader   219
Ginther, Ronald   *238f*
Glaser, Rob   323

Gleason, Caroline (Sister Miriam Theresa)
      220–221, *221f*
Glines Canyon Dam, removal of   337
global conflict   **255–277**
   American "neutrality"   256
   Cold War defense work   270–272
   employment discrimination regulation
         263
   federal spending for   255, 276–277
   Japanese-American internment
         266–270, *270f*
   labor shortages   262–266
   Pearl Harbor bombing   257
   women in defense work   273–275
   World War II defense work   257–262
Goethals, George W.   246
gold
   California discoveries   89, 184
   Chinese immigrants attracted by   184,
         187–188
   Klondike gold rush   141–142
   Native Americans removed for   78
   Rogue River site   77
   trespassing/raping by miners   100
Goldschmidt, Neil   309
gold standard   156
Goll, Norman   246
Gorgas, William Crawford   197
Gorton, Slade   337
Gotcher, Emma   218
Grand Coulee Dam
   construction of   *229f*, 243–244, 246–248
   Roosevelt's promise of   238, 246
   view of   *247f*
Grand Staircase-Escalante National
         Monument (Utah), as example   335
Grant, Ulysses S.   125
grape boycott pressure   297–299
Gray, Robert   5, 10–13, 37–39
Gray, W.H.
   A History of Oregon   93, 94
Grays Harbor shipyards   158
Great Depression   **231–248**
   about   231
   earlier recessions. *See* economic
         recessions
   post-World War I economy   232–233

Great Depression (*Continued*)
  after stock market crash
    about 233–234
    Hooverville 234–236, *236f*
    New Deal programs. *See* New Deal
  World War II as recovery for 244–245, 256
  See also Civilian Conservation Corp;
    Works Progress Administration;
    specific federal programs
Greater Sage-grouse 334
Great Northern Railway
  Coeur d'Alene mining district service 129
  Hill's controlling interest in 139–140
  to Seattle 141
  survival of 136
Greeley, Horace 88–89
Greenwald, Maurine Weiner 202, 203–204
Griggs, Everett 155
Grimm, Warren 162
Griswold, James *217f*
Groves, Leslie 259–260
Guerrero, Julio César 303

h
habitat protection, as treaty requirement 337
Hall, Delores *314f*
Hall, Fort 42–43
Hall, Wendy 205
Haney, John M. 162
Hanford (WA) 260
Hanford Nuclear Reservation
  about 259–260
  during Cold War 271
  Kennedy at 255
  sexism at 273
  women's roles at 274
Hanna, James 37
Hara, Lloyd 306
Harmon, Alexandra 47–48, 64, 97
Harney County (OR), decline of 329, 330
Harriman, E.H. 139, 140
Harrington, Mike 323
Hartley, Roland 237

Haugen, Gilbert 233
Haywood, William D. (Big Bill) 153, *164f*, 167
HBC (Hudson's Bay Company). *See* Hudson's Bay Company
health care providers
  acupuncturists 171, 190
  healers 24, 73
  herbalists 192–193
  Native revenge on 66, 73
  Sisters of Providence 104–105
  Whitman (Marcus) as 66, 73
Heceta, Bruno de 4, 73
Hen Lee 190
Henry J. Kaiser Shipyards 257, *258f*, 273–274
high-tech industries 322–324
hiking trails, as CCC legacy 240
Hilgard, Ferdinand Heinrich Gustav. *See* Villard, Henry
Hill, Edwin 179, 239–240
Hill, James J. 139–140, *139f*
Hill, Joe 150, *151f*
Hine, Robert V. 202
Hines, Donald 73
Hirabayashi, Gordon 269–270
Hiroshima, bombing of 260
Hispanics
  embracing their identity 288
  as farm labor during World War II 265, *290f*
  "illegal status" of 289
  pesticide exposure of 297
  working conditions/poverty of 289–291, *292f*
A History of Oregon (Gray) 93, 94
HIV 310–311
"hobo orators" 154–155
Hogness, John R. 302
Holder, Eric 311
Holladay, Ben 124
Homer, Benjamin 47
homesteads 96
Hoover, Herbert 232, 234
Hoover, J. Edgar 268
Hooverville 234–236, *236f*
Hopkins, Edna 274

hops, UFW targeting of   295
horses
   canoes vs.   100
   Lewis and Clark's use of   29
   in Native lifestyle   17, 23
   payment with   24
   saddle train use of   121
   theft of   59, 66, 71–72
   as valued items   19
hostages, after Whitman massacre   74
housework   200–201
housing
   discrimination in   313
   of Hispanics   291, *292f, 298f*
   of Native Americans   8–9, 12, 22, *25f,*
      79f
   ordinances governing   *314f,* 315
Howe, Daniel Walker   61, 78, 216
Hubbard, Dale   162
Hudson's Bay Company (HBC)
   Christian proselytizing by   60–61
   Clallam conflict fatalities   48–49
   diversification of   36
   dominance of   39–40, 41–44
   emigrant assistance from   51, 92
   environmental impact of   46
   exclusion laws, non-enforcement of   180
   hostage intervention by   74
   opposition to provisional government
      93–94
   recruiting flyer from   *44f*
Huerta, Dolores   295
Humbarger, I.G.   158
Hume, Robert Deniston (R.D.)   169–171
hunger marches   237
Hutton, May Arkwright   213, 216
hyphenation, minority use of   293

i
Idaho
   politics of   331
   views on immigrants   332
   white environment of   211
   See also Boise
Idaho City   188, 190
Idaho Health Freedom Act   331
Idaho Tri-Weekly Statesmen   121

Immigration Act (1917)   289
Immigration and Naturalization Service,
      raids by   303
Immigration Reform and Control Act
      (1986)   303
important dates and events, summary of
      115–116, 227–228, 348
income gap
   early 20th century   152
   Sawant's position on   330
   of urban/rural areas   272, 329–330
   after World War I   232
Indian Civilian Conservation Corps   242
Indian Removal Act (1830)   78
Indian Reorganization Act
      (Wheeler-Howard Act)   242
Indians. *See* Native Peoples/Native
      Americans
Indian Territory   78
individualism   152
Industrial Revolution
   environment of   168
   gender roles in   200
   inequities from   150
Industrial Worker   154
Industrial Workers of the World (IWW).
      See IWW
infrastructure, WPA construction of   241
Ing Doc Hay   192–193, *192f*
Inslee, Jay   331
Intel   324
intellectual/social opportunities, women's
      201–202
International Association of Machinists,
      discrimination by   263
international commerce   322, 326
Interstate Commerce Commission   134
intertribal warfare   17–18
Irish community, women's role in
      208–209
Iroquois as Catholic missionaries   60
Issei   267
Italian prisoners of war, preferential
      treatment of   264
IWW   **149–171**
   in Aberdeen   157–158
   in Centralia   160–163

IWW (*Continued*)
  in Everett   158–160
  formation of   152–153
  job-shark employment agencies
    153–155
  membership recruiting by   157
  music/songbooks used by   150, *151f*
  outcome of   163–168
  Progressive Era   151–152
  resurgence of   243
  in Spokane   149–151
  in Wenatchee   158
  in Yakima   158

j

Jackson, Andrew   78
Jackson, Henry M. (Scoop)   276–277
Jackson, Jesse   234–236
Jackson, Mance   313
Japanese-American internment   266–270,
  270f
Jefferson, Thomas
  instructions on interactions with Native
    Americans   13, 14
  Lewis and Clark expedition and   5,
    13–21
  Louisiana Purchase   13, 17
  "yeoman farmers'" vision of   89
Jeffrey, Julie Roy   73
job-shark employment agencies   153–155
Joe, Andrew   265
Johnson, Lyndon B.   292, 331
Johnstone, James   7
Jones, Robert L. and Eda   313
J.R. Simplot   260

k

Kaiser, Henry J.   257
Kalama-Tacoma railroad link
  completion of   119
  funding of   120, 123, 126
Kamiakin   100, 101
Kam Wah Chung Company   192–193
Kane, Paul
  paintings/sketches by   *24f, 25f, 42f, 49f,*
    63f
  travels of   49

KDNA radio station   302–303
Keen Footwear   334
Kelley, Hall   88
Kendrick, John   11, 37
Kennan, George   271
Kennedy, Anthony M.   311
Kennedy, John F.   255
Kepner, Harry L.   141
King, Martin Luther, Jr.   308
King County Council   314
Kinsey, Alfred
  Sexual Behavior in the Human Female
    (1953)   308
  Sexual Behavior in the Human Male
    (1948)   308
Kinsey, Darius   107
Kitzhaber, John   331
Klamath Falls' Hooverville   236
Klondike gold rush   129, 141–142
Knight, Philip   328
Knights of Labor   157, 170, 181,
    186–187
Kootenai Pelly   61
Kopay, Dave, coming out   310
Korematsu, Fred   269–270
Ku Klux Klan   211, *233f*
Kullyspel House   40

l

labor
  binary pay system   169–170, 179
  Chinese as low-wage drivers   188
  Fair Labor Standards Act. *See* Fair Labor
    Standards Act
  Hispanic   265
  IWW. *See* IWW
  on-the-job injuries   153, 156–157
  job-shark employment agencies
    153–155
  layoffs/wage cuts
    at Boeing   271
    copper prices and   209
    during economic recessions   153,
      156
    in Everett   159
    by Hill (James)   140
    in the timber industry   156, 159

minimum wage. *See* minimum wage
Native Americans as source of 97–98, *98f*
overtime pay 219
power saw hazards 156, 157
protests. *See* protests
shortage of 262–266
Starbucks/Nike practices 327–328
strikes. *See* strikes
unemployment. *See* unemployment
unions. *See* unions
War Department improvements 165
worker conditions
  in coal mines 181–182, *182f*, 184
  in the timber industry 156–157
World War II as labor drain 262
See also El Movimiento
Labrador, Raul 332
Lady Washington (ship) 11
Lamb, John 163
Lamb Machine Company 158
land ownership
  by the federal government xvii
  land grants 120, 140
  Native conflicts
    with missionaries 59–60, 71
    with reservations. *See* reservations
    with settlers 97
  Northern Pacific land sale 133
Lane, Joseph 95, 96
Langley, Fort 44, 46
Langlie, Arthur 263
language barriers
  Catholic mastery of native languages 69
  in treaty signing 100
  at Waiilatpu (Whitman mission) 64–65
Lapwai
  damage to 73
  Native farming at 70
  site selection 64
  Spalding's departure from 74
Lassiter, Tom 160
Lee, Jason 63, 64, 74
Lee See How 208
"legal" marriages for Native couples 205–206

Lemos, Jesus 293–294, 298
Lend-Lease Act 256–257
Lend-Lease depot 259
lesbian, gay, bisexual, and transgender community. *See* LGBT community
Leschi 100
Lewis, Meriwether 13–21
Lewis and Clark expedition
  about 5, 13–21
  centennial poster *21f*
  Mackenzie's influence on 40
LGBT community
  as McCarthy-era target 307
  relationships 306–312
  same-sex marriage legislation 331, 332
"Liberty" ships 257, *258f*
Lighty, Jane Abbott 306, 311
Limerick, Patricia Nelson 179
Lindeberg, Jafet 142
The Little Red Songbook 150
livestock, shipping 131
Livingston, Robert R. 13
Locke, Gary 311
logging
  camp conditions 156
  by Hudson's Bay Company 44
  photo of *117f*
  railroads/technology advances in 155
  restrictions on 329
  by soldiers *261f*
  transportation challenges of 122
  during World War II 260
  See also timber industry
"long-short" hauling 133–134
Lord, Alice 204, *215f*
Louisiana Purchase (1803) 5, 13
Lower Elwha Klallam Tribe 337
Loyal Legion of Loggers and Lumbermen (4-L) 165
loyalty oaths 166
loyalty-related offenses 165
Luark, Michael 89
lumbering. *See* timber industry
Lung On 192–193
Lydia (ship) 38
lynching of IWW members 162, 166

m

Mack, Gilbert F.   158

Mack, Mable   *263f*

Mackenzie, Alexander   40, *40f*

MacLachlan, Mary   197–198

Magnuson, Warren G. (Maggie)   276–277

mail order shopping   127

Main-Traveled Roads (Garland)   201

Maldonado, Carlos S.   289

Maleng, Norm   306

Malheur County Cattlemen's Association   335

Malheur National Forest   329

Malheur National Wildlife Refuge, standoff at   xv, 339–340

Manby, Thomas   7–8

Mangun, Kimberly   210

Manhattan Project   259–260

Manion, Katherine   197–198

manufacturing

  airplanes. *See* aircraft production; Boeing

  efficiency increases   257

  post-World War I growth of   232

  ship building. *See* ship building

Manweller, Matt   339

marijuana legalization   331, 332

marriage equality law (2012)   306

married working women   202–203

Marshall, Beatrice   274

Marshall, Thurgood   263

Martin, Charles   243

Martínez, Don Esteban José   5, 60

Martínez, Ricardo   337

Martínez, Samuel   294

massacres

  along Oregon Trail   92

  in Centralia   160–163

  of Chinese   186, 188

  in Clallam-Hudson's Bay Company conflict   48–49

  in Everett   158–160

  at Whitman Mission   74–77, 103

  See also altercation fatalities

Mattachine Society   308

Matthias, Franklin   260

maximum work hours

Fair Labor Standards Act, requirements of   220, 243

laws regulating   *203f*, 204

Supreme Court decision on   219

Waitresses Union in Labor Day parade   *215f*

McCall, Tom   *324f*

McCarthy, Eugene   276

McCarthy, Joseph   307

McDonnell, J.W.   155

McDougall, Duncan   35

McElfresh, Arthur   162

McGerr, Michael   152, 153

McHurin, Richard   236

McInerney, James C.   163

McKay, Kathryn   10

McLoughlin, Fort   43

McLoughlin, John   48, 50, 67

McMichael, Alfred   141–142

McNary, Charles   233

McNary Dam   247

McNelis, Mary   209

McPherson, James   62

McRae, Donald   159

media   308, 309–310

Medicine Creek Treaty (1854)   98, 100, 106

Meinig, D.W.   123

mental disorders list, homosexuality changes   309

Menzies, Archibald   5, 7, 9

Mercier, Laurie   209

Methodist missionary work   62, 66

Mexicans/Mexican Americans. *See* Hispanics

Michigan Mill Company   133, 155

Micron Technology   *323f*, 324

Microsoft   322–323

middle-class activism   151

Milken Institute   322, 324

minerals

  in Coeur d'Alene area   129

  gold. *See* gold

  Hume's claim on   170

  price fluctuations of   232, 234

  shipping costs of   122

Minidoka Relocation Center   269, *270f*

minimum wage

Fair Labor Standards Act, requirements
of   219, 243
in Oregon   *200f,* 204, 220
in Washington   204, 330, *330f*
mining
of coal   181–183, *182f*
in Coeur d'Alene district   129
of defense-related metals   260
during Great Depression   234
minimal contributions of   329
prospecting cautionary advice   142
missionary work   **59–80**
Catholic-Protestant competition
66–73
conversion work   60–64
emigrant assistance   71–72, 92
Sisters of Providence role in   104–105
sketches. *See* Point, Nicholas
teaching tools of   69–70
at Waiilatpu (Whitman mission)
about   59–60, 64–66
massacre at   74–77
monument to   *76f*
Sager children at   71, 74
site selection of   63–64
Missouri Gazette   87
Modocs, massacre by   92
Modoc War (1872–1873)   *93f*
Mondale, Walter   276–277, 331
Monroe, James   13
Montgomery Ward   127
Morales, Rosa   302
Morgan, Murray   125, 246
"mosquito fleet"   131–132
Mother Joseph   104–105
Mountain House   325
El Movimiento   **287–315**
about   287–289
braceros' war on poverty   289–292
on campus   297–302
Chávez, César   294–297
federal war on poverty   292–294
Spanish-language radio station
302–303
United Farm Workers Union   294–297,
303–304
victories of   303–305

Muckleshoot reservation   100
Muller, Hans Curt   218
Muller v. Oregon   204, 218–219
Munson, Curtis   267
Murphy, Mary   202
Murray, Patty   333
music as a tool   150, *151f*

n
NAACP   210, 212, 313
Nagasaki, bombing of   260
Napoleon, Louisiana Purchase and   13
Nash, Gary   10
National American Woman Suffrage
Association (NAWSA)   214
National Guard, role in restoring order
162, 183, 237, *242f*
National Industrial Recovery Act   243
National Labor Relations Act (1935)   295,
304
National Organization of Women, support
for gay rights   309
National Women's Party   216
Native Peoples/Native Americans
agriculture as impact on   97
assistance to emigrants   91
balance of power changes   17, 23
boarding schools   106–107, 205, 206
Boldt decision   337
burial practices   9–10
as Christians   61, 64, 75
conquest of   88
dam removal support   337–338
in defense work   264–265
disease. *See* disease
dress style   8–9
early Euro-American encounters with
altercation fatalities. *See* altercation
fatalities
before 1804   3–13
Lewis and Clark expedition   13–21
embracing their identities   288–289
environmental changes by   96
fishing rights   98–99, 260, 335
food   22–24
gender norms   50
gift-giving among   48, 49

Native Peoples/Native Americans
(*Continued*)
  Grand Coulee Dam impact on   229f,
    243–244
  housing
    Gray's destruction of   12
    types of   8–9, 12, 22, 25f, 79f
  hunting and gathering vs. farming
    70–71
  intermarriage   49–50
  intertribal power structure   46–47
  Jefferson's instructions/outlook on   13,
    14, 17
  as labor source   97, 98f
  as Lewis and Clark expedition guides
    15–18
  recreation   24, 24f
  religious leaders' apology to (1987)
    77
  Siberia as origin of   22
  slaves   38
  spiritual life of   24–26, 64, 65
  traders' interaction with   46–50
  treaties with   77, 98–102
  as U.S. military scouts   93f
  villages
    along Columbia Gorge   12
    along Puget Sound   8–9
    Coast Salish   22–23
    on Warm Springs Reservation   93f
  women's employment   207f
  See also *specific people*; *specific tribes*
Native rights   91
Nativists   211
Naturalization Act (1790)   267
natural resources, private-versus-public
    ownership of   169
Nature Fountain Farms   304
NAWSA (National American Woman
    Suffrage Association)   214
Nazi Party comparisons   299
Negro Repertory Company   241
Nelson, Hellen   262–263
New Deal
  about   238–239
  evaluation of   243–245
  programs of

  Civilian Conservation Corp (CCC)
    231–232, 239–240, 239f
  Works Progress Administration (WPA)
    240–241, 241f
  other programs   241–243
Newell, Gabe   323
New Northwest   212
Nez Perce
  Christianity and   61
  Lewis and Clark interaction with   18, 20
  region-wide power of   48
  treaty resistance by   101–102f
  See also Lapwai
Nike   325, 327
Nineteenth Amendment   212, 216
Nintendo   324
Nisei   267
Nisqually
  Methodist Mission for   87
  traditional village locations   22
  treaty with   98–100
Nisqually, Fort   45, 45f, 46, 47
Nixon, Richard   276
nontraditional families   309
non-violence   295
Nootka Sound   60
Nootka Sound Convention (1790)   5, 6
Norling, Ernest   241
Northern Pacific Railroad
  bankruptcy of   136
  Chinese labor for   184
  Coeur d'Alene mining district
    connections   129
  Hill's controlling interest in   140
  Kalama-Tacoma railroad link   119–120
  last spike ceremony   123f, 125
  role in African American emigration
    181–182
  to Seattle   141
  Stampede Pass tunnel   129
  "Suffrage Special"   216
  transcontinental line completion   123
  Villard's controlling interest in   125
  Weyerhaeuser land purchase from   155
Northwest Chicano Radio Network   303
North West Company   40, 41, 49, 60
Northwest Ordinance (1787)   90

Northwest Passage   4, 6
Northwest Territory ("Old Northwest")   90
nuclear reactors
   Japanese disruption of   262
   N reactor dedication   255
   plutonium production of   271
   waste cleanup from   271–272

o

Odegaard, Charles E.   299
Ogden, Peter   74
O'Hearn, Frederick   294
OIC (Oregon Improvement Company)
      181, 182–183
Okanagan, Fort   48
Okanagan region, mineral strikes in   129
Olivotto, Guglielmo   264
O'Meara, John   313
*O'Meara v. Washington State Board Against
      Discrimination*   313
"One Big Union"   *154f*, 157, 163–164
on-the-job injuries. *See* labor
open housing   313–315, *314f*
opium   188
Ordinance of 1787   90
Oregon
   Black exclusion laws   94–95
   Japanese attacks on   261–262
   polarized politics of   331
   promotion of   87–88
   provisional government of   96, 97
   slavery ban in   94–95, 98–102
   territory status (1848)   77
   See also exclusion laws/practices impact;
      Portland
Oregon and California railroad   124–125
Oregon Bureau of Labor, investigation by
      290
Oregon Central Railroad   124–125
Oregon City, Chinese expulsion from
      186–187
Oregon Council of Churches   290
Oregon Equality Act (2007)   311
Oregon Freeze Dry   325
Oregon Improvement Company (OIC)
      181, 182–183
Oregon Natural Desert Association   334

Oregon Railroad & Navigation Company
      123, 125, *127f*, 132
Oregon Steam Navigation Company
      119–120, 121
Oregon Trail
   emigrant assistance
      from Hudson's Bay Company   51, 92
      from missionaries   71–72, 92
      from Native Americans   91
   emigrant experiences   89–93, 103
   role in fur trade termination   50
Oregon Treaty (1846)   90
Otter, Clement Leroy (Butch)   322, 331,
      332
Otto (Hawaiian Islands boy)   12
outdoor recreation   324–326, 332–335
ownership rights, court nullification of
      171
Owyhee Canyonlands Conservation   333,
      334

p

PACCAR (Pacific Car and Foundry)   259
Pacific Aero Products Company. *See* Boeing
Pacific Fur Company   41
Pacific Northwest settlement
   overview   **87–105**
      agriculture introduction   95–97
      Indian treaties and reservations   77,
         97–102
      Mother Joseph's role in   104–105
      opposing views of   87–89
      Oregon Trail experiences   89–93, 103
      provisional government of   93–95
      state borders   1863, *95f*
      See also Oregon Trail
   climate as factor in   89
   countries of origin   *191f*
   economic impetus for   89
   emigrant arrivals   71
   by foreign-born Americans   128
   as invasion/conquest   88
   Klondike gold rush   129, 141–142
   railroad marketing as driver for
      125–128, 129
   women's rights leadership in   198
   during World War II/Cold War   255

Pacific Pine Manufacturers' Association 155–156

Padilla, Gary 302

Palmer, Joel 91, 92, *92f*

Panic of 1873 119–120, 122–123, 124, 128, 136

Panic of 1893 135–136, 183

Pariseau, Esther. *See* Mother Joseph

Parker, James 260

Parker, Samuel 63

passenger transportation 122

Patagonia 333, 337

patriotism, as settlement motivation 89–90

Patterson, James 307

Paul, Alice 216

PCUN 297, 304–305

Pearl Harbor bombing 257

Pérez Hernández, Juan José 4, 36

Perkins, Frances 239

pesticide exposure 297, 304

Peterson, Pete-e 306, 311

Philadelphia and Reading Railway Company 136

Pinchot, Gifford 135

Pineros y Campesinos Unidos del Noroeste. *See* PCUN

place name conventions 7, 10, 100–101

plutonium production 255, 259–260, 271

Point, Nicholas
about 79–80
drawings by *67f, 69f, 72f, 79f*

police brutality, in Tacoma 186

politics
conservative backlash against LGBT 310
left to right polarity 330–332
outlook on Hooverville 236
shift to the left 237–238
wilderness preservation, for/against 332–335

polygamy 66, 205

PopCap Games 324

Pope and Talbot 132, 155

population declines
from disease 6, 23, 50, 73
during economic downturns 233

population growth
in Oregon 71, 121
from railroad construction 123, *128f*
railroad marketing as driver for 125–128, *128f*, 129
during World War II/Cold War 255

Portland
economy of 325
growth of 128–129, 328
night clubs for LGBT community 307
overwhelmingly white environment of 211
post-World War I economy 232
Seattle vs. 142
ship building in 256, 257–258, *258f*
view of *324f*

Port of Seattle 325–326

possession-taking practices formalized 5

potatoes, Idaho as leader in 329

poverty, causes of 290–291

Pratt, Richard Henry 106

Prentiss, Narcissa. *See* Whitman, Narcissa

Presbyterian missionary work 66

price fluctuations
of coal 183, 232
of copper 209
of food 232–233, 234
of furs. *See* fur trading
during Great Depression 234
Native bargaining power 20
of timber 135, 155–156
during World War I/II 232, 262

Pringle, J. Arthur 297

private-versus-public ownership 169

Progressive Era 151–152, 167–168

prohibition laws 94

property defense, stand-your-ground laws and 166

Protestant Church
antipathy toward Catholicism 67–68
influence of 200
See also missionary work; *specific missionaries; specific missions*

protests
anti-war movement 308
by Black/Hispanic students 297–302
Free Speech Fight. *See* Free Speech Fight

hunger marches as   237
at Malheur National Wildlife Refuge   xv,
    339–340
for minimum wage   *200f*, 330, *330f*
at Seattle City Council meetings   *314f*
Stonewall riots   308–309
strikes. *See* strikes
by unpaid railroad workers   119, 120
WTO   326–327
Providence Health & Services   105
provisional government   93–95
Prucha, Francis   60, 75
public-speaking ordinance. *See* Free Speech
    Fight
Puget, Peter   xv, 3, 5, 7, 9
Puget Sound   xv, *4f*, 6–9
Puget Sound Agriculture Company (PSAC)
    45
Puyallup Indian School   106
Puyallup reservation   100

q
Quiemuth   100

r
racial hierarchy/discrimination. *See*
    discrimination
Racialist theory   177–178
radiation risks   260
radical politics   237–238
radioactive waste cleanup   271–272
Radio KDNA   303
railroads
    overview   **119–140**
    city growth with   128–131
    construction of   119–121, 122–124
    as extraction industry driver   131–133
    failure of   135–138
    Hill's role in   139–140
    need for   121–122
    public relations/marketing by
        125–128, *127f*, 129
    as unregulated monopolies   133–135
    Villard's monopoly   124–125
    completion of   89
    construction cost over-runs   119–120
    livestock, liabilities for   131

price wars   132–133
profitability problems   125–126
rate disparities   133–134, 140
regional   123–125, 129
short-line   129
transcontinental
    Central Pacific   120, 132
    Great Northern. *See* Great Northern
        Railway
    Northern Pacific. *See* Northern Pacific
        Railroad
    Southern Pacific   123, *127f*, 136
    Union Pacific   123, 140
    See also Kalama-Tacoma railroad link;
        specific railroads
Rainier, Mt.   *4f*, 7, 101, *333f*
Ramón, Rosa   303
Randolph, A. Philip   263
R.D. Hume and Company   169
Reagan, Ronald   270, 277, 303, 331
Real Networks   323
Red-baiting   307
Reed, William (Mike)   236, 237
REI   325, *325f*, 333
relief measures
    federal
        clergy's opinion of   244
        Coolidge/Hoover opposition to   233,
            234
        New Deal programs. *See* New Deal
        Pacific Northwest growth from   180
    local   234–235, *235f*
remote areas, decline of   329
reparations, for Japanese-American
    internees   270
reservations
    battles as resistance to   100–102
    treaties for relocation to   77, 98–99
Reynolds Metal Company   259
Richland (WA)   260
Richmond, John   87
Riley, Glenda   198
Ringle, Kenneth   267
road-building rights, on reservations   98
Robal, Dan   303
Roberts, John G., Jr.   311
Roberts, Loren   163

Rockefeller, John D.   152
Rocky Mountain Fur Company   42
Rogers, Cornelius   74
Rogers, T.C.   162
Rogue River tidelands/river, purchase of
      169
Ronda, James P.   17–18, 27
Roosevelt, Franklin Delano (FDR)
      on American "neutrality"   256
      discrimination barred by   263
      election of   237–238
      at Grand Coulee Dam   *229f*
      Japanese-American internment order
            267–268
      support for   243
Roosevelt, Theodore   135
Ross, Ben   237
Round Valley Reservation   205–206
Rousseau, Louis-Pierre   69
Royer, Charles   309
Rural Electrification Program   242
Russia
      claims relinquishment   41
      fur trading by   36
Russian-American Company   36, 44,
      45

S
Sacagawea   15, 27–29, *28f*
Safeway, picketing of   *300f*
Sager children
      adoption of   71
      death of   74
      Oregon Trail story   90, 91, 103
Sagstad Shipyard   264–265
Sahaptin language group   23
St. Mary's Mission   *67f, 69f*
St. Paul & Pacific Railroad   133, 139,
      155
Salish   22–23, 69, 79
salmon
      canning/shipping   131–132, 169
      Chinese labor for   *185f*
      decline of   135
      Grand Coulee Dam impact on   *229f*
      during Great Depression   234
      packing   44

Salvation Army   150, 154, 158
same-sex relationships/marriage
      306–312, 331, 332
Sam Sing   190
Sánchez, Juan   302
Sauls, James D.   94
Sawant, Kshama   330, *330f*
Scalia, Antonin   311
Scandinavian settlers   128, 191, *191f*,
      208
Schell, Paul   327
Schlesinger, Arthur, Jr.   307
Schwantes, Carlos
      on fur deserts   43
      on fur trading   4
      on "love-hate relationship" with railroads
            133
      on Oregon Steam Navigation Company
            121
      on railroad lines   124
      on shipping costs   121
Scroggs, William Lee   91
Sea Otter (ship)   37
Sears Roebuck   127
Seattle
      anti-Chinese sentiment in   186, *189f*
      economy of   322–326
      gay counseling and support services in
            309
      growth of   128–129, 328
      Hooverville in   234–237, *236f*
      Klondike gold rush impact on   141–142
      LGBT community in   306–312, 331
      Negro Repertory Company   241
      overwhelmingly white environment of
            211
      post-World War I economy   232
      ship building in   256, 257–258
      view of   *326f*
Seattle & Walla Walla Railroad   128–129
Seattle Central Labor Council   167
Seattle City Council, open housing
            ordinance   *314f*, 315
Seattle Electric Company   *166f*
Seattle Gay Alliance   309
Seattle General Strike (1919)   166–167
Seattle streetcar strike (1903)   *166f*

Seattle-Tacoma Shipbuilding Company 257–258

Seattle Union Record 203–204

Seattle Waitresses Union 204, *215f*

Second Great Awakening 61, 75

Sedition Act (1918) 165

sedition laws, Washington State 165–166

See-pay, Chief 42

segregation. *See* racial hierarchy/ discrimination

Seminole 78

Sexual Behavior in the Human Female (Kinsey; 1953) 308

Sexual Behavior in the Human Male (Kinsey; 1948) 308

sexual harassment 273

sexual identity 306, 307

sexual liberation 308

Shaw, Willis 103

Shawaway, Ira 264

Sheehan, Michael 163

Shepro, Theresa de 302

Sherman Anti-Trust Act (1890) 140

ship building
   female employees in 262
   wages in 273
   during World War I/II 232, 256, 257–258, *258f*

Shirtwaist and Laundry Workers Union 218

Shoshone
   Lewis and Clark interaction with 15–18
   Sacagawea as 27–29

Sicade, Henry 106

Simer, Jeremy 297–298, 299

Simpson, Asa 155

Simpson, Elmira 220

Simpson, Fort 43

Simpson, George 41–44, 46, 47, 48, 50–51

Simpson, Mike 322

Singer, John 306, 312

Sisters of Providence 104–105

Skinner, Bob 335

Slater, James H. 188

"slave bill" 296–297

slavery
   division over 179

Hudson's Bay Company tolerance of 48
   Native Americans practice of 38
   Oregon's ban on 94–95, 98–102

Slickpoo, Allen P., Sr. 71

Smith, Aza 73

Smith, Britt 163

Smith, Edmund A. 132

Smith, Elmer 162, 163

Smith, Jedediah 88

Smith, Sam 315

Smith Tower 142

Social Darwinism 156

Socialism
   art reflecting *238f*
   attitudes toward 163
   during Great Depression 237–238

software industry 322–323

Sohon, Gustav 79

"Solidarity Forever" *164f*

Sone, Monica 267, 268, 269

Sorenson, S. 149

Southern Pacific Railroad 123, *127f*, 136

Spain
   claims 3–5, 41
   trading by 36

Spalding, Eliza (daughter) 74

Spalding, Eliza (wife and mother) 63–64, 69–70, 74, 198

Spalding, Henry 63–64, 69–70, 74

Spanish-language radio station 302–303

Speck, Gordon 11, 12

Spence, Infanta *314f*

Spokane
   Free Speech Fight in 149, 153–155
   growth of 129–130
   IWW convergence in 149–151
   railroad rate disparities as disadvantage for 134

Spokane Garry *51f*, 61

Spokane House 40

Spotted Owl, protection of 329

Sprague, Charles 269

stagecoaches 122

Stamper, Norm 327

stand-your-ground laws 166

Stanford, Leland 139

Starbucks 327

state parks, as CCC legacy   240
steamboats, portages required by   121
steam donkeys   133
stereotypes
   of Chinese   188
   of gay men   308
   of Irish   208–209
   shedding   288–289
   of women   198
Stettler, Frank C.   220
Stevens, Isaac   98–100, *99f, 101–102f,*
   127
Stevens, John F.   140
Stewart, Helen   91
Stewart, Samuel   190
Stikine, Fort   43
Stimson, Charles   133, 155, 156
Stimson, Henry   267
stock market crash   233–234
Stonewall riots   308–309
strikes
   at Amalgamated Sugar Company   290
   by braceros   266
   against Chateau Ste. Michelle winery
      303–304
   at coal mines   181–183, *182f*
   at Delano Farms   295
   Free Speech Fight. *See* Free Speech Fight
   during harvest season   296–297
   by Hispanics   266, 290, 295
   of hop growers   295
   by IWW. *See* Free Speech Fight
   laws regulating   296–297
   for minimum wage   *200f*
   National Guard role in   *242f*
   National Industrial Recovery Act and
      243
   in Portland   157
   region-wide   157
   scab labor
      African Americans as   181–183, *182f*
      Chinese as   184–185
      women as   202
   in Seattle   166–167, *166f, 330f*
   of Seattle Education Association   *330f*
   Seattle General Strike (1919)   166–167
   Seattle streetcar strike (1903)   *166f*

Shirtwaist and Laundry Workers Union
   218
sympathy strikes   167, 183
   in Tacoma   *242f*
suffrage   212–216, *213f, 217f*
Supreme Court decisions
   Brown v. the Board of Education   288
   Communist Party First Amendment
      rights   237
   Fair Labor Standards Act (1938)   219
   on Japanese-American internment   270
   on minimum wage laws   220
   Muller v. Oregon   204, 218–219
   on public school attendance   233
   on same-sex marriage   311, 332
   on sodomy laws   309
Swinomish Reservation, Sagstad Shipyard at
   264–265
sympathy strikes   167, 183

t

Tacoma
   Chinese expulsion from   177, 186–187
   Hooverville in   236
   as railroad terminus   119, 120, 123, 126,
      128
   ship building in   257–258
Tacoma expulsion method   177, 186–187
Tacoma Mill Company   132
Taiping Rebellion   188
Taku, Fort   43
taxes, directed at Chinese   187
Taylor, Quintard   313
teaching opportunities, women's role in
   201
Ten Commandments as the bar   65
theft accusations   19, 65–66
Third Reich comparisons   299
Thompson, David   40
Thompson, James P.   154
Thoreau, Henry David   133
Thorne, William A.   158
Thurston, Samuel   88–89, 94
Tiloukaikt   59–60, 74
timber industry
   in Aberdeen   157–158
   decline of   329

environment of   155–156
in Everett   158–159
during Great Depression   234
IWW focus on   153
minimal contributions of   329
over-production by   155–156
price fluctuations of   135, 232
shipping of   122, 132
worker conditions in   156–157
during World War II   260, *261f*
See also logging
Tocqueville, Alexis de   78
Told by the Pioneers (Federal Writers'
Project)   241
Tolmie, William Fraser   47
Tonquin (ship)   41
Tootiscootsettle (chief)   12
tourism   *137f*, 322, 325–326, 332–335
Tracy, Thomas   160
trading
overview   **35–51**
background   35–36
fur trading. *See* fur trading
product diversification   44–46
along Oregon Trail   91
Christian proselytizing during   60
Gray's altercations during   11, 12
intertribal   18, 23–24
Native initiation of   7
peaceful   6
prices. *See* fur trading; price fluctuations
sexual favors during   19
tribal balance of power changes with
17
Trading with the Enemy Act   165
"Trail of Tears"   78
treaties
boarding schools as outgrowth of   106
with Native Americans   77, 98–102
to squelch immigration   178
violations of
dams as   337
Indian Removal Act as   78
Trevino, Roberto and Carlos   295
Tri-Party Agreement   271–272
Truman, Harry   260, 271
Tyler, Robert   164–165

U

UFW (United Farm Workers Union)
294–297, 303–304
UMAS (United Mexican American
Students)   298–299
Unemployed Citizens' League   237
unemployment
cycles of   179
during Great Depression   231
after New Deal   244
during Panic of 1893   135–136
during stock market crash   234
after World War I   232
Union Pacific Railroad   123, 140
unions
American Federation of Labor (AFL). *See*
American Federation of Labor
blacklisting as risk of   295
Central Trades Council   160
collective bargaining rights   295, 297
Everett as regional nerve center of   159
grower capitulation victory   295
IWW. *See* IWW
Knights of Labor   157, 170, 181,
186–187
limited effectiveness of   165
race/sex/skill-level discrimination by
152–153, 274
right to organize   *242f*, 243
Shirtwaist and Laundry Workers Union
218
unemployment. *See* unemployment
United Farm Workers Union   294–297,
303–304
workers turning to   167
United Air Lines   *241f*
United Farm Workers Union (UFW)
294–297, 303–304
United Mexican American Students
(UMAS)   298–299
United States
Civil War debt   120
claims of   35–36
Convention of 1818   88
in fur trading   39
immigration laws of   185–186, 190
"joint occupancy" with Britain   41

United States (*Continued*)
  military use of Native scouts   *93f*
  See also armed forces; federal
      government
United States Army
  Fort Lawton racial tensions   264
  gender restrictive policies of   197–198
  Supreme Court ruling against   270
  tribal wars with   77
  See also armed forces
University of Washington
  boycott pressure on   297–299
  Chicano demands at   301–302
Unruh, John   91–92
urban pioneers, women as   202

V

Valve   323
Vancouver (WA)
  high-tech industries in   324
  ship building in   257–258, 262
Vancouver, Fort   42, 45, 50–51
Vancouver, George
  logbooks of   5
  on Native burial practices   10
  place name conventions of   7
  Puget Sound exploration   xv, 3
  Discovery, grounding of   *1f*
Vanderbilt, Cornelius   136
Van Dong, Susan   *314f*
vaqueros   289
Vaughan, Delia   209
vertical integration schemes   169
Vibert, Elizabeth   48
Victor (Flathead chief)   79
Victoria, Fort   47, 50–51
Victorian standards for Native couples
      205
Villanueva, Tomás   294, 295
Villard, Henry   124, 139
Vinson, Carl   256
vitrification plant   272
voting rights   212–216, *213f, 217f*

W

wage concessions   295
Waiilatpu (Whitman mission). *See*
      missionary work

"Waitresses' Bill"   204
Walden, Greg   339
Waldo, America (slave's daughter)   180
Waldo, Daniel (master)   180
Walker, Elkanah and Mary   66
Walker, Joel   89
Walker, Mary Richardson   198
Walla Walla
  growth of   129
  missions in proximity of. *See* missionary
      work
Walla Walla Savings and Loan Association
      180
Walla Walla treaty council (1855)   *101–102f*
Walla Walla-Wallula railroad   122
Walsh, J.T.   150
Wanapum Dam   247
Wanapum fishing rights   260
War Department, labor improvements
      165
Ward Massacre   92
war hysteria   166
War of 1812   41
war on poverty   289–294
War Relocation Authority (WRA)   269
Wartime Civil Control Administration
      269
Washington Citizens for Migrant Affairs
      (WCMA)   292
Washington Equal Suffrage Association
      216
Washington Mill Company   132
Washington State
  economy. *See* economy; manufacturing;
      timber industry; wheat
  marriage equality in   311, 331
  political polarization of   331
  sedition laws   165–166
  See also Seattle
Washington State Federation of Colored
      Women (WSFCW)   215
Washington statehood   *130f*
water transportation, portages required by
      121–122
Watt, John   162
WCMA (Washington Citizens for Migrant
      Affairs)   292
Weatherwax, James M.   158

Wedderburn 169
Weisbach, Jacob Robert 186
Welch, Mary Josephine (Chicago Joe) 198
Welter, Barbara 199
West, A.J. 158
Weyerhaeuser, Frederick 133, 155
Weyerhaeuser forest practices 135
wheat
    from the Palouse 191
    price fluctuations of 232–233, 234
    reputation of 131
    shipping of 121, 122
    stability of 329
Wheeler-Howard Act (Indian
        Reorganization Act) 242
Whidbey, Joseph 3
Whidbey Island 97
White, Richard
    on dark skin 289
    on federal anti-poverty programs 294
    on Native-fur trader interaction 48
    on suffrage success 217
    on transcontinental railroads 136
    on Villard 125
    on women as moral authority 199
White Bluffs (WA) 260
white paranoia/superiority 177–178, 188
White-Parks, Annette 207
Whitman, Alice Clarissa 65
Whitman, Marcus
    adoption of Sager children 103
    anti-Catholic views of 70
    death of 74
    lobbying for missionary position 61–62
    mass migration led by 89
    mission direction change 72
    sketch of *63f*
Whitman, Narcissa
    adoption of Sager children 103
    anti-Catholic views of 68
    in benevolent work 62
    birth of daughter 65
    continental divide crossing 198
    death of 74
    sketch of *63f*
    Til-au-ki-ak's exchange with 59–60
Whitman Mission. *See* missionary work
Wickananish 38

Wickersham, James 188
Wild Olympics and Wild and Scenic Rivers
    Act (2012) 333, *334f*
William, Fort 42–43
Williams, Dorothy *274f*
Wilsey, Belle 206
Wilson (Woodrow) administration 165
Wilson, Thomas B. 206
Winship, Abiel 47
Winship, Fort 47
Winship, Jonathan 47
Winship, Nathaniel 47
Wobblies. *See* IWW
wolf population restoration 321–322
Women's Land Army *263f*, 265
Women's National Indian Association 206
women's roles
    overview **197–221**
        African American 209–212
        in canneries *203f*
        in changing work settings 200–204
        Chinese 207–208
        early rights/recognition for 216–217
        Gleason's role in 220–221
        Irish 208–209
        liberation, need for 197–199
        for minority women 205–206, *207f*
        as moral authority 199–200
        Muller v. Oregon 218–219
        occupations for 200–202
        as scab labor 202
        suffrage 212–216, *213f*, *217f*
        wages/work hours for 204–205
    in defense work 273–275
    as early pioneers 63, 198
    government protection of 204,
        218–219, 220
    as missionaries 75
    in overcoming discrimination 259
    in Point's drawings 79
    in religious revival 61–62
Wood, A.D. 158
Woods, Rufus *247f*
worker mutualism/reciprocity/
        confederation 152
worker protection
    Fair Labor Standards Act (1938) 219,
        220, 243

worker protection (*Continued*)
  Muller v. Oregon   218–219
  See also labor
work/home life balance   273–274
working women   200–202
Works Progress Administration (WPA)
  240–241, *241f*
World Trade Organization (WTO)
  conference   326–327
World War I
  economic boom during   232
  female doctors' rejections in   198
  free speech suppression during   165
  women in men's jobs during   202
World War II
  beginning of   256
  economic revival during   244–245,
  256
  female layoffs after   274
  Grand Coulee Dam's role in   247
  as LGBT coming out experience   307
WPA (Works Progress Administration)
  240–241, *241f*
WRA (War Relocation Authority)   269
WSFCW (Washington State Federation of
  Colored Women)   215
WTO (World Trade Organization)
  conference   326–327
Wyeth, Nathaniel   42–43

y

Yacolt Burn   135
Yakama reservation   100
Yakima
  Chávez in   *296f*
  IWW in   158
  Northern Pacific interaction with   123,
  130–131
  UFW boycott in   *300f*
  YVCC student demands in   300–302
Yakima County Housing Authority   291
Yakima Signal   130
Yakima Valley Community College,
  Chicano/Black education requests
  at   300–301
Yakima Valley Council for Community
  Action (YVCAA)   292
Yakima Valley Farmworkers Clinic
  292–293
Yakima Valley growers, charges against
  295
Yakima War (1855–1858)   77
Young, Claudell   301
Young, Ewing   93
Young Republicans, boycott opposition
  299
Yukon, Klondike gold rush   129, 141–142
YVCAA (Yakima Valley Council for
  Community Action)   292